SHIPWRECKS

SHIPWRECKS
OF THE
REVOLUTIONARY &
NAPOLEONIC ERAS

TERENCE GROCOTT

CHATHAM PUBLISHING

LONDON

To Doctor Jacqueline Hart MB, BS
Derriford Hospital, Plymouth

Copyright © Terence Grocott 1997

First published in Great Britain by Chatham Publishing,
1&2 Faulkner's Alley, Cowcross St, London EC1M 6DD

Chatham Publishing is an imprint of Gerald Duckworth & Co Ltd

British Library Cataloguing in Publication Data
A catalogue record for this book is available from the
British Library

ISBN 1 86176 030 2

Typeset by Eden Valley Press, Kirkby Stephen
Printed and bound in Great Britain by Bookcraft (Bath) Ltd

CONTENTS

ACKNOWLEDGEMENTS

The author wishes to express his gratitude to the many librarians and others, in several different countries, who have given freely of their time, assistance and knowledge, over a period of more than seven years, and whose help in the compilation of this work has been greatly appreciated.

In particular, the writer would like to thank the following:

From beyond these shores:

Mrs Louise de Wet, Bredasdorp Public Library, Cape Town Province

Mr G J D Wildeman, Rijkmuseum, 'Nederlands Scheepvaart Museum', Amsterdam

Mr Pierre Waksman, Chef du Service des Archives et des Bibliothèques de la Marine, Château de Vincennes (Pavillon de la Reine), Paris

Senor Jesus Gaite, Pastor, Archivo Historico Nacional, Ministerio de Cultura, Madrid

Dr Leon Allen, Mount Lawley, Perth, Western Australia

From these sceptred isles:

Dr Ray P Fereday, Plymouth, Devon

Mr Breeda O'Loghlin, Burt House, Speenoge, County Donegal

Commander John Smith RN (Ret'd) of the Naval Historical Section, Plymouth Public Library

The ladies of Plymouth Public Library

ABBREVIATIONS

AR	Annual Register
Capt	Captain
Cdr	Commander
Chr	Chronicle (Annual Register)
EI	East Indies
Lt	Lieutenant
Lt Cdr	Lieutenant Commander
MC	Mariner's Chronicle
NC	Naval Chronicle
P & DT	Plymouth and Dock Telegraph
SNC	Steel's Naval Chronologist*
SNL	Steel's List of the Royal Navy
Sub Lt	Sub-Lieutenant
SYM	Sherbourne and Yeovil Mercury

* Sometimes, but not always, embodied in *Steel's List of the Royal Navy*.

PREFACE

This work, written in its entirety from contemporaneous publications, is essentially a chronicle of maritime tragedies, which for the greater part have been forgotten, yet at the time of occurrence cost the lives of countless seamen. Every important shipwreck which appeared in a British newspaper or other publication of the period will be found in this volume, together with many other lesser accidents; yet every shipwreck, great or small, represented a major tragedy for all concerned. For Great Britain alone, Sir G J Dalyell, a contemporary authority, claimed in 1812 that 'perhaps not less than five thousand natives of these islands yearly perish at sea'.

Listed are some 1500 ships, vessels of many nations, naval and mercantile, the result of many years of research, yet they make up a very small proportion of the disasters of the 1793-1815 period. It cannot be truly comprehensive, for it has been estimated that more than 2000 shipwrecks occurred world-wide during each of these years.

From 1 January 1793 to 31 December 1799 alone, it appears from *Lloyd's Lists* that 4344 British ships were captured by the enemy, and of these 705 were recaptured. During the same period 2385 ships were lost, and 652 driven on shore, out of which 70 were eventually refloated. Thus 3639 ships were lost to the enemy and 2967 lost through perils of the sea. (*NC* vol 17, p369). The ratio of the Navy's losses was reversed: a modern study by David Hepper (*British Warship Losses in the Age of Sail*, Rotherfield [1994]) estimates that during the period 1793-1801, 62 ships, or 27 per cent of total losses, were to enemy action but 152 vessels or 67 per cent to the perils of the sea.

Many of the articles are presented with only minor alterations to grammar and syntax, having been taken from two or more contemporary sources, whilst other articles are quoted verbatim – as they appeared in the original publications. Repetition has been studiously avoided, whilst original spellings are generally retained, except where clarity requires modernisation: as in place names, for example.

Wherever possible, the *Times* references are given in preference to such local papers as the *Sherborne and Yeovil Mercury*, the *Globe*, or the *Plymouth and Dock Telegraph*, not necessarily because the *Times* articles are more accurate – far from it – but because microfilms of the *Times* made that source more readily accessible. The writer has found that articles which appeared in the *Times* or the *Annual Register* were often copied verbatim from *The Naval Chronicle*, the *Globe* or the *Sherborne and Yeovil Mercury*, or vice versa. Similarly, Duncan's *Mariner's Chronicles*, written between 1805 and 1812, often copied the *Annual Register* or *Naval Chronicle* articles verbatim. Evidently, it was often the case that one person wrote an article and all the rest copied it (see, for example, the entry for 20 November 1808).

Sir G J Dalyell, in his three-volume *Shipwrecks and Disasters at Sea*, published in 1812, wrote up the same incidents with a considerable depth of nautical knowledge, but in the lurid style later adopted by the 'Penny Dreadful'. Yet because his writing was contemporary it is today valuable for comparison, although it must be taken with a large pinch of salt. Some of his work was pure fiction and is criticised for being so in Volume 32 of *The Naval Chronicle* (p212 et seq). Even so, Dalyell's work was published in Boston, Massachusetts, in 1812, under the name of Thomas Bingly, whom we may assume pirated the text whilst the war with Britain was being fought. There was, of course, no law of international copyright: American authors received no remuneration from British publishers, and British authors were treated likewise by the Americans. At a public dinner held in New York on Friday 18 February 1842 Charles Dickens complained bitterly of the lack of international copyright.

The book contains numerous dramas, some sensational, which illustrate the perils and hardships of the age of sail. It represents not only the range of maritime tragedies, but also the contemporary view of such disasters in a society with widespread and sometimes intimate connections with the sea. Although it is not entirely exhaustive, no other work contains so much non-technical information on the maritime disasters of the period 1793-1815, and the writer hopes that his labours will prove of value to students of naval, mercantile and world history.

Terence Grocott
Plymouth, 1997

INTRODUCTION

Shipwrecks occur relatively rarely today and usually there is no comparison with the scale of the disasters which befell seamen two hundred years ago. There were then no weather reports to forewarn ships, no radios for distress calls, no rocket apparatus for life-saving, no emergency lighting, no life jackets, no life rafts and often only one or two boats to a ship, and those not dedicated lifeboats.

Ships' boats were intended for auxiliary duties, such as carrying stores, laying out kedge anchors or towing the ships in calms, while those of warships were used for landings or cutting-out operations. A warship might have a 'seaboat' under davits prepared for quick release to recover a man or men in the water, but it was not specifically intended to preserve life after the ship herself had been lost. As a result, ships' boats were not regularly equipped with all the necessities for survival; oars, sails and masts may have been kept in the boat, but not navigational equipment, nor water and certainly not food. Most necessities had to be found and loaded after the ship had sprung a leak or been wrecked, and quite often it was then too late.

Despite such drawbacks, boat voyages made under these circumstances were almost unbelievable. Captain Austen Forrest and the crew of the *Sydney* had to journey 4000 miles, which will probably remain for all time the greatest voyage ever undertaken by shipwrecked mariners (see entry for 20 May 1806). Yet Captain Forrest and his crew were very fortunate: not only did they have time to equip the boats fully, but the complete voyage was sailed in warm tropical seas. There are examples of other seamen, less fortunate and therefore more impressive in their achievements, who had to suffer the Arctic ocean (*Ann*, 30 July 1807) or the far south Atlantic (*Isabella*, 8 February 1813), both of whom covered approximately 1400 sea miles.

Even if there was time to prepare for abandoning a ship, naval or merchant, the means of salvation for the crew were usually totally insufficient. The 100-gun *Queen Charlotte* was perhaps the finest ship in the British Navy (*NC* vol 3, p302), yet when she caught fire and blew up (see entry for 17 March 1800) within easy reach of shore, more than 700 lives were lost; the boats of the vessel could not accommodate more than a quarter of her complement (*AR* 1800, Chr, p9), and shore boats would not approach because of the danger of explosion. Other ships carried boats sufficient to accommodate the crew, but without provision being made for passengers, who upon occasion would be left to perish with the wreck, as was the case with the *St Patrick* packet on 25 January 1794; or if the passengers were accommodated, the crew would be left to perish, as happened with the *Charles Baring* on 24 October 1800. These were not isolated cases, such instances occurring with amazing frequency. Some merchant ships actually sailed the Atlantic without boats or life-saving equipment of any description; the *Diana* of the *Convert*'s convoy was apparently one such vessel (8 February 1794). Rafts had to be constructed after disaster had occurred (see under 24 October 1800).

The labour of seamen came cheaply – just a few shillings per week – and for that meagre pittance their lives were fraught with peril. Despite low labour costs, merchant ships invariably carried small crews (about one man or boy for every twenty tons of burthen), and during a gale if three or four of the crew were washed overboard, the remainder might not have sufficient strength to launch a boat; that is, assuming the boats had not themselves been washed away, wrecked by falling masts or spars, or frozen in situ (which was not as uncommon as one might think). Sometimes the crew might not even be able to venture on deck, compelled by stress of weather to remain below, in an unmanageable hulk, and pray for the best (*Solomon*, 26 October 1811). Boats slung under davits for lowering directly into the sea became more common in the 1790s, but the vast majority of ships still kept their boats on the spare booms in the waist of the spar deck, with the outside chance of floating off complete with occupants as the ship went down (*Athenienne*, 20 October 1806). But in the case of the *Penelope*, 30 April 1815, it would appear that the jollyboat was frozen to the booms and could not be freed; a very common occurrence in high latitudes. Ships were entirely at the mercy of the weather, which given the usual rigs of those days they found it difficult to contend. An extreme example was the 74-gun *Cumberland*, which arrived at Portsmouth on the 30 December 1796, after taking seventy-three days from Gibraltar, seven of which were spent beating up from Start Point to Spithead (*Times*, 2 January 1797).

The causes of shipwreck

Of all the reasons for shipwreck – and a nineteenth-century journal listed fifty (see Appendix A) – one of the most common was navigational error. At this period many ships were lost because of the inability of their masters to correctly determine their longitude. Thus during the night of 2 April 1804 the *Apollo* was wrecked with most of her convoy a few miles to the north of Cape Mondego, when by dead reckoning they had thought themselves to be more than 100 miles to the westward of that Cape (*NC* vol 11, p392 et seq); a list of the thirty-one merchant ships lost out of forty appears in the *Times* of Saturday 28 April 1804.

Hydrography was also in its infancy. Marine charts of the time were more notable for their omissions than for their accuracy (see under 13 December 1800). Many rocks, atolls, islands and reefs were omitted simply because cartographers were unaware of their existence. Yet even if charts had been more accurate, the problems associated with longitude remained unsolved; for many ships sailed without chronometers, half-hour glasses being the only timekeepers in use well into the nineteenth century (*NC* vol 2, p250).

Weather-related risks were naturally increased by sailing in winter. In earlier times late-season voyages were avoided wherever possible, and the navy's 'Great Ships' were never risked in winter campaigns. However, ships had become somewhat more seaworthy and the Royal Navy in particular had become more adventurous in the employment of its capital ships throughout the year, but it occasionally had to pay the price. The worst example was the loss of the 74-gun *Defence* and the 98-gun *St George*, both of which struck the sands at Nissum, with the consequential loss of more than 1300 lives, while attempting a late voyage home from the Baltic (24 December 1811). But a whole catalogue of disasters was caused by ships sailing during the months of winter: to give just one more instance, the *Boadicea*, *Lord Melville*, and the *Seahorse* were carrying troops returning from the battlefield of Waterloo when they were lost on 30 January 1816. Even where there were no losses, winter voyaging could be both dangerous and tedious: on 23 December 1814 the *Times* had reported from Cork, 'The Bermuda fleet with its escort have put back for the fifth time.'

It was not only the land that posed a threat to ships; there was also the danger of other vessels. In wartime, merchant ships usually sailed in convoy, but during a gale, even in daylight, such close proximity was dangerous (see under 30 July 1803 and 21 February 1811). Sometimes as many as five or six hundred vessels sailed in one convoy, as when the fleets for the Cape, West Indies and the Mediterranean sailed together as far as the coast of Portugal, to gain the trade winds (*NC* vol 4, p521). Occasionally the outbound fleets found themselves on a collision course with the homeward bound fleets, as occurred on the night of 13 December 1795, when the *Leander* ran aboard and sank the *Commerce*. Nor was it much safer in the escorts, a number of small naval vessels being run down and sunk, especially at night or in fog, by the very ships they were supposedly protecting (see *Calypso* 30 July 1803).

Besides 'Acts of God' and pure accidents, there were occasions where human agency played a part. Merchant ships, completely rotten, were often sent to sea when they should have been broken up, and it was not until Samuel Plimsoll took up the issue of safety in the 1870s that any practical improvement came about. The British Admiralty were also much criticised for the state in which many ships were sent to sea, and many an officer blamed poor workmanship in the Royal Dockyards – or, even more commonly, in contract-built ships – for the weak or leaky state of his ship. In wartime during periods of extreme danger when every possible ship was required at sea, standards were lowered and extreme measures accepted. The best example of this is the pre-Trafalgar programme to 'brace and double' some laid-up ships, where a girdling of extra planking and some internal strengthening made barely seaworthy warships of a useful number of old and decrepit hulks.

The exigencies of war often led to decisions of disastrous consequence, but often in circumstances where there was little practical alternative. The rotten ships of Admiral Graves's fleet, which sailed from Bluefields, Jamaica, on 25 July 1782, were in a terrible state, and the *Centaur*, *Glorieux* and *Ville de Paris*[1] foundered in a hurricane when 2000 sailors lost their lives (*NC* vol 5, p396 et seq). They had been involved in Rodney's long and strenuous campaign against de Grasse – indeed the last two had been captured at the Battle of the Saintes – but because there was no major dockyard in the West Indies the strained and damaged ships had to be sent home. Another ship of the fleet, the 74-gun *Hector*, was in an equally deplorable condition and became so leaky that it was impossible to keep her above water. A snow then took off about 200 of her crew, including Captain Bourchier, who had been severely wounded in action; the remainder of the crew could not be taken off and went down with the ship (*AR* 1782, Chr, p226). The *Blenheim* and the *Java* (ex-*Maria Reijgersbergen*) were two more examples of naval 'floating coffins', and when these ships vanished in the Indian Ocean about 1 March 1807 at least another nine hundred seamen perished (*NC* vol 17, p506).

The last resort of a ship which could not make safe headway was to anchor – assuming she was in water shallow enough – but even then she was not necessarily safe, being very dependent on the quality of her ground tackle (the anchors and cables), and the type of ground in which she was anchored. Although many French ships of the period were anchored by means of mooring chains,[2] the view of most British officers was that the iron of the time was too brittle to withstand the violent snubbing action of a ship anchored in heavy weather. Extensive postwar trials were necessary before the Royal Navy was prepared to give up the tried and tested hemp cable. However, British naval ships often served abroad for several years at a time, at the end of which their cables were frequently little more than junk, in the original sense of the word.[3]

Vessels, apparently securely moored, often drove with disastrous consequences during a gale. The *Queen* transport on Trefugis Point, the *Arniston* on the Aghulas, and the *Sceptre* in Table Bay are but three examples of major disasters caused by ships driving during onshore gales. Even if the cable did not part, the anchor might drag, and there are instances on record when to prevent this a cannon was lashed to two small anchors in a bid to gain more holding power. In earlier years, this expedient had been successfully used by Anson in the *Centurion*, and by a warrant officer on the 74-gun *Terrible*, Captain Richard Collins, when that ship was attached to the squadron under Admiral Saunders, at the taking of Quebec, and was driving in the St Lawrence (*AR*, 1759, vol 2, p126).

Several ships were lost by settling on their own anchors: the *Regent*, 29 October 1812; and the *Prince of Wales* packet, the crew of which actually got off the vessel and walked about on the sands waiting for the tide to return, without apparently realising that the vessel would be driven upon her anchor (14 September 1806). Or an earlier shipwreck, 'a great quantity of ice cut the cable of the *Duke of Edinburgh*, bound to the Straits, and she dropped upon her anchor, which made a hole in her bottom and sank her. Her lading consisted of bale goods to the amount of £20,000 which were considerably damaged'. The locality and date were not given in the article (*AR*, 1767, Chr, p48).

Other perils of the sea

Among the commonest of cargoes were those of whale and seal oil, cork, timber, masts and staves, the latter being in very great demand for the manufacture of casks for the storage of food and liquids on land and sea. Some timber-laden ships were to prove almost unsinkable, in any weather, being kept afloat by the buoyancy of their lading (see entry for 7 August 1809). The most tragic example of such unsinkable ships must surely be that of the brig *Polly* which sailed from Boston, Massachusetts, on 12 December 1811, for Santa Cruz, and overset three days later. Six months later, on 19 June 1812, the two survivors were taken off the timber-laden hulk, 600 leagues west of Marrakesh (see under 15 December 1811). Unfortunately, waterlogged ships became mere floating hulks and a menace to other vessels. Survivors who had to keep the deck, once the masts were cut away, then had for company the surviving rat population which the men were afraid to kill in case they were needed later, to serve as food for the human survivors (*NC* vol 34, p487). Almost all ships had their quota of rats, cockroaches and lice. The *Euros* store ship, armed *en flute*, had to leave her station in Bantry Bay and return to Plymouth, in order to get rid of the numerous rats with which she was infested. 'The quantity of flour and provisions they destroyed was immense, and notwithstanding every effort of Captain Innes and his crew to kill them, they increased to such a degree as to baffle all ordinary means' (*Times*, 28 August 1804).

Sailors who escaped the ravages of scurvy, had to be doubly fortunate to avoid flea, tick or mite, and typhus, for which there was no remedy. The entries for *Intrepid*, 6 December 1793, and the *Raisonnable*, 24 December the same year, are but two examples of many. This was an entirely international problem. After the failure of the French invasion of Ireland in December 1796 due to the storms, General Harty reported that the *Eole*, a 74-gun ship, had been making water everywhere, and his troops were wet to the skin and eaten alive by vermin[4] throughout the crossing; furthermore the ship sailed from Brest with 200 smallpox cases on board, whose condition did not improve with travelling (*Archives de la Marine*, BB4 102).

Many ships were kept at sea quite unnecessarily: transports returning from Copenhagen were kept off Yarmouth for three weeks without the troops, their wives and children being allowed to land. As a direct consequence of this order, more lives were lost than in the battle itself (see under 10 October 1807). We may at this juncture notice that naval casualty lists omitted women and children, so that all such lists are apt to err on the conservative side. We may also note that early editions of *Steel's Navy Lists*, included neither transports nor merchant vessels, although those editions did include the East India Company's ships, hired armed vessels and packets.

Early developments in rescue

Many people were now becoming aware of the need for rescue equipment to be based on shore as well as on board ship, and in the year 1806, Captain George W Manby,[5] a militia officer of Norfolk, invented a life-saving apparatus, essentially a mortar firing a lead ball with a line attached, by means of which communication with a vessel was achieved. However, many years were to pass before it became generally available around the coasts of Britain (see entry for 20 January 1814).

While such praise is due to Captain Manby, it may be remembered that as far back as 1792 a bounty of fifty guineas was awarded to Mr John Bell, then sergeant, afterwards lieutenant of the Royal Artillery, for his invention of throwing a rope on shore by means of a shell fired from a mortar on board a vessel in distress (*Transactions of the Society Instituted in London, AD 1754, for the Encouragement of Arts, Manufactures and Commerce*, vol 25, 1807).

This period also saw the first experiments with purpose-built shore-based lifeboats. In 1785 Lionel Lukin modified a Norwegian yawl with buoyancy chambers, which he called his 'insubmergible boat', and a similarly modified coble was employed on the Northumberland coast for a period. However, the best known of the early lifeboats was a design by a South Shields boatbuilder, Henry Greathead, which was a very seaworthy hull form combined with buoyancy arrangements, and a number were built from the late 1790s onwards (see under *Ajax*, 27 December 1799, for example). Nevertheless, by the end of the Napoleonic War there was no systematic rescue service around the coasts of Britain, and it was not until 1824 that the first steps were taken that eventually led to the establishment of the Royal National Lifeboat Institution.

In most cases, however, the crew of a ship facing destruction had to use their own resources, but the formidable ingenuity of the seaman could sometimes contrive a mode of escape. Robert Hay, for example, describes (and illustrates) the apparatus by which he escaped from the wreck of the *Amethyst* frigate in Plymouth Sound in February 1811 (*Landsman Hay*, edited by M D Hay, London, 1953). It comprised a hawser from the ship's bowsprit cap to the shore, from which was suspended a hatch grating running on a thimble. *Amethyst* was undoubtedly lucky in running ashore bow-first on a populated and friendly shore, so could benefit from a co-operative shore-party, but not every shipwrecked crew was as fortunate.

Salvage

We now come to the question of salvage, and in shallow water it would appear that little was too difficult for the salvors of the time. The Dutch frigate *Ambuscade*, which went down on 9 July 1801 at Sheerness, was weighed four days later; and within a fortnight of the *Hindostan* East Indiaman going down on the Wedge Sand, twelve miles offshore, on 11 January 1803, eleven of the thirteen chests of bullion had been recovered. All sixty-two chests of dollars which went down with the *Earl of Abergavenny* on 5 February 1805 had been salvaged by 17 May 1806; and some of the Elgin Marbles[6] which went to the bottom with the brig *Mentor*, at Cerigo, were salvaged within two years (see entry for 17 September 1802).

An interesting account of diving and salvage efforts of an earlier date by John Lethbridge of Wolborough, and others, and the diving machine Lethbridge invented as early as 1715 appears in *Reports of the Devonshire Association*, vol 12, 1880.

Survivors

In wartime many of the shipwrecked found themselves cast up on the enemy shore, and consequently having escaped death faced the prospect of life as a prisoner of war. In Britain the majority of French, Dutch and prisoners of other nationalities were sailors, but whether merchant seamen or naval made little difference. Manpower shortages led to attempts to recruit among prisoners, particularly in instances where political differences could be exploited. French Royalists or Dutch Orangists were induced to serve against the revolutionary regimes in their home countries. For example, on 12 February 1798, the *Times* (a paper supportive of the government) noted, 'The plan of engaging Dutch prisoners of war in our service is not new. During the late war several of them enlisted in the marine corps, and though not very expert soldiers, they were orderly and obedient. Eight hundred of the men who composed the crews of the ships taken by Lord Duncan (at Camperdown) have been embarked on the Isle of Wight, with numerous other foreigners for the new battalions of the 60th reg. of foot, which is always to do duty in the West Indies.'

Clearly imprisonment was an unattractive alternative, and there is plenty of evidence of why British prison hulks or camps were avoided at all costs. On 29 December 1800 the *Times* reported, 'A number of French prisoners of war have died lately, in consequence of the very scanty allowance of their own government. The Transport Board has ordered them some relief.' This admission by the editor of the *Times* actually meant that a great number of prisoners of war had starved to death in England. However, we know that some British prisoners of war were treated as badly in France, particularly during the early years of the Revolutionary War when political fervour was at its height.

The 74-gun *Alexander*, Captain Richard Rodney Bligh,[7] was taken on 6 November 1794, and carried into Brest:

'Officers and men shared the same lot and were reduced to starvation. A wretched dog that had crept into the cells was killed and his head alone sold for a dollar. A prisoner, in a state of delirium, threw himself into the well within the prison walls, and his dead body, after lying sometime, was taken out, but no other water was allowed the people to drink. An English lady and her daughters, confined along with the men, had no separate apartment, and all their privacy was supplied by the generous commiseration of the British sailors, who standing side by side close together, with their backs towards the fair captives, formed a temporary screen while they changed their dresses. These facts were supplied to the author (Captain Brenton) by the officers who were present.'

This story occurs in Marshall (p702), Brenton (vol 1, p364) and (Ralfe, 1828, vol 2, p520) but they are obviously from the same source. By contrast, in *NC* vol 13, p427-428 a letter signed by Captain R R Bligh ends with '...I have hitherto been treated with great kindness and humanity, and have no doubt but that I shall meet with the same treatment during my captivity.' Captain Bligh was returned to England on parole in May 1795, which was the fate of most officers, if not always of their men.

The pages which follow run the whole gamut of maritime tragedies – the bizarre, curious and quirky, as well as the familiar – and in all their inconsequential detail. Alongside stories of daring rescues and astounding ordeals will be found strange facts, like the fate of the oldest Freemason in Britain; unlikely events such as the flogging round the fleet which hurt the spectators more than the punished; examples of the casual cruelty of the age, like the seamen marooned on buoys in depth of winter by an irate press gang; and many a horrifying tale of hardship and death, perhaps none more so than that of the captain trapped on a beach beneath the cargo of his wrecked ship awaiting inevitable slow death as the tide came in. Through the medium of the reporting of the time, what is here presented is a truly contemporary perspective on events, in itself a fascinating revelation of the mores and attitudes of the late eighteenth and early nineteenth centuries.

PART ONE

THE

REVOLUTIONARY

ERA

1793 – 1801

On 1 February 1793 the National Convention at Paris declared a State of War existed between France on the one hand, and Great Britain and the United Netherlands on the other.

This was followed on 11 February by a Counter Declaration.

On 4 March France also declared a State of War existed against Spain; a war in which Portugal was involved.

1793

16 February, Nautilus, 16 guns   HM sloop *Nautilus*, 16 guns, was chased into Plymouth Sound by two large French privateers of 28 guns each; and at Plymouth on the same date, a French privateer with 16 carriage guns and some swivels came within a league of Penlee Point, although in the Sound were two line of battle ships, a 50-gun ship, two sloops of war and a cutter. The privateer then tacked about and stood to the east-south-east. (*Times*, 27 February 1793)

20 March, Pelican, privateer   At 2pm, as the *Pelican* privateer of Liverpool was cruising in the Mersey, by a sudden gust of wind she overset and instantly went to the bottom. The vessel was manned by 94 seamen and had on board 40 passengers at the time of the accident. Of this total, 102 lost their lives. The accident was said to have been caused by the guns being loose and when the ship heeled over, the weather guns ran across the deck and broke through the lee ports, when the ship immediately went to the bottom, in shallow water, as her masts were partially visible at low tide. (*Times*, 23 March 1793)

12 April, small boat at Newhaven   'The following melancholy and distressing catastrophe happened at Newhaven. As thirteen men, artificers and labourers, employed on the new piers at that place, were crossing the river, the rapid and resistless current overset their boat, when six of them were drowned. The other seven were with great difficulty saved.' (*AR*, 1793, Chr, p17)

13 May, George's boat   At 10pm, at Dock (Devonport), as a boat belonging to the *George*, from Milford, was going from North Corner to Keyham Point, where the magazines were situated, the shifting thwart of the boat on which a man was sitting gave way and the end of it went through her bottom. As there was a 3-pounder gun in the boat, she sank at once and one man lost his life. (*Times*, 17 May 1793)

17 August, Southampton's boat   This evening, at 7.30pm, a six-oared cutter belonging to HMS *Southampton* was going from the ship in Plymouth Sound with a westerly gale blowing and a heavy sea running, when she got amidst the breakers near the Cobbler's Reef and soon filled. The boat's crew, consisting of two midshipmen, captain's steward, coxswain and six seamen, were all washed out of her by the violence of the sea before any assistance could be given them, but the six seamen got hold of the gunwale of the boat and held on till rescued. The two midshipmen, Mr Grant and Mr Godfrey, together with the steward and coxswain, were all drowned. (*Times*, 21 August 1793)

27 August, Tweed, merchantman The *Tweed*, Captain Pinter, from Sunderland to Bridport, ran on shore on the Shingles, between Hurst Castle and the Needles, and was lost during a gale. (*Times*, 28 August 1793)

27 August, Westbury, merchantman News arrived in England that the *Westbury*, Captain Fisher, from Archangel to Bristol, was lost on Archangel Bar during a gale. The crew and some cargo were saved. (*Times*, 28 August 1793)

9 November, Madona, East Indiaman At 1am, the *Madona*, an East Indiaman, of London, Captain Allardice, from Ostend in ballast, with a lieutenant of the navy, his wife, three passengers and a crew of sixteen, struck on the Goodwins and soon went to pieces. One man was taken up by the *Flora*, of Broadstairs, and carried in there; he had lashed himself to a hen coop and part of the mizzen mast, and by that means was saved. He stated that the pilot and the captain were both drunk when the ship ran aground, but this was later denied by other survivors. These twelve men and a boy were taken up at sea, floating on a piece of the wreck, by a Yarmouth lugger and carried into that place. (*Times*, 15 November 1793)

20 November, Le Scipion, 74 guns Le Scipion[8] was taken on 29 August 1793 by Lord Hood at Toulon, and with the British squadron, under the command of Rear-Admiral Cosby, was in Leghorn harbour to take on provisions and livestock for the populace of Toulon. The ship was captained by M de Goy, and had a crew of 600 Frenchmen, who had come away from Toulon and the Republican cause; but many of the 600 were invalids and, most unfortunately, the entire crew were on board at the time of the accident.

At 3pm, large volumes of smoke were observed issuing from various parts of the ship, followed shortly after by flames which caught the rigging and sails; the crew then began jumping overboard, everyone striving to escape with his life. Boats belonging to the British, Spanish and Neapolitan men-of-war picked up many of those in the sea, but the invalids were not so fortunate; of the 600 members of the crew on board when the fire started, 390 perished. Captain M de Goy died with his ship. To this loss must be added a great quantity of livestock and all manner of provisions destined for Toulon. The ship was reckoned to be worth one million piastres.

By 4pm, all the rigging and masts were seen to be on fire; the gunports resembling so many furnaces. The guns, loaded with grape or roundshot, were continually going off, and the whole threatened to set fire to the rest of the shipping in the harbour. Rear-Admiral Cosby, aware of the danger to his ships and aware also that the magazines of *Le Scipion* contained 300 barrels of gunpowder, immediately put to sea with the squadron. Shortly afterwards, the French ship, completely on fire and fanned by a strong offshore breeze, drifted past the other ships and out to sea. About 8pm, *Le Scipion* was four Italian miles[9] from the port when the magazines blew up and the ship disintegrated. The next morning the only thing to be seen was a part of the hull, afloat, full of coals and covered in bodies.

The accident was said to have been caused by a barrel of brandy being set on fire by a candle which was burning near it. Within a few days, workmen began sweeping for the cannon, for which they were allowed one-third of the value of those they could recover. (*AR*, 1793, Chr, p54)

2 December, fire at Wapping At 4.30pm, fire broke out on a ship laden with wine, lying at Hawley's wharf, not far from Hermitage Stairs, at Wapping. The fire soon communicated to two other vessels, and the three ships then burnt to the water's edge. Several other ships were anchored nearby, and although it was low water, yet from the exertions of the fire engines, no further losses occurred. The fire was so great that it was clearly visible from Maidenhead Bridge, 29 miles away. (*Times*, 3 December 1793)

6 December, Intrepid, 64 guns *Intrepid*, a 64-gun ship, Captain Carpenter, arrived at Dock (Devonport) from Corunna after a rough passage. The following day 160 crew were taken to the naval hospital, probably suffering from louse typhus. (*Times*, 10 December 1793)

Intrepid was old, built at Woolwich in 1770. (*NC* Vol 1, p551)

9 December, Severn, 44 guns The *Severn*, 44 guns, Captain Minchin, sailed from Quebec on 10 November and arrived at Plymouth on this day. During her voyage she met with severe gales and had to throw overboard fourteen guns and cut two anchors from her bows to prevent foundering. (*Times*, 13 December 1793)

15 December, Pigmy, 14 guns 'His Majesty's cutter *Pigmy*, of 14 guns, Lt Pulliblank, sailed from Torbay on the morning of the 15th, with the wind at SSW bound to Plymouth. In the course of the day, the wind veered farther south, and increased to a violent gale, attended with very hazy weather. About six o'clock in the evening they found themselves very near the shore, abreast of Motherbank [Mothecombe], a small inlet 12 miles east of the port of Plymouth, dividing it from Dartmouth, which place it is said they mistook for the entrance of Plymouth Sound. The sea running very high, and the wind right on the shore, they were under the necessity of letting go two anchors to prevent her drifting on the rocks; the anchors held fast for about two hours, at which time the cutter began to drive; one of the boats with five people on board then put off from her, and fortunately reached the shore, though one of the seamen was drowned in the attempt.

'At nine o'clock the cutter drifted to the rocks, and fell broadside on, when the crew began cutting away the mast, which very providentially fell towards the shore, and afforded an opportunity for the officers and crew to save themselves, the greater part of whom, by all means, reached the rocks in safety. The commander, Lt Pulliblank, as the crew report, could not be prevailed on to leave the cutter, though by tarrying he had nothing but inevitable destruction before him, and this officer, with about eleven others (the number not exactly ascertained), were unfortunately drowned, and the cutter by eleven o'clock at night was dashed to atoms. The crew, when the cutter sailed from Torbay, consisted of 65 persons; there was also on board a woman, the wife of one of the sailors, that had the day before been delivered of a child, who together with the infant was miraculously saved.[10]

'The country people, on hearing signal guns of distress, went down the Roads with lanthorns, and gave every assistance in their power towards saving the crew, but the cutter was so situated that nothing could prevent her from being totally destroyed.' This article is copied verbatim from *The Times*, 19 December 1793.

The *Sherborne and Yeovil Mercury* article which follows is also given verbatim:

'Sunday evening HM cutter *Pigmy*, commanded by Lt Abraham Pulliblank, was lost at the entrance of Arm harbour,[11] near the village of Mothecombe, in Bigberry Bay; she was one of Macbride's squadron, whom she parted with at Guernsey the preceding day, and arrived at Torbay the Sunday morning, from whence she sailed for this port (Plymouth). But the weather being extremely hazy all day, and the wind foul, the pilot mistook Bigberry Bay for the entrance of the Sound, and before the mistake was discovered, the cutter was too near the shore to preserve her; two anchors were however let go, but to no purpose, as she struck, and before eleven o'clock went to pieces. The commander and five others perished in her, as they positively refused to quit her. The remainder (about sixty in number) were saved on the mast and in the boats; very little of her materials are saved.' (*SYM*, 23 December 1793)

The *Pigmy* had been built at King's shipyard at Dover and launched in February 1781. Commanded by Lt Thomas Dyson, the vessel was driven on shore at Dunkirk during a gale and there taken possession of by the French on 22 December 1781. She was retaken in July 1782 and renamed *Lurcher* on 31 May 1783. Just two months later the name reverted to the original. (*SNL*, 31 January 1783)

24 December, Raisonnable, 64 guns The 64-gun *Raisonnable*, Captain Lord Cranstoun, had been at sea for six months prior to her arrival at Falmouth on this Christmas Eve. One hundred and eighty of her crew were ill and taken to hospital. The vessel was old, built at Chatham and launched in 1768; because she had been so long at sea, and her crew numbered 500, it is reasonable to assume that the ship, like the *Intrepid* eighteen days earlier, had some form of typhus. (*Times*, 30 December 1793)

1794

7 January, Betsey, collier; Abigail, slaver; Concordia, merchantman The *Betsey*, Captain Hutcheson, was a collier laden for Aalborg, Denmark, when she was driven ashore during a gale and wrecked near Als, about 15 miles south of the Lim fiord, the passageway to Aalborg. A slaver, the *Abigail*, from Africa for Jamaica, was taken by a French privateer and carried into Martinique. The *Concordia*, Captain Brower, from St Petersberg for Spain, went on shore near Lessoe, in the Kattegat, and was completely wrecked. (*Times*, 15 January 1794; dates not given or known)

25 January, St Patrick, packet From Liverpool for Ireland, the *St Patrick* packet was wrecked during a gale at Amlwch, Anglesey, where, although the twenty-eight passengers all lost their lives, the crew managed to save their own. Nevertheless, when they made land, they were robbed by the miners of the Parys copper mine who had gathered for that purpose. (*Times*, 5 February 1794)

29 January, Hope, privateer A cutter privateer mounting 10 guns, the *Hope*, Captain Neale, sailed from Liverpool for Gibraltar with a crew of forty, but was totally wrecked near Stanner Point on the day she sailed. The entire crew perished on the sands, where five of them were cast up lashed together. (*Times*, 31 January 1794)

30 January, Amphitrite, 24 guns A 24-gun vessel, the *Amphitrite*, Captain Anthony Hunt, was lost in the Mediterranean by striking on a submerged rock near Elba, off the coast of Tuscany. The crew were saved. (*SNL*, 1799; and *NC* Vol 1, p347)

8 February, Convert, frigate and convoy Captain Thompson, of the merchant ship *Diana*, arrived in the Downs from Jamaica on 16 March 1794, and wrote to his owners on the following day: 'I arrived here in thirty-six days from Jamaica. I left the island on 6th February under convoy of the *Convert* frigate, with about fifty sail. I am sorry to add that my time under her protection was of short duration, as the frigate with nine sail of the convoy was unfortunately wrecked between twelve and one o'clock on the morning of the 8th. At daylight I was a spectator of their total destruction on a reef that lies to the east of Grand Cayman. The fleet stood on and off until three o'clock in the afternoon, endeavouring to get the people off, but I having no boats could give no assistance and immediately set sail. I cannot give you the names of any but the *Sally* of Kingston.' (*Times*, 18 March 1794)

The *Convert*, Captain John Lawford, was formerly *L'Inconstante* and was taken from the French by the *Penelope* and the *Iphigenia* in the Bight of Leogane, St Domingo, on 25 November 1793.

10 February, Property, merchantman The *Property*, Captain Boden, from London for Newcastle and Teignmouth, was wrecked near Blyth, Northumberland, and all the crew perished. (*Times*, 12 February 1794)

12 February, Spitfire, schooner The *Spitfire*, an 8-gun schooner, Lt T W Rich, commander, overset at 7am on 12 February in the Canal de la Mona, off the east end of San Domingo. Four seamen were the only survivors; they were picked up by the sloop *Saucy Tom*, Captain Edmonson, after four hours in the water. (*Times*, 19 April 1794)

4 March, Ann, collier The sloop *Ann*, a collier of Fowey, Captain Mills, laden with coals from Wales, was wrecked during a gale near Bantham, in Bigbury Bay. Although the vessel and cargo were completely lost and the crew were several times washed overboard, even so they managed with difficulty to save themselves. (*Times*, 11 March 1794)

? April, Ardent, 64 guns The exact date during April when the *Ardent* was lost appears to be unknown. The *Ardent* was a Third Rate 64-gun ship, built in 1782, and captained by Robert Manners Sutton. The ship was stationed off Villefranche-sur-Mer, between Nice and Monaco; her duty was to watch two French frigates and the convoy they were protecting. It was while the *Ardent* was engaged on this duty that she was assumed to have caught fire and blew up. [Her quarterdeck was found with some of the gun-locks sticking in the beams; and the marks of the splinter netting deeply impressed on the deck left no doubt that the whole was the effect of explosion (Brenton, ed, 1837, p302-303).] Of the crew, who totalled more than 500, there were no survivors to relate the unfortunate circumstances of the *Ardent*'s loss. (*SNL*, 1794)

30 April, Commerce, merchantman A fine copper bottomed merchant ship mounting 16 guns, the *Commerce*, Captain Bell, was on passage from Jamaica for Liverpool when, on this day, the vessel was wrecked on St Mary's Cape, Placentia Bay, Newfoundland, yet only one person was lost. The captain, mate and passengers took their passage on board a cartel with 250 French prisoners of war, and were taken out by the *Two Friends*, an American ship, and carried to Falmouth. The survivors, prior to being rescued, were eight days on the rocks, with only a pig, also a survivor, albeit an unfortunate one, to sustain them. (*Times*, 15 July 1794)

1 June, Battle of 'Glorious First of June' The *Brunswick*, Captain John Harvey [made post 1777], and *Le Vengeur*, Captain Renaudin, each of 74 guns, were part of the British and French fleets, when for more than two hours on this day they fought an action at close quarters, which left both almost complete wrecks. At 1.30pm the *Brunswick*, with her mizzen mast gone, 45 dead and more than 100 wounded, ceased firing and steered to the north for a British port. *Le Vengeur*, with her fore and main masts over the side, continued to wallow until 7pm, at which time, with her colours flying, she foundered, taking with her 625 brave French heroes. (*SNL*, 1794)

James, in his 1826 edition, states that at 6.15pm *Le Vengeur* was approached by boats of the *Alfred, Culloden* and *Rattler*, which saved about 400 of *Le Vengeur*'s crew. Captain Harvey was wounded by a splinter, had an arm amputated, and died. (James, p164)

British losses on this 'Glorious' day: 296 killed, 844 wounded.

28 June, Rose, 28 guns   The *Rose*, a 28-gun Sixth Rate, Captain Matthew Henry Scott, was wrecked on Rocky Point, south-east Jamaica; her crew were saved. (*SNL*, 1794)

14 July, Hound, 16 guns   A 16-gun sloop of war, the *Hound*, Commander Richard Piercy, was returning from the West Indies when she was taken by two French frigates, *La Seine*, 42 guns, and the *Galatee*, 44 guns. Although the *Hound* was not wrecked, the sequel is interesting, for both the French ships eventually were.

La *Seine* was taken by the British ships *Jason* [Captain Charles Stirling], *Mermaid* and *La Pique* [Captain David Milne], off the Saints in the Passage Breton, on 29 June 1798, and was taken on the strength of the Royal Navy; the vessel was wrecked during the night of 21 July 1803 (*qv*). The *Galatee* was wrecked near the Penmarks on 23 April 1795, but of this French vessel, little information is forthcoming. The *Galatee* should not be confused with the British 32-gun frigate, built at Portsmouth in 1794 and named *Galatea*. (*SNL*, 1799; Norie, 1827, p409)

19 July, Sarah and Elizabeth, whaler   The *Sarah and Elizabeth*, a Greenlander, was returning from whaling in the Davis Strait, when about 4pm, then being about nine leagues off St Abb's Head, she was fired on by the *Aurora* frigate, Captain William Essington, when she hoisted her colours and, being to windward, at the second shot bore down on the frigate.

Most of the crew had in the meantime got between decks and secured the hatches to prevent being impressed. A boat's crew from the frigate then went on board, followed shortly after by another of armed men, when one of the frigate's men took the helm. About 5pm the *Aurora* went alongside, and as the crew would not come on deck, the boatswain of the *Aurora*, holding a grenade in one hand and a lighted match in the other, asked Captain Essington if he should fire the grenade amongst the people, which his captain then ordered him to do; but on being told by the master of the *Sarah and Elizabeth* that the ship was full of oil and would blow up, he desisted. They then commenced to break up the hatches with crows, but the men still refusing to come on deck, the *Aurora*'s captain ordered the eighteen marines to fire down the hatchway, by which fire one man was killed and three badly wounded. The crew of the ship asked for quarters long before the marines ceased firing, yet ordered by their officers to do so. The greater part of the crew of the *Sarah and Elizabeth*, together with the wounded men, were taken on board the *Aurora* and put in irons, and were still in irons on 1 August.

The *Sarah and Elizabeth* arrived at Hull on Wednesday 23 July, when the body of the dead man, Edward Begg, carpenter's mate, was landed and a verdict was taken before William Watson Bolton, coroner. The jury were unanimous in bringing a verdict of wilful murder [see also 30 November 1794] against the captain and part of the crew of the *Aurora*; whereupon the owners of the *Sarah and Elizabeth* instituted a prosecution against them. The wounded men were Hugh Brooke, boatswain, William Barker, line coiler, and Richard Hubey, seaman.

Captain Essington wrote a letter[12] to the Mayor of Hull, defending his action. He stated that the crew of the merchantman were in a state of mutiny and fired at one of the officers first. (*Times*, 1 August 1794)

Captain Essington became Sir William Essington and was promoted to Rear-Admiral of the Blue on 23 April 1804. (*NC* vol 11, p343)

8 August, overcrowded boat Many men lose their lives at sea, more from sheer recklessness than from misadventure; probably the most unfortunate example of this occurred on this day at Cowes. One would have thought it impossible for twenty-eight men to crowd into a 14-foot boat, yet on this day, it actually happened.

At 8am on this summer morning, a party from one of the transports, under convoy of the *Nonsuch*, 64 guns, lying at anchor at Cowes for Jersey, obtained permission to land so that they might bathe from the shore. Returning to their ship, with the wind blowing strong from the north, and the tide on the ebb, the small boat in which they were not being more than 14 feet long, and they totalling twenty-eight persons, overset, when sixteen soldiers of the 32nd Regiment and two seamen were drowned; the others were picked up with difficulty by harbour boats. (*Times*, 11 August 1794)

29 August, L'Impetueux, 74 guns *L'Impetueux*, one of the six prizes taken by Lord Howe's fleet on the 'Glorious First of June' this year, was lying out of commission in Portsmouth harbour when she accidentally caught fire and was burnt to the water's edge. At Portsmouth on 31 August an enquiry was held, as it was suspected that some Spaniards or Toulonese had deliberately fired the vessel. However, it was proved to have been an accident, caused when these same people were shovelling damaged powder out of the magazine; they were using iron-bound shovels which struck the nails and sparks set the powder on fire. (*Times*, 1 September 1794)

13 October The *Bud*, Captain Matthews, arrived at Liverpool on 4 November, when the captain reported the following. On 19 September he spoke the *Orion*, Captain Cooke, from Jamaica for London, in latitude 30°. On 13 October he saw a yellow-sided vessel, bottom up, which appeared to have been lately overset as there were several casks floating around her, and the bottom appeared to have been newly payed [tarred]. There were apparently no survivors.

Captain Matthews also reported that the ship *Maryford*, from Tobago for London, was found at sea off the Newfoundland Banks with no-one on board, by the *George* of Boston, from Virginia for Amsterdam. The *George* put some men on board and sent the *Maryford* to Boston. (*Times*, 5 November 1794)

26 November, Southampton, merchantman At 10am, as the ship *Southampton* was warping from the Catwater into Plymouth Sound, she went ashore on the Cobbler's Reef and as the tide ebbed she fell on her starboard side. The crew cut away the masts to ease the ship, but to no avail; the ship's back was broken with the sea making a clear breach over her, so that she shortly became a complete wreck. (*Times*, 29 November 1794) [The article also stated that the *Southampton* was of 300 tons burthen and at the time of her going ashore the wind was very moderate at WNW and the sea smooth.]

26 November, Pylades, 16 guns Lt Thomas Twysden of the *Pylades*, 16 guns, sailed from Leith Roads to watch the French squadron at Bergen, but two days later, during a gale, the *Pylades* lost her main yard and suffered other damage. However, once the gale had passed, Lt Twysden proceeded to carry out his orders and for some days cruised off Bergen. On his return from there, being overtaken by a southerly gale, he was obliged to bear away for the Shetlands, but being unable to gain Lerwick, he could only make Haroldswick Bay on the Isle of Unst, where he failed to get into any harbour because of the sea that was running. Together with the lack of daylight at that season of the year, and having thrown all the guns of the *Pylades* overboard and being so very unfortunate as to lose his bower cables and anchors, he was then lucky enough to ride to a small anchor till a pilot came on board by whose direction the *Pylades* was swung upon a sandbank which was the only means left of saving the lives of those on board, as there was a reef under her stern which she was then drifting upon. On the 26th all the crew got safely on shore but the ship was a total wreck. (*Times*, 16 December 1794)

26 November, unknown wreck The *Times* reported that the Dutch galliot *Zee* had arrived at Plymouth on Saturday 22 November with the following news:

'On the previous day when about eight leagues south of the Scillies, the *Zee* passed the wreck of a wine laden vessel with many pipes of wine floating near her.' (*Times*, 26 November 1794)

26 November, Virginia, merchantman On Thursday 11 December arrived at Port Glasgow, Captain George Price of the ship *Virginia*, of Peterburgh, Virginia, with his second mate, the ship's carpenter and three seamen, they being the only survivors of the crew of this vessel lately lost on her passage from the Clyde to America. Captain Price related their misfortunes as due chiefly to the bad weather the ship encountered.

On 19 November the *Virginia* sailed from the Clyde in ballast and with seven passengers on board, namely a Mr Murdoch of Paisley, his wife, two children and a sister-in-law, together with a maidservant and a Mr Dixon as well as the captain and crew, altogether twenty-two souls; and by Monday the 24th had got as far on her passage as position 56°N 19°W, when about 6pm they discovered that the ship had sprung a leak, and soon after had five feet of water in her hold. This induced the master to bear away for Ireland, the wind blowing hard from the NNW, but though both pumps were constantly going, the water gained on them until the following Wednesday about 3pm, when it had increased to seven feet and was still rising. The passengers and crew, so fatigued by the pumping, could continue no longer, and as the ship must inevitably sink in a short while, they resolved to take to the longboat.

Having provided themselves with a few necessaries such as bread in bags and some barrels of porter (for all the water casks were stove), they all embarked in the boat, but less than fifteen minutes later they shipped a sea and in a moment of panic they threw all the provisions overboard to prevent her sinking. Four hundred miles from land the prospect was bleak. They continued scudding with one sail before the wind which blew excessively hard but always from the west and continued to do so until about 2pm on the Saturday afternoon when they saw the Irish coast and made every effort to gain it, but the wind shifting to the southward they were forced to bear away for Islay. During the night they suffered extreme hardships from hunger and the cold, as well as being soaked by the spray, and on Sunday morning the servant girl and one of the seamen were found dead, Mrs Murdoch nearly so and Dixon the passenger and three of the seamen bereft of reason. About noon on Sunday they saw Islay and about 4pm they nearly gained the shore and attempted to land on the north-west side. But a strong ebb tide and heavy surf swept the boat upon a reef where they all perished except those mentioned earlier who managed to save themselves by scrambling up the rocks. In a few moments the boat was smashed to pieces and those who had survived endeavoured to save others not so fortunate; but they were too weak and the surge too rough so that the task was beyond them.

When hope for the others had gone the six proceeded a short way from the shore where they came to a house which proved to be that of

Alexander Campbell of Ormsey. They stayed eight days, during which time all the bodies but one were found and decently buried.

When last seen from the boat, the *Virginia* was lying over with her lower yards in the water. (*Times*, 24 December 1794)

29 November, Wildman, West Indiaman   The *Wildman*, Captain Cundall, from London for Jamaica, took the ground at the back of Ramsgate with eight feet of water in her hold. On 1 December the ship caught fire and was burnt to the water's edge. It was believed that the *Wildman* caught fire in consequence of the large amount of lime in her hold, which the generality of West Indies merchantmen always carried and which heated by the sea striking the vessel and the water entering the hold.

The *Wildman* was one of the finest vessels engaged in the trade, being a new ship of three decks and capable of carrying 800 hogsheads of sugar. (*Times*, 1, 3, 6 December 1794)

30 November, Maria, merchantman   The *Maria*, Captain Randle, from Newfoundland, arrived in Steedland Bay (Studland Bay) having some passengers on board as well as the crew. The officers of the Impress Service, expecting to meet some resistance, had called for the military and twenty armed soldiers went on board the tender which went down the harbour to meet the vessel, upon which, when going alongside the *Maria*, and finding the people [crew] obstinate, orders were given to fire, which they did. The pilot (then at the helm) and two other men were killed instantly, and several others were so dangerously wounded that two of them died shortly afterwards.

The town of Poole was in a state of uproar; Lts Glover and Phillips, together with all on board the tender, were taken into custody and an inquest was held on the body of the pilot, when a verdict of wilful murder was returned. (*Times*, 3 December 1794) (*SYM*, 8 December 1794)

6 December, Success, merchantman   The *Success*, Captain Coutts, from Norway for Cork, was lost on the Isle of Skye; a part of the cargo was saved. (*Times*, 3 January 1795)

10 December, Diana, merchantman   The ship *Diana*, Captain Walker, from Martinique for Lancaster, was taken in the North Channel by a French privateer and sunk; the crew were taken to France. (*Times*, 1 January 1795)

17 December, Ceres, transport   The *Ceres* transport, of North Shields, Samuel Fisher master, sailed from Martinique on 22 October with thirty-one other ships in convoy, and arrived at Plymouth on 17 December.

On the voyage home, 22 men and 12 women and children died. (*Times*, 20 December 1794)

21 December, Mary, merchantman The *Mary*, Mahony master, was laden with butter for London when she was wrecked a short distance outside Cork harbour. There were no survivors. (*Times*, 1 January 1795)

22 December, Countess of Findlater and Lady Jane, merchantmen The *Countess of Findlater*, from London for Banff, was wrecked in a gale 18 miles to the north of Aberdeen, near the Kirkton of Slains. (*Times*, 1 January 1795)

    Also on this day, the *Peterel* sloop of war was cruising off Ostend when she fell in with and retook the *Lady Jane*, of Hull, Wray master, from Danzig for London, which ship had been taken by the *Nice*, a French brig, ten days previously. The *Peterel* put on board the *Lady Jane* Mr Soames, their master, a midshipman, Mr Melville and ten seamen. Bearing away to gain the land, the vessel that night struck on the Shipwash, 15 miles east of Harwich. The *Lady Jane* was seen to break up and all on board perished. (*Times*, 5 January 1795)

? December, Express Lottery, packet About the third week in December, the Irish *Express Lottery* boat was presumed lost in crossing from Dublin, when she was run foul of by the *Carolina* packet, which carried away one of her masts; and not very long afterwards, was run foul again by the *Liverpool* packet which carried away her other mast and bowsprit and otherwise damaged her.

    In that condition, the only hope for her was to drift down to the Isle of Man, which fortunately she did; some fishing boats put off and towed her to the Skerries lighthouse [Rockabill, Co Dublin] and from thence to Dublin. The crew experienced the greatest hardship, due not only to short allowance, but also to the severe gales that were encountered. (*Times*, 5 January 1795)

30 December, Apollo, 38 guns The *Apollo* frigate, 38 guns, put into Yarmouth with the loss of her rudder, after being on the Leman and Ower sandbank [north-east of Cromer], during which time the crew had to throw overboard several of the guns.

    The *Apollo* was a new vessel and had been built at Woolwich just a few months prior to the accident. (*Times*, 1 January 1795)

1795

19 January, Prince of Wales, coaster A small vessel of 50 tons burthen, the *Prince of Wales*, of St Ives, laden with copper ore for the smelter at Neath, came to an anchor about a league off Swansea harbour on Sunday evening, 18 January. From some unknown cause, the vessel foundered about 7am on the following morning, when Captain Simcock and his crew all perished. (*Times*, 31 January 1795)

25 January, the French Brest fleet   On this day one of the most disastrous weeks in the history of the French Marine commenced. After the series of battles from 28 May until 1 June 1794, with the English fleet under Lord Howe, the greatest part of the French fleet returned to Brest for necessary repairs, etc, but the Committee of Public Safety [a nine-person body created 6 April 1793] soon insisted that the fleet, commanded by Admiral Villaret-Joyeuse, put to sea again. At the beginning of December, the government decided to send six ships, under the command of Rear-Admiral Renaudin, to Toulon; the Brest squadron was to sail with this division.

The Minister, M d'Albarade, wrote several dispatches to hasten the repair work, but the port authorities encountered great problems in getting the ships ready for sea, due to lack of materials and supplies. Difficulties were such that the administration of the port of Brest had to overcome the greatest obstacles in order to supply a month's provisions to all the ships; even so, some sailed with only fifteen days' supplies. The ships of Admiral Renaudin were the only vessels to have provisions for several months; yet not a single detail of this state of affairs reached the Minister. Some officers who had been ordered to Paris and consulted on the possibility of a new sortie had strenuously protested against all such ideas. It was then that the Committee of Public Safety, displeased with the opposition it encountered and wanting to prevent all further objections to the proposal, sent Admiral Villaret the peremptory order to sail.

On 24 December the 110-gun *Revolutionnaire*, a three-decker, trying to get under way, struck on the Maingan Roche and became a complete loss. The 74-gun *Redoubtable*, had it not been for the skill and presence of mind of her captain, M Moncousu, would have shared the same fate; as it was, the latter ship lost all her boats and anchors.

On 29 December Admiral Villaret-Joyeuse led his fleet into Camaret Roads, from whence they sailed next day. With the loss of the *Revolutionnaire*, the Brest fleet now consisted of 34 ships of the line (four three-deckers, three 80s and the remainder 74s), 13 frigates and 16 corvettes, avisos and tenders, making the whole 62 ships of war.

The dispatch of the Brest squadron at this season exhibited a complete ignorance of their business on the part of the naval directorate, for some ships had received very incomplete repairs to the battle damage of the previous June, due largely to the inadequacy of the port's resources. Several vessels were only jury-rigged and the rigging in very bad condition. Some ships were old: the *Revolutionnaire*, formerly the *Bretagne*, was launched on 24 May 1766, then rebuilt and relaunched on 7 April 1777; and the *Scipion*, formerly *St Esprit*, was launched on 12 October 1765. Even if we exclude battle damage, many of these old ships no longer had the strength to withstand rough seas and should have been placed in reserve.

Whilst Admiral Villaret had intended to keep in the offing of the French coast, once at sea, the squadron experienced several easterly gales which drove the ships off the coast and by 25 January the fleet had fetched 150 leagues from Brest. Damage rapidly increased on those ships which were already in an unseaworthy condition. The gales worsened and in the storm which raged from 25 to 29 January, three of the largest vessels foundered. First to go was the *Neuf Thermidor*, formerly the *Jacobin* of 80 guns, which went down with nearly the whole of her crew, many of them on account of the fore and main masts falling on the quarterdeck. The following day, the 26th, the 80-gun *Scipion* with a crew of 970 foundered, but by good fortune nearly all were saved. The third vessel to founder was the 74-gun *Superbe*, Captain Colomb; formerly named *Temeraire*, the ship had been launched on 21 November 1784. On 26 January Captain Colomb informed Admiral Villaret that his ship was taking on more water than the pumps could free her of. The guns and shot were jettisoned but to no avail and Admiral Villaret ordered the evacuation of the ship. The crew of 800 were taken off by three vessels – *La Montagne*, the 74-gun *Montagnard* and *Le Papillon*. On 30 January, when the water was up to the orlop deck, Captain Colomb quit his ship and within five minutes of his leaving, the vessel foundered. Twenty-one of the crew perished because the ship overset before they were clear of her.

On 30 January the wind backed to north-west which permitted some of the fleet to return to Brest; others were not so fortunate. The 74-gun *Neptune* only escaped foundering by the crew running the ship aground on the mud flats of Perros-Guirec, from which she could not be refloated. The 74-gun *Temeraire* succeeded in reaching St Malo when on the point of going down. The 74-gun *Fougueux* put into port on the Ile de Groix. The 74-gun *Convention* reached Lorient with great difficulty. The 110-gun *Majesteux*, a three-decker, was so leaky that she could hardly be kept afloat, even at her moorings. This vessel and the 80-gun *Revolutionnaire* both had seven feet of water in their holds. If the north-west winds had blown for a day longer, these ships would also have disappeared.

The 20-gun *Daphne*, Captain William Edward Cracraft, seventy British merchantmen and 1500 British prisoners were the trophies taken from the British blockading fleet during this terrible winter. [The *SYM* for 26 January 1795 reads: 'Sir Joseph Bankes's and Dr Garthshore's glasses agree in having fallen to 23, by far the lowest freezing point ever known in this climate. *Note that 23 inches of mercury represents a barometric pressure of 778...* The Thames is frozen over at Battersea Bridge and at Execution Dock, so as to admit persons to cross backwards and forwards on the ice... The tide rose to such a height on Thursday (22nd) as to do considerable damage to the shipping below London Bridge, from the ponderous ice floes.

At Limehouse, 200 vessels were driven ashore and damaged. One lighter laden with coals was entirely lost'.] Such advantages as were obtained were feeble compensation for such a great disaster. (O Troude, *Batailles navales de la France*, Paris, 1867, vol 2, pp404, 407; E Chevalier, *Histoire de la Marine Française*, Paris, 1886; Captain E P Brenton, *The Naval History of Great Britain*, London, 1823/24; *SYM*, 26 January and 16 February 1795)

1 February, unknown West Indiaman   Malbay in west County Clare is six miles long and when the wind is in the south-west quarter presents a lee shore with no shelter. On this day a large ship, supposed to have been a West Indiaman, was lost with her entire crew. Several puncheons of rum and hogsheads of coffee and sugar floated ashore, but nothing to indicate the name of the vessel. (*Times*, 11 February 1795)

7 February, West India convoy   Often, waiting for a ship was more danger-ous than being involved in a shipwreck, as this article in *The Times* proves.
     The report is dated Plymouth, 7 February: 'The troops which have been here so long waiting for the West India convoy, have suffered consider-ably; a great number have died and last week seventy were buried in one day.[13] At Stock (Stoke), about half a mile from Plymouth, one regiment of six hundred has lost four hundred dead and the remainder not fit for duty.
     'The 2nd and 45th Regiments of Foot, that arrived here last night from Yarmouth to join the troops here, have been ordered to Portsmouth. They are sickly owing to the miserable and unhealthy state of the bedding on board, which is certainly infected.' (*Times*, 10 February 1795)

9 February, West India convoy   Another report from Plymouth: 'At six o'clock this evening orders were given to disembark all regiments that cannot muster four hundred duty men. The seven hundred merchant ships at Plymouth are ordered to Portsmouth, to shelter till the Grand Fleet can sail.' (*Times*, 12 February 1795)

14 March, Illustrious, 74 guns   The British and French fleets fought an action in the Gulf of Genoa after which the British bore away for Spezia, leaving the *Meleager* towing the *Illustrious* (Captain Thomas Lenox Fred-erick). However, the two ships soon ran into very rough seas which caused them to anchor in Valence Bay, near Avenza, where the *Illustrious* parted her cables and drifted on shore. Although every attempt was made to get the ship off, her crew were eventually forced to abandon and set fire to the vessel. (*SNL*, 1795)

1 May, Boyne, 98 guns   At 11am of 1 May, a fire broke out on board the *Boyne* of 98 guns, commanded by Captain George Grey, at Spithead. The flames burst through the poop before the fire was discovered and spread so rapidly that in less than half an hour the vessel was completely on fire. Every effort by the crew to extinguish the blaze was futile, but as soon as the other ships in the harbour became aware of the situation, boats were sent to her assistance, by which fortunate circumstance most were rescued, only eleven persons losing their lives. (*Times*, 4, 15, 27 May 1795)

All the guns on the *Boyne*, being loaded, went off as they became heated, some shot falling amongst the shipping whilst other shot reached the shore at Stokes Bay. Two men on board the *Queen Charlotte* were killed and another wounded.

About 1.30pm the *Boyne* burnt her cables and drifted to the eastward till she grounded on the Spit, opposite Southsea Castle, where the vessel continued to burn till 6pm when the fire reached the magazine and she blew up. It was never ascertained exactly how the fire originated; the most probable cause appeared to be that part of the lighted paper from the cartridges of the marines, who were exercising and firing on the windward side of the ship, blew into the admiral's cabin and set papers or other materials on fire. (*NC*, vol 6, p269 et seq)

? May, Mount Pleasant, transport   A large fleet sailed from England on 14 May, destination the West Indies, but on the 18th when off the Bay of Biscay, the fleet was overtaken by a violent south-westerly gale when most of the ships were dispersed, yet sixteen managed to keep together and joined by the 64-gun *Sampson*, reached Kingston on 10 July. One of the fleet that left England on 14 May was the *Mount Pleasant*, a government transport, carrying in addition to her crew 100 dragoons.[14] It was believed at the time that she foundered during the gale of the 18th, or shortly afterwards. There were no survivors. (*Times*, 7 September 1795)

12 June, fire in Paimboeuf harbour   Paimboeuf, situated a few miles east of St Nazaire, was in 1795 an important rope manufacturing town. On 12 June a fire broke out on the *Aurora*, an American ship lying in the harbour, surrounded by other vessels which also caught fire. The *St Nicholas*, *Young Charles*, *Simple Alexander* and the *Mere Cherie* all burnt to the water's edge. Four American sailors died in the blaze which was fanned by a strong NE wind. (*Times*, 1 July 1795)

15 June, Thomas, slaver   The *Thomas*, Captain Millar, was a slave ship trading between the coast of Africa and the West Indies when on her outward voyage she was driven by gale force winds onto the island of Sal, one of the Cape Verde Islands, in daylight. The crew were saved. (*Times*, 31 October 1795)

20 June, Juno, country ship   The *Juno*, Captain Alexander Bremner, was an old ship of 450 tons in a very bad state of repair. The ship was lying at

Rangoon to load teak for Madras. The crew numbered 53, of whom not less than 45 were lascars and the remainder Malays to assist in working the ship. The captain's wife and her maid together with a few Europeans brought the number up to 72.

The *Juno* sailed on the afternoon of 29 May with the young ebb, and almost at once found herself in five to seven fathoms with soft mud and at 6pm the water suddenly shoaled to a quarter less four fathoms. The helm was put sharp a-lee but the ship struck on a hard sandbank where she remained for hours until she floated off with the next tide and no apparent damage.

On 15 June the ship encountered a violent storm which continued for several days during which time the *Juno* sprang such a leak that no amount of pumping was able to free the vessel, although the two pumps together could rid the ship of 50 tons of water an hour. The water increased so much that by the 20th of the month, when in latitude 17°10′N, the water was over the main deck and the crew were of necessity forced to seek refuge in the tops, after they had cut away the main mast to steady the ship. The *Juno* carried two boats, but like the ship herself, they were completely rotten, leaked and were useless for such an environment as the Indian Ocean.

The seas continually sweeping the deck forced the people to remain aloft where most of them were crowded into the mizzen top with little room to spare; several tried to swim to the fore mast to gain that top but four or five died in the attempt and several others, the captain included, died of exposure.

The crew realised that the *Juno* was not going to sink, being kept afloat by the timber cargo, so that their only worry besides hunger and thirst was the fear that the waterlogged ship might take the ground some distance from the shore, because her draught was effectively increased by the height of the vessel.

Several days were to pass before the *Juno* eventually drifted ashore near Cox's Baza [Cox's Bazaar on the south side of the mouth of the Ramoo river]. The crew landed at high tide on the edge of the jungle about six days' travel from Chittagong, although they did not reach the latter place until 28 July. [All of the coastline between Cox's Bazaar and Chittagong is barely above sea level and during the monsoon season is subject to much flooding.]

Before the *Juno* grounded, she had drifted more than 600 miles across the Indian Ocean. (Dalyell, 1812 ed, vol 3, p259)

12 July, boat on Lough Derg   Lough Derg is situated in the south of County Donegal, about four miles to the north of Pettigoe. The lough itself contains several small islands, on one of which, Station Island, is St Patrick's Purgatory, a place of pilgrimage for the faithful.

On this day a boat laden with pilgrims on their way to visit the purgatory, capsized, and 74 poor country people perished. The Roman

Catholic Prelate of Clogher had tried in vain to dissuade the people from the pilgrimage, probably because he was aware the boat was overloaded. (*Times*, 27 July 1795)

13 July, L'Alcide, 74 guns L'Alcide, a French 74-gun ship of the line, fought a running battle with two ships of Admiral Hotham's fleet, the *Culloden* and the *Victory*, off the Hyeres Islands about forty miles from Toulon. The *Culloden* lost her top mast and the *Victory* had her fore topsail yard shot away; *L'Alcide* was so much disabled that by 2pm she ceased firing and was approached by the two French frigates *Alceste* and *Justice* to take her in tow. Yet before this could be effected, *L'Alcide* caught fire, and although every effort was made to save the vessel she soon blew up.

Of *L'Alcide*'s crew of 650 men, only 300 were saved. Combustible materials had been placed in her shrouds, but it was afterwards ascertained that the cause of the tragedy was that the ash from the forges used for heating the cannon balls, had ignited some loose powder which communicated to the magazine. (*Times*, 4 and 11 August 1795; *SNL*, 1795)

23 October, small boat accidents On this Friday night, as some of the musicians of the North Devon regiment of militia were returning to Dartmouth from Totnes, where they had been to attend a ball, the boat upset and eight of the musicians as well as two boatmen were drowned.

This same night two men in a stone boat sailing from Exmouth to Topsham, by carrying too great a press of sail, ran the vessel under water and they also were lost. (*Times*, 4 November 1795)

14 November, disaster off Calais A letter from Calais of the 16th contained the following melancholy intelligence: 'Last week we had six colliers on shore near this harbour. Their captains were allowed to take with them all their personal property and cabin furniture, and were conveyed into private hotels, and four days afterwards they were sent back to England. On Saturday morning, the 14th, at day-break, three ships came on shore with troops; they prove to be Hanoverians and emigrants, and were part of a fleet, seventy in number, bound from Hamburgh to Portsmouth, one of these vessels is supposed to be totally lost, with every soul on board; the second lost fifty men and forty horses; the third lost but little. On board these vessels were about seven hundred men, French and Hanoverians, and near fifty distinguished emigr- ants, among whom are the Duke de Choiseul and M. de Montmorency. It was a shocking sight to see so many fellow-creatures perishing, and not to be able to save them, on account of the high sea. The sands are covered with corpses and dead horses. Had darkness continued for half an hour, half the fleet would have been on shore. Three or four more were on shore, but got off and saved themselves; many women were with the troops.' (*Times*, 20 November 1795)

18 November, Daniel, sloop This was the day a great storm was raging in the Channel, when at 7am the *Daniel*, a sloop of Mevagissey, Captain Pallot, ran foul of the transports in Plymouth Sound, which carried away the sloop's mast, bowsprit and sail, and it was with difficulty that the crew saved the ship from foundering.

Some time later, the spars and sail were seen to drift near the entrance to the Catwater and it was proposed to make an attempt to recover them. Mr Pallot, Mr Elson and Mr Ellis, all masters, together with Mr Davis and Mr Duncalf, both of the Excise cutter of Plymouth, embarked in a boat and made for the place where the spars were floating.

The wind was blowing a gale, the sea running very high, and within a few minutes of the boat leaving the pier it shipped a sea and overset. Three of the men managed to clamber on to the bottom of the boat but a second sea washed them all off again and the five men all drowned within full view of a number of spectators who were unable to render any assistance. (*SYM*, 23 November 1795)

18 November, Mary, brig The brig *Mary* of Plymouth, Captain Hill, laden with salt and coal from Liverpool, went on shore at 11am near Polhawn Cove in Whitsand Bay, and was totally lost. As soon as the ship struck, Captain Hill was washed overboard and drowned, but the rest of the crew managed to save themselves. The shipwreck was caused by the mainsail splitting and the rudder becoming choked. (*SYM*, 23 November 1795)

18 November, Maria Carolina, transport The transport *Maria Carolina*, Captain Prehn, from Hamburg with troops, was wrecked in the storm at Spithead. ['It is said another troop-ship is also totally lost on the Isle of Wight, and only two persons saved.' (*SYM*, 23 November 1795)] (*Times*, 25 November 1795)

18 November, Arethusa's boat A boat belonging to the *Arethusa* frigate, 38 guns, was swamped and foundered on The Bridge, between St Nicholas Island and the main in Plymouth Sound. The seven men on board lost their lives. (*Times*, 19 November 1795)

18 November, Admiral Christian's convoy On Sunday evening 15 November, the outward bound fleet of some 200 ships under the command of Rear-Admiral Christian sailed from St Helens with a favourable wind and on Tuesday the 17th were observed off Exmouth Bar, but the wind shifting to south-south-west the fleet could not then fetch Torbay and had of necessity to put about for Weymouth. The wind increasing to gale force, several of the transports were unable to stand out to sea sufficiently far for them to weather the Isle and Race of Portland, and on the ensuing day, at high tide, several of the vessels struck on the Chisel Bank, a dangerous lee shore, when the wind is in the south-west quarter.

The *Catherine, Piedmont, Thomas* and *Venus* were all wrecked nearly opposite the villages of Langton, Fleet and Chickerell, about four miles to the west of the Passage House; the *Hannah* was driven on shore near Hill's harbour, whilst the *Aeolus* and the *Golden Grove* were both wrecked against part of the Passage House, near where the French frigate *Zenobie* had been wrecked in 1762.[15] The *Commerce* transport, Captain Robinson, with many troops on board was driven on shore near Cumberland Fort and totally lost. The known facts about the ships wrecked on the Chisel Bank are as follows.

The *Catherine of Montrose,* Cromey master, had sailed from Southampton to join the fleet at St Helens, but three of the intending passengers, Cornet Stukely Burns, aged 24, of the 26th Light Dragoons, together with his wife and Lt Stephen Jenner, aged 31, of the 6th West India Regiment, had missed the ship at Southampton and had hired a hoy to enable them to embark at St Helens. Also on board were Lt Stains of the 2nd West India Regiment and Mr Dodd, surgeon, as well as two women and twenty-eight dragoons with their horses as well as the ship's crew.

There were only two survivors. The wife of Cornet Burns and a ship's boy who had been below decks when the ship struck. Mrs Burns, ill in her bunk, had been washed through a port when the ship struck high on the bank; being ill had saved her life. All the rest had either been lost trying to swim ashore or washed off the deck before the *Catherine* had taken the ground. Mrs Burns was taken to Fleet farm, the residence of Mr Abbot, where she was cared for by his sister with kindness for several days.

The *Piedmont* transport went to pieces soon after she struck. On board were 138 soldiers of the 63rd Regiment of light infantry with their officers, Captain Ambrose William Barcroft, Lt Harry Ash and Mr Kelly, the regimental surgeon, together with the crew.

There were sixteen survivors, Serjeant Richardson, eleven privates and four seamen who were all accommodated at Chickerell where they were seen in the morning of the 19th by an officer of the Gloucester Militia, accompanied by Mr Bryer, a surgeon of Weymouth. They had both ridden out to the villages to render such aid as was possible to render. Two of the privates had broken limbs, whilst all had some kind of injury.

The *Thomas* of London, laden with masts for Oporto, burthen 350 tons, also went to pieces and the master, Thomas Brown, his son, three women and seven seamen all died. The mate and four seamen were saved, as also was Mr Smyth, a young lad on his way to Lisbon, who had saved his life by remaining on the ship when all the rest had been swept away. The *Thomas* was driven high on the Bank, when he leapt out and walked ashore.

The *Venus*, a transport with 96 people on board, was carrying important passengers to the West Indies, amongst whom were: Major John Charles

Ker, Military Commandant of Hospitals in the Leeward Islands; his son Lt James Ker, aged 14 years, of the 40th Regiment of Foot; Cornet Benjamin Graydon, Adjutant of the 3rd West India Regiment; Lts B Chadwick and James Sutherland, both of Colonel Whyte's West India Regiment; and Mr Darley of the hospital staff. There were nineteen survivors: Mr Darley, Serjeant-Major Hearne, twelve soldiers, four seamen and a boy. In common with others, Mr Darley had waited till the ship was driven high on the bank and the tide had ebbed.

The *Hannah*, Hickman master, 300 tons burthen, for Martinique, was driven on shore near Hill's Harbour after being run foul of by the *Harmony* transport [see entry for 17 December 1795], also for the West Indies, Alexander Wilson, master, who was believed to have been the only seaman on board. The entire crew of the *Hannah* were saved, as also the cargo of ordnance stores, but several horses were drowned and the *Hannah* herself finally went to pieces on 25 November.

The ship *Aeolus* of Whitby, Isaac Duck master, laden with masts and naval stores, was driven to the top of the Chisel Bank where 'she sits like a whale'. Once again, those who stayed with the ship saved their lives, whereas those who endeavoured to swim ashore, perished. Lt Mason of the Royal Navy; his brother, a midshipman; and seven seamen died, but the master and eight seamen were saved.

On 3 December three members of the crew of the *Aeolus*, William Lloyd, James Hannah and Samuel Cock, wrote a letter to the papers, 'Having had the misfortune to be wrecked in the *Aeolus* transport and being informed of scandalous articles in the papers concerning the people of Portland plundering bodies washed up on the Bank, we wish it to be known that we received the most hospitable treatment and kindness from everyone we met, and never will we forget it.'

The *Golden Grove* of London, Robert Bole master, was laden with bale goods for St Christopher (St Kitts) and went to pieces soon after she struck. Doctor Stevens and Mr Burrows, both of St Kitts, the master and two boys were lost. Lt Col Ross and seventeen seamen escaped with their lives.

The ship *Pitt* of London, John Horn master, was another of the West India fleet; laden with military stores and provisions, the *Pitt* was driven on shore near Encombe, to the westward of St Alban's Head, where the crew were rescued.

The *Firm* of London, Joseph Heakston master, for Martinique with ordnance stores, was dismasted but managed to make Weymouth Bay.

The *Hope* of Bristol, with troops for the West Indies, lost her main and mizzen masts on the 18th but was back in Weymouth Bay on 23 November.

On 24 November burial services took place for the eighteen officers and nine ladies whose bodies had been recovered from the wrecks on the Chisel Bank.

Seventeen of the officers were buried with military honours, by 50 members of the Gloucester Militia, in a mass grave in the churchyard at Wyke, to the north of the tower, whilst Lt Ker was interred on the south side. His father's body was neither found nor recognised. The nine ladies were also laid to rest, in the churchyard upon the same occasion. The seamen who had lost their lives numbered about 300; they were buried on the Fleet side of the Chisel Bank, in mass graves beyond the reach of the sea, the graves being marked by cairns.

All the transports listed above were part of Rear-Admiral Christian's fleet and were conveying the troops and supplies of General Sir Ralph Abercromby's army to the West Indies. The transports were for the greater part most wretchedly manned and the case of the *Harmony* was certainly no exception.

The ship was crewed by landsmen who would never dream of climbing a ship's rigging during a gale. It was said that the best sailors, if not the only sailors, had been taken by the press gangs for the Navy, for of all the ships wrecked on the Chisel Bank, not one was a naval vessel. (*SNL*, 1795; *SYM*, 23 and 30 November 1795; *AR*, 1795, Chr p44 et seq; *Times*, 21 November 1795; Dalyell, 1812 ed, p298 et seq; *NC* vol 21, p181 et seq)

21 November, Bee, merchantman The *Bee*, Captain Battison, in ballast from Dublin to Whitehaven was lost in a violent gale on this Saturday night, upon Langness Point on the Isle of Man, when all on board perished. The body of an elderly gentleman was washed ashore the next day and in his pockets were found forty guineas and a gold watch. (*Times*, 7 December 1795)

? November, Le Droit du Peuple, 36 guns Le Droit du Peuple, a French frigate of 36 guns with a crew of 300, was in chase of some merchantmen near Drontheim in Norway, when she struck upon a ledge of rocks, was wrecked, and 200 of her crew perished. (*Times*, 18 December 1795)

? November, Peggy, brig The brig *Peggy* of Greenock, Captain Williamson, on a voyage from Halifax, Nova Scotia, to Boston, New England, struck upon a sandbank a few miles from Boston during a violent storm. Only one man, a Mr Cameron, survived. He got into the boat, when the painter broke and he drifted to leeward leaving all the rest to perish in the storm. The captain, mate and carpenter were all married, their families living at Greenock. (*Times*, 22 January 1796)

10 December, Concord, merchantman During a south-westerly gale off the Bay of Biscay, the *Concord* of London, laden with wines was lying to under a storm foresail when she shipped a heavy sea which carried away her masts, everything on her deck and all the crew, except for two men; the vessel becoming waterlogged with her gunwales even with the water. Nine days later when in position 48°46′N 11°14′W the ship, *Thomas and Mary*, Captain O'Bryan, from Cadiz for Dublin, fell in with the wreck and took off the two survivors who had lived for nine days on the afterpart of the vessel. (*Times*, 31 December 1795)

11 December, Leda, 36 guns   The *Leda* frigate, 36 guns, Captain John Woodley, sailed from Cork with a crew of 250 men, as convoy to twenty-five victuallers and storeships for Martinique. The convoy had reached position 37°56′N 17°30′W, with the wind blowing a gale from the south-west and with a broken sea, when at midnight one or two of her cabin guns broke loose and went through her sides. The *Leda* filled in about ten minutes; many seamen being lost between decks but about forty got into the pinnace while another seven launched the jollyboat. It was afterwards supposed that the pinnace went down with the *Leda*, the only survivors being seven private seamen in the jolly boat. Why the *Leda* was carrying merchant seamen is unknown but the seven were providentially picked up by the brig *Brownlow* of Belfast, Penterk master, who deserved great praise for his kindness and humanity; on hearing of the accident he hove his vessel to in the hopes of picking up some more of the crew, but in vain.

At Madeira, three of the survivors were taken on board the *Bulldog* sloop of war while the other four were taken on board the *King George*, West Indiaman, which latter ship arrived at St Thomas on 2 January 1796. (*Times*, 8 February; 3 and 17 March 1796)

12 December, Neily, sloop   The sloop *Neily* of Lerwick, William Fullerton master, with a cargo of sundries from Shetland for Leith was in a most violent storm driven ashore on the sands on the south side of Sinclair's Bay, in Caithness. The master and two boys were drowned, the ship completely wrecked and the cargo lost. (*Times*, 31 December 1795)

12 December, Admiral Christian's convoy (ii)   After the failure of the fleet to proceed to the West Indies, due to the gale in the Channel on 18 November, Admirals Christian and Pole were back in St Helens on the 19th with as many ships as could be collected together, after the dispersal of the fleet. By the end of November damage to the ships had been made good, the fleet was ready to sail once again, and on 3 December Admirals Christian and Pole boarded their respective flagships, the *Glory* and the *Colossus*, to await a break in the weather, which occurred on 9 December. (*NC* vol 21, p181)

The transports and merchant ships carrying 16,000 troops of Lt Gen Sir Ralph Abercromby's army, had for their protection, two 98-gun ships, the *Glory* and the *Impregnable*; three 74-gun vessels, *Colossus*, *Alfred* and the *Irresistible;* as well as three 64-gun ships and several smaller vessels. Yet the danger was not from the French, but from the weather. It was too late in the year to embark on such an adventure and the ships were once again caught in a gale and dispersed on 12 December, when sixty leagues west of the Scillies.

13 December, Commerce, transport During the night of 12 December the outward bound West Indies fleet had the misfortune to fall in with the returning Lisbon fleet which had also dispersed and, at 2am on Sunday the 13th, when in position 48°30′N 9°41′W, the *Leander*, 50 guns, Captain Delparno, from Lisbon steering before the wind which was blowing a gale at south-south-west, ran aboard the outward bound *Commerce*,[16] an ordnance transport, having on board a crew of thirteen and laden with government stores and ammunition. The *Leander* stove in the larboard side of the *Commerce* by the after part of the fore chains, and the *Commerce* went down almost immediately.

John Gibson the chief mate, and Sebastian Tulloch the second mate were the only survivors; probably at the wheel, they saved themselves by grabbing hold the wreck of the *Leander*'s main topmast and getting on the yard of that ship. Captain Glynn and the rest of his crew were probably in their hammocks when the *Leander* struck the vessel. When the *Leander* hove in sight, the *Commerce* was on a wind under fore sail and mizzen staysail and from that time till she sunk did not exceed seven minutes. (*Times*, 21 December 1795; *SYM*, 4 January 1796)

15 December, Alfred, 74 and Undaunted, 38 guns The *Alfred*, 74 guns, Captain T Drury, arrived at Dock (Devonport) with the loss of her main, mizzen, and fore topmasts, occasioned by the gale of the 12th. Sixteen men who were on her yards went overboard with the main mast and of these only nine were picked up, the other seven lost their lives.

On this day also arrived at Dock the *Undaunted*, 38 guns, less all her masts and bowsprit. (*Times*, 19 December 1795)

17 December, Crache Feu, gunbrig, and Harmony, storeship The gunbrig *Crache Feu*, Lt Mortlock, carried away her rudder head which obliged the crew to steer the vessel with tackles hooked to a sweep that they fastened to the after part of the rudder. The brig arrived at Milford on 17 December. *Crache Feu* had been taken from the French on 9 May 1795 by Captain Sir Richard Strachan's frigate squadron off Cape Carteret. (*SNL*, 1795)

Also on this day, the *Harmony*, an ordnance storeship, arrived at the Cove of Cork dismasted; she had fallen in with the *Glasgow*, another storeship also dismasted. Admiral Kingsmill the commander-in-chief of the Irish Station, immediately dispatched four frigates under Captain J Faulkner of the *Diana*, to cruise for the protection of the scattered fleets. (*Times*, 22 December 1795)

18 December, West India convoy On this day, when in position 49°00′N 11°27′W, the fleet hove to and Captain Sparkes of the *Thetis*, a West Indiaman, went on board the *Trident*, 64 guns, to receive from Captain Edward O Osborne, the Commodore, sealed instructions in case of dispersal of the fleet, there being 183 ships in sight, so that 35 were missing.

The *Thames*, Captain Fotherly, and the *Arethusa*, both transports, returned to the Bristol Channel with much damage.

19 December, mishaps to transports The armed transport ship *L'Etrusco*, 24 guns, Captain Hanson, was fifty leagues south-west of Cape Clear when she rolled away her masts and laboured so hard that the crew had of necessity to throw all the guns overboard except three. The next day *L'Etrusco* fell in with an American ship which towed her to Milford, where they arrived on 19 December. (*Times*, 23 December 1795) See under 25 August 1798 for her loss.

The *Lord Hood* transport had on board 178 men of the 28th Regiment of Foot. On the 14th the ship had so much water in the hold that she was ordered to England. On that day she saw a merchant ship drifting with no-one on board, either abandoned or washed overboard. About 6pm hailed her several times but no answer and no-one appeared on deck. The *Lord Hood* arrived at Plymouth on the 19th. (*Times*, 22 December 1795)

The *Aid* transport, with all her boats stove and six feet of water in her hold, bore away for Plymouth, but when five leagues west of the Scillies she fell in with a French 12-gun privateer. During a chase of six hours the *Aid* had five wounded, one of whom had to have a leg amputated when the ship arrived at Plymouth on the 19th. The *Aid* was saved by the soldiers she was carrying, a truly varied lot, who kept up a vigorous musket fire. They included Captain Lightbourne of the 81st Regiment; Captain de la Cour, 1st Royals; Lt White, 22nd Regiment; Lts Piers and Edie of 4th and 6th West India regiments respectively; and Doctor White and Ensign Hall, both of 41st Regiment. (*SYM*, 28 December 1795)

24 December, Terror, bomb The *Terror* bomb vessel and her tender arrived at Plymouth during the night of 29 December while a westerly gale was raging. The ships had parted from the fleet during a gale on the 24th when seventy leagues west of the Scillies. The *Terror* was quite waterlogged, the sea making a clear breach over her, which forced overboard one of the 6-pounders in her waist; had she not been a tight ship she must have foundered, as she carried the standard bomb vessel armament of a 13-inch and a 10-inch mortar. On the 25th the fleet then consisted of 110 sail. (*Times*, 4 January 1796)

24 December, ordeal of the John and Elizabeth 'On this day one hundred and twenty persons were discharged at Jersey from two fencible regiments; they were eighty-six Somersets, twenty-nine Suffolks and five women, who were put on board the *John and Elizabeth*, a boat belonging to Cowes, but of only thirty-five tons burthen, by an army officer whose name the master did not recollect. The officer saw and approved of the vessel, and paid the master five shillings per head to land the people in England.

'On 26th December the vessel sailed from Jersey and put into Guernsey for water and to enable the passengers to obtain provisions. The next morning at ten o'clock the vessel sailed with a favourable wind at west-south-west, but at six o'clock it had increased to gale force. The crew took in three reefs in the mainsail and set the storm jib, but by three o'clock on Tuesday morning, the 29th, the wind blew so hard and the weather was so thick that they could not see the land so lay to from four o'clock until eight, when they bore away and made the land at ten o'clock, but still being hazy were unable to tell where they were. At noon, the crew set the trysail and then lay to, at which time there were then no hatches on, although the seas were running very high, with the boat shipping much water that the pumps could not free her of. At eight o'clock that evening the master called to the people below that the hatches must be battened down or the ship would inevitably founder; it was impossible to leave them open, but as many as chose could run the hazard of coming on deck, which seven actually did, although one of the seven was to die of exposure later. At midnight, the weather getting even worse, it became necessary to lay tarpaulins over the hatches, and it was about this time that the master was alarmed by a cry of fire. He dashed to the fore hatchway and tore off the tarpaulins and hatch and then the main hatch also, from which there ensued a most offensive odour.

'On Wednesday morning, about two o'clock, the wind shifted to north-west and eased, and when daylight came the hold was examined, when forty-seven men and three women were found dead, all of whom were thrown overboard. One other man died after being landed at Cowes. The master William Mitchell, and his brother the owner of the vessel, made an affidavit which threw the blame for the tragedy entirely upon themselves and exculpated every other person. They admitted that the violence of the gale did not oblige them to fasten the companion, and that they did not think it proper to knock down the bulkhead, in consequence of which all circulation of air was cut off from the people below. It was to this circumstance that the loss of fifty-one lives was attributed.' [This is an authentic copy of a letter from an agent of transports dated Cowes 3 January 1796. (*Times*, 5 January 1796)]

The *Times* likened the disaster to the 'Black Hole of Calcutta', and on 4 January 1796 printed: 'It is to be hoped that the government will institute an immediate investigation into the conduct of those who have caused the loss of so many lives.' (*Times*, 2, 4 and 5 January 1796). See also entry for 3 July 1811.

29 December, Hercules, merchantman The *Hercules* of New York, a large ship of some 500 tons burthen laden with deer and bear skins, pitch, tar, potashes and staves, was driven on shore at Gunwalloe Cove, about five miles south of Helston. The vessel came in on a sandy beach and by good fortune all on board were saved, then, by the appearance of the military from Helston, the countrymen were prevented from boarding and plundering the ship and at low water most of the skins and staves were saved. The ship was lying exposed to the south-west gale and at high tide that night with a very heavy sea the vessel broke into two parts with the stern portion driven underneath the cliffs with the remainder of her cargo. The staves were washed up on the shore but the casks in the bottom of her hold were soon covered by the sand; the following morning the whole beach resembled a dockyard.

The tinners were soon on each part of the vessel, and with their axes and hammers were ripping her to pieces; many of them to get at a bolt of iron, not worth twopence, ran the most dangerous risks of losing their lives, as the waves every time they hit the vessel shook her as if she would have fallen to pieces. On Thursday morning 31 December, one man lost his life when the remainder of the wreck finally broke up.

The *Hercules* was a prize, carried into Halifax, Nova Scotia, and for some unknown reason, sent to England for condemnation. On Monday 28 December (the day prior to grounding) the *Hercules* was boarded by a French privateer, who refused to capture her on account of her being an American. (*Times*, 11 January 1796)

29 December, Amethyst, 36 guns The *Amethyst* frigate, 36 guns, Captain F T Affleck, sailed from Torbay during the afternoon of Monday 28 December, in company with the *Trusty*, 50 guns, on a cruise in the Channel. Early that evening she missed the Commodore's lights, and by the storm which then raged the *Amethyst* was driven on to the Hannouaux reef, near Guernsey, where she struck at 4am on Tuesday the 29th, then having got off thence, the vessel was driven upon the Island of Alderney, and at 9.30 that morning, ran on shore in the Bay of Praye. It was luckily near high tide and by waiting for the ebb the crew landed safely with no loss of life. The ship lost her three masts and bowsprit, but most of her stores were saved. The sea ran so high that the people of Alderney could not get near her, except one boat, which got under her quarter and near enough to catch a rope, but was then overset and two of the men drowned, the four others were saved by the great exertions of their friends on shore, who made a chain of persons through a most tremendous surf to rescue them. The sailors' clothes and bedding were all saved, but having their pockets full of prize money, little discipline could be exercised.

On 8 March 1796 Captain Affleck was tried by Court Martial for the loss of the *Amethyst*. He was dismissed the service, put at the bottom of the list and rendered incapable of ever serving again.

The *Amethyst* was formerly *La Perle*, taken at Toulon on 29 August 1793 by Lord Hood. (*SNL*, 1793; *Times*, 5 January and 11 March 1796)

1796

5 January, Leighton and Fowler, transports   The *Leighton* transport of London, Captain Hamilton, was one of the dispersed West Indies fleet, and on this day the ship arrived at Plymouth with 200 of the Royal Irish Artillery, commanded by Captain Swaine. The *Leighton* had twice parted from the fleet during heavy gales and the last time she saw them was on 22 December in the evening, in position 49°28′N 10°44′W, and the next day fell in with four other transports, also from the fleet. The name of one of the four was *Fowler*, of Scarborough [see also 25 January]; the names of the others it was not possible to discover, but with these she kept company till the 30th, during all of which time they continued beating up to regain the fleet, but on that day another gale parted the *Leighton* from the others and Captain Hamilton thought that they had borne away for Ireland.

The gale with great violence had forced the *Leighton* to bear away also, as she was very leaky and had sprung her bowsprit.

Unknown to the crew of the *Leighton*, the *Fowler* was still beating about until three weeks later, when she was either wrecked or foundered near Cuddan Point. There were no survivors. (*Times*, 8 and 11 January 1796)

11 January, Aurora, transport   The *Aurora* transport with German troops outward-bound to the West Indies, was another of Admiral Christian's convoy, that had sailed from St Helens on 9 December.

The fleet was lying-to in the Bay of Biscay during a gale when the *Aurora* was seen to hoist signals of distress; the ship had lost her masts and rudder and lay like a log in the water, yet no assistance was possible. Boats of the men-of-war were hoisted out, to take out the people on board the *Aurora*, but had to be hoisted in again or would have been staved by the heavy sea. (*Times*, 8 February 1796)

On 15 January Captain Smith of the ship *Mary*, another of the convoy, saw a large part of a ship floating, on which was painted *Aurora* of London. (*Times*, 3 February 1796) In the meantime, the *Aurora* was being kept afloat by the efforts of the people at the pumps, which efforts they had to maintain until 2 February, on which date the *Aurora* was then about ten leagues to the west of the Lizard, where she fell in with the American ship *Sedgely* of Philadelphia, Captain Hodges, who at the hazard of his own life, and the lives of his crew, rescued 160 persons from the *Aurora*. The troops, all Germans, tendered Captain Hodges 1000 guineas in gratitude which he nobly refused, saying he had sufficient remuneration in his own mind for the risks he and his crew had undergone. [The *Times* article stated: 'It should be recorded to his honour that his humanity, aided by nautical skill, triumphed over the danger that awaited his exertions in the boat.' From this, it would appear the *Sedgely* lay to and Captain Hodges manned his own boat.] (*Times*, 9 February 1796)

On the same day that Captain Hodges and his crew were performing deeds of valour, a large ship, copper bottomed with her keel upwards, was seen from Penlee Point in Plymouth Sound drifting eastwards. (*Times*, 5 February 1796)

22 January, Garland's launch   The launch of HMS *Garland*, on her way from Sheerness to the Nore, unfortunately foundered, and the 1st Lt Mr Watson, Mr Steward and Mr Thompson, masters' mates, all young officers, together with five seamen and a woman, were all lost. Ten men, the remaining part of the crew were saved. The launch had taken on too many stores and was overladen. (*Times*, 28 January 1796)

25 January, Fowler, transport   Ships of the West Indies fleet, which had left St Helens on 9 December, had been dispersed by winter gales of the utmost severity and were foundering in the Channel at the end of January. On the 25th the coastline four miles east of Marazion, near Cuddan Point, was littered with great quantities of wreckage from ships of the fleet. Scores of horses with D26 (the brand mark of the 26th Light Dragoons) burnt on their hooves, and about 150 men, women and children were washed ashore. On the blade of an oar was stamped, *Fowler* of Scarborough. (*Times*, 30 January 1796)

26 January, Dutton, East Indiaman   The *Dutton*, East Indiaman, Captain Sampson, was one of Admiral Christian's fleet which had left St Helens on 9 December and after seven weeks at sea, was on the afternoon of 25 January driven by stress of weather into Plymouth Sound where the ship was brought up, the tide then being too low for the ship to enter the Catwater. During the course of the night the wind veered around to south-south-west and blew a very heavy gale with a tremendous sea. The *Dutton* rode well until 9am on the 26th when the vessel started to drive and was so near the rocks at Mt Batten, that it was thought necessary to slip the cables and run for the Catwater; the fore topsail and the staysail were both let go, but unknown to the pilots, the buoy at the west end of the Cobbler's Reef had moved during the gale and the ship touched on the tail end of the reef and lost her rudder. Unmanageable, the *Dutton* stood on till she reached the rocks abreast the Citadel flagstaff, when her masts were cut away, and although they fell towards the shore, were useless as a bridge, being broken by the heavy sea. Yet only two men were believed to have lost their lives: one was hanging by ropes under the main chains, and when a mast was cut away, it fell upon him; the other was struck by an axe during the cutting away of the mast. All the active and able people, including the captain and officers, got safe on shore, but Captain Sampson was hauled on board again at 2pm, by a rope lashed around his waist. About 3pm the storm abated and shore boats went to the seaward side of the ship and took out about 300 soldiers, grenadiers of the 2nd, 3rd, 10th and 37th Regiments, as well as 80 sick together with some women and children. (*Times*, 29 January and 12 February 1796)

On the following day the *Dutton* was seen to have driven further up on the rocks, with her head to the south, her bottom out and parted in the middle. Two days later, on Friday 29 January, the wreck and materials were sold by public auction for £850. (*Times*, 1 February 1796)

On 19 August 1802 the remains of the *Dutton* were buoyed up and taken into Sutton Pool to be sold. (*NC* vol 8, p171)[17]

26 January, Pomone, 44 guns At 1pm in Plymouth Sound, while the *Dutton* was on shore on the Hoe, *La Pomone*, 44 guns, was at anchor in another part of the Sound when she was struck by lightning, which shivered her fore mast and injured ten men. (*Times*, 2 February 1796)

28 January, Prins Carl von Hessen, transport The *Prins Carl von Hessen*, Captain Ahrens, from Hamburg, had been beating about in the North Sea and the Channel for fifteen weeks prior to arriving at Ramsgate at 1am on 28 January during a gale. The ship struck against the east pier and received considerable damage before finally running on shore near the bathing rooms. The vessel had on board 180 men, emigrants, who were hussars and part of the Regiment of Rohan. Although they had been afloat for so many weeks, yet they all appeared to be very well and, furthermore, luck was with them, for having survived such a voyage, they also survived the loss of the ship. (*Times*, 2 and 3 February 1796)

2 February, Stag, cutter The *Stag* cutter was lost on the rocks of Crosshaven, about four miles from Queenstown. (*Times*, 13 February 1796)

4 February, Sally and Jenny, sloop The *Sally and Jenny* was a sloop of 70 tons burthen, and was laden with butter for the Plymouth market, when on Thursday 4 February the vessel became embayed in Whitsand Bay during the strong south-westerly gale of that night; it was conjectured at the time that the sloop struck between Queener Point and Rame Head.

The sloop from Cork also carried passengers, and the next day a lady's body, finely dressed, was found on the rocks near Rame Head. (*Times*, 9 and 12 February 1796)

10 February, Clementina, transport The *Clementina* transport with troops on board, had sailed from Cork on 9 February and the next day was run on board by the *Hercules* of Bristol, also with troops.

The main mast of the *Clementina* was carried away as also was the head and bowsprit of the *Hercules*. While the *Hercules* put into Waterford to refit, the *Clementina* continued on to Bristol where she arrived on 17 February.

The *Clementina* lost two lieutenants and sixteen privates of the 14th Dragoons, who were unfortunately drowned. (*Times*, 20 and 24 February 1796)

24 February, Lynn ferry As the ferry boat was crossing the river from Common-staithe quay to Old Lynn at 7pm, with about thirty persons on board, it ran foul of the cable of a barge and was overset; by which accident more than twenty persons lost their lives. Four more would have shared the same fate, but for the heroic exertions of one of the passengers, John Price, a sailor, who at the hazard of his own life rescued four other passengers. A fifth passenger, a woman, was torn from his grasp by the rapidity of the tide and he nearly met the same fate himself.

A similar accident happened at the same ferry in 1630 when eighteen persons were drowned. (*AR*, 1796, Chr p7) See also 5 October 1811.

25 February, Devonshire, collier The *Devonshire*, a collier, struck upon the Whiting sandbank (in Hollesley Bay, Suffolk) where she beat off her rudder, and after remaining there about four hours, floated off, but soon sank in five fathoms. The crew took to the boat and after rowing for several hours, were taken up by a Harwich smack and carried into that place. (*Times*, 1 March 1796)

8 March, Bellisarius, transport The *Royal Sovereign*, 110 guns, Admiral Cornwallis, sailed from Portsmouth on 1 March with a squadron and a large convoy for the West Indies, but returned to Spithead on the 15th, owing to the *Bellisarius* transport running her on board, by which she had received much damage.

The accident occurred when the convoy was in position 42°00'N 14°30'W, and was said to have been occasioned by an argument between the master and the second mate, by which, not paying attention when wearing the ship, she fell athwart the *Royal Sovereign*, when the latter's jibboom and bowsprit took the main mast of the *Bellisarius* and struck her amidships, causing her to founder in a very short space of time.

The troops on board the *Bellisarius* were all Hessians, and though they totalled more than 300, yet those saved amounted to less than half that number; they included Captain Barge of the transport, 16 of his crew, 5 women and 120 soldiers, some of whom were injured and died later.

A woman had tried to throw a child on to the *Royal Sovereign*, but it fell between the two ships and she was said to have then fallen between the vessels herself. (*Times*, 16 and 17 March 1796)

11 April, Ça Ira, 80 guns Ça Ira, a French 80-gun ship, was taken off Genoa on 14 March 1795 by the fleet of Vice-Admiral W Hotham. On 11 April 1796 the ship, then commanded by Captain Charles Dudley Pater, was cruising in San Fiorenzo Bay, Corsica, when she caught fire and was lost; yet of the 600 men on board, only 4 lost their lives. (*SNL*, 1796)

29 April, Asia, 64 guns Extract from a letter from Port Royal, Jamaica, of this day's date:
'I am sorry to inform you of a most shocking accident which happened on board His Majesty's ship *Asia* of 64 guns. This morning at nine o'clock as Captain Home, myself and several other officers were parading the quarter deck, part of our lower gun-deck blew up close by the grand magazine, where we had taken in, but the day before, 300 barrels of powder; a sight, the most shocking I ever beheld, to see 300 of the crew jump into the sea, thus to avoid one dreadful danger by rushing into another. As soon as the shock was over Captain Home, myself and several of the officers, with a few remaining seamen, went down and extinguished the fire, with the loss, happy I am to say, of only eleven men killed and wounded.' (*Times*, 2 August 1796)

13 May, Salisbury, 50 guns The *Salisbury*, 50 guns, Captain William Mitchell, was another old ship, having been built in 1769. On this day at 4pm, an open boat with the first lieutenant and four seamen of the *Salisbury* arrived alongside the *Africa* at Port Royal, Jamaica, with news of the loss of the *Salisbury* on a reef near the Île de Vache, off the coast of Hispaniola (SW Haiti).
When the boat left the *Salisbury* she was filling fast but the crew were all safe and were eventually taken up by a schooner, Lt Man, dispatched from Port Royal, to render assistance. (*Times*, 5 July 1796)

10 June, Arab, 18 guns The *Arab*, 18 guns, Captain Stephen Seymour, was originally *Le Jean Bart* and was taken from the French on 29 March 1795; this ship is not to be confused with a vessel of the same name taken eighteen days later, on 15 April, off Rochefort, and afterwards renamed *Laurel* (26 guns). (*SNL*, 1796)
The *Arab* was cruising off the Penmarks when she was becalmed, drifted ashore and was wrecked [on the Îles Glenans, 12 miles SSW of Concarneau]. She became a total loss and her crew were taken prisoner, that is, the eighty who survived. Among those who lost their lives were the captain, the surgeon and twenty seamen.

The officers who survived were very fortunate, for only five weeks later, on 13 July, the French cartel sloop *Displai* arrived at Cawsand Bay in Plymouth Sound, encumbered with seven of the *Arab*'s officers on exchange; they had been paroled and included the 1st Lt Sir John Colyton, the 2nd Lt Mr Steward and the purser Mr Stanford. (*Times*, 16 July 1796)

The *Displai* also brought from France living proof that regardless of what Edmund Burke thought, the age of chivalry was not yet extinguished. The *Displai* brought over from Brest Citizen Bergeret, a Capitaine de Vaisseau, the late commander of *La Virginie*, a 44-gun French frigate, taken by Sir E Pellew's squadron, forty leagues SW of the Lizard, 22 April 1796. (*Times*, 18 July 1796)

Capitaine Bergeret sailed from Plymouth for France shortly after he was taken, on parole to exchange Captain Sir Sydney Smith in lieu of himself; on failure of which he pledged his honour to return to this country. The Convention would not exchange, therefore he returned.

16 June, Hercules, merchantman Captain Benjamin Stout of the American ship *Hercules* chartered his vessel, then at Bengal, to the East India Company, and took on board 9000 bags of rice for London. The *Hercules* sailed from Diamond Harbour, Sagar Roads, on 17 March with a cosmopolitan crew of sixty-four persons.

On 1 June it began to blow a gale which increased until the 7th, when a sea struck her aft, tore away her rudder, started the stern post and shattered the whole of the stern frame. The pumps were sounded, and within a few minutes the water had increased to four feet, though the pumps (made by Mann of London) were discharging fifty tons an hour. To get at the leak, between 300 and 400 bags of rice were taken from the run of the ship (the lower part of the hull aft) and thrown over the side, then when the leak was found, everything at hand was rammed into the opening to try to stem the onrush of water. Next day the *Hercules* was two hundred leagues off the east coast of Africa and, although the gale had eased, the swell was so great that the long boat was put over the stern to keep the ship's head to the wind. Captain Stout later said he would have put a cable over the stern to act as a sea anchor if he could have spared men from the pumps to prepare it.

['Letters from New York mention the lucky thought of a negro in saving a ship in distress, by launching a 150 fathom hawser with a spare boom fastened to it; the ship by this means, riding head-a-wind during the storm as at anchor, after having cut away the main mast.' (*AR*, 1763, Chr p110)]

On the 16th with five feet of water in her hold, the ship was only two miles off the coast, when the longboat was brought up and into her were taken the ship's papers. The second mate and three seamen were then given orders to remain in the offing while the ship was run on shore. The *Hercules* took the ground about two cables out and just a few leagues from the Infanta

(Breede) river. Two rafts of spars and casks had already been constructed, but the larger grounded a cable's length from the shore; the smaller raft was then floated from the vessel and with its aid all were saved.

On the journey to Cape Town, 150 miles, which had to be walked, the men split into groups and most found work with Dutch settlers, so that by 30 July, when Cape Town was reached, Captain Stout was almost alone. There he found passage on the *St Cecilia*, Captain Palmer, and arrived at Crookhaven, Ireland, the middle of November. (Dalyell, 1812 ed, vol 3, p314 et seq)

17 June, Washington, American Indiaman The *Washington*, an American East Indiaman of 750 tons burthen, was esteemed the finest ship in the service of the States, but on this day she ran ashore on Lizard Point during a gale and was beyond recovery. Although the vessel was lost, nevertheless, some of the cargo was recovered from the wreck; bales of silk, muslin and Indian hemp, were brought ashore and taken to Falmouth, but 300 tons of sugar and a great quantity of rice were beyond recovery.

The whole cargo was valued at £55,000, but this included sugar that the captain had on board to the value of $14,000, and this was not insured. The ship had come from Calcutta, but whether for the account of the East India Company or not, could not be ascertained. The pilots absconded. (*Times*, 25 June 1796)

15 July, Trompeuse, 18 guns La *Trompeuse*, 18 guns, was taken off Cape Clear on 12 January 1794, by the 20-gun *Sphynx*, Cdr R Lucas, and on this 15 July was wrecked on the Farmer Rock, Kinsale. Cdr Joshua Rowley Watson and his crew were saved. (*SNL*, 1794 and 1796)

16 July, Commerce, merchantman At 6am on this Saturday, as the American ship *Commerce*, Captain Delano, was sailing down the river at Liverpool in order to get out to sea, she was discovered to be on fire. The flames spread with such rapidity that it was with difficulty that the forty passengers could be got off the ship. The crew then ran the vessel on shore and scuttled her, after which the fire was extinguished, but the cargo was very much damaged. No lives were lost. (*Times*, 21 July 1796)

30 July, Active, 32 guns The *Active*, 32 guns, was launched at Northam, Devon, in 1780, and on 16 April that year was in action at Porto Praya Bay, St Jago, in the Cape Verde Islands, where a French squadron under Commodore Suffrein had surprised the British, 'anchored in slovenly confusion', and made an unpleasant example of Commodore Johnstone.

Following the Treaty of Versailles, the *Active* was laid up for the greater part of ten years, when the ship was once again commissioned for active service, which, however, was cut short, as the ship, commanded by

Captain Edward Leveson Gower, was lost on Anticosti in the St Lawrence river at the end of July. The crew were saved. (*SNL*, 1796; *Naval and Military Record*, 8 November 1894)

13 August, Middlesex, West Indiaman   On this Saturday evening the *Middlesex* West Indiaman, from Barbados, ran ashore in Erith Long Reach at low tide, and quickly bilged. The accident was said to have been caused by the pilot who had been admonished by the officers of the ship that there was not a sufficient depth of water to float the vessel, but a major cause of the grounding was a want of hands on the ship, for most of the crew, even including the ship's carpenter, who was an officer, had been pressed. The few crew members who were on board, did not abandon the ship until the water came over the deck, for at one time it was thought the *Middlesex* would hold together till the tide rose. The cargo of sugar and cotton was saved by the timely assistance of various small craft. (*Times*, 16 and 17 August 1796)

On Wednesday 7 September, at a sale held in Lloyd's Coffee House in London, the remains of the hull were knocked down for £270, and the remainder of the cargo for £190. (*Times*, 9 September 1796)

27 August, Undaunted, 38 guns   After Captain Roberts of the *Undaunted*, 38 guns, was taken ill at Kingston, Jamaica, his ship was taken over by Lt Robert Winthrop of the 16-gun *Albacore*, who then became the acting captain, in Commodore Duckworth's squadron.

In company with the 74-gun *Leviathan* and the 26-gun *Jamaica*, the *Undaunted* was on passage to Irvis when she ran ashore on the Morant Cays and became a complete wreck. The officers and crew were all saved, as well as the guns and most of the rigging; the whole being taken aboard the *Leviathan*, Commodore Duckworth's flagship.

About the same time that his late ship was wrecked, Captain Roberts died at Kingston. (*Times*, 14 December 1796)

The *Undaunted* was formerly the French frigate *L'Arethuse*, taken at Toulon by Lord Hood in 1793. (*SNL*, 1799) [This ship should not be confused with *Bienvenue*, a French 28-gun storeship, taken by the squadron of Vice-Admiral Sir J Jervis at Martinique on 17 March 1794, and afterwards renamed *Undaunted*.]

? August, Sirenne, 16 guns   *La Sirenne*, a 16-gun sloop of war, was taken from the French off San Domingo, during the month of August 1794, by the *Intrepid*, 64 guns, Captain C Carpenter, and the *Chichester*, 44 guns, Captain R D Fancourt.

La Sirenne was cruising in the Bay of Honduras, when from some unknown cause the sloop was either wrecked or foundered; because her commander David Guerin and his entire crew of about 100 men perished, the exact date or place of loss was never ascertained. (Norie, 1827 ed, pp407, 453; *SNL*, 1799)

7 September, yellow fever in the West Indies The *Times* printed the following:
  'The pestilence continues to scourge Europeans in the West Indies. At Cape Nicolas Mole (Haiti) yellow fever has swept away one half of the officers and seamen of the different ships of war and the mortality among the land forces is in greater proportion. The *Swiftsure*, 74 guns, and the *Raisonnable*, 64 guns, have lost 800 and amongst these, in the *Raisonnable* alone, 32 from the quarterdeck. There are few instances of persons recovering and Mr Melville, the surgeon of the *Raisonnable* is the only one to survive two attacks... The day previous to the *Swiftsure* sailing, seventeen lieutenants were made, nearly the whole without the necessary etiquette (Time served).
  'Between the 24th July and the 28th August ten died on the *Grantham.*'
  Swiftsure was captured by the French 24 June 1801; and retaken at Trafalgar 21 October 1805.

13 September, Cormorant, 16 guns The *Cormorant*, a 16-gun sloop of war, Lt T Gott, was launched on the Thames in 1794, of 427 tons burthen, and had a crew of 125 men. The sloop was lying at Port-au-Prince in the Island of Hispaniola, when she accidentally blew up. Lt Thomas Gott died with 100 of his men, for only twenty were saved. (*SNL*, 1796)
  On 19 October the *Philadelphia Gazette* stated that Lt Gott was giving a party to celebrate his appointment, a few days previously, to the command of the *Cormorant* when the accident occurred. (*Times*, 26 November 1796) [It may be noted here that both Lecky (*The King's Ships*) and Laird Clowes each give the date of the accident as 24 December, which is quite wrong, apparently copied one from the other. Later sources have also followed this mistake.]

22 September, Amphion, 32 guns The *Amphion* frigate, 32 guns, Captain Israel Pellew, anchored in Plymouth Sound on the evening of 19 September and went up harbour at 7am the following morning.
  On the 22nd, at 4.30pm, a violent shock was felt as far away as two miles distant at Stonehouse, then when the alarm and confusion had subsided it became known that the *Amphion*, which had more than 400 people on board, had blown up. The frigate was manned by a Plymouth crew of about 300 men, and also on board were about 100 men, women and children who were visiting their friends and relations, as the ship was to sail next day. Because there were so many visitors on board the actual number of people on the *Amphion* could not be exactly known, yet it was believed at the time

of the accident that not less than 350 lost their lives. Perhaps the most fortunate were the men who were working aloft, for when the masts went they fell into the sea and were picked up very little hurt. The boatswain (Mr Montandon) was standing on the cathead; the bowsprit had been stepped for three hours, the gammoning and everything on, and he was directing the men in rigging out the jibboom when suddenly he felt himself being driven upwards, and he fell into the sea; he then perceived he was entangled in the rigging, and had some trouble to get clear; when taken up by a man-of-war's boat, his arm was found to be broken.

A young midshipman in the *Cambridge* guardship, lying not far distant from the *Amphion*, was watching the taking in of the bowsprit and he said that the *Amphion* suddenly appeared to rise altogether from the surface of the water, until he nearly saw her keel, the explosion then succeeded; her masts seemed to be forced up into the air, and the hull instantly to sink, all happening within seconds.

Dining with Captain Pellew in his cabin were his first lieutenant and Captain William Swaffield of the Dutch prize *Overyssel*, 64 guns, who was also due to sail the following day. They were drinking their wine when the explosion threw them off their seats and struck them against the carlings of the upper deck. Captain Pellew had the presence of mind to dash to the cabin window where looking out he saw two hawsers, one slack in the bight and the other taut, upon which he threw himself, and by so doing saved his life. The 1st Lt did likewise; but Captain Swaffield, being as supposed more seriously injured, did not escape, his body not being found until 22 October. He was buried with military honours at Stonehouse Chapel. The sentry at the cabin door happened to be looking at his watch; how he escaped no-one could tell, but he felt his watch dashed out of his hands, after which he was no longer sensible of what happened to him. He was, however, brought ashore very little hurt.

At low water the next day about a foot and a half of one of the masts appeared above the water, and on the 29th, part of the fore-chains was hauled up, as well as the head and cutwater. The wreck itself was weighed on 14 November 1796 by Mr S Hemmans, Master Attendant of the dockyard. (*SNL*, June 1797, p17)

On 23 June 1797 the *Times* published a Plymouth report of the 20th which read:

'On Saturday last the wreck of the *Amphion* was turned bottom upwards by the person who weighed her, notwithstanding she had in her hold between 200 and 300 tons of iron and shingle ballast besides shot and other weighty material. Believed the first instance of a ship being weighed by mechanical means.'

It was the fore magazine which took fire, but the reason for it doing so was never discovered; the 1st Lt stated that to his certain knowledge the key of the magazine was hanging in his cabin at the time. It was conjectured by many naval people that, contrary to rule, all the fires had not been extinguished, though the dinners were over. (*SYM*, 26 September 1796; *NC* vol 3, p197 et seq)

? September, Bermuda, 18 guns The *Bermuda*, an 18-gun sloop of war built the previous year, was commanded by Lt Thomas Maxtone when she was presumed to have foundered in the Gulf of Florida; the exact date and position unknown. Lt Maxtone had been promoted only a few months previous to the disaster which cost him and his crew of 120 men their lives. (*SNL*, 1796)

16 October, London, West Indiaman 'This evening a ship named *London* from St Christopher (St Kitts), having on board about three hundred blacks (French prisoners of war), was driven on the rocks near the pier at the entrance to the harbour of Ilfracombe during a violent gale, by which about fifty were drowned.

'The two hundred and fifty who got on shore exhibited a most wretched spectacle, the scene too shocking for description. The wind was blowing fair into the harbour.' (*SYM*, 24 October 1796; *AR* Chr p38)

25 October, Union, packet On this Tuesday, two packet boats were ordered from Yarmouth for Dover to take messengers to Calais. One of them, the *Union*, Captain Osborne, in sailing around the coast to Dover, was driven by the gale on to the French coast between Gravelines and Calais and wrecked. Every assistance was given by the French, who not only rescued all on board, but also immediately returned the crew to England, where they arrived on 27 October, within 48 hours of leaving Yarmouth. (*Times*, 28 October 1796)

? October, Barrington, West Indiaman The *Barrington*, Captain Stewart, was a West Indiaman and was on passage from Leith for New York when she foundered off Cape Sable (the southernmost point of Nova Scotia). The crew were saved but the ship and cargo lost. (*Times*, 6 January 1797)

31 October, Curlew, 18 guns With a crew of 125 men and boys the 18-gun *Curlew* was commanded by Cdr Francis Ventris Field when she vanished in the North Sea. There were no known survivors from this vessel which had been built in 1795. (*SNL*, 1796)

3 November, Helena, 14 guns The *Helena*, Cdr Jermyn John Symonds, was a 14-gun sloop of war built in 1778. Cruising off the coast of Holland, the vessel was caught in a sudden squall and foundered with all on board, about eighty men and boys. (*SNL*, 1796)

4 December, Queen, packet   A packet boat with passengers from Parkgate for Dublin, the *Queen* was wrecked near Formby Point on the Lancashire coast; crew and passengers were saved. (*Times*, 12 December 1796)

7 December, Reunion, 36 guns   La *Reunion*, 36 guns, Captain William Bayntun, with a crew of 250, from Sheerness for Yarmouth, struck on the Sunk Sandbank, 13 miles SE of Harwich and bilged soon after she took the ground; even so, boats that were fishing nearby managed to save all the crew, three excepted. At the time the vessel was wrecked, there was no light on the Sunk Sandbank although one was ready for placement. The reason given was the enemy may have used it for directional purposes.

   La Reunion was one of the swiftest frigates in the navy and had been taken from the French off Cherbourg on 20 October 1793. (*Times*, 14 December 1796; *SNL*, 1793)

11 December, Dover, 44 guns   On this Sunday morning the *Dover*, a 44-gun ship, Lt H Kent, was an armed transport belonging to the Transport Office, when she sailed on to the Owers Bank and beat off her rudder. Nevertheless, with the assistance of other vessels she got off and arrived at Portsmouth on the morning of the 13th. (*Times*, 14 and 16 December 1796) [The Owers Bank is in the English Channel, extending from seven miles SE of Selsey Bill, Sussex. It is not to be confused with the five-mile long Ower Shoal, which lies in the North Sea, outside the Leman Sand and twenty miles NE of Cromer.]

16 December, Seduisant, 74 guns   A fleet comprising seventeen sail of the line, thirteen frigates, six corvettes, seven transports and a munitions ship, the whole carrying 17,500 troops for the invasion of Ireland, left Brest this day for Bantry Bay. The fleet was commanded by Vice-Admiral Morard de Galles, who had decided to sail via the Passage du Raz, the better to conceal his movements from the British who were cruising off Ushant. However, at 4pm, with darkness approaching and the wind becoming variable, the signal was given for the fleet to steer for the Passage du Iroise, directly in front of the port of Brest, but few ships saw the signal and the greater part of the fleet sailed on the course as decided previously.

   Near the entrance to the Passage du Raz lies the Grand Stevenec rock and upon this the 74-gun *Seduisant* struck. Within a few hours the ship was transformed into a complete wreck, and of the 1300 soldiers and sailors on board, it was believed that 680 men, including Captain M Dufossey, lost their lives. (*SNL*, 1796; E Chevalier, *Histoire de la Marine Française*, 1886) [The *Naval Chronicle*, vol 27, p229 states that the rock upon which the *Seduisant* struck was the Govivas, a small sunken rock which has at low water only 4½ feet.]

18 December, Courageux, 74 guns The *Courageux* was launched in October 1753 at Brest. The *Courageux* was a 74-gun vessel commanded by
Captain M Dugue-Lambert and was returning from San Domingo when
she was taken off Vigo by the *Bellona*, 74 guns, Captain Robert Faulknor,
on 14 August 1761; during this action Captain M Dugue-Lambert was
killed.

The *Courageux* was therefore a very old ship when Captain Benjamin
Hallowell was given command in the absence of Captain Waldegrave who
had been sent to England with dispatches. On 9 December Captain Hallowell was not on board as he was sitting at a court martial in Gibraltar; several
of his officers were also not on board as they were on shore leave as a
consequence of which the watch on deck that night was entrusted to a young
midshipman, while the command of the *Courageux* devolved upon Lt John
Burrows.

During that night a levanter (a violent easterly wind) sprang up and
caused the *Courageux*, which was at anchor in Gibraltar Bay, to drive nearly
under the guns of the Spanish batteries on the north-west side of the Bay.
The next morning the crew got the ship under sail to work her into a safe
anchorage, but the wind increasing, the crew had to close reef the topsails,
they being afraid to anchor in case the vessel drove again. That evening the
levanter blew with increased force, so as to cause the crew to hand the
topsails and keep the ship under her courses, so as to be far enough to
windward to get into Gibraltar. Unfortunately the weather became thick
and hazy accompanied by incessant rain with thunder and lightning, and
for eight days the *Courageux* was at the mercy of the weather which caused
them to stand too far towards the south.

The wind was at east-south-east and at 9pm on 18 December, the ship
was discovered to be among the breakers before the land was seen. An
attempt was made to wear ship but the decision was taken too late and the
Courageux struck and fell broadside on to a precipitous shoreline close to
Apes' Hill. Many seamen jumped overboard and attempted to swim ashore
but were lost between the side of the ship and the rocks; and of the 600 men
and boys on the vessel, 470 perished.

The survivors lived for the first six days upon dried beans, and were
then marched through the country for another six days, during which time
the Moors gave them as much bread once a day as they could eat, and after
which time they were sent back to Gibraltar. [The food was most probably
locust beans, fruit of the ceratonia or carob tree. James' *Naval History* (1826
ed, p451) states that of about 593 officers and men who were on board the
Courageux, only 129 effected their escape; five by means of the launch that
was towing astern and the remainder by passing along the fallen main mast
to the rugged shore.]

Apes' Hill was the Mount Abyla of the ancients and was one of the
reputed Pillars of Hercules, as Calpe, now Gibraltar, was the other. Today,

Apes' Hill is known as Mount Hacho, at the foot of which lies the Spanish town of Ceuta on the coast of Africa. (*Etat-Major Service Historique; Ministère de la Défense (Marine); NC* vol 3, pp202 and 203; *MC,* 1808,vol 6, p206 et seq)

21 December, *Bombay Castle, 74 guns* Sir John Jervis arrived at Lisbon with ten sail of the line and lost one 74-gun ship immediately. Entering the River Tagus, the *Bombay Castle,* Captain Thomas Sotheby, with a crew of 590, in avoiding the *Camel* 26-gun storeship, was swept by the current on to the South Catchup sandbank, near Bouge Fort. Although the ship built in 1782 was lost, the crew were saved. (Norie 1827; Brenton 1837; *SNL,* 31 January 1783)

22 December, *Elizabeth and Peggy storeship* On 25 November the two ships, the *Elizabeth and Peggy* and the *Peggy* were both laden with government provisions and sailed under convoy of *La Vipere,* an 18-gun sloop of war, Cdr Henry Harding Parker, and the *Beresford* cutter, then on 20 December the convoy dispersed upon seeing the French fleet off Bantry Bay. On 22 December the *Elizabeth and Peggy* was taken by the French frigate, *La Charente,* 44 guns, but the *Peggy* bore away for Valentia and eventually arrived at Tarbert.

The cargo of the *Elizabeth and Peggy* was 1100 casks of butter and 230 tierces (casks equivalent to 42 gallons, or one-third of a pipe) of beef.

La Charente also took the *Alfred* from Bristol for Cork, laden with glass, bark and sundry goods, which vessel she sunk; and a sloop from Bideford laden with bricks and tiles which she then ransomed for 250 guineas. (*Times,* 11 January 1797) See also 2 January 1797.

25 December, *Amity, West Indiaman* The *Amity,* a West Indiaman, Captain Burdon, from Martinique for London, sprang a leak this day which increased so much that by 29 December, when in position 35°49'N 50°14'W, the ship had seven feet of water in her hold and the crew exhausted by the need for constant pumping, abandoned her and boarded the *Guardian,* Captain Beaton, which was in company and arrived on 24 January at Dover. (*Times,* 25 January 1797)

29 December, *Impatiente, 44 guns* An American ship, *Ellis,* Captain Harvey, arrived at Cork on 4 January 1797, when Captain Harvey reported that while a gale was raging on Thursday 29 December, in the evening he was hailed by a French ship of 74 guns, dismasted, and in great distress. On her deck he saw a number of dead seamen and soldiers, and shortly after she had hailed him and before he could approach close enough to render any assistance, the vessel foundered.

Captain Harvey was mistaken. It was not a French 74-gun ship, but rather was it a 44-gun frigate, *L'Impatiente*, which was lost near Crookhaven and, regrettably, of the 250 soldiers and 300 seamen on board the ship, only seven survived. (*SNL*, 1796) [In the *Gazette* account she is said to have carried only 20 guns, and was therefore probably armed *en flute*. (Norie, 1827, p412)]

Captain Harvey was a fine seaman. Owing to unfavourable reports respecting the *Ellis*, the underwriters had refused twenty-five guineas per cent for insuring her, yet she had arrived safe off Land's End from New York, just two days after leaving Cork. (*Times*, 7 January 1797)

30 December, Scaevola, 44 guns Captain Harvey, the American mentioned above, saw on fire this morning a vessel of 'great force' which a short time later blew up. The ship he saw was *La Scaevola*, a 40-gun French frigate with a crew of 420, and carrying 400 soldiers for the invasion of Ireland. [*La Scaevola* was a *razee*, a battleship cut down by a deck but retaining its heavy lower deck gun battery. She was one of half a dozen vessels which had proved crank (*ie* lacking stability) but which as cut down gave some further, albeit limited, service as very powerful frigates. The British followed suit with three *razees* of their own: *Magnanime, Anson* and Pellew's famous *Indefatigable*.]

La Scaevola was a very old ship, quite unsuited for winter gales in the North Atlantic, and was in a sinking condition when a French 74, *La Revolution*, Captain Dumanoir-le-Pelley, approached and took off all the 820 men, without losing one, and that, while a gale was blowing. A truly remarkable and never to be excelled feat of seamanship. *La Scaevola* was then set on fire and this was shortly before Captain Harvey saw her and after *La Revolution* had left the scene. *La Revolution*, now with 1600 men on board and short of provisions returned to Rochefort, which she reached on the afternoon of 14 January. (James' *Naval History*, 1837 ed; *Journal de Morard de Galles* [commander of the French invasion squadron]; Archives de la Marine, BB4 102)

30 December, Cumberland, 74 guns The *Cumberland*, 74 guns, Captain B S Rowley, anchored in Portsmouth harbour at noon with the loss of her main topmast. The ship had taken seventy-three days from Gibraltar and parted from Admiral Mann's squadron, consisting of six sail of the line, on the 23rd off the Start during a gale.

The *Cumberland* had 150 of her crew sick with typhus and dysentery and was put under quarantine at the Mother Bank. They reported that the whole of Admiral Mann's squadron was much infected with dysentery, but expected them in port before the *Cumberland*. (*Times*, 2 January 1797)

The latter part of December was noted for the violent gales which swept the coasts of Britain, and the same gale that caused the *Cumberland* to take seven days from Start Point to Portsmouth, also caused much damage to other ships.

The *Prince*,[18] 98 guns, Captain Larcom, going down to St Helens, ran foul of the *Sans Pareil*, 80 guns, Captain W Browell, when the *Prince* carried away her jibboom, sprang her bowsprit and became leaky, while the *Sans Pareil* received much damage about the main chains. The *Atlas*, 98 guns, Captain Dod, ran on to the Mother Bank, and the *Formidable*, 98 guns, got on board the *Ville de Paris*, 110 guns, and carried away her bowsprit. On the latter ship at the time of the accident was Admiral Earl St Vincent, and Captain G Grey. (*Times*, 28 December 1796 and 2 January 1797)

? December, Shah Munchah, East Indiaman   The *Shah Munchah*, of 1000 tons burthen, had been built at Bombay for the East Indies and China trade when on a voyage from Canton to Bombay the ship was lost on the island of Pedro Branco in the Strait of Singapore. The crew managed to launch the ship's boats in which they eventually arrived at Malacca. (*NC* vol 15, pp465 and 466)

It may be noted here that in *Findlay's Directory*, 1870, the island is called Pedra Branca, and upon this rock, which is 450 feet long and 200 feet broad, was built the Horsburgh Lighthouse. It was determined on in 1847, after years of arguing, and the deaths of countless seamen. The funds for its construction were partially raised by liberal subscription in China and Singapore.

One other important shipwreck occurred during the latter half of 1796, yet unfortunately neither the name of the vessel nor the date of misadventure are given in the article which follows; taken verbatim from the *Times* of Tuesday 30 May 1797:

'Captain Mackie, of the *Young William* from South Georgia is arrived at Scilly, wholly laden with Sea Elephants' oil; he took from Desolation Island the entire crew of an American vessel that was lost there when on the eve of sailing with 30,000 seal skins on board; they had for months subsisted on particular parts of the seals and elephants; and not one had died.

'Two of Captain Mackie's crew have remained on that dreary un-inhabited spot to await the next vessel that shall make the voyage, to return.'

? December   On 16 December the *Times* printed the following article which unfortunately gave no dates: 'Captain Saul of the *Mary and Jane* arrived at Waterford from Barbadoes. In position 50°00'N 12°00'W he fell in with the wreck of a vessel, polacre (polacca) rigged and on going on board he found that she was laden with oil. Her two masts were over her side and her hold full of water. He saw the corpses of five men and a large Newfoundland dog on board; but did not take anything out of her.'

The given position is about 300 miles west of Land's End. The vessel had probably been caught in a storm and her unfortunate crew, unable to reach their supplies, had perished from lack of food and water.

1797

2 January, Vipere, 18 guns La Vipere had been taken in the Channel from the French by the 36-gun frigate *Flora*, Captain Sir J B Warren, on 23 January 1794.

    After the dispersal of the convoy on 20 December *La Vipere*, Captain Henry Harding Parker, in company with several other ships had borne away for Valentia harbour, but had been driven by gales and the French fleet farther to the north, to the Shannon, where although the French had reached as far as Scattery Island, several of the British convoy had made Tarbert and were safe. Not so *La Vipere*; off the estuary of the Shannon she capsized and took with her the entire crew of 120 men. (*SNL*, 1797)

2 January, Daphne, merchantman The *Daphne*, Captain Ohman, from Oporto for Hamburg, went ashore in Bigbury Bay, about fifteen miles to the east of Plymouth and became a total wreck. Her crew were saved. (*Times*, 4 January 1797)

2 January, Surveillante, 44 guns A 44-gun French frigate the *Surveillante* was one of the fleet that had left Brest on 16 December for the invasion of Ireland. On board the vessel was General Mermet, the cavalry commander, with 250 of his men. On this day during a westerly gale the ship was driven ashore (or scuttled according to *SNL*, 1799) in Bantry Bay, and although many were rescued by the boats that were in company, yet not a few who had managed to get ashore were made prisoners of war by the British. (James' *Naval History*, 1837)

3 January, Liverpool boat On this Tuesday about noon a tragedy occurred in the harbour of Liverpool. As Mr Slack the deputy constable was conveying a party of volunteers raised in Manchester and the adjacent parishes for the navy, the boat in which they were proceeding to the tender overset and before any assistance was forthcoming twenty-five men had lost their lives. (*Times*, 10 January 1797)

6 January, Fille-Unique, transport Another vessel of the French invasion fleet, *La Fille-Unique*, a transport conveying 300 soldiers foundered in Bantry Bay, but of all those on board, how many were lost or saved, or became prisoners of war, appears today to be quite unknown. (James' *Naval History*, 1837 ed.)

7 January, Betsy, transport The *Liberty* transport, Captain Harrington, arrived at Plymouth from Gibraltar. At sea Captain Harrington spoke to the brig *Lewis*, seven weeks from Malaga, the master of which informed him that in position 44º30'N 17º30'W he boarded a wreck called the *Betsy*, in the transport service with all her masts gone and with no-one on board. It appeared by papers found in the cabin that the master's name was Brown, and it was from these papers also that the ship's name was obtained. (*Times*, 10 January 1797)

10 January, St Lawrence, merchantman The storms that had dispersed the French fleet at the end of last year had also dispersed the homeward bound West Indies and Quebec fleets, and several of these ships were taken not only by the French fleet but also by French privateers that were cruising in the area to the southward of Cape Clear. The *St Lawrence*, Captain Shaw, from Quebec for London, was found at sea with no-one on board and with seven feet of water in her hold, by the *Stag* frigate. This ship had been taken and scuttled by the French privateer *L'Eclair*, of 18 guns and 150 men, which privateer was herself taken a few days later by the *Doris*, 36 guns, Captain C Jones, and by the *Unicorn* frigate, 32 guns, Captain Sir Thomas Williams, when sixty leagues south-west of Cape Clear. (*Times*, 23, 25 and 27 January 1797)

11 January, Baillies, merchantman During a gale at south-east the ship *Baillies* of London, Symes master, from London for San Domingo laden with government stores, struck on the Horse Bank (Horse Island) quite violently, and the wind soon after veering to the south-west and the weather becoming thick she drifted off and ran on to the Woolsners, or Chichester shoals, at the entrance to Langston harbour, where although the ship soon went to pieces, yet the crew managed to save themselves in the longboat. By the following morning the vessel had completely vanished. (*Times*, 14 January 1797)

It was on the Woolsners that the *Impregnable* was lost on 19 October 1799 (*qv*).

12 January, Thetis, merchantman On 2 January the ship *Thetis* of Whitby from Memel for London, laden with timber, was wrecked during a gale upon the coast near Sunderland and ten days later a great tragedy was enacted at the scene of the wreck.

Captain Irvine was one of the twelve survivors of the shipwreck and on this Thursday 12 January, while he was assisting to salvage the cargo, a tier of the timber that had been stacked on the shore suddenly fell down upon him and imprisoned him by the thigh. Every endeavour was used to extricate him but in vain, and before a surgeon could arrive to cut off the imprisoned member the tide flowed in and ended all hopes of relief. In this terrible situation and under the most excruciating tortures from the pressure upon his fractured limb the poor man remained, recommending his wife and children to the agonized spectators on the strand, till the water reaching his head closed the afflicting scene. Captain Irvine left a wife and two children. (*Times*, 24 January 1797)

14 January, Droits de l'Homme, 74 guns The *Droits de l'Homme*, 74 guns, Commodore Jean Raimond L Grosse, was returning from Ireland, and in addition to her crew was carrying General Humbert with 600 of his troops when at 3.30pm on 13 January, Ushant bearing north-east about fifty leagues, two British frigates were observed, the *Indefatigable*, a *razee* of 44 guns, Captain Sir E Pellew; and the *Amazon*, 36 guns, Captain Robert Carthew Reynolds.

The French ship had been constructed on a new principle, much longer than most ships of her rating, with two tiers of guns, but unfortunately for her crew the lower deck ports and sills were thirty inches lower than usually was the case with ships of her rating so that with the heavy sea then running the ports had to be kept closed, thus depriving the ship of the use of her main armament, 32-pounders (equivalent to about 39 English pounds).

At 4.15pm, during a heavy squall, the French ship was seen to lose her fore and main topmasts, and at 10.30pm the Frenchmen were obliged to cut away their mizzen mast. The action continued throughout the night and at daylight it was seen that both the *Droits de l'Homme* and the *Amazon* had gone ashore in Audierne Bay. The *Amazon* lost only six of her crew, the remainder, being rescued by the French, became prisoners of war; but the French ship was not so fortunate and out of the 1300 on board more than 700 were said to have lost their lives. Norie states that the French loss was 170 men, but this may have referred to the crew but not the troops.

On 25 September 1797 a court martial was held on board the *Cambridge*, 80 guns, in the Hamoaze at Plymouth, when Captain Reynolds and his crew were tried for the loss of the *Amazon*. They were all honourably acquitted. Captain Pellew claimed Head Money for 1750 men. (*NC*, vol 8, p465 et seq)

14 January, Sincerity, sloop The sloop *Sincerity*, Captain Seville, arrived at Plymouth from Wales laden with culm and slate, but waterlogged; then in turning to go up the Catwater she missed stays and went on shore on the Cobbler's Reef. Two pilot rowing boats at great peril to themselves put off from the pier and rowed around the breakers which broke over them several times, yet they managed to save all on board and landed them at the Barbican. (*Times*, 17 January 1797)

15 January, Draper, merchantman The *Draper*, from Oporto for Dublin, drifted into Bantry Bay on this Sunday morning without a soul on board. It was believed that the *Draper* had been taken and then scuttled by the

French, who had made Captain Madden and his crew prisoners. Although scuttled, yet the ship had been kept afloat by the buoyancy of the cork, wine and fruit, of which the cargo was comprised. (*Times*, 23 January 1797)

18 January, Indian Chief, merchantman The American ship *Indian Chief*, Captain Shaw, was lying in Falmouth harbour where she had taken on board fourteen hundred hogsheads of pilchards with which she was bound for Genoa. At 9pm the ship caught fire and, fuelled by the oil in the pilchards, within four hours was burnt to the water's edge. (*SYM*, 23 January 1797)

21 January, Thomas and Alice, collier As the *Hindostan*, an East Indiaman, was navigating Blackwall Reach on the Thames, she ran foul of the *Thomas and Alice*, a collier of Blyth, and sank her. (*Times*, 23 January 1797)

? January, Hermes, 12 guns The *Mercury*, a Dutch 16-gun brig, was taken by the 18-gun brig *Sylph*, Lt J C White, off the Texel, on 12 May 1796.

    Eight months later, now renamed *Hermes*, and commanded by William Mulso with a crew of eighty, the ship vanished at sea, date and place unknown. (*SNL*, 1797)

1 February, Ocean, East Indiaman Some time after 3am, during a gale, the East Indiaman *Ocean* was wrecked on the Paternosters to the northward of the island of Kalaotoa, position 7°19'S 121°00'E.[19] For the next two hours the ship lay motionless as if on a bed of rocks, it being to all appearances low tide. At 9am the cutter was manned and sent with two officers to negotiate with the natives and while they were away the ship lost her rudder and heeled to starboard. The crew then got a spare topmast over the side to prop her up. At 2.30pm, the jollyboat broke adrift and upset in the surf; the cutter and yawl which went to assist the men in the water, likewise upset, yet only three men lost their lives; two were saved by a raft, while the rest managed to gain the shore. Tents were put up on the land and some provisions saved from the ship which, however, soon went to pieces.

    A fortnight later on the 15th an affray took place between the ship's crew and the natives, when seven of the crew were killed and four were wounded. On 18 February in three proas hired for the purpose and the *Ocean*'s longboat, the captain and the rest of the crew, about 100 men, left Kalaotoa for Amboyna, one of the Moluccas in the East Indies, position 3°41'S 128°10'E. This entailed a journey of some 500 miles in shark infested waters, yet the four boats arrived at Amboyna on 28 February, all well. (*Times*, 5 February 1798)

11 March, Aurora's boat A boat in which there were two midshipmen and six sailors belonging to the *Aurora*, a Russian warship at Chatham, coming from Sheerness was overset by a sudden squall; by which unfortunate accident one midshipman and four sailors were drowned. The others were taken up by a sailing barge and put on shore in the marsh, near the Folly-house, but not knowing the direct path and the tide making very fast, they were soon cut off and the two sailors lost their lives, leaving the midshipman the sole survivor to tell the shocking story, from his bed on board the *Archipelago* Russian frigate, where he was taken. (*AR*, 1797, Chr, p14)

27 April, Albion, floating battery   The *Albion*, 64 guns, was built at Deptford in 1763 and in 1794 was converted into a floating battery for the defence of the River Thames. For this purpose the ship was positioned in the Middle Swin, seven miles north-east of Foulness Point, Essex.

On this April day the *Albion* was driven ashore in a gale and wrecked on a sandbank, yet Captain Henry Savage and his crew were all saved by the crew of the 32-gun frigate *Astrea*. (*SNL* 1797)

['The crew of the *Albion* has been transferred to the *Lancaster*, 64 guns, now fitting out at Deptford.' (*Times*, 5 May 1797)]

? April, Tartar, 28 guns   The *Tartar*, 28 guns, Captain the Hon Charles Elphinstone, had a crew of 200 when the vessel was wrecked coming out of Puerto Plata on the north coast of San Domingo. The crew were all saved by the *Sparrow* cutter, Lt J C Peers. The *Tartar* was a very old vessel, having been built by Randall of Rotherhithe and launched on 3 April 1756. (*SNL*, 1797)

10 June, Three Sisters, merchantman   The ship *Three Sisters*, Captain Nazby, sailed from Liverpool for Onega 15 May for a cargo of timber. All went well till 8 June when the ship was in position 71°00'N 4°00'W, about 250 miles east of Jan Mayen Island, when the ship became trapped in the ice and held for two days, then when it opened the ship foundered.

In the meantime Captain Nazby and his crew had placed some provisions and water in the boat together with some spars and planks torn off the quarterdeck. They formed a kind of deck to the boat like the flat roof of a house which they covered in canvas to throw off any water that was shipped and to protect them from the weather (they were in the Arctic Ocean). With the help of two poles set up as masts the sixteen men and boys reached Shetland on 19 June, greatly distressed for want of water; then having had refreshment and rest they set sail the following day for Liverpool which they reached on Saturday 1 July. (*Times*, 8 July 1797)

16 July, the Taylors' wherry   About 11am as the three Mr Taylors, two of whom were clerks in the office of foreign affairs, the other ADC to the Duke of York, were going into London from Richmond in a small wherry with a sail, which they had built themselves for their own amusement, the boat overset near Kew, by striking against a barge and all three fell overboard. Mr B Taylor got on shore unhurt. Mr Herbert Taylor was carried on shore with little signs of life, but recovered, and Mr William Taylor who had recently returned from Vienna with Mr Hammond, to whom he had acted as secretary, was unfortunately not found. (*AR*, 1797, Chr, p38)

23 August, Thames boat accident   Where the Thames joins Barking Creek thirteen persons returning from on board a vessel stopped to take a child on board. The tide flowing strong, the boat was carried a little way from the ship when some of the party endeavouring to reach the child dropped it into the water. Everyone attempting to save it ran to the side of the boat which caused it to upset and six persons including the infant were drowned. (*Times*, 29 August 1797; *AR*, 1797, Chr, p44)

? August, Seton, country ship   The ship *Seton* of Bombay, about 600 tons burthen, from Bombay bound to Canton, was perceived to be on fire when near the coast of China, which could not be extinguished by the crew; but a strong breeze being favourable for running towards land, they were enabled to run her on shore near Macao, which saved her crew. (*NC* vol 15, p466)

2 September, Thomas, slaver   'The *Thomas* was a slave ship belonging to Liverpool; trading from Barbadoes to the coast of Africa for slaves, and after buying a cargo in August 1797 sailed for that island. Because the coast of Africa was infested with French privateers Captain M'Quay had thought it expedient to teach the slaves the use of firearms, as he had had frequent skirmishes with the French on his last voyage. But instead of becoming auxiliaries in his defence they took advantage of his instructions, and seizing the ammunition chest on 2 September very early in the morning about two hundred of them appeared on deck, accoutred, and fired on the crew, some of whom fell; others taken by surprise and with no means of defence jumped overboard, whilst others escaped through the cabin window and took refuge in the boat which was astern. The remainder still continued to try and quell the slaves, but with no other arms than those usually kept in the cabin they could entertain no hope of success; but the captain observing that some of the crew were in the boat and ready to desert, he remonstrated so warmly as to induce them to return, but yet again convinced that they were over-powered and could not regain the ship, twelve once more secured the boat and quitted the *Thomas*.

'They had escaped one tragedy for another more dreadful. At the mercy of the elements they suffered hunger and thirst for several days, when they providentially took a small turtle, floating on the surface of the water asleep. Raw turtle did not last long among so many and again driven to distress for want of food they soaked their shoes and two hairy caps in the water, which being rendered soft, each partook of them. Several days later with the pangs of hunger pressing hard upon them they fell upon the dreadful expedient of eating each other. To obviate all contention they cast lots to determine who should suffer and he then only requested that he might be bled to death. The surgeon of the *Thomas* being among them, had his case of instruments in his pocket when he quitted the vessel, and the request was not denied. No sooner had he divided the vein than he pressed his lips to the cut and drank the blood as it flowed, while his comrades anxiously watched the victim, that they might prey upon his flesh. Of those who glutted themselves with human flesh and gore some perished with raging insanity whilst others who had refused to eat their comrade still preserved theirs.

'On 10 October, their thirty-eighth day in the boat, two men and a boy, the only survivors, saw the island of Barbadoes, but having no helm with which to steer, had to wait until they were washed ashore. The boy having fallen into the surf and unable to save himself was drowned. The two men exerting what little strength they had crawled to the mouth of Joe's river on the north-east coast, where they were found by a Mr Mascoll.' (*NC* vol 20, pp133 and 134; Dalyell, vol 3, p355 et seq)

[The *Naval Chronicle* and Dalyell each gave the same version, taken from an unnamed Barbados newspaper. The *Times* also printed the story on 18 December 1797, calling the slaves 'Insurgent Blacks'. The *Times* also queried the disposal of the ship; but this appears to be unknown. This was not the first time slaves had taken over a slaver; the ship *Delight* was taken over in 1769. (*AR*, 1770, Chr, p98)]

12 October, Monnikendam, 44 guns A 44-gun frigate, the *Monnikendam*, was one of the Dutch ships taken by Admiral Duncan on 11 October off Camperdown. On board the ship was placed an English prize master, a Lt with a midshipman and 33 seamen, with orders to take the vessel to England. Jury masts were rigged but were soon lost as the ship laboured heavily with fourteen feet of water in her hull, and the situation became so bad in an ensuing gale that the prize master, in order to save the lives of all on board, was compelled to ask a Dutch boatswain to run the ship on shore, which he did at West Cappel. The 35 British were put on board the *Walcheren*, then lying at Flushing. (*Times*, 2 November 1797)

16 November, Tribune, 36 guns Much has been written about the loss of *La Tribune* on 16 November 1797, yet the stories all emanate from the same source. Volume 1 of the *Naval Chronicle*, has the story on p468 et seq; while Duncan has the same version in vol 2, p342 et seq. But Captain Edward Pelham Brenton RN, in his *Naval History of Great Britain* 1837, vol 1, p269, has written a neat precis of the same article and it is this, with a few minor alterations, which is printed here:

'*La Tribune*, 36 guns, Commodore Moulston, was taken from the French on 8 June 1796 by the *Unicorn*, 32 guns, Captain T Williams. The ship was commanded by Captain Scory Barker when she sailed from Torbay on 22 September 1797 as convoy to the Quebec and Newfoundland fleets, which she lost during a gale on 10 October when in position 46°16′N 32°11′W.

'The ship reached the entrance of Halifax harbour at eight o'clock on the morning of 16 November with the wind at ESE, when Captain Barker proposed to the master to lay the ship to until they could obtain a pilot, but the master assured the captain that he had been frequently there and had a good knowledge of the harbour; so a pilot was dispensed with and Captain Barker went below to prepare for the landing. In the meantime the master placing dependence on the judgment of a negro named John Cosey, who had formerly belonged to Halifax, took upon himself the pilotage of the ship.

'The master with an ignorance only excusable in a boy ran the ship on the Thrum Cap Shoal, which lies on the starboard or right-hand side going in. Lt Haliburton, the officer of the guard at Fort Sandwich, instantly saw her situation, and very soon got on board, when he advised the captain to provide for the safety of the crew, the ship being irretrievably lost; Captain Barker, unwilling to give her up, made signals of distress but refused to let the boats which had come to his relief quit the ship. Mr Haliburton, however, finding him obstinate, contrived to get away and thus saved himself and his boat's crew from the fate that awaited the people of *La Tribune*, and many others that went to her assistance. At this time the day was clear and she had all her sail set, with a light breeze from ESE which leads directly up the harbour. In winter the wind from this quarter invariably increases to a gale before nightfall, and it was from a knowledge of this fact that Lt Haliburton foretold the destruction of the ship. Boats from the dockyard reached her with labour; all the guns were thrown overboard, the mizzen mast was cut away, and about nine o'clock she floated off with the loss of her rudder, the gale increased, it was perfectly dark, and they contrived to keep her head to the westward, and run towards the harbour; but she could not be brought to steer and at half-past ten sank within pistol shot of the shore in thirteen fathoms, in Herring Cove, a rocky bay on the south side of the channel.

'With the ship died the captain and about two hundred of the crew; the survivors about one hundred, clung to the fore and main rigging, and got into the tops which remained above water; about midnight the mainmast fell, taking with it all those unfortunate people who had prolonged their wretched existence for one hour in the top; nine of them reached the foremast, but by six o'clock the whole number living was reduced by cold and fatigue to seven men. At daylight a boy came off by himself in a boat and took away two of them, which were all he could carry. How it happened that this poor child, only thirteen years of age, should have been the first to reach the ship after the calamity was impossible to learn; the fact is however, as certain as it is disgraceful to those concerned. The others were rescued during the course of the morning.'

Captain Brenton then goes on to state that he had been accused of treating the memory of a fellow officer with severity, but that he himself had piloted a frigate into Halifax harbour, and had never refused a pilot when he could obtain one. By his obstinacy Captain Barker had cost more than 300 men their lives, for of all those on board, only seven escaped.

1 December, Eagle and Chance, Grand Banks fishing vessels At Harbour Grace, Newfoundland, a gale drove on shore many ships that had been fishing on the Banks. At Carbonear Bay the *Eagle*, Captain Graves, was wrecked with 4000 quintals of cod, whilst the *Chance*, Captain Green, was wrecked with 1600 quintals on board, also of cod. (*Times*, 8 January 1798)

16 December, Worcester, West Indiaman The *Marquis of Worcester*, West Indiaman, carrying thirty passengers in addition to the crew, was driven on shore during a south-westerly gale, at Burton Bradstock in Dorset. Only one person survived, a seaman who was so unfortunate as to die on shore of injuries he had received from floating wreckage. (*Times*, 28 December 1797)

17 December, Thames boat A ship's boat in which were fourteen men employed in towing Indiamen up the Thames, overset in Long Reach, between the Dartford and West Thurrock marshes when regrettably eleven of the men lost their lives. (*Times*, 18 December 1797)

20 December, Ariadne, merchantman Not all misfortunes happened on board ships; some took place in the insurance field.

The *Ariadne*, a fur ship from Quebec valued at £170,000 had been missing for some days when the vessel was insured for £100,000 at 50% at Lloyds. Just a day or so later it was learned that the *Ariadne* had been taken by a French privateer and carried into Bordeaux. (*Times*, 27 December 1797)

21 December, Viceroy, packet About this date Mr Handy and his troop of equestrian performers, altogether twenty-five men, women and children, with their horses boarded the *Viceroy*, the Liverpool packet for Dublin. Also on board were the two sons of Sir John Pownall, Chancellor of the Exchequer in Ireland; making a total of about fifty persons in all, as well as more than sixteen horses, not all of which however belonged to Mr Handy. (*Times*, 3 January 1798)

When the *Viceroy* left Liverpool it was observed that she was too heavily laden, being nearly gunwale deep in the water. From this circumstance and having put to sea with only four points of the wind in her favour and a gale blowing, it was presumed that the vessel foundered with all on board, for after leaving Liverpool, she was neither seen nor heard of again. It was thought at the time that the horses may have contributed to the loss of the ship, by their rolling to one side when the vessel heeled. (*Times*, 9 and 12 January 1798)

30 December, unknown, ?privateer   The *Carteret*, a packet-ship sailed from New York on 9 December 1797.

On 30 December at noon she was chased by a ship which gained upon her very fast. By two o'clock she was within a mile when the *Carteret* hoisted her colours and fired a gun to leeward, which the chasing ship answered. Her colours were observed to be more of a crimson colour than English colours generally are; and the manner of working her and her manoeuvres convinced all on the *Carteret* that she was an enemy.

A squall coming on carried away some of the top halliards of the packet but she kept her topsails secure. The same squall took the other vessel also, she heeled extremely and the people on board her took in their main topgallant sail and spanker, but too late, for she upset and went down almost immediately. She was full of men, many of whom appeared on her broadside for a moment, but were carried down by the vortex occasioned by the sinking ship. The *Carteret* shortened sail and put about in the hope of saving any of the unfortunate men, but in vain, as not a vestige remained above water. (*Times*, 6 January 1798)

1798

4 January, Pretzler, whaler   This Thursday at 6pm a large ship, the *Pretzler*, belonging to the South Seas whale fishery, laden with blubber, was stranded near Beachy Head during a gale. The crew had barely time to get into the longboat before the ship sank, and they having no oars on board, were at the mercy of the seas. Eventually they drifted into Providence Bay near Rye harbour, where they got safe on shore, all except the captain who was drowned. A part of the cargo amounting to some 200 butts was saved. (*Times*, 8 and 11 January 1798)

9 January, Hawk, merchantman   In rough weather, a fishing smack arrived at Harwich from the Dogger Bank. The master of the smack spoke to a Dutch Dogger at sea, about fifteen leagues from the Texel, who informed him that he had picked up a boat marked *Hawk*, of Newcastle, James Bay master. As Capt Bay would have made every effort to recover his boat, it can only be assumed that the *Hawk* went down with all hands. (*Times*, 11 January 1798)

11 January, Cerberus, 32 guns   The *Cerberus*, 32 guns, Captain John Drew, arrived in Plymouth Sound from Cork and came to an anchor in Cawsand Bay. The wind blew fresh from the south, attended by a confused sea, and continued so until 1.30pm when the wind abated.

At that time, Captain Drew; his nephew Mr James Drew, acting Lieutenant of the *Cerberus*; Captain John King Pulling of the Cork station; Mr Poore and Mr Daly, both midshipmen; Captain Drew's boatswain and a black servant belonging to Captain Pulling; together with a boat's crew of six sailors left the *Cerberus* in the captain's barge and steered for the Hamoaze. Captain Drew was carrying letters from Admiral Kingsmill, the commander-in-chief at Cork, for the Port Admiral at Plymouth.

By 2pm they were passing the Bridge, a narrow channel between Mount Edgcumbe and St Nicholas Island; the swell there was very heavy with a strong ebb tide running counter to the southerly wind and sea, with the bottom rocky and the water shoal. The barge shipped a sea and Captain Drew, becoming alarmed, took off his coat and advised everyone to be prepared for the worst. His fears were soon realised for the barge shipped two or three seas and immediately foundered. Of all those on board only two survived, both were seamen and strange to relate neither could swim, yet each managed to hold on to an oar and by so doing were driven on to the rocks of Mount Edgcumbe.

Captain Pulling had only recently married a daughter of Admiral Kingsmill, and had taken passage in the *Cerberus* to enable him to take up his appointment as captain of the *Hindostan* fitting out at Plymouth as a storeship.

Just a few months later on 25 May (*qv*), Captain Drew's brother Cdr James Drew of the *De Braak*, was drowned with part of his crew when his vessel capsized in the Delaware.

The family home of the Drews was at Stockaton near Saltash in Cornwall. (*SYM*, 15 January 1798)

17 January, launching mishap   Two ships, one the *Kent*, a 74-gun Third Rate, and the other an East Indiaman were launched at Perry's shipyard at Blackwall. The East Indiaman was launched first, then when the *Kent* was launched, it collided with the other which lost its figurehead, whilst the galley of the *Kent* was stove. (*Times*, 19 January 1798)

3 February, Raven, 18 guns   The 18-gun brig *Raven*, Cdr John William Taylor Dixon (see also 2 April 1804), was lost on the Middle Ground sandbank in the mouth of the Elbe, near Cuxhaven, during the night of the 3/4 February. Except for one man, all the crew and officers were saved, after suffering the most severe fatigue and distress. Part of the ship's stores were also saved. It may be noted that the *Raven* was built in 1795 of fir (deal) a soft and useless wood for shipbuilding. (*SNL*, June 1797; *Times*, 26 and 28 February 1798)

3 April, Thames boat accident   A small boat with a sail attempted to pass the middle arch of London Bridge but by some misfortune the mast touched the arch and the boat overset, when five of the eight people on board perished. (*AR*, 1798, Chr, p26)

4 April, Pallas, 32 guns   The *Pallas*, a 32-gun frigate, was commanded by Captain Hon Henry Curzon, when she arrived at Plymouth Sound on Tuesday morning 3 April from a cruise off the coast of France.

Soon after the vessel had anchored a heavy gale came on from the south-west attended by a tremendous sea which continued with increasing violence until about 7am on Wednesday, when the *Pallas* parted from one of her anchors and drove much nearer to the shore before her other anchors could bring her up. The yards and topmasts were then struck and she rode with an apparent degree of safety until 8.30 when she again began to drive. The crew now cut away her masts to prevent her holding so much wind; but notwithstanding all their exertions, she did not bring up, even though with three anchors ahead, until the afterpart struck on the rocks in the bay between Withy-Hedge and the Cobbler's Reef. The tide by this time was strong ebb and the ship remained with her head to the sea, being kept in that situation by means of her cables and anchors until 3.15pm, the sea making a free and tremendous break over her. Though now quite aground abaft, the sea raised her forepart so much that the cables parted and the surf heaving her broadside round beat against her with so much fury that she was every minute completely hid from the view of the spectators. While the *Pallas* remained in that situation every hope for the crew seemed ended; yet providentially, because she drew less water forward than abaft, every su ceeding sea forced her head neared the land until she got nearly end on with her stern to the sea. Hopes for the crew now revived, especially as the tide was ebbing very fast. The ship being quite aground fore and aft she was then made to heel towards the shore and the crew therefore sheltered from the worst of the elements. In this state the ship lay until 11pm, when the crew were out of danger, and by noon [presumably the same day] the tide had left her so as to enable the officers and men to get ashore safely. The greater part of the stores in the ship were taken out by men from the dockyard.

Although only one man on the *Pallas* lost his life by the falling of the mainmast, yet a boat belonging to the 74-gun *Canada*, in attempting to go to the relief of the *Pallas*, was upset, and Mr Massey, acting Lieutenant of the *Canada*, and three seamen were drowned.

Much gratitude was owed to the officers and the men of the *Busy* revenue cutter for their exertions in endeavouring to save the crew of the *Pallas* and for preserving the baggage and clothes of the officers after they were taken from the ship. (*Times*, 7 April 1798; *AR*, 1798, Chr, p24)

4 April, French chasse-marée   A French *chasse-marée*, laden with brandy and wine, a prize to Sir J B Warren's squadron, was lost in Bigbury Bay. Although the vessel was completely wrecked, the crew were saved as was a small part of the cargo. (*Times*, 10 April 1798)

5 April, Princess Amelia, East Indiaman An East Indiaman, the *Princess Amelia*, Captain John Ramsden, was burnt by accident off Pigeon Island (14°01'N 74°19'E) on the Malabar coast, when about forty persons lost their lives. (*Times*, 22 August 1798)

12 April, Lively, 32 guns The 32-gun frigate *Lively*, Captain James Nicholl Morris, stood in too close to the shore and ran aground off Rota Point, near Cadiz, during a night of poor visibility. Next morning, shore batteries opened fire on the British boats engaged in rescuing the crew, yet only one man lost his life. Before the ship was finally abandoned, the crew set it on fire. (*SNL*, 1798; *Times*, 18 May 1798)

20 April, Raymond and Woodcote, East Indiamen Two East Indiamen, the *Raymond*, Captain Smedley, and the *Woodcote*, Captain Hannay, were at anchor in Tellicherry Roads on the Malabar Coast, when they were surprised by the French 46-gun frigate *La Preneuse*, Captain L'Hermite; after some resistance, both the British ships were captured, but the *Woodcote* foundered from damage received in the action. The *Woodcote* had been unable to use her guns as her deck was lumbered with the cargo she had taken on board, 100 tons of pepper.

Of the 46 guns mounted on *La Preneuse*, thirty were supposedly 24-pounders, eight were 9-pounders and the remainder were 30-pounder carronades (actually 40 guns, 12- and 9-pounders). The *Raymond* mounted 26 guns, some of which were 9-pounders, the remainder 3-pounders. (*Times*, 22 and 23 August 1798)

25 May, De Braak, 18 guns The following article appeared in the *Times* of 4 July 1798: 'Philadelphia, May 28. By Mr Vincent Low, who arrived from Cape Henlopen yesterday afternoon, we have received the melancholy news of the loss of his Britannic Majesty's sloop of war *De Braak*, Captain Drew, which overset in Old Kiln Roads about four o'clock last Friday afternoon; she was at the time under the mainsail and reefed topsails, just about to cast anchor, a mile from the lighthouse, her boat alongside waiting for the captain, who intended to go on shore at Lewes Town; a sudden slew of wind laid her down on her beam-ends; she immediately filled and went down, with Captain Drew, his Lieutenant, 38 officers, seamen and marines. The rest of the ship's company, about 25, including the boatswain, escaped in the boats and several were taken up by a pilot boat.

'The *De Braak* parted with the fleet off the Western Islands (Azores) in chase of a strange sail and was unable to rejoin the convoy.

'The crew of the *De Braak* consisted of 83 persons, about half of whom were saved, including those who were in a prize she had taken. The officers left alive are the Prize-master, a Midshipman, and the Boatswain. The accident, a most melancholy one, is greatly heightened by the circumstance of the Captain's lady being so near as New York. The prize lies at the fort.'

De Braak was formerly a Dutch 14-gun cutter, detained by the 16-gun *Fortune*, Lt Wooldridge, at Falmouth, 20 August 1795. (*SNL*, 1799)

24 July, Resistance, 44 guns   The *Resistance*, 44 guns, Captain Edward Packenham, came to an anchor early in the evening of 23 July in the Strait of Bangka (Banca). At 4am, for no apparent reason (although lightning was suspected), the *Resistance* took fire and blew up, then an hour later when daylight came all that remained of the ship was a part of the netting just visible above the water on the starboard side. At that time there were 12 survivors, but this number reduced to 4 as a consequence of injuries received by the explosion. [More than 300 perished in the disaster; including all the officers, about 250 seamen, 30 marines, 3 married English women, a Malayan woman of Amboyna and 14 Spanish prisoners of war, taken in a prize brig. (Duncan, 1812 ed, vol 2)] One of the four was a seaman, Thomas Scott aged twenty-two, a native of Wexford, who survived because as the night was so fine he did not retire to his berth below, but instead slept on the larboard side of the quarterdeck where he was awakened by a fierce blaze, followed by an explosion when he found himself precipitated into the sea. When the explosion occurred the weather was mild and the sea smooth, but of the original group of survivors only four were able to set about the task of constructing a raft from floating debris, the other survivors being too injured to assist, and one of the latter group, Robert Pulloyne, died during that first day. The men were fortunate enough to gain the main yard which with its rigging provided the foundation and lashings for the raft, although it was 1pm before the makeshift raft complete with a mast and rough sail was finished. They were three leagues from the coast of Sumatra, but at 7pm it started to blow fresh; the sea ran high with a strong current setting against them, and while yet a considerable distance from land the lashings of the raft began to give way and itself to part.

The four strongest, the men who had constructed the raft, with survival of the fittest in mind, took to an anchor stock which had been part of the raft, and to it they lashed two spars to stop it from rolling; 'within an hour they lost sight of the forlorn companions of their distress, and never heard nor saw them more.'

At 9pm on the 25th the four made land on the north coast of Sumatra; and the next day when straggling wearily along the shore they discovered five pirate proas lying in a bight, part of a fleet of about twenty vessels on the lookout for trading ships from China or Java that they could plunder.

But the British were well treated by the pirates although they were sold as slaves, and some months were to pass before they were bought by the Sultan of Lingga. The first to be acquired were quartermaster Alexander M'Carthy and John Hutton, to be followed by Joseph Scott, who had been ransomed by some Timormen for 15 rix-dollars.[20] The Sultan of Lingga then provided a proa, and believing that the three men were the only survivors of the *Resistance*, had them taken to Penang. Thomas Scott was brought up in Penobang and sold in the market place of the town of Lingga for 35 rix-dollars. His relief was obtained in an unexpected manner. Major Taylor, the commander of the British garrison at Malacca, had sent a proa with a letter to the Sultan of Lingga, asking for his help in locating any survivors and to assist them.

Thomas Scott arrived in the proa at Malacca on 5 December and some months later boarded the *Carysfort* frigate, 28 guns, Captain J Alexander. (*NC* vol 2, pp159 and 539; vol 4, pp160, 209 et seq)

['Portsmouth, October 6th. Yesterday arrived the *Carysfort* frigate from the East Indies, last from Ireland.' (*Times*, 8 October 1799)]

26 July, Garland, 28 guns   The 28-gun *Garland*, Captain James Athol Wood, ran ashore off Madagascar, bilged and sank. The crew salvaged guns, sails and provisions, and, not molested by natives, formed an encampment during their stay. Four months later they were taken off by the 18-gun brig *Star* brig, Cdr D Atkins, and carried to the Cape. (*NC* vol 1, p259; *Times*, 16 February 1799). See also Appendix G.

27 July, a hanging offence   Two friends, Lt Edward Dawson of the *Grace* gunboat, and Lt John Matthew Miller, the commander of the *New Betsy* gun-vessel, dined with their families and other officers on board the *New Betsy*, at Sheerness on the evening of 10 July when they imbibed too freely of the wine. A Lt Forth fell asleep and Dawson picked up a speaking trumpet to blow into Forth's ear. Miller objected and an argument ensued. Dawson left the ship and made his way to the beach. About 10pm the party came ashore and Miller stepped off the boat to assist the ladies. Dawson, already on the beach, incensed by the supposed insult, immediately drew his hanger and ran it through Miller's body, which occasioned his death.

On 25 July, at Maidstone, Dawson was tried before Mr Justice Buller for the wilful murder of Miller. The jury, out for a quarter of an hour, returned a verdict of guilty. Just two days later Dawson was hanged on Pennenden Heath. (*Times*, 3 August 1798; *SYM*, 6 August 1798).

Note: *Grace* and *New Betsy* were river barges bought in 1794, each mounting 3 guns. (*SNL*, June 1797)

7 August, Royal Charlotte, East Indiaman   Two East India Co's ships, *Britannia* and *Royal Charlotte*, lay three or four cables apart at Culpee, fifty miles from Calcutta. In addition to their crews, the vessels had taken on board many passengers including women and children, and as part of the cargo, each ship was laden with about 500 barrels of gunpowder for the Cape.

The ships were without lightning conductors and on this day during a thunderstorm the crew of the *Britannia* were employed placing wet swabs around the foremast and pumps when they were shaken by the explosion of the *Royal Charlotte*.

'The magazine ill constructed, the foremast running through it; hence lightning in the magazine.' (*Times*, 17 December 1799)

Of the 140 persons, including about 50 women and children and 75 lascars on board the *Royal Charlotte*, there were no survivors. (*AR*, 1798, Chr, p68)

7 August, John and Thomas, sloop   The sloop *John and Thomas*, Captain Kessick, sailed from Liverpool on 6 August and the next day at 7pm during a storm was forced on shore almost at low water, near the north wall at Whitehaven. The tide was rising and the sea so rough that no boats could go to the aid of the people on board. The sailors had lashed two women with infants in their arms to the mast and all went well until midnight, but just when hopes were entertained that all would be saved, a heavy sea washed the two infants and a fourteen-year-old girl overboard and they were lost. The rest of the people on board were all saved during the next few hours. (*AR*, 1798, Chr, p68)

10 August, Terpsichore, 32 guns   The sentinel at the cabin door of the *Terpsichore*, then stationed at Messina, fired a musket cartridge into a box of gunpowder which blew up. The wounded amounted to twenty-four persons, and among those injured were the Captain, Richard Bowen, the first lieutenant, the doctor and the master as well as twenty seamen, four of whom died later. (*Times*, 19 October 1798)

24 August, Commerce, merchantman   On 18 September the ship *Isabella* arrived at Plymouth from Demerara bound for London and laden with coffee, cotton and sugar; a few days previously she had parted from the West Indies fleet under convoy of *L'Aimable*, 32 guns and the *Beaver*, an 18-gun sloop.

On 29 August the *Isabella* fell in with and spoke the ship *Commerce* belonging and bound to Newburyport (Massachusetts), from Liverpool, totally dismasted, and the captain washed overboard in a gale on 24 August in latitude 41°20'N, after which Benjamin Heard the chief mate took the command of the ship.

On 15 September the *Isabella* spoke the *Sarah* of Liverpool bound to Africa and took out of her the captain, doctor and five seamen of the ship

Kitty, which vessel was lost on the Tuskar Rock, off the coast of Wexford and the crew taken up by the *Sarah*. See also 12 May 1812. (*Times*, 21 September 1798)

25 August, L'Etrusco, armed transport L'Etrusco, an armed transport of 24 guns, Captain George Reynolds, was purchased by the government in 1794. Returning from the West Indies the ship foundered in the Atlantic, her crew being rescued by ships in company. See also 19 December 1795. (*SNL*, 1798)

1 October, Amelia and Eleanor, slaver Extract of a letter from Captain A Spiers of the slave ship *Amelia and Eleanor* to his owners in Liverpool, Messrs W Brettagh and Co, dated Barbadoes 26 October 1798.

'We sailed from London bound to Angola. On 1st inst. I fell in with a French privateer, 18 guns, 6 and 9 pounders, in position 3°30'S 22°00'W. At eleven the action commenced and continued till half-past two in the afternoon. Early in the action I lost my bowsprit and foremast close by the rigging; when he found I was disabled, he renewed the action with double vigour and hoisted the bloody flag at his main top-gallant mast head, sheered alongside within pistol shot and hailed me, "Strike you —, Strike!" which I answered with a broadside, which laid him on a creen; he then stood away to the northward to plug up his shot holes, as I could see several men over the side. In about twenty minutes he came alongside again and gave me a broadside as he passed; he then stood to the southward and got about a mile to windward, gave me a lee gun and hauled down his bloody flag, which I answered with three to windward. I have received a deal of damage in my hull; on my starboard bow, two ports in one; several shot between wind and water; I lost all my head sails and my after sails ruined.

'I lost one slave and four wounded; four of the people wounded, two are since dead of their wounds. I shall not be able to proceed from hence till January, as my hull is like a riddle.' (*NC*, vol 1, p171)

13 October, Jason, 38 guns The *Jason*, 38 guns, Captain Charles Stirling, was cruising off Brest on this Saturday when five *chasse-marées* under convoy of a French lugger were sighted. The French ships stood towards the land, and at 3pm when the *Jason* gave chase, after prize money (the contemporary Golden Fleece), she struck on a submerged rock between Brest and Cap du Raz and soon started to fill.

The British had of necessity to surrender but not all did so. Whilst some members of the crew were making their way ashore to the prison camps, six others of a more resolute turn of mind took a piece of beef, a cheese, a bottle of Geneva, and a compass, put the lot in the six-oared cutter and set out for England. The following day it blew a gale with a heavy sea and was still blowing on the Monday morning when the mariners arrived at Plymouth. (*Times*, 18 October 1798)

But they were not the only members of the *Jason*'s crew to do so. With the French soldiers already on board the *Jason*, six other seamen, under the pretence of rowing ashore to join the other prisoners, took the jollyboat which had no compass and instead of rowing ashore, stood out to sea. Their voyage was the more perilous, for without a compass it was longer, they had no water and only a handful of biscuits when they left the *Jason* at 7pm, not long after the cutter had departed. Two days later at 6pm the jollyboat with its crew was taken up six leagues from the Start by the Danish brig *Speculator* of Altona, Captain C Courier, for Lisbon, who brought them down Channel to Plymouth Sound where they once again got into their own boat, but with the sea then running they were driven into the river Yealm where they landed and made their way to Plymouth on foot. (*Times*, 20 October 1798)

During the two days these men were afloat they experienced only bad weather and saw no other vessel till they fell in with the Dane. (*SYM*, 22 October 1798)

19 November Britannia, packet   Some ships were no more than floating 'charnel vaults' and one such vessel was the *Britannia*, a packet which plied between Cork and Bristol.

The *Britannia* sailed from Cork on Monday 19 November with a fine breeze at north-west, to arrive at Bristol the following day. The vessel was laden with skins, in addition to which in the hold were 45 recruits for the Prince of Wales' Fencibles; 15 women with 7 children and 18 other passengers and 4 horses. That evening the wind shifted to the east and increased to a severe gale; and with only 40 gallons of water on board, each person was rationed to a half-pint per diem with none for the horses, which rationing continued until the Thursday evening. On that night, from the heat in the hold (the hatches being kept on to prevent the vessel from foundering), the smell of the skins and the lack of water, the poor horses became wild and injured some of the 85 men, women and children, who were confined in the hold with them, so that the men had perforce to knock them down. On Friday morning one of the women passengers died, but on this day the gale began to moderate so that the captain stood the vessel to the north with hopes of making the land near Dunmanus Bay, but to the surprise of all on board, they made the Skillegs and Dursey Island. If the gale had lasted another day they would have been lost in the Atlantic. On the Saturday evening two of the children died; and on the Sunday morning the vessel reached Crookhaven.

The following day the *Britannia* once again sailed for Bristol, but without the troops, for Captain Harding thought the better of it and marched his men to Cork. Whether the cabin passengers remained on board is today unknown, but they included Colonel Munro and Captain Kennedy, both of the Caithness Legion. (*NC* vol 1, p84)

23 November, Britannia, merchantman   On Sunday 18 November the *Britannia*, Captain Caleb Watson, sailed from Shields laden with lead, bacon, butter and bale goods for London; the vessel also was carrying eleven passengers. On the Monday the wind shifted to the east bringing on a heavy sea, which continued until the 23rd during which time the vessel beat about and was driven to the northward on the Staples, near the Farne Islands, opposite Bamburgh Castle, where she was totally wrecked and the twenty-one people on board all lost their lives. Amongst those lost were Mr Thomas Heron, cabinet maker (son of the late Major Heron of Newcastle), his wife and two children; Thomas Scott, a shipwright of Newcastle, who left a wife and three young children; Andrew Ferguson, a private in the Perthshire Fencible Cavalry who was stationed at Newcastle, and the mate of the *Britannia*, Mr John Watson, who was a brother of the captain. (*NC* vol 1, p83)

24 November, Margaret, tender   The *Margaret*, a hired tender, Lt John Pollexfen, was sent from Cork by Vice-Admiral Kingsmill with dispatches for the squadron under the command of Captain Roddam Home of the 80-gun ship *Caesar*. News of the loss of the *Margaret* was given by a gentleman residing near Dunfanaghy who wrote to Admiral Kingsmill acquainting him of the loss of the vessel.

'I feel much concern at being obliged to give you the melancholy information of the loss of the *Margaret* tender, with all her crew (25 in number) on this coast, in the late violent storm. On Saturday night last, the 24th November, in a dreadful gale of wind at north-west about nine o'clock, a gun was heard, supposed to be from a vessel in distress, and soon after a brig was driven upon a ridge that runs out from the mainland to the island of Ennisboffin [now usually spelt Inishbofin] and almost instantly went to pieces, as I believe this place is one of the most dangerous for a vessel to touch upon in any weather. The wreck was so complete that when I got to the shore the next morning, the stern of the vessel was lying a considerable distance from the wreck of the ship, and the whole altogether broke into different parts. From a piece of paper taken up along the shore, only can it be known what the vessel was. One paper mentions the *Margaret* tender, John Pollexfen, Lieutenant and Commander; Colin Ross, Master and Commander; it seems to be a return of the men on board.

'The bodies of nine men and one woman have been driven on shore and buried here: scarce anything from the wreck has been saved.' (*NC* vol 1, p83)

27 November, Rose, brig   On this Tuesday morning the brig *Rose*, of Plymouth, Captain George Cooper, laden with sundry goods from Bristol for Plymouth, was driven by a south-westerly gale onto the rocks in Bigbury Bay, about twenty miles to the east of Plymouth Sound, where the vessel was completely lost with all the cargo, yet the crew were saved. (*Times*, 1 December 1798)

9 December, Henry Addington, East Indiaman, and others   The East Indiaman *Henry Addington* from Portsmouth for India struck on Bembridge Ledge off the Isle of Wight during a thick fog at high tide; then when the tide left her at 5am on the 10th, the vessel which was laden chiefly with guns, shot, shells and anchors, soon bilged. Five of the crew were drowned in trying to reach the shore on a raft, while a young boy was killed by the falling of one of the blocks from the head of the main mast. Although the main and mizzen masts were cut away there was no hope of saving the vessel and by 16 December the only part of the ship that was left standing was the forepart of her upper works.

Some dry goods floated ashore and several large cases were saved by revenue officers of the custom house, but most of the heavy cargo seemed then to be irretrievably lost.

The *Henry Addington* was not the only vessel grounded by the fog. The *Taunton Castle* went on shore in Sandown Bay but got off with little damage. The *Thames* West Indiaman, however, was stranded on the Owers off Selsey Bill, but much of her cargo was taken out and brought ashore by several small vessels. The ship was bilged and could not be saved. (*Times*, 14 and 18 December 1798)

10 December, Colossus, 74 guns   On Friday 7 December the *Colossus*, 74 guns, Captain George Murray, arrived in St Mary's Road in the Scilly Isles with a direct contrary wind, having under her convoy eight vessels from Lisbon, that arrived at the same time, the rest of the fleet having parted two days before for Ireland and the northern ports. In the evening, the wind increasing to a gale, her cable parted, and all attempts to secure the ship failing, she drifted onto a ledge of rocks, called Southern Wells, near the island of Sampson, which rocks are from eighteen to twenty-four feet under water, all the convoy riding in safety then and since, notwithstanding the wind had risen to a perfect tempest. Only one life was lost, QM Richard King, who was so unfortunate as to fall overboard when he was in the act of sounding. The inhabitants of the islands exerted themselves to the utmost of their ability in cutters and open boats, and by Tuesday evening every person had been taken out and safely landed, the sick and wounded first, whereof many were from the Battle of the Nile, the most worthy captain, and most to be commiserated, remaining to the very last. The following night the ship fell on her starboard beam ends; and so violent was the continuing gale that nothing could approach her. The ship was said to have been distressed, in order to supply other vessels of the fleet, and also to have been in a bad state before, and a worse state since she left Lisbon. By 15 December the main mast and the bowsprit had gone over the side; and on

29 December the *Fearless* gunbrig, Lt John Manderson, sailed from Dock with two naval transports for the Scillies to bring away the stores that had been salvaged from the wreck. (*NC* vol 1, pp86 and 165)

Note: 'On 29 December the remains of Admiral Lord Shuldam, brought over in the *Colossus*, lately lost in the St Mary's Road, Scilly, being rescued from the wreck, after remaining for some time in the Citadel at St Mary's, were interred on 9 January 1799 in Wyredsbury church-yard, Buckinghamshire.' (*NC* vol 1, p176)

11 December, Mars, 74 guns The *Mars*, 74 guns, Captain J Manley, was built at Deptford in 1794 and on this Tuesday was moored in Cawsand Bay in Plymouth Sound. Two seamen were being 'flogged around the fleet' (from ship to ship), and when alongside the *Mars*, while the delinquents were receiving their punishment, the greater part of the crew were leaning over the rail (as is usual upon these occasions), when the stanchions gave way and nearly 200 fell over the side. Although there were many broken limbs, there were no deaths, that is unless the poor devils being flogged died of their injuries, which often happened. (*Times*, 24 December 1798)

14 December, Coquille, 44 guns, and Endeavour, brig La Coquille, a French 44-gun frigate, was taken on 12 October by the squadron under the command of Sir J B Warren off the coast of Ireland.

Two months later on 14 December the vessel was moored at the foot of Millbrook Lake in the Hamoaze at Plymouth, when at 4pm a fire was discovered to proceed from about the gunroom in the after part of the ship. In less than five minutes an explosion occurred which blew up the quarter-deck, and the mizzen mast fell over the side; the flames then spread along the main deck and caught the main mast and the standing rigging, and from thence the fire extended itself to the fore mast and forecastle so that within half an hour the ship was wholly in flames, driven along by a strong easterly wind. As *La Coquille* was surrounded by a number of other ships it became necessary to cut her from her moorings, after which the ship was towed to the mud-flat to the north-east of Southdown, not far from the victualling office brewery. The *Endeavour* brig of Scarborough, laden with coals, bound to Guernsey, had unfortunately grounded on the mud, close to the spot where *La Coquille* first brought up, by which means she caught fire, and together with her cargo was totally destroyed.

La Coquille continued burning with incredible fury till the ship was destroyed to the surface of the water, which was about 11pm; but the fire was not wholly extinguished until the next morning at 9am; and the coals in the bottom of the brig were even then still a strong body of fire.

The crew of the *Endeavour* were all saved yet there were many casualties in *La Coquille*. Missing were three midshipmen, Mr Drury, Mr Evanson and Mr Bate; ten seamen, a woman and a custom-house officer Mr

John Jellicoe, who were all believed to have been in the gunroom at the time the accident happened.

La Coquille was a very large handsome frigate, only three and a half years old, and the fire caused a loss of £10,000 to her captors.

On Monday 24 December 1798, auctioned at noon at the Crown Hotel and Tavern, Cowley's, near the Theatre, Dock, 'the remains of the hull of *La Coquille* to be sold in one lot as she lies on the West Mud, near Millbrook Lake in Hamoaze; is an object well worth the notice of the public, being coppered and of immense length; at low water she is quite dry. Immediately afterwards will be sold in separate lots, some pieces of masts, bowsprits, &c,&c.

'Lot 2. One piece of main mast with 11 stout iron hoops and cap.

'Lot 3. One bowsprit with 16 iron hoops.

'Lot 4. One topsail yard with 16 iron hoops and one gaff.

'All lying at Mr Dunstervilles, Ship builder's yard, Stonehouse.

Peter Symons, Broker.' (*NC* vol 1, pp85 and 86; *SYM*, 24 December 1798)

Note: For *Ambuscade* captured by the French on 14 December 1798, see 26 August 1799.

24 December, Mariner, merchantman   The ship *Mariner*, Captain Chivers, from London bound to Nevis in the West Indies, with horses and various merchandise, arrived at Plymouth on 24 December. On the 6th of the month when in the Bay of Biscay, during a violent gale, a tremendous sea had struck her on the quarter, which threw her on her beam ends, carried away her mizzen mast and washed everything off the deck, together with the whole watch, consisting of seven men, two only of whom were able to regain the ship; the other five poor fellows, after a long time using every exertion among the floating wreckage to save themselves, perished in the sea. The ship lay on her beam ends many hours and eight of the horses were drowned in the hold before the vessel was again on her bottom.

The *Venus*, 32 guns, Captain Graves, fell in with the *Mariner* off the Start and escorted her into Plymouth. (*NC* vol 1, p165)

? December, Ontario, merchantman   During this month of December, exact date unknown, the American ship *Ontario*, about 600 tons burthen, from Canton for New York, was wrecked on a hitherto unknown rock in the clear channel near Karimata, on the south-west coast of Borneo. The crew were saved and taken on board the American ship *Swift*, which was in company. (*NC* vol 15, p466)

31 December, two colliers   This year ended on a tragic note. On this Monday morning two colliers were stranded on the sands outside Yarmouth, in consequence of which the launches of the fleet were ordered to go to their assistance, regardless of the weather. Unfortunately, not only were the colliers lost but the launches also, and with them all on board. (*Times*, 3 January 1799)

1799

7 January, Apollo, 38 guns The *Apollo*, a 38-gun frigate, Captain Halkett, arrived at Yarmouth on 1 January with men who had been injured when one of the capstan pawls broke as the anchor was being weighed causing men on the other bars to lose control, and the capstan then running free, the remaining bars knocked down and injured about thirty men.

On 5 January the *Apollo* sailed once again, probably short of her complement, to cruise off the coast of Holland, but only two days later in thick weather at 7am the ship struck on the Haak Sandbank off the Texel and could not be relieved. It was late in the afternoon when a small wine laden Prussian galliot appeared which stood by till it was decided to abandon the *Apollo*, then to accommodate the 250 men, the greater part of the galliot's cargo had to be thrown overboard and at 9pm the *Apollo* was finally abandoned.

The galliot had water enough only for her crew so that the men of the *Apollo* were perforced to drink wine during the three days and nights that they were on the galliot where class distinction prevailed; the twenty-two officers of the *Apollo* all crowded into the cabin of the galliot, where they ate, drank and slept, as never since, for it was only eleven feet square and six feet high, whilst the unfortunate sailors had to share the hold of the vessel with the remainder of the wine!

On 11 January the galliot arrived at Yarmouth followed three days later by a cutter belonging to the *Apollo*, the captain of which stated that he went on board the *Apollo* after the vessel was abandoned. There was no water between decks nor in the cabin; that he had taken away his things out of the wardrobe and brought away a goat that was standing upon the deck; the masts were all standing, the sails furled and twenty guns abaft.

On Tuesday 15 January on board the *Monmouth*, 64 guns, lying at Yarmouth, Captain Halkett and his crew were tried by court martial for the loss of the *Apollo* when, although the captain and the remainder of the crew were acquitted, the pilot was broke. (*NC* vol 1, p168; *Times*, 14 and 16 January 1799)

11 January, Ganges, armed schooner The *Ganges*, an armed schooner belonging to the East India Company, came to an anchor to the eastward of Lacam's Channel in the mouth of the Hooghly river and the *Laurel*, another of the East India Company's ships, was then about four leagues farther in the offing, in a south-easterly direction. About 8pm while Captain Wade and his officers were walking the deck of the *Ganges*, a disagreeable smell of burning oil and smoke came from the cabin, and upon their going below the smoke appeared to be coming from aft. The gunroom was immediately cleared and upon opening the scuttle of the after gunroom the smoke rushed out and plainly indicated that to be the quarter where the mischief lay. Captain Wade directed all the powder that was in the gunroom to be quickly removed, whilst he himself together with his officers and some crew members were employed in throwing water into the after gunroom. But their efforts were impeded by the smoke and the fire-fighters had to retreat to the deck. The *Ganges* carried only one boat and as a measure of prudence Captain Wade ordered the boat out and to be kept a little ahead of the schooner; but this was no sooner done than thirty or forty of the crew jumped into it and the officers found it necessary to push off in order to prevent the boat from becoming overloaded. Those left on board had not only now to fight the fire, but also had of necessity to construct rafts and to achieve this end the captain, two boatswains and some crew members who had all been crowded forward, were going towards the mainmast to cut it away, that it might serve as a spar when the magazine exploded, tearing up the deck from the tafferel to several feet before the main mast, by which accident eight men were killed and the second boatswain had a leg broken. Although the fire had been mostly blown out by the explosion, yet it had caught the rigging which falling down from time to time rekindled the flames on the deck. With no hope left of saving the ship, whatever things could be met with to answer the purpose were hastily lashed together and put over the side as a raft to which all the men on board, amounting to fifty-nine, were obliged to commit their safety. But before the last of the crew left the *Ganges* the cable was cut, that as it was ebb tide, the wreck of the schooner and the raft would drift together towards the *Laurel*, that the sight of the burning wreck might guide boats from that ship in the track to find them. The raft and the wreck continued drifting with the ebb tide within pistol shot of each other for the next two hours, when the wreck suddenly went down and their situation caused them great anxiety, yet they were very fortunate for after a lapse of six hours on the raft, they were found by the boats of the *Laurel* and carried safely on board.

The cause of the fire on board the *Ganges* was ascribed to spontaneous combustion of a small quantity of wood oil, contained in a dubber or leathern jar which was stowed in the after gunroom. A fire originating from a like cause occurred in the arsenal in Fort William about the year 1794. (*AR*, 1799, Chr, pp25-26)

13 January, Mariam, West Indiaman   The ship *Elizabeth*, Captain Dickson, one of the Windward Island fleet, fell in with the barque *Miriam*, Captain Frost, from Martinique for London on 8 December last in position 44°00′N 26°00′W; nearly sinking, and took out of her the captain, crew, and two lady passengers, fifteen in all; they left the *Miriam* under sail and supposed she went down soon after.

The *Elizabeth* after making the north-west coast of Ireland, was driven by foul winds and storms as far away as latitude 60°00′N longitude 17°00′W, which reduced the people to great straits for bread and water, having a number of passengers on board as well as the crew of the *Miriam* and it was not until 13 January that the *Elizabeth* made Liverpool. (*Times*, 18 January 1799)

31 January, Bee, cutter Early this morning a small cutter called the *Bee*, John Nation master, from London for the West Indies went on shore on the sands near Poole, Dorset, in a heavy gale blowing from the east. There was a tremendous sea running and a heavy snow falling which rendered it difficult and hazardous to render any assistance to the unfortunate crew. Boats from the gun-vessel *Tickler* as well as several other boats attempted it without success, and the poor fellows, after cutting away the masts and otherwise doing all in their power to relieve the vessel, were left without hope, expecting at any minute to be overwhelmed by the sea. But always in these moments of great distress men appeared who would risk their lives in the cause of humanity, and one such man was Charles Sturt, Member of Parliament for Bridport, of Brownsea Castle and of Crichel House Dorset, who was then thirty-five years old. About the middle of the day Mr Sturt with a makeshift crew boarded his sea-going yacht and although the shoal on which the *Bee* was stranded was very dangerous to approach with the seas then running, yet the gallant Mr Sturt and his crew managed to take off everyone on board the *Bee* and carry them to his hospitable mansion where they received every attention that their state required. See also 20 September 1800. (*AR*, 1799, Chr, pp5-6; *MC*, Duncan, vol 2, p75 et seq)

1 February, Hope, snow The snow *Hope*, of Liverpool, Captain Anyon, from Riga for Lisbon, laden with hemp and iron, put into Hull for repairs and sailed from thence on Tuesday 29 January with the wind at north-west, and her crew consisting of the master, mate, four seamen and three boys, one of whom, the cabin boy, was only twelve years of age. The vessel proceeded southward until 3am the next day when the wind came on to blow a hard gale from the south-east, which increased to such a degree that they were obliged to lay-to under reefed foresail, the wind and sea raging with such violence that notwithstanding every exertion the ship was driven to the northward labouring and straining very much. The gale continuing its force, with heavy snow and total darkness, they could neither make the Humber nor were they able to perceive the land, but they fell in with a brig cutter, whom Captain Anyon hailed, and requested the assistance of a pilot; no answer however attended the application as the cutter soon after parted company and the *Hope* continued to drive to the northward at the mercy of the wind and waves. About midnight on Friday 1 February she unfortunately struck the ground, the sea at that time running so high as to make an entire passage over her; and at that instant the cabin boy was washed from the deck. The mate was of the opinion that they were not far from land and signified his intention to make it, although the snow was descending in clouds and the darkness prevented him from seeing the length of the ship. The captain and Carl Ehric, a Prussian seaman, delivered their watches and money to the mate who jumped into the boat which still remained upon the deck; but a heavy sea at that moment breaking over her swept away the boat and he preserved himself by catching hold of the main stay: the next sea however proved too strong and he lost his life. The rest of the crew sought shelter in the rigging, one man in the fore top, and the rest in the main top. In this situation they held their grasp on life for some hours but from the extreme severity of the night and their benumbed and exposed position the captain with two of the seamen were all three washed out of the main top, probably almost dead from exposure. The vessel had now driven nearer to the shore and another heavy sea breaking over her carried away the main mast with the Prussian, another seaman and Swain, a young boy, upon it. The Prussian tried to save the boy but for his own preservation was obliged to quit his hold and the poor boy was drowned.

The main mast still being entangled with the rigging of the fore mast, the Prussian remained in his perilous situation for some time, till the mast drifted nearer the fore mast and he was enabled to lay hold of the fore topsail yard, from whence he got to the fore topmast head, where he found the man before mentioned still alive. By this time the *Hope* had drifted close to Dimlington high land on the Holderness coast, about eight miles to the north of Spurn Point. The Prussian perceiving the cliff and supposing it to be attainable from the topgallant masthead, prepared to ascend it, and was solicited by his shipmate to lend him assistance to ascend it also, but the Prussian declared that it was not in his power to do so and exhorted his ship-mate to follow, being the only means left for preservation; to which the other replied that being frozen stiff with the cold he was unable even to move. This poor fellow being never afterwards seen it was supposed that he shared the fate of the rest of the crew. The Prussian, watching an opportunity, dropped down the side of the cliff, which from being frozen hard was exceedingly slippery and rendered it difficult to prevent himself falling into the breakers. However, he got safe to the top, a solitary survivor of the crew. The Prussian arrived at Hull on Tuesday 5 February. (*NC* vol 1, pp255-256)

1 February, Proserpine, 28 guns   The *Proserpine*, 28 guns, Captain James Wallis, in company with the *Prince of Wales* packet, Captain Dean, sailed from Yarmouth for Cuxhaven at noon on Monday 28 January having on board the Hon Mr Grenville, Foreign Secretary, and his retinue on passage to the Court at Berlin. The ship which had a complement of 200 was carrying two pilots when on Wednesday morning, then being close in with Heligoland, a signal was made for a local pilot, who soon came on board and as it was such a fine day with a light breeze at NNE the ship proceeded for the Red Buoy to anchor for the night. It was there that they discovered that all the buoys in the river had been taken up but nevertheless it was decided that if they proceeded between the half ebb and half flood all the sandbanks would then be visible and because the pilots knew their marks well there would be no danger – or so they thought. On the Thursday morning the ships got under way with the *Prince of Wales* keeping a little ahead. It was a fine day with the wind still in the same quarter, but from 4pm when the vessels were then within four miles of Cuxhaven it began to snow and came on very thick which obliged them to anchor. At 9pm that evening the wind shifted to east by south and blew the most dreadful snowstorm that could be imagined and with the ebb brought down such torrents of heavy ice that with all hands on deck it was only with great difficulty that they preserved their stations. At 8am on Friday, perceiving that the flood tide had carried most of the ice away, which left a little opening ahead; seeing also the *Prince of Wales* on shore, it was decided to turn around and make some part of the coast of Jutland, but in this design they were foiled, for the ship struck at 9.30am on the extremity of a sandbank (Schamhorn Island) stretching out from Neuwerk Island, it blowing a heavy gale at that time, the vessel drove on with great force although the only sail set was the fore topmast staysail; it was high tide and under the fore part of the ship there was only ten feet of water. Because of the amount of ice around the vessel the boats could not be used to carry out an anchor, so all hands turned to, to shore the ship for her to heel towards the bank and not the stream. In this they succeeded, for as the tide ebbed she took to the bank; the next run of the tide, however, brought down so much ice that the shores were carried away, tore off all the copper from the starboard quarter, cut the rudder in two, the lower part of which lay under the ice under the counter, and in the hope of getting her off with the next tide, the stores and guns were thrown overboard, where the ice was so thick that the guns actually rested upon it. At 10pm on Friday, it being high water, the gale at south-east kept out the tide to that degree, that under the fore part was three feet of water less than when the vessel got on, so that all hopes of getting her off were ended. On the Saturday morning, with the ice up to the cabin windows, the stern post broken in two and the ship otherwise irreparably damaged, it was proposed by Mr Grenville and the officers to try to get over the ice to Neuwerk Island, two leagues distant, as the only means of saving the lives of the ship's company; although doubtful of success, Captain Wallis agreed.

At 1.30pm the ship's company commenced their march on the ice in sub-divisions, attended by their respective officers, in such good order as could only reflect the highest honour upon them. At 3pm the captain, accompanied by Lt Ridley of the marines, after seeing everyone out of the ship, followed; and at 6.30pm after a journey of six miles in the severest weather and often up to their waists in snow and water, they arrived at the island. But on the trek to the island a dozen people lost their lives, while others suffered frost-bitten feet and hands.

The snowstorm continued without intermission until the night of the 5th when it began to moderate. The next morning at 8am 1st Lt John Wright and one half of the officers and men with Mr Grenville, Mr Wynne, Mr Fisher (secretary of the embassy), the three messengers (Messrs Shaw, Detry and Mason), with local fishermen as guides, set off and providentially arrived at Cuxhaven after a passage as dangerous as that from the ship to the island.

Of those who remained behind, six men including Mr Anthony the master and Mr Kent the surgeon, returned to the wreck on the 10th, and when they did not return to the island were presumed lost; for on the morning of the 11th the ship had completely vanished; but the ice had been set in motion, and freezing hard had supported the ship until she was eventually cast up on the island of Baltrum, from whence the six made their way to Cuxhaven, arriving at that place on 22 February, just one day ahead of Captain Wallis and the rest of the crew.

In the 1802 Civil List Mr Grenville was awarded £1086 for his loss sustained by the loss of the *Proserpine*. The sailors got nothing. (*MC* vol 2, p84 et seq; *Times*, 22 and 27 February, 1799; *Times*, 23 March; *NC* vol 1, p332 et seq)

2 February, Penguin, letter of marque, and others The *Penguin*, a letter of marque sloop, drove from her anchors in Dublin Bay during a severe gale on this Saturday morning, and was completely wrecked on the North Bull, where the Bull Wall lighthouse now stands. All on board perished; and at the same time an East Indiaman and another Liverpool ship were both wrecked at the entrance to the River Liffey, where all on board those perished also.

On Sunday morning 65 bodies were washed ashore. (*Times*, 9 and 16 February 1799; *AR,* 1799, Chr, p6)

2 February, Nautilus, 16 guns The *Nautilus*, a 16-gun sloop of war, Cdr Henry Gunter, had been built at Itchenor in 1784 and carried a crew of 125 men. The ship was convoy to twenty-two sail from Christiansand and had nearly reached the Humber at the time she was wrecked. The violence of the storm caused the vessel to touch the ground off Speeton Cliff on the south side of Filey Bay at 6am. The difficulty of seeing the land was such, owing to the incessant drifts of snow, that she was in the midst of the breakers on a lee shore before her real condition could be discovered.

Two attempts were made to clear the land on each tack, by standing to the northward and to the south, but without success. A few minutes later, finding she touched and every possibility of getting her off being lost, the best means were taken to lay her in a good position for preserving the lives of all on board. In the course of two hours this was happily effected, to the astonishment of the people on the coast who were competent judges of the difficulty of accomplishing it under the circumstances in which the *Nautilus* was placed. (*NC* vol 1, pp291, 292, 346)

3 February, Lt Jones oversteps the mark Lt Jones of the *Sensible*, a 36-gun frigate, was tried by court martial at Portsmouth on a charge of taking 50 seamen who had been sent to him to weigh the anchor of the Danish ship *Gross Redustross* in the Tagus with orders not to take them over the bar of the river. He did. In returning they were run down and 43 of the men were drowned. He was also charged with embezzling part of the cargo of a prize at Falmouth.

He was found guilty in part: that he took them over the bar and did not return them as soon as directed; for leaving the convoy and going into Falmouth with a prize, when there was a fair wind up the Channel instead of proceeding to Spithead or the Downs, and also for embezzling part of the cargo of the prize. He was sentenced to be dismissed from His Majesty's service, rendered incapable of ever again serving as an officer and mulct of all his prize money. (*Times*, 31 January, 5 February 1799)

11 February, Weazle, 14 guns A 14-gun brig *Weazle* was classed as a sloop of war, commanded by 23-year-old the Hon Henry Grey, 4th son of the Earl of Stamford and Warrington. During the afternoon of Sunday 10 February the vessel came to an anchor in Croyde Bay with the wind from the north. As people were going to church seafaring men felt some anxiety that the wind would shift a point and blow, which it afterwards did. As the day wore on the wind increased to gale force and veered to NNW and although every effort was made to get her out to sea yet the vessel struck and foundered on the south side of Baggy Point, where she became visible at low tide.

Although all the 105 persons on board lost their lives yet there was one survivor, Mr Simon Haly the purser, who happened to be on shore that afternoon. (*NC* vol 1, pp253, 256, 291, 292 and 348; *Times*, 18, 21 and 25 February 1799)

11 February, Beckford, Economy and Diligence, merchantmen On the same day as the *Weazle* was wrecked, further down the coast in St Ives Bay the *Beckford* and the *Economy*, both from Yarmouth, and the *Diligence* from Ilfracombe, were all three lost with their entire crews, excepting the mate of the *Economy* who managed to save himself by clinging to a piece of wreckage. (*Times*, 28 February 1799)

21 March, Mr Brace's shells At public auctions anyone could purchase barrels of gunpowder, cannon, shells or other warlike stores; there were no restrictions and a Plymouth man Mr Brace (who may have owned a privateer) went to a public sale where he purchased a quantity of fixed 6-inch bomb-shells, removed from French prizes brought into Plymouth. The shells were lying in the shell magazine at the gun-wharf, in the arsenal at Keyham Point, Devonport. Mr Brace and his twelve-year-old son, together with G Newman, R Herdon and G Searles were employed in removing the shells and to save the labour of carrying them the men rolled them on the stone floor, when the sparks ignited the fuses of several and a violent explosion took place which was heard all over the Plymouth area. Mr Brace and his son were killed outright; G Newman lost his right leg at the thigh and died soon afterwards; while Messrs Herdon and Searles were both dangerously wounded, and several others had left the scene only minutes before the explosion and therefore escaped. (*Times*, 26 March 1799; *AR*, 1799, Chr, pp10-11; *NC*, vol 1, p440)

22 March, a gunpowder accident   A young midshipman of the 32-gun *Castor* was taken to the Royal Naval Hospital Stonehouse, a most pitiful sight. He had let off some loose glazed powder (see Glossary) from a priming horn and being careless the horn had exploded and burnt his face dreadfully, as well as mutilating both his hands. (*NC* vol 1, p440)

30 March, lifeboatmen rewarded   His Grace the Duke of Northumberland gave twenty guineas (exclusive of his annual contribution) to be distributed to the crew of the Northumberland lifeboat at North Shields as a testimony of his approbation of their conduct in going off at imminent peril through a vast quantity of floating ice and a very high sea, and thereby safely bringing to shore a number of shipwrecked seamen, as there were at that time four ships upon the Herd Sand at entrance to River Tyne. (*AR*, 1799, Chr, p11)

4 April, Life. . .   'A woman was delivered of three children on board the *Kent*, a 74-gun man-of-war, all of whom are in a fair way of doing well.' (*Times*, 13 April 1799)

12 May . . .and death   On 28 February John Haines, a currier, was hanged in chains on Hounslow Heath at a cross-roads for shooting at Henry Edwards, a police officer.

On 12 May eight men belonging to the Walton Association formed a party to go and see Haines. On their way home they stopped at the Flower Pot at Sunbury till ten at night, then when they were crossing the Thames at Walton the boat upset and three of the eight were drowned. (*AR*, 1799, Chr, p21)

14 May, explosion aboard the Theseus, 74 guns   The *Theseus*, a 74-gun Third Rate, was employed in the defence of Acre, and on this day at 9.30am twenty

36-pound shells and fifty 18-pound shells had been got up and prepared for service by Captain Ralph Willett Miller's order, the ship then on her own at Caesarea; when in an instant the whole was on fire and a most dreadful explosion took place; the ship was immediately in flames in the main rigging and mizzen top, in the cockpit, the tiers and various parts of the ship; but with great exertions on the part of the crew, and more particularly by Lt Summers and Mr Atkinson the master, the fires were got under control.

The loss from the calamity was great: Captain Miller was one of the 26 killed by the explosion, while 45 were wounded and 10 were drowned. The whole of the poop and after part of the quarterdeck were blown to pieces and all the beams destroyed; eight of the main-deck beams falling down, jammed the tiller, and the bedplace and bulkheads were likewise destroyed and the ship left a perfect wreck. (*AR*, 1799, App Chr, p98)

The shells had been taken from French ships captured at the Battle of the Nile in the previous August.

10 June, Hoefnung, merchantman A large Danish ship, *Hoefnung*, from Altona for Malaga with a cargo of staves, went on shore on the Goodwin Sands and a Ramsgate mackerel boat observing her distress made for the sandbank to render assistance. The crew of six hands with some difficulty got on board the Dane; but they had not been long there before their own boat anchored near the ship broke away and was lost. It then blowing a very hard gale, they were left on board the wreck together with the ship's crew, thirteen men and a boy, and they remained all Monday night expecting every moment to be swallowed up by the waves or buried in the sands. About 6am on Tuesday the ship broke into five parts but all the persons in her, twenty in number, providentially preserved themselves on the different pieces of the floating wreck to which they clung for some time. A boat was seen at some distance, by which their signal was observed; she proved to be a Deal boat which after much difficulty picked up the whole and landed them at Dover. (*NC* vol 1, p158)

28 June, Earl St Vincent, privateer The *Earl St Vincent*, Captain Smith, was a schooner privateer belonging to Falmouth and on this day when six leagues south-south-east of Cape Spartel fought an action with two French privateers supported by four Spanish gunboats. On finding that he could not weather them, he bore down on the privateers, to disable them before the gunboats could get up, but they each carried from 60 to 80 men and mounted from 8 to 12 guns and after a close action of one hour the gunboats came up and the whole commenced a heavy fire of great guns and musketry upon him. Finding it useless to contend with such superior force he ordered his stern and quarters to be cut and made a battery of his stern chase, from which he kept up a constant fire upon the enemy making at the same time all the sail he could to reach Tangier Bay, which he did after an action of five hours and a quarter. The *Earl St Vincent* carried 18 guns, 4- and 6-pounders, and had a crew of 40 men. During the action she had 3 men wounded but no-one killed. (*NC* vol 2, p251)

4 July, Townley, merchantman   The *Townley* of Liverpool was on 4 July captured by a French privateer of 14 guns, which took out her crew except Mr W Atkinson the chief mate and Mr John Overton, and put six men on board her. On the 7th Mr Atkinson assisted by Overton took an opportunity to fasten three of the Frenchmen below and attacked the rest; the prize master fired his pistols without effect and fell in the conflict when his men submitted; and on the 14th the two English took their ship safe into Viola (Vaila) Sound in Shetland. (*NC* vol 2, p251)

7 July, Fortitude, merchantman   The *Fortitude*, Captain Kearney, from India for New York, ran aground on the rocks of Ascension Island, knocked off her rudder and false keel and drifted off making much water. Two boats with seventeen men landed on the island but Captain Kearney and twenty men who remained on board were lost. (*Times*, 11 December 1799)

10 July, Planter, merchantman   Copy of a letter from Captain John Watts of the American ship *Planter* dated off Dover 15 July:
     'I sailed from Hampton Roads June 18th and nothing particular occurred for 24 days: but when in position 49°20'N 17°30'W on 10th July at two pm espied a lofty ship to the southward in chase of us. By her appearance we were all fully convinced she was an enemy, and being certain we could not outsail her, at four pm had all ready for action, down all small sails, up courses, spread boarding nettings etc.[21] At half-past five pm we backed our main topsail and laid by for her, all hands giving three cheers, she then bore down upon our starboard quarter, fired one gun into us and showed national colours; we found her to be a privateer of 22 guns, twelves, nines, and sixes, with small arms in the tops and full of men. We immediately rounded to, and gave her a broadside, which commenced the action on both sides; the first broadside we received cut away all our halyards, top-sheets, and braces, and killed three men on the quarterdeck. We kept up a constant fire for two glasses and a half, when she steered off to repair damage; and in about one glass returned to board us, with his bloody flag hoisted: we were all in readiness to receive him, got our broadsides to bear upon him and poured in our langrishe and grape shot with great success. A heavy fire kept up on both sides for three glasses this second time; in all the engagement continued firing for five glasses; at last he found we would not give out and night coming on sheered off and stood to the south-west.
     'When he sheered off, saw him heaving dead bodies overboard in abundance; we had four killed and eight wounded.
     'My passengers Mr M'Kennon and Mr Hodgson with small arms

stood to their quarters with a degree of noble spirit; my two lady passengers Mrs M'Dowell and Miss Mary Harley kept conveying the cartridges from the magazine to the deck, and were very attentive to the wounded, and administering every comfort the ship could afford, in which we were not deficient for a merchant ship.

'The merchants of Whitehaven, to which town the ladies went, acknowledged their services in the handsomest manner.' (*NC* vol 2, p250)

26 August, Ambuscade, 32 guns The *Ambuscade*, a 32-gun frigate, Captain Henry Jenkins, was taken by *La Bayonnaise*, rated by the French as a 20-gun corvette, on 14 December 1798 after an action fought with some desperation for several hours, during which time the fore mast of the *Ambuscade* fell across the French ship and served as a bridge for the French soldiers to pass over. At the time of the action *La Bayonnaise* had on board more than 200 French troops independent of her full complement of seamen, which gave her a decided advantage over the British vessel. The *Ambuscade* was sent into Rochefort.

On Monday 26 August 1799 a court martial was assembled on the *Gladiator* in Portsmouth harbour for the trial of Captain Jenkins, his officers and men, for the loss of the *Ambuscade*. After three days of enquiry Captain Jenkins and his officers were all acquitted for having their ship captured, which was occasioned by a most rapid succession of unfortunate events; by having the mizzen mast carried away by the enemy's bowsprit; by the wheel being rendered useless and the tiller ropes broken; by the bursting of a gun which wounded eleven men; by the blowing up of some powder and cartridges, which blew out the stern of the ship, carried away the jollyboat which was hung over it, and wounding seven men; by the Captain being most dangerously wounded; by the 1st Lt being killed, also the master and eleven men; by the Lt of marines being twice wounded together with thirty-nine men; by the ship being on fire; by the 2nd Lt being away in a prize with several men, and the ship already many short of her complement.

After paying a just tribute to part of the ship's company for their heroic exertions, particularly Mr Penny a midshipman, about fifteen years old, the Court passed some censure on the other part of the crew for not having shewn that intrepidity so deservedly the characteristic of British seamen, and so conspicuously shown by some of their own men, Mahony, Hodgson, and a few others. But as the evidences could not well establish those who did not behave well, and the Court fearful of involving the innocent with the guilty, acquitted the whole ship's company. Poor Captain Jenkins, from the dreadful wound he received, looked extremely ill. (*NC* vol 1, p170; vol 2, p354)

[Captain Henry Jenkins was awarded a pension of £200 per annum. (*SNL,* 1 October 1811, p61)]

28 September, Blanche, 32 guns   The *Blanche*, a 32-gun frigate, Captain John Ayscough, was being used as a transport in operations against Holland, and with only 18 guns mounted was armed *en flute*. The vessel grounded on a sandbank in the Scalp Gat in the Texel and although no lives were lost yet the vessel was.

On Friday 1 November a court martial was held on board the 44-gun *Expedition* in Sheerness harbour to enquire into the cause and circumstances of the loss of the *Blanche* and to try Captain Ayscough, his officers and crew for their conduct on that occasion. After due deliberation the Court reached the conclusion that the loss of the ship was entirely the pilot's fault and therefore acquitted Captain Ayscough, his officers and crew. (*NC* vol 2, pp537 and 634; *Times*, 21 October 1799)

28 September, Fox, schooner   The armed schooner *Fox*, of eighteen 18-pounders, Lt James Wooldridge, sailed from Jamaica on 5 September with General Bowles, Chief of the Creek Indians; she was destined to land him in the Gulf of Mexico and then to proceed on a cruise. The *Fox* touched at the Isle of Providence for a pilot but could not procure one and then sailed for her destination. On 28 September, the master then sounding, about three leagues from shore, she struck a sandbank close by a coral reef or quay [*ie* key], in shoal water, bilged and fell on her larboard side. The officers and crew remained all night in the rigging expecting every moment she would go to pieces; to add to their distress the boats were all stove. When morning appeared they got out a little pork upon the reef, and fortunately every officer and man was safe from the wreck at noon, when the *Fox* fell over and went to pieces.

In this melancholy situation, with a small pittance of pork, without any water but what they dug for in the sand, they remained 32 days without any prospect of relief. On the 33rd day they descried a sail and making signals which were answered, the sail neared them, sent boats to the reef, which took off safe though very weak for want of provisions, Lt Woold-ridge, General Bowles and the officers and crew. She proved to be the *Providence* privateer, and was on her way to Jamaica. In the Gulf she met the *Thunderer*, 74 guns, Captain T Hardy, who took the *Fox*'s officers and crew on board, and landed them with General Bowles, all safe at Port Royal on 1 December. At a subsequent court martial Lt Wooldridge together with his officers and crew were all most honourably acquitted of the loss of the *Fox*. (*NC* vol 3, p235)

23 September, Hillsborough, transport   The *Naval Chronicle*, vol 3, p324, quotes a letter from Botany Bay of this date: 'The mortality on board the *Hillsborough* transport on her voyage from England was very great; no less than ninety-six of the convicts having died during that period.'

9 October, Lutine, 32 guns La Lutine, 32 guns, Captain Lancelot Skynner, in company with the *Arrow*, sloop of war, Captain Portlock, sailed from Yarmouth Roads on the morning of 9 October and twelve hours later, during a heavy gale at north-north-west, was wrecked on the outward bank of the Fly Island Passage (Vlieland), off the coast of the Netherlands. A strong lee tide prevented any assistance being given by the crew of the *Arrow* or from the shore, where several schoots were in readiness to go to her aid.

La Lutine was carrying several passengers for the Texel, in addition to which the vessel was also carrying specie to the amount of $600,000, equal in 1799 to about £140,000. Much of the bullion has since been salvaged. [See, for example, S J Van der Molen, *The Lutine Treasure*, London 1970.]

When the dawn broke, *La Lutine* was looked for in vain; she had been under a press of sail when she struck the sandbank at about eight knots, and immediately overset. The cutter *L'Espiegle*, picked up at sea, near Borkum, two men floating on oars, the sole survivors of the *Lutine* frigate, who were taken to Yarmouth, where one of the men was so unfortunate as to die, probably from exposure. The other man, now the only survivor of the wreck left alive to tell what really happened, was not a member of the crew; he was Mr Schabrack, a notary public. (*Times*, 26 October 1799; *NC* vol 2, pp441, 535 and 538)

10 October, boat of the Resource, 32 guns During the past few days, several newspapers carried a story of the loss of a boat from the *Raisonnable*, 64 guns, Captain Charles Boyles, which was purported to be at the Downs.

However, this was not so. The boat which unfortunately foundered with the loss of ten men including a captain of marines and a purser, belonged to the *Resource*, a 32-gun frigate, Captain Crispo, which was still in the Downs on this date, whereas the *Raisonnable* remained at Spithead. (*NC* vol 2, p430)

12 October, Countess of Leicester, packet As the *Countess of Leicester* packet, Richars (*sic*) commander, was sailing out of Waterford harbour she ran on a sandbank and was totally lost. Passengers, crew and mails were all saved. (*Times*, 18 October 1799)

12 October, Trincomalee, 18 guns, and Iphigene, privateer [This article is taken from a letter written by Mr Cramlington of the *Pearl* to India House and dated Muscat 10 November 1799. According to Smyth's *Sailor's Word Book* of 1867, the 'seacunnies' mentioned below were helmsmen in lascar-crewed ships.]

The *Pearl* East Indiaman, Captain Fowler, left Bushire on 4 October with light winds from the west and north-west. On the 7th at 8.30am the Great Tomb[22] bearing south about two miles distant the *Pearl* was surprised by the appearance of a ship right-ahead and close to them, which it afterwards appeared had been lying at anchor under the Great Tomb, and had seen the *Pearl* at sunset, but was concealed from the *Pearl*'s view by the land and the hazy weather. After hailing, the enemy (for so he proved to be) instantly hauled his courses up and discharged a broadside and a volley of musketry into the *Pearl*, which was returned as soon as possible and Captain Fowler gave orders for getting the tacks down, to trim the sails on a wind, and thus endeavour to escape; with which view Captain Fowler took the helm himself, but was unfortunately soon afterwards killed by an 8-pounder shot which struck him in the chest; the main topsail tye was shot away about the same time, and the ship taken aback; on which the crew, mostly lascars, sepoys, horsekeepers and seacunnies, all quitted the deck. The chief officer Mr John Cramlington had no alternative but to surrender the ship, having previously thrown the government packets and mails overboard. The *Pearl* suffered six men killed and several wounded. On the following day the freight and bullion was removed into the privateer, which proved to be the *Iphigene*, Captain Malroux, from the Isle of France, mounting 22 guns, four of which were 48-pounder carronades, the rest 12s and 6s, and carrying a crew of 200 men. Mr Cramlington together with the gunner and some of the crew were shifted into the privateer and Captain Malroux then decided to quit the Gulf in company with the prize. Two days later on the 10th at midnight, being off the Coins (Quoins), the *Pearl* about two miles ahead of the privateer fell in with HM sloop *Trincomalee*, 16 guns, and the *Comet*, a cruiser (probably belonging to the Bombay Marine, the East India Company's private navy) who upon hailing the *Pearl* and not receiving a ready reply, fired into her, on which the privateer fired two guns in that direction then put about, judging one of them to be an English frigate, and that the *Pearl* was retaken. This was not the case and next morning the *Pearl* and *Iphigene* were together and to leeward of the English, when a few shots were exchanged. Baffling winds and calms succeeding it was not until 10pm on the 12th that a close action was fought. *Trincomalee* and *Iphigene* then fell on board each other, the privateer having her studding-sail boom rigged out, with grappling irons fixed in their extremities when she engaged. The number of her crew encouraging them to place great confidence in boarding, they were in the act of making the attempt when the *Trincomalee* blew up. Of her crew of 100 save for an English seaman and a lascar, all on board perished. The ships touching each other at this time the shock stove in the side of the privateer and forced the main and mizzen masts clear of the ship. Mr Cramlington was then on the orlop deck, which was reserved for the wounded and prisoners. He therefore had two decks over his head with the hatchway choked with lumber, at this time the *Iphigene* was going forward but Mr Cramlington and about thirty Frenchmen managed to jump overboard through the wreckage of the ship which foundered about four minutes after the explosion, the men in the water supporting themselves on pieces of the wrecks. The *Pearl* and the *Comet* were in the meantime firing at each other which precluded their sending immediate relief to the sufferers; but at length, the *Comet* made sail and boats from the *Pearl* picked up the survivors.

The privateer lost about 115 men, 12 of whom were officers, including the captain, surgeon and boatswain. A Jewish passenger whom the *Pearl* had received on board at Bussora (Basra) and several of the *Pearl's* crew went down in the *Iphigene*. The *Pearl* anchored at Muscat on 15 October and after landing the native crew members but retaining the gunner and carpenter sailed for the Ile de France (Mauritius). (*NC* vol 3, pp149, and 513; *NC* vol 4, p319 et seq)

19 October, Impregnable, 98 guns   Arrived late last night and early this morning twelve merchant ships from Lisbon for Portsmouth, under convoy of the 98-gun *Impregnable*, Captain Jonathan Faulknor. However, although the merchant ships made Portsmouth harbour the *Impregnable* did not. At the time of her arrival there was a strong gale blowing and the ship standing rather too far to the eastward ran on shore on the Chichester Shoals. All her masts were cut away and vessels from the dockyard, victualling office and gun-wharf, as well as launches and boats from the men-of-war at Spithead, went to the assistance of the crew, who were all rescued.

On Wednesday 30 October a court martial was held on board the *Gladiator* in Portsmouth harbour when Captain Faulknor and his officers were tried for the loss of the ship. It appeared that her loss was occasioned by running upon Chichester Shoals whilst in charge of Michael Jenkins the master; and afterwards beating a considerable way upon the mud flats so that it was impossible to get her off. The evidence imputed the disaster to the negligence of the master, he having run beyond the proper distance before he hauled in for St Helens and not having anchored the ship at the time when the men at the leads declared there was a material difference in the soundings; but those men differed in their reports. The evidence respecting Captain Faulknor and his officers was highly creditable to themselves and to the discipline of the ship. The Court adjudged the said Michael Jenkins, in consideration of his having been deceived in the soundings, only to be dismissed from his Majesty's service; and the said Captain Faulknor and his officers to be honourably acquitted. (*NC* vol 2, pp446, 534, 545 and 658)

25 October, Nassau, 64 guns   The *Nassau*, 64 guns, but mounting 36, was commanded by Captain George Tripp when she sailed from Deal on Sunday 20 October for the Texel. The vessel was being used as a store ship and carried a crew in excess of 300 men. On the night of Thursday the 24th the vessel was hit by a violent gale and at 12.30am on the Friday she struck on the Haak sandbank, a little to the north of the Texel; the breakers were so high that it was impossible to approach for the rescue of the crew. (*Times*, 6 November 1799)

All hands were employed making a raft to save their lives when at about 11am a brig was seen making sail towards them, but she could not venture within a mile and a half of the *Nassau*, and it continued blowing so hard that it was impossible to live in that sea. However, as the day wore on, hopes began to revive as they sat down on the quarterdeck and forced down a few mouthfuls of mutton and a glass or two of wine.

An officer reported, 'I think I shall never forget the serious countenances of all present at this repast. We sat upon the quarterdeck as the water had driven us from every other part and even there the sea washed over us. About three o'clock we hoisted out one of the boats and the Captain of Marines, Purser and a midshipman, along with the boat's crew went in her to try if they could make the brig; but alas they had not gone ten yards from the ship when the boat upset and all hands perished. [Lost in the boat were: Andrew McIntosh, Captain of Marines; Mr F Bennett, Purser; Hugh Owen, Midshipman; Charles Youle, Captain's Coxswain; Robert Chambers, Boatswain's mate; Dan McNeal, Sailmaker; Patrick Helmsley, Captain of forecastle; Mr Gammel, as previous; Thomas Searles, Thomas Lowe, John Coleman, boy; John Gent, Warranted Caulker.] (*NC* vol 2, p537)

'After the accident happened there was not a word to be heard in the ship; all hands again despondent till about five o'clock when the wind began to moderate and the brig sent her boats to and fro loaded with our people; and I had the good fortune about six o'clock in the evening to get into one of the boats and was put safe on board the brig *Jealous*. I had hardly got on board when it again blew a hurricane, which prevented any more boats going to the assistance of the rest; 205 had by this time been taken off the *Nassau*. Next morning with more moderate conditions the remainder of the crew were taken off by shore based boats.'

Of the survivors, the *Jealous* arrived at Yarmouth on the afternoon of the 30th, and landed the 205, the remainder being left on board the 32-gun *Juno* at the Texel. Men who had jumped overboard from the *Nassau* at 5pm, just as it was getting dark, were picked up by the *Jealous*'s jollyboat but they had a rough night in front of them. The boat had lost an oar and with the three oars that were left it was not possible to fetch the ship so they had to stand to sea all night. At 10am next morning in a very high sea and out of sight of land they had the good fortune to be taken up by a Prussian galliot. It was afterwards reckoned that 42 of the crew of the *Nassau* had perished.

It may be noted that the *Naval Chronicle*, vol 2, p537, gives the date of loss as Thursday the 14th whereas the 14th was a Monday; *SNL* of March 1800 also states the *Nassau* was lost on the 14th. The articles should have read Thursday 24th.

The *Times* of 22 October has a Deal report: 'Deal, October 20th 2pm *Nassau* under weigh for the Texel.'

30 October, unidentified transport A transport with stores and troops foundered on Scroby Sand (to the east of Yarmouth Roads), by which 74 artillery men and officers were drowned. The crew of five were saved. (*Times*, 11 November 1799)

1 November, Guernsey Lily, transport The *Guernsey Lily*, an ordnance transport, sailed from the Texel on 30 October for Yarmouth Roads, which she reached on 1 November, and foundered there the same day. The ship brought over Maj-Gen Farringdon of the Royal Artillery who was saved, as were the crew. (*Times*, 5 November 1799)

3 November, Brothers, merchantman The ship *Brothers* ran ashore near Blackpool, Lancs and soon went to pieces. A part of the stern on which was the name was washed ashore as also were nine bodies of the crew. (*Times*, 15 November 1799)

3 November, unidentified schooner Lt Elliot of the *Plymouth*, a lugger, arrived at Plymouth on 9 November from a cruise. She experienced dreadful weather at sea. On the 4th she spoke to a fishing vessel in the Channel which had picked up the master, his wife and children and the crew of an American schooner from Surinam, laden with cocoa, which was in the frightening gale of Sunday the 3rd, struck by lightning, which drove through her bottom and she went down. Providentially the smack was at hand and saved all on board. (*NC* vol 2, p544)

3 November, unnamed sloop At Hull a sloop of which John Darling was the master, drove against another sloop, on board of which was the master Thomas Marshall, his wife and three children. Marshall, because his sloop had shipped water, had the impression she was going to founder, where-upon he put his wife and children on the other vessel. Shortly afterwards he had the mortifying experience of seeing the other sloop capsize and take his family to the bottom. (*Times*, 12 November 1799)

5 November, Orestes, 18 guns The 18-gun sloop *Orestes*, Cdr William Haggitt, was formerly the Dutch 24-gun *Hercules* taken by the 40-gun *Artois*, Captain J MacBride in the North Seas in 1781. With a crew of 120 the ship was lost in a hurricane in the Indian Ocean. There were no survivors. (*SNL*, 31 January 1783; *SNC*, October 1801)

5 November, Swallow, brig On Thursday 7 November two pilot boats belonging to Ilfracombe carried into that harbour the brig *Swallow* of Jersey, from Liverpool for Plymouth, laden with staves. They fell in with her about one mile from the north-east end of Lundy Island. The crew were supposed to have abandoned her on the 5th near the Milford Islands and taken to the boat, but from the violence of the gale and the heavy seas then running, they were presumed to have lost their lives. (*Times*, 15 November 1799)

5 November, Beaufoy, merchantman   The *Beaufoy*, Atkins master, from Dover, arrived at Plymouth with wines for the victualling office. She was captured on 30 October by a French privateer, who put seven men on board and sent Captain Atkins and his mate below; they perceived through the grating that five of the enemy had got into the boat that was alongside, whereupon they cut the lashings, got on the deck and seized from the binnacle a pistol each and drove the other two Frenchmen overboard. They then cut the boat adrift with the other five in it, then steered for Plymouth and arrived safely. (*NC* vol 2, p544)

6 November, Malvena, brig   A Portsmouth report stated: 'The brig *Malvena* of Shields, Bell master, from Riga with hemp for Lisbon, caught fire owing to the length of time the cargo was on board; near five months, half of which time the brig has been lying at this port for a convoy. She was taken up the harbour and scuttled to save both vessel and cargo.' (*Times*, 8 November 1799)

10 November, Valk, 20 guns   On 20 November the *Pelter* gunbrig, Lt John Walsh, arrived at Portsmouth from the Texel for refitting, having been ashore on the Dutch coast. The *Pelter* brought over Lt Hill of the Welch Fusiliers. He was the only officer saved and was one of 25 persons the only survivors of the 529 people who were on board the *Valk* (*Voolk*),[24] when she was wrecked during the night of 10 November on the island of Ameland. Among the passengers on board the ill-fated vessel were three companies of the above regiment. [Also reported was the sad case of Lieutenant Hogart who having got to safety on a piece of the wreck, died instantly in a state of delirium, caused by excess of joy, after exclaiming 'Thank God, my lads, we are once again safe on shore.'] (NC vol 2, p546)

10 November, Roebuck, troopship   The *Roebuck* troopship arrived in the Downs from the Helder having on board the 2nd Battalion of the 20th Regiment under the command of Lt Col Brooke. When the regiment went out they were 1600 strong; they returned with less than 500 and they mostly sick and wounded. The ship was twelve days on her passage from the Helder, the troops under continual apprehension of the vessel being lost. Some of the grenadiers assured the *Times* reporter that they had had no change of clothes for ten weeks. (*Times*, 13 November 1799)

Also arrived in the Downs on this same day the *Lord MacArtney* mast ship and the *Lynx* sloop of war of 16 guns, Captain Hall, from Halifax in sixteen days, the shortest time ever known.

11 November, Dolphin, cutter   The *Dolphin* cutter was a new vessel launched in June to take troops to the Helder; her task this voyage was to bring them back. Captain Johns sailed from St Ives for Holland, but in the gale then blowing the vessel grounded a few miles off Fairlight. The crew in an endeavour to get her off cut away the mast, but no sooner done than the gale lifted the vessel off and drove her ashore. Three of the crew, Roger Holman the mate, the cook and another man, lost their lives and were buried in Rye churchyard on Tuesday 12 November. (*Times*, 16 November 1799)

16 November, Espion, troopship   *L'Atalante* a French national frigate of 38 guns was taken by the *Swiftsure*, 74 guns, Captain Charles Boyles, near Cork on 7 May 1794. The vessel was taken on the strength of the Royal Navy and renamed *L'Espion*.

On this November day the vessel was engaged with scores of other ships in bringing troops back from the Helder, and commanded by Captain Jonas Rose, was armed *en flute* to make room for them. *L'Espion* was returning from the Helder with 400 Russians when she got on the Goodwins and became a total loss, all those on board being rescued by ships in company.

On 25 November a court martial was held on board the *Overyssel* at Deal to try Captain Rose, his officers and crew for the loss of the ship; they were all honourably acquitted except the pilot, who was given six months and one day in the Marshalsea prison, and rendered incapable of ever again serving as an officer in the navy.

L'Espion was lost because she struck at high tide and although shored up when the tide left her the ship nevertheless soon bilged and was lost. (*NC* vol 2, p658)

23 November, Marquis of Granby, merchantman   This morning the *Marquis of Granby* of Sunderland, Stephen Urwin master, was captured in crossing the Kentish Knock sandbank by a French lugger privateer. The captain and two men were put into the Frenchman's boat in order to be conveyed on board the privateer, which was giving chase to another vessel, and by carrying a press of sail, in a short time left the boat nearly five miles astern; this circumstance induced Mr Urwin to conceive it practicable to retake his own vessel, and wrestling a sword out of the hands of the officer of the boat he compelled the French sailors to row him back to the *Marquis of Granby*. He gallantly boarded her sword in hand and soon cleared the deck of the Frenchmen, who precipitately plunged into the sea and were picked up by their countrymen in the boat. The captain proceeded on his voyage; but what became of the French sailors and the boat is unknown. The Committee of the *Navigation Policy Company*, with which the vessel was insured, have 'with that liberality and laudable forwardness which have ever characterised the port of Sunderland, when bravery and merit claimed respect, presented the captain with a piece of plate with a suitable inscription.' (*NC* vol 3, p76)

5 December, Sceptre, 64 guns On the afternoon of 4 December the *Sceptre*, 64 guns, armed *en flute*, Captain Valentine Edwards, was at anchor in Table Bay (Cape of Good Hope) alongside the *Jupiter*, 50 guns; the *Oldenborg*, a 64-gun Dane; together with some other vessels, the sea then being calm.

Table Bay is open to the north-west and on the morning of Thursday the 5th a gale from that quarter blew directly into the Bay in which there was no shelter. At 12.30pm the ship parted from her best bower cable and the sheet anchor was then immediately let go and the cable veered away to twenty-eight fathoms. At 2pm the *Sceptre* again parted a cable and this time the crew let go the spare anchor, in fact they really let it go for in veering it away they slipped the cable, the end of it not being secured.

The launch was now hoisted out to endeavour to get to the end of a cable from His Majesty's ship *Jupiter*, but the launch was unfortunately upset and lost as also was every man in her. At 7pm the ship parted from her sheet anchor and at once the utmost confusion prevailed on board, from a too precipitate order for every man to provide for his own safety. The vessel continued to drive for about ten minutes when she struck upon a reef, and although broadside on to the shore she unfortunately heeled over on her larboard side towards the sea which broke and swept over her incessantly. At a little after eight the orlop deck suddenly gave way and the larboard side of the vessel fell in, when the crew were obliged to retreat to the starboard broadside, from which many were swept off and drowned. About 9.30pm the poop was washed away and seventy or eighty men who were upon it had nearly reached the shore when it went end-over-end and every man upon it perished. The wreck soon afterwards heeled in towards the shore and upon heeling off again it rent fore and aft parting in two places before the main-chains and abaft the fore chains. It was at this moment that the captain and a great number of the crew lost their lives. One of the survivors, Mr Buddle a midshipman, struggling only to keep above water, floated on a piece of timber in a direction parallel to the shore and thus escaped wreckage, by which others who made directly for the shore were injured and drowned.

The *Naval Chronicle*, vol 3, p147, gives the number of those lost in the wreck as 10 officers and about 280 seamen and marines; whilst those who survived totalled 128, of whom many were on shore at the time of the tragedy. Three wagon loads of the dead were next morning taken to a place near the hospital and there interred; whilst another hundred bodies that were unrecognisable were buried in a communal grave on the beach.

A complete list of the officers and men of the *Sceptre* who were either saved from the wreck of the ship or who were on shore at the time of the disaster appears in the *Times* of 12 February 1800, which article is duplicated verbatim in the *Times* of 15 February 1800.

The *Sceptre* had on board trophies taken at Seringapatam,[25] which were consequently lost with the ship. The wreck drifted on shore at Hottentot Holland about two miles from the place where she had anchored.

Few of the vessels lying in Table Bay escaped damage during the gale. The Danish ship *Oldenborg* was driven on to a sandbank from which most of the crew escaped to the shore, whilst eight other vessels, among which was a large American ship from Bombay, laden with cotton, were likewise driven on shore and totally lost. (*MC* vol 1, p222 et seq)

It should be noted that *SNL*, 1799 (contemporary with the tragedy) gives the date of loss of the *Sceptre* as 5 December as does Norie, p456; yet the *NC* vol 3, p147, published in 1800, states the ship was lost on 5 November. Duncan, vol 1, p222, 1812 edition has the ship lost on Friday 5 November, but the 5th was a Tuesday; and if we turn to December, the 5th was a Thursday. It would appear that Duncan did not check his facts.

Furthermore, the courts martial took place on 14 December 1799, and because courts martial always took place as soon as possible after the events which caused them to be held; it would appear that the *Sceptre* was lost on 5 December, which date the writer believes to be correct. It is also the date adopted by official Admiralty records.

21 December, crime and punishment Cases which came before the Admiralty Sessions 200 years ago must be seen as events of that day and age, with sentences far removed from those given today. An interesting case occurred at the Admiralty Sessions held in December at the Old Bailey.

François Antoine Sauvajot who had accidentally killed a man named Mootoo on board the *Triton* East Indiaman, was found guilty of manslaughter and pursuant to sentence was burnt in the hand in open court. This was the first conviction under Lord Chancellor Sir W Scott's bill. (*Times*, 23 December 1799)

25 December, Ethalion, 38 guns The *Ethalion*, a 38-gun frigate, Captain John Clarke Searle, was wrecked off Pt de Penmarch on this Christmas Day and Captain Searle's narrative of that day's events is given here abridged from vol 3 of the *Naval Chronicles*, pp74 and 75.

'On the 24th at four o'clock in the afternoon, Point Le Cleure bore SE by E three or four leagues; standing off and on, off St Matthew with an intention of beating to windward in the morning. At eight o'clock I gave the usual necessary directions and precautions to the officer of the watch and to the pilot for keeping the ship in a proper situation during the night; and to inform me if any change of wind or weather took place; and whenever the pilot wished the ship to be put on the opposite tack; and at the end of each watch to acquaint me, as was the custom every night, with the situation of the ship with respect to the distance from the land, St Matthew's light then (at eight pm) bore E by N about three leagues; the ship then standing to the southward under her treble reefed topsails, fore topmast staysail, with the wind SE and lying up SSW going a knot and a half. At midnight the light bore NE by E three or four leagues at which time Lt [H F] Jouncey told me there was then not much wind, and I directed a reef to be let out of the topsails, and the jib to be loosed to be in readiness to make sail at a moment's warning, which order was complied with. At half-past one in the morning, the light bearing ENE between five and seven miles, Lt Quillam the officer of the watch acquainted me it was the desire of the pilot to wear again and stand to the southward till four o'clock as there was little wind; but at ten minutes past three, although the ship had not gone more than two miles from the time of her being wore and the light was then in sight and bearing NE by E (the night very dark), the rocks were discovered close ahead; and in attempting to wear clear of them the ship struck, when I ordered the hands to be turned up, and got the pumps to work and the boats out: sent the master to sound; started the water, threw the guns overboard and used every exertion to get the ship off. At four she struck very hard and knocked away the sternpost; made signals of distress to the *Sylph*. At six she fell over on her starboard side and bilged. At daylight saw the *Danae*, *Sylph* and *Nimrod* cutter; made the signal for boats to assist: finding she had bilged in several places and parted on the starboard side amidships, and seeing the impossibility of saving any of the stores, sent away the idlers and first division of seamen in our own boats to the *Danae*, *Sylph* and *Nimrod*. At nine Lord Proby [Captain of the *Danae*, 20 guns] came alongside and also another boat from the *Danae*, followed by one from the *Sylph*. The water was now over the lee gunwale and the greater part of the stern totally under water; and it was at this time difficult and dangerous for boats to approach the ship owing to the very great surf among the rocks.

'At eleven o'clock, having got all the people out of the ship, the first lieutenant by my directions set fire to her remains; and Mr Ballinghall the master's mate cut away her lower masts, which being done, and after I had seen all the commissioned officers and master into the remaining boat I was then under the painful necessity of abandoning her.'

Captain Searle then went on:

'I wish it was in my power to describe the very great merit of all the officers and the ship's company; sure I am, their exertions, their promptness in executing my orders, and the steady perseverance they shewed, was never on any other occasion exceeded: for in no similar instance was there ever less confusion.'

27 December, Ajax, collier   In a strong gale of wind at east-south-east accompanied by much sea the ship *Ajax* parted from her anchors in Sunderland Roads and grounded near the bar. It being quite low water and the ship having twelve keels of coals on board, her situation was viewed by those on shore with much anxiety; but being a new vessel (this was her first voyage) hopes were entertained that she would hold together till the tide came, and beat upon the beach so that the crew would be safe. By 12pm the sea had increased so much with the coming tide that it seemed impossible the ship would hold together much longer, and no boat daring to approach her a messenger was sent off to Shields for their lifeboat as the only means of saving the lives of those on board. The sea making a free passage over the vessel, the crew were seen to be upon the masts and in the rigging expecting the ship at any moment to capsize. About 1pm the ship hove with her broadside to the sea; the crew expecting her masts to go were seen to descend and try to hold on to the fixtures upon deck. Soon after this the ship lay down and almost at once broke up. Men were seen at intervals holding fast to portions of the wreck, and at this time two cobles put off to the wreck and succeeded in bringing off four men. Undaunted they returned, and the foremost, having taken off the captain, shipped a sea and sank; her crew and the captain were at once picked up by the other coble and brought safe on shore. By this time four other cobles and a boat, stimulated by the efforts of their companions, ventured off and with great difficulty saved the remainder of the crew except for one man who was drowned in the wreck.

The inhabitants of Sunderland and the Wearmouths made a collection for the men who had saved the crew. One hundred and fifty-eight guineas were divided amongst them; some assistance was given to the widow of the drowned seaman, the balance to be used to purchase and maintain a lifeboat. (*Times*, 9 January 1800)

1800

5 January 1800, Mastiff, gunboat   Refer to article of 7 April for *Mastiff* wrecked at Winterton.

8 January, Bruille Guille, 20 guns   The *John and Sarah* cartel arrived at Plymouth from Brest on 29 January with twenty English prisoners, amongst whom were Mr Joad, Mr Fisher and Mr Hare, passengers in the *Generous Planters*, Captain Smith, with a valuable cargo of naval stores for Jamaica.

She was captured on 1 January in position 49°00′N 13°00′W by *L'Eole*, a privateer of Bordeaux, with 26 guns and 160 men. *L'Eole* was to cruise for six weeks between 51°00′N and 47°30′N and from 15°00′W to 20°00′W. As the *Generous Planters* was going into Brest on the 8th (after beating about for seven days), *La Bruille Guille* (*Brule Guele* is the correct spelling), a French corvette of 20 guns and 170 men from the Ile de France, with nearly a million of specie, struck on some rocks and bilged. She soon capsized, broke up, and 132 of her crew were drowned; thirty-eight of the officers and crew being saved by the exertions of Captain Smith and the people of the *Generous Planters*.

This gallant conduct struck the French commandant at Brest so much that he at once ordered the officers, passengers and crew of the *Generous Planters* for England on exchange. (*NC* vol 3, p151)

10 January, Venerable's boat At Portsmouth a boat with eighteen persons on board was on passage to the *Venerable*, 74 guns, lying at St Helens, when the boat unfortunately overset near the White Buoy.

Those who perished were: Lt B C Meredith of the marines; Mr Stokes a midshipman; ten seamen; three boys and one woman, all belonging to the *Venerable*. Of the two survivors, one preserved himself by means of a trunk belonging to an officer, who avoided sharing the fate of the others by getting out of the boat only a few minutes before it left the sally port. (*NC* vol 3, p148)

17 January, inhumanity of the press gang Press gangs were very active in Plymouth on the night of 16 January, many useful hands being picked up. The next morning at about 2am a boatload of armed men boarded the merchantman *David* which had just arrived from Oporto with wines. They started two butts and drank their fill, then took out the mate and two seamen, carried them into the Sound, put the mate on the red Spill buoy, and the two seamen on another, they all three remained exposed to the wash of the sea until day-break, when the master of a stone barge going down the harbour for Catwater saw their distressed situations and sent his boat to take them off, almost benumbed with the cold, it being January. No idea was ever formed of who the inhuman villains were who could have been guilty of such an atrocity. See also 14 August 1811. (*NC* vol 3, p150)

26 January, Brazen, 18 guns At 5am this morning the *Brazen*, an 18-gun sloop of war, Captain James Hanson, was driven on to the Ave Rocks, near Newhaven, when of the whole crew of 106 men, merely one man was so fortunate as to survive. He was Jeremiah Hill, who had been drafted from the *Carysfort* frigate to the *Brazen*, upon the latter sailing from Portsmouth only ten days before she was wrecked.

Hill on the night of the 25th had the middle watch and was relieved about 2am on the 26th, but did not go to his hammock till 4am. At 5am he was alarmed by the striking of the ship (but had heard no soundings called) and hastened on deck with his jacket and trousers in his hand, which, on seeing the state of the ship, he cast away, and assisted in cutting the weather shrouds to release the main and mizzen masts, which went over by the board, but without any good effect, as the ship was by the violence of the sea almost instantly hove on her side and completely wrecked. He then got on the main mast and retained his situation until a carronade gunslide presented itself to his reach, which he embraced, and clung to it until it floated him on shore. It was remarkable that although he could not swim yet he managed to save himself whilst the most expert swimmers in the ship were drowned. At day-break the ship was seen about half a mile from the shore with her masts all gone yet many of the crew were still hanging on to those parts that were out of the water; although nothing could be done for them, for the *Brazen* had struck at low water and within a few hours the sea was breaking nearly fifty feet up the cliff's face.

The sternpost with two of the guns drifted on shore on Wednesday the 29th and while a small part of her side was carried by the tide beyond the eastern pier yet the fore part remained on the rocks where the vessel had been wrecked.

It would appear that the *Brazen* was on her maiden RN commission, Captain Hanson having been appointed to her in November, whilst the crew consisted of seamen drafted from ships that had been paid off and who were believed to have been possessed of not less than £5000 in cash and bills.

Captain Hanson had sailed around the world with Captain Vancouver during the years 1791 to 1794. (*NC* vol 2, p547)

A monument in Newhaven churchyard records the whole tragedy. (*NC* vol 3, pp147-148)

19 February, legality of pressing upheld At the Admiralty Sessions held on Friday 21 March John Salmon, midshipman, of the *Dromedary*, 24 guns, was tried for the murder of William Jones, a sailor belonging to a transport in the river (Thames), and Lt William Wright for assisting. They had pressed Jones and he had endeavoured to resist, when John Salmon drew his dagger and stabbed Mr Jones to death. Lt Wright upon producing his Admiralty warrant authorising him to impress seafarers, was acquitted and Salmon was later pronounced 'Not Guilty'. This decision established the legality of Impress Warrants. (*NC* vol 3, p234)

28 February, Britain's oldest Freemason 'Mr Lewis, aged 80, the oldest Freemason in Great Britain, accidentally slipped his foot on the gunwale of a vessel in Hamoaze, fell overboard, and was drowned. His remains were picked up this morning: Verdict, Accidental Death.' (Copied verbatim from *SYM*, 3 March 1800)

10 March, Repulse, 64 guns A 64-gun Third Rate ship of the line, the *Repulse*, Captain James Alms, was one of the ships belonging to the Channel fleet, but had been detached by Sir Alan Gardner to cruise off the Penmarks for the purpose of intercepting supply vessels going into Brest. On Sunday 9 March a violent gale and the rolling of the ship caused an accident to befall Captain Alms, who while standing near the companion ladder was thrown down it, by which accident one of his ribs was broken and he was disabled from doing any further duty on the ship's deck.

For two or three days the weather had been so thick that it was not possible to make any observation and the current had driven the ship so far out of her reckoning that about midnight on the 10th the *Repulse* struck on a sunken rock, supposed to be the Mare, twenty-five leagues south-east of Ushant. She was then going about six knots and continued striking about three-quarters of an hour before she could be brought to wear, and the water rushed in so fast that the lower deck tier was soon flooded. By great exertions the ship was kept afloat long enough to be enabled to approach the coast near Quimper and at 10.30am Captain James Alms and the ship's company quitted her and made good a landing on one of the Glenans Islands (or East Penmark), about two miles from the continent.

In the confusion of getting on shore one of the ship's boats upset with five seamen who were drowned. Two others were drowned owing to drunkenness; and four more were so drunk they could not disembark.

The first and fourth lieutenants, two midshipmen and eight seamen, preferring the risk of getting to England safe, to the horrors of a French prison, betook themselves to the large cutter and having got a small supply of provisions and bread steered for Guernsey. They had got within eight leagues of the land on the first day when a gale of wind came on, which drove them towards the French coast; and it was not until the fourth day that they reached Guernsey, after having undergone the most severe hardships, the seas breaking over the boat so incessantly that four of the seamen were constantly employed in bailing her. (*NC* vol 3, p233)

On 26 June at Portsmouth a court martial was held to try Captain Alms, his officers and men for the loss of the *Repulse*. Mr Rothery the 1st Lt, and Mr Finn the master, were found guilty of disobeying the captain's orders and were sentenced to be dismissed His Majesty's service and rendered incapable of ever serving again; whilst the rest of the ship's company together with Captain Alms were honourably acquitted. (*NC* vol 4, p74)

[He was treated badly by the Admiralty, missing out on Prize, Head and Gun Money. Although he died, in 1816, as a Vice-Admiral of the Red, James Alms had not been employed since he was wrecked in the *Repulse*. (*Steel's Navy List*, June 1816)]

17 March, Queen Charlotte, 110 guns   The *Queen Charlotte*, 110 guns, Captain Todd, was cruising under easy sail between the islands of Gorgona and Leghorn when at 6am the ship, which was carrying a crew of 837 men, was discovered to be on fire, occasioned it was believed by the fire of a match which was kept lighted for the purpose of firing signal guns communicating with some hay which was lying under the half deck. The fire spread rapidly, and bursting through the portguns and the hatchway of the ship soon caught the shrouds, and regardless of every exertion the ship burnt to the water's edge and then blew up. It was believed at the time that upwards of 700 lives were lost as the boats could not contain one quarter of the men on board the ship. (*AR* 1800, Chr, p9)

Mr John Braid the carpenter of the *Queen Charlotte* made the following statement, dated 18 March 1800:

'Mr John Braid, Carpenter of the *Queen Charlotte* reports, that about twenty minutes after six o'clock in the morning as he was dressing himself he heard throughout the ship a general cry of 'Fire' on which he immediately ran up the fore ladder to get upon deck, and found the whole half deck, the front bulkhead of the Admiral's cabin, the main mast's coat, and boats covering on the booms, all in flames; which from every report and probability he apprehends was occasioned by some hay, which was lying under the half deck, having been set on fire by a match in a tub, which was usually kept there for signal guns. The mainsail at this time was set and almost entirely caught fire; the people not being able to come to the clue garnets on account of the flames.

'He immediately went to the forecastle and found Lt Dundas and the Boatswain encouraging the people to get water to extinguish the fire. He applied to Mr Dundas, seeing no other officer in the fore part of the ship (and being unable to see any on the quarterdeck, from the flames and smoke between them) to give him assistance to drown the lower decks and secure the hatches to prevent the fire falling down. Lt Dundas accordingly went down himself with as many people as he could prevail upon to follow him; and the lower deck ports were opened, the scuppers plugged, the main and fore hatches secured, and water drawn in at the ports, and the pumps kept going by the people who came down, as long as they could stand at them.

'He thinks that by these exertions the lower deck was kept free from fire and the magazines preserved for a long time from danger; nor did Lt Dundas or he quit this station, but remained there with all the people who could be prevailed to stay till several of the middle-deck guns came through that deck.

'About nine o'clock Lt Dundas and he finding it impossible to remain any longer below went out at the foremost lower-deck port and got upon the forecastle; on which he apprehends there were then about 150 of the people drawing water and throwing it as far aft as possible upon the fire.

'He continued about an hour on the forecastle and finding all efforts to extinguish the flames unavailing, he jumped from the jibboom and swam to an American boat approaching the ship, by which he was picked up and put into a tartan, then in the charge of Lt Stewart who had come to the assistance of the ship.'

It appears that the *Queen Charlotte* was dispatched by Lord Keith to reconnoitre the island of Cabrera, about ten leagues from Leghorn, which island, then in the possession of the French, Lord Keith had determined to attack. When the fire was discovered the ship was about three to four leagues from Leghorn and although assistance was promptly sent, two or three hours must have passed before relief reached the vessel; and even then a number of boats were deterred from approaching the ship in consequence of the firing of the guns, which were shotted, and which when heated by the fire discharged their contents in every direction.

Captain Andrew Todd, who according to the report shot himself, was amongst the 700 persons who lost their lives in the disaster. (*NC* vol 3, p299 et seq; *The Naval Magazine* or *Maritime Miscellany*, vol 2, p216, May 1800)

7 April, Mastiff, gunboat The *Mastiff* gunboat, 12 guns, Lt James Watson, was lost with eight of her crew on 5 January on the Cockle Sands, near where the Cockle Light Ship now is, between Yarmouth and Winterton.

On 7 April the Lords of the Admiralty gave 150 guineas as a reward 'to the humane and intrepid exertions of some fishermen who at Winterton in Norfolk, at the risk of their lives, saved upwards of thirty of the crew of the *Mastiff* gun-vessel, wrecked near the Cockle Sands; Abel King and William Pile each receiving 25 guineas for their first volunteering in that service of danger and humanity.' (*AR* 1800, Chr, p9)

20 May, Cormorant, 20 guns The *Cormorant*, 20 guns, Captain the Hon Courtenay Boyle, ran on shore about three and a half miles from the Bogaz of Rosetta and although the crew were saved the vessel herself became a total loss. The ship was formerly *L'Etna*, built at Havre de Grace in 1793 and taken by the British on 13 November 1796 off the coast of France. (*NC* vol 4, p254)

7 July, a drunken accident A boat in which were eight or nine lumpers was on this Monday 7pm overset near Execution Dock. They had been working on board a West India ship and it was supposed that they made too free with the rum, which cost them all their lives. (*Times*, 9 July 1800)

9 July, Queen and Kent, East Indiamen The following is an extract from a letter sent by an officer from on board the *Kent* Indiaman at St Salvadore on the coast of Brazil and dated the 17 July 1800:

'We should have left this place ere now, but for a melancholy accident which has befallen the *Queen* Indiaman, which had put in here with us a few days since, for want of water. On the 9th between 2 and 3am our officer who had the watch on deck discovered a smoke issuing from the gunroom ports of the *Queen* which was moored a little way from us. Immediately we called the captain and officers, for although no alarm was given from the *Queen*, yet she was evidently on fire, so every exertion was made to man our boats with the fire-engines, buckets, &c for their assistance; but within a few minutes of our discovering the smoke she was completely in flames from stern to stem, and in a few minutes more the three masts were overboard. Unfortunately it blew very fresh and a current of three or four knots rendered it very difficult for the boats to get alongside to save the people; and so rapid were the flames that about thirty soldiers perished below decks, being unable to get up the hatchways. All the officers of the ship were saved and fortunately for us the current carried her clear of the Bay, and she drove a considerable distance before she blew up, about 7am. The cause of the fire is not ascertained as no person had been in the gunroom after 8pm; and although several people slept over the gun-scuttle the smoke was not discovered till near three o'clock. The scene was dreadful, from the cries of between 200 and 300 men, and many perishing in the flames or sea. Those that are saved are almost entirely naked from being hurried out of their beds. The remaining troops and all the passengers, about 300, proceed in the *Kent* to India. There are five ladies, and General St John and family, are accommodated by the captain of the *Kent* with his cabin apartment.

'Most of the passengers, Captain Craig, and some of the officers, were ashore at the time. Unfortunately six of the passengers and seventy of the crew perished. The only way in which this dreadful disaster can be account-ed for is that immediately upon arrival of the *Queen* at St Salvadore a guard of Portuguese were sent on board to prevent so they said smuggling, and a gunboat at the same time was laid alongside of her, the crew of which kept a fire of wood constantly burning; some of it, it is supposed, they threw in at the scuttle hole of the gunroom, for it was there the fire was first discovered, and no one of the ship's company had been near it with a candle.'

The *Queen* had more than fifty barrels of gunpowder on board at the time of the fire.

The remaining troops and passengers totalling 300 proceeded to India in the *Kent*, which now had more than 600 persons on board; but there was a sequel which occurred on 7 October; and is here taken from the *India Telegraph* of 18 October 1800:

'On Tuesday morning the 7th instant, a strange sail was discovered in the north-west quarter; the *Kent* at that time was lying to off the Sand Heads, near the mouth of the Hooghly, awaiting a pilot, and Captain Rivington conceiving the vessel in sight to be a pilot schooner immediately bore down, hoisted his colours and made a signal for a pilot; the stranger, upon this made sail and hauled up towards the *Kent*. It was soon discovered that she was a ship; the hands were immediately called to quarters and the ship prepared for action; upon her approach to the *Kent*, as she showed no colours, a shot was fired at her from the larboard side, which was followed up, as she passed upon the opposite tack, by a broadside, and a constant fire was kept up while she was within reach of the guns; the privateer *La Confiance*, for it was now ascertained to be, soon afterwards tacked, came up on the larboard side and commenced the engagement within about musket-shot, but without doing much injury, although she continued in this position for some time. She then shot ahead, and passing around the bow of the *Kent*, renewed her engagement on the other side, nearly at the same distance and for the same length of time, but with as little effect as

before. She afterwards made sail ahead, as if with the intention of relinqu-
ishing the attack and making off, which she could easily have done, having
greatly the superiority in sailing; when she got about the distance of half a
mile ahead of the *Kent* she was however observed to haul her mainsail up
and wear around for the *Kent*, and for the first time hoisted her national
colours. (Surcouf afterwards declared that he had forgotten to hoist them
previously). *La Confiance* then fired a broadside and a volley of musketry
from every part of the ship, which was returned by the *Kent* for as long as
her guns would bear; the privateer then wearing around her stern, ranged
close up alongside and received a full discharge from *Kent*'s starboard guns;
at this moment the privateer fired a whole broadside and threw a number
of hand grenades from her tops into the *Kent*, some of which penetrated the
upper deck and burst on the gun deck, at the same time a fire of musketry
was kept up from her tops, which killed and wounded a number of the
passengers and recruits that were on the quarterdeck and poop; when the
ships were completely locked with each other, Captain Surcouff entered at
the head of about one hundred and fifty men, completely armed for boarding, having each a sabre and a brace of pistols. The contest upon the deck
lasted about twenty minutes, until the French took possession.

'From the commencement of the action until the French were in
possession of the ship was about an hour and forty-seven minutes; and from
the gallant manner in which the officers and crew of the *Kent* behaved while
the ships were clear of each other. there is not much doubt but that she
would have overcome the privateer; but there being a very great deficiency
of small arms they had no means of repelling such a number of boarders, so
well prepared for close action; and Captain Surcouf acknowledged that had
he not succeeded in carrying her his own ship must soon have sunk
alongside.

'It is with extreme regret we add that Captain Rivington after the
most manly conduct in the defence of his ship fell by the musketry from the
tops of the privateer while Surcouf was in the act of boarding.

'General St John and his family were on board the *Kent*, and appear
to have been particularly unfortunate. All his jewels, plate and baggage, had
been aboard the *Queen*, when the vessel was burnt in St Salvadore in July.'

The loss on board the *Kent* during the action amounted to 11 killed
including Captain Robert Rivington; Mr Findlay the carpenter; and the
third and fourth officers; while the wounded totalled 44 and included
Captain Pilkington, Aide-de-Camp to Hon Gen St John. The casualties on
board *La Confiance* are unknown. (*NC* vol 4, p344; vol 5, p257 et seq, p368;
AR 1800, Chr, p35 et seq)

7 July, King George, merchantman The *King George* merchantman sailed
in convoy from Jamaica for London about the beginning of July. The vessel
was one of the finest in the West Indies trade and at 700 tons was laden on

this day with 400 pipes of Madeira, and also on board were many invalid soldiers.

Before the ship had cleared the island she ran aground, and in firing signal guns of distress the fire by some means communicated with some loose powder and the train ignited the magazine which blew up and the greater part of those on board perished in the explosion. (*Times*, 2 September 1800)

8 August, Insurgent, 36 guns The United States ship *Insurgent*, a 36-gun frigate captured from the French, Captain Patrick Fletcher, sailed on this day from Norfolk, Virginia, for the West Indies with a crew of 340 men. She was never seen again nor was any apparent trace of her ever discovered. (J Fenimore Cooper, *History of the Navy of the USA,* 1839, vol 1, p365)

10 August, Dromedary, storeship The *Dromedary* storeship, 24 guns, Captain Bridges Watkinson Taylor, was endeavouring to pass through the Abacus (Dragon's Mouth), one of the entrances to the Gulf of Paria, when the ship was carried by the current on to the Desert Rock, at 10pm on 10 August. The *Dromedary* was driven upon the rocks in such a situation that her bowsprit approached a rock which a man gained by swinging from a rope. He was quickly followed by several others and a spar was then launched from the bow, by which means everyone on board the vessel escaped to the shore. In addition to the crew the ship was carrying a great number of soldiers of the 2nd West India Regiment under the command of Lt Col Carmichael; together with some wives and children, so that the total number of persons on the vessel amounted to more than 500.

Fifteen hours later they had once again to board the wreck, for boats which had been sent by Governor Keton to their relief, could not, because of the breakers, approach the rocks, but come only as close as the *Dromedary*, which was used as an embarkation pier. It was remarkable that although on the ship were more than 500 people yet not a single life was lost. (*NC* vol 4, pp516 and 517)

20 August, Pickering, 14 guns The United States ship *Pickering* was a 14-gun sloop of war and with a crew of 90 sailed from New Castle, Delaware, for Guadaloupe on this day. The vessel never arrived, nor was any trace of her ever discovered. (J Fenimore Cooper, *History of the Navy of the USA,* 1839, vol 1, p365)

20 August, Caledonia, extra ship The *Caledonia*, an East India extra ship, Captain Stephen Haweis, from China and Bengal, arrived at Plymouth on 26 August. This ship put into the Cape of Good Hope, homeward bound, on 19 March, in great distress, having lost her masts and been rendered a complete wreck by several furious storms which she encountered on her passage from Bengal. After temporary repairs the *Caledonia* sailed from the Cape on 20 May and from St Helena on 17 June; at which time she made 12 inches of water an hour, which during her voyage home increased to 30 inches, so that the ship was only kept above water by continual pumping. The vessel arrived at Plymouth on 26 August after a passage of eleven weeks and sailed for the Downs on the 28th. (*Times*, 30 August; *SYM*, 1 September, 1800)

6 September, Stag, 32 guns The *Stag*, 32 guns, Captain Robert Winthrop, had been built at Chatham in 1794 on a larger scale than frigates of that class generally were. (*NC* vol 1, p559) On 6 September the ship was at anchor in Vigo Bay when during a gale of wind she dragged her anchors and ran ashore. It was found impossible to get her off and the officers led by Mr Pym, the 1st Lt, destroyed the vessel after the crew had first been taken off by boats of the fleet and distributed among the various ships. (*NC* vol 4, p254; *Times*, 4 October 1800)

14 September, boat accident off Ostend At 7.30pm a vessel in crossing the channel of Ostend as the tide was coming in was overset and of the estimated 200 persons on board only twenty were saved. It was a beautiful summer's evening, a Sunday, and there was at the time a festival at Slykens, about half a league from Ostend, to which about 4000 of the inhabitants of Ostend had gone.

Santhonax the Commandant of Artillery lost his four young children; an officer of artillery with his wife and son were lost and the wife, son and niece of a Captain of Artillery were also lost. The latter swam and saved three persons but not his own relatives. The whole town of Ostend was a scene of weeping for the loss of a relative or friend. (*Times*, 29 September 1800)

20 September, Cambrian, frigate Charles Sturt of Brownsea Castle, Member of Parliament for Bridport, was the owner of a fast sea-going cutter, which was kept in Weymouth Bay.

On this morning, the King and Queen with the Royal Family boarded the *Cambrian* frigate, and at 10am the *Cambrian* stood out to sea, followed a little later by Mr Sturt, who had made a match, his cutter against that of Mr Wield of Lulworth Castle.

Mr Sturt's cutter having the boat fastened astern, which he thought impeded her sailing, he ordered a young lad to get into the boat and take her to Weymouth; but the lad declined as did the men, for the sea was running high and they were two leagues from the shore. Mr Sturt then got in himself but having underestimated the strength of the tide he was driven towards the Shambles and a broken sea, by which his boat was several times overset, and each time with failing strength he had to swim back to the boat, sometimes to get on her keel and at other times to get inside her. Being a good sailor he used a spar as a sea anchor and fastened the painter to her broadside by means of which, each time a sea came, he holding the rope got out to leeward and then hauled himself back again, and by so doing saved himself from many a heavy sea. (*AR* 1800, Chr, pp38-39)

Being driven still farther from the land, a gale of wind coming on, and the tide carrying him on to the Portland Race, he took a diamond watch out of his fob, tied it securely round the waistband of his trousers, pulled them off and tied them round the thwart of the boat. When he had done that he made a running knot with the painter intending to put it round himself in his last moments, knowing that his boat from the direction of the wind would be driven near his house or Bridport and that his watch and seal would lead to the discovery of who he was.

But these precautions were not needed because eight sail of transports for Guernsey were obliged to put back by contrary winds, and one transport the *Middleton*, Captain Rankin, with troops of the 85th, lowered a boat and Mr Sturt was taken up after five hours in the sea.

'On 23rd September Mr Sturt accompanied by Col. Jackson of the 85th went on board the *Middleton* and distributed fifty guineas amongst the crew. Ten guineas and a silver cup to Captain Rankin; five guineas each to John Jones, John Dayly, James Napier and John Woolman, they being the four resolute fellows who dared all, in the boat to save him; and twenty guineas amongst the rest of the crew.' (*MC* vol 2, p75 et seq)

26 September, Hound, 16 guns   On 25 September the *Hound* sloop of war sailed from Brassy Sound, having in company the *Eliza* of Lerwick, with the mail for Aberdeen. The *Eliza* returned to Brassy Sound on the 27th, wind south-south-east blowing a storm with heavy rain. It was then reported from the island of Unst that several articles had been washed up in Balty Sound with the word *Hound* upon them. It was likewise reported that a cow which was sold by Mr Thomas Edmonstone of Bunes to the purser or some other gentleman of the *Hound*, the last time she was in the Balty Sound, was found among the wreckage, and by marks cut on the horns it was known to be the same cow that was delivered on board the *Hound* by Mr Edmonstone. All the reports added together spelt a disaster. The *Hound*, probably driven far to the north, had then tried to make for Balty but failed to do so; she had gone down and taken with her Captain William James Turquand, his crew of 120 men and 45 poor Dutch fishermen who were being held as prisoners of war. (*NC* vol 4, p337)

7 October, Plymouth boat accidents   A boat belonging to the *Saturn*, 74 guns, at anchor in Cawsand Bay, was going from the ship to the Hamoaze and in doing so had to cross the Bridge, a dangerous and narrow channel between Redding Point and St Nicholas Island in Plymouth Sound. A strong gale at south-west was blowing at the time with the tide on the ebb and when crossing the Bridge the boat overset, and of the twelve men on board only one lived to tell the tale.

On the same day, just a few miles away, a boat was going from North Corner at Dock (Devonport) to Torpoint when it overset, and of the eight persons on board the only survivors were a woman with an infant, which she held providentially supported by a small plank until a boat could put off and rescue them. (*Times*, 14 October 1800)

9 October, Chance, 18 guns   El Galgo, a Spanish *corveta* of 18 guns, was taken by the *Alarm*, a 32-gun frigate, Captain Edward Fellowes, off Grenada on 23 November 1796, reportedly carrying specie worth $80,355. The ship was added to the strength of the Royal Navy and renamed *Chance*.

The vessel had a crew of 125 men and had apparently made or was going to make several calls in the West Indies, for on board were passengers belonging to Martinique, Antigua and Jamaica, as well as several soldiers of the 11th Regiment of Foot, when on this day she foundered in the West Indies after leaving Port Royal, Martinique, and of all the people on board only two officers and twenty-three men survived. Captain Samuel George Stoven perished with his ship. (Norie, p457; *NC* vol 4, p517; *Times*, 29 December 1800)

24 October, Charles Baring, West Indiaman   The ship *Charles Baring*, Captain John Aris, sailed from Port Royal, Jamaica for London on the evening of 6 September with a good westerly wind and on the 8th weathered the Morant Cays and the following day made Navasa and Hispaniola.

Nothing material happened until about 15 October when the ship was found to be making a considerable quantity of water, which increased so much that by the 17th the pumps could scarcely free her, and in that condition they continued until the morning of the 20th, when they found five feet of water in her hold. The captain immediately ordered the gundeck to be scuttled that they might get to the pump well; that being done two large casks were slung on tackles which answered their purpose so well, that by 12pm there was only three feet of water in the hold. The crew kept her from gaining on them until the morning of the 21st, when the pumps were rendered almost useless by the quantity of coffee and cocoa which continually got into them. The danger of their situation increasing, the guns were thrown overboard and also a quantity of wood from the fore peak. At dusk the pumps were quite choked and entirely useless and the leak gained considerably, all hands that could be spared from bailing were employed in clearing the fore hatch-way, which by daylight was so far completed that two more casks were got to work. At this time the water was up to the orlop deck but by the unremitting exertions of the passengers and crew it was kept from gaining until the night of the 23rd, when it came to blow a heavy gale of wind which heeled the ship so much that the greater part of the water they bailed returned to the hold. The water gaining so fast, the people almost tired to death, and the gale increasing, there was then no hope of saving the ship, their only care was saving themselves. With the dawning of the 24th the main mast went over the side and it was with difficulty that it was cleared from the ship. The water had by this time reached the gun deck and no time was lost in providing for their safety. The boat (the *Charles Baring* only carried one) was got out and at 8am Captain Aris remarked that as the boat could not contain everyone he advised all hands to set to and construct a raft of spars and bags of cotton; but before this was accomplished the ship foundered and twenty-seven of the people perished. Three days later, although there was a heavy sea running at the time, the survivors were taken up by the ship *Harriot* of New York, which landed them at Cork on 8 November. The survivors included General and Madame Le Grande, Captain Aris and Madame Bauvois and her two daughters. General Bauvois was lost with the ship. (*NC* vol 4, p441)

? October, Earl Talbot, East Indiaman, and Chinese tchuan The *Naval Chronicle*, vol 15, p466 lists two shipwrecks that were believed to have occurred this month.

The *Earl Talbot*, an East India Company's ship, burthen about 1500 tons, which sailed from Bombay for Canton on 17 August, was supposed to have either foundered or been wrecked on the Pratas shoal, about 300 miles to the east of Hong Kong, during a gale. The crew and passengers, in excess of 150 persons, perished; included was the second officer Sir James Dalrymple, Bart. of Hailes. (*NC* vol 8, p345)

A Chinese tchuan from Java for Borneo foundered near the Pratas shoal in the gale which occasioned the loss of the *Earl Talbot*. The crew saved themselves in their launch. (*NC* vol 15, p466). But this is surely wrong. The Chinese ship would have had to be more than 1000 miles out of her track and that would be most unlikely. (See also entry of 21 August 1801 for *Abkar* and the *Feroze*.)

4 November, Marlborough, 74 guns The *Marlborough*, 74 guns, Captain Thomas Sotheby, was wrecked during a severe south-westerly gale on a ledge of rocks near Isle Grouat (*sic*) – actually the Beridaur shoal off Point Beguelon. The ship struck during the night of the 3rd and for several hours the situation of the crew was precarious, the weather blowing a perfect hurricane with the sea making a clear breach over the ship; but by throwing the guns overboard, clearing some of the wreckage and putting everything movable over the side, the ship lightened a little, yet still stuck fast in a kind of cove on some sharp rocks, with the water up to her orlop deck. In the morning the weather moderated somewhat and the boats of the *Captain*, 74 guns, Sir R Strachan, pushed through the surf with great perseverance and gallantry, and to their everlasting credit, took off all the 600 men on board, so that no lives were lost. (*Times*, 19 November 1800)

The *Marlborough* was one of the old class of 74s, had been built at the Royal Dockyard, Deptford in 1767 and was of 1642 tons burthen. (*NC* vol 1, p549)

9 November, hurricane in the Channel   The weather on this day and the previous night was the worst of the year, and the Plymouth report in the *Naval Chronicle*, vol 4, p435 states:

'Wind west by south. Blows an hurricane with rain. The gale of last night and this morning was awfully grand, accompanied by a heavy rolling sea; the most tremendous this season. It blew with incredible fury till seven this morning when in a moment the wind shifted from south and south-west directly to north-west, by which means the shipping in Catwater broke adrift by the crosscut of the sea and wind, which laid them athwart-hawse; all of them came to in safety, except the *John* of Boston, an American ship from the Straits with wines for the navy. She parted both cables and went on shore on the rocks of Deadman's Bay, Catwater; they cut away her mizzen mast, and she now lies bilged with a hole in her bottom. Providentially the crew were saved, but had the accident happened in the night every soul must have perished.'

But it was not only the Plymouth area that was affected by this gale of the 9th; it also caused great havoc amongst the shipping on the French coast and in the Channel Islands. The Plymouth report of the 12th, which is here given in full, tells of its effect at Jersey.

'Plymouth, 12 November. Wind WSW Cloudy. Arrived a brig from Jersey. The account she brings of the effects of the late hurricane on that coast are dreadful; *La Loire*, 48 guns, Captain Newman, parted all her cables and anchors; at high tide she passed over a ledge of rocks the night being pitchy dark, yet got safe to Spithead after they had given themselves up. The *Havick*, 18 guns, Captain Bartholomew; *Pelican*, 18 guns, Captain Thicknesse; *Lion*, 14 guns, Lieutenant Tathum; and a Guernsey privateer, were all driven from their anchors on to the rocks where they lie bilged. The officers and crews with difficulty saved their lives. The tide rose several feet in the height of the gale. The *Redbridge*, a 16-gun schooner, Lt Lempriere, drove to sea and was supposed to have foundered; since arrived at Spithead with the loss of all her guns. The *Telegraph*, 18 guns, Lt Corsellis, brought up with her best bower anchor, and was saved by cutting away her main mast. Arrived the *Providence*, Captain John, smuggling lugger, of Polperro, with 970 ankers of brandy, and three tons of tobacco, sent in by *L'Oiseau*, 36 guns, Captain Linzee; since restored, being taken out of the limits.' (*NC* vol 4, p436)

On 23 November *L'Ambuscade*, 40 guns, Hon Captain Colville, arrived at Plymouth with the crews of the *Havick* and *Pelican*, wrecked in

St Aubyn's Bay on the 9th of the month. They said that for nearly six hours after all their masts were gone they were exposed to the drifts of a sea running mountains high, which made so clear a breach over each ship that all on board expected every moment would be their last. Providentially the tide which had risen thirty-two feet, suddenly receded, and the officers and crews saved their lives but lost all their property.

The *Havick* became a total wreck and a write-off, while the *Pelican* was towed alongside the pier at St Helier, although apparently not repairable. [*SNL* May 1803 shows the *Pelican* as being on the Jamaica station and so she must therefore been repaired; in fact, she was not broken up until 1806.] (*NC* vol 4, p518)

20 November, Flora, armed ship The *Flora*, a hired armed brig of 14 guns, Lt Carpenter, was at anchor in the Hamoaze when she drifted on to the rocks between Mount Wip and the old gun-wharf. Then, to prevent her falling over, the crew cut away the masts, yet she soon afterwards hauled off and sank in deep water on her larboard beam ends. She was a well equipped brig, sound in all stores, and bound for the Straits.

On 1 December the *Flora* was weighed up by means of casks and lighters, then towed to the Catwater to be repaired.

On 3 December a Court of Enquiry was held to enquire into the circumstances which led to the upsetting of the *Flora* when, after due consideration of all the factors, Lt Carpenter was honourably acquitted. (*NC* vol 4, p520)

13 December, America, 64 guns A court martial was held on board the *Carnatic* in Port Royal harbour, Jamaica on Saturday 27 December 1800 to try Captain Bingham, his officers and ship's company, for having got the 64-gun *America* on the Formigas [18°26' to 18°34'N 75°41' to 75°51'W] shoal at 2pm on 13 December.

The Court was of the opinion that the sole cause of the accident was the great errors in the charts on board the ship; particularly two charts, one published by Hamilton Moore in 1784 and the other a French chart published in 1787.

And it appeared to the Court that Captain Bingham was proceeding perfectly consistent with the order produced and that the courses steered were such as would have taken His Majesty's ship a considerable way to the northward of the Formigas had that shoal been situated nearly as laid down in the charts above mentioned. (*NC* vol 5, p278)

30 December, a shoreside tragedy 'Tuesday a most shocking accident happened at a public-house at Plymouth Dock in North Corner Street, kept by Mr Jackson: as their daughter, a fine girl of thirteen years old was taking a book out of a chest of drawers in the bar, a spark from her candle fell into a part of the drawer accidentally, which communicated to a cannon cartridge of powder of six pounds, which blew up with a terrible explosion, and with such violence as to force her and the bow window into the street: she was taken up directly, but although every means was used to recover her, she expired, much scorched, in great agonies. A little infant in a cradle near the bar was providentially saved. Her father and mother were absent on business when the accident happened.' (*SYM*, 5 January 1801)

1801

1 January, Highland Lass, West Indiaman, and Requin, 10 guns   At 5pm this evening the ship *Highland Lass*, Captain Druce, from Demerara for London, laden with cotton, coffee and sugar, ran upon the South Goodwin sands and although the masts were soon cut away the ship quickly bilged and became a total wreck. (*Times*, 5 January 1801)

Also lost on the 1st was the 10-gun brig *Requin*, Lt Samuel Fowell, which was wrecked near Quiberon, where although the crew of some 55 men were saved yet 20 of them became prisoners of war. This vessel was originally French, having been taken on 20 February 1795 by the 36-gun frigate *Thalia*, Captain Richard Grindall in the Channel. (*SNL*, 1799, p38; Norie, 1827, p408)

4 January, Dictator, merchantman   The *Dictator*, Captain Lovelace, was a Liverpool ship on passage from Berbice, where she was laden, for London; but on this day the vessel was driven by one of the worst storms of the winter into Dingle Bay where she was wrecked on or near the Inch Peninsula, and sad to relate of the entire crew only three survived.

The shores of the peninsula were covered with cotton, coffee and puncheons of rum, as well as the country people keeping a weather-eye open for *God-sends*. Four days later with the arrival of Mr Marshall, the late high-sheriff of the County of Kerry, 'scranny picking' had of necessity to cease. He recovered many important letters as well as £20,000 in London bank-notes and bills; from one country man alone, who could not read, he recovered £12,000 in bills which belonged to Mr James Frazer of Berbice, a passenger who was drowned.

In consequence of a large reward offered by Mr Marshall, Mr Frazer's body was found by some country people several miles from the scene of the wreck, and being identified by the three surviving sailors was interred in the church at Inch. (*AR* 1801, Chr, p4; *Times*, 21 January 1801)

7 January, boat of the Nemesis   The *Nemesis*, 28 guns, built at Liverpool in 1780, had a chequered career. The ship was taken by the French at Smyrna on 9 December 1795, when commanded by Captain Samuel Hood Linzee; and retaken by the *Egmont*, 74 guns, Captain John Sutton, on 9 March 1796.

On this day the *Nemesis* was part of the North Sea Fleet and was at anchor at Deal, when a boat belonging to her returning to the ship was overset and the seven men on board were all said to have lost their lives. (*Times*, 10 January 1801)

11 January, complaint against factory 'This Sunday morning at three o'clock a scandalous piece of cruelty was practised on the inhabitants of Goswell Place, by the workmen of the foundry for melting down cannon. They had a loaded 18-pounder from which they could not draw the charge, and not choosing to put it in the fire in that state, for their own safety, they fired it off in the yard. The ball passed over the field, cleared the tops of the houses in Brick Lane and then fell in Bridgewater Square.

'The foundry working nights and Sundays had long been complained of and now magistrates may do something.' (*Times*, 13 January 1801)

2 February, Legere, 22 guns *La Legere*, a French 22-gun corvette, was captured by two 36-gun English frigates, the *Apollo*, Captain J Manley, and the *Doris*, Captain Hon C Jones, south-west of the Scilly Isles, on 22 June 1796. (*SNL*, 1796)

Five years later on 2 February 1801 *La Legere*, commanded by Captain F Cornelius Quinton, was wrecked twelve leagues to the north-east of Cartagena, Columbia, where the crew had tried to beach the vessel to enable essential repairs to be carried out. The captain and crew were saved only to become prisoners of war. (*Steel's Naval Chronologist*, 1801)

It may be assumed that the *Legere* struck on the Palmarita Shoal, position 10°51.45'N 75°16.25'W, yet this is not certain.

3 February, Denton, troopship At the end of January two transports, the *Polly* and the *Denton*, carrying detachments of the 49th and 85th Regiments, left Guernsey for Portsmouth under convoy of the *Rambler* cutter. During a violent storm on 3 February the *Denton* lost her masts and foundered, yet the crew together with the officers and men of the 85th were all taken on board the *Polly* and the *Rambler*, which both arrived at Plymouth on 12 February. (*NC* vol 5, p182)

10 February, sheltering at Plymouth The Plymouth report for this day included the following:

'Came in *La Juste*, a most beautiful French privateer of St Maloes, of 16 guns and 120 men. In a fog chase in with the coast of France she fell in with and ran foul of the *Amelia*, 44 guns, Hon. Captain Herbert, and carried away her fore topmast and bowsprit, and struck directly. She is supposed to be the fastest sailer out of France. Also came in the schooner *Hamilton*, Captain Hinderman, from Falmouth for New Providence; she sailed under convoy of the *Fly*, 18 guns, Captain Duval, with twelve others, and on the 1st inst. fell in with a French squadron of five sail of the line and two frigates in latitude 43°00′N. [This may have been the last sighting of the *Fly*, since the ship was believed to have foundered off the Newfoundland coast; Captain Thomas Duval and his crew of 120 all perished.] They separated by signal from the *Fly* and on the 3rd inst. came on a dreadful gale of wind, which almost water-logged the *Hamilton*, and choked the pumps so much that with the utmost difficulty she was kept afloat till her arrival here.' (*NC* vol 5, p182)

14 February, Telegraph, armed brig On 25 March 1799 the *SYM* published a Plymouth report of the 23rd, which stated that on the 18th the *Telegraph*, armed brig of 16 guns and 60 men, commanded by Lt James Andrew Worth, fell in with and captured off the Île de Batz after a severe action of nearly four hours, the French national brig corvette *L'Hirondelle*, of 16 guns and 72 men, commanded by Captain La Porte. [This ship is not to be confused with a vessel of the same name, a 20-gun corvette taken four months earlier on 20 November 1798 by the three British frigates *Phaeton*, 38 guns; *Ambuscade*, 32 guns; and *Stag*, 32 guns. (*SNL*, 1799)]

On 8 April the *SYM* quoted a Plymouth report of the 6th which read: 'Lt Worth, who captured *L'Hirondelle* in the *Telegraph*, after a gallant action in excess of three and a half hours, is promoted by the Lords Commissioners of the Admiralty to the rank of Master and Commander.'

The *Telegraph* may have been badly damaged during the action, for whereas the ship went up harbour (the Hamoaze), on 22 March (*NC* vol 1, p440), yet it did not come down into the Sound until 26 April. (*NC* vol 1, p536)

Command of the vessel was now given to Lt Caesar Corseillis, who had received his lieutenant's commission as far back as 21 November 1790, and who we may therefore assume was a very experienced naval officer. There is some reason to believe that the *Telegraph* may have been at least a little crank (unstable). Perhaps whilst in harbour the top hamper had been replaced by heavier masts, and yards; or some of the ballast may have been removed, and not all of it replaced (see entry for 1 April 1803); for only a year later, on 21 May 1800, it was reported: 'Arrived the *Telegraph*, 18 guns, Lt Corsellis. She experienced great distress in the late gale of wind. She was on her beam-ends for some minutes, with the water up to the combings of her hatchways, when the fore topmast and bowsprit both went and she righted. (*NC* vol 3, p509)

Then again in the gale of 9 November 1800 we read that the ship once again suffered some damage. 'The *Telegraph* brought up with her best bower anchor and was saved by cutting away her main mast.' (*NC* vol 4, p436)

On 23 January 1801 the *Telegraph* arrived at Plymouth from a cruise during which she detained six ships; the last three being two Danes and one

Swede, which ships she sent into Dartmouth. The Swede, for Stockholm, was laden with tobacco from Baltimore. (*NC* vol 5, p179)

One of the three, the *General Wraigh*, arrived at Plymouth on 26 January (*Times*, 29 January); whilst another of the three, the *Catherine Margaretta*, from Seville to Altona with fruit, did not arrive at Plymouth until 4 February. (*Times*, 7 February)

We next learn of the *Telegraph* from a Plymouth report, dated 18 May, which stated that fears were ascertained for the *Telegraph* which sailed with Vice-Admiral Sir R Calder, and went up the Straits with dispatches, but had not been heard of for three months. (*Times*, 21 May 1801)

A further report from Plymouth dated 25 May (*NC* vol 5, p462) stated that the *Argo* transport which had just arrived from Malta brought news that the *Telegraph* (supposed lost), had passed the island with dispatches for Egypt, yet nothing was ever heard of her again. Lt Corsellis with his crew had perished. It may be noted here that the writer after extended research, has read nothing to indicate that the *Telegraph* actually called at Malta; certainly the Plymouth report does not say it did; nor has he discovered anything to indicate how the crew of the *Argo* knew the vessel was carrying dispatches for Egypt.

So we may now pass on to *Steel's Naval Chronologist of the War, February 1793-1801*, which publication was contemporary with the events; it states on p44 that the *Telegraph* 'parted in a gale off Cape Ortegal 14th February and had not since been heard of.' (Norie, 1827 ed, p458, concurs)

4 March, mutiny in the Marianne The following article has been taken from the *Naval Chronicle*, vol 6, p427; and is a copy of a report from Fort William, (Dum Dum), Calcutta, dated as above.

'We have received the following melancholy account of the massacre of Captain George and his officers on board of his own ship near the Sand Heads [off the Hooghly, the approach to Calcutta], by four of his own crew. The ship *Marianne* was bound from Prince of Wales Island to this port, and had nearly completed her voyage, when four of the seaconnies [see 12 October 1799] rose upon their officers, murdered the captain, his first and second mates, and a native woman; gaining over the lascars they proceeded for Chittagong when getting sight of land they hoisted out the ship's boat, laid a train of gunpowder between decks and were in the act of pushing off from the vessel and to set fire to her, when a Tindal, plucking up courage, jumped into the boat alongside, plunged his knife into one of the seaconnies, and himself being wounded, they both fell into the sea and were drowned; the lascars upon this attacked, and killed two of the remaining three seacunnies; the survivor took refuge on the main topmast head, being armed with a brace of pistols and a large knife, where he remained for two days. He was at length persuaded by fair promises to come down, and having been plentifully plied with liquor he fell asleep, when he was secured in irons by the lascars, his arms taken from him, and in this state the ship arrived back at Prince of Wales Island.'

11 March, Triton, 32 guns Accidents associated with guns and powder were of frequent occurrence, often caused by double or treble shotting and one such accident happened on board the *Triton* frigate, 32 guns, Captain Gore, which arrived at Plymouth on the 11th and immediately went up harbour to refit. The story is here taken from the *Naval Chronicle*, vol 5, p274, dated 12 March.

'A most melancholy accident happened on board the *Triton* during her late cruise off the Penmark Rocks in chase of a cutter; as the *Triton* was firing at her the eleventh gun abaft on the larboard side unfortunately burst, by which accident the 2nd Lt, Mr Alford, and a gunner's mate were killed, and eighteen seamen and marines badly wounded; the deck ripped up and the Captain's cabin much damaged. Captain Gore had Lt Alford, Lt Thompson and the purser dining with him; on this gun being reported ready, Lt Alford just went out of the cabin door when the explosion so dreadful in its operation took place, and forced in the lifeless trunk and separated the head of Lieutenant Alford on the cabin floor; Captain Gore was providentially saved in the midst of pieces of the gun and splinters flying about him; one officer was forced into the quarter-gallery, but was otherwise unhurt. The man who fired the gun escaped almost unhurt. The wounded men were conveyed to the Royal Naval Hospital to receive that care and attention so congenial to the feelings of those gentlemen employed in the cure of the sick or wounded seamen and marines of the Royal Navy. Lt Alford was the son of the Reverend the Dean of St Burian's.

'On the morning of the 13th the remains of Lt Alford and the gunner's mate were conveyed from the Naval Hospital to Stonehouse chapel-yard and interred with military honours; Captain Gore and the officers attended in deep mourning. The service was performed by the Rev J Bidlake, A B Chaplain to the Duke of Clarence.'

14 March, lucky escape for Urania In going up the Hamoaze the *Urania*, 44 guns, Captain Towry, by means of the current at half tide off Devil's Point, struck on the German Rock and swung quite round, but the tide flowing she soon got off and anchored safe in Barnpool. (*NC* vol 5, p274)

The vessel had been the French *Uranie* (ex-*Tarta*), taken 5 January 1797.

14 March, James, packet The *James* packet, Captain M'Intosh, sailed from Whitehaven for Liverpool about 1pm on Saturday the 14th and about 5.30pm made the lower end of Walney, it was then blowing hard with sleet. About 8.30pm Captain M'Intosh said they would lay her to but at that instant she struck upon a sandbank on the main about four miles from

Lytham. The stroke knocked off her rudder, whereupon they let go the anchor; but she made so much water that they cut the cable intending to run her up, but she filled with water and laid down on the lee side. The confusion and alarm upon deck was very great and six persons were almost instantly washed off the ship and no more seen. The remaining twelve climbed into the shrouds; but benumbed by the weather nine of these dropped off one after another; the surviving three remained in the rigging till about 5am on Sunday, when the vessel ebbed dry and they walked ashore. (*NC* vol 5, p366)

16 March, Invincible, 74 guns The *Invincible*, 74 guns, a very old ship built on the Thames in 1765, was of 1631 tons burthen, and on this day was commanded by Captain John Rennie and wore the flag of Rear-Admiral Thomas Totty. The ship sailed from Yarmouth on this Monday morning for the Sound to join the fleet under the command of Admiral Sir Hyde Parker, but shortly after 2pm the ship struck on Hammonds Knoll, off the Norfolk coast, where she beat most violently for more than two hours, when the mizzen mast went by the board and the main mast was immediately cut away. The ship then dropped from three and a half into seventeen fathoms where she lost her rudder and becoming unmanageable was again driven upon the sandbank. A fishing smack now approached the wreck, when two of the *Invincible*'s boats were got out and in one of these the Admiral, purser, four midshipmen and some seamen reached the fishing smack in safety, as did the other boat also full of people. Both of them immediately returned to the ship, but on approaching the smack once more one was forced away and all on board would have perished had not a collier which happened to be passing at the crucial moment picked them all up; this vessel afterwards afforded every assistance that she was capable of giving, and was the means of saving the lives of many of the crew. The fishing smack, with the Admiral on board, although unable to afford the least assistance to the ship, nevertheless remained at anchor during the whole of Monday night, and when daylight came, proceeded towards the ship. But to the dismay of all on the smack, the *Invincible* once again drifted off into deep water and gradually sinking, took with her more than 400 persons.

While the ship was thus going down the launch was hove out and as many as she could possibly hold jumped into her; others who attempted to get on board the already overladen launch were struck away with the oars, to prevent the certain loss of the whole. About 70 of the crew were saved in the launch, the whole of whom had assembled upon the forecastle; but all those who had remained in the poop were lost. A total of 196 people were saved from the ship which was carrying about 50 passengers in addition to the crew of more than 600.

The *Invincible* represented Captain Rennie's first appointment since being made post captain; it was regrettable that he was amongst those who lost their lives.

At Sheerness on 31 March a court martial was assembled on board the *Ruby*, 64 guns, to try the survivors for the loss of the ship. All the evidence went to prove it was solely owing to the ignorance of the pilot and the master; the latter himself a North Sea pilot; for from Yarmouth Roads, or rather after getting through the Thackle, the ship was steering with a free wind, and till half an hour before she struck they had the advantage of the land in sight to assist them. When she struck, both the pilot and master each asserted that it must be on a bank unknown, or on a knowl (*sic*) that had recently been made by some convulsion. However, they were deceived, for it proved to be no other than Hammond's knowl, on which they were drawn by a most rapid tide, allowance for which they had not made.

Rear-Admiral Totty, the surviving officers and crew, were all acquitted, the pilot and master both perished with the vessel.

(*AR* 1801, Chr, p9; *Times*, 20, 21, 24 March 1801; *NC* vol 5, p261 et seq; Norie, 1827 ed, p180)

25 March, Scout, 18 guns   The *Scout* was an 18-gun sloop of war, commanded by Captain Henry Duncan, when she was lost on the Shingles, Isle of Wight.

On 1 April a court martial was held on board the *Gladiator* in Portsmouth harbour, to try Captain Duncan, his officers and ship's company, for the loss of the *Scout*, in her passage through the Needles. After hearing the narrative of Captain Duncan the court was of the opinion that the loss of the *Scout* was occasioned by her being drifted on to the Shingles by the rapidity of the tide, after she was tacked, and before she got headway through the water, the ship having been put in stays, by the pilot's directions, whilst the proper mark (being the light of Hurst Castle), was in sight, and that no blame was imputable to Captain Henry Duncan, his officers, the pilot or to the ship's company, for their conduct upon that occasion. (*NC* vol 5, pp367-368)

10 April, Centaur and Mars, 74 guns   During the night of 10 April, while cruising off the Black Rocks, the *Centaur*, 74 guns, Captain Littlehales, was run foul of by the *Mars*, also of 74 guns, Rear-Admiral Thornborough, by which accident two members of the crew of the *Centaur* were killed and four were injured, occasioned by the falling of the main mast. But the crew of the *Centaur* rigged up a jury main mast and bore away for Plymouth, where the ship arrived on 14 April.

In the meantime after the accident in which the *Mars* had carried away her head, bowsprit, fore mast and main topmast, she was taken in tow by the *Canada*, 74 guns, Hon Captain de Courcy; but from her disabled state, the wind blowing a squall at north, right on to the French shore, then but three leagues distant, and not a creek to run into should she get embayed, her main yard having been carried away in the slings, the *Canada*'s three topsails split to rags, and fearing the *Mars* would run aboard her and disable both ships, Captain de Courcy cut the tow line. He determined however to stay by the *Mars* to the last, and was getting ready to take out her officers and men if she should drift near the shore [the shoals of the Ile de Batz], which she was approaching fast; when the wind lulled at north and shifted round to east-north-east, by which providential change, and getting up a sail on the stump of the jury fore mast the *Mars* hauled off shore and the *Canada* was once again enabled to get a tow cable on board by which she was towed safe to Plymouth, where they arrived on the morning of 20 April, the very day when the *Centaur* was taking in her new main mast, in Cawsand Bay. (*NC* vol 5, pp366 and 371)

On 29 April a court martial was held on board the *Cambridge* flagship in Hamoaze to try Captain Lloyd of the *Mars*, and Lts Burnet and Davis of the *Centaur*, for those ships running foul of each other on the night of 10 April. Captain Lloyd and Lt Burnet were both honourably acquitted, but Lt Davis was sentenced to lose six months seniority and dismissed his ship. (*NC* vol 5, p457)

30 April, Dragon, merchantman Two ships, the *Elizabeth* and the *Dragon*, each laden with flour, sailed from Southampton for Plymouth during the preceding week. On the 30th the *Elizabeth* arrived at Plymouth with 270 sacks of flour; she also brought news that the *Dragon* had foundered and taken with her the entire crew. (*Times*, 14 May 1801)

23 May, Highland Chief, extra ship The *Highland Chief*, 28 guns, extra East Indiaman, Captain Greenaway, from Bombay, last from St Helena, put into Plymouth in great distress on the 24th. The ship was run aboard by a frigate in a fog off the Lizard which stove in her bows and carried away the fluke of her anchor which lodged in the bows of the frigate. The ships having much way through the water, the cable fastened to the anchor ran out end for end after it; very fortunately it was not secured to the mast as is usual or the consequence might have been fatal to both ships.

The *Highland Chief* brought Governor Brooke and his suite from St Helena. (*Times*, 26 May 1801)

9 June, Meleager, 32 guns A 32-gun frigate, the *Meleager*, Captain Hon Thomas Bladen Capell, struck on the Triangle Bank in the Gulf of Mexico, and became a total loss; the crew, however, managed to scramble on to some low lying coral islets, where they existed for fourteen days until rescued by the *Apollo* frigate. (*Times*, 28 October 1801)

10 ? June, Forte, 44 guns The French 44-gun frigate *Forte*, Captain Beulieu le Long, was captured on 1 March 1799 at 2.30am by the 38-gun frigate *Sibylle*, Captain Edward Cooke. The French vessel had to supply crews for seven prizes and was therefore short of hands and unable to man all the quarterdeck and forecastle guns. Captain Beulieu le Long was killed in action and Captain Cooke, mortally wounded, died at Calcutta on 25 May 1799, after suffering three months of great pains. During the action, after Captain Cooke had been carried below, command of the *Sibylle* devolved upon Lieutenant Lucius Hardyman who was eventually promoted and given command of the *Forte*, which ship was however wrecked off Jeddah during June 1801. The exact date of loss appears to be unknown, even in official Admiralty records, yet the *Times* carried an article: 'The navigation of the Red Sea has proved fatal to several of the ships on that part of the expedition to Egypt, which was sent from Bombay. The following is an extract of a letter dated Jaddah (*sic*), Red Sea, 24 June 1801: On the 8th inst. the *Rockingham*, Captain Butter, struck on a sunken rock and will be obliged to return to Bombay to repair; the *Susannah*, from Bombay is lost near this place; *La Forte* frigate is wrecked here and two other ships have been lost in these seas.' (*Times*, 21 November 1801)

7 July, Augustus, gun-vessel The *Augustus* gun-vessel, Lt James Scott, this morning got under weigh in the Catwater for Cawsand Bay, but in turning into the Sound, missed stays, and went on shore east of the two gun batteries under the lower fort of the Citadel, and although every assistance was given by Captain Hawker and boats of the *Fisgard*, etc. and casks ready to buoy her, she went to pieces during the night; nevertheless, the crew and part of the cargo were saved. (*NC* vol 6, pp79-80)

9 July, Ambuscade, 32 guns At 8am this morning the Dutch frigate *Ambuscade*, 32 guns, Captain Van Voss, left her moorings in Sheerness harbour on her way to the Downs. Her foresail, topsails and topgallant sails being set, with the wind blowing fresh WNW when she was perceived, a little before 9am, to be nearly on her beam ends, just beyond the Middle Sand about three miles from Sheerness and in the Fair Channel to the Nore. On board the ship, it was first discovered by some women on the lower deck, who seeing the water rushing in at the hawse holes, ran upon deck and gave the alarm, but too late. The crew had no time to clew up the sails, for within five minutes of the women rushing on deck, the ship went down, and 22 of the crew were drowned.

This accident was owing to the hawse holes being extremely large and low, the hawse plugs not being in, and the holes being pressed under water by a crowd of sail on the ship, through which a sufficient body of water got in, unperceived, to carry her to the bottom.

The instant she sank, she rolled over to windward across the tide, and lay on her beam ends; so that at low water the muzzles of the main deck guns were a little out of the water, and pointed to the zenith, with thirty-two feet of water round her.

The *Ambuscade* was an old frigate; and had been ordered to join the three other Dutch ships at Ireland. (*NC* vol 6, p67)

Only four days after foundering the ship was weighed and towed into Sheerness harbour where she was grounded on the west side, and on 21 July was warped alongside the *Drochterland* hulk, to be once again fitted out for sea. (*AR* 1804, pp851-852 [contains a complete account of the salvage of the *Ambuscade*, written by Joseph Whidbey, Master Attendant in Sheerness Dockyard])

21 July, Jason, 36 guns   Today at Plymouth the wind was variable, the weather sultry, and the thermometer in the shade stood this afternoon at 75°. On this beautiful day a hundred or so miles to the south-east of Plymouth, the *Jason*, a 36-gun frigate, Hon Captain John Murray, was wrecked near St Malo, but no lives were lost and the crew, saved by the local people, became prisoners of war.

On 5 August an attempt was made by Lt Ross of the *Weazle* to burn the wreck, to prevent its being of use to the enemy, but he was defeated by the rising tide. The next day, however, he was aided by men from the boats of the *Insolent* and the *Liberty*, and this attempt was successful. (*NC* vol 6, pp81, 166, 250 and 251)

21 July, Iphigenia, 32 guns   About this date the *Iphigenia*, a 32-gun frigate armed *en flute*, Captain Hassard Stackpoole, was burnt by accident at Alexandria. She had been to Cyprus to fetch wood and water, and had not been long at Alexandria when she was discovered to be on fire. The amount of wood the vessel had on board rendered every effort to save her ineffectual; yet the crew were saved. (*NC* vol 6, p250)

22 July, Bahamas hurricane   At Nassau in the Bahamas a hurricane came on at noon blowing from the north-north-east and increasing in violence as it gradually became due north. With a flowing tide the north wind drove all the vessels, about 120, on to the town side of the harbour, a string of them along the shoreline. An ebb tide together with a change of wind and they would have been driven out to sea, for by 3pm there was scarcely a vessel in the harbour.

The British ship *Echo* had captured a Guineaman, a slaver, which lay up the harbour; but she parted from her anchors and drove towards the town, struck the ground, and got on her beam ends: the seamen got to leeward on her sides, but 250 slaves on board, and between decks, were in the most imminent danger. After a short time the vessel fortunately righted and drove on shore, where the crew and slaves were unexpectedly preserved. Another Guineaman, named the *George*, which only arrived the previous day, got on shore, and was in the greatest danger, but the crew and slaves were fortunately saved.

At about 4.30pm the wind got around to the east, and kept veering about with the sun; a sure prognostic that the gale would not be of long continuance: but still its violence continued unabated until 8 or 9pm when the sun set, and it had resolved into a fresh gale. (*AR* 1801?, Chr, pp31-32)

? July, Intrepid and Comet, Bombay Marine cruisers   The *Intrepid*, a ship, and the *Comet*, a schooner, both of Bombay and belonging to the Hon East India Company's marine service, were dispatched to the South China Sea to survey various shoals and islands which were known to be improperly charted. At the end of July both vessels were observed to pass out of Sincapour (*sic*) Strait, but what happened then is unknown, although at the time they were presumed to have been lost on one of the Paracel Shoals, together with their crews, amounting to nearly 100 men. (*NC* vol 15, p466)

29 July, boat accident at Harwich   A boat with eleven men on board belonging to a ship employed to take invalid soldiers to Hamburg was upset by getting across the hawser of a vessel lying in Yarmouth Roads and ten were drowned. (*Times*, 3 August 1801)

11 August, Lowestoffe, 32 guns   The *Abigail*, a merchantman, Captain Bradley, arrived at Liverpool from Jamaica and reported the loss of the *Lowestoffe*, a 32-gun frigate, Captain Robert Plampin.

The *Abigail* joined the fleet for England, which consisted of about 100 sail of vessels, on 28 July off Port Antonio, and at 8pm made sail under convoy of the *Acasta* and *Lowestoffe* frigates, *Bonetta* sloop of war, and *Musketo* and *Sting* schooners.

On 11 August at 5am the *Lowestoffe* was seen on shore with her masts gone and bilged on the north-east end of Heneager (Great Inagua). Four ships and a brig were also on shore and only twenty vessels were then in sight; with the *Acasta* and *Bonetta* lying-to. At 5pm the *Acasta* took charge of the ships then in company and left the *Bonetta* and her three boats to assist the vessels on shore. On 7 September the *Abigail* parted from the fleet in a gale of wind at north-west in position 43°49'N 39°06'W and arrived at Liverpool on Tuesday 22 September. (*NC* vol 6, p250; *Times*, 28 September 1801)

21 August, Spitfire, schooner   In the Indian Ocean the *Spitfire*, Lt Campbell, was wrecked on a reef off the southern part of some low-lying islands, situated about six leagues to the north of the bank which surrounds the Amirante, or Admiralty Islands. The ship, when she struck at 5.10am, was then running at about four knots under her fore topsail, and had sounded often during the night with no ground with twenty fathoms line a short time before she struck. On her striking the masts were immediately cut away to prevent her oversetting, and soon afterwards she was driven over the reef into a kind of sandy basin, and at low water her crew were able to walk ashore; most of her stores and provisions were saved. On 27 August Lt Campbell with four men quitted the islands in a small boat to procure relief from the Seychelles. On the 29th at 9am they saw the principal island but did not arrive there until 5pm on the 31st; being then in urgent need of water, of which they had only one bottle left. Lt Campbell having landed and procured some coconuts quitted the shore and soon after saw and went on board *La Sybille* in Mahé Roads. (*NC* vol 7, p357)

The *Spitfire* was on passage from Bombay for the Gulf of Aden and the Red Sea, from which it may appear that the ship was a thousand miles off her track when she was wrecked, but this was not so: she was sailing the southern passage. Findlay's *Indian Ocean Pilot* (1870 ed), has the following on pp166 and 167: 'It is useless to attempt the direct passage from Bombay to the Gulf of Aden during the SW monsoon months, or from early in June to the end of August, either for steamers or sailing vessels. There is no record of any vessel having succeeded, though some have tried it. The East India Company's steamer *Abkar*, tried the direct passage in June 1846 but was obliged to bear up for Bombay with her cutwater damaged. The East India Company's steamer *Feroze* attempted it in July 1849 but finding the wind and sea increase as she advanced to the westward, so as to require four men at the helm, and the decks being constantly flooded, after four days she bore up to the southward and made the southern passage.'

4 September, Proselyte, 32 guns The *Proselyte*, a 32-gun frigate, Captain George Fowke, was formerly the *Jason*, a Dutch frigate taken into Greenock by a mutinous crew on 8 June 1796. (*SNL*, 1799)

Whilst cruising off Great Bay, St Martin, one of the Lesser Antilles, the *Proselyte* struck the Man-of-War reef and was lost, her crew being saved. (*Times*, 29 October 1801)

1 October, peace with France The preliminaries of Peace with France were signed this day in London.

4 October, Extraordinary Gazette announces peace Arrived at Plymouth this morning at 9am, the mail coach decorated with laurels and the coach-man, guard and horses with blue and gold favours, on delivery of the Extraordinary Gazette of Peace with France.

9 October, celebration of the peace The *NC* vol 6, p343 gives the Plymouth report for this date, which is given here in part, verbatim. 'Wind SW, Rain. In consequence of the Peace with France a bonfire was exhibited on the Hoe, composed of eight hundred large barrels of tar, oil, pitch, etc., with faggots and firewood, sixty feet high and two hundred and forty in circumference, it had a grand effect, though it rained incessantly and blew a hurricane; there was also a general illumination and the men-of-war in Cawsand Bay had up their top-lights and threw up signal rockets and blue lights, which were answered from the Hoe.'

12 October, hostilities cease This was the day hostilities actually ceased and the Plymouth report had the following: 'This morning the mail coach covered with laurels and flags brought the Gazette with the ratification of the preliminaries of peace; the populace saluted it with nine cheers, took out the horses, and drew it towards Dock (Devonport), amidst the acclamations of thousands of people.' (*NC* vol 6, p344)

In such a manner was ending the Revolutionary Era.

With the advent of peace the number of vessels at sea dropped dramatically owing to the consequential laying up of many naval ships and privateers; and therefore the number of shipwrecks also diminished.

We may also vouchsafe the number of human wrecks diminished with the paying off of the press gangs.

PART TWO

THE ERA OF
THE
PEACE OF AMIENS
1801 – 1803

1801

17 October, paying off the press gang   This was a day of south-west gales
and hard rain; the Plymouth report read: 'The Press Gang of Lieutenant
John Newton, forty-one years a lieutenant in the Royal Navy, was this day
paid off here and at Oreston; it is but justice to state there never was a more
orderly set of men than the seamen and landmen belonging to Lieutenant
Newton's rendezvous; the gallant veteran has raised for the naval service, at
this port, nearly three thousand seamen and landmen during a period of nine
years.' (*NC* vol 6, p345)

? October, Cockatrice, cutter   The *Cockatrice* cutter was built at Mr King's
shipyard Dover in 1781. *SNL* of June 1797 shows the *Cockatrice* in ordinary
(reserve) at Portsmouth, where she probably remained until 1801, when
completely rotten, she was allowed to sink at her moorings (exact date
unknown). A year later the vessel was raised and sold out of the service.

   The ship was then cut in half and lengthened, brig rigged and hired
out to the navy! The burthen of the vessel had increased from 181 to 195
tons, and the hiring rate by 120 guineas per annum!

   On 7 May 1808 Lt William Balfour, the new commander of the vessel,
wrote from Dock (Devonport), where the ship then was, to his uncle John
Balfour at Curzon Street, London:

   '*Cockatrice*, Plymouth. My dear uncle, I arrived here this morning
having come by water from Portsmouth, and after waiting on Admirals
Young and Sutton, I proceeded to join the never to be forgotten *Cockatrice*,
of which the following is a description. She has been an old smuggling cutter,
cut and lengthened, brig rigged, pierced for 16 guns, mounting 14; allowed
a complement of 45 men of which the owners are seldom able to procure
one half. At present we have 30 on the books including myself and servant.
She is old and extremely leaky but I have a very tolerable cabin and the
greater part of my servant's wages are paid by the owners. I understand that
Captain Bolderson, who commanded her 16 months, made upwards of two
thousands prize money... I shall do the best I can in the hope of promotion.
I think the Admiralty... took advantage of my being at such a distance as to
prevent my receiving any information respecting her; to give me what they
could get no-one else to take.' (*Orkney Archives* D2/27/12)

   On the 21st of the same month he wrote to his uncle: '...the vessel
must be taken out of service... she leaks most abominably... the present
owner having given her some repair, had interest[26] enough to get her hired
into the service at 15/- per ton per month (she measures 195 tons), and £5
10s each for 45 men per month.'

25 October, Bonetta, 18 guns   On 11 August the *Bonetta* had been left at
Great Inagua to assist the stranded ships of the *Lowestoffe*'s convoy. On 25
October the 18-gun *Bonetta*, Captain Thomas New, grounded on a shoal

near the east end of the Jardines de la Reina, which lie off the south coast of Cuba, where she bilged and overset, but although the vessel was lost the crew were saved.

On 12 January 1802 a court martial was assembled on board the *Cumberland*, Captain Bayntun, in Port Royal, Jamaica, to try Captain New, his officers and crew for the above accident, when they were all acquitted except Lt Goakman who had the charge of the watch at the time the ship was grounded.

On 17 January, and continued by adjournment until the 19th, Mr Goakman the 2nd Lt of the *Bonetta* was tried by court martial for being the cause of the loss of the sloop by sleeping on his watch and disobeying the orders he had received from his captain. The charge being proved, he was adjudged to be dismissed His Majesty's service, rendered incapable of serving His Majesty as an officer, mulcted of all his pay, and to suffer two years imprisonment. (*NC* vol 7, pp271-272)

28 October, Margaret, brig The brig *Margaret*, Captain Hicks, bound from Swansea to Falmouth with coals, foundered in Bead's Bay, when the captain and six men perished, a boy being the only survivor. (*Times*, 6 November 1801)

2 November, Atlantic storms The ship *Elizabeth*, Captain Lowe, arrived at Hull on 20 November and brought news that the storm of the 2nd had been very destructive to shipping on the coasts of Norway, Sweden and Denmark. The *Elizabeth* on her passage from Elsinore to Anholt (in which harbour she remained during the storm), being about 150 miles, observed fourteen vessels of different descriptions stranded and completely wrecked, six of them bottom upwards. During the storm a Dutch hoy was thrown upon the rocks of Anholt and dashed to pieces, only two of the crew being saved, who were found on the rocks after the gale had subsided, almost perished with cold and hunger; her cargo consisted of deals, staves, etc, name unknown. The *Flaxton* of Hull, upset in the gale and was totally lost; the crew got upon her keel, from whence they were taken up by a Prussian vessel, and distributed amongst the ships bound for England; four of the crew arrived in the *Elizabeth*. Two English vessels were observed to founder at their anchors on the coast of Norway and all their hands were lost, names unknown. The *Dash*, Captain Hill of Hull, was reported to have foundered at sea. (*NC* vol 6, p426)

The same storm also affected shipping in the Channel area and the Plymouth report for 2 November (*NC* vol 6, p429) stated: 'Wind SW. Blows an hurricane. Last night and this morning the hurricane at SW and NW was the most dreadful seen for many years; the sea ran mountains high. Several boats broke adrift and a large American ship went ashore on the Bear's Head, Catwater, where she lies bilged. A man-of-war's cutter was found upset under Withy Hedge, with her oars and boat hooks floating alongside, all hands supposed to have perished.' [The American ship was the *Roba and Betsy* of Norfolk, Virginia, which received much damage to her hull but was got off the same day. (*SYM*, 9 November 1801)]

The storm of the 2nd was also fraught with trouble for many ships in the Channel Islands. The gunboat *Friendship*, Lt Astley, was driven out of Guernsey Roads and was supposed to have been lost with her crew. But not so; the vessel was driven ashore near St Malo where the crew managed to get on a rock, and when the tide receded on the morning of the 3rd they waded up to their waists in water and got ashore. They were humanely received by an officer and some soldiers who conducted them to a barn about two miles in the country, where they were treated very kindly. Ten days later the commandant sent them in an open boat with a flag of truce to the Prince de Bouillon, captain of the *Bravo* at Jersey. (*Times*, 25 November 1801)

The *Galatea*, 32 guns, Captain Byng, nearly foundered in the Bay of Biscay. Her mizzen mast was carried over the side and at the same time the main and fore topmasts were carried away although there was not a rag of sail set. One seaman went over with the mizzen mast and several were injured. The gale lulled on the 3rd and after clearing the wreckage the *Galatea* bore away for Cork, where she arrived on the 9th, to rig jury masts. The ship then sailed for Plymouth where she arrived on the 21st to refit. (*NC* vol 6, p432)

4 November, Margate pilot boat   At 7pm this evening Captain Palmer, his eldest son, Captain Harman's eldest son, a Mr Smith and three others went in a Margate pilot boat in quest of a vessel to get her into the harbour. In going off strong winds swamped the boat when Captain Palmer of the *Rose in June*, his son, Captain Harman's son and Mr Smith, mate of Captain Hilliard's packet, were all four drowned. (*AR* 1801, Chr, p36)

5 November, L'Utile, 18 guns   *L'Utile*, a French 16-gun privateer, was taken on 1 April 1799 by the 32-gun *Boadicea*, Captain R G Keats, in the Channel. The vessel was then bought into the Royal Navy. Refitted now with 18 guns, *L'Utile*, Captain Edward Jekyll Canes, sailed from Gibraltar on 5 November for Minorca with £27,000 for the payment of the garrison, but at which place she did not arrive; nor was any intelligence ever received respecting the vessel or her crew of 120 men. It was assumed that she upset soon after leaving Gibraltar when all on board perished. Captain Canes, a native of Portsmouth, left a wife and three children. (*NC* vol 7, p172)

26 ? November, Sophia Magdalena, East Indiaman   The Swedish East India Company's ship *Sophia Magdalena* from China with 7000 chests of tea went ashore near Kingsdown on the South Foreland; her masts soon went, she bilged and was full of water so that only 200 chests were undamaged. The decks had to be cut up to get at the remainder and at a public auction on 21 December at Deal the remains of the ship were knocked down for £307. The *Eugenie* sloop of war, Captain Sommerville, together with the *Anacreon* brig had dropped down from the Downs to the Foreland, where they anchored as near as possible consistent with safety, to the *Sophia Magdalena*, and rendered all possible assistance. (*Times*, 1 and 23 December 1801)

30 November, Newfoundland convoy Last night and this forenoon it blew a terrible gale from the south-west, the wind then shifting to west-north-west and increasing with a heavy rolling sea. Fourteen sail of the Newfoundland fleet which sailed from St John's three weeks since under convoy of the *Aurora*, Captain Caulfield, put into Plymouth, not being able to weather the Start, and anchored under Withy Hedge about 7am this morning. The gale increased most violently, when four Newfoundlanders parted their cables and anchors and went plump ashore between Mount Batten reef and the Leek Beds. (*NC* vol 6, p512)

? November, Generous Friends, country ship The ship *Generous Friends* of Madras, burthen about 400 tons, was wrecked on her passage from Canton about 10pm on one of the shoals of the Paracel group. One European and about fourteen lascars were saved by the freebooters who visit the shoals for plunder and to fish. The commander, officers and passengers, as well as the principal part of the crew, who left the wreck on rafts and in the jollyboat, believed to have totalled about forty persons, were supposed to have perished. A few others were said to have been killed in an affray with the Chinese freebooters. (*NC* vol 15, p466)

? November, Industry, brig The *NC* vol 7, p269 quotes a letter from Halifax, Nova Scotia, dated Saturday 12 December. It states:
'By a small schooner which arrived here on Tuesday last from Yarmouth, we learn that the brig *Industry*, Captain Matthews, which sailed from this port a few weeks since, bound for St John, New Brunswick, unfortunately caught fire and was consumed near the mouth of the Bay of Fundy. Besides the captain and crew there were on board the *Industry* Mrs Bradley, wife of Mr Leverit Bradley of St John, her three children and several seamen, intended for another ship, twenty-four in all; who finding it impossible to extinguish the flames were compelled to quit the vessel and betake themselves to the boat, with one barrel of biscuit and a keg of rum. In this forlorn situation they made Mount Desert Island, Maine, on the third day, and flattered themselves that they should reach the shore, but a heavy gale coming on drove them quite across the Bay, and it was not until five days later that the boat was driven on shore at Tuskett [the Tuskett Rocks lie about twenty miles SE of Yarmouth, Nova Scotia]. In the meantime Mrs

Bradley, her three children, the mate and fourteen seamen perished with fatigue, cold and hunger; the bread being unfortunately washed away on the second day after leaving the brig. Captain Matthews and the four surviving seamen were carried to Yarmouth where they received every attention from Dr Bond and the humane inhabitants of that town.'

? November, Le Babet, 20 guns   On 23 April 1794 the squadron of Commodore Sir J B Warren cruising off the Île de Batz took two French ships; one *Le Babet*, and the other *La Pomone*. Both were taken on to the strength of the Royal Navy and both were eventually to be lost; *La Pomone* on 8 September 1802 in St Aubin's Bay (*qv*). But the end of *Le Babet* (*The Betsy*), was to be more tragic.

Le Babet, 20 guns, Captain Jemmett Mainwaring, was cruising in the West Indies in late November when from some unknown cause the vessel vanished taking with her the entire crew of 140 men and boys. No trace of her was ever found, nor was any wreckage ever discovered. (Norie, 1827, p458 and *SNL* 1801)

26 December, Sally, sloop   The smuggling sloop *Sally*, Captain Hicks, from Guernsey for Lisbon with brandies, was forced into Plymouth by stress of weather during a violent gale in which she shipped a sea which washed four men overboard and who were, by the returning wave, washed on board again and saved. (*NC* vol 7, p89)

27 December, boat accident   At Plymouth during a gale, as five seamen in a boat were trying to get off with an anchor and cable to a vessel then driving in the Catwater, the boat shipped a sea astern, and not being able to cut the stopper of the anchor, the boat went down and they were all drowned. (*NC* vol 7, p89)

✳✳✳✳✳✳✳✳✳✳✳✳✳✳✳✳✳✳✳✳✳✳✳✳✳

1801, East Indiamen's defences   The *NC* vol 6, p251 gives the following:

'The ships taken up this season for the service of the Hon. East India Company are proposed to be armed as follows: Vessels of 1200 tons burthen to carry thirty-eight pieces of ordnance, each of which is to be an eighteen-pounder; twenty-six whereof are to be mounted on the principal battery; ten to be carried on the upper deck, and two in the after ports, eight feet in length, to serve as stern-chasers. The vessels of 800 tons are to carry thirty-two pieces of ordnance, twenty are to be mounted on the principal battery, or gundeck, ten on the upper deck, and two carronades, eighteen pounders, in the after ports as stern-chasers. The ships are all to be fitted with boarding nettings, at least half mast high, and close round the quarters. The men to be stationed in the tops are to be armed with swivels, musquetoons and pole-axes. A Master at Arms is to be carried in each ship in order to teach the crew the exercise. The former method of defence in general practice on board East India ships was twenty guns on the principal battery and six on the quarterdeck. Their weight of metal was limited to twelve and nine pounders which was very inadequate to the defence proper to be made by ships of so respectable a construction and equipment; hence the losses which have been sustained by captures this war. The *Pigot*, taken in Bencoolen Roads; the *Princess Royal*, captured in the Straits of Sunda; the *Triton*, taken by a pilot schooner in the Bay of Bengal; the *Raymond* and the *Woodcote* [20 April 1798 *qv*] taken by the French on the Malabar coast; and lastly, the unfortunate *Kent*, captured off the Sand Heads by Surcouff [9 July 1800 *qv*]. This last capture was avowedly owing to a want of a means of defence.' (*NC* vol 6, p251)

? 1801, Scout, 18 guns One other Royal Naval vessel was lost either during late 1801 or early 1802. When the *Scout* sloop was lost on 25 March 1801 (*qv*), Captain Duncan was given immediate command of an ex-French privateer *Le Premier Consul*, taken on 5 March 1801 by the 36-gun *Dryad*, Captain Mansfield of the Irish Station and renamed *Scout* (Norie, 1827, p503). It was an unfortunate appointment for Captain Duncan; he had survived one disaster to lose his life, ship and crew in another. The *Scout* with a crew of 120 vanished somewhere in the North Atlantic, date or place unknown for there were no survivors; naval opinion at the time was that the *Scout* had gone down off Newfoundland.

1802

4 January, Atlantic gales The gales of this and the following day raged in areas as far apart as the North Sea and the Bay of Biscay.

Nine vessels sailed from South Shields on 4 January and during a gale on the 5th they were driven ashore on Seaton Sands, near Seaton Carew. Three of the vessels were completely wrecked but the others were expected to be got off.

On the 4th also the ship *Omnibus*, Captain Conradus, from Rotterdam for Leghorn, was lost near Calais; and again on the 4th the ship *Jerusha*, Captain Massey, from Charleston, South Carolina, for London, put into Cherbourg in great distress after throwing part of her cargo overboard. (*Times*, 27 January 1802)

5 January, Magnanime, 44 guns The *Magnanime*, 44 guns, Captain Taylor, arrived at Plymouth from the Leeward Islands after a passage of fifty-two days; during which time twenty-two of her crew died, most from overwork.

The ship had dreadful weather on her passage, the pumps being continually choked; when the crew had perforce to bale out the water from her numerous leaks. Constantly wet between decks, so that of 300, only eighty-four were fit for duty; the ship then could not come to in the Sound, but had to be rowed up the harbour. The sick men, mostly with typhus, scurvy and dysentery, were landed at the hospital stairs in Stonehouse Creek and conveyed to the different wards. (*Times*, 7 January 1802)

The *Magnamine*, built at Deptford in 1780, was a *razee*, cut down from a 64-gun vessel during September 1794. (*NC* vol 1, p555)

When the frigate left the islands, Guadaloupe was completely in the possession of the blacks and mulattoes, who had driven away all the whites in circumstances of great distress. (*NC* vol 7, p90)

6 January, Urania of London   On 13 January the *Times* printed a report from Harwich dated 11 January, which read: 'On Friday the stern of a ship with the words *Urania of London*, together with the long boat with the same name and T Robinson, master, on the inside of the stern, were cast up at Walton within this port and also three pieces of Geneva. Several pieces were cast up at Languard Fort and on the Suffolk coast.' There were apparently no survivors.

21 January, worst storm for years   The worst storm for many years occurred throughout the British Isles on this day and shipping suffered severely.

The *Peggy* of Greenock, from Cork for Liverpool, foundered at Liverpool and only one man was saved. (*Times*, 27 January 1802)

The *Swallow*, Captain Westcott, from Newfoundland for Dartmouth, was run down by the *Lord Duncan* from the Leeward Islands, and foundered, but her men were saved by the *Lord Duncan*'s crew. The *Rio Douro*, from Oporto for Newcastle, laden with wine, went ashore on the Cockle Sand near Yarmouth, then drifted off and grounded on the Outer Barber shoal off Caister. The master, Captain Garcia, together with his crew managed to get ashore in the evening and sometime later, several pipes of wine were recovered from the wreck. The *Industry*, W Hopkins master, from Shields for Liverpool, laden with glass bottles, was abandoned at sea and afterwards towed into Yarmouth. The ship *True Friend* of Lynn ran on shore at Southwold where she caught fire and burnt to the water's edge. Her crew were saved.

The brig *Newcastle*, Thomas Dixon master, from Sunderland with coals and goods for London, went ashore in Hollesley Bay and afterwards when the tide came she drifted off and went down in deep water. Once again, the crew were saved. (*Times*, 23 and 27 January 1802)

1 February, Isabella, merchantman   The ship *Isabella*, Captain Edward Brown, was freighted at Natal (0°33'N 99°05') on the west coast of Sumatra for Bombay. Early on this day, in the tremendous swell then prevailing, she was seen hove to leeward as far as Malabar Point, about 5 or 6 leagues off shore. Then after riding to her sheet anchor for some time, she parted her cable and endeavoured to run ashore, with a view to save the lives of the crew, who were without any hope of getting assistance, owing to the state of the weather. She soon struck and her masts went overboard with the sea breaking completely over her. In a short time she bilged and was totally lost with a valuable cargo; but the crew were with the utmost difficulty saved. (*NC* vol 8, p256)

8 February, Margate hoy   Between 2 and 3am this morning one of the Margate hoys belonging to Mr Sackett, heavily laden with corn, which was stowed both in the hold and on deck, and with thirty passengers on board, besides the crew, consisting of the master and four seamen, was overtaken by a gale between Birchington and Reculver; she first lost her rudder, when becoming unmanageable, she shipped several heavy seas and was carried towards the beach. To preserve the lives of the women and children, the hatches were battened down. Shortly afterwards the vessel struck and filled; the sea breaking over her washed nearly the whole of those upon deck overboard and twenty-five persons were said to have perished. Nine bodies were picked up on the shore and fourteen were found in the cabin of the hoy.

The most unfortunate sufferers must surely have been the Thornton family of Margate; Mr Thornton, his wife and son, were going to town to put the son out as an apprentice, but they lost their lives and most regrettably the other six Thornton children who had remained at Margate became orphans. (*AR* 1802, Chr, p366)

A subscription was raised for the sufferers. (*Times*, 23 March 1802)

13 February, Sir Edward Hamilton, merchantman   The *Sir Edward Hamilton*, rice ship, Captain Robertson, on its voyage to Bengal when in latitude 46°44′S longitude 40°E was struck by lightning which carried away the fore topgallant mast, and went through the deck abreast of the fore mast. It then spread below, setting fire to the sailors' hammocks, wrenching all the ironwork from their chests and then taking a direction aft into the cabin went off among the arms which were in that part of the ship and caused an explosion. Captain Robertson and his crew were on deck furling the sails and had lucky escapes. The given position would place the ship not far from Prince Edward Island, about 700 miles to the south-east of Port Elizabeth; yet the *Guardian*, 44 guns, Lt Riou, was damaged by an iceberg in almost the same position when some of her crew were out in boats collecting ice for water on 23 December 1789.[26] (J Forbes, 1790)

25 February, Suffolk, 74 guns   A rumour persisted on this day in London, that the *Suffolk*, a 74-gun Third Rate ship of the line, Captain Curtis, was missing. However, on 29 March the *Suffolk* arrived at St Helen's Roads, where she brought to for a few hours and then proceeded to the Nore. The ship arrived at Deal on 1 April and then sailed for the river, arriving at

Sheerness on 3 April after eight years in the East Indies. Going into harbour she got aground (*Times*, 6 April 1802) but by assistance from ships' boats she got off and proceeded to Chatham without material damage. [This source also stated that the *Suffolk* had in her convoy from Bengal, a rice ship named *Prince*, with 400 French prisoners of war, which ship parted company and was missing; it was believed that the French rose on the crew and took over the vessel, but she may have simply foundered. (*Times*, 26 February 1802)] This ship had probably been confused with another of the same name, a rice ship from Bengal which had, so far as could be ascertained, sailed in the same convoy from Bengal; a letter from St Ives dated 4 March 1802 gives the following: 'The *Suffolk* came on shore in a shocking and distressed condition, having split all her sails to pieces the night before; and of twenty-one hands on board six only were able to do duty, the rest being sick; the ship proving very leaky and the water continuing to gain on them they were obliged to let her drift before wind and sea. The crew remained on board in a perilous situation for some hours but by the vigilant exertions of the people on shore (who always in such cases distinguish themselves by manly alacrity), having got boats from the creek of Hayle, and a large eight-oar boat carried from St Ives (three miles) by land, and being well manned they attempted at all hazards to get to the ship. In the meantime the captain and crew on board fastened a line to a keg and let it drift from the ship; the boat's crew got hold of it and by that means hauled the people on shore one by one until they were all safely landed, except two who were so ill as not to be able to struggle, and so died in their hammocks. The weather next day proving favourable all the bale goods, which consisted of raw silk and muslins, with some hundred bags of rice, were brought to St Ives by boats; and yesterday the ship with part of the cargo of rice was got off and brought into St Ives pier much damaged.' (*NC* vol 7, p269)

3 March, La Sensible, 36 guns   *La Sensible*, a 36-gun frigate, was taken from the French in the Mediterranean on 21 June 1798 by the *Seahorse*, 38 guns, Captain E J Foote. The two vessels were to meet again in rather different circumstances. *La Sensible* was cruising off the coast of Ceylon when at 2am she struck on a coral bank a few miles southward of the Molliwally shoal and about twenty miles to the southward of Moldavia. (*NC* vol 8, p343). The accident was said to have been caused by a strong westerly current for which an allowance had not been made in the dead reckoning. The ship quickly bilged and at 8pm, after a fatiguing eighteen hours at the pumps, Captain Robert Sause gave the order to abandon ship. A cable's length in any direction from where the wreck occurred and all must have been lost. (*Times*, 26 August 1802)

A few days later Captain Foote, of the *Seahorse*, was ordered by Admiral Rainier to go to the scene of the disaster and salvage whatever he could; and then although the ship had filled with water up to the gun deck yet Captain Foote and his crew managed to recover the masts, stores and everything else of any value. (*NC* vol 8, p339)

29 March, Assistance, 50 guns A 50-gun Fourth Rate the *Assistance*, with a crew of 330 men and boys, was on passage from the North Sea to Portsmouth when she ran on to the banks between Dunkirk and Gravelines, then after beating over them was entirely lost. The captain and crew, except for two marines, were saved by a Flemish pilot boat and some fishing boats which went to their assistance, and with great difficulty and hazard landed them at Dunkirk where a vessel was hired and landed them in England. (*NC* vol 7, p357)

On Thursday 8 April a court martial was held on board the *Brilliant* at Sheerness to try Captain Lee, his officers and crew for the loss of the ship. Captain Lee was admonished not to trust pilots so much in the future. The two pilots, Watson Riches and Edmund Coleman, were each mulct of their pay and given six months in the Marshalsea prison. (*Times*, 12 April 1802)

7 April, Juliana, brig Many shipwrecks of the period were not well documented, not only because there were very few survivors, but also owing to the remoteness of the area in which they occurred and the length of time information took to arrive at the ship's home port.

One such vessel was the brig *Juliana*, Captain Stalymane, which foundered near Benkulen (3°47′S 102°10′E), Sumatra, on 7 April; news of which did not arrive in England until the following October. Whilst twenty-two sailors perished, the captain, seven crew members and Mr Morelli, a passenger, were saved. (*NC* vol 8, p431)

11 April, seamen's revenge At Plymouth a boatswain's mate from one of the ships paid off during this last week was waylaid by some of the ship's company, who seized him, cut off his ears, and actually put them in one of his pockets; they then made good their escape. (*Times*, 14 April 1802)

16 April, Nymph, schooner The *Nymph* schooner, Captain Corlet, laden with flour and maize, having been out four days from Philadelphia bound to Charleston, South Carolina, had the misfortune to run aground off Cape Lookout[28] shoals on the night of 16 April, the wind being north-by-east. After being bilged, in about half an hour she went to pieces, all her cargo having been previously washed overboard. The captain and crew had cut away her main mast, in the fall of which a great part of the larboard side of the wreck was carried along with it and the boat entirely lost. The crew consisted of eight and one passenger all of whom, except one John Kelly, a young Englishman, perished. The captain betook himself to a piece of the mast and the rest to the spars, oars, etc. Kelly who still hung to the main wreck got off nearly an hour later, during which time he was endeavouring to procure from the wreck some part most likely to effect his safety. He passed by all his fellow sufferers but the cook, who did not go through the breakers; when he had gone some distance by the captain, he looked back and waved his hat, which was only answered by a shake of the head. He never saw one of them after. Floating on, for two days and a night, and often overwhelmed by the breakers, he got within two miles of the shore, when the wind shifting, he was again driven to sea, above six miles; thus wafted at the mercy of the waves, he was at length discovered about a mile off, by Captain Dudley of the schooner *Hannah*, from Beaufort, North Carolina, who humanely put about, and was fortunate enough to snatch this hapless victim from a watery grave. (*NC* vol 8, p76)

23 April, Princess, merchantman   The large ship, *Princess* of London, W Lee master, from Smyrna with a cargo of cotton, drugs, etc valued at over £80,000 was driven ashore near Beachy Head at 5am on this Friday, but by the exertions of the crew and the tide flowing, she was got off at 3pm. But not long afloat when she unshipped her rudder and quite unmanageable was once again driven on shore and completely wrecked. (*Times*, 28 April 1802)

30 August, explosion at Madeira   About 12.45am on this Monday morning, the inhabitants of Madeira were alarmed by a dreadful explosion, which shook every house and broke several windows, but providentially did no other damage in the town. Immediately after the explosion, the large Portuguese ship *Aurora*, Captain Fabricio Jone dos Santos, was discovered to be on fire. Being in the dead of night, little or no assistance could be given by the people on shore. His Majesty's ship *Woolwich*, commanded by Captain Ulick Jennings, was at that time anchored nearby, and at the first alarm, Captain Jennings had all his boats manned to render assistance. All the people, thirty-four in number, perished by the explosion, except two, who were saved by the boats of the *Woolwich*; one of them was very little hurt, but the second had one of his legs broken, the other much shattered and he had contusions to his head also. The people saved could give no account of what had happened, but probably someone was careless with a light near the powder magazine. (*Times*, 18 October 1802; *NC* vol 8, p339)

3 September, Nimble, packet   During this night in a heavy gale of wind at south and then at south-west, with a pitching and rolling sea, the *Nimble*, a packet boat from Plymouth for Portsmouth, foundered off the Bolt Tail, and although there were more than eighty people on board, yet there was only one survivor, a seaman who had taken to the boat; but how he managed to do so, when no-one else did, is unknown. He arrived at Plymouth on 26 September, where he related his story in a deposition before the justices (*SYM*, 20 September 1802): 'The *Nimble* was run foul of by a large ship off the Bolt Tail, and started a butt end when she was at some distance from the land; she then parted in two and he was so lucky as to take to the boat. He tried to save the master of the *Loire*, of 44 guns, who held as long by the stern as his strength would permit, but being quite exhausted, at length went down.' Among those lost were Mr Bennett the captain of the *Nimble*; the master of the *Loire*, his wife and four children; Lieutenant Kelly of the Royal Navy, son of the Hon Mrs Kelly (aunt of Lord Boringdon); as well as sixty-seven other persons who were discharged sailors with their wives and children. By 24 September the *Nimble* had been weighed and towed into Salcombe. (*NC* vol 8, pp260, 345 and 349)

4 September, double tragedy at Plymouth A large barge, Hicks master, in turning down Hamoaze with a cargo of staves missed stays between Mount Edgcumbe and the rocks of Devil's Point battery; she was then driven on to the rocks of the latter place where the vessel bilged and filled, the cargo was lost and Mr Hicks drowned, being knocked overboard with the jerk of her striking on the rocks. (*NC* vol 8, p259)

    Also at Plymouth on this same day a trawl boat (belonging to Mr McAughland, a pilot to the East India Company, in working into Catwater from fishing, and trying to weather Victualling Office Point [see under 1 July 1806] now called Fisherman's Nose), she missed stays, and was driven amongst the breakers off Deadman's Bay where she bilged, but it was expected if the weather moderated that she would be got off. (*NC* vol 8, p259)

4 September, mutiny in the Thomas, Guineaman 'Came into Cawsand Bay, forced in by contrary winds, the *Thomas*, Guineaman, Captain Martin, bound to Senegal and Goree, with a cargo and for slaves. Captain Martin went ashore in the afternoon of Sunday the 5th to procure fresh beef and vegetables. While absent six of the sailors (lately paid off from a man-of-war), being rather in liquor, refused to furl the sails or go aloft, on which Mr Scott, chief mate, remonstrated. Fup and Arthur, two of the ringleaders and the most active in the mutiny, with the others, rushed aft, knocked down Mr Scott, and used him very roughly indeed, till rescued by the better disposed part of the crew. During the mutiny Captain Martin came on board and ordered them to do their duty, which they refused, and Fup gave the captain so violent a blow on his neck as brought him to the deck, on this they kicked him as he lay senseless. The mate being on the forecastle hailed *La Venturiere*,[29] 18 guns, lying abreast of the *Thomas*, when a boat well manned and armed with Royal Marines, with a midshipman, pushed off and got alongside the *Thomas*, when the mutineers took shot and axes, and swore they would sink the boat before any marine would come on board the ship, swearing they would have their blood for supper, and that of their captain and his mate. By this time the Royal Marines rushed up the side, boarded, and charged with bayonets on the mutineers, who were soon overpowered, handcuffed, and sent on board the flagship in Hamoaze, and put in irons for the night, but still behaved very disorderly and riotous. On the 8th the seamen handcuffed and guarded were taken in the morning to the Guildhall, where the depositions of Captain Martin, Mr Scott and the midshipman, were taken before the mayor and deputy town clerk. It was supposed they would be committed for trial at the Admiralty Sessions.' (*NC* vol 8, p260; Plymouth report 8 September 1802)

8 September, La Pomone, 44 guns   On 23 April 1794 two French naval vessels, *La Pomone*, 44 guns, and *Le Babet*, 20 guns, were both captured by the squadron of Sir J B Warren off the Île de Batz channel. *La Pomone*, 1239 tons burthen, 'was esteemed the finest frigate afloat'.

Yet at 8pm this evening *La Pomone*, Captain Hon Edward Gower, broke her back and foundered when she ran on to the rocks as she was beating into St Aubin's Bay, Jersey. Even so by 24 September the ship had been weighed and towed into harbour, where after some repairs had been effected she sailed with *La Revolutionnaire*, 44 guns, Captain Locke, and arrived at Portsmouth on 25 October. Two days later, on board the *Neptune* lying in Portsmouth harbour, a court martial was convened to try John Geram the pilot of *La Pomone* for the loss of the vessel. Blame was attributed to him for attempting to enter the Bay of St Aubin at night, when the ship might have remained with safety at sea until dawn. He was adjudged to be mulcted of all the pay and allowances due to him for services done as a pilot on board that ship; and to be imprisoned in the Marshalsea for three months from that day. (*NC* vol 8, pp349, 430 and 437)

17 September, Mentor, brig   'The brig *Mentor* foundered at Cerigo on her passage from Athens to Malta. She was laden with sculptured marble of unequalled beauty and workmanship from the Temple of Minerva at Athens, and other monuments of antiquity belonging to Lord Elgin, our Ambassador at Constantinople. Mr Hamilton, his Lordship's secretary; Captain Leake of the Artillery; and Captain Squire of the Royal Engineers, were passengers in the vessel on their return from a very interesting tour through Syria and Greece.

'It is entirely owing to Mr Hamilton's indefatigable exertions that any part of this truly valuable cargo has been recovered; he remained some weeks on the island of Cerigo to try if it were possible to get up any of the property; and after having employed various means, he at length sent for divers from the island of Samos, who succeeded in the undertaking.' (*Times,* 26 February 1803)

On 27 February 1805, more than two years after the event, the *Times* printed: 'Letters from Corfu of the 27th December 1804, advert to the loss of the brig *Mentor*, in September 1802, in thirteen fathoms at the entrance to the port of Cerigo (the ancient Cytherea). On board were ten cases of marble, all attributed to Phidias; among the rest, the marble seat of the

Prytaneum at Athens. Shipped by Lord Elgin for London, the then Ambassador at the Porte. His Lordship on hearing of their loss charged Doctor Calucci, the British vice-consul at Cerigo, to use every possible method to recover these curiosities. The doctor after two years has succeeded; thanks to the swimmers of Calimno in getting up all that was desired without injury to any divers. (*Preface*, p5)

19 September, lightning strike   An electrical storm occurred at Gibraltar. The first ship struck was the 80-gun *Gibraltar*. A flash of lightning struck the fore topgallant mast, split the fore topmast and shivered the fore mast, driving large splinters as far as the quarterdeck. From the fore mast it passed into the light room close to the magazine, shivering the strong plate glass to pieces; from thence to the gunner's store room where it destroyed several boxes of grape shot. Only two men were hurt, one being badly burnt. A flash struck the *Active* frigate, split the topgallant mast, several feet of which completely disappeared. The ship's butcher, standing near the main mast with his cleaver in his hand, was killed. The *Superb* and the *Dragon* were also struck; the former had her main topgallant mast as well as the binnacle on the quarterdeck carried away; whilst the latter vessel was not damaged, though the lightning passed all round the captain's cabin via the bell wires. (*Times*, 18 October 1802)

23 September, female transportation   'The *Glatton*, 54 guns, Captain James Colnett, has dropped down to St Helens. She has 170 female convicts for Botany Bay, 27 of whom are not 20 years of age.' (*Times*, 21 September 1802). The *Glatton* was originally an East Indiaman purchased by the government in 1795. She sailed for Botany Bay on 23 September. (*SNL*, May 1803)

8 October, Flora, brig   The brig *Flora*, Mr Soper master, sailed from Plymouth during September with a cargo of pilchards for Venice and to load back on freight for Plymouth and London. In the night of 8 October, in a violent gale of wind, the vessel struck on a reef of rocks on the extremity (compass position not given), of the island of Majorca; she was soon fast with a heavy sea breaking over her, yet nevertheless the crew got with difficulty on shore, there to await the dawn to see if they could save any papers or perhaps part of the wreck. In the morning there was not a vestige of the *Flora* to be seen, so completely was she knocked to pieces. After performing quarantine in a hut for seven days the crew were escorted by Spanish troops to their part of the island, from whence the vice-consul returned them to England. (*NC* vol 8, p517)

13 October, Earl St Vincent, West Indiaman   The Plymouth report of today's date read: 'Came in, after a long passage of ten weeks, the *Earl St*

Vincent, of this port, from Jamaica. She experienced very bad weather and was given up as lost by her owners here, and 25 per cent premium for insurance was actually offered and refused, as she was supposed to have foundered on her passage.' (*Times*, 16 October 1802)

28 October, Juno, 34 guns   The Spanish frigate *Juno*, 34 guns, Captain Ignacio Bostillos, having on board at least $100,000 and 420 persons, was lost on her passage from Porto Rico to Cadiz.

The *Favourite* schooner, Captain Pourland, from Madeira for Boston, fell in with the *Juno* in latitude 36°40′N longitude 67°16′W. The *Juno*'s captain informed Mr Pourland that she was in great distress and that the water gained so fast that their utmost exertions were necessary to keep her free; he at the same time requested that the *Favourite* would continue in company until he could make land, and received on board three officers and four marines. Nothing occurred for four days when it blew a gale from the north-west and Mr Pourland observed signals for abandoning the frigate, and for the *Favourite* to run as near as possible under her lee. At 9am the main mast went over the side and the fore mast fell alternately from side to side. Every effort was made by the *Favourite* to afford her assistance, but in vain. A heavy fog ensued and continued half an hour; when it cleared away the frigate was no longer to be seen.

The *Juno* had left Porto Rico with 413 persons on board, including many women and children, and went down twenty miles east of Cape May, in 180 feet of water. There were apparently no survivors. (*AR* 1802, Chr, pp471–472)

18 November, Nautilus, merchantman   The *Nautilus* was a ship of about 400 tons burthen of and from Calcutta for Canton when she was wrecked on the Iron Island,[30] near the Great Lema off Hong Kong in a typhoon. The official account of the loss of the ship was probably written by the ship's second officer who was a known survivor. It is here given verbatim from the *Annual Register* of 1803, Chr, pp441–442:

'On 16th November we had fine pleasant weather; observed in 22°15′N at sunset a ship bearing WSW pleasant through the night. On the 17th in the morning saw land bearing WSW soundings sandy bottom. At seven A.M. saw Padra Branca bearing NW by W from the fore-top, hazy looking weather. At noon came on a hard squall – had no observation; ship steering to the northward and westward. At one o'clock the squall clearing up a little saw Padra Branca bearing N by E about two or three miles distance; and also a great number of fishing boats going in different directions, and seemingly in great confusion; hauled more to the westward; still squally with heavy rain. At eight o'clock at night, the squall increasing, and dismal-looking weather, handed our topsails and courses, and lay-to under the mizzen staysail, heaving the lead through the night; at midnight, blowing hard with rain, the wind about NE. At three o'clock next morning wore ship to the southward and eastward, blowing furiously, and a tremendous sea. At four o'clock wore ship again. At daylight saw an island under our lee; let go both the bower anchors; but at this time the wind being so very violent the anchors had no effect on the ship, and she drove bodily on the island and went to pieces shortly after she struck. In the evening we mustered eighteen men on shore; came to us two China men, from the top of the island, and brought with them some roots: in return we gave them some liquor; they behaved very well and went again to the place they came from. This night we remained among the rocks; the next morning found one lascar dead. This day went on top of the island where we found two or three huts but no people. A little while after came some men women and children and conducted us to a place where we found a mandarin and many inhabitants: this man treated us with great civility. On the 21st sent us to Maeno [Macao?], where we arrived in the evening and staid in the boats all night. The next day about noon I went with the gunner on shore but the China men would not allow the lascars to be landed. I went and reported this to the governor and he got them released. I suppose 27 of the crew to be lost, together with the captain and chief mate. Nineteen are saved including myself and the gunner.' (See also *NC* vol 15, pp466-467)

18 November, Spanish frigate The same night in which the *Nautilus* was wrecked a Spanish frigate from Manilla, bound to Canton and freighted with dollars, was wrecked in Brandon's Bay on the coast of China near Hong Kong. The crew were saved, but most of the treasure (said to have amounted to more than $800,000) was lost. (*NC* vol 15, p467)

23 November, Melville Castle, East Indiaman The *Melville Castle* was an East Indiaman, which being found unseaworthy, was sold to some Dutch merchants who traded to the East Indies. At Amsterdam, the ship ostensibly repaired, was chartered by the Government of the Batavian Republic to carry troops to the Cape and Jakarta. (*MC*, 1812 ed, p210 et seq)

On 20 November 320 soldiers of the 2nd Marine Battalion, who had marched from Rotterdam, boarded the ship, to be followed on the morning of the 21st by the admiral, colonel and officers together with their families. The ship, renamed *Vryheid* (Liberty), and her convoy got under way and sailed with a variable wind till early next morning when it blew a heavy south-westerly gale. (On the 21st and 22nd the weather was extremely tempestuous. *NC* vol 8, p515.) As the day opened the wind blew with increased violence and the most serious apprehensions began to be entertained for the safety of the vessel, and these fears certainly increased when about 3pm on this Monday afternoon the main mast went by the board, and in so doing swept several of the crew overboard whilst other seamen were injured. A signal of distress was now hoisted and after great exertions the ship came to anchor off Hythe Bay and it was at this time that a Dover pilot boat as well as two Deal boats endeavoured to reach the vessel but owing to the rough seas she could not be boarded. After several hours in this situation, about 6am on Tuesday the vessel parted her best bower anchor and it appears that Captain Scherman and his crew twice attempted to put the ship about and stand to the east but were unable to do so. The ship now drifted towards Dymchurch Wall where she took the ground at the first groyne at a place called Brookman's Barn about half way between Hythe and Dymchurch. After she struck the first sea filled the ship to the lowest deck, full of water and drove her on her side, when also the ladders between decks were washed away so that people below could not get on deck in consequence of which many drowned before she went to pieces, which being a crazy old ship, she did almost at once. (*NC* vol 8, p428; *Times*, 27 November 1802)

Of the 472 people on board the *Vryheid* only 8 marines and 10 seamen survived the shipwreck, which was one of the most disastrous ever to occur on the coast of England.

Perhaps the most illuminating account of the tragedy was that given by a young gentleman who was residing at Folkestone; it was given in a letter which he wrote to his father and was dated 24 November. After stating that he beheld the waves running mountains high, he then goes on: 'About one o'clock I observed many casks floating and the people running along the beach towards the rock to procure whatever might fall in their way; before I could get to the point which is about a quarter of a mile from where I live, the body of a fine young woman was driven upon the rock; she was entirely naked except for one stocking and a leather garter which was buckled below her knee. About a quarter of an hour after another female came in with many different articles, such as cartouche-boxes, puncheons, canteens and soldiers caps. I heard the wreck was at a place called Brookman's Barn, so I rode over there and beheld such a spectacle as I hope I never shall witness again. The ship had passed Dimchurch (*sic*) about eight in the morning, yet appeared to be all well; about half an hour after she was driven on shore on the sand, and almost instantly parted, the sea driving the upper part farther in the land.

'I rode for two miles along the coast from the wreck towards Margate, which was covered with puncheons, musical instruments, muskets, &c. as also dead bodies of men; the soldiers appear to be principally marines, by having two anchors crossed on their buttons. There has been a great number of them carried away to Hythe church: in a mile and a half's ride I counted the bodies of one hundred and twenty. The seamen were observed handing seven or eight females up the shrouds, that being the most probable means of saving them; but shortly after the mast went by the board and they were all plunged in the devouring element. There were near one hundred poor fellows on a piece of wreck and very near shore when a sea came and swept them off. A Mr Kemp of Hythe saved one of them from death by running into the sea. He was very near an officer and had just got hold of him when he perceived a swell approaching, with a large piece of the wreck, and had only time to save himself, for immediately the timber knocked out the brains of the officer. On my return to Folkestone I found two more women and two or three infants had come ashore; I also saw a little girl this morning about eight months old. Not an officer or female is saved: every person here is busy on the beach picking up what they can: some find watches, money, skins, &c.' (*Times*, 27 November 1802)

27 November, Adventure, brig Captain Codling was hanged at Execution Dock for the scuttling of his vessel the brig *Adventure* (*NC* vol 9, p84) [The complete story of the scuttling, at Brighton, and the trial of Richard Codling, and the two owners of the vessel, George Easterley and William Macfarlane, on 26 October 1802, appears in *AR* App. to Chr, p568 et seq, and *NC* vol 8, pp168, 403-424]

2 December, Flora, merchantman The *Flora*, Captain Sanson (Sampson?), of Plymouth, with a cargo of deal, balk and spars, from Danzig for Plymouth, was wrecked in a gale during the night of Thursday 2 December. The ship had been six days on her passage from the Straits of Dover and was taken aback off Beer Seaton Cliffs, and it being a lee shore, as the wind then was, the vessel became embayed, parted her best bower and went plump ashore. In endeavouring to reach the beach Mr Sanson and three of the crew were drowned, but the rest got safe on shore. (*NC* vol 8, p517)

11 December, London Bridge mishap While it was blowing strong from the west-north-west four barges about to shoot the centre of London Bridge were by the violence of the wind forced into the draught of the lock together, in consequence of which they were jammed together in their passage through the arch and continued in that state until the centre one (which was carrying 21,000 bricks, and was a new barge) sunk; as also did two of the others, also deeply laden, when they got clear of the bridge, but luckily no lives were lost. (*Times*, 15 December 1802)

25 December, storm off Honfleur This was not to prove a happy Christmas for many of the residents of Honfleur which 200 years ago was a small town where most of the populace existed by fishing.

Many of the boats which sailed on the evening of the 24th were caught in a storm on Christmas Day when two of the vessels foundered. Eighteen men and boys, the crews of both the boats, perished. Other vessels which ran for shelter were more fortunate, but nevertheless lost a total of about forty nets. (*Times*, 4 January 1803)

29 December, gale in the western approaches   Whitsand Bay in Cornwall has a dangerous lee shore when the wind is in the south-west quarter, which is the prevailing wind for that area.

This morning, during high tide and a dreadful gale, the sloop *Unanimity*, from Cork for London, laden with butter and dairy products, was driven ashore in Whitsand Bay, where the vessel, cargo and crew were all lost, except for one young black seaman. (*NC* vol 9, p75)

In the same south-westerly gale, and also in Whitsand Bay, at the village of Wrinkle, a fine American ship, the *Juno*, Captain Lionel Clarke, becoming embayed, was driven on to the sands where she immediately bilged and settled, very fortunately at high tide. Captain Clarke had then coolly collected his owner's and his ship's papers and swam ashore; he gallantly returned against the surf and with the seamen saved a gentleman, his wife and children, on their passage to London, and then the remainder of the crew. The *Juno* had struck at 9pm during a December gale, and for Captain Clarke to swim ashore from the wreck and then back again in the dark showed courage of a very high order. (*NC* vol 9, p75 et seq)

The *Juno* was bound from Philadelphia for London and had sailed from the Delaware on 24 November with a cargo of various timbers, furs, coffee and cotton, as well as pearl and pot ashes in hogsheads. At an auction of the wreck and cargo held at Tregantle in Whitsand Bay on Friday 14 January 1803, one of the men assisting in getting out the timber injured a hand so severely that it had to be amputated. It was said afterwards that much credit was due to R Pole Carew of Anthony, who with his troop of yeomanry cavalry protected the property of the ship and passengers.

At 8am on this same day, 29 December, in a heavy gale at south-south-west, the brig *Frederick*, from Cork for Workington, struck on the North Bull in Dublin Bay one and a half miles west of Sutton, and in less than an hour went to pieces. The passengers together with the crew of twelve all perished except for one man. Washed ashore were the bodies of two sailors, two women and three children, all of whom the magistrates ordered to be decently interred. (*Times*, 5 January 1803)

? December, Mapaphema, merchantman   A very large ship, presumed a Dutch or Danish East Indiaman, was lost near Peterhead, when all the crew perished. However, by some wreckage and papers which came ashore, the ship proved to be the *Mapaphema*, a Russian in ballast. (*NC* vol 9 pp83-84)

30 December, Junge Jan Swaartz, galliot   This afternoon as a Dutch galliot *Junge Jan Swaartz*, the weather having moderated, was working out of Plymouth Sound on her passage from Amsterdam for Bayonne, laden with butter and cheese, a squall came on by which she missed stays and was then driven on to the rocks to the east of the Sound, where although she quickly beat to pieces, yet Captain Soers and his crew all survived. (*NC*, vol 9, p75)

31 December, small boat tragedy at Plymouth   The year was to end tragically; three boats belonging to people living at Dock and Stonehouse, were out under the cliffs of Staddon Heights, where they were endeavouring to salvage some of the wreckage of the *Junge Jan Swaartz*, when the surf dashed them against the breakers and the whole upset. Of the fifteen persons who had been on the three boats, nine were drowned. (*NC*, vol 9, p75)

1803

4 January, Hero, merchantman   The ship *Hero*, Captain Deane, from Newfoundland for Lisbon, with wet and dry fish for a market, appeared off the bar of the River Tagus near Lisbon and, in endeavouring to work up the harbour, the wind being scant, the current forced the ship on to the South Catchups (38°42'N 9°09'W) where she bilged and became a total loss. It was regrettable that after such a long voyage the captain, crew and passengers were all to lose their lives. (*Times*, 28 January 1803)

8 January, unknown French ship   On this day near Portland the ship *Eliza*, of London, Captain Donaldson, from Rotterdam for Bristol, picked up eight hogsheads of French wine floating on the sea and passed through upwards of a hundred more of the same sort, from which it was conjectured that some French ship must have been lost near that island. The crew also took up the figurehead of a ship with netting attached. (*NC* vol 9, p77)

9 January, Neptune's boat   This afternoon a boat belonging to the 98-gun *Neptune*, Captain W O'Bryen Drury, with eight persons in it, five boatmen and three passengers (two of them young gentlemen of Gosport, who were going to the *Neptune*, lying at Spithead, to see their brother), was overset in a gust of wind near the hospital and all drowned, except three of the boatmen. Four bodies were immediately picked up; two of them young gentlemen aforementioned, who had held by the boat till exhausted, but driving on the shore, were beat off and perished. (*AR* 1803, Chr, p354)

10 January, Hussar, 38 guns   Late this evening during a heavy easterly gale the 38-gun *Hussar*, Captain Wilkinson, lying at Blackstakes (above Sheerness), caught fire by accident in the gunner's storeroom, close to the magazine; and from the explosion of some combustible matter the ship's company rushed on to the quarterdeck and thence into a boat which was hanging in the tackles astern; and from too great a number getting into her for the purpose of saving themselves, the davit by which she was hoisted up gave way and threw the whole of the people into the sea; through which unfortunate accident, two masters' mates, one midshipman, fourteen seamen and one woman were drowned. By the exertions of the captain, officers and the remaining part of the crew, the fire was soon extinguished without much material damage to the ship. (*AR* 1803, Chr, pp354-355)

10 January, Meanwell and the lifeboat   The ship *Meanwell*, Captain Holiday, was on passage from Bordeaux to Hull and Newcastle when she ran ashore a mile or so to the northward of St Andrews. The accident and circumstances relating to it were given in a letter from Camborough, which presented 'a most satisfactory statement of the efficiency of that inestimable invention, the lifeboat.'

'I have the satisfaction to inform you that our St Andrews lifeboat performed wonders last Monday the 10th in saving the crew of twelve persons of the *Meanwell* of Scarborough. I happened to be in town that day when it blew a tremendous storm from the north-east with the seas running mountains high, and thick weather. About two o'clock a ship appeared so near the shore that she could not possibly clear the land. Hundreds of people turned out to give assistance, every signal was made for the harbour and the life-boat in readiness. Unfortunately, just as the ship was entering the harbour, a heavy sea made her strike the ground and hove her out of the channel among the breaker's rocks, from whence the lifeboat soon brought the crew to safety. Had I not been an eye witness to it, I could not have believed that any boat could have lived in such a sea and surge. The storm was so violent that the fishermen could not be persuaded to enter into the boat till Mr Dempster, one of the magistrates, and a Major Horsberg, volunteered their services; also a shipmaster David Stewart, who made great exertions indeed. The famous and enterprising Mr Honey was on the beach, also ready for exertions. Please intimate this to the committee at Lloyds for encouraging the building and keeping of lifeboats on different parts of the coasts of the United Kingdom.'

Although the bottom of the vessel was out, yet a part of the cargo was saved and landed at Dundee. (*AR* 1803, Chr, pp355-356)

10 January, Active, West Indiaman   At 6pm the *Active* of Greenock, Captain Hornby, a fine new West India ship of 350 tons burthen and laden with 300 hogsheads of sugar, etc, bound to Greenock, parted from her anchor in the Margate Roads and went ashore at the pier-head where she soon foundered. After the sea had made a complete breach on her weather-side, she drove in shore, with her fore and mizzen masts standing, upon the Nayland Rock, at 3am; to which fortunate circumstance may be attributed the safety of part of the passengers and crew who, had she remained where she first struck, would in all probability have perished. They consisted of nineteen persons and from lashing themselves in the shrouds ten out of the nineteen were saved. Five perished in the main top by the falling of the mast; one lad was washed overboard, and three were taken from the rigging, who perished by the spray of the sea and from the inclemency of the weather. Every means of resuscitation on them was used by Mr Slater, a surgeon of Margate, without success. Among the survivors were the captain, mate and pilot. (*NC* vol 9, pp70-71; *AR* 1803, Chr, p354)

11 January, Hindostan, East Indiaman   On 4 January the purser of the *Hindostan* attended India House and received his final dispatches for the Cape, Madras and China, but unknown to him at the time the voyage was to prove of short duration.

The *Hindostan*, an East Indiaman of 1248 tons burthen, Captain Edward Balston, sailed from Gravesend on her fourth voyage on Sunday 2 January and brought to in the Upper Hope Reach near Hope Point, probably to await the purser; the company then received their river pay as well as two months pay in advance, and all the women were sent ashore. On this day, the 4th, with a foul wind the ship proceeded and having passed the Nore came to an anchor with her best bower in the Queen's Channel off the Wedge Sand on the 9th, the wind then being east. On Tuesday 11th, although the weather was clear, yet there was a strong easterly gale blowing; the *Hindostan* had rode out the lee-tide, and in tending to windward the pilot thought it necessary to heave in the cable to prevent the ship tailing on the sand. The capstan bars were manned but in heaving taught, a violent squall came on and the ship taking a sudden range the cable parted and within minutes she was on the sandbank (between the Tongue and Margate Sands), twelve miles from shore. The fierce north-easterly wind blew so violently towards the river, raising a tremendous sea, that several ships returned to the Hope, but the *Hindostan* was fast aground; and from the moment of her striking it was only too evident that the ship must be lost; she had taken the ground at 4pm and within half an hour it was quite dark with heavy seas breaking over the vessel and a freezing easterly wind, so that doubts were raised about saving the lives of all the 120 persons on the ship. The main and mizzen masts soon went by the board whereupon the boats, all except the launch, were hoisted out, but the cutters were quickly stove against the side of the ship by the violence of the sea and she began to part about the main chains. Two rafts were quickly constructed and several people committed themselves to them with the hope of floating ashore, but by the violence of the sea the rafts were dashed against each other and although most of the persons on them were washed off and drowned yet a few did manage to survive. Many others had ascended the fore rigging and most of these people also survived, although several froze to death or dropped from the rigging as they became benumbed; yet it was remarkable that of all those on board only about 30 were to lose their lives. About 9am on the 12th approximately 80 of the crew were taken off by a Margate Hoy and the remainder by the *Liberty* pilot sloop, of which latter vessel Mr Thompson was the master; his journal reads as follows: 'Tuesday 11th. During a heavy gale but with clear weather, saw the *Hindostan* with ensign half up at the peak and firing minute guns. I weighed and proceeded to the ship and at five-thirty came close to her and found her aground on the Wedge Sand, all masts gone except the foremast. Sounded close to the ship's starboard side and found three and a half fathoms and ahead of her three and a quarter fathoms. I sheered off and anchored in six fathoms about a cables length from the *Hindostan*. Could not get near her with the boat as heavy seas were breaking over the boat and right over the ship and it was with great difficulty that I got back to the *Liberty* at about eight-thirty. The *Hindostan* fired directly at the boat and at the same time we thought we saw two boats (no doubt the rafts) put off, and they, judging from the ship they could not fetch me, was I thought the reason for their firing directly at me. Immediately I slipped leaving a whole cable with the anchor and steered in the direction that we supposed the boats had gone but could not find them, the tide was too strong so at midnight anchored two miles to the west of *Hindostan*. At four o'clock weighed again and at seven anchored close to the ship and assisted in getting men out of her. At nine o'clock took out Mr Turner the 2nd officer and twenty men, the last to leave the ship, and anchored at Gravesend at two o'clock.'

The cargo of the *Hindostan* was valued at £100,000, of which the greater part was made up of bales of wool or woollens. The ship was also carrying 45,000 ounces of silver, private venture bullion in thirteen chests, of which eleven were salvaged by 24 January as also were 100 bales of woollens. The East India Company had no bullion on the vessel. It was on this day, the 24th, that it was decided to abandon the wreck; what with the continuing easterly gales and the rough seas the *Hindostan* had sunk so far forward that it had become not only too perilous to approach the vessel, but also far more dangerous with all the wreckage inside the ship for anyone to descend the hatches on the gun deck, which were now at a steep angle, just to salvage woollens, and the East India Company's officers left the scene, to be followed by the two gun brigs that had been stationed there to protect the wreck. (*Times*, 15 January 1803, et seq; *NC* vol 9, pp69-70; *AR* 1803, Chr, p355)

12 January, Vaasa Wall, merchantman　A Swedish ship *Vaasa Wall* of Vassa (now Finland), Frederick Calumnius master, from Cadiz for Rotterdam laden with salt and a small quantity of fruit and wine, was lost off Caister near Yarmouth during a gale. Three of the crew were lost but the other seven were saved by a brig lying in Yarmouth Roads. A few pipes of wine were picked up at the time. (*NC* vol 9, p83; *Times*, 15 and 17 January 1803)

17 January, Hector, merchantman　The ship *Hector* of and from New York for Hamburg, laden with tobacco, etc, drove on shore on Flamborough Head where she soon went to pieces. The crew and passengers totalling nineteen persons were all rescued, except the cook, who lost his life while trying to swim ashore. (*Times*, 25 January 1803)

26 January, Hope, collier　The collier *Hope*, Captain Hodgson, from Whitehaven for Dublin, was driven by a gale on to the Muglin Rock, about a quarter mile to the east of Dalkey Island (Thorn Island) in Dublin Bay, where she soon went to pieces. Sometime later, wreckage together with bodies of some of the crew floated ashore at Dun Laoghaire, whilst other bodies were cast up at Merrion Strand. It would appear there were no survivors. (*Times*, 3 February 1803)

29 January, Canadian schooner A schooner belonging to St John's, Newfoundland, George Gempton master, laden with fish and oil from St John's, ran in the dead of night during a snowstorm on to Goodrington Sands in Torbay, where she soon went to pieces. The schooner and cargo were lost but the crew were saved. (*NC* vol 9, p160; *Times*, 1 February 1803)

31 January, Pandora, merchantman A ship, the *Pandora*, Captain Bienvenue, from Philadelphia for Guernsey laden with tobacco, imprudently attempted the passage of the Bridge, between St Nicholas Island and Redding Point in Plymouth Sound. As was expected, she stuck fast in the Middle Passage, where she lay till the top of the tide, when she swung off with great violence, though with little apparent damage and proceeded on her outward bound voyage. (*NC* vol 9, p160; *Times*, 3 February 1803)

8 February, Supply, brig *NC* vol 9, p83 gives the following: 'The *Supply*, Captain Johnson, from London for Pensacola, is put into Margate with loss of an anchor.' This was followed by an article in the *Times*: 'The brig *Supply* was lost on the Brake, one and a half miles from Ramsgate. The master, six seamen and a passenger got upon the topmost shrouds; with the sea making a clear passage over the vessel. In this precarious situation they remained throughout the night, and the next morning at daybreak a boat put off to their relief; but at this time the sea beat the brig into deeper water and she foundered, only one man being saved.' (*Times*, 14 February 1803)

19 February, Trelawney The *Trelawney*, Captain Affleck, from Baltimore for Liverpool was actually seen off Liverpool on this day, but with the gale then blowing the ship could not fetch the port and was driven to the northward where she took the ground about sixteen miles from Whitehaven (north or south unknown [but probably struck near Ravenglass, which has a lee shore in a SW gale]) and went entirely to pieces. (*NC* vol 9, last page)

17 March, Isabella and Antoinette The Dutch frigate *Isabella and Antoinette* on her passage from St Domingo for Holland was lost on the Mayaguana Reef in the Caicos Passage. The crew who were fortunate enough to be saved numbered amongst themselves seven Americans who had been impressed by the Dutch captain. (*Times*, 30 May 1803)

22 March, accident on Lake Lucerne This was the day when a tragic accident occurred to a boat that was transversing Lake Lucerne; as well as the crew the vessel was carrying 60 passengers who were going to assist in the procession of St Nicholas when as a consequence of it being overloaded the boat suddenly foundered and all on board perished. (*Times*, 14 April 1803)

26 March, La Determinee, 24 guns   La Determinee, a 24-gun corvette, Captain Alexander Becher, was lost near Normont Point as she was working into the harbour at Jersey, and on 30 March Captain Becher wrote to Sir Evan Nepean, for transmission to the Lords of the Admiralty, his account of the loss of the vessel. It is here given verbatim, from SNL of 1803.

'In pursuance of orders received at Spithead from Admiral Milbanke dated 23rd March, to receive on board a detachment of the 81st Regiment and proceed without loss of time to Jersey; *La Determinee* being in all respects ready for sea I sent an officer on shore on the morning of the 24th, to Commissioner Sir Charles Saxton, to request his assistance towards obtaining a pilot; but his not being able to send one, occasioned me to make application to the flagship, where I was equally unsuccessful.

'The troops being all embarked by three o'clock in the afternoon of that day, *La Determinee* sailed, in company with the *Aurora*, for Jersey; and as the ships were going through the Needles Passage I had hopes of getting a pilot either at Cowes or Yarmouth.

'Being nearly off Cowes about six o'clock in the evening I made the signal with a gun for a pilot and about forty-five minutes after seven both ships anchored at Cowes.

'In the morning at daylight I repeated the signal with two guns but no pilot appeared; and at five o'clock the ship weighed anchor and followed the *Aurora* for the Needles.

'Falling little wind as we approached Yarmouth I sent an officer on shore at that place to endeavour to get a pilot, and at the same time repeated the signal with guns for that purpose; but these efforts proving as ineffectual as the former we sailed through the Needles and no chance was left but to obtain one at Guernsey, or on the Jersey coast.

'The ships went through the passage of the Great Russel [between Herm and Sark] the next day about two o'clock pm; the signal for a pilot was constantly abroad and many guns were fired.

'Unable to obtain a pilot I resolved to follow in the *Aurora*'s wake; the weather was fine and moderate and it appeared to me a strict attention to and that ship's motions would render it far from being unsafe to adopt a measure for which a general signal is established.

'The master acquiescing with me in this proposal, orders were given to keep immediately in the *Aurora*'s wake.

'About a quarter past four being close upon the wind and nearing the harbour the *Aurora* was observed to be in stays; every thing was of course prepared and in momentary readiness for that purpose; in about five minutes after, judging *La Determinee* as near the place as possible, I ordered the helm a-lee; the ship came instantly to the wind and the after-yards were hauled about; the mainbrace was scarcely belated when she struck on the rock, and in less than three minutes the water inside of the ship was of equal height with the surface of the sea.

'Being apprehensive that the ship might fall into deep water from the strength of the tide I ordered both anchors to be let go, which was done and the cables bitted and stopped.

'The panic which prevailed over the women and children threw the ship into a scene of confusion hardly to be described, in spite of every effort to suppress it.

'Notwithstanding, the sails were clued up, and topgallant sails handed, and the men in the topsail yards in the act of furling the topsails; but thinking their weight aloft might tend to upset the ship, I called them down to get the boats out. The large cutter was soon out; but the hurry and fear of the people who crowded into her, plainly foretold their fate. In vain I remonstrated on the impropriety and folly of their quitting the ship, and solicited them to let the women and children only go into the boat; but both reason and persuasion had lost their influence; and in this moment the ship fell on her broadside.

'Myself with many others were by this change thrown into the sea; and it was not without difficulty after being near ten minutes in the water, that I regained a dry situation; but at last having reached the mizzen-top I had once more an opportunity of advising towards saving the lives of those left with me on the wreck, though still unable to prevent many from jumping into the sea.

'Too much praise cannot be given to all the officers and men assisting upon this unfortunate event, who by their exertions in the course of three hours and a half, in a tide running near six knots, had taken every man from the wreck, which when I had seen done I went with my officers on board the *Aurora*.'

At a court martial held on board the *Gladiator* in Portsmouth harbour on 4 and 5 April 1803, Captain Becher, his officers and men were all honourably acquitted for the loss of the ship; and the court was of the opinion that Captain Becher 'used every means in his power to obtain a pilot for Jersey, both before he sailed from Spithead, and during the voyage, without effect; that he was actuated by commendable zeal for the service in attempting to enter the harbour by endeavouring to follow the *Aurora*'s track; and that his cool and officer-like conduct, after she struck, was highly meritorious, especially in ordering the anchors to be let go, to prevent her drifting into deep water, by which means many lives were in all probability saved.'

Those lost with the ship were a midshipman and one seaman belonging to the ship, ten soldiers, two women and three children, of the 81st Regiment, and a woman and child of the invalids.

26 March, pressing activities in Bristol Although it was ostensibly a time of peace the press gangs were as active as ever and on this Saturday evening at Bristol they were uncommonly numerous and attended by the military. It was a time of gang warfare with press gangs fighting gangs of civilians who had no true representation in Parliament. Shooting, killing, wounding and shanghaiing were the order of the day. At every avenue in the city of Bristol parties of soldiers were stationed to prevent any escape, and upwards of 200 men were picked up, many of whom not being seamen were discharged the following day.

On the Sunday afternoon as the press gang and a party of marines were conducting the pressed men to Lamplighter's Hall in order to put them on board a frigate lying in King Road, they were violently assaulted by a large mob in Hotwell Road who flung mud and stones, which so irritated the military that they fired among them and killed a boy and wounded several others. (*Times*, 30 March 1803)

2 April, L'Aigle's press gang 'A Fifth Rate, the 36-gun frigate *L'Aigle*, Captain Wolfe, was ordered to Portland Roads on impress service, and on this Saturday evening Captain Wolfe ordered his press gang to board vessels lying in the Roads and impress seamen, who however did not hang around and escaped on shore. Later that same night a press gang consisting of Captain Wolfe, Lt John Hastings and John Fortesque Morgan, together with twenty-seven marines and as many sailors, proceeded to the village of Chesilton where they impressed Henry Wiggot and Richard Way, without any interruption whatever, Nevertheless, the people of the village took fright and fled to the hamlet of Easton near the centre of the island where they made a stand at the pond. The press gang followed them the two or three miles to Easton where the captain took a man by the collar. The man pulled back at which the captain fired his pistol, at the sound of which the lieutenant of marines ordered his men to fire, which being done, three fell dead, being all shot through the head; they were Richard Flann, aged 42, a quarryman; Alex Andrew, aged 47, a quarryman and William Lang, aged 26, a blacksmith. Another man was shot through the thigh and a young woman was shot in the back from which the ball could not be extracted and who was believed to have had little hopes of recovery. Poor Lang was at the door of his smithy when he fell. [On 19 April the *Times* denied the authenticity of this version of what happened on the night of the 2nd.] (*Times*, 13 April 1803)

At the coroner's inquest held a week later at Weymouth the jury returned a verdict of wilful murder against Captain Wolfe, his officers and those men who had been members of the press gang on that occasion.

On 27 April Mr Jervis on the part of Captain Wolfe, Lt Hastings, John Fortesque Morgan and seven others, moved their lordships for a writ of *Habeas corpus*, to be directed to the gaoler at Dorchester to bring up these three gentlemen and also for a writ of *Certiorari* to bring up the depositions that had been taken before the coroner in this case. Furthermore, he stated that he had the affidavit of the surgeon of the ship stating that the men on board who were wounded, had received gun shot wounds, and that the mob was previously armed with guns, swords and pistols, with the intention of resisting these gentlemen in the execution of their duty, and that the resistance with guns, etc first began on the part of the mob.

On 10 May Captain Wolfe and his gang were bailed in the sum of £400 each with four additional sureties of £100 each. At the beginning of August at Dorchester Assizes, Captain Wolfe, his officers and seven men were tried for the murder of those who were killed by his press gang. They were all honourably acquitted. (*Times*, 3 August 1803)

11 April, East India convoy   About 8pm five East Indiamen, part of the homeward bound East India fleet, under convoy of the *Romney*, 50 guns, and *Daedalus* frigate, arrived off the Eddystone, where finding the easterly wind too strong to enable them to beat up the Channel, they were compelled to lay-to and were then boarded by armed press gangs who took from them nearly 300 seamen; then short of men, the East Indies ships bore away for Plymouth Sound, there to be manned by men from the ships in ordinary (reserve) to navigate them to the Thames. Eventually sailing from Plymouth on the 17th, they were once again under convoy of the *Romney* and *Daedalus*, even though war had not yet been renewed. (*NC* vol 9, pp331-332)

14 April, Thomas, brig   Robert Scotney, the second mate of the brig *Thomas*, Captain Gardner, was a native of Spalding, Lincolnshire, who survived by himself seventy-five days in a perfect wreck. His case was recorded in a letter from Mr Paulin, 4th officer of the *Europe* East Inidaman, to his father, dated Madras Roads 8 September 1803.

'On 29th June, about half-past eight a.m., we saw a small boat on our starboard bow, which upon nearing we discovered to have only one sail set, and otherwise to be a perfect wreck. No-one was observed to be on her deck until hailing her a wretched object presented himself, apparently in a most distressed situation, and in the posture of imploring our assistance. A boat was immediately sent on board her with Mr Mackeson the second officer, who returned with him, having sent the wreck adrift.

'By the poor man's account it seems he sailed from London as second mate of the brig *Thomas* of London, commanded by Captain Gardner, and belonging to Broderick and Co. of Wapping, on 4th March 1802, bound to the Southern Ocean, on the whale fishery. On their outward bound voyage they arrived at Staten Island [Strait of Le Marie, Patagonia], where they continued six or seven months, and got about seven or eight hundred skins. In the course of that time they rose upon their longboat, lengthened and decked her and converted her into a shallop, of which they gave him the command, and put three seamen on board under him, with orders to accompany the brig to the island of Georgia to procure seals and sea elephants.

'They accordingly left Staten Island the end of January in company with the brig, and after eleven days' passage arrived at the island of Georgia, where they remained two months, and left it the beginning of April, with their own brig and another brig, the *John* of Boston in company, and stood for the island of Tristan da Cunha.

'On 14th April they were parted from their consorts in a heavy gale of wind, in which gale he lost his three hands, who were washed overboard by a tremendous sea, from which he himself narrowly escaped, having the moment before gone below for a knife to cut away some rigging.

'At that time he had on board only three pounds of flour and three and a half of meat, six pounds of bread and two hogsheads of water, which were all more or less damaged by the gale. some whale oil remaining in the bottoms of some of the casks, and a small quantity of salt. On this scanty pittance, and without any means of dressing even that, he prolonged his existence for the surprising period of seventy-five days.

'He likewise emptied a medicine chest he had on board and got out of it some burning medicine, which he found made his body a little comfortable and warm, as he never got his clothes off. He was almost constantly wet.

'When we fell in with him he was shaping a course for the Cape of Good Hope, having missed the island of Tristan da Cunha, to which it was his intention to have proceeded for the purpose of rejoining his consort, whom he expected to have found there. His debility was however so great that he had been for several days previous incapable of going into the hold of the vessel for what little sustenance then remained, or of shifting his helm should a change of wind have happened.

'He then lived mostly on tobacco, which he took an amazing quantity of; and when he came on board both his cheeks were swelled out amazingly with the ruinous quality he had in his mouth, and which he seemed to suck with convulsive agony.

'The appearance of this poor wretch when he was hauled up the side (for he could not walk) deeply affected everyone; he had entirely lost the use of his extremities – his countenance was pallid and emaciated; and it was the opinion of our surgeon that he could not have prolonged his existence two days longer.

'It is not necessary to enlarge upon the thankfulness of the poor fellow for his preservation, or that he experienced every possible assistance which his situation required, and which I make no doubt, you will hear with pleasure, proved successful.' (M C Duncan, 1811 ed, vol 4, p217 et seq)

19 April, Reliance, merchantman This morning on the Gardenstown coast a tremendous gale blew from the west-south-west which increased towards the afternoon to a complete hurricane, abating only at short intervals throughout the ensuing night.

The next morning some young men finding wreckage on the beach proceeded westwards and from the top of More head discovered a mass of wreckage in a small bay called Walcove. They, climbing down the five hundred foot cliff not far from St John's church, found Colin Burn, a native of Montrose and the only survivor of a crew of eleven. The wreck proved to be the *Reliance* of Newcastle, William Allen master, of 198 gross register-ed tons, the vessel had sailed from Shields on the 17th laden with coal for Jamaica. Mr Burn engaged with Captain Allen on the 16th, so was little acquainted with his shipmates but thought that three of them hailed from Aberdeen. Six bodies were recovered and interred, probably at Gardens-town. (*AR* 1803, Chr, p382)

28 April, Indian Ocean pirates The *Bhowany Pattamar*, a boat mounting four carriage guns, arrived at Calcutta and reported that on her passage along the coast she was attacked by six piratical boats off Severn Droog (Suvarn-drug),[31] and beat them off when they hauled their wind and stood to the westward, but soon after tacked and stood in apparently for Severn Droog. They appeared to be of fifty or sixty tons burthen and besides swivels and muskets, each vessel carried a heavy bow chase gun and many men. (*Times*, 21 December 1803)

7 May, altercation with press gang On this Saturday afternoon two rowing galleys, each containing an officer and a press gang, arrived at Hungerford Stairs, and in endeavouring to impress several people, they were resisted by a party of coal heavers belonging to the wharf adjoining, who assailed them with glass bottles and coal, when several of the gang were cut in a most shocking manner. The impressed men, for whom there was no room on the *Enterprise* (a tender), were put in the Tower and the gates shut to prevent their escape. (*Times*, 9 May 1803)

? May, Bellerophon, 74 guns The following appeared in the Obituary List of the *NC* vol 9, p423; yet the article advanced no dates: 'We are extremely concerned to learn that a letter received from an officer on board the 74-gun *Bellerophon*, Captain Loring, at Jamaica, states that a dreadful mortality had raged on board that ship. She had lost several officers and upwards of one hundred of her crew.' The most likely cause would have been yellow fever or typhus.

PART THREE

THE
NAPOLEONIC
ERA
1803 – 1816

1803

16 May, renewal of war with France The Peace of Amiens proved to be of short duration, for on this day Britain once again declared war on France, and on 18 May this was published in the *Gazette*. Next day, the 19th, King George's declaration occupied the whole of the front page of the *Times*, which also issued a supplement of several pages.

18 May, first action of the Napoleonic War The 18-pounder 36-gun frigate *Doris*, Captain Richard Henry Pearson, fought an action off Ushant with *L'Affronteur*, a French hired lugger of fourteen 6-pounder guns and 92 men, commanded by M Latoye, Lt de Vaisseau, the crew of which fought with great courage against overwhelming odds; and had their captain and eight men killed, as well as fourteen wounded, before they surrendered. It was said at the time that the crew of *L'Affronteur* mistook the *Doris* for a West Indiaman and hauled close under her quarter for the purpose, it is supposed, of boarding; in which situation she fired three broadsides into the *Doris*, the last being so close the *Doris* could not bring her guns to bear. The date of this action remains open to question; it may have occurred before war was declared. (*NC* vol 9, p418)

31 May, Resistance, 36 guns A 36-gun frigate, the *Resistance*, was built by R Parsons of Bursledon and launched on 29 April 1801. On 31 May 1803 the vessel captained by the Hon Philip Wodehouse was en route for the Mediterranean, when early in the morning she struck a few miles to the northward of Cape St Vincent and could not be saved. The crew were all rescued. (*SNL*, 1803)

On this same day, but twelve hours later, an affray occurred on the Barbican at Plymouth, where a press gang being beset by a mob of two or 300 people opened fire and Mr Rokestrew, the master of a fishing smack, was killed on the spot. The jury at the coroner's inquest returned a verdict of wilful murder. (*Times*, 6 June 1803)

28 June, Lady Hobart, packet On 22 June 1803 the *Lady Hobart*, a packet of 179 tons burthen, Captain William Dorset Fellowes, sailed from Halifax, Nova Scotia, for England, the vessel steering to the southward and eastward to clear Sable Island, and on the 24th hauled to the northward to pass over the north of the Great Bank of Newfoundland, and also to avoid the French cruisers. On 28 June it was blowing from the west with a heavy sea and intervals of thick fog, when about one hour after midnight the ship then going at seven knots struck an iceberg with such violence that several of the crew were thrown out of their hammocks. The vessel then struck a second time, upon the chess-tree, and then swung around upon her heel, the stern post being stove in and the rudder carried away before anything could be done; the iceberg meanwhile was overhanging the ship about twice the height of the masthead and was estimated to have been about a third of a mile long. (Since it was 1am and foggy, this is probably no more than an educated guess.)

The guns were thrown overboard and the two bow anchors cut away; two sails were got under the ship's bottom, the two pumps kept going while others baled at the main hatchway with buckets. Their efforts availed them nothing, and within minutes the ship had settled to her forechains; the cutter and jollyboat were hoisted out, with the ladies being placed in the cutter, the size of which was 20ft long, 6ft 4in beam, and 2ft 6in deep, and into this eighteen persons were crowded. The jollyboat was smaller, being 14ft long, 5ft 3in beam and 2ft deep, and into this were crowded the other eleven persons. The cutter towed the jollyboat, and later on, during the same morning while standing to the northwest, they passed two more icebergs, nearly as large as the first.

At noon, by observation, they found themselves to be in latitude 46°33′N, St John's, Newfoundland, bearing west ¼ north, distant 350 miles. This was the only observation that they were able to make during the whole time they were in the boats.

While the cutter had been getting out, one of the seamen, John Tipper, was seen emptying a demi-john (a 5-gallon bottle) which contained rum, when asked by the captain why he was doing so, he replied he was emptying it for the purpose of filling it with water from the scuttle-cask on the quarterdeck, which was the only fresh water that could be got at. This proved afterwards to be their principal supply.

Seven days later on 4 July they saw the land about a mile distant, between Kettle Cove and Island Cove, in Conception Bay about fourteen leagues from St John's and about 4pm had the good fortune to be towed into Island Cove by a fishing vessel. After the people had rested for two days, Captain Fellowes hired a schooner into which the ladies and the most infirm were placed, and at 2pm on the 7th, the schooner towing the jollyboat with the cutter in company, left Island Cove for St John's, which was reached a few hours later.

The garrison commander Brigadier-General Skerrit provided beds and necessities for the crew, several of whom required surgical attendance, being so much frostbitten.

On 11 July Captain Fellowes, his wife, Lt-Col George Cooke of the 1st Regiment of Guards, Captain Richard Thomas of the navy, and several others embarked in an Oporto-bound vessel in which they had engaged a cabin, this being the only available ship and most probably laden with salt fish.

On 26 July in mid-Atlantic they fell in with an American ship, the *Bristol Trader*, from New York for Bristol. The captain and owner, Mr William Cowley, learning who they were, hove to and according to Captain Fellowes, received them on board 'with a benevolence and humanity that reflect honour on his character.' They arrived safely in England, at Bristol, on 3 August 1803. (Duncan, *Mariner's Chr*, 1812 ed) [The article written by Captain Fellowes was copied verbatim by both Duncan and Dalyell, in each case covering more than 20 pages; of necessity, given here abridged.]

Exactly one year after the boats of the *Lady Hobart* reached Island Cove, one of her crew died. The *NC* vol 12, p87 recorded:

'Obituary. Suddenly, in Falmouth on Wednesday 4th July, John Tipper a seaman, who had been married sixteen days. This is the same John Tipper whose name is so honourably recorded in Captain Fellowes narrative of the loss of the *Lady Hobart*.'

2 July, Minerve, 38 guns   The French 40-gun frigate *La Minerve*, Captain Perree, was taken near Toulon on 24 June 1795 by the two British frigates *Lowestoffe*, 32 guns, Captain B G Middleton, and *Dido*, 28 guns, Captain George H Towry. (*SNL*, 1799)

In the evening of 2 July *La Minerve*, Captain F Jahleel Brenton, grounded on a sandbank near Cherbourg during a thick fog. The crew were rescued by the French and although made prisoners of war were nevertheless treated in the kindest manner by their captors. (*NC* vol 10, p260)

La Minerve had a chequered career: she was refloated and taken once again into the French navy, being renamed *Canonnière*. She was captured a second time by the British on 3 February 1810 by the *Valiant*, 74 guns, and then renamed *Confiance*. (*SNL*, December 1812)

21 July, La Seine, 38 guns   *La Seine*, a 42-gun French frigate, was taken by the *Jason* and *La Pique* frigates off the Saintes on 29 June 1798, and by coincidence all three were sooner or later to be wrecked. During the action in which *La Seine* was taken by the British, *La Pique* ran aground on the Saintes and was wrecked; but the crew were saved. Captain David Milne of *La Pique* was then given command of *La Seine*, and five years later was the commander when the ship grounded on a sandbank to the northward of Terschelling during the night of 21 July. The vessel could not be got off and the crew, who incidentally were all saved, eventually set fire to the ship, to prevent its falling into the hands of the original owners.

On Thursday 4 August 1803 a court martial was held at Sheerness to try Captain Milne, his officers and ship's company for the loss of the vessel, when they were all honourably acquitted, except however the pilots, who both being found wanting, were sentenced to be mulcted of all their wages and to be imprisoned in the Marshalsea for two years. (*Times*, 26 July and 6 August 1803)

29 July, Caledonia, merchantman   The *Caledonia*, Captain George Thomas, left Balasore Roads (near the entrance to the River Hooghly) on 18 May for Bombay with many passengers on board, including thirty-seven men of the 78th Regiment, four women and several children. On 29 July, when running in for the land, they struck soundings and found forty-five fathoms, it then blowing very fresh with a heavy sea. About 11am, Captain Thomas was looking out for a double altitude of the sun, when smoke was observed to be coming up the fore hatchway, then, when the cover was removed, fire broke forth with such violence as to preclude any hope of saving the ship, and it was soon realised that the hold was on fire so that saving the lives of the passengers and crew became of paramount import.

Embarked in the longboat were Captain Thomas, his wife, Colonel Paterson, Mr Rose, Mrs Joyce, wife of a Sgt-Maj of the Bengal artillery at Tannah, and Mrs Fraser and child, she the wife of a private of the 78th, in all fifty-six people. In the pinnace were ten sea-cunnies and lascars, of whom seven were lost on the rocks when trying to land; while in the jollyboat was the gunner (an officer), and fourteen lascars, of whom four were lost in the surf on Malabar Point.

Soon after quitting the ship, those in the boats observed the main mast go over the side and the ship which was carrying fourteen barrels of gunpowder was seen to blow up abaft.

The total number of persons on board the *Caledonia* were 157, of whom 86 lost their lives. (*Times*, 2 February 1804)

30 July, Calypso, 16 guns A 16-gun sloop of war, the *Calypso* was built in 1783 and twenty years later was commanded by Captain William Venour. On 30 July the ship was on escort duties acting as convoy to the West Indies fleet sailing from Jamaica for England, when during a violent storm a heavily laden West Indiaman ran foul of the *Calypso* which immediately foundered. All 120 of the *Calypso's* crew perished.

Captain Venour was a very good officer, was sometime attached to the Hon Admiral Waldegrave's flag (Lord Radstock), and sailed from Portsmouth as 2nd Lt of the 74-gun *Theseus*. (*NC* vol 10, p175)

4 August, Redbridge, schooner Taken by a squadron of French frigates off Toulon the *Redbridge*, Lt George Lempriere, was a 16-gun schooner, whose crew were to suffer eleven years as prisoners of war, and a court martial on 4 June 1814; they were released after the abdication of Napoleon at Fontainbleau, 20 April 1814. (*SNL*, 1803, 1814)

17 August, Flinders' odyssey Early in the year 1801 the ship *Investigator*[32] was fitted out on the Thames and put under the command of Lt Matthew Flinders (hereafter known as Captain Flinders), for the purpose of exploring the coasts and interior of New Holland (Australia); besides the crew the vessel carried artists, scientists and naturalists, and on 18 July 1801 the *Investigator* sailed from Spithead on her voyage of discovery. (*NC* vol 6, p83)

By February 1802 the ship had reached Nuyt's Land, having cruised down the coast of Western Australia and into the Great Bight when, in need of supplies and repairs, they proceeded to Port Jackson, arriving there on 5 or 6 June 1803. It was then discovered that the vessel was so rotten as to be unfit for further service. It was therefore determined that the *Porpoise*, a small armed vessel under the direction of Governor King should complete the voyage of discovery, but this vessel also was found to be unfit for such a voyage and it was then decided that the *Porpoise* should proceed to England with the officers of the *Investigator* and as many scientists as the ship could accommodate, the remainder to await other transport or for Captain Flinders to return with another ship.

On 10 August 1803 the *Porpoise*, commanded by Lt Robert Fowler with Captain Flinders as a passenger, in company with the *Cato*, Captain John Park, and the *Bridgewater*, Captain Edwin Hanker Palmer, sailed from Port Jackson, the *Porpoise* for England, the *Cato* and *Bridgewater* for Batavia. The *Porpoise* was formerly a Spanish packet, the *Infanta Amalia*, mounting ten 6-pounder guns which had been taken by the *Argo* frigate of 44 guns, Captain James Bowen, off the coast of Portugal on 6 August 1799. The vessel was purchased from its captors by the British Government and converted into a storeship for use of the colony of New South Wales, but being out of England for three years was very much in want of repairs. The *Cato* was a much smaller vessel, not more than 90 tons burthen; nevertheless, she was a more sturdily built merchant ship, as was the *Bridgewater*, but all three were eventually to be lost, the *Bridgewater* apparently in 1806 with all hands.

At 1.15pm on the 17th, seven days after leaving Port Jackson, the *Cato* observed a dry sandbank (now called Cato Island, 23°28′S 155°49′E) bearing south-west about three leagues, whereupon she signalled the *Porpoise* which then stood towards the bank after which she resumed her former course. At 9.45pm the crew of the *Cato* saw breakers ahead, all hands were called and attempted to get aboard the main tack, but the *Bridgewater* having hauled to the wind on the opposite tack, the *Cato* was obliged to bear up to avoid running against her, and the *Cato* then struck the reef about a cable's length from the *Porpoise*, which had been ashore some time. The *Bridgewater* stood on to the southward and fortunately cleared the breakers. The *Cato*'s situation was desperate, for whereas the *Porpoise* had run on to a level shelf, and then heeled away from the surge of the sea, the *Cato* heeled towards it, and the surf broke violently over the ship and filled her. The crew cut away the lanyards of the inner shrouds and the masts went by the board, after which the crew took to the inner fore-chains, which were their sole refuge, in order to prevent being washed overboard by the violence of the surf, and in that situation they had to cling all night with the sea making a free passage over them.

In the morning, about 9am, the *Bridgewater* hove in sight to the southward and stood towards the wrecks so as to show her courses above water; at 9.30am she tacked, stood to the southward again and they never saw her more.[33] At 10am the *Cato* began to part at the larboard gangway, (previous to which her decks were all blown up), which obliged them to attempt getting through the surf to the *Porpoise's* boats, which lay to leeward ready to receive them. The *Cato's* decks being copper-fastened, the nails all drew and whole planks came up together. On these they ventured through the surf, two or three on a plank, and by 2pm on the 18th, were all away from the ship. It was however regrettable that three seamen, Robert Kay, William Tindall and George Philliskirk, were lost in the surf. The next landed in safety, but naked, and joined the crew of the *Porpoise* upon a sandbank, about 250 yards long and 100 yards broad, and about a quarter of a mile from the wrecks. The officers and men of the *Porpoise* humanely shared their clothes and blankets with the crew of the *Cato*, and after getting on shore some provisions and water from the *Porpoise*, they all lay down to sleep with some little comfort and 'except from a few of the *Cato's* men who were bruised among the rocks, not a complaint was heard on the bank.'

The survivors from the two ships, eighty altogether, were fortunate; they were wrecked in the vicinity of a coral bank that was permanently dry and from where at low water they had easy access to the *Porpoise*, which although a crazy old ship held strictly together, while of the *Cato* which was a stout merchant ship there was hardly a vestige to be seen. By the 24th all the provisions, enough for three months, and everything of use had been taken out of the *Porpoise* and on 26 August the decision was taken for the cutter to sail to Port Jackson for assistance. The six-oared cutter, 26ft in length, was prepared for the 800-mile journey by being partly decked (*NC* vol 16, p226) and on 27 August the cutter with fourteen men on board sailed from the reef for Port Jackson. Those on the cutter included the best seamen: Captain Flinders of the *Investigator*, and Charrington, the boatswain of the *Investigator* as well as Captain Park of the *Cato* and Mudie his second mate. Within a day or so of arriving at Port Jackson on 8 September the men were returning to the reef on board the convict ship *Rolla*, accompanied by two small colonial schooners, the *Frances* and the *Cumberland*. On 7 October when they arrived back at the reef they were surprised to find that those left behind had in the meantime constructed a 20-ton schooner from the wreckage of the *Porpoise*, and that with a minimum of tools.

On 10 October the four ships departed the reef with the officers and crew of the *Porpoise* sailing for Canton in the *Rolla*, a dangerous voyage in those days, yet even so on 17 November they saw Tinian and Saipan in the Marianas, and made Macao Roads on the morning of 4 December. (Duncan, 1808 ed). Those who wished to return to Port Jackson did so in the *Frances* and the *Resource*, the latter being the vessel they had themselves constructed, while the 29-ton schooner *Cumberland* sailed for England with Captain Flinders, and after a voyage of some 4000 miles, called at Mauritius for supplies. It was not to be: the French Governor De Caen imprisoned Captain Flinders as a spy, and allowed the *Cumberland* to rot and fall to pieces. Flinders was not released until the British took Mauritius in 1810 and he returned to England in November of that year.

It should be said here that in the writer's opinion the Frenchman did not act unreasonably; there was a war on and Captain Flinders had taken soundings on his way into an enemy harbour, and being a very good navigator would have carefully plotted them. Although he had a safe conduct passport from the French Government, it would not have given permission to take soundings in their harbours in time of war; Captain Flinders should have signalled for a pilot. (*NC* vol 12, pp143-144, 302-304 and 450; vol 16, p223 et seq; Duncan, MC, 1808 ed)

A noteworthy article appears in volume 16 of the *Naval Chronicle*, p225, which says: 'I have heard that the *Bridgewater* has been missing for a length of time and apprehensions are entertained for her safety.' Volume 16 was printed during the latter part of 1806 and p225 about September of that year. An error occurs in *Steel's Navy List* which shows the *Porpoise* as being lost in 1804. No dates were given but 1804 was the year the news arrived in England. The *Times* dated 26 May 1804 has an article.

? August, Houghton, East Indiaman   During the month of August, exact date unknown, the East Indiaman *Houghton* of 700 tons burthen, built on the Thames, of and from Bombay, bound for Canton, was believed to have foundered in a typhoon off the coast of China, where the entire crew of 120 persons perished with the ship.

In the same typhoon that the *Houghton* suffered, three Chinese tchuans from Java, Borneo and Siam, all or in part from those countries, homeward bound to China, foundered near that coast. In those vessels were about 500 men, out of whom 12 or 14 were seen floating in a tank, and were taken up by the Hon East India Company's ship *Warren Hastings*. (*NC* vol 15, p467)

20 September, Victory, merchantman   The ship *Victory*, Captain Morrison, sailed from Liverpool at 7pm of the 20th during a severe gale and was driven on to the West Hoyle sandbank at the mouth of the Dee, where she completely went to pieces at 10am the following morning. The main mast was cut away and five of the crew who had lashed themselves to it were picked up by a fishing boat, while another seventeen managed to save themselves in the ship's boat. Thirty-seven people died including Captain Morrison, who the ship's carpenter stated received a severe blow on the head from a falling spar and was then washed overboard just before the vessel went to pieces. (*AR* 1803, Chr, p437; *Times*, 1 October 1803)

23 September, Anstruther, East Indiaman   The East Indiaman *Anstruther*,

600 tons burthen, of Calcutta, Captain William Richardson, was fitted out as an armed ship at Malacca on the coast of Malaya, being equipped with twenty-four carriage guns, some 12- and the remainder 9-pounders. The vessel was carrying European infantry and artillery with native troops as marines bound for the island of Balambangan, lying in the Balabac Strait between North Borneo and Palawan, but a strong south-west gale drove the vessel past the northern end of Balambangan and amongst the shoals near the north-west of the island of Banguey where the vessel was wrecked. Many of those on board were said to have perished. (*Times*, 13 October 1804; *NC* vol 15, p467)

9 October, Jason, brig   Early this Sunday morning the brig *Jason*, Vasey master, from Sunderland for Exeter laden with coal, ran on to the Goodwins and could not be got off; the crew were saved by some boats from Deal which went to their assistance. The crew of the *Jason* reported that a sloop went on to the Goodwins, near them and soon went to pieces when all the crew drowned. The name of the sloop is unknown. (*Times*, 11 October 1803)

29 October, General Baird, East Indiaman   The ship *General Baird*, Captain Fleming, was of the same squadron as the *Anstruther*, lost on the 23 September (*qv*). The vessel registered at Calcutta had been used as a troopship to ferry troops to Balambangan and was in that harbour when she caught fire and was burnt to the water's edge. (Ref. as *Anstruther*)

31 October, Philadelphia, 44 guns   The *Philadelphia*, Captain William Bainbridge, was an American frigate of 44 guns and 350 men, engaged in maintaining the blockade of the port of Tripoli, when during a westerly gale the ship was driven a considerable distance to the eastward of her station. On Monday 31 October as the *Philadelphia* was running down to her station, about 9am, a vessel, believed to be a corsair xebec, was seen inshore and to windward, standing for Tripoli. Sail was made to cut her off and Captain Bainbridge believing himself to be within long gun shot, opened fire at 11am; the lead constantly giving from seven to ten fathoms. At 11.30am, Tripoli then being in plain sight, distant a little more than a league, satisfied that he could neither overtake the chase, nor force her ashore, Captain Bainbridge ordered the helm a-port, to haul directly off the land into deep water. The next cast gave but eight fathoms, immediately followed by casts of seven and then six and a half. At that moment the wind was nearly abeam and the ship had eight knots on her when the shout of 'half-six' was heard, the helm was put hard down, and the yards were ordered to be braced sharp up. While the ship was coming fast to the wind, and before she had lost any of her way, she struck a reef forwards and shot up on it, until she lifted between five and six feet.

This was an appalling accident to occur on the coast of such an enemy at that season of the year, and with no other cruiser near! It was first attempted to force the vessel ahead, under the impression that the best water was to seaward; but on sounding around the ship it was found that she had run up with such force as to lie nearly cradled on the rocks, there being only fourteen feet of water under the fore-chains, while the ship drew, before striking, eighteen and a half feet forward. Astern there were only seventeen feet of water whereas the frigate needed twenty and a half. Every effort was used to get the vessel off; the guns were run aft and the yards braced aback, most of the guns were then thrown overboard together with most of the shot and all the anchors except the larboard bower; the water butts in the hold were all started and the water pumped out, then the foremast was cut down, but probably because of the angle the ship was resting at, in its fall it also brought down the main topgallant mast. Notwithstanding all this, the vessel remained as immovable as the rocks on which she lay; the ship had struck at the top of the tide and probably on the crest of a swell.

The enemy in the meantime had sent out nine gunboats which stationed themselves on her weather quarter where it was impossible for the American ship to bring a single gun to bear and at 5pm the flag was hauled down. One report stated that the number on board the ship totalled 315 of whom 22 were officers; they all became prisoners of war.

On 2 November the north-west wind blowing fresh forced the water up on the African coast, and bearing on the larboard quarter of the ship her stern was driven around and she floated in part but continued to thump as the seas left her. The Turks put out anchors and cables astern and on the 5th managed to get the vessel into deep water within two miles of the city where they had to anchor because of the weather. The scuttling was not well done, only a few holes bored instead of cutting the planks through. The Turks quickly plugged the holes and relieved the ship of the water inside her; furthermore they then recovered almost everything that had been thrown overboard including the guns and anchors, which were later reported to have been replaced on the *Philadelphia*. Partially repaired, the ship was then moored about a quarter of a mile from the Bashaw's castle.

The Americans could not allow their ship to remain in the hands of the Turks and decided to do something about it. Captain Bainbridge, now a prisoner of war, managed on 5 December to pass a letter written in lime juice (which becomes visible when heated) to Mr N C Nissen the Danish consul at Tripoli, to be delivered to Captain Edward Preble, the commander of the American fleet at Syracuse, suggesting that the *Philadelphia* be re-taken. Lt-Cdr Stephen Decatur, aged 24, was chosen for the mission. With his ship the 12-gun *Enterprise*, he had previously taken a small ketch of some 45 tons, the *Mastico*, from the Turks. The Americans renamed the ketch *Intrepid*, and on 16 February 1804 the *Intrepid* with Decatur and 82 fellow American sailors, escorted by the 16-gun *Siren*, entered the harbour of

Tripoli. They could not recover the *Philadelphia* as the corsairs had not replaced the fore mast and furthermore not a sail was bent nor a yard crossed; nevertheless, they fired the frigate and then beat a successful retreat from the harbour. (J Fenimore Cooper, *The History of the Navy of the United States of America*, 1839 ed)

16 November, Circe, 28 guns   The *Circe* frigate, Captain Charles Fielding, was a 28-gun ship of 598 tons, launched at Dover in 1785, and was manned by a crew of 200 men when on this Wednesday afternoon at 3pm, in chase of a French privateer, she ran on to the Leman and Ower sandbank about twenty-five miles north-east of Cromer. As the sea rose and fell, the frigate thumping several times, lost her rudder and damaged her keel but she beat off the bank into deep water, where for want of her rudder she was entirely unmanageable. The vessel was almost twenty years old, very leaky, and the crew were already at the pumps when the accident occurred. Now the officers as well as the men had to man them, and man them incessantly, until about 7pm the following evening, when all were exhausted and despaired of saving the ship or their lives. It was at this time that the crew were taken off by three fishing smacks that could not approach earlier owing to the weather. They did not depart at once; at Captain Fielding's request they waited to see her go down, which occurred at 7.30pm that evening. The crew lost everything, except the clothes on their backs, but not a man was lost or injured.

On Friday evening the 18th they were landed at Yarmouth Roads where they were taken on board the *Repulse*, 74 guns, Admiral Russel, and a day or so later transferred to the *Galgo* armed ship and taken to Sheerness.

A few days later a court martial was held on board the *Winchelsea* in Sheerness harbour, when Captain Fielding, his officers and crew were tried for the loss of the *Circe*. They were all honourably acquitted. (*NC* vol 5, p560)

16 November, Scillies pilot disaster   During a severe gale, seven pilots belonging to the island of St Agnes perished near the Land's End. A Guernsey cutter privateer, with a rudderless Dutch East India ship, her prize, approached the islands where they took pilots on board, but because the wind and tide were not favourable it was not practicable that day to fetch any harbour in the Scilly Islands, they therefore came to and anchored as close as possible. During the night the wind became even more adverse, so that they were constrained to slip or cut their cables. Nevertheless, each vessel now had a pilot on board and the pilot boat with five other pilots maintained a close company. The gale increasing and shifting a point, the three vessels were driven to the eastward where fortunately both ships and the cutter made the harbour of St Ives in safety. The two pilots now left the ships and rejoined the other five in the cutter with hopes of getting home;

the weather, however, getting worse and they not being acquainted with that part of the coast, were observed from the land, all to perish without the least possibility of receiving help. (*AR* 1803, p460)

17 November, Jussrow Rebec, merchantman A ship was driven on to the rocks on the north part of the coast of the island of Yell in the Shetlands and just before she struck a total of sixteen people were observed to be not only on the deck, but also in the shrouds. In the gale then raging no boats could be launched to render assistance to those unfortunates on the ship and consequently they all perished. Seven bodies, including a woman's, were later washed ashore and interred.

On a part of the wreckage appeared the name *Jussrow Rebec* of Bremen, and it was believed that the ship hailed from Archangel. The cargo of oil, rye and wheat was entirely lost. (*Times*, 7 December 1803)

22 November, Hecate, bomb vessel The boat of the *Hecate*, a 14-gun bomb vessel, overset on the Reculver, near Margate, in consequence of which accident Lt Parsons, the master and four seamen were drowned. Mr Parsons had been with the *Hecate* only three months, having been appointed to the vessel in the preceding August. (*NC* vol 10, p174; and vol 11, p67)

26 November, Fanny, country ship The ship *Fanny*, Captain Robertson, sailed from Bombay for Canton on the morning of 8 August 1803, on what was not to prove a pleasant voyage. Misfortunes started in the Malacca Strait when the vessel tailed on a reef and lost her rudder, yet she was soon fitted up again and proceeded on her voyage.

On 16 September the appearance of the moon foretold blowing weather and by the 19th the beginnings of a typhoon were only too apparent. From noon on the 21st till midnight on the 22nd the storm raged with unparalleled ferocity so that no sail could be carried; yet even so, at 9am on the 22nd the fore mast went and in going astern it tore away the rudder and left the ship wallowing with three feet of water in her hold, yet at this very time from 9pm for half an hour there was a dead calm and then it started again. At midnight on the 22nd the storm abated and the morning of the 23rd brought some relief with only nine inches of water in her hold.

It was at this time that the first mate was later said to have gone raving mad, at the same time as the captain's spirits were at a low ebb, so that the safety of the vessel and crew devolved upon the second mate Mr Page. The ship was now in the area of the Paracel islands and with insufficient sail and the loss of her rudder rolled excessively and continued to do so until 10pm that evening when the main topmast went overboard, and in so doing killed one man and injured five others. The voyage continued and on the 13 October the ship made Hainan where the first mate and five others left the vessel.

The ship eventually made Canton where she loaded rice and set about her return voyage. At 1pm on 26 November 1803 the vessel struck on one of the shoals in the south-east part of the China Sea, her position then being given as 9°44′N 113°51′E, which would place the ship as being between Fiery Cross Reef and Sin Cowe, which however is doubtful, the longitude given being exactly ten degrees east of Singapore is probably no more than an educated guess. Nevertheless the crew were good mariners and boat-builders also; the fifty-six men who were now stranded on the reef managed to cut the poop off the ship (a 600-ton vessel), and build two flat-bottomed boats that were to stand the rigours of a thousand mile voyage. With some provisions obtained from the hold of the vessel the lascars embarked in one boat with the Europeans in the other. On the morning of 8 January there was no sign of the lascars' boat and the Europeans believed it to have foundered; they continuing on their thousand mile trip, made Malacca on 4 February.

Soon afterwards a vessel arrived at Malacca with a lascar on board belonging to the other boat which was thought to have foundered. The lascars had steered right before the wind and made the Malacca Strait where they went ashore on a small island for water, where being weak from hunger and exposure they were murdered by the Malays excepting for one man who escaped, stole a canoe and reached Rhio, off the west coast of Bintang, where he obtained a passage in a ship to Malacca. (Dalyell, vol 3, 1812 ed; *NC* vol 15, p467; Findlay's *Directory for the Navigation of the China Seas*, 1870 ed)

? November, Mercury, West Indiaman The *Mercury*, Captain Sowden, was a West Indiaman taken during September 1803 by the French 36-gun frigate *L'Egyptienne*, one of four French privateers that had been seen cruising off the island of Madeira. The *Mercury* sent into Teneriffe was purchased by the Portuguese who allowed Captain Sowden to proceed in her to Madeira, where he hoped to procure a passage in a neutral vessel for England. The ship had scarcely reached Madeira Roads when a storm arose and she was driven from her anchorage upon the beach where the *Mercury* soon became a total wreck; yet of her crew only one man was lost. (*Times*, 2 February 1804)

? November, Garland, 22 guns Formerly a French privateer named *Le Mars*, the 22-gun Sixth Rate *Garland*, Captain Frederick Cottrell, was wrecked on one of the reefs off Old Cape Francais on the north side of St Domingo, position 19°40′30″N 69°55′W. The crew were saved. (*SNL*, 1803)

5 December, Avenger, sloop A 16-gun sloop of war the *Avenger*, Cdr Francis Jackson Snell, was formerly the French *Le Vengeur*, taken on 17 March 1794 at Martinique by Vice-Admiral Jervis's squadron.

During a gale on 5 December the *Avenger* foundered in Heligoland Bight, off the Weser; the crew were saved.

On 18 January 1804 a court martial was held at Sheerness to try Captain Snell, his officers and crew, for the loss of their ship. They were all acquitted, save the pilot, who was reprimanded for his ignorance. (*NC* vol 11, p76; *SNL*, 1803)

10 December, Minx, 12 guns The *Minx*, Lt Manderston, was a gunbrig mounting 12 guns, built at Pitcher's Yard, Northfleet, and launched on 14 April 1801. The brig was anchored off Dover in the Road from the Downs to take on provisions, the wind then blowing fresh from the north-east. By 2pm the wind had shifted to the south-west, increasing with a heavy sea, and at 2.30pm the *Minx* started to drive. More cable was quickly veered away and a spring[34] put on it; everything was tried to prevent the ship from drifting ashore, all to no avail, the *Minx* taking the ground beneath Dover Castle. Fortunately the vessel was driven over the rocks and on to the beach where she was left quite dry at low tide, so was easily patched up and put into condition to float, then at 9pm on 12 December at high tide the ship was refloated and towed into Dover harbour.

Almost six years later on 2 September 1809 when commanded by Lt George Le Blanc the *Minx* was stationed off the Scaw, as a lightship, when she was taken by six Danish gunboats. (*Times*, 12 December 1803; *SNL*, 1803 and 1809)

10 December, Shannon, ex-Pallas, 36 guns Always reckoned as unlucky to change a ship's name, the *Pallas*, while it was building, was renamed *Shannon*, and within three months of being launched on 2 September 1803, at Brindley's yard, Frindsbury, she was lost and her crew prisoners of war.

The *Shannon* was a 36-gun frigate, commanded by Captain Edward Leveson Gower, when during the night of 10 December she was driven by a gale on to rocks under the batteries of Cap de la Hague, where the crew were rescued by the French. The *Shannon* was destroyed some time later when boat crews from the *Merlin* sloop of war landed and set fire to the wreck to prevent its being of use to the enemy.

It may be noted that whereas *SNL* of 1803 gives the locality of the wreck as being off Cap de la Hague, the *NC* vol 10, p515 states the ship was lost to the eastward of Cap Barfleur.

More than four years later on 18 March 1807 Captain Gower, his officers and crew, were tried by court martial for the loss of the *Shannon*; they were all honourably acquitted. (*Times*, 20 March 1807)

14 December, Grenada, sloop The *Grenada* sloop, a tender to the *Amelia*, 44 guns, Captain Young, bound for Grenada, was lost at Cowes. (*NC* vol 10, Marine List)

19 December, Mary, merchantman The *Times* of 3 January 1804 printed an extract of a letter received from Aberdeen dated 25 December:

'I procured a berth in a ship called the *Mary* of London, Captain Wrongham; we accordingly sailed from Elsineur [Elsinore] on 13 December, under convoy of the *Carysfort* frigate. The second day after we left Elsineur it began to blow very fresh, which terminated in a very heavy gale of wind. Our ship being leaky at the best now got so bad that we were obliged to pump night and day; and the ship being waterlogged it was determined to take to the longboat. We got accordingly what things we could out of the cabin, it being half full of water, such as bread, two hams, some liquor, a compass and quadrant. We had not time to put the things in the longboat when the ship upset. Four of the people [the crew] were drowned, and the rest of us got upon her bottom where we remained about an hour and a half, expecting every minute to be washed away. There was a ship close to us but could render no assistance, but God was with us, for a heavy sea struck and carried away the three masts which were under water when the ship instantly rightened and we got on her deck. Nothing was to be seen but the wreck of the masts which the rigging held, but the deck was completely cleared. In this situation we remained four days and three nights without as much as a biscuit, an ounce of beef or a drop of water and constantly wet.

'On the third day one of our men died of hunger and cold and on the fourth day another. We were reduced to the necessity of eating two small cats which had clung to the wreck. On the fourth night we got among the breakers and the second time she struck, she knocked her bottom from her topsides. We now lashed ourselves to the bowsprit with ropes and in about two hours got on shore, but our legs and hands so swelled that we could hardly crawl to a small house which stood on the beach.

'The next day people came from miles around to see us, indeed we were most lamentable objects. The people behave uncommonly kind to us; we have been in bed two days but I can now walk a little. It will be a poor Christmas but I did not expect to see one at all. The ship upset on the nineteenth at 8 or 9 am. The hands were twelve in number of whom four were drowned, two died of exposure and six got on shore, of whom two poor fellows will lose their toes.'

19 December, Thomas, Tagus and Hamburgh Packet, merchantmen This evening between 4 and 5pm as it was getting dark the brig *Thomas* of North Shields, laden, was driven ashore among the rocks in the Bay of Nigg. The master and six of the crew were on the yard handing the sails when she struck, and the mast giving way, they all perished; four others were saved. (*Times*, 28 December 1803). The same newspaper carried the following article:

'The *Tagus* of London came on shore half a mile south of Whiteness.

It is only known to be that vessel by pieces bearing her name, floating on shore, for there is hardly a vestige of her to be seen, of course, all hands perished. A great deal of wreck has come on shore in the different creeks.'

The same day there was another shipwreck in the same locality; the *Times* of 30 December printed the following letter dated Arbroath, 20 December:

'The storm had been truly dreadful since Saturday 17th. Yesterday at three o'clock in the afternoon a large vessel appeared off here and soon afterwards foundered in eight fathoms, off East Heaven (East Haven) about four miles to the westward, all perished. By the captain's desk coming ashore, and the papers found in it, she appears to be the *Hamburgh Packet*, Robert Couch master, from Danzig.'

20 December, Nancy and New Greenwich, merchantmen A large brig was seen to founder a few miles to the southward of Arbroath and by some wreck which floated ashore she was believed to be the *Nancy* of London. There were no survivors. (*Times*, 28 December 1803) The *Times* of the 28th also printed a letter received from Johnshaven dated 22 December, giving details of a further shipwreck on the 20th:

'On the morning of the 20th the brigantine *New Greenwich* of London, laden with barley, was cast on shore on the rocks about a mile south of Bervie. All perished and the vessel was a mere wreck. Mr David Scott, merchant of Johnshaven, took charge of the wreck and a part of the Mearnshire Volunteers, under the command of Walter Thom assisted to secure the property and prevent depredations. Two bodies were washed ashore.'

22 December, Wadewood, merchantman On the morning of the 22nd the *Wadewood*, Captain Melboom, from the Isle of Rhe with salt, was totally lost at Cowie near Stonehaven, fifteen miles to the south of Aberdeen. The captain, mate and five seamen were saved while seven other poor sailors lost their lives. (*Times*, 29 December 1803).

The *Wadewood* was probably embayed between Cowie and Garron Point.

23 December, Lady Saltoun, sloop During the night of the 23/24 December several pieces of a large vessel were washed ashore on to the sands of Belhelvie, and from a board with the letters *Lady Saltoun of B—*, it was supposed to be the sloop *Lady Saltoun of Banff*. Nothing was known of the fate of her crew. (*Times*, 28 December 1803)

25 December, Les Deux Amis, merchantman In the course of the night of 24/25 December several ships that had arrived at Plymouth Sound for shelter ran foul of each other while others were driven ashore.

Les Deux Amis from Martinique for Bourdeaux, a prize to the *Malta*, 80 guns, Captain Buller, went ashore in the Catwater near Deadman's Bay during a violent storm. Her cargo was 178 hogsheads of sugar and 38 casks of coffee. She was an old ship, twenty-two years since she was launched, and was safely moored when the storm began, with anchors and cables ahead. After she parted, struck and bilged, at 5pm her stern frame came out bodily and she soon went to pieces, but as the cargo was floating in shore, and the weather had moderated, a guard of Colonel Longmead's battalion of Plymouth Volunteers, consisting of a captain, two subalterns and forty rank and file, were turned out and did duty with great alacrity all night over the remains of the wreck, though the sentinels were obliged to fire several rounds of ball cartridges to keep off the water pirates' boats which were skulking in shore to plunder; but they thought proper on being struck to sheer off.

The sea ran so high at 11am that although 100 guineas were repeatedly offered to any pilot to carry off to *Les Deux Amis*, a spar, cable and anchor, no-one would venture. (*NC* vol 11, p76)

25 December, La Suffisante, 14 guns   *La Suffisante* was a 14-gun sloop of war taken from the French on 25 August 1795 by the squadron of Admiral Duncan at the Texel. (Norie, p410; *SNL*, 1799)

On the evening of Christmas Day the vessel commanded by Cdr Gilbert Heathcote was acting as a tender, conveying volunteer seamen and soldiers to England, but the storm which was raging over the whole of the British Isles on this day prevented the vessel, which had weighed anchor, from leaving the port and she came to an anchor at the entrance to Cork harbour. At 7pm that evening the ship started to drive and shortly afterwards grounded on the bank between the Spit and Spike Island. Two hours later the vessel fell on her broadside and remained in that position the entire night. Next morning the vessel was seen to have parted in two but as the weather moderated the local whaling boats managed to take off all the survivors, about ninety crew members and forty or fifty others. Seven of the people were lost overboard while three others were killed by the falling of a mast.

At Plymouth on 14 January 1804 a court martial was held to try Cdr Heathcote for the loss of his ship. He was honourably acquitted.

We may note that *SNL*, and Clowes, each give the date of the loss as 15 December. The *NC* vol 11, p76 and the *AR* 1803, Chr, p467, each give the date of loss as 25 December. The *Times*, 4 January 1804 printed a report from Cork, dated 26 December, which stated *La Suffisante* was wrecked the previous evening. The Cork report is given above. The court martial report makes the date of loss the 25th.

It may also be noted that *SNL*, 1803, p54 states the ship was taken in 1792, yet this is another error; the countries were at peace.

26 December, L'Atalante, 16 guns *L'Atalante*, a 16-gun sloop of war arrived at Brixham with loss of her main and mizzen topmasts; Captain Masefield had also been obliged to order all the guns thrown overboard to lighten the vessel. They had tried to make Plymouth but were driven by the gales to the eastward where they fetched Torbay. (*SYM*, 2 January 1804)

28 December, Friendship, brig The American brig *Friendship*, Captain John Ingraham, from New York, arrived at Plymouth with tar and turpentine; she had lost all her boats and other stores that were movable, having had them washed off the deck on Christmas Day during the gale. She also experienced other damages by an almost continual gale from the time she left New York. (*NC* vol 11, p78)

29 December, aground off Lesso This day the *Times* printed a letter from Captain Williams of the merchant ship *Argo*, on shore at Lesso, a Danish island in the Kattegat: 'I am sorry to add, there are nine sail on shore around us, besides seven sail more on the north end of the island, two of which have gone to pieces. Some have lost a great part of their crew.'

31 December, Grappler, 12 guns The *Grappler* gun-vessel mounted 12 guns and was commanded by Lt Abel Wantner Thomas when she grounded on the Îles Chausey, and was there taken possession of and burned by the French. The crew were to suffer eleven years as prisoners of war. (*SNL*, 1803)

? December, York, 64 guns The *York*, 64 guns, was built at the yard of Barnard and Roberts, Deptford, where she was launched on 24 March 1796. The vessel had been ordered by the East India Company and named *Royal Admiral*, but while still on the stocks had been purchased by the government. The ship mounted 26 guns on each gundeck, 24- and 18-pounders, as well as twelve 12-pounders. The *York* with a crew of 500 men and boys sailed on 26 December into the North Sea and was never seen again; nor does it appear that any wreckage, bodies or survivors were ever found. With the poor communications that existed in 1803 it may have been the case that the ship was lost somewhere off the Norwegian coast. (*SNL*, 1803)

As late as 22 February 1804 the *Times* printed: 'Some hopes are entertained of the safety of the *York*, 64 guns, whose loss in the North Seas has been seriously apprehended for some time past.'

However, it was not to be: Captain Henry Mitford, his officers and crew had perished.

1804

2 January, La Creole, 44 guns *La Creole* was a French 44-gun frigate apparently armed *en flute* in order to accommodate 530 soldiers who were on board when the ship was taken off San Domingo by ships of Commodore Bayntun's squadron on 1 July 1803. The command of *La Creole* was given to Cdr Austin Bissell of the *Racoon* and in company with other vessels the ship sailed from Jamaica sometime during December 1803, bound for England. On 2 January 1804 *La Creole* foundered in the Atlantic, where the crew were rescued by the 74-gun *Cumberland*. (*SNL*, 1803 and 1804)

On 29 January 1804 a court martial was held on board the *Gladiator* in Portsmouth harbour to try acting Captain Bissell, his officers and ship's company, for the loss of *La Creole*. The Court being fully satisfied that her loss was occasioned by her leaky condition, they were all honourably acquitted. (*NC* vol 11, p166)

Ostensibly repaired at Port Royal, yet still unseaworthy, if the weather had been bad, her crew could not have been taken off, and all would have perished; as it was, on board the *Cumberland* they were all but eaten alive by vermin. Then when the ship arrived at Portsmouth on 24 January it was learned that on her passage home 26 of her crew had died. (*NC* vol 11, p172)

Captain Bissell was to lose his life in yet another unseaworthy ship, the 74-gun *Blenheim*, on 1 March 1807 (*qv*).

8 January, unknown sloop A sloop which sailed for Guernsey was wrecked under the rocks of Plymouth Citadel. The only remains of the vessel were a few pieces of wreckage and some empty ankers of seven gallons and a half that were washed up. Every soul perished. (*NC* vol 11, p80)

8 January, Liberty, merchantman A Penzance pilot boat fell in with a wreck off Land's End and towed it in. On the stock of the anchor, which was still fast to the wreck, was burnt the name *Liberty* and the letters W M. Some time later two boats were washed ashore and on the stern of each were the words *Liberty*, Great Yarmouth. (*SYM*, 16 January 1804)

9 January, Cecilia, extra ship During a gale at Madeira Roads the *Cecilia*, an East India extra ship, bound for Bengal, dragged her anchors and was driven between two rocks where the ship became wedged; then when the main mast went overboard on the landward side the crew and passengers used it as a bridge to gain the shore in safety. Two people lost their lives, one of whom was called Tierney, the other's name unknown. During the ensuing night the *Cecilia* was beaten to pieces, and not a vestige was to be seen the following day. (*Times*, 2 February 1804)

11 January, Aid, merchantman The *Aid*, William Cranetch master, from Bristol for Dublin, was wrecked during the night of the 11th on Wicklow Bank; the wreck being later towed on shore about three miles to the northward of Wicklow. The captain's nine year old son and wife were lost, together with three other women. (*Times*, 20 and 23 January 1804)

16 January, Elizabeth, merchantman The *Elizabeth*, Captain Murphy, and eleven other vessels from Wexford for Dublin were driven on shore (locality not given) and three of them were completely lost. (*Times*, 24 January 1804)

19 January, Flora and Jason, merchantmen The *Times* contained articles of two shipwrecks. The *Flora*, Captain Carpenter, from Newfoundland for Poole, was lost on Portland beach where three of the crew perished.

    The *Jason*, Captain Taylor, belonging to Bridlington and bound to London, was lost near Bridlington. Captain Taylor was lost with his ship. No dates given for either wreck. (*Times*, 19 January 1804)

19 January, Jane, merchantman Laden with tar, turpentine, etc, the *Jane*, a Plymouth vessel, from thence for Liverpool, was wrecked in Stoke Bay between Netton Island and Stoke Point, to the eastward of Plymouth. Captain Weyers and his crew drowned. (*NC* vol 11, p82)

19 January, unknown brig A brig was seen waterlogged off Whitsand Bay, Cornwall, with four men lashed to the stump of her mast above water, with signals of distress flying; but due to the violence of the storm no assistance could be rendered and she foundered with all hands. (*NC* vol 11, p82)

19 January, rescue in Cawsand Bay The *Fearless* gunbrig, Lt George Williams, and a dockyard lighter were obliged to cut from Cawsand Bay and were then both driven on the rocks near Redding Point, where all hands must have perished but for the assistance of some Cawsand fishermen with ropes and lanthorns. They saved not only Lt Williams and his wife but also two children belonging to a mate, as well as the officers and crew, altogether thirty-two persons. They then rescued the crew of the lighter and took them all safe to Cawsand. The vessel had struck at 11pm during a raging gale, yet not a life was lost. (*Times*, 25 January 1804)

19 January, Vanderzee, privateer The *Vanderzee*, a Dutch privateer of 9 guns and eighty-seven men, was lost in the North Sea. Nineteen of her crew died. (*Times*, 23 January 1804)

19 January, unknown brig At Thurlestone near the Bolt Tail the remains of a large brig were washed ashore on the sands and all hands perished. Several chests of books, mostly good editions of the classics, were washed ashore as well as several boxes of gilt paper. There was no trace of where the vessel came from nor was her identity discovered. (*NC* vol 11, p83)

25 January, boat accident in Cawsand Bay Coming from Cawsand Bay the pinnace of the *Prince*, 98 guns, Captain Crindall, with a lieutenant and eight men, together with a shore boat, to save going around the eastern rocks of

St Nicholas Island, fatally attempted the passage of the Bridge. They were under a press of sail when a sudden squall gybed the sails of both boats and they overset. The men tried to swim ashore but with the great run of the tide and a heavy sea, except for one man, they all perished. (*SYM*, 30 January 1804)

27 January, Franklin, merchantman On 2 January 1804 the *Courageux*, 74 guns, Rear-Admiral Dacres, sailed during the morning with a large fleet for the West Indies, to be joined later by another forty ships from the Downs. (*NC* vol 11, p84)

The ships experienced gales all the way as far as Cape Ortegal, and on 27 January the *Courageux* ran down the *Franklin*, of London, when the ship immediately foundered and all on board the *Franklin* perished. (*Times*, 6 February 1804)

The weather was so bad that out of the 150 ships that had set sail on the 2nd, by the 28th only 73 were in company, and on the 29th only 43 were in sight. Many of the ships bore away for Cork, whilst others made Falmouth and Plymouth, at which latter place the *Courageux* arrived on 1 February with only 30 ships in company. (*NC* vol 11, p169)

? January, Sovereign, merchantman The *Cumberland*, 74 guns, Captain Searle, and the *Chichester*, 44 guns, Captain Spears, arrived at Portsmouth on 24 January from the West Indies after a rough passage of nine weeks. Of the forty-eight ships that had sailed under their convoy, they arrived with only one, the rest being dispersed by the gales. (*NC* vol 11, p172)

One of the dispersed ships was the *Sovereign*, from Trinidad for London. She was wrecked during a gale near Youghal, about twenty-six miles east of Cork and sad to relate, her captain and twenty-eight crew members perished with their ship. The exact date the *Sovereign* was lost appears to be unknown, but it was most probably Christmas Day. (*Times*, 1 February 1804)

12 February, Hussar, 38 guns A 38-gun ship, the *Hussar*, Captain Philip Wilkinson, was built at Woolwich dockyard and launched on 1 October 1799. The ship was cruising off the coast of France, near the Saints, when she struck on the Home Reef. The officers and crew were saved by boats of the fleet and Captain Wilkinson escaped in the ship's cutter. With his boat's crew he arrived at Plymouth on board the *Sirius*, a 36-gun frigate, on 28 February. (*NC* vol 11, p258)

13 February, Centurion's centenarian George Gregory died today at Kingston at the advanced age of 109. He was believed to be the last survivor of the crew of the *Centurion*, which ship bore Lord Anson in his circumnavigation of the globe. He never knew a day's illness since he went to sea in 1714. (*AR* 1804, Chr, p371)

19 February, Cerbere, gunbrig   La Cerbere, a French gunbrig mounting seven 18-pounder carronades and a crew of 87 men, was cut out from under the batteries of Port Louis, Mauritius, by acting Lt J Coughlan (of the *Viper* cutter), in a ten-oared cutter belonging to *L'Impetueux*, 78 guns, with only 20 men, 29 July 1800. (Norie, 1827)

At 2pm on 19 February the *Cerbere*, Lt Joseph Patey, got under weigh from Brixham quay; with the wind at north-east the vessel stood on to the southward, but when she approached Berry Head and endeavoured to get on the other tack, the *Cerbere* missed stays, took the ground and was wrecked. The crew were saved by spectators on the shore and the vessel itself was weighed up shortly afterwards. (*Times*, 22 February 1804; *SNL*, 1804)

Cerbere was one of those vessels without a keel and only drew six feet of water. (*SYM*, 27 February 1804)

22 February, mistaken identity   The *Ceres*, a 32-gun frigate, sailed from Cork and on the morning of the 22nd, before daylight, fell in with the *Sylph*, an 18-gun brig. The *Ceres* immediately commenced an action which lasted for two hours, yet no lives were lost. The *Ceres* arrived at Portsmouth on 23 February, the *Sylph* at Plymouth on 3 March. (*NC* vol 11, p258; *Times*, 25 February 1804)

? February, Curtis, merchantman   The American ship *Curtis*, from Virginia for Rotterdam, was lost at the entrance to the harbour of Brouwershaven on the Isle of Schouwen. There was one survivor. (*Times*, 25 February 1804)

25 March, Magnificent, 74 guns   Between 8 and 9am the 74-gun *Magnificent*, Captain William Henry Ricketts Jervis, lying off the Saints (the Black Rocks), in the act of getting under weigh, struck on an unknown shoal. The boats were hoisted out and the pumps kept in full action, but to no purpose. In less than an hour the water was up to her orlop deck. Nothing remained but to preserve the crew and signals were made accordingly. *L'Aigle* and the *Indefatigable* both anchored off the bows of the *Magnificent*, with the *Pickle* schooner and the *Fox* cutter on her starboard quarter. Everyone had left the vessel by 10.30am, at which time she foundered. The crew of 650 men and boys were all rescued by the boats of the inshore squadron, but nevertheless some were even yet unlucky. The officers of the marines, together with about 80 men and boys, in the hurry of trying to save themselves, got on board the large launch of the *Impetueux*. It was blowing hard with a heavy sea and the men were seen baling out water; but as there was a small island leeward of the launch hopes were entertained that they might reach it, though become prisoners. That in fact is what actually happened; 86 became prisoners of war for ten years. (*SNL*, 1808)

Magnificent was an old ship, built at Deptford in 1766, but about five years prior to being lost, the vessel had undergone a major repair at Plymouth, which took two years to complete.

It was said that Captain Jervis suffered a great loss in a complete service of plate, worth £1500, which went down with the wreck.

Great credit was due to Lts Nicholson of the *Fox* and Lapenotière of the *Pickle* who with their crews had saved the people of the *Magnificent*. (*NC* vol 11, pp293 et seq, and 339-340)

On 5 April the *Times* printed a letter from an officer of the *Magnificent*, dated at sea 26 March: 'At eight o'clock yesterday morning we rounded the Black Rocks under a press of sail with an ebb tide under our lee, we had completely weathered the Black Rocks, when twenty minutes later the ship struck an unknown shoal[35] and swung head to wind and could not be backed off. The leak gained two inches in every minute and was soon up to the orlop deck. While rescue work was proceeding, *L'Impetueux*, *Colossus* and *Montague* kept plying to windward.'

2 April, Apollo, 36 guns On Monday 26 March the *Apollo*, a 36-gun frigate, Captain John William Taylor Dixon, sailed from the Cove of Cork in company with the *Carysfort* frigate and sixty-nine sail of merchantmen under their convoy, the greater number for the West Indies but others for Lisbon and Madeira. By the next day they were out of sight of land, with a fair wind blowing a strong gale, and steering about WSW, which course they continued, with the same weather, until the 31st, when the wind came more to the westward, yet more moderate. On Sunday 1 April at noon they observed in position 40°51'N per account (dead reckoning) 12°29'W. At 8pm on Sunday the wind shifted to SW blowing fresh; their course SSE. At 10.30pm it became squally and at 11.30pm the main topsail split; they furled it and the main sail, so that the ship was now under her foresail, main and mizzen storm staysails; the wind blowing hard with a heavy sea.

About 3am on Monday the 2nd the *Apollo* struck the ground, to the astonishment of everyone on board, and by the above reckoning they then conjectured upon an unknown shoal. The vessel continued striking the ground, very heavy several times, by which her bottom was materially damaged and making much water; the chain pumps were rigged with the utmost dispatch and the men began to pump; but in about ten minutes she beat and drove over the shoal. On endeavouring to steer her the rudder was found to have been carried away and the ship then got before the wind. The pumps were kept going, yet from the quantity of water she shipped there was every probability of her soon foundering, as she was filling and sinking fast.

After running for five minutes the ship struck the ground with such tremendous shocks that the crew were fearful she would instantly go to pieces; she kept striking and driving further on the sands with the sea making complete breaches over her. The rigging was cut away and the masts fell over the larboard side, while the ship herself fell on her starboard side with the gunwale under water. The violence with which she struck and the weight of the guns, those on the quarterdeck tearing away the bulwark, soon made the ship a perfect wreck abaft: only four or five guns could be fired to give the convoy warning of the danger. To prevent being washed overboard by the surges or hurled by the dreadful concussions overboard, the crew held fast by the larboard bulwark of the quarterdeck and in the main channel, while Captain Dixon stood naked upon the cabin skylight grating, holding fast by the stump of the mizzen mast, and making use of every soothing expression to encourage the men in such a perilous situation. Most of the officers and men were entirely naked, not having the time to slip on even a pair of trousers. About 4.30am when daylight first appeared the land was discovered about two cables distant, a long sandy beach reaching to Cape Mondego, three leagues to the southward, and when the daylight actually came in, the crew could perceive between twenty and thirty sail of the convoy ashore, both to the northward and to the southward, and several of them perfect wrecks. [The *Times* for 28 April 1804 contains a list of 31 ships lost.]

Of the six boats that the *Apollo* carried not one was saved, all being stove and washed overboard with the booms. By Monday evening many of the crew had perished in trying to reach the shore and the morning of Tuesday brought no better prospects. On Tuesday afternoon Captain Dixon and three seamen ventured on the jibboom to reach the shore but they were washed off and perished. After this tragedy, the crew without food and water since Sunday, had to endure a second night on the wreck, living with the apprehension of the remaining part of the wreck going to pieces at any moment. Had the *Apollo* not been a well built ship the small part of her that was left could never have resisted the elements so well, as all the after part from the chesstrees was gone, the starboard bow under water, the forecastle nearly perpendicular, the weight of the guns hanging to the larboard bulwark on the inside, and the bower and spare anchors on the outside, which it was not prudent to cut away, as they afforded resting places to a considerable number of men, there being only the fore channels and cathead where it was possible to live in, and about which were stowed upwards of 150 men; it being impracticable to continue any longer in the head, or upon the bowsprit, by reason of the breakers washing completely over these places. This second night, the wind increasing with frequent showers of rain, and the seas breaking over them every two minutes, the men clinging on for dear life, their condition was pitiful in the extreme. Some unfortunate wretches drank salt water, others chewed leather whilst many more chewed lead, from which they conceived they found relief by reason of its drawing the saliva which they swallowed.

Among those who had managed to reach the shore were Lt Harvey and Mr Callam, master's mate, and about 3pm on Wednesday the 4th they, together with some of the men of the merchant ships and some Portuguese who were encouraged by Mr Whitney, the British Consul from Figuiera, managed to launch a merchant ship's boat against the surf and all the crew remaining on the wreck were brought safe on shore. Some men died soon after getting on shore from imprudently drinking too large a quantity of spirits, whilst many others had suffered injuries from floating wreckage.

About forty ships of the convoy were lost at the same time as the *Apollo*, but because they drew less water they were mostly driven close in shore and no person remained on them after the first night. Some merchant ships were however lost with all their crews, whilst almost every ship lost some men. Sixty-one of the *Apollo*'s crew lost their lives; every day bodies were floating ashore and the beach for ten miles was littered with wreckage.

The masters of the merchant ships had erected tents upon the beach and generously shared the provisions they had salvaged from their ships.

On Tuesday 22 May a court martial was held at Portsmouth to inquire into the loss of the *Apollo*, when the Court agreed it was due to an error in her reckoning. The officers and crew were acquitted. (*NC* vol 11, p392 et seq; *AR* 1804, App. Chr, p530 et seq; *NC* vol 12, p57)

2 April, Hindostan, storeship   The *Hindostan*, constructed as an East Indiaman, was purchased by the government in 1795 and mounted 54 guns. The *Hindostan* was then converted into a storeship. She sailed from the Downs on 4 January for Portsmouth where she took on board hospital supplies for the British in the Mediterranean including Malta. On 6 February the *Hindostan*, Captain John Le Gros, and the 28-gun *Thisbe*, Captain Shepherd, sailed from Portsmouth with a large fleet for the Mediterranean, and all went well until the evening of 29 March, when the *Hindostan* in company with the *Phoebe*, 36 guns, and a transport, was caught in a violent north-west gale when off Cape St Sebastian. (*NC* vol 11, p173)

It took all hands to secure the mortar raft which fetched away, part of it being secured above the quarterdeck, and effect repairs to the sails and rigging.

On 2 April, about 7am, smoke was observed from below and it was soon evident that the fore-hold was on fire. It was now supposed that during the gale of 29 and 30 March some of the eleven medicine chests in the hold had been broken by the working of the ship and that spontaneous combustion had been caused by some of the materials which the chests might have contained. Every effort was made to smother the fire, the lower deck hatches were laid on, ports lowered down and the scuttles were choked up, then at 9.15am the crew wore ship to the north-west and made all sail for the land.

As there was no cock to flood the magazine, the carpenters and shipwrights cut scuttles through two of the cabins to get at the powder and enable the crew to throw it overboard through the scuttle in the captain's after cabin.

At noon the land was seen bearing north-west by west; latitude 41°59′N distant three or four leagues. Because of the smoke not all the powder could be jettisoned, nor was it possible to save the ship's books. By 1.30pm the fire had gained to such an extent that it was no longer possible to approach the fore part of the vessel, but a few minutes after 4pm, the *Hindostan* ran aground in the Bay of Rosas, half a mile out from the shore and three miles north-north-east of the town of Ampurius La Escala.

At 9.30pm the *Hindostan* blew up some distance from the shore having drifted as she became lighter. On 9 April the wreck was discovered lying in nine and a half fathoms and the place marked by a buoy.

Saved from the *Hindostan*, mostly by Spanish boats, were 259 men, women and children, so that only three persons were missing: two supernumerary boys John Colquhoun and William Montgomery and an able seaman James Key. (*MC* vol 3, p1 et seq)

On Thursday 19 April 1804 a court martial was held on board the *Royal Sovereign* at sea to try Captain John Le Gros for the loss of his ship; the Court pronounced him to be honourably acquitted, and gave him great credit for his conduct in smothering the fire at a distance of twelve leagues from shore, which saved the lives of the people on board. (*NC* vol 12, p58)

19 April, Anne, country ship   At 11pm the sea-cunny of the watch called out that he saw the land and before anyone could distinguish it breakers were seen ahead; the helm was put down but before it could be effective the ship *Anne*, Captain Knight, struck on a reef five leagues to the northward of the southernmost Souheli Par island (in the Laccadives). The sails were furled and the stream anchor run out. The small bower was let go in four fathoms and a strain put upon it, yet the *Anne* did not get off.

The shingle ballast was heaved out and the salt water casks forward were staved. The sails were again hoisted and strain put upon the small bower but to no avail. The people below, instead of exerting themselves for the safety of the ship began to plunder whatever they could lay their hands upon, saying that as the land was near there was no danger. Finding the *Anne* could not be got off, the crew started pumping but by daylight the water had gained on the pumps to eight and a half feet. A heavy swell now set in and the ship began to strike very hard; several large pieces of sheathing and other parts of her bottom came up alongside; at 5am the rudder unshipped and carried away the greater part of her stern, stove in the counter on the starboard side; the water was now within a foot of the twin decks. At 5.30am, the ship being bilged, fell on her starboard beam ends and nothing further could be done to save the vessel.

Captain Knight now ordered the syrang (a native boatswain) and lascars to get the masts and sails in the boats as well as some rice and water for the people; this however they refused to do, saying that there was plenty on the island; instead, they began to plunder the ship. This resolved the captain to take as many of the other party as the boat could carry and to leave the pinnace for the rest; in the meantime the sea-cunnies had got the longboat's sails and masts in and a small quantity of water and biscuit, and at 7am they quitted the ship and made for the Malabar coast.

The people saved in the longboat were: Thomas Knight, captain; John Wheattall, pilot for the Red Sea; Edward Greaves, 2nd officer; John Lunardy, gunner; four seacunnies and six natives. (*NC* vol 13, p59 et seq)

29 April, press gang death This evening about 10pm, a young seaman named Stoddart was pursued by a press gang down Broad Chare in Newcastle. To escape he jumped into the Tyne and tried to swim to Gateshead on the opposite bank. One of his pursuers threatened to shoot him if he did not return. The boy drowned. (*AR* 1804, Chr, p382)

29 May, Phantom islands The following article, furnished by Captain Candler, who arrived at Boston on 8 August in the schooner *Betsey* from Madeira, is taken from the New York papers: 'On 29 May I was running for the Western Islands [Azores], on passage for Madeira, when I made something which appeared like a sail; but as I approached it nearer, discovered it to be a rock, the top of which was nearly one hundred feet out of the water, and from appearance deep water all round about it. It blowing very hard I was not able to sound or examine the rock any further than by running within a cable's length of it on the northern side. By observations, I found it lay in latitude 37°47'N and by calculation (dead reckoning) in longitude 34°29'W. The situation of this stupendous rock may be relied on as I was very particular in my course and distance till I made the land, which was the third day after; I then made Fayal. As I never saw a rock laid down in this situation, I think it is my duty to give this information to the public.' (*NC* vol 12, p453; *Times*, 16 October 1804)

It may be of interest to recall at this juncture an article on p667 of Findlay's *North Atlantic Memoir*, 'Reported Reefs.' It reads:

'Between Fayal and Flores, and off the latter, it is stated that some rocks exist. They were announced by M M Ferreira of the Brasilian brig *Constante*. The first showed above water, at low water, in position 37°56'20"N 33°04'08"W, and has been named *Constante Reef*. The second, *Ferreira's Reef*, is nearer the islands and in position 38°26'44"N 30°25'10"W; the sea broke on this. Nearly on the same reported position as the first reef, another announcement, under the name of the *Rhoon Rocks*, was issued in the *Nautical Magazine*, July 1844. This was an extensive group of rocks, some of them more than sixteen feet above water; position 38°32'N 33°16'W. Again, a rock called the *Atila Rock*, was announced in 1857 to lie in position 36°31′N 32°24′W, or 200 miles WSW of Fayal, and a singular warm mist and boiling sea was passed through on 13th November 1857 by the *Estremadura*, in 39°57′N 25°50′W. All these reports seem to indicate a series of dangers which are very perplexing to deal with, for after repeated searches they have not been again met with. But the notice of them here will attract attention and induce caution.' (Findlay, 1870 ed)

9 June, Captain Baker of the Pelican   The following is an extract of a letter received by the publishers of the *Naval Chronicle*, from Jamaica.

'His Majesty's Sloop *Pelican*, Port Royal 10th June 1804:

'Sir, with the greatest respect I take the liberty of informing you that yesterday evening at five o'clock, Morant bay NE four or five leagues, seeing a Spanish schooner bearing down before the wind, made sail to speak her. At half-past five Captain Baker hailed her and told them to put their helm a-port and heave to; they either not understanding or not wishing to obey the command put the helm the contrary way. Our heaving all back to keep clear of her, rendered our ship ungovernable; in which situation the schooner unfortunately fell on board our starboard bow, where she remained for several minutes, carried away our spritsail yard, her own bowsprit, and her larboard stove to the water's edge. Captain Baker jumped on board the schooner, followed by Lt Davis, Mr Butts, the gunner and several of the seamen. The vessels separated and with their assistance every person belonging to the schooner got safe on board the *Pelican*. On the vessels separating the schooner dropt (*sic*) astern; I immediately sent a boat on board to bring them from the schooner, she having apparently at that time sunk more than one half her topsides in the water. Captain Baker, anxious to see every person safe before he quitted the vessel, sent the whole of the people in our boat except himself, Lt Davis, and four men, whom he desired to immediately launch the schooner's boat over the side, which they did and all got into her. At the moment of shoving off, the schooner gave a heavy roll, filled, and in the act of sinking caught the boat Captain Baker was in under her main stay, and took her to the bottom; although every effort was made on my part, and every other person on board the *Pelican*, no signs of them could be seen afterwards. Thus ended the life of that most worthy and promising officer, whose loss will ever be regretted by, Sir, with the greatest respect, your devoted humble servant.' (W S Foley, 2nd Lt)

Obituary. Captain Baker was a son of Mr W Baker, late Member for the County of Herts; he was the second son of Mr Baker to be lost in the West Indies. (*NC* vol 12, p87)

11 July, Cornelia, merchantman   At 11pm in position 46° 40°W the ship *Cornelia* under full sail with a fair wind, going about seven knots, struck on what was supposed to be a vessel, bottom up, with such violence that it was sometime before she could recover herself. The pumps were immediately set to work while the remainder of the crew set about clearing the forepeak, by throwing the staves overboard, when to their astonishment they found the stem started and several hoodsends opened so as to admit of several thicknesses of blanket. By 4am the crew discovered the gripe carried away, hanging by some of the lower bolts only; and after five hours' very hard pumping found four feet of water in the hold. The situation was now hopeless and some hands were employed in preparing the boats. At 10am the crew, after all their exertions at the pumps, finding six feet of water in the hold began to be disheartened and low-spirited, yet when all seemed lost two ships were descried from the masthead, but being to windward it was 2pm before they came up with the *Cornelia*, at which time there was eight feet of water in her hold. They proved to be the *South Carolina*, Captain Steele, for New York; and the *Vigilant*, Captain Prentiss, bound for Portland. Captain Steele having a great number of passengers on board, the *Cornelia*'s crew concluded to go on board the *Vigilant*; and with both ships hove to, by 7pm Captain Bliss and his crew of thirteen had shifted most of their provisions and water on board the *Vigilant*, and the *South Carolina* left the scene while the *Vigilant* lay to until the next morning in hopes of saving something from the wreck. This hope however proved abortive; the wind blowing fresh from the south-west and the ship lying over very much, the boats were ordered to leave her and at 8.30pm the *Cornelia* capsized. (*NC* vol 12, pp474-475)

22 July, St Antonio, merchantman   The ship *St Antonio*, burthen about 500 tons and belonging to Macao, was returning from Saigon in Cochin China to her home port, when she was wrecked on one of the shoals of the Paracel group in latitude 16°45′N. The shoal consisted of a high sand bank, with a single high Palmyra tree in the centre of the bank, which was surrounded by a coral reef. The captain and crew constructed rafts and in three days made Manchow on the east side of Hainan.

The cause of the loss of the ship was a westerly gale which drove her to the eastward amongst the shoals; the ship not being able to carry sail. (*NC* vol 15, pp467-468)

28 July, Candidate   The *Times* stated: 'The ship *Candidate*, Captain Fell, was lost in the Indian seas on 28th July last. Captain and Mrs Fell; Mr Ball 2nd officer; Doctor Anderson of the 75th Reg; and ninety other persons all perished. Decre. Jones and Fox, mates; and ten lascars were saved in the jollyboat.'

2 August, Active, merchantman   The ship *Active*, Captain Irvine, was lost on her passage from London to Perth, her home port. She sailed on Sunday 29 July and on the Thursday following it was seen that she had sprung a leak and had five feet of water in her hold, which was hourly increasing. A Shields vessel hove in sight and the master, whose name was Hind, effected a rescue of the crew who were landed at Shields on 5 August. Shortly after the rescue a fog came on and the *Active* was seen no more. (*Times*, 14 August 1804)

8 August, Ranger, West Indiaman   One of the West Indies fleet, the *Ranger*, arrived home under convoy of the *Romney*, then in going up the Thames the vessel ran aground on the Nore sandbank and could not be got off. Although a part of the cargo was saved the *Ranger*, being completely wrecked, was lost. (*Times*, 15 August 1804)

21 August, Cornwall gale   A boat of Gorran (Cornwall) was forced ashore during a westerly gale when two of the crew managed to leap onto the rocks, but five who did not perished with the vessel. A spectator who leaned too far over the cliff lost not only his footing but his life also. (*AR* 1804, Chr, p412)

1 September, seditious music   A court martial was held on board the *Salvador del Mundo*, 112 guns, in Plymouth Sound (Hamoaze?) to try a seaman for distributing seditious songs, etc, on board the ship to which he belonged, while at sea; J Liddle acted as judge advocate. The sailor, whose name does not appear in the newspaper, was awarded 500 lashes on his bare back, around the fleet at different periods, to be followed by two years' solitary in Marshalsea prison. He was of a respectable family in Ireland and was bred to a liberal profession. (*SYM*, 10 September 1804)

3 September, De Ruyter, storeship   *De Ruyter*, 64 guns, was taken from the Dutch on 30 August 1799 by the joint Russian and British expedition to the Helder. The vessel was being used as a storeship, commanded by Lt Joseph Beckett, when she was lost during a hurricane at Antigua, yet only one man lost his life. (*SNL*, 1804)
　　De Ruyter was on passage from English Harbour, to become a prison ship at Falmouth, Jamaica; but getting to leeward anchored near the Fire Islands, she parted her anchor, grounded, and went to pieces. (*NC* vol 12, p493)

3 September, Drake, 16 guns   On the same day that the *De Ruyter* was lost, the *Drake*, a 16-gun sloop of war, Captain William Ferris, was driven by the hurricane on to a shoal off the island of Nevis where the vessel was wrecked but the crew saved. (*SNL*, 1804)
　　Note: In the hurricane of 3 September ships lost totalled at St Bartholomew's 56; Antigua 59; St Thomas's 44; Dominica 27; and St Kitts at least 100. (*NC* vol 12, p493)

25 September, Georgiana, cutter   The *Georgiana* was a hired armed cutter, commanded by Lt Joshua Kneeshaw, when she ran aground on one of the banks near Harfleur, when reconnoitring that harbour. (*SNL*, 1804)

Every effort to get her off proving ineffectual, owing to the ebb tide, and being on the enemy's coast, the crew set fire to the vessel to prevent her falling into the hands of the French, after which they were taken up by boats of the Havre squadron, notably the *Trusty*, 50 guns, and the *Locust* gunbrig. (*NC* vol 12, p506) The *Times* of 3 October 1804 calls the vessel *King George*, her original name.

At a court martial held on 17 November at Portsmouth, Lt Kneeshaw and his crew were praised for their highly meritorious conduct, and were all honourably acquitted for the loss of the *Georgiana*. (*NC* vol 12, p509)

Lt Kneeshaw was an old serving officer who had lost an arm in the service of his country; he received a pension of £200 per annum. (*NC* vol 35, p287)

27 September, magazine explosion This morning as W and T Ash (father and son), W Arnold and J Fowler, shipwrights, were working in the magazine of the *Bellerophon*, lying in dock at Portsmouth, a candle (the place being secluded from light) communicated itself to some loose powder, and they were killed by the explosion. (*AR* 1804, Chr, p418)

30 September, Sea Nymph The Portsmouth report of this date contained the following: 'The *Sea Nymph* transport is come into harbour to put the remainder of the French St Domingo prisoners, which she brought from Jamaica on board the prison ships. Of about three hundred who embarked at Jamaica one hundred and five died on their passage, and fifteen more since her arrival, of dysentery, scurvy, etc. Such was their inhumanity to each other that the unhappy creatures, the moment they were indisposed, were carried to the deck and left without the most trifling assistance, to die.' [The article contained nothing to indicate why the crew of the *Sea Nymph* allowed this to happen.] (*NC* vol 12, p506)

1 October, recruiting emigrants The Plymouth report for this day gave the following news item: 'Came in a large Hamburg ship with a cargo of poor German emigrants going to Baltimore as indentured servants; but a great many on coming ashore have entered into the Navy at this port, and many of them into the Plymouth Division of the Royal Marines, preferring our service to the chance of crossing the Atlantic; they are most of them from the interior of Germany and good looking strong men.' (*NC* vol 12, p429)

4 October, Two Brothers, schooner The schooner *Two Brothers* of Sunderland was wrecked turning out of the Bay of Wick when all on board, consisting of four hands and three passengers, perished. (*Times*, 16 October, 1804)

6 October, Princess of Wales, West Indiaman   A fleet of eighty-one merchantmen sailed from Martha Brae, on the north coast of Jamaica, on 27 July, under convoy of the *Elephant*, 74 guns, Captain Dundas, and the *Urania*, 40 guns, Hon Captain Herbert. After more than nine weeks at sea the fleet had nearly fetched Cork, when they were dispersed by a violent gale on 2 October.

One of the fleet was the *Princess of Wales*, bound to Greenock, and first news of the vessel arrived at Liverpool when the American schooner *Hope*, Captain Stanton, docked there after a voyage from New York of eighteen days. Captain Stanton's letter dated 11 October stated: 'On 9th inst., between 11 and 12 am, Beachy Pool Head bearing E by S distant about 6 leagues, fell in with part of a wreck and took therefrom from Hugh Rankine, seaman, who informed me he belonged to the *Princess of Wales*, Captain Colin Campbell, from Martha Brae bound to Greenock, with rum, sugar, cotton, etc, that was cast away on Saturday last, about five pm, in thick foggy weather, on the [Codling] shoals between Wicklow and Dublin; does not know if the captain is saved, as the last he saw of him was on the poop-deck attempting to get into the boat. The first and second mates, two passengers, and eleven of the crew, remained on the wreck without provisions or water; they secured a small keg of spirits which floated out, and was all they had to subsist upon. On Monday morning the poop-deck separated: Mr Hunter, Mr M'Millan, and Rankine, got thereon; the first two died, and were washed off about two hours before the latter saw the *Hope*, which took him up. Several vessels passed very near the wreck in the morning but took no notice.' (*NC* vol 12, p476)

The *Times* printed the following: 'Six of the unfortunate sailors of the *Princess of Wales* have arrived in an open boat at a place called Gwydir in the county of Caernarvon. There were twenty-six hands on board at the time of the wreck, of whom the six, plus two taken up by an American ship are all that are saved. The captain was one of the six. They spent three nights and four days in the boat in a violent storm. In the launch at the time the ship was lost were a goat and sheep which they slaughtered for the express purpose of quenching their thirst with blood.' (*Times*, 22 October 1804)

8 October, Speedy, schooner   The supposed loss of the *Speedy* schooner in government service on Lake Ontario is taken from the *Upper Canada Gazette* of 3 November 1804.

'The *Speedy*, Captain Paxton, left this port [unspecified] on Sunday evening, the 7th October, with a moderate breeze from the NW for Presque Isle, and was descried off that island on the Monday, before dark, when preparations were made for the reception of the passengers; but the wind coming around to the NE, it blew with such violence as rendered it impossible for her to enter the harbour and very shortly after she disappeared.

'A large fire was then kindled on shore as a guide to the vessel during the night; but she has not been seen or heard of; and it is with the most painful sensations we have to say, we fear she is entirely lost. It is concluded that the vessel either upset or foundered. Several articles, such as the compass box, hen-coop and mast, known to have belonged to the *Speedy*, have been picked up on the opposite side of the lake. The passengers on board the ill-fated vessel, as near as we can recollect, were Mr Justice Cochrane, Robert J D Gray Esq. Solicitor General and Member of the House of Assembly, Angus Macdonnell Esq. Advocate and also a Member of the House of Assembly; Mr Jacob Herchmen (*sic*) merchant, Mr John Slegman Surveyor, Mr George Cowan Indian interpreter, Mr John Fisk High Constable, all of this place. The gentlemen were proceeding to the district of Newcastle in order to hold the Circuit and for the trial of an Indian (also on board the *Speedy*) for the murder of John Sharp, late of the Queen's Rangers. Also on board were two children, passengers, of parents whose indigent circumstances necessitated them to walk. The crew of the *Speedy* totalled five seamen and Captain Paxton; they all left large families.' (*NC* vol 13, pp58-59)

10 October, Spanish brig 'On this Wednesday night a Spanish brig ran ashore on the west side of Dungeness and by Thursday afternoon had completely gone to pieces. The vessel was bound from Cadiz to Antwerp with a cargo of indigo, hides and sugar, of which cargo very little was saved. The captain's name was Marquinez, but the name of the vessel the writer was unable to learn. The mate lost his life, but the rest of the crew were saved.' (*Times*, 16 October 1804)

13 October, Flora, whaler The following distressing particulars of the loss of the brig *Flora* of Philadelphia, T Burrows master, on a whaling voyage to Cayenne, were extracted from the *New York Chronicle*:

'The *Flora* sailed from Philadelphia in good order and well conditioned on 28th September, with a crew consisting of Thomas Burrows master; Jacob Olderburg mate; William Davidson supercargo; John Nevan, Samuel Badcock, William Story, Joseph Wilder, seamen; Josiah Smith, James Cameron, boys; and Josiah Anderson, steward. Nothing particular happened till Friday 12th October when they were in position 28°50'N 54°W [roughly 700 miles E by S of Bermuda], the wind began to blow hard from the NE, the gale continuing to increase, accompanied by thunder, lightning, rain and a heavy sea, the pumps constantly going.

'Next day at two am, finding it impossible to lie-to any longer, determined to cut away the main mast and scud before the wind; but before that could be done, was struck by a whirlwind, which hove the brig on her beam ends. Joseph Wilder, being in the forecastle, was drowned; the main mast went by the board, the hatches burst off, the vessel filled with water, and the cargo was floating out at each hatchway: for their preservation they endeavoured to lash themselves to the main chains, but a heavy sea breaking over them, carried away William Davidson, William Story, and the two boys. The fore mast now went by the board, and day coming on, they beheld a most awful sight, mast and spars hanging to the wreck, and the cargo coming out of the hold washed over them. At this time the *Flora* shipped a sea, which stove in the stern, and the cargo broke out of the cabin; they remained on the main chains until nine am, when they took to the bowsprit, thinking that to be the safest part of the wreck. At this time William Story, and the boy Cameron, drifted on board on the caboose house, but about noon the boy died of exposure. The latter part of the day the gale moderated but a heavy sea continued. On the 15th William Story died and the mate (Jacob Olderberg) actually devoured a part of his flesh. On the 19th they discovered a large ship to leeward and made all the signals they were able, but in vain; for she passed without taking the least notice. On the 20th several kegs of butter came up from the forecastle, one of which they opened and ate, but being salt, increased their thirst. On the 21st a schooner passed to leeward, within a mile, they could see every man on the deck, yet they took no notice. The mate now became delirious, in which state he continued till the 23rd, when he died; his blood they drank and devoured part of his flesh; with the remainder they caught a large shark, which proved a great relief to them.

'At sunrise on the 24th they saw a brig standing towards them and at ten am she hove-to and hoisted out her boat to their assistance. She proved to be the snow *Thames* of London, Charles Burton master, from Madeira for New Providence; then in latitude 25°05′N by observation and fortunately eleven miles to the northward of their account. The four survivors were taken up and given every human attention, for which they publicly expressed their gratitude.' (*MC* vol 5, p171 et seq; *NC*, vol 13, pp122-123)

13 October, Firebrand, fire brig The *Firebrand*, Lt McLean, was a fire brig that sailed from the Downs on the afternoon of the 13th, to deliver ordnance stores. The crew saw a light which they thought was a ship at anchor, but was actually a light on the beach near Dover, and the *Firebrand* ran ashore. A boat went to her assistance but could not get the vessel off and the wind and sea increasing, together with the tide flowing, the ship lost her rudder, bilged and filled with water and by the next morning was a complete wreck. (*Times*, 16 October 1804)

16 October, Melcombe, merchantman The *Melcombe*, a coaster of Weymouth, laden with stone for Southampton, ran on the Shingles about 9pm. The master Miles Prouse, aged eighty-seven, his son and one other man were the whole of the crew. The son lost his left hand, but by great exertions dragged his father up the shrouds and held him there for several hours, when the old man was beat off by the violence of the sea and perished, as did the other man. The son was discovered at day light hanging on the mast and was saved by a boat belonging to a frigate, lying off Hurst Castle, and landed there. Soon after the *Melcombe* beat off and sank in deep water. (*Times*, 20 October 1804)

24 October, Conflict, gunbrig The *Conflict*, a 12-gun brig, Lt Charles Cutts Ormsby, grounded near Nieuport (not Newport, Isle of Wight, as in Clowes), when in chase of the enemy. The Dover report of 28 October gives the following: 'The *Griffin* hired cutter of this place arrived here today; she had been trying to get off the *Conflict* gunbrig, on shore near Nieuport; but the French had got such a number of guns on the shore, and flying artillery, and such a heavy fire of musketry, that they were obliged to give up and sheer off; the cutter is much shattered, several large shot having gone through her, a shell in her hold and one just over their heads, she had two men killed and eight wounded: the Lt of the cruiser lost a leg; two shrouds were shot away, and the mast wounded; they were within pistol shot of the enemy's guns.' (*NC* vol 12, p429)

30 October, Ceres, merchantman A ship ran on shore this morning at Yarmouth without any person on board and then went to pieces. On her boat was marked *Ceres* of Sunderland, Will. Scroub; her crew were probably washed overboard. (*Times*, 1 November 1804)

2 November, Adder gun-vessel The *Adder* gun-vessel got under sail from Folkestone at 5pm and at 10pm that evening went aground on Romney Flats, about three miles to the eastward of Dungeness Light, where it was thought to have been beyond recovery.

The vessel was however a very tight ship and was still whole on 16 November when Captain Bolton of *L'Aimable*, the commanding officer of Romney Bay, ordered the *Vesuvius*, Captain Lillicrap, and the *Biter* gun-brig, at anchor in Romney Roads, to attempt a salvage operation. They succeeded and the *Adder* came away under her own sails. (*NC* vol 12, p429) (*Times*, 20 November 1804)

3 November, Eurydice, brig The *Eurydice*, Captain Gebroelson of Gesse, a Swedish brig laden with brandy from Valencia for Emden, went ashore at Dungeness Point, and although the vessel was lost, yet a great part of the cargo was saved.

At the same time as the *Eurydice* was lost, a recaptured light collier went ashore about a mile to the eastward of Dungeness and three of the crew perished. (*Times*, 9 November 1804; *NC*, vol 12, p429)

19 November, Romney, 50 guns The *Romney*, Captain Hon John Colville, was a 50-gun Fourth Rate, built at Woolwich in 1762. The ship sailed from Yarmouth Roads on Sunday 18 November to take bullocks and vegetables to the fleet of Admiral Russel at the Texel; the vessel was also carrying the mail for the fleet.

During the first night at sea a gale came on and the *Romney* which had sailed from Yarmouth Roads with the 50-gun *Adamant*, parted company. *Adamant* veered away to three cables and rode out the storm; *Romney* was not so fortunate and at 9am on the Monday took the ground on the Zuider Haak sandbank from whence she could not be got off. During the afternoon all her masts went by the board. [The stranding was said to have been caused by mistaking three American ships, wrecked the previous night on the Haak sandbank, for part of the British Texel fleet at anchor. (*SYM*, 3 December 1804)]

Early on Tuesday morning, when no doubt remained that the ship must be totally lost, the crew constructed several rafts of the studding-sail, yards, booms, etc, and about seventy men took to them at the hazard of their lives, yet all were to be eventually rescued, one raft with a dozen men by the *Alert* cutter. These men were most fortunate for the wind blew fresh, the sea ran very high, and their raft was being driven out to sea when they were taken up at 10pm, in the dark, by the *Alert*; all the rest, except for twenty-eight, were rescued by the Dutch. The twenty-eight were lost when the *Romney* struck about two leagues from the land, then when the boats were hoisted out they overset almost at once.

Rear-Admiral Kilkkert of the Dutch navy ordered Captain Gerrit Verdooren to conduct the rescue operations from Kijkduin by using seven rowing and sailing shallops. The operation proved so successful that not only were all the people on the *Romney* rescued, but those on the rafts also. Captain Verdooren landed 91 British at the Helder; Captain S O Pool landed 110 and Captain Duynkerk saved 56 sailors from the rafts. Altogether 280 men were landed at the Helder, although at the time the sea was so rough that Captain Verdooren's shallop half filled with water.

The British were treated with great humanity by the Dutch who lodged the officers in two houses and the men in the church. On the 23rd Captain Colville and his officers were invited to dine on board the *Brutus* where upon arrival their sidearms were returned to them. Next day the British officers, Rear Admiral Kilkkert and several captains of the Dutch navy, dined with Captain Verdooren on board the *Doggersbank*.

Shortly afterwards Captain Colville and his officers were sent back to England on their parole by Admiral Kilkkert; and on 28 March 1805 the *Boadicea* frigate arrived at Yarmouth with 250 men, the remaining part of the *Romney*'s crew, who spoke in high terms of their hospitable treatment by the Dutch.

By the 22nd, only three days after grounding, the *Romney* had gone to pieces, and it may have been the case that the ship from which the crew were lucky to have escaped with their lives was not a very sound vessel, being 42 years old. (*Times*, 29 November and 10 December 1804; *AR* 1804, Chr, pp433-434; *NC* vol 12, p472)

20 November, Three Sisters, smack Early this morning the smack *Three Sisters* of Penzance, Jones master, from Gibraltar, was wrecked at the east end of Hayling Island near the entrance of Chichester harbour and Lt Bennett of the Royal Garrison Battalion, his lady, his daughter of about twenty-two, one of twelve and two infants were washed overboard and drowned. The vessel entirely went to pieces. The two daughters and one of the infants were washed up at Hayling and interred. Another passenger Mr Laurence Calahan and his wife, the master and three of the crew were saved but a boy of the vessel was drowned.

It appeared that the passengers hired this little vessel of 36 tons at Gibraltar for 180 guineas to take them to England to escape the dreadful ravages of the plague and left Gibraltar on 9 October. She put into Falmouth but was obliged to depart though in a leaky state; that she afterwards had a heavy gale of wind off the Lizard, and was driven back to Penzance where she lay a fortnight under quarantine and was then again ordered to Standgate Creek (on the Medway), and it was in pursuance of these orders that she was lost and so many of her passengers drowned. The Collector of the Customs at Chichester put several persons under quarantine in Chichester harbour who had had communication with the survivors; and the Collector of the Customs at Portsmouth on the 20th went to the wreck, secured all the baggage that had been preserved and put the survivors into a vessel of Mr Lindegren's for quarantine. (*Times*, 23 November 1804; *SYM*, 3 December 1804)

23 November, fever in the Amelia The following extract of a letter from an officer of the *Galatea* off Antigua to his mother, dated 23 November 1804, was published in the *NC* vol 13, p165:

'I embrace the opportunity of this *Packet*, to prevent any uneasiness on your part, or any of our family, as to my death, which I understand is enclosed in the report of those officers who died on board the *Amelia* while I belonged to her. We had the misfortune to lose in the course of ten days the captain, fourteen other officers, and about eighty men, of a malignant fever [possibly yellow fever]; few of them lived thirty-six hours after the first attack. I had a very severe attack but, thank God, am now recovering.'

24 November, Venerable, 74 guns This Saturday evening, about 5pm, in consequence of the wind suddenly springing up from the NE a signal was made for the fleet (at anchor in Torbay) to get under way, which all did except the *Goliath*, 74 guns, and *Impetueux*, 80 guns, both having grounded. In consequence of the darkness of the night there was great confusion in the fleet and unfortunately his Majesty's ship *Venerable*, 74 guns, Captain John Hunter, in fishing the anchor, the fish-hook gave way, when a master's mate and a seaman fell overboard and were drowned. A boat and crew were instantly lowered down to endeavour to save them, but in the hurry the after-tackle gave way and the boat filled, consequently the crew were floating, which threw the people into the utmost confusion. Another ship being almost aboard of them, owing to the darkness of the night, and the *Venerable* getting stern away, they endeavoured to stay her, but the ship refusing stays, and not having room to wear her, she went ashore on the north part of Torbay at Roundham Head, Paignton. This happened about 8pm, and on the signal of distress being made his Majesty's cutter *Frisk*, Lt Nicholson, immediately stood towards her and on hailing to know in what manner she could be useful, she was requested to anchor as near as possible to receive the men, the ship being at this time bilged. Lt Nicholson immediately complied, assisted by the boats of the *Goliath*, *Impetueux* and *Venerable*, as well as those of the *Frisk*. When Lt Nicholson saw the *Venerable*, which was not till sometime after, there being but little light, she appeared to be nearly upright with the water even with the upper deck ports.

The sea being very high and at times making a breach over her, no boat could lie alongside, so that the men were retrieved down from the stern with ropes. Being near the rocks, and having a rope from the shore to the vessel, several got on shore by that means; but a little midshipman in endeavouring to land in this manner quitted his hold and was drowned. Besides the mate and midshipman, the master and ten or twelve seamen were also lost. Four or five sailors were seen at times looking out of gunports, and notwithstanding her jollyboat hung to her quarter, yet the people on shore could not by their gestures and hallooing persuade them to lower the boat down and quit the ship. It was supposed they were ill, or had more probably got to the spirit-room, and were intoxicated. (*NC* vol 12, p497)

At midnight the *Frisk*'s cable parted and she was very near sharing the fate of the *Venerable*; but the precaution of having kept the mainsail up prevented it, for had it been to hoist after the cable had parted, with 400 men on board of a vessel barely 100 tons, when every part of her upon deck and below was full, her destruction would have been inevitable; but having only the foresail and jib to hoist, and the vessel being very manageable, as soon as she gathered a little way, they stayed her, and most fortunately she came round. (*MC*, 1805 ed, vol 3)

On the evening of the 27th two respectable farmers, out of curiosity, walked near the wreck, and were challenged by one of the guards twice, but by mistake the marine fired at them and wounded one, it was feared mortally, as the ball fractured the bone of the arm and lodged in his breast. Five surgeons were employed to amputate the arm and extract the ball. (*NC* vol 12, p497)

A further paragraph on p497 then stated: 'The total borne on her books the day she grounded was 555; the following day the number mustered was 547; but of the missing only four are known to have suffered.'

On the morning of 11 December 1804 a court martial was held on board the *Salvador del Mundo* in Hamoaze to try Captain Hunter, his officers and ship's company for the loss of the *Venerable*. They were all honourably acquitted, except for one man, who was found guilty of drunkenness, disobedience of orders and plundering the officers' baggage. He was adjudged to receive 200 lashes around the fleet, as an example. (*NC* vol 12, p505)

2 December, Cameron, merchantman　This morning were released from quarantine at Plymouth the mate and two American seamen belonging to the late American schooner *Cameron* of Boston, bound from Barcelona to Boston with a cargo of wines and brandies. After experiencing dreadful weather a few weeks since, off the Banks of Newfoundland, the *Cameron* started a plank and went down so suddenly that the master, a passenger, and the crew had just time to take out a little wine, get into the jollyboat, which was leaky, and commit themselves to the mercy of the seas. After beating about the ocean for twelve days and being almost exhausted, having had nothing to subsist on but a little wine, mixed with salt water, which brought on great debility, the master, a passenger and one seaman expired under the pressure of hunger and inanimation, the boat having been half full of water from the time they left the schooner, besides being nearly swamped from several heavy seas, which kept them constantly employed in bailing the water out. The remains of their companions were committed to the deep. On the 13th day, almost perished with cold, weak with hunger and fatigue, the surviving mate and two men gave themselves up for lost, and were perfectly resigned to their melancholy fate, as the boat was filling fast, and they had scarcely strength to bail out the water, when to their great joy they espied a sail and making a signal as well as they could with their handkerchiefs, the vessel bore down towards them. The boat was hoisted out immediately and they were with difficulty got on board the ship, which proved to be the *Rover* transport from Jamaica, with French prisoners. These men speak very highly of the great humanity of the master of the *Rover*. (*NC* vol 12, p504)

6 December, Morne Fortunee, 6 guns　The *Morne Fortunee* schooner, mounting six 12-pounder carronades, was a French privateer taken on the 16 September 1803 by the 74-gun *Blenheim*, Captain T Graves, off Port Royal, Martinique. (Norie, 1827 ed, p505)

On 22 September 1804 *Morne Fortunee*, commanded by Lt Alfred Dale, sailed from Plymouth at 7pm, with dispatches for Jamaica and the Leeward Islands, possibly notifying of an intended breach with Spain, as the ship was a fast sailer. (*NC* vol 12, p338)

On 6 December, within two days sailing of Jamaica, *Morne Fortunee* struck a reef off the west coast of Attwood Cay in the Crooked Island Passage where she was completely wrecked. The crew were saved by the boats of the *Pelican*, after remaining eight days on the reef without provisions, and enduring every hardship. (Norie, 1827 ed, p461)

We may note here that the *NC* vol 13, p242 states that the ship was lost on Crooked Island; while *NC* vol 35, p248 states the vessel was lost on Ackland's (Acklin's) Island. However, if the ship had been lost on either of these islands the crew would not have been without provisions, the islands being populated. But Attwood Cay is a barren place, with only a little samphire and wild grass; a most inhospitable environment.

12 December, Rover, packet Five persons were lost when the *Rover* packet was wrecked on the rocks of Yealm Point, east of the Slimer Rocks in Wembury Bay. Two men and the mate jumped from the bows but were drowned, as was the mate's wife. Captain Rutledge, with the mate's child in his arms, was washed ashore senseless and the child perished. (*NC* vol 13, p79)

20 December, Blonde, 32 guns At Brixham at daylight, the *Blonde*, a 32-gun frigate, Captain Faulknor, was discovered in great distress, riding to her sheet anchor, her colours hoisted union downwards; yet no boat could venture off to assist her. About 9am the crew cut away the main and mizzen masts and ran the ship into Goodrington Sands within a mile of Roundham Point, where the *Venerable* was lost a month earlier. Some scores of Brixham men hastened to assist and took two large lively smuggling boats, which would live in almost any sea, and dragged them around from Brixham, four miles. Then seven daring Brixham sailors, much to their praise, ventured off in the midst of the breakers, took out the captain's lady with all the rest of the women and children first; altogether they saved 114 men and 18 women. The greatest praise was due to the seven who had a medal struck for their courage.

Captain Faulknor had run his ship in on the sands and laid her athwart.

On 18 January 1805 the *Blonde* was got off with very little damage, having knocked away her gripe and part of her keel aft. (*NC* vol 13, pp77 and 328)

20 December, Tartarus, bomb vessel The *Tartarus*, Captain Thomas Withers, was a bomb vessel which mounted 12 guns, a converted merchantman purchased in 1797. At 6pm whilst at anchor in Margate Roads during a heavy squall the vessel parted her cable and drove upon a sandbank from which no vessel had ever been known to be saved.

The ship's signals of distress were plainly heard in Margate, but it being low tide with a strong ENE gale blowing, no boats could get off till midnight, when two luggers each with twelve men approached the *Tartarus* about 1am, but on account of the heavy surf could not remain and anchored at some little distance in two fathoms. The *Tartarus* lowered one of her boats, into which were put the sick, as well as the women and children, to the number of twenty; but the boat, in endeavouring to reach one of the luggers, the *Lord Nelson*, grounded on the sand. The other lugger, the *Queen*, at the imminent hazard of the lives of her own people immediately slipped her cable and ran alongside the boat, in six feet of water and had the good fortune to save the whole. Another boat, this time loaded with prisoners, was sent off from the *Tartarus* and reached the *Lord Nelson* in safety. A rope was carried with her to draw her back to the ship; but she was dashed to pieces in the attempt. Another (the remaining boat) was then lowered from the ship, with two men in it, and immediately sunk; one of the men was drowned, and the other, with great difficulty, was saved.

It was now 3am and the luggers returned to Margate to procure further assistance, and land those they had saved. It was not until 2pm that the luggers returned with two other boats and the weather having moderated, they took out the remainder of the crew, to the number of seventy, who were obliged to be slung by ropes from the yardarms into the boats.

On the morning of the 22nd there was nothing to be seen but her masts. (*NC* vol 13, pp57 and 58)

20 December, Severn, 44 guns The *Severn*, 44 guns, armed *en flute*, Captain Philip d'Auvergne, Prince de Bouillon, was at anchor in Grouville Bay, Jersey, on 19 December when a violent gale set in from the NE and blew directly on shore; a lee shore, void of shelter and full of dangerous rocks.

During the night, at 1am on the 20th, the crew cut away her main mast to ease the ship and a few hours later cut away the mizzen also. About noon the vessel was observed to be driving on shore, having parted her anchors. The tide was out, which left a strand of a mile from the redoubts. About this time two boats from the *Alcmene*, which was riding the storm out to windward, reached the *Severn* and with their aid ropes were got ashore and by 5pm upwards of 300 people were landed in safety.

The commander on board the *Severn* was Lt d'Auvergne (brother of the Prince), who had tried all possible means to save the ship but to no avail; she had struck and was held fast until 11pm when the spring tide lifted the vessel and carried her close inshore.

The next day, the 21st, parties from the 18th and 69th Regiments were employed in getting her stores out; she was a complete wreck, but was quite dry when the tide was out. (*NC* vol 13, pp56-57)

21 December, Nabby, merchantman On 19 December the ship *Nabby*, Philip Crandell master, sailed from Liverpool for Boston with a cargo of salt, crates, dry goods, etc, with the wind at ESE. On the 21st the ship sprung a leak which continued to gain upon them, notwithstanding both their pumps were kept constantly going. Finding the leak still increasing they hauled their wind in order to gain a port. Standing along by the wind, they made Mizen Head, on the western coast of Ireland. Not being able to gain to windward of it, and then having six feet of water in the hold, and the men fatigued with three days and nights' incessant pumping, they tried for Berehaven in Bantry Bay. By this time the ship became waterlogged, and the wind still ahead, they determined upon gaining the shore, and saving if possible, part of the cargo. Accordingly on the morning of the 25th they ran into a small cove on the south side of the Bay and let go their anchors in eight fathoms, about twenty-five yards from the shore. They then loaded their boat with provisions and part of their effects, and sent them on shore, where they were left in the care of the mate and one man.

While they were loading a second boat the country people began to collect on shore, to the amount of 200 men and women. Immediately on the arrival of the boat again on shore, which contained all the effects of the officers and crew, together with all the ship's papers, the inhabitants attacked the defenceless crew, and inhumanly robbed them of all their clothes, papers and money, and from some of the crew, their hats from their heads and shoes from their feet. Not content with this, they proceeded on board the ship, where all they could lay their hands on fell a prey to their rapacity, threatening those who opposed them with instant death. About dark the robbers left the ship and carried their spoils into the mountains, when the crew left her also and proceeded to a miserable hut where they spent the night.

Early in the morning of the 26th Richard Donovan, a gentleman living eight miles from where the ship was lost, came to their assistance and conducted the whole ship's company to his house; to his benevolence the crew owed their lives. Early on the morning of the 28th Captain Scott with a party of forty soldiers went from Bantry in order to search for the stolen property, when upon the approach of the soldiers the country people left their huts and fled into the mountains. (*NC* vol 13, p120 et seq)

'The *Nabby* was an American ship belonging to Portland, Mass., the crew managed to save themselves in their boats, but to the indelible disgrace of Ireland, were plundered on their landing by the savages of the place, five of whom died of their avarice, for they were on board when she went down.' (*Times*, 11 January 1805)

Maine was a part of Massachusetts from 1651 to 1820 after which it became a separate state.

1805

7 January, Sheerness, 44 guns   The *Sheerness*, a 44-gun ship, Captain Lord George Stuart, was at anchor at Trincomalee, Ceylon, when at 5.30pm a gale sprang up, which by 7pm had increased to storm force, blowing from the NW and attended by heavy rain. In another half hour the wind veered to NE at which time the *Sheerness* parted all her cables and drove on shore on the SW end of York island.

The situation then became most perilous for the crew; the ship laboured so violently, that until the main mast went by the board, and the mizzen mast was cut away, it was impossible to stand on the deck. However, the top weight (occasioned by the masts, and the great hold the wind had upon them) being removed, the ship became more steady, but heeled very much on the larboard side. In a very short space of time the water in the holds rose above the orlop deck and pumping proved ineffectual, as the water gained until it became equal with the surface of the sea.

Guns were fired throughout the night, as signals of distress, but no assistance could possibly be obtained from the shore; for the captain who was there with his 1st Lt Mr Bean and the Master Attendant, used every possible means to get aboard, but their boat was swamped when near the ship, and a heavy squall drove them again on shore. As an instance of the impossibility of any boat gaining the ship, the launch of the *Sheerness* was sent to their assistance, when she shared a similar fate with the loss of the crew, who were drowned. (*NC* vol 14, p255)

8 January, Alexander, brig The government brig *Alexander* left Tutucoryn (on the Carnatic coast of India) on Sunday 6 January, bound for Colombo, with about 700 bags of rice for the government. The following day they made the island at about 9am between Chilaw and Negumbo; and Captain Stephany, finding he could not get into Columbo Roads before night, judged it prudent to anchor at 6pm, in ten fathoms, off Chilaw (about 40 miles north of Colombo), where he intended to remain till daylight next day.

At 3am on the 8th, Captain Stephany perceiving that the anchors did not hold, cut his cables and stood to sea; at 5am several succeeding seas breaking over the vessel, filled it with water; and notwithstanding every exertion to pump the water out, she foundered at 10am, distance about four miles from the shore.

S Fretes, the sole survivor, was saved on a grating of the vessel, and cast on shore in the mouth of the Negumbo river; he stated having seen several attempting to save their lives, on casks and hencoops, but did not think that one of them succeeded in the attempt, having seen Captain Stephany go down with a hencoop.

Lt Anselm of the Wurttemberg Regiment, and inhabitant of Columbo, who was the only passenger on board the *Alexander*, shared the same fate as the rest of the ship's company; his body was cast up near Colpetty. (*Ceylon Gazette*, 16 January 1805)

12 January, Doris, 36 guns   As the *Doris*, a 36-gun frigate, Captain Patrick Campbell, was proceeding to Quiberon Bay, through the Benequet Passage, she struck upon a sunken rock called the Diamond Rock, and in consequence made so much water that Captain Campbell was obliged to throw all her guns, and every weighty article, overboard. During the 13th it blew a tremendous gale at SW, but the weather moderating on the following day they gained upon the leak,which was under the fore-foot, and in the evening she sailed for England with a fine breeze, accompanied by the *Felix*. During the night however it blew hard from the NW with a heavy sea, which tore off the soldering which had been put under her bottom to stop the leak, and the water gushed in with such violence, that every exertion to keep it out proved ineffectual; she became water-logged, would not answer her helm, and had drifted considerably to leeward during the night. In this predicament Captain Campbell, finding it impossible to keep her above water, determined to abandon the ship, and accordingly on this day, the 15th, she was brought to an anchor, 'between a reef of rocks' off Crozie (near the mouth of the Loire) called Le Four, and a rock called the Turk; there was an excessive heavy swell running, and the breakers could be seen directly astern, about three miles distant. Happily the wind abated or all on board must have perished. At this time a Danish brig was drifted in by the tide, and part of the crew put on board her, with orders to proceed for England; the rest, including the captain and most of the officers, in all 117, got on board the *Felix*, an armed sloop of 14 guns, commanded by Lt Bourke. The *Doris* was set on fire, and in a short while the after magazine blew up (the fore magazine had been drowned) and she immediately went down.

On the 16th the *Felix* fell in with the squadron under the orders of Sir T Graves, and delivered some of the *Doris*'s people on board the *Tonnant*, which ship left that station for England on the 21st. [It may be noted that *SNL* and Clowes each give the date the *Doris* was lost as the 21st, which is patently wrong.] (*NC* vol 13, pp123-124)

16 January, Tonnant's boat   Some few days after the *Doris* struck there was a tragic sequel. Captain William Henry Jervis of the 80-gun *Tonnant*, together with Captain Campbell of the *Doris*, were going in a four-oared gig from the *Tonnant* to visit Sir Charles Cotton, then senior Admiral in the *San Joseph*, when a heavy sea broke over the bow of the boat and upset her, yet even so, only one man was lost. Captain Campbell sustained himself on an oar, while Captain Jervis was supported by the coxswain until the latter's strength was exhausted and he had to save himself.

Captain Jervis was the heir and nephew of Earl St Vincent; one of the verdurers of the New Forest and Treasurer of Greenwich Hospital. He left a wife and two daughters. (*NC* vol 13, pp165-166)

16 January, coble at Blyth   About 2pm on this Wednesday at Blyth, a ship wanting a pilot to bring her into the harbour, made the accustomed signal; upon which four men put off to her in a coble. As they approached the ship, which was going very swiftly before the wind, and the sea very high, they were dashed with violence against her and the coble was overset; notwithstanding every possible assistance was given, they all perished. They all left widows and amongst them twenty-one small children to lament their loss. (*NC* vol 13, p165)

17 January, Constance, cutter His Majesty's hired cutter *Constance*, Lt Duncan Menzies commander, was lost in Roundstone Bay, County Galway, during a violent gale, which after carrying away almost everything on her deck, dashed her on a rock where she was totally lost. Two of her crew died but the rest were saved by the neighbourhood peasants. (*AR* 1805, Chr, p356)

24 January, Fame, privateer Four reports related to the loss of the *Fame* privateer. 'Sailed [from Plymouth, 21 January] for Guernsey to take in her sea stock and proceed on a lucrative foreign station, that crack privateer, the *Fame*, 32 guns, Captain Hosier, and 150 men'. (*NC* vol 13, pp240-241)

The *SYM* dated 28 January stated: 'Sailed for Guernsey, the *Fame*, 32 guns, and from thence after completing her stores, on a voyage to the South Seas, to enrich her owner and jolly crew of fine fellows with Spanish dollars.'

The Torbay report of 29 January stated: 'By a sloop which arrived here last night from Guernsey, I have learnt the sad effects of the tremendous gale of last Thursday, in which a number of vessels suffered, but most particularly that beautiful ship privateer, *Fame* (late *La Blonde*),[36] of 38 guns and 240 men, Captain Hosier, belonging to H C Blewett Esq. of Plymouth, and which sailed from thence last Monday. She parted one cable in the gale and dragged the other two anchors, till she went ashore against the castle, and is become a mere wreck. She had previously cut her mizzen mast away to ease the ship, but it availed nothing. She had her commission [a Letter of Marque] and was to have sailed the next day.' (*NC* vol 13, p328)

The final report is dated Plymouth 31 January; it follows: 'Letters received from Guernsey state the *Fame* was found on shore on some rocks in Guernsey Roads and totally wrecked in a violent gale of wind at ENE. The entire crew were saved but it is feared they will not save many of her stores. She went to Guernsey to take in additional stores and more hands, and was to have sailed for the South Seas therefrom, as an annoyance to the French in that quarter. Her shipwreck may be considered as a national loss and a serious misfortune to her public-spirited owners, who had fitted her out at a great expense in the most complete style as a private ship of war.' (*NC* vol 13, p242)

29 January, Raven, 18 guns The *Raven* brig, mounting 18 guns, Lt William

Layman, acting commander, by an error in their account, thought themselves to be 25 miles from Cadiz, yet before midnight on the 28th they found themselves to be in Cadiz Bay among the rocks and shoals and at dawn on the 29th their situation appeared most distressing with a tremendous sea and shoals on either hand. At 10am the gale increased and they anchored and remained so until 8pm when the *Raven* parted her cables and took the ground, yet only two men were lost, a seaman and a marine. The next morning at daylight the crew were made prisoners by the Spanish soldiers, but were treated extremely well; the officers being at liberty to move as they pleased within a twenty-mile radius of Cadiz, whilst they awaited to be exchanged on parole. (*NC* vol 13, p386)

5 February, Earl of Abergavenny, East Indiaman On Friday 1 February the *Earl of Abergavenny*, an East Indiaman, Captain Wordsworth, sailed from Portsmouth in company with the *Royal George, Henry Addington, Wexford* and *Bombay Castle*, under convoy of the *Weymouth* frigate and all destined for the East Indies. However, immediately after sailing, the ships ran into foul weather and after floundering about for four days, on the morning of the 5th, at 10am, the Commodore made a signal to bear up for Portland Roads, they then being ten leagues to the westward of Portland.

The story is now taken up by Mr John Clark, 5th mate of the *Earl of Abergavenny*: 'We bore up accordingly; at this time having main topgallant mast struck, fore and mizzen ditto on deck, jibboom in, and the wind about west-south-west. At three p.m. got a pilot on board, being about two leagues to the westward of Portland: ranged and bitted both cables. At about half-past three called all hands and got out the jibboom at four o'clock. While crossing the east end of the Shambles [about 3 miles east of Portland], the wind suddenly died away, and a strong tide setting the ship to the westward, drifted her into the breakers; and a sea striking her on the larboard quarter, broached her to with her head to the northward, when she instantly struck, it being about five o'clock; let out all reefs, and hoisted the topsails up, in hopes to shoot the ship across the Shambles. The wind shifting to the northward, the surf driving us off, and the tide setting us on alternately, sometimes having four and a half, at others nine fathoms. Continued in this situation till seven o'clock; at about half-past seven she got off. During the time she was on the Shambles, had from three to four feet water, pumps constantly going. Finding she gained on the pumps, it was determined to run her to the nearest shore. At eight o'clock the wind shifted to the eastward. The leak continuing to gain upon us, having ten or eleven feet water, found it expedient to bail at the fore scuttle and hatchway. The helm being hard a starboard, the ship would not bear up, she being waterlogged; but still had a hope we could keep her up till we got her on Weymouth sands; cut the lashing of the boats, could not get the longboat out without laying the main topsail aback, by which our progress would have been so retarded, that little hope would have been left us of running her aground; and there being several sloops in sight, one having sent a skiff on board, and took away two ladies and four or five passengers, but finding much difficulty in getting back to their sloop, did not return, although having promised to do so. About this time the third officer Mr Joseph Wordsworth and the purser Mr Stewart were sent ashore in the cutter with the ship's papers and dispatches and to obtain assistance. The crew continued pumping and bailing until eleven o'clock when she went down. The last heave of the lead was in eleven fathoms. The tops of all the masts were above water, when at two o'clock in the morning boats came and rescued about seventy people from the wreck.'

The ship's cargo, estimated to be worth about £200,000, was made up of porcelain, together with £70,000 in specie; and on board were upwards of 400 persons, as follows: seamen, etc., 160; troops (King's and East India Company's), 159; passengers at the captain's table, 40; passengers at the third mate's table, 14; Chinese, 32. The number of persons saved totalled between 90 and 100, so that those who perished with the ship exceeded 300. (*NC* vol 13, p124 et seq, and p386 et seq; *AR* 1805, Chr, p360 et seq; *Times*, 8 February 1805)

'Weymouth, 18th May 1806. Last night was landed at the Custom House, the last chest of dollars from the wreck of the *Abergavenny*, which completed the sixty-two chests recovered by Mr Braithwaite, who with much ingenuity has succeeded. The total value was £70,000.

'He is now going to proceed immediately on the cargo.' (*AR* 1806, Chr, p409)

'Weymouth 11th October 1807. Almost the whole of the valuable property of the *Abergavenny* has been recovered from the wreck, near the Race of Portland.

'Thirty pipes of wine have also been weighed from her during the course of the late summer.' (*AR* 1807, Chr, p498)

'*Abergavenny* has since been blown up, under water, so as to prevent the wreck from forming a dangerous shoal.' (*SNL*, September 1812)

2 March, Fly, 18 guns [Although *SNL* of 1805, Norie of 1827, and Clowes of 1905 all give May as the month of loss of the *Fly*, we may observe that the vessel was not lost during May; that was the month news of the loss of the vessel arrived in England. The ship was wrecked on 2 March and the court martial took place on 17 April 1805.] The 18-gun sloop of war *Fly*, Cdr Pownoll Bastard Pellew, was lost on the Carysfort Reef in the Gulf of Florida; her crew were saved. (*SNL*, 1805)

19 March, Candidate, merchantman The *Times* stated: 'The ship *Candidate*, Captain Fell, was lost in the Indian seas on 28 July last. Captain and Mrs Fell, Mr Ball 2nd officer, Doctor Anderson of the 75th Reg, and ninety other persons all perished. Decre, Jones and Fox, mates; and ten lascars were saved in the jollyboat.

21 March, Antelope's boat   This afternoon, as the boat belonging to the 50-gun *Antelope* was coming to the jetty at Yarmouth, she overset, and out of eleven men who were in her, five were drowned within 100 yards of the shore. The mother of one of the unfortunate sufferers had come sixty miles to see him, and was on the jetty when he was drowned. (*AR* 1805, Chr, pp374-375)

12 April, Terror's boat   Lt J Eades Baker, who had lately been appointed to the 32-gun *Winchelsea*, at the Nore, endeavouring to join his ship, from New Southend, Essex, this morning at about 2am, was unfortunately upset in a jollyboat belonging to the 10-gun *Terror* (repeating signal ship) and himself, Mr Day the gunner, four seamen belonging to the *Terror*, and a person supposed to be Lt Baker's servant were all drowned. The lieutenant was highly respected and had lost a leg in the service of his country. (*NC* vol 13, p335; *AR* 1805, Chr, p376)

? June, Nymph, merchantman   About the first week of June the brigantine *Nymph* of Montrose, Captain W Barclay, was lost near Domesnes Point at the entrance to the Gulf of Riga. She was caught between two pieces of ice, which in ten minutes laid her on her broadside and five minutes later she went down with all hands. Two other Montrose vessels in company witnessed the accident, but from the close proximity of the land and the gale then blowing, no assistance was possible. Five of the crew were the captain's nephews, and one other his intended son-in-law. (*Times*, 24 June 1805)

? June, loss of three naval brigs   This was a bad month for British seamen in the English Channel; three naval vessels vanished without trace and another 350 sailors had perished.

The *Hawke*, an 18-gun brig, Cdr James Tippet, was originally a privateer purchased by the Navy in 1803. The vessel was last sighted during May, but never seen again.

The *Sea-Gull*, Cdr Henry Burke, was also an 18-gun brig which went down in the Channel; date and position unknown.

The *Mary*, Lt T S Pacy, was a hired 16-gun brig, which sailed from Plymouth to join the Fleet off Ushant and vanished. (*SNL*, 1805)

19 June, Lochgilphead, packet   The *Lochgilphead* packet sailed from Ardrisshaig Point for Greenock with the master, a boatman and twenty-four passengers. The vessel refused stays off Ardlamont Point, fell into confusion and was overset. Some time later, a boat put out from Ettrick Bay and picked up ten survivors who had been in the water for two hours, probably clinging to the upturned vessel. (Letter of 24 June, quoted in *Caledonian Mercury*, Monday 1 July 1805)

25 June, soldiers lost overboard During a storm at Yarmouth Roads, three soldiers were leaning over the side of a ship, when a heavy sea washed them overboard. A boat was launched to their assistance, but a sudden squall upset it and seven sailors shared the fate of the soldiers. (*AR* 1805, Chr, p401)

19 July, Blanche, 36 guns The *Blanche* was a 36-gun frigate, launched in 1801, and on this day was captained by Zachary Mudge.

The *Blanche* was in position 20°N 66°W (about 100 miles to the northward of Puerto Rico) when she fought an action with a French squadron consisting of two frigates and two sloops and was taken after a most gallant resistance, but being unseaworthy, the French took out the crew and burnt the ship.

One of the French squadron was the *Le Faune,* and she was carrying 22 British prisoners when she was herself taken on 15 August by the 74-gun *Goliath* and the 20-gun *Camilla.* (*SNL*, 1805)

On 14 October 1805 a court martial was held on board the *Salvador del Mundo,* in Hamoaze at Plymouth, to try Captain Mudge, his officers and crew for the loss of the *Blanche.* It was stated at the court martial by Mr Hughes, the 1st Lt, that *Le Topaze* and *La Torche* came into action together, and *Le Departement des Landes* eight minutes later. Captain Zachary Mudge, his officers and crew were all honourably acquitted. (*NC* vol 14, p341)

On 15 October 1805 the *Times* printed an article copied from an American newspaper, which is given here verbatim; it should be noted however that in two instances the American captain is named Lark and in another instance Lake. It follows: 'Captain Lark, of the schooner *Sally*, on 27th July in position 22°11′N 63°W at four p.m. fell in with the main mast of a large ship which he supposed had been blown up, as part of the rigging and sails were much burnt; picked up part of an English pendant and a number of blocks stamped with an arrow; saw another mast about a mile distant with all the yards and other spars attached to it, and one of the bower anchors, with a cable to it, hanging under the maintop. There being a high swell, and the weight of the anchor keeping the mast nearly upright, Captain Lark could only save a few spars and blocks. On one of the topgallant yards *Blenheim G R* is cut with a penknife.

'HM ship *Blenheim* of 74 guns was commanded by Captain Bland; she does not appear to be annexed to the fleet under Lord Nelson. From the circumstance of her having her colours flying (which Captain Lake could plainly discern underwater), it is conjectured that the ship must have been in action when the accident occurred.'

On 16 October the *Times* printed: 'The account given in the American papers of the probable loss of the *Blenheim* is not credited at the Admiralty. The wreck seen by the American ship was, we have no doubt, that of the *Blanche*, which was burnt by the French, after having been so gallantly defended by Captain Mudge.'

9 August, Montezuma, merchantman The American ship *Montezuma*, Captain Ives, from the coast of Africa for Charleston, South Carolina, was taken by a French privateer, *Regulateur*, Captain Savourme, when sailing in position 32°12′N 76°20′W. The *Regulateur*, mounting one brass 24-pounder and four 6-pounders, was crewed by 100 men; she had been out three days from St Jago [de Cuba], and had been cruising off Charleston Bar when she took the *Montezuma*, which was carrying 348 prime slaves. (*NC* vol 14, p337)

9 August, Pigmy, schooner The *Pigmy*, a 12-gun schooner, commanded by Lt William Smith, was wrecked in St Aubin's Bay Jersey, the crew being saved. On 19 August 1805 a court martial was held at Portsmouth to try Lt Smith, his officers and crew for the loss of the vessel. Excepting the pilot, who was reprimanded, Lt Smith, his officers and the ship's company were all honourably acquitted. (*NC* vol 14, p173)

? August, Althorpe, cutter The *Althorpe* was a hired cutter mounting 16 guns and commanded by Lt William Scott when she foundered in the Channel. Because there were no survivors, the date the ship was lost and why she went down is unknown. (*SNL*, 1805)

11 September, Experiment, merchantman 'The ship *Experiment*, Captain Wethers, from Botany Bay and China, sailed from China about six weeks before the fleet which has just arrived, in company with the *Ocean*, and parted from her off the Cape of Good Hope, since whence she has not been heard of.' (Copied verbatim from the *Times* of 11 September 1805)

22 September, Brodren Erento samt Lorenz, brig At 9am the Danish brig *Brodren Erento samt Lorentz*, Severt Hansen With master, burthen 240 tons, last from London for Plymouth and Leghorn, went ashore on a sandbank two leagues from Margate. The vessel struck during a heavy gale, went on her starboard side, her main mast washed overboard, her keel gave way and she was seen reeling on her gunnel, yet the crew were saved. The brig was in ballast. The sails, anchors and cables were mostly saved as well as other valuables and on the 30th the crew were employed in landing her stores and conveying them in waggons to the warehouses. (*Times*, 2 October 1805)

28 September, excessive punishment 'The body of John Archer, late a seaman on board HMS *Theseus*, was on Saturday last taken up at Chatham after it had been buried; a consequence of suspicion having arisen that he died from excess of punishment. The jury having since met, have been adjourned several times, and have examined a number of witnesses whose evidence appears contradictory. A serjeant of marines has gone so far as to state that the man was very seriously and repeatedly punished and that at the time punishment was inflicted upon him the man could not walk, but was brought up from below and laid across a gun, not being able to stand upright, and he was flogged in that position. The surgeon of the ship, on the contrary, states that the man had not been severely treated and that when he was called to see him his case appeared so lenient that his attendance was not required. The jury met again on Thursday evening at six o'clock to examine the remaining witnesses, and about nine o'clock not being able to form an immediate opinion they withdrew into a separate apartment and were locked in nearly three hours when they requested the presence of the coroner and delivered the solemn verdict of *Wilful Murder* against Captain Temple.' (*Times*, Saturday 5 October 1805)

2 October, Barracouta, schooner The *Barracouta* was a 4-gun schooner, launched in 1804 and commanded by Lt Joel Orchard, when she ran aground on Jordan Cay off the coast of Cuba. The crew were saved and held in Cuba as prisoners of war. (*SNL*, 1805)

Obituary. 'A few months since, Mr Thomas Ross, a prisoner of war in the island of Cuba. He was Sub-Lt of the *Barracouta* schooner and eldest son of Mr Charles Ross, Purser of the *Maida* [74 guns].' (*NC* vol 17, p352)

4 October, press gang violence 'James Fair the master of a press gang was indicted for a violent assault upon Mrs Anne Harvey, the owner of a public house in East Smithfield, on the night of 4th October.

'Mrs Harvey proved that the defendant, accompanied by his gang, came to her house in quest of seamen. There were two men sitting in the bar; one the mate of a merchant vessel, the other an old man, formerly a sailor. The prisoner upon inquiry from them learning they were seafaring men, insisted on their going along with him; they refused. The prisoner and his gang endeavoured to force them; a tussle ensued and the prosecutrix, rather alarmed for the security of those rather fragile utensils of glass and china, in which the honour and interest of her bar were so materially involved, ventured to step between them and danger; in which effort she happened to get in the way of the prisoner, who not very punctilious in his regards for the tenderness of her sex, struck her a very unmerciful blow with his brawny fist, nearly tantamount to the kick of a coach horse, upon her side. Then in some other exertions of his violence, he pulled down a shelf in the bar upon which was sustained a five gallon cask of Hodges high flavoured cordial gin, which being precipitated upon the exterior of the prosecutrix's head, laid her as prostrate and senseless upon the floor, as if the violence of the material had acted *Ab Interiori*. The prisoner, seeing the mischief he had done, cut and ran to avoid the consequences, but was afterwards brought before a magistrate and consigned for trial. Mr Mainwaring in summing up the evidence for the jury, reprobated such acts of outrage, as wholly incompatible with the necessary duty of the Impress Service. The prisoner was fined forty shillings.' (*Times*, 4 December 1805)

6 October, Baltic convoy   The Baltic fleet (merchantmen) sailed from St Petersburg on 10 September for England under convoy of the *Rosina* armed ship. On 6 October, during a gale, thirty vessels were driven ashore on Riga Bar, eleven of which were transports laden with a vast quantity of stores. Only one vessel was English, which was supposed to have been the *Cusino* of Liverpool, the crew of which all perished except the captain. (*Times*, 6 November 1805)

22 October, Two Friends, transport   The *Two Friends* transport with part of the 100th Regiment sailed from Falmouth on 29 August for Quebec. On board the ship was the quartermaster and his family, with all the regimental stores and baggage, a lieutenant and thirty men as a guard, and about forty sick and lame. Until the Banks were reached the ship experienced the most atrocious weather, several of the ships in company losing their masts, while others ran foul of one another. It was now 12 October and their sea-stock, for which they had paid fifteen guineas a piece, was quite exhausted and for the rest of the voyage there was nothing but salt pork and biscuit.

On 22 October the ship under a press of sail was making eight knots; the night was dark and hazy and the passengers were retiring when the vessel struck. It was high tide and the ship passed over the outer reef and then came up in two fathoms. The masts were cut away and an anchor let go to prevent her drifting off into deep water; the ship kept beating all night with seven feet of water in her hold and the seas making a clean sweep over the deck. At daylight an attempt was made to launch the jollyboat, but it was quickly stove on the rocks. At 10am their hopes began to revive with the appearance of a man on the shore, who later brought a very small boat which held four persons and with its aid about half the people were landed before dark, the rest landing the next morning. Only three people lost their lives, a lieutenant and two privates; they had tried to get ashore with the aid of a rope attached to the ship but the breakers had cost them their lives.

The *Two Friends* had struck within one and a half miles of Louisburg position 45°46'N 60°W on Cape Breton Island, but north or south is not given in the article. (*MC*, Duncan, 1812 ed, vol 2, p364 et seq)

23 October, Aeneas, transport The *Aeneas* transport was one of the fleet that sailed from Portsmouth on 21 August for Quebec, but was more unfortunate than the *Two Friends* in the same convoy. The *Aeneas* also was carrying part of the 100th Regiment, but of 347 persons (including many women and children) who were on board when the vessel sailed from Portsmouth, only seven survived to tell what actually happened after the ship was wrecked near the Port aux Basques to the east of Cape Ray, and most probably at the Îles aux Mortes.

About 4am on 23 October the *Aeneas* struck with such force that it was at once realised the ship must become a wreck. The deck quickly crowded with men, women and children, who in a short space of time were hit by a sea which came with such violence as swept very many from her deck, and the rock on which the vessel had struck forced its way through all the decks.

By 8am the ship had entirely gone to pieces, yet thirty-five survivors had by that time managed to float on pieces of wreckage to a small island, about a quarter of a mile from where the vessel had struck. Of those who landed on the island seven were seamen and the remainder, men of the 100th, two of whom were officers, Lt Dawson and Ensign Faulkner; they had the misfortune for the wind to change as soon as they landed so that everything from the wreck was driven out to sea and nothing saved.

That night four of them died and the next morning about thirty reached the mainland on a raft they constructed. The greater number then directed their course to where the sun rose, leaving behind three who were unable to walk; but were nevertheless fortunate enough to be found by a hunter, Michael Gillam, who occupied a fishing post during the summer months and shared a hut with four or five other hunters during the months of winter. Gillam also found two sailors who had split from the main party; they were of the opinion that Mr Faulkner and his party had perished in the timber.

Previously, Lt Dawson being unable to keep up with the main party, two soldiers were detailed to remain with him; they afterwards stated: 'We staid by him till we knew not whether he was alive or dead.' Then after leaving him the two were lucky enough to be found by a hunting party of five or six men, yet could give no directions to the hunters in their quest for Faulkner's party, for they knew not where they had been.

In the spring Michael Gillam took the five men he had rescued to Fortune Bay, where they embarked for Quebec. Of the thirty-five who had survived the wreck, only the five soldiers and two sailors were ever found. [On 26 August 1806 the *Times* article included: '...Thus, melancholy to relate, were about 230 souls, the greater part in the prime of life, full of health, comeliness, vigour and spirits, suddenly ingulphed in the briny waves, a prey to the voracious monsters of the deep.'] (*NC* vol 22, p381 et seq; *Times*, 26-27 August and 10 September 1806)

24? October, Donegal, 80 guns   After the Battle of Trafalgar the *Donegal*, 80 guns, Captain Pultney Malcolm, was employed to secure a Spanish prize, when Mr Ellis the ship's carpenter was severely injured by the falling of a mast. Captain Malcolm had a boat launched to convey Mr Ellis to a Spanish hospital, but the boat was swamped and Mr Ellis and twenty-five of his comrades perished. He left a widow and four children wholly unprovided for; since Mr Ellis nor the seamen were not killed in action, the families received nothing. (*Times*, 6 December 1805)

1 November, King George, transport, and Britannia, East Indiaman   'At half-past three in the morning the officer of the watch on board the *Leda* frigate, Captain Honyman, observed breakers ahead yet the frigate wore quickly and cleared the dangers, but in so doing the boats over the stern actually hung over the rocks. The signal gun for the convoy to tack was fired but when daylight came it was seen that one ship, the *King George* artillery transport, was ashore on the Rocas [3°51'27" 33°48'57"]; and the *Britannia* East Indiaman, when on the point of tacking had been run foul of by a larger East Indiaman, the *Streatham*, when the *Britannia* had her bowsprit and fore topmast carried away and then drifted on to the Rocas where she lost her rudder and bilged. The *Europe, Comet,* and *Veruna* (*sic*) Indiamen, sent in their boats and took off Captain Birch of the *Britannia*, his entire crew and the East India Company's recruits, altogether about four hundred persons. As the leak increased the *Britannia* drifted about seven miles from the rocks and went down in deep water. It was said at the time that of one hundred and sixty chests of dollars on board only twelve were brought away, so quickly did the *Britannia* go down.

'Meanwhile the *Leda* was employed sending her boats to a sandy isle from which they took off the entire crew of the *King George*, as well as the artillery troops that had been embarked therein, that is all except Brigadier-general York who was the only person to lose his life. The women and children were all slung from the spritsail yard, on to a rock which was close by and then taken again to an island which was high and dry to await other boats from the Indiamen. The general however, being the oldest among them, they wished to do the same for him, which he indignantly refused; he therefore went to the spritsail yard to get on the rock without being slung by a rope, regardless of the entreaties by one of his gunners, who perceiving his situation, again expressed a wish to sling him with a rope, to ensure his safety, which he would not suffer. He sometime afterwards remained on the yard, unresolved to venture down, which obliged those few remaining behind him to let themselves down from the jibboom. At last the general either let himself down or lost his hold, and falling in the surf had not the strength to hold on the rock against the back-water and disappeared beneath the ship's bow.

'The loss of the general seemed the more melancholy; he being the only person to perish; yet a woman who had been delivered of a child not more than three or four hours was received on board the *Leda* with her infant; and a man who had broken his leg two days previously was also got safe on shore without injuring his new set leg.

'On the shore were found three anchors laid across each other, without stocks, and near the part of the wreck of a ship. From the appearance of age it was conjectured to have been the remains of the *Cato* man of war of 50 guns, Admiral Hyde Parker, lost on her journey to India.' [This was not so. The *Cato*, lost in 1783, sailed from England on 13 October 1782 via the Cape of Good Hope. (*SNL*, 31 January 1783)] (*NC* vol 23, p483 et seq)

7 November, Orquijo, transport The *Orquijo* was an 18-gun Spanish sloop, taken by the *Pique*, 40 guns, Captain Charles Ross, on 8 February 1805. The command of the vessel passed to Lt Charles Balderson, then acting commander, who was fortunate enough not to be on board this day; he was on the *Penguin*, 18 guns, formerly the Dutch *Comet* (*Komeet*).

The *Orquijo* was employed as a transport and on board, as well as the crew, was a detachment of three officers and thirty men belonging to the 6th Battalion of the 60th Regiment, bringing the total on board the sloop to 136 persons. The ship was off Port Antonio on the north-east coast of Jamaica when she went down during a violent squall. Thirty-nine men were rescued but four died of their injuries later, so that a total of 101 persons lost their lives. (*SNL* gives the number who died as 95)

On Monday 11 November a court martial was held on board *L'Hercule* in Port Royal harbour, Jamaica, to try Commander Balderson, his officers and ship's company for the loss of the vessel. They were all honourably acquitted. (*Times*, 14 January 1806)

21 November, Betsey, schooner The *Betsey*, a 75-ton schooner, sailed from Macao for New South Wales on 10 November 1805 with a crew of ten men: William Brooks commander; Edward Luttrell mate; one Portuguese seacunny; three Manilla and four Chinese lascars. All went well until 2.30am on the 21st, when the vessel going at the rate of seven and a half knots struck upon a reef in the South China Sea in position 9°48′N 114°14′E.[37] The boat was instantly lowered and a small anchor dropped astern, but on heaving the cable parted and both were lost. At daybreak they found that the vessel had forged upon the reef four or five miles, not having two feet of water under her, the reef extending nine or ten miles to the south and four or five miles east and west. For three days and nights the crew tried to get her off, but to no avail, and they had become so weakened by their efforts that they could scarce be persuaded to construct a raft, the ship being at this time bilged on the starboard side.

However, by the 24th a raft had been constructed and with the jollyboat in company a course was set for Balambangan. In the boat were

Captain Brooks, the mate, the gunner, and three sea-cunnies, who had to share six bottles of water and a small bag of biscuits, while those on the raft were better provided for, but during the night a brisk gale from the north-west parted the boat from the raft which was seen no more; it was conjectured to have drifted to the island of Borneo which lay to the south. At dawn on the 29th land came in sight, supposed to be Balabac Island which they could not fetch, and the people nearly exhausted by rowing under a burning sun, in a perfect calm, were obliged to drink their own urine. That night it blew so hard from the north-east that they were obliged to bear up for Banguey Island, which they discovered next morning and instantly went in search of water, when meeting with natives they exchanged spoons for sweet potatoes and coconuts. But two days later a group of eleven natives appeared on the shore and after some conversation, Captain Brooks and the gunner were killed. The others fled to the boat and shaped their course for the Straits of Malacca. All went well until 15 December when they fell in with a group of islands and were attacked by two proas and one sea-cunny was killed. Their sextant, logbook and boat, even their clothes were taken from them and for three days they were kept on board a proa under a burning sun with no covering and only a little sago to eat.

They were landed on the island of Soebi (largest island of the South Natuna group) where they were kept in a state of slavery, entirely naked and subsisting on sago, until 20 April when they were taken in a proa to Rhio, where they arrived after a passage of twenty-five days, nearly famished.

Their distresses however were alleviated by Mr Koek of Malacca, who treated them in the kindest manner; and by the ship *Kandree*, Captain Williamson, arriving next day, bound for Malacca, they obtained passage for that port. (*NC*, vol 17, p321 et seq; Dalyell, 1812 ed, vol 3, p424 et seq)

? December, Weser expedition   On Tuesday morning 10 December the 50-gun *Leopard*, together with the *Fury* and *Furious* gunbrigs, having 120 sail of transports under their convoy, sailed from the Downs for the Weser. On board the transports were troops of the second division of the expeditionary force who had embarked at Deal, Dover and Ramsgate and included amongst them were, the 3rd or Old Buffs; 8th or King's Own; 7th and 9th Fusiliers; 26th or Cameronians; 4th or King's Regiment; the 1st battalion of the 89th; 2nd battalion of the 95th or Rifle Corps; and the 91st, a regiment of highlanders; as well as the 28th, 30th, 34th, 35th, 36th, 40th, 46th, 87th, and 88th Regiments, altogether about 21 battalions. (*Times*, 12 December 1805)

The left wing of the 87th did not arrive at Deal till 8pm on the 9th. 'From the miserable state of the roads, the poor fellows are dreadfully jaded, all over mud and dirt; so bad has the weather been of late that for several days past, troops have come in literally drenched. The officers are worse off;

they have to wait for baggage trains but privates carry a change of clothes.' (*Times*, 13 December 1805)

Unknown to all, worst was yet to come. The Dover report of 12 December stated: 'The wind blows very hard from the NNE with hard showers of hail and rain.' (*Times*, 14 December 1805)

On 14 December the *Jenny*, transport No 365, was driven ashore near Gravelines but was got off by the French National Guard who found on board her a crew of 11 seamen, 115 soldiers of the 30th Regiment, 4 officers, 12 women and 6 young children, one of whom was born the night before. They were taken to the barracks and on the 16th removed from Gravelines to Valenciennes, whereupon the captain of the *Jenny* and the army officers wrote to the Mayor of Gravelines thanking the people for their kind and humane treatment. (*Times*, 11 January 1806)

On 14 December, also, the *Hope* transport, Captain Varrely, arrived at Dover with loss of anchor, cable and boat. On board were 320 soldiers, being 210 more than her complement. (*Times*, 17 December 1805)

Then again, on 14 December the *Derwent* and four other sail returned to Harwich after 17 days at sea with the German Legion cavalry on board. They had sailed with the first division (that of the 10th was the second). The first two days out the weather had been tolerable, the wind fair and only one heavy gale, but on the night of the second day the wind had gone around to the north-east and a dreadful and dangerous gale had ensued. The Commodore had signalled to put about for England but about half the ships did not see the signal and it became every ship for itself, although according to the captain of the *Derwent*, less than one half the captains knew the Dutch coast. (*Times*, 17 December 1805)

These were not the only ships which arrived back on 14 December; the *Mary*, transport No 374, arrived at Dover during the night, having on board 83 horses and 30 dragoons of the German Legion. This ship had also parted from the convoy during the gale of the 11th. (*Times*, 18 December 1805)

On the 15th the *Fury* with several transports including the *Commerce* arrived back at Deal with men of the 8th, 28th, 30th, 36th and 89th Regiments; while the *Leopard* and *Furious* together with the greater part of the transports arrived at Dover. (*Times*, 17 and 18 December 1805)

The gale was apparently a continuing one and on 16 December the *Ariadne* transport foundered to the west of Calais where all on board were rescued by the French. The crew of 26 men, 300 soldiers of the Fusiliers, 11 officers (including 2 colonels), 20 women and 12 children were taken to Calais and then on to Valenciennes. (*L'Moniteur*, 21 December 1805)

L'Moniteur also reported the unfortunate circumstances of two other English ships. The *Atalanta*, a 12-gun brig on board of which were 12 seamen, 28 cavalry and 34 horses was seen to go down from Calais yet no help could be rendered; and an English ship of about 500 tons was also seen to go down off Calais and once again there were no survivors.

The Portsmouth report of 17 December read: 'The brig *Commerce*, a transport, arrived this day; the fleet separated during the night of the 11th when several were driven near the French coast off Calais. (*Times*, 19 December 1805)

At this time also great fears were entertained for the *Maria* transport with more than 200 men of the 26th Regiment, as a vessel exactly answering her description was seen dismasted off the Texel. (*Times*, 21 December 1805)

It would seem that the convoy of the 10th included two vessels named *Maria* and two named *Commerce*, for the Deal report of the 23rd stated: 'Just arrived from Portsmouth, the *Commerce* and the *Maria* which sailed on the 10th with part of the 30th Regiment of Foot.' (*Times*, 25 December 1805)

Yet a transport named *Commerce* had arrived at Deal on the 15th and most unfortunately the report from the Texel was only too true; the *Maria* of London, Captain Scott, a transport with 270 troops on board and bound to Emden, was on the morning of the 15th driven by a violent snowstorm and gale upon the Haak sandbank, off the Texel, then when she struck the ship immediately bilged and went over. Of the above number, only one officer, Captain Jones, 14 privates, the assistant surgeon of the 26th, and 4 seamen were saved by clinging to the rigging though constantly in fear of being washed off by the breakers running over them. When the day dawned it presented a dreadful spectacle of their drowned comrades, wives and children. At length a Dutch schuyt put off from the shore and conveyed them as prisoners of war to the *Brutus*. (*Times*, 14 February 1806)

A few miles from where the *Maria* was wrecked, during the same night, the English transport *Isabella* of Liverpool, Captain Laybert, was wrecked in the Texel and of the 300 troops on board only 165 were saved. (Amsterdam report 21 December 1805; *Times*, 10 January 1806)

Captain McLeod of HM sloop *Cygnet* arrived at Deal on 19 December. On Monday the 16th, off the Goodwins, he fished up the main mast, yards and bowsprit of the *Aurora* transport. He also picked up the adjutant's chest and another large one with a buoy and buoy rope attached but with the bottom out and which had probably contained the money to pay the troops. The *Aurora* had sailed on the 10th with the entire staff of the Cameronians; the commanding officer, a major; the surgeon and adjutant, the grenadier company and the band, as well as 250 men. Captain McLeod was firmly of the opinion that the ship had gone down and that all on board had perished, as indeed they had; including the crew, about 300 men died on the *Aurora*; probably, women and children also. (*Times*, 21 December 1805)

On 22 December the convoy once again set sail for the Weser and once again the ships were dispersed by a gale. Several, including the escorts, returned to the Downs where the *Leopard* ran aground on the Brake, off Sandwich, for one and a half hours and received much damage. (*Times*, 7 January 1806)

Several of the vessels that had managed to proceed had been unable to land their troops owing to icing in the Weser, and on 17 January transports were arriving at Ramsgate after almost a month at sea. Included were the *Vigilant* with 147 men of the 26th; *Derwent* with 115 men of the 8th; *Adventure* with 125 men of the 30th; *True Briton* with 95 men of the 30th; *Vestal* with 146 men of the 89th; and *John and Thomas* with 107 men of the 28th Regiment of Foot. Also arrived at Ramsgate were the *Crescent*, *Theresa* and the *Mary*, with 91 horses of the King's German Heavy Horse and about 100 men. The remainder of the 89th were landed at Bremen on Christmas Day. (*Times*, 20 January 1806)

In the meantime, on the morning of 30 December, an express reached Ramsgate from the government with orders for all troops on board transports to disembark and the empty ships to sail for the Elbe to bring back the troops sent to Hanover. This very unexpected order to Captain Raines, the naval officer in charge of transports, was nevertheless obeyed with alacrity and by 4.30pm all available ships had sailed for the Downs. (*Times*, 1 January 1806)

The following day, 31 December, the *Adamant*, *Diligence*, and the *Pincher* sailed from Deal with a convoy of empty transports. (*Times*, 2 January 1806)

In all about 1000 men, women and children had perished with the transports and the expedition had never even reached its destination.

14 December, Lord Eldon, East Indiaman An East Indiaman the *Lord Eldon* laden with pepper from Benkulen, Sumatra, struck on the sands off the Nore and could not be got off. (*Times*, 16 December 1805)

24 December, Helder, transport Originally named *Heldin*, the *Helder* was a Dutch 28-gun vessel captured in the Texel on 28 August 1799 by the British. The ship, sold out of the Navy in 1802, was renamed *Helder*.

During the night of 24 December the vessel was being used as a transport and was probably overladen. On board were 600 men of the 5th Regiment of Foot together with 40 crew members when the *Helder* was wrecked near the Helder. All on board were rescued by the Dutch and taken safely into the Nieuwe Diep in the Texel. (*Times*, 16 January 1806)

1806

2 January, Captivity, prison hulk Built at Bucklershard in 1774 the 64-gun *Vigilant* for at least ten years prior to 1806 had been a prison hulk lying at Portsmouth. (*SNL*, June 1797; *NC* vol 5, p552). The ship was then repaired and renamed *Captivity*. The Portsmouth report of 2 January reads: 'This morning at 3 o'clock the *Captivity* which was taken out of dock a few days since, fitted to receive prisoners of war, sunk at her moorings at the entrance to Porchester Lake. There were but the usual number of persons on board which belong to a ship in ordinary (reserve); they were all saved. It is imagined she broke her back from being moored improperly and went down in four minutes after the crash was heard.' (*Times*, 4 January 1806)

3 January, punishment for aiding desertion   A waterman of the name of Giles was whipped through the streets of Sheerness for aiding and abetting in the desertion of a seaman from the 44-gun *Magnanime*, after which an officer and a party of marines took him on board the flagship to serve His Majesty. (*Times*, 8 January 1806)

9 January, Cecilia, merchantman   A vessel sailed from Dublin for Barbados previous to which she was to join a convoy at Cork. She was unfortunately overtaken by a dreadful storm, driven on the Welsh coast, and foundered at the back of Holyhead where all on board perished. Several boxes of soap and candles having been driven on shore, there is reason to believe she was the *Cecilia* of Dublin, Captain Browne, which sailed that day. (*Times*, 21 January 1806)

11 January, typhus at Plymouth   'Typhus exists on several ships at Plymouth; particularly *Formidable, Pompee, Salvador del Mundo* (the flagship), and *Resolue*. The hospitals are crowded; some ships send thirty men a day and many have died.' (*Times*, 13 January 1806)

? January, Le Papillon, 6 guns   *Le Papillon*, a French 6-gun corvette, pierced for 12 guns, was taken by the *Vanguard*, 74 guns, Captain James Walker, off St Marcs, San Domingo, 4 September 1803.
      The vessel commanded by William Woolsey was on passage from the Jamaica station when she foundered in the Atlantic during January, exact date unknown. Of her crew there were no survivors. (*SNL*, 1806)

14 January, privateers   The Dover report of 17 January contained two interesting articles:
      'The enemy's privateers, constantly at low water infest our coast and so daring are they that two of them came to anchor abreast of our harbour on Tuesday evening the 14th. The Sea Fencibles went to the batteries but were prevented going to the guns by the sentinels, who alleged that no persons should touch the guns without an order from Lord Forbes, the Commanding General, who was at Canterbury.
      'The *Nile* cutter commanded by the intrepid Thomas Johnson is lying in our harbour. Johnson on being asked by a gentleman of Dover why he did not see after these privateers replied: "My brave commander is gone on

another station, but I expect orders to sail very soon, when be assured the cutter shall not disgrace her name." The *Nile* is manned by a very brave set, who although they may not have particularly attended to the revenue of the country, would not suffer her honour to be tarnished; and when they have smuggled spirits to quaff the king's health would draw their swords and protect him with their lives.' (*Times*, 20 January 1806)

? January, Neptune's crew A shocking occurrence took place a few days ago at a public house along shore below Liverpool. Several men, part of the crew of the ship *Neptune*, which had run ashore a little below the fort, had been employed in getting her off. They had left the vessel for refreshment when a person came to request their immediate attendance at the ship, yet not being able to prevail upon them to leave the house instantly, he had recourse to the dreadful stratagem of scaling the roof of the house and dropping a cartridge of gunpowder down the chimney; in consequence of which one man was killed and another's arm so badly shattered that amputation was necessary. Several others were severely hurt and the house shaken of its foundation. (*Times*, 31 January 1806)

16 January, Namur's cutter During a dreadful gale the launch of the *Namur*, 74 guns, lying at St Helens, broke adrift with two men in it. Two cutters were manned and sent after it, one of which returned with the launch, but the other, with Lt Smith and seven men was suddenly lost sight of; from which it was conjectured that she struck on the Woolsners and overset, when attempting to enter Langston harbour, and that all had perished. A cutter with six oars and the body of a seaman drifted on shore at Hayling Island. (*NC* vol 17, p87)

18 January, Hibernia's launch A most melancholy accident occurred at Plymouth during the hurricane of 16 and 17 January. The launch of the 120-gun *Hibernia*, Admiral Douglas, was sent ashore with old stores and to receive new, manned with a lieutenant, a midshipman and forty-three seamen: after having loaded the launch they went off to join the *Hibernia*, in Cawsand Bay, it blowing then hard; but before the launch could near the Indiamen in the bight of Cawsand Bay it was found necessary to bear away, and endeavour to weather the Mew Stone, and get into Yealm river for the night, but in doing this the mast went over the side; the launch missed weathering the Mew Stone, and got it being near the high water, between the Shag Rock and the land. She then struck on the deceitful Rennie Rocks between the Shag stone and the land and overset. The lieutenant and eighteen men were by some providential means washed ashore, but the midshipman and twenty-three seamen were unfortunately drowned. The poor young midshipman and sixteen bodies were washed ashore, and decently buried together in Wembury churchyard. One seaman with his leg broke, and jammed to pieces, contrived to crawl up a rock, and his comrade, almost exhausted, crept to his side for warmth. In the morning when the quarry men came to their assistance the wounded man was found still alive, but his companion, a lifeless corpse. The wounded man was conveyed to the Royal Naval Hospital.[38] (*SYM*, 20 January 1806; *AR* 1806, Chr, p361; *NC* vol 17, p87)

22 *January, Pallas, transport*   About 26 horses and men of the German Legion were landed at Chatham from the *Pallas* transport after three weeks in the North Sea. The horses had stood so long that as soon as the slings were removed from their bodies they laid down at once and were only got up with difficulty. (*Times*, 25 January 1806)

? *January, Berbice, schooner*   A 6-gun schooner, *Berbice*, built in 1804 was commanded by Lt James Glassford Gooding when she foundered in the Demerara river. Although the crew were saved the date of loss remains unknown. (*SNL*, 1806)

6 *February, Pomona, merchantman*   As five boys were coming on shore at North Shields, from the ship *Pomona*, the boat unfortunately got upon a ship's hawser and upset. Four of them got hold of the rope but the fifth, who was a Scots lad (to whom they had given passage from Mona Island where he had been shipwrecked and suffered many hardships), went to the bottom, and before assistance could be rendered the others, one of them a London boy, let go his hold and was likewise drowned. One body was found two days later. (*AR* 1806, Chr, p367)

6 *February, Isabella, West Indiaman*   The ship *Isabella*, a West Indiaman of some 600 tons burthen, went ashore on the Horse Sand at Portsmouth, where she was nevertheless soon weighed by persons under the direction of a Mr Heather a merchant of Portsmouth, and taken to a place close to the harbour. (*NC* vol 15, p260; *Times*, 7 February 1806)

? *February, Seaforth, 16 guns*   The *Seaforth* was a fairly new 16-gun vessel purchased in 1805 and was commanded by Lt George Steele when she capsized in a squall on the Leeward Island Station. Except for two men the captain and entire crew of one hundred perished with the vessel. (*SNL*, 1806)

18 *March, murderous punishment*   At 2pm a special Privy Council was held, which was attended by the Lord Chancellor Sir William Scott and the judge of the Admiralty Court; Mr Grey, the Master of the Rolls; Lord Minto, the Attorney General; Mr Wickham; Mr Graham, the magistrate belonging to Bow Street office; and Mr White, Solicitor to the Treasury likewise attended.

The business for which the Council was assembled was to investigate a charge against Lt Stephens of the Royal Navy on suspicion of assisting in the wilful murder of Nichols, Smith and Jeremiah Dause, three seamen under his command in the East Indies. The Court sat upon this extraordinary business until 6pm; and during their sitting John Firzching and several other sailors, who were under the command of Lt Stephens, gave evidence.

In the year 1800 the prisoner was 2nd Lt on board the *Trident*, 64 guns, bound for Bombay under the command of Captain John Tanner. On 1 January 1801 the captain died, when the command of the ship devolved upon Lt George Rutherford the 1st Lt; the prisoner then became the second in command.

In the month of March following the officers and crew were on shore at Butcher's Island in Bombay, when a charge of a private nature was made against the three men deceased; the consequence was they were ordered to run the gauntlet between about 400 men. They were stripped naked, except for their trousers, lashed upon gun carriages and underwent the punishment which was inflicted from 10am until nearly 1pm. It is hardly necessary to say that their bodies presented a most horrid spectacle after they had undergone this severe punishment. They were afterwards drawn to a pest house where surgical assistance was refused them; they then requested some drink which was likewise refused. The consequence was that one sailor died two hours after the flogging, the second lived until 7pm, while the third died at 6am the following morning. The flogging was inflicted without a court martial.

Six years after the men died the ship returned to England and the witnesses gave the information which led to the Privy Council meeting. The prisoner, since his return to England, was employed on the *Fame*, 74 guns, which was lying at Chatham. Mr Gray gave instructions for a telegraphic dispatch to be sent to the Port Admiral on the 1st inst, for the prisoner to be discharged and delivered into the custody of two messengers.

On 18 March the Gazette contained an offer of a reward of £200 for the capture of Lt George Rutherford. It stated that he was charged with the murder of three seamen of His Majesty's Ship *Trident*, whilst he was commander of that ship at Butcher's Island in March 1801, and that he escaped on 12 March 1806, by jumping overboard from the *Salvador del Mundo*, on which ship he was being held at Plymouth. (*Times*, 19 March 1806)

On 25 March Lt Stephens gave evidence before the Privy Council, at the Council Office, from noon until 4pm, when Mr Burrows surgeon of the *Trident* gave evidence. The Lord Chancellor, Mr Grey the Master of the Rolls and most of the Ministers were present. (*Times*, 26 March 1806)

On 22 April the *Times* stated that Lt Rutherford of the *Trident* had been secured in the neighbourhood of Scarborough.

On Wednesday 14 May 1806 the *Times* contained the following article: 'The method of punishing seamen on board men of war by running the gauntlet is ordered to be immediately discontinued.'

Despite extended research the author was unable to discover what happened to either Rutherford or Stephens; he would be pleased to learn.

18 March, Mary, merchantman   The ship *Mary* of Boston, Iben Trescoff master, sailed from Canton on 9 February and all went well until 18 March at 2pm in position 15°30'S 93°30'E, when a violent and sudden squall came on and upset the ship. The crew cut away the masts and the ship partly righted but filled in such a manner that for seventeen days the twenty-six crew members subsisted on two gallons of water. On the eighteenth day the weather moderated and the sea being smooth the men cut a hole in the upper part of the main deck by which means they procured some provisions that floated; after which they built a raft on the weather quarter and remained fifty days in that dreadful situation; when they were picked up by a ship bound from Batavia for Philadelphia. At the time they were picked up they supposed that one third of the cargo had been washed out. (*Times*, 21 August 1806)

? March, Agnes, lugger   An 8-gun hired lugger *Agnes* was believed to have foundered off the Texel during March. Fate of her thirty man crew unknown. (*SNL*, 1808)

9 April, French officers   On the morning of Saturday 5 April Admiral Villeneuve of the *Bucentaure*; Captain Lucas of the *Redoubtable*; Captain Infernet of the *Intrepide*; with a physician and two lieutenants; all officers who had fought at Trafalgar,[39] left Reading for Plymouth to embark in a cartel for Morlaix, where they were going on their parole. (*Times*, 11 April 1806)

Upon arrival at Plymouth the French officers were accommodated in Murche's Hotel until the morning of 9 April, when they embarked for Morlaix from the pier heads in the *Union*, Captain Stebbe, an English cutter cartel, lying off the victualling office (where Phoenix Wharf now is). Captain Cotgrave the Commissioner for prisoners of war accompanied Admiral Villeneuve in a man of war's boat to the cartel. (*SYM*, 14 April 1806)

On 17 April the *Union* arrived back in Plymouth from France, where as soon as the cartel arrived soldiers were placed on board and remained till she sailed, so as to prevent any communication with the shore. (*Times*, 21 April 1806; *SYM*, 21 April 1806)

The *AR* 1806, Chr, p529 contains an error. It states that Admiral Villeneuve was known to have landed at Morlaix in the night between 22 and 23 April, yet we have seen that the *Union* arrived back at Plymouth on the 17th.

12 April, Le Brave, 74 guns *Le Brave,* 74 guns, was taken at the Battle of San Domingo on 6 February 1806 by the squadron of Sir John Duckworth.

Two months later on 12 April *Le Brave,* Captain Edmund Boger with a scratch crew foundered off the Western Islands (the Azores) when on passage from Jamaica, yet except for three men, the entire crew were saved. (*SNL*, 1806)

20 April, Lady Burgess, East Indiaman On 31 March the 50-gun *Leopard* sailed from Portsmouth with a convoy of six East Indiamen, the *Asia, Lady Burgess, Melville, Nelson, Sovereign,* and the *Walthamstow,* and cleared the Lizard on 1 April. By 13 April the convoy had made the Salvage Islands and on the 14 the Island of Palma. All went well until 20 April when at 2am signal guns were fired by one of the convoy.

The remainder of the ships immediately hove to and at daylight discovered the *Lady Burgess,* dismasted on a reef, between Boa Vista and Sao Tiago in the Cape Verde Islands. Boats were sent at once to the aid of the people on the ship, but by 9am she was a complete wreck and the heavy surf breaking over her made the approach of the boats not only difficult but also extremely dangerous. in spite of all the exertions of the boats' crews, of the 184 persons on board the *Lady Burgess* 34 people lost their lives, including Mr Cock, the chief mate; Mr Dick, the purser; three East India Company cadets and eighteen of the ship's crew. (*NC* vol 16, pp109-110; *AR* 1806, Chr, p416)

29 April, Montrose, packet The *Montrose* packet from St Michaels for London was taken by *Le Topaze,* a French 40-gun frigate and burnt; the crew were taken as prisoners of war to Brest. (*Times,* 30 May 1806)
Note: St Michaels, otherwise Sao Miguel, Azores.

30 April, Beaver, merchantman The *Beaver,* Captain Linesley, from Waterford for Newfoundland, was also taken by *La Topaze* and burnt; the crew again being taken to Brest. (*Times,* 30 May 1806)

18 May, Schrikverwekker, 68 guns The *Schrikverwekker* was a Dutch 68-gun ship of the line with a complement of 450 men, and captained this day by Hendrik Alexander Ruysch (1767-1839). The vessel was built in 1798 to the design of the shipwright Mr R Dorsman in Amsterdam.

Visibility was so bad in the early morning of the 18th that the lookouts did not see the breakers until it was too late, and the ship ran aground on the reefs of the Agnieteneilanden (Angenieten) Islands (6°10′S 106°48′E), a group of small islands to the north-west of Batavia Roads in the Thousand Islands Sea.

It is not known how many people were on the *Schrikverwekker* when she struck, although what is known is that only two men drowned, all the rest being rescued. (G J D Wildeman, Librarian, Nederlands Scheepvaart Museum, Amsterdam)

20 May, Sydney, East Indiaman The *Sydney*, Captain Austen Forrest, left Port Jackson on 12 April for Bengal; Captain Forrest intending to proceed through Dampier's Straits as close as possible in the track of Captain Hogan of the *Cornwallis*, which appeared to be a safe passage. However, on the morning of 20 May at 1am in position 3°20′ 146°50′E the *Sydney* ran upon a shoal, and as it was not noticed in any charts, they happened to be the unfortunate discovers of it. The ship had struck at high water and when soundings were taken over the taffrail they found twenty-five fathoms, yet over the bow only two fathoms. One of the boats was immediately got out with a bower anchor, but on sounding ten fathoms distance from the ship found no ground at sixty fathoms. By 3am the ship which had been striking very hard began to sue (*ie* to be left high and dry) forward; small black rocks began to appear and six feet of water in the hold began to increase rapidly. Then by 5am the ship was setting aft, her topsides parting at the floor-heads.

With the ship irrecoverably gone all hands were employed in getting the boats ready to receive the crew of 110 persons, which the three boats could barely hold, and at 5pm on 21 May, when there were three feet of water on the orlop deck, the crew abandoned the ship. The captain, with Mr Trounce the second officer, and seventy-four lascars took to the long-boat; Mr Robson first officer, Mr Stalkart the third, and sixteen lascars were in the cutter; while the jollyboat was allotted to fifteen Dutch Malays and one sepoy; they faced a voyage of almost 4000 miles in open boats.

That first night they shaped their course for the Admiralty Islands, the three boats keeping in close company, with the longboat towing the jollyboat. At daylight, finding the cutter sailed better, Captain Forrest directed Mr Robson to take the jollyboat in tow. This was to prove disastrous; the wind increased as the morning advanced and a heavy swell rising at 10am, the jollyboat sunk while in tow of the cutter and the sixteen men on board all perished. It was lamentable to witness their fate as it was not in the power of the others to render the least assistance. At noon on the 22nd the Admiralty Islands were seen bearing NNE distant three or four leagues, the boats having run fifty-eight miles.

The two boats now stood to the westward and on the 25th made a small island (probably Durour), where about twenty landed in search of water but were driven off by the natives who threw about 200 spears at them. Continuing westwards they fetched the north-west extremity of Ceram on 9 June, where Mr Robson and many of the lascars landed and from whence they could journey to Dutch-held Amboyna in two or three days.

It may here be noticed that from the Admiralty Islands to the north-west of Ceram, keeping the coast of New Guinea in view during the hours of daylight, is something like 1500 miles, so the boats had averaged three and a half knots, day and night.

The number in the longboat was now reduced to seventeen from the *Sydney* and some others picked up en route; but how many, or who they were is today quite unknown. (*NC* vol 29, p93). The men now continued their passage through the Banda and Flores Seas into the Sape Strait, between Komodo and Soembawa, and from whence they passed into the Indian Ocean, along the southern coast of Java and made Java Head on 4 July, by which date they had voyaged considerably more than 3000 miles.

On 9 July at midnight they came to off Pulo Penang 5° 10′S 103°59′E, on the west coast of Sumatra but at daylight were too weak to get up the anchor and had to make a signal of distress; whereupon a sandpan (*sic*) with two natives came off and as Captain Forrest was the only person with strength enough to move, took him ashore where they carried him to an adjoining house. Such refreshments as the place afforded were immediately sent off to the longboat and they recovered so quickly that two days later, on 12 July they weighed, and on 19 July anchored off Rat Island, at Benkoelen.

Those members of the crew of the *Sydney* who arrived at Benkoelen, including Captain Forrest, Mr Trounce and Mr Stalkart, had completed what must for all time remain the longest voyage ever undertaken by shipwrecked mariners, almost 4000 miles.

On 7 August Captain Forrest left Benkoelen for Penang, where he arrived on the 28th and was surprised to meet his late chief mate Mr Robson, who with the lascars landed at Ceram, had safely reached Amboyna, where the Dutch Governor Mr Cranstoun supplied them with all their needs as well as money, at the same time refusing to take any receipt for the amount. Such honourable conduct from the governor of a foreign country, with which England was at war, was widely promulgated.

Captain Forrest was married to Miss Matcham Pitt, cousin to the late Lord Nelson. His death was occasioned by a fall from his horse, near his own seat, Swilly Farm, New South Wales, 24 December 1811. (*AR* 1807, p907 et seq; *NC* vol 28, p440; *NC* Vol 29, p89 et seq)

20 May, Lilly, merchantman A raft with seven seamen on it was on Friday 23 May picked up and taken into Dover. They were part of the crew of the American ship *Lilly*, which on the evening of Tuesday 20 May struck on the Kentish Knock, a sandbank fifteen miles north-east of the North Foreland, and was wrecked. (*Times*, 26 May 1806)

5 June, Eliza, merchantman The ship *Eliza* of London, Bx Cheppenier master, struck on the Spaniard Shoal in the Thames estuary, about six miles north of Whitstable, where she foundered. The ship had an unknown number of people on board but including many women and children, and although several boats put off to their rescue, yet many drowned, probably owing to the length of time the boats took to reach the wreck.

The captain lashed his wife, another woman and himself to the rigging, and were four hours in the water before being rescued, although the other woman died soon afterwards. Fifty men, mostly naked, were also rescued. The *Eliza* was on passage from London for Dover to pick up more passengers when she struck. (*Times*, 9 June 1806)

21 June, Warren Hastings, East Indiaman   The *Warren Hastings*, Captain T Larkins, an East Indiaman of 1200 tons burthen, mounting forty-eight 18-pounders, sailed from China, last from Penang, in company with the *Ganges*, Captain Harrington; *Surat Castle* and *Dorsetshire*. A few days later the *Warren Hastings* and *Ganges* parted from the other ships, perhaps because of the leaky condition of the *Ganges*, but from whatever cause the *Ganges* made for Bombay for repairs, after first transferring packets and letters entrusted to Captain Harrington to Captain Larkins, who also accepted some stores for St Helena. (*NC* vol 16, p343)

The *Warren Hastings* was now alone and at 7.30am on 21 June when in position 26°12'S 53°21'E the ship was seen by the French 40-gun frigate *La Piemontaise*, Captain L J Epron, and an action commenced at 12.10pm, which lasted until 4.45pm when the *Warren Hastings*, by this time a complete wreck, was forced to strike her colours. (*NC* vol 16, p479 et seq)

On 7 January 1807 the Court of Directors of the Hon East India Company awarded Captain Larkins 500 guineas and the crew 2000 guineas for their gallant defence of the *Warren Hastings*. (*AR* 1807, Chr, p355)

1 July, Nayaden, merchantman   Mr John McAughland was not only the owner of several trawl boats at Plymouth, he had also been for many years a pilot to the Hon East India Company at that port. His end was to be tragic as was that of a fellow pilot Mr Mann.

A Swedish ship *Nayaden*, Carl Danerward master, arrived at Plymouth from Corunna during the evening for orders and was being piloted to her anchorage by Mr Aughland and his partner Mr Mann. The ship's captain asked the two pilots if he could fire off one of his guns, a 4-pounder, which had been loaded for a considerable time and which the crew were unable to draw. The two pilots agreed and when it was fired it burst into several pieces. Mr McAughland had his legs blown off and was killed as was Mr Mann. Two Swedish sailors died the next morning; the mate had both his legs broken and the captain was injured in the groin.

The loss of Mr McAughland and Mr Mann was severely felt at Plymouth as they were excellent seamen and very good pilots. (*SYM*, 7 July; *Times*, 5 July 1806)

20 August, Dover, accommodation ship   The 44-gun *Dover* lying off Deptford in ordinary (reserve), was formerly a prison ship, and had been prepared as a floating barracks for a new division of marines to be called the Woolwich Division. The ship was moored alongside the upper end of that town near the mast houses, close to the quay. From the quay to the ship was a platform which gave easy access and in every sense the ship was as commodious as land barracks.

About 12.30am on this Wednesday the sentinel on the poop of the ship gave the alarm of fire, which was passed to the dockyard. The fire-bell was rung and immediate relief and assistance were afforded to those on board, who were in number about 120 men, 50 women, and half as many children. About 2am the *Dover* was in flames from stem to stern and by 3am had burnt to the water's edge. Such a scene of distress had been seldom witnessed; men dragging their wives out of the ports and mothers screaming for their children; others jumping from the ship into the mud, it being low water at the time and generally confusion prevailed.

Nevertheless only two people lost their lives; both were men. One had been seen on shore and it was supposed that he returned to the ship; but the other poor devil was most unfortunate, he was in the hole for neglect of duty and was also in irons; he was burnt alive.

At the time of the fire the *Dover* was not exactly an old ship by naval standards. She had been built at Parson's Yard at Bursledon, and was launched in the month of May 1786. (*NC* vol 1, p554; *NC* vol 16, pp160-161; *Times*, 21 August 1806)

? August, Heureux, 22 guns The *Heureux*, mounting twenty-two 12-pounder guns was formerly a French privateer, taken on 5 March 1800 by the 36-gun frigate *Phoebe* in the Channel. The Plymouth report of 29 March states: 'Eleven British seamen who were found in arms on board *L'Heureux*, when captured by the *Phoebe*, ...are now in irons, they pretend to be Americans.' (*NC* vol 3, p326). The vessel was shortly afterwards purchased by the British government from its captors.

The *Heureux*, Captain John Morrison, was on passage from the West Indies to Halifax, Nova Scotia, when she foundered with all the crew of 150 men. (*SNL*, 1806)

5 September, Wolf, 18 guns The 18-gun *Wolf*, Commander George Charles MacKenzie, was a sloop of war built at Tanner's Yard, Dartmouth, of deal, a soft wood, and was launched on 4 June 1804.

The vessel struck on Great Inagua in the Windward Passage on 5 September and was completely wrecked although the entire crew were saved. (*SNL*, 1806)

14 September, King George, packet The *King George* packet, Captain Walker, bound from Parkgate to Dublin, sailed from Parkgate at noon on

Sunday 14 September 1806, full tide, weather hazy, drizzling rain and the wind nearly directly south. At 1pm she struck on the Salisbury sandbank (in the Dee estuary) and remained nearly four hours dry, with part of her crew on the sands waiting for the next tide. No apprehensions were then entertained of her having received any injury. On the return of the tide, the wind veered round to the west, and she received the wind and tide right on her side, resting on her anchor. As the tide came in she filled rapidly with water; the night was dark with rain. Her passengers, mostly Irish harvest-men, above a hundred in number, who were going home with the pittances of their labours to their families, were under the hatches. The pumps were soon choked and the water came in so fast on the men in the hold that they had to fight their way upon deck. Her cable broke and she was drifted around with her head towards the tide, and lay upon her side. They were three miles from any vessel and could not, or at least did not give any signal that was heard. The boat was launched and ten of the crew, among which was the captain, and an Irish gentleman, got into it. Her captain seeing some of the best sailors still with the vessel and hoping she might remain with the tide, which had nearly an hour and a half to flow, went again on board; the Irish gentleman and three others followed him. One of the sailors in the boat, seeing a poor Irish sailor boy clinging to the side of the vessel, pulled him by his hair into the boat, cut the rope that fastened it to the vessel, and the tide drove them away. At this time great numbers ran screaming up the mast; a woman with her child fastened to her back, was at the topmast head; the masts broke, the vessel being on her side, and they were drowned.

Only those in the boat, four seamen, a woman and the boy saved their lives, the rest amounting to 106 persons lost theirs.

The packet was formerly a privateer carrying sixteen guns and was afterwards employed as a Harwich packet. This was her second voyage to Dublin for which service she had been lately repaired; yet still considered as too sharp built for the sands. (*NC* vol 17, p72 and vol 22, p384; *AR* 1806, Chr, p444; *MC* vol 6, pp314-315; *Times*, 14 October 1806)

? September, Serpent, 16 guns The *Serpent*, a 16-gun sloop of war, Commander John Waller, was built at Portsmouth dockyard and launched on 3 December 1789. The vessel based at Jamaica foundered with the entire crew, the exact date and place unknown. (*SNL*, 1806)

? September, Martin, 18 guns The 18-gun sloop of war *Martin*, Commander Thomas Prowse, was a new vessel, built at Tanner's yard, Dartmouth, and launched on 1 January 1805. The vessel was on passage to Barbados yet never arrived; she was presumed to have foundered somewhere in the Atlantic and another hundred sailors perished. (*SNL*, 1806)

2 October, Hawthorn, passage boat The *Hawthorn* was a passage boat that plied between Poole harbour and Wareham and was generally known as the market boat.

On Thursday 2 October the *Hawthorn* laden with corn and perhaps overladen left Poole quay between 5 and 6pm. The vessel was carrying twelve passengers as well as Mr Gillingham the owner and two boatmen. Between 6 and 7pm the weather began to freshen with thick fog and small rain that made it extremely dark and about midway on their passage, when just in stays, the skid[40] took the ground which with the pressure of the sails laid her down so that she took in a quantity of water. The place where she grounded being steep she slipped off into deep water and instantly went down.

There were only two survivors: a Mr Everett and a poor woman called White. Although he was wearing a heavy coat he managed to take hold of an oar and then helped the woman to hold one end of it while he held the other and after floating for two miles they came into shallow water. Mr Everett then walked into Wareham and having related the accident to Captain Bartlett they arrived back in a post chaise and Captain Bartlett took the woman into his own house for the night.

On Sunday 5 October seven of the bodies that had been recovered were interred in the churchyard at Wareham. (*SYM*, 6 October; *Times*, 10 October 1806)

12 October, La Constance, 22 guns   La Constance, 22 guns, was taken off Brest on 9 March 1797 by the frigate *San Fiorenzo*, 36 guns, and the *Nymph*, 36 guns, Captains Sir Harry B Neale and John Cook.

La Constance, Captain Alexander Saunderson Burrowes, grounded on 12 October near Cap Frehel (15 miles west of St Malo), after a continued fire of four hours from a battery which was seconded by a number of field pieces in the engagement maintained with *La Salamandre* against an inequality of force which establishes this contest as an illustrious example of valour. (*La Salamandre* was armed *en flute*.) (*SNL*, February 1807)

La Salamandre was also driven on shore and burnt during the engagement; the French salvaged the *Constance*.

Captain Burrowes lost his life in the engagement and those of his crew who survived became prisoners of war. (*SNL*, 1806)

20 October, Athenienne, 64 guns   His Majesty's ship *Athenienne*, 64 guns, commanded by Captain Robert Raynsford, was formerly the French (ex-Maltese) *L'Ateniene*, taken by the British on 4 September 1800 at the surrender of Valletta.

On 16 October 1806 the *Athenienne* with 470 men aboard sailed from Gibraltar for Malta with a fair wind, and on the 20th when they passed Sardinia everyone was in high spirits not doubting but they would arrive at Malta the next day. Yet at 9.30pm that very night when going fully nine knots the *Athenienne* struck on Keith's Reef, not on the Esquerques or Skirky Bank as many historians would have us believe. The rocks were completely underwater and sixty miles from the nearest shore.

Confusion was rife; every soul instantly upon deck, most of them naked, and in such a state of despair as to be unable to make the least exertion to save themselves.

It became immediately necessary to lighten the ship to prevent her falling over on her broadside and the masts were cut away for that purpose; but in less than half an hour after, from the violent concussion of the rocks against her bottom, she filled to the lower deck ports and fell on her beam ends on the larboard side.

Captain Raynsford, who from the first foresaw the total loss of the ship, ordered the boats to be hoisted out, with an idea that they would be useful in towing a raft that was constructing to leeward; but as soon as the two jollyboats were lowered from the quarters and clear of the ship, the men (for there were no officers with them), bore up, and were no more seen by their unhappy shipmates who were left on the wreck. The cutter and barge, in hoisting out, were stove and swamped, and thirty men unable to regain the ship perished. By the fall of the masts several were killed and others injured. Two midshipmen were killed by the spanker boom crushing them between it and the side.

An officer (name not given) takes up the story: 'There now remained only two boats; one had her side knocked in by the falling of the fore mast; the other, the launch, was the only remaining hope. She was still nearly amidships in her station and crowded with men so it was impossible to shove her afloat. However, I leapt into her and was soon followed by Brigadier General Campbell. I made to shove her off, but in vain, even though I leapt out myself as an example, very few followed me. I therefore again took my place in her and after remaining there full half an hour a wave washed us out of the wreck. We had oars all ready and immediately pulled from her, and although we had a hundred on board yet we rowed under her stern thinking we could take in a few more men. But so great was the anxiety of those on the poop to join us that we were in the most imminent danger of being overwhelmed by numbers jumping into her. We had to pull off after taking in only two officers who had jumped from the stern gallery into the sea.' One of these officers had tried in vain to persuade Captain Raynsford to swim to the launch but he refused to quit his post while a man remained.

Captain Raynsford perished with 346 of his crew, only 121 men and 2 women being saved.

The launch steering for Maritimo fell in with a Danish brig early the next morning and put two officers and twenty seamen on her to beat to windward to endeavour to save as many people as might still be clinging to the wreck. It appears that the wreck had broken up during the night, for they found nothing. (*Times*, 22 December 1806; *MC* Duncan, 1808 ed, vol

5, p28 et seq; *NC* vol 16, p493 et seq and vol 17, p57 et seq; Norie, 1827 ed, p463). Note: Norie and *SNL* each state *Athenienne* was lost on 27 October.

30 October, the Jamaica fleet The *AR* 1806, Chr, p452 reported: 'We are sorry to record the serious disaster which has befallen the fleet from Jamaica. The following have foundered:

	Tons	Men	Saved
Pallas	233	12	1
Rashleigh	232	11	all
Forty-second	266	12	1
Ann	220	11	all
Coverdale	385	25	all
Nutwell	426	29	all
Herculean	646	25	22
Frances	326	13	all
Exeter	503	22	2
Erin	290	18	none
Achilles	267	14	all
African	374	20	11
Cumberland	251	—	—

'Seventy people drowned, exclusive of passengers. The *Cora*, 155 tons, and the *Sally*, 263 tons, were abandoned by their crews during the gale. They have since been found at sea and the former carried into Philadelphia. The *Union* is put into Virginia dismasted. The *Jane* sprang a leak and bore away for America. Seven sail bound to America parted for their destination; four of them were known to be arrived. The *Minorca* for London parted off the Havannah. Thirteen parted during the gale, seven of which have arrived; and five remain unaccounted for, viz. *Jean*, 184 tons; *Concord*, 315 tons; *Acteon*, 260 tons; *Pursuit*, 302 tons and *Aurora*, 267 tons.

'Recapitulation: 13 foundered; 2 abandoned; 2 gone to America; 7 parted, bound to America; 1 parted without leave; 71 arrived with *La Franchise*, 44 guns, and the *Penguin*; 7 arrived before; 5 unaccounted for; 1, the *Carmathen* for London, put into Bermuda. Total 109.'

31 October, Wakefield, merchantman The *Wakefield* of Hull, Captain Bruce, lost sight of her convoy on the night of 30 October 1806. On the following morning they hauled in for land, being nearly in the latitude of Oporto, wind about N by E thick and hazy with heavy rain.

A little past 5pm it cleared up; no land was in sight, and they were by reckoning upwards of eight leagues distant. About 6pm, it then being very dark and raining hard the mate went on deck, while the captain changed his clothes, and in a few minutes the ship struck. Captain Bruce then ran upon deck and found her surrounded by rocks; the first heavy sea struck in her stern and hove the ship on her broadside; a second tore away Captain Bruce from the mizzen rigging and he then caught hold of the main topgallant masthead where he hung until he was so much bruised by the floating wreck that he was compelled to let go his hold and endeavour to reach the shore by swimming; which, after having been tossed about in the surf a considerable time and repeatedly carried back again from the beach, he at length accomplished, but so much exhausted that he could only crawl on his hands and knees.

In this manner, with no clothes excepting a coat and shirt, a pair of drawers all torn to pieces, and one stocking, with neither hat, trousers, nor shoes, he reached a ruined hut where he lay about six hours. Finding himself a little refreshed he set out to reach, if possible, some place of shelter; and following the marks of cartwheels about half a mile on the sand he found Thomas Homan, one of the boys, lying there unable to proceed any further.

About a mile and a half from thence Captain Bruce came to a house, but was refused admittance, and compelled to spend the night in the open air; about 8am the next morning he was more favourably noticed, carried to a hut, and supplied with warm clothes. After obtaining refreshment he returned to the place where the ship was wrecked, a ledge of rocks a little to the southward of Ville de Conde; and one of his legs was so severely cut and swollen that he was obliged to be carried back, and for some time was unable to walk. He was carried in a litter to Oporto.

Except for the captain, the boy mentioned above, and a Portuguese sailor, all the crew perished. (*NC* vol 16, p496; *MC* Duncan, 1808 ed, vol 5, p176 et seq)

3 November, Byng's executioner 'Last week in Pontefract workhouse a pauper named Venn, aged 84 years, hung himself.

'The deceased was one of the six marines selected to shoot Admiral Byng and often said that he was sure his ball killed him.' (*AR* 1806, Chr, p453)

4 November, Redbridge, schooner The *Redbridge*, a 12-gun schooner, Lt Edward Burt, was stationed at Nassau on New Providence Island in the West Indies, when she was wrecked on one of the Cays. The crew were saved. (*SNL*, 1806)

10 November, Thames boat accident This was the day of the Lord Mayor's procession, when the chief magistrates went by water to the Court of the Exchequer at Westminster Hall to swear in the new Lord Mayor.

During a fog, as the city procession was passing Hungerford Stairs, a boat, on board of which were fifteen persons, men, women and children, upset, as a consequence of which four persons were drowned. (*Times*, 11 November 1806)

17 November, Glasgow, packet The *Glasgow* packet, Captain Johnson, sailed from Leith on 16 November at 5pm having on board twenty-one passengers. With a fresh leading breeze the vessel continued scudding before the wind till about 2am of the 17th, at which time the captain, whose watch it was, went down below, not to bed but sleeping in his cabin. Previous to his going below he left orders with the watch, consisting of two sailors and an old man at the helm, to give him immediate notice when they came in sight of the Farne Island lights. Yet when they came in sight of them the man at the helm refused giving the captain notice, swearing he knew the navigation as well as any man living, having sailed on that coast for twenty-five years; thus obstinately persevering until the awful moment arrived when the vessel running before the wind at the rate of eight knots struck upon the breakers with a most tremendous shock. Instantly all hands were alarmed, but the vessel being strong built, they had time to gain the deck and fire a few guns, as signals of distress.

The vessel bilged and blew up the hatches and light part of the cargo with great destructive force; she at length settled lower on the rocks and compelled them to stand four feet in the water, while every alternate wave embroiled them ten feet deep. The first boats to arrive at the scene could neither approach nor afford the smallest relief, having no ropes on board. After eight hours in the water and eight persons washed off the rigging, a fishing boat captained by Ralph Wilson arrived from Holy Island and was instrumental in saving the lives of the survivors.

With respect to the crew, the captain excepted, they behaved in a most disgraceful manner; instead of aiding the women and children or any other passengers they secured the boat for themselves and rowed off, quite unmoved by the cries and entreaties of those left on board.

The survivors were at length landed at Bamburgh Castle and one of the survivors, Mr Swanson, continues: 'We were received with the most exemplary attention and humanity by Archdeacon Thorp and his amiable and good family whom I shall ever remember with the most lasting and unbounded gratitude. He clothed those who were nearly naked, gave us every necessary assistance, and even provided us with money to proceed on our respective journeys. To the inhabitants of Holy Island also our praise is due for their good and humane conduct upon this distressing occasion.' (*MC* Duncan, 1808 ed, vol 6, p325 et seq)

24 November, Diana, 38 guns A court martial was held at Portsmouth to try Patrick Hinds, a seaman of HM ship *Diana*, a 38-gun frigate, for writing an anonymous letter to the Admiralty against his captain and officers.

He was sentenced to receive 500 lashes, to be followed by twelve months in the Marshalsea prison. (*NC* vol 16, p513)

9 December, Adder, gunbrig On 27 May 1814 a court martial was held on board HM ship *Gladiator* in Portsmouth harbour to try Lt Molyneaux Shuldham for the loss of the *Adder* gunbrig on 9 December 1806 on the coast of France near Abrevack (Abreval).

It appeared that from lying-to, the vessel had drifted and an error occurred in her reckoning, which was not sufficiently explained to the Court, that in the night time she drifted over a ledge of rocks and could not get out; that Lt Shuldham with great judgement steered her through numerous rocks and breakers (placing himself at the fore topmast head, whence he could clearly see the dangers above and below water) into a small cove, where all the people were rescued; to serve eight years as prisoners of war.

The Court censured him for neglecting to heave the lead during the time the *Adder* was lying to, but in consideration of his judgement in steering her ashore, by which the lives of the crew were saved, only admonished him to be more careful in future. The crew were acquitted. (*NC* vol 31, p486)

12 December, Fort George ferry   A lamentable accident occurred this evening to the ferry which plied betwixt Fort George and Fortrose in the Moray Firth. For some unknown reason the ferry foundered and the four boatmen together with nine or ten passengers lost their lives. (*Times*, 27 December 1806)

25 December, Elgin boat tragedy   'Among the many calamitous occurrences which happened on the 25th ult. we have to mention the loss of three boats with their crews, consisting of eighteen men and three boys, belonging to Stotfield near Elgin. By this unfortunate calamity eighteen widows and about fifty children are left destitute'. (*NC* vol 17, p75)

25 December, Conway ferry   In consequence of a heavy swell in the river Conway the boat carrying the Irish mail coach, with eight passengers, the coachman and the guard, a youth of fifteen, together with the boatmen, fifteen persons in all, was upset and all except two persons perished. (*Times*, 29 December 1806; also in *AR* 1807, Chr, p354)

? December, unknown ship   There was lately driven into the Bay of Donbeg in County Clare the deck of a large vessel to which were fastened by ropes five dead bodies. It was supposed the unfortunate sailors had lashed themselves to the rings of the deck during one of the tremendous storms, and the ship encountering a very heavy sea was dashed to pieces. (*NC* vol 17, p74)

? December, Clinker, gunbrig   The *Clinker* gunbrig, mounting 14 guns, Lt John Salmon, foundered during December, when on a cruise off Le Havre. There were no survivors, and consequently the exact date the vessel was lost is unknown. (*SNL*, 1806) (See 19 February 1800.)

1807

5 January, Nautilus, 18 guns   A letter written by Mr Chillingsworth, the master of the *Nautilus* 18-gun sloop of war, to his mother, dated Zante 21 February 1807, provides an eye-witness account of the loss of the *Nautilus*, and relates also his previous good fortune of not being on board the *Athenienne* when she was wrecked on Keith's Reef on 20 October 1806, (*qv*). It is given here in part:

'In no instance of my life have I ever felt myself more uneasy than these three months past. You no doubt heard of the dreadful misfortune which befell the *Athenienne* in October last. I was providentially saved from the fate of most of my shipmates. Myself and a midshipman were sent on shore at Gibraltar in search of some deserters when unexpectedly our signal was made to get under way, which our ship immediately did, and left us behind as well as others working in the dockyard. I at once applied to the captain of a packet lying there for a passage for ourselves and people to Malta, which he granted; and the next morning we got under way, but upon our arrival at Malta we were surprised to find that the *Athenienne* had not arrived, and the first news we heard of her, which was three days afterwards, was an account brought to Malta by three of the survivors, viz. the purser, doctor and master, who were passengers.

'On the arrival of Sir Thomas Louis' squadron at Malta, I joined HM ship *Standard*, 64 guns, Captain Harvey, as second master; whence we proceeded up the Archipelago to the Dardanelles, where we lay some time, anxiously expecting a war with the Turks. On 2nd January, through the goodness of Captain Harvey, I was appointed master [*ie* the sailing master or navigator] of HM ship *Nautilus*, Captain Palmer.

'On 3 January we left the admiral at the Dardanelles, charged with dispatches of importance for England. On Monday morning the 5th at four o'clock, just as I came on deck to relieve the watch, I was surprised at hearing the man looking out on the forecastle cry out, rocks ahead; it being very dark and hazy they could be seen only a short distance; so that in less than two minutes the ship struck, when she bilged and was almost completely filled to the orlop deck with water. Our only hope was to endeavour to get upon the rocks, which with great difficulty we almost all did, by means of our masts, which providentially fell that way; but the greater part were most dreadfully bruised and lacerated, it blowing very hard and a heavy sea running and breaking over them, so that many of our people weakened by fatigue and benumbed with cold were swept away and perished; and those that remained had no prospect before them.

'Some of our people, as soon as the ship struck, lowered down a boat from the quarter and made the island of Cerigotto, about three leagues distant, where they found a few poor inhabitants who could give us no help on account of the bad weather. It continued blowing with very little intermission till the fifth day, when we gave up all hopes. The captain, first lieutenant and the doctor, and about one half of the people perished of cold and hunger, whilst others yet alive resorted to the dreadful expedient of eating their dead companions and drinking their own urine. On the sixth day about noon the weather became more moderate, when we had the satisfaction to see the boats of the island coming to our deliverance.'

The survivors spent eleven days on Cerigotto from whence they were taken to Cerigo where there was a British Consul, a Greek, 'and a more hospitable, attentive and humane man never lived'. From Cerigo they proceeded to Morea, about twelve leagues distant, and there procured passages on board a Russian frigate, which put to sea on 15 February for Corfu, but on the 18th was driven by bad weather into Zante, from which island Henry Chillingsworth sent the above letter to his mother. (*NC* vol 23, p481 et seq)

The official complement of the *Nautilus* was 121, yet on board at the time of the shipwreck were 122 persons, of whom 62 perished. (*SNL* and the *Times*, 30 March and 18 April, both 1807)

Dalyell, 1812 ed, vol 3, p441 et seq gives what is essentially the same version as above but adds that when the vessel struck turmoil ensued because the ladders below gave way.

12 January, gunpowder explosion at Leiden   A major disaster occurred at Leiden in the Netherlands, where scarcely a single house or building escaped without some damage, and alongside the Rapenburg canal where it happened the houses to a large extent were levelled to the ground.

Many families were sitting down to dinner at the time and all were hurried to one promiscuous grave. Several of the most respectable families in the city, as well as visitors, lost their lives. Several professors of the university were stated to have been killed, but as it was vacation time most of the students were absent. Property to a large extent was lost and showers of glass filled shops and apartments and injured many people.

It seemed that the cause of the tragedy was a vessel laden with five tons of gunpowder, from Amsterdam for Delft. The vessel was lying in the Rapenburg canal when it apparently caught fire and exploded. Of the ship, on board of which were the owner's two sons and a servant, not an atom was visible.

Close to the vessel which blew up lay a yacht, on board of which were from fifteen to twenty persons, not a vestige of whom was to be found.

On Friday 16 January the King visited the injured at Leiden for the second time. He empowered the magistrates of the unfortunate town to make a generous collection throughout the whole kingdom, and ordered that 100,000 guilders out of the treasury be left to the deposition of the Minister of the Home Department for relieving the most pressing necessities of the poor and those who lost their all. (*AR* 1807, Chr, p360 et seq)

20 January, Rotherhithe accident An accident occurred at Rotherhithe. As Captain W Welden of the *Weymouth*, well known as a trader to the Mediterranean, was coming from the ship *Eliza*, then repairing alongside a wharf, a loose plank gave way, when the tide being out Captain Welden fell and hit his head against a timber of the wharf and was killed. Captain Welden was going home to dinner, which he was giving to a Captain Williams, who had just married his eldest daughter. A few years ago his wife fell down the main hatchway of a ship he commanded and was killed. (*Times*, 24 January 1807)

22 January, Felix, 10 guns The 10-gun *Felix*, Captain Cameron, was formerly a French privateer, taken, and purchased by the British government in 1804. The vessel was being used as a cartel for the exchange of prisoners of war when she was lost at Santander in the most distressing manner. Here follows Henry Ellard's affecting narrative, written in one paragraph by himself:

'Honoured captain, I take the liberty of sending you these few lines, to inform you of our misfortune of being cast away in your schooner on the night of 22nd January last, between twelve and three in the morning, on the coast that lies opposite the fort at the entrance of Santander, where every soul perished but me [*SNL*, 1807 says there were three survivors], being 79 in number, including nine prisoners that we got exchanged, being sent here for them as cartel. We arrived here on the 18th of said month, got our prisoners on board on the 19th after twelve; when it came on to blow so strong right in the harbour, that we could not put to sea, being at anchor under the fort from which they hailed us, ordering us to put to sea. We told them we could not as the wind was right in the harbour; that if we did we should be in great danger, as the weather looked bad and the wind was right ahead on the shore. They told us if we did not get out immediately they would fire upon us, which they did at eight o'clock, and at twelve in the night gave us another shot; at four in the morning a third, it then blowing a gale; and at eight in the morning fired again at us, so was forced to weigh anchor, but it was impossible to get out, the wind blowing so strong from the north-west with a terrible sea, which obliged us to anchor at the entrance to the bay, the sea breaking over us every instant, and the gale still increasing. We rode out all that day in the greatest danger, were forced to haul down our cartel flag, and hoisted the English flag union downwards and fired a number of guns in distress; but no assistance attempted to come near us; though a French brig as I have since heard, and several American merchantmen offered to assist us, but the heads of Santander would not permit them to come near us.

We stood in this state all the night of the 20th, the gale continually increasing: and on the 21st we hove eight guns overboard; the sea running so high that it washed our boat overboard, together with a great number of our hands, no one remaining on deck but was lashed to different parts of the ship in which we stood until the 22nd, not knowing what to do, the sea running mountains high, nothing but death before our eyes. The captain, Lieutenant Mitchell, the pilot, and myself, were all that could be seen aboard; the bulwarks being all stove in, we were lashed to the ring-bolts on the quarterdeck, the sea flying over us every instant. About twelve a sea carried away our masts and bowsprit, so that nothing remained but clear decks and a bare hull; we lay lashed until two in the morning when a sea parted our cables, so we did not know what to do. I spoke to Captain Cameron and persuaded him to jump overboard, that in five minutes we should be all to pieces on the beach and murdered by the wreck; we immediately unlashed ourselves and jumped overboard, until the pilot or Mr Mitchell laid hold of my leg, at which time I was obliged to let go of Mr Cameron to clear myself; at length the sea hove me on shore, where I crawled upon my hands and knees, not being able to walk, until I was clear of the sea; where I lay until half-past six the next morning, almost dead, no person being there to assist me. I rose and went towards the hills; but being so weak from the blood I lost from a dreadful wound I received on my head and several parts of my body, so that I could not go any further. At length a Spaniard took me up and dragged me to his house, where I lay for some time bleeding; at light they sent for a doctor who dressed my wounds and ordered me to be put to bed. In this situation I lay for several days, until I was a little recovered, when they took me from thence and put me in prison, where I remain, naked, half starved to death and eaten up with dirt and vermin, no one to assist me, the English agent was once to see me, and told me he could not assist me; as the Spanish Government had me in their charge, and only allows 5d per day, which scarce keeps me alive. I should be happy to be able to relate to you all this; but I am afraid it will be a long time, as I am kept close confined. I should have sent you this account before now, but had no opportunity; at length a friend has offered to deliver this to our ambassador at Lisbon, to have it sent to you.' (*AR* 1807, Chr, p507 et seq)

23 January, Orpheus, 32 guns   The *Orpheus*, 32 guns, Captain Thomas Briggs, was stationed at Jamaica and on this day was wrecked on an uncharted coral bank. The crew were saved. (*SNL*, 1807)

13 February, Woodcock, schooner   The *Woodcock*, a 10-gun schooner built in 1806, was commanded by Lt Isaac Charles Smith-Collett, when she was wrecked on St Michaels in the Western Isles. The crew were saved. (*SNL*, 1807)

13 February, Wagtail, schooner   The *Wagtail*, 8 guns, Lt William Cullis, built the same year as the *Woodcock*, 1806, was lost the same day and at the same place, St Michaels; and once again the crew were saved. (*Times*, 15 April 1807)

14 February, Ajax, 74 guns The 74-gun *Ajax*, Captain Hon Henry Blackwood, accidentally caught fire and was burnt to the water's edge with the loss of approximately 267 lives; only 383 persons being saved out of the 650 on board the vessel at the time of the disaster. The survivors are listed in *NC* vol 17, p424. At a Board of Inquiry, held on board the *Canopus*, by order of Vice-Admiral Sir John Thomas Duckworth KB, dated 16 February 1807, Captain Blackwood of the *Ajax* gave his evidence as follows:

'At 9pm on 14 February 1807 at anchor off the mouth of the Dardanelles, in company with the squadron under Vice-Admiral Sir J T Duckworth KB, just as I had gone to bed, the officer of the watch ran into my cabin and acquainted me there was a great alarm of fire in the after part of the ship: I immediately ordered the drummer to beat to quarters, which was effected; and instantly, as I came out of my cabin, I directed the signal No.12 to be made; which was made and repeatedly enforced by my guns at intervals; I called some of the senior officers of the ship, who went down with me to the after cockpit and the lower deck, from whence the smoke issued; I immediately ordered as much water as possible to be thrown down and the cock to be turned, which I found had been previously done. When I made the signal No. 12 I ordered a boat, with Lieutenant Wood, a midshipman, and a boat's crew, to go and inform all the ships near us of the unfortunate situation of the *Ajax*. I had scarcely been three minutes on the lower deck when I found the impossibility of any officer or men remaining in the cockpit, to endeavour to extinguish the fire; perceiving from the quantity and thickness of the smoke that several men fell down with buckets in their hands, from suffocation.

'To obviate this I desired the lower-deck ports to be hauled up to give air; but very soon finding the harm it produced, I directed them to be lowered down, and the after-hatchway to be covered up, in order to gain time, by stopping the vent of the smoke, for the boats to be hoisted; which measure I was induced to adopt, finding that the fire was of that nature that the ship must soon be in flames. Owing to there not being any cock leading to the after magazine, I ordered the carpenter with his screw to scuttle the after part of the ship; but by this time (a period from the commencement of not more than ten minutes, as near as I can judge) the smoke, though endeavoured to be stifled, had gained so much that though it was bright moonlight we could not distinguish each other, even on deck, by speaking or feeling, consequently all attempts to hoist the boats out were ineffectual, except in the case of the jollyboat, which began to take up the men who had jumped overboard. Immediately as the flames burst up the main hatchway which divided the fore from the after part of the ship; as all hopes were at an end of saving her; I called to everybody to go to the foremost part of the ship; I desired every one to save himself as fast as he could. I had scarcely reached the forecastle when I saw all parts from the centre of the booms aft in a raging flame. When the fire had reached the other part of the forecastle, after exhorting the officers and ship's company to the amount of four hundred, and about the bowsprit, to be cool, and depend on the boats; and also seeing all hopes of saving the ship in vain, I jumped overboard, from the spritsail yard, and being about half an hour in the water, I was picked up by one of the boats of the *Canopus*, and taken on board that ship much exhausted.'

Captain Blackwood then goes on: 'I derived much assistance from all the officers, but particularly from Lieutenants Proctor, Brown, Mitchell and Sibthorp and also the master and Captain of Marines.'

The names of Mitchell and Sibthorp did not appear in the official list of survivors; nor did those of Captain Boyd of the Royal Marines; Mr Owen the surgeon; and Mr Donaldson the master.

The fire, it appeared, had for some time (comparatively speaking) been alight in the breadroom before the alarm was given; for when the first lieutenant and many others broke open the door of the surgeon's cabin the after bulkhead was burst down by the accumulated flames and smoke abaft it, and so rapidly made its progress through the cockpit that it was with difficulty he could regain the ladder, and most of those who accompanied him were suffocated in the attempt.

The *Ajax* had been built at Randall's yard, Rotherhithe and was launched on 3 March 1798, so was not an old vessel. Blackwood, who commanded the *Euryalus* at Trafalgar, became a Baronet in 1814, and a vice-admiral before his death in 1832. (*MC Duncan*, 1808 ed, vol 5, p306 et seq; *NC* vol 17, p319 et seq; and p378 et seq; *NC* vol 1, p547)

18 February, gale in the Downs   The Deal report for 19 February stated: 'At the close of yesterday's letter I anticipated a dreadful gale but about seven in the evening it began to moderate and remained so until eleven o'clock, when it rose again and continued to blow with violence until three a.m. and at daybreak a scene of devastation presented itself. Out of 150 vessels in the Downs prior to the gale, not more than thirty remained; of these, five had lost one or other of their masts or bowsprits, and four had neither stump of a mast nor bowsprit left; but floated on the water as quite sheer hulks. Two vessels, one a man of war, are reported as foundered. A line of battle ship has had her main topmast carried away and is at anchor in a SE direction, distant about six or seven miles. The number of vessels on shore between the south end of Deal and St Margaret's Bay is 13.

'The particulars of nine are as follows: Brig *George* 180 tons, Captain R Burnett, of and from London for Lisbon with iron, hemp and sundry merchandise, on shore near Walmer Castle; ship *Alexander* of Norfolk, Captain W Foster, from London to St Ube's in ballast on shore near Walmer

Castle; sloop *Hope* of Deal, John Moore owner, for Lisbon from Deal with grocery and sundry items, on shore near Walmer Castle; *Holy Christina* of Pappenburgh, 130 tons, Captain J Phillips from London for Charante, in ballast, near Deal Castle; ship *Isis*, 397 tons, copper bottomed, of and from London bound to Grenada with sundry valuable merchandise, on shore near Deal Castle; ship *Griffin* of London, Captain G Dunkin, bound to Demerara on shore near Old Stairs; ship *Vincent* of London, outward bound, on shore near Kingsdown; brig *Providence* of Exeter, Captain George Stable from London for Poole in ballast, on shore near Kingsdown; ship *St George* of London, Captain Palmer, copper bottomed bound to Jamaica, on shore near St Margaret's Bay. The above vessels will be totally lost, three or four have already gone to pieces. The brig *Regard*, Captain Gales, laden with King's slops, bound to Portsmouth is also lost.

'The whole of these ships, entirely lost; little or nothing will be saved.' (*Times*, 21 February 1807)

The storm of the night of 18/19 February was also fraught with peril for ships of the Channel fleet off the coast of France; and while several were driven by stress of weather into French ports where the crews became prisoners, other vessels were unfortunate enough to founder with all hands. The *Ignition* excepted, the following are taken from the Navy List of 1807:

Prospero, bomb vessel, Commander William King, foundered off Dieppe; seven of the crew drowned, the rest made prisoners.

Inveterate, gunbrig, 14 guns, Lt George Norton, wrecked off St Valery en Caux, four of the crew died, the rest became prisoners. (See also 24 March 1807 and 31 May 1814.)

Speedwell, gunbrig, 14 guns, Lt William Robertson, founded off Dieppe. The crew perished.

Griper, gunbrig, 14 guns, Lt Edward Morris, foundered off Ostend. The entire crew perished.

Ignition, fire vessel, 4 guns, Lt Philip Griffin, wrecked off Dieppe; the master, a midshipman and four seamen died; sixteen were saved and made prisoners of war. (*Times*, 24 March 1807)

Magpie, a 14-gun schooner, Lt Edward Johnson, was driven into Perros-Guirec by the storm and there taken possession of, with the crew becoming prisoners of war.

19 February, aftermath of the gale 'At Dover, the gale having abated this morning, the shore was lined with people a-wrecking. The beach for several miles between Dover and Deal is covered with pieces of ship timber, soldiers' belts, cartouche boxes, hats, shoes, empty casks and remnants of wearing apparel.

'Among the fragments of the wreckage I found some beams of a ship which appeared to be of a large size, as they were 26 and 27 feet long, some large knees, copper bolted, were also lying near them. Shortly after the body of a lad apparently between fourteen and fifteen years of age, with a fresh complexion and blue eyes, was found. The stern piece of a boat shortly washed on shore marked *St George* of London, Captain S Palmer, was marked inside. The shore further on was strewn with salted herrings, salt beef, pork, coals and some crucibles. Some of the crew are saved at St Margaret's, but of the crew of the ship which foundered off here, we can hear nothing.' (*Times*, 21 February 1807)

26 February, Utrecht, 44 guns A messenger arrived at Thurso on 3 March from Kirkwall requesting volunteers to be sent to the island of Sanday where a Dutch 44-gun frigate, the *Utrecht*, Commodore Baron de Castreo, was wrecked on or near the Holms of Ire on 26 February during a violent snowstorm, the worst for twelve years. The vessel drove on shore during the morning yet it was 6pm before the crew were all landed, and by that time of the 500 men on board a hundred had perished through exposure.

The *Utrecht* had been seen on Sunday 22 February before the storm, with two other frigates lying with springs on their cables in a Dutch port, when they each had 200 troops on board. At 3am on 7 March Colonel Sinclair with 400 volunteers embarked on board eight smacks, which had been detained by contrary winds, and sailed with a westerly wind and full of martial ardour for Kirkwall. A major of the line who was at Thurso with a recruiting party offered to take command of the volunteers but was refused. He was much displeased and left at once with his small party in order it was supposed that he might raise a few hands elsewhere, and be beforehand with the volunteers in making prisoners of the Dutchmen.

The bustle created by the landing of so many men from the wreck had subsided by 12 March, by which date 300 of the volunteers had returned to Thurso, leaving behind the remainder to assist the inhabitants to take care of the Dutch, who had given themselves up prior to the arrival of the volunteers. The *Utrecht* had on board a great quantity of provisions, such as cheese, potatoes, brandy and gin, and was bound for Curacao. The dispatches on board were sent to London.

Thirty-six of the Dutchmen joined the Royal Navy and were put on board the *Texel* in Leith Roads. (*Times*, 17, 18, 24, and 25 March 1807)

? February, L'Atalante, 16 guns L'Atalante, a 16-gun sloop of war, was taken by the *Phoebe*, 36 guns, Captain Robert Barlow, eighteen leagues south-west of Scilly on 10 January 1797.

Ten years later the *Atalante*, commanded by Lt John Bowker, was wrecked off Rochefort during a gale and although the crew were saved yet several became prisoners of war.

Atalante was not a seaworthy vessel and when the wind blew fresh she made twenty inches of water an hour, yet when Lt Bowker applied for the ship to be surveyed, it was refused. In parliament Sir Samuel Hood declared that he had the word of Commodore Keats that the ship was fit to go to any part of the world. (*SNL*, 1797 and 1807)

? February, Busy, 18 guns   The *Busy* brig sloop, 18 guns, Commander Richard Keilly, upset and foundered on the Halifax station. Of the crew who numbered 120 there were no survivors. (*SNL*, 1807)

? March, Blenheim, 74 guns   The *Blenheim* was built at Woolwich in 1761 as a 90-gun Second Rate ship of the line. By the end of the century she was an old ship that had the additional misfortune to be so wretchedly hogged that the builders strongly remonstrated against her proceeding to sea. (*NC* vol 38, p358). But instead of being broken up the vessel was cut down a deck to a 74 during the years 1801-1802, and the Portsmouth report of 22 October 1802 (*NC* vol 8, p436) stated that the *Blenheim* was in a state of forwardness and ordered to be fitted with four months stores. A few days later on the evening of 7 November, having taken on board Captain Samuel Hood of the navy and other commissioners appointed to make commercial arrangements at Trinidad, the *Blenheim* sailed from Portsmouth and made Barbados on 8 December after a passage of 30 days, under the command of Captain Bover (*Times*, 31 January 1803). On 18 September 1804 the *Blenheim* was back in Portsmouth from Barbados, and commanded by Captain Bland. (*Times*, 20 September 1804)

In 1805 Captain Austin Bissell was appointed to the *Blenheim* as Rear-Admiral Sir Thomas Troubridge's flag captain, and the ship sailed for Madras, at which place in 1807 the rear-admiral received orders to take command at the Cape of Good Hope.

On 12 January 1807 the *Blenheim*, with a crew of 650 men, sailed from Madras in company with the *Harrier* sloop of war, commanded by Rear Admiral Troubridge's son; and the *Java*, 32 guns, Captain George Pigot. At this point it is worth recalling the condition of the *Java*. The ship was formerly the *Maria Reijgersbergen*, a Dutch 36-gun frigate taken by the *Caroline*, 36 guns, Captain Peter Rainier off Batavia (Jakarta) on 18 October 1806 and renamed *Java*. The vessel then sailed approximately 2500 miles to Madras, during which voyage it became obvious that the *Java* was an old vessel and alarmingly crank (unstable) and quite unfit for a 5000-mile voyage. (*NC* vol 38, p358)

The best account of what happened on the voyage of 12 January is that given on p4 of the *Naval and Military Record* of 3 January 1895, and although written nearly ninety years after the event it was nevertheless taken from an unknown contemporary account and remains the most complete record, at least so far as the present author has been able to discover; it follows, verbatim:

'This is what is on record of her (*Blenheim*) sailing from Madras Roads.

'Utterly unseaworthy and required constant pumping even when in harbour. Her back was broken, her frame shaken to pieces and she was hogged excessively. In fact her head and stern fell so much that she rose like a hill amidships, to such an extent that a person at the door of the poop cabin could not see the sentry on the forecastle below his waist. Sir E Pellew had entreated Rear-Admiral Troubridge to select any other ship on the station for his flag but Sir Thomas refused. He had every confidence in his own ability to keep the *Blenheim* afloat; perhaps mindful of the way he had saved the *Culloden* when aground at the Battle of the Nile. His own flag captain Austen Bissell formally reported the condition of the *Blenheim* to Rear Admiral Troubridge, who told him that if he was afraid he might go ashore, a taunt that compelled the unfortunate officer to sacrifice himself with his ship's company. Admiral Troubridge thought to force the broken keel back into its place by getting put in an extra heavy main mast, and could not be convinced that he was increasing the danger. The distinguished officer who supplied these particulars [possibly Pellew himself] went on board the *Blenheim* on the day she sailed, in order to take leave of the captain. He found Captain Bissell had just written a last farewell to his wife, from his conviction that the *Blenheim* must inevitably founder.

'On 12th January 1807 the *Blenheim* sailed from Madras Roads with the *Java* frigate and the *Harrier* sloop of war. On 5th February the *Harrier* parted company off Rodriguez Island in a very heavy gale in which the *Blenheim* and *Java* (with 300 crew) were seen to be making repeated signals of distress. They were never seen again.

'All that was heard more about the *Blenheim* and her consort was this. The captain of a French frigate, the *Semillante*, gave information many years afterwards when at Plymouth that he had sighted the *Blenheim* near Rodriguez, in a heavy gale of wind on 18th February 1807.

'News also came, more than a year after the event, by way of Calcutta (to which place it had been brought by a frigate which had touched at the Island of Sainte Marie, off the north east coast of Madagascar), that in February 1807, two vessels had arrived in distress, had put in for repairs and sailed again; the description of the officers given, exactly answering to Sir T Troubridge and his companions. The inhabitants of the Isle of Bourbon (Reunion) had also according to the same authority caught sight after the gale of a line of battle ship in distress with a rear-admiral of the white's flag flying.

'A special search was also made with the sanction of the French authorities in the various French possessions in that part of the Indian Ocean, by Captain Edward Troubridge of the *Harrier*, the missing admiral's own son, but Telemachus could find no tidings of Ulysses.

'No other news of the *Blenheim* ever reached England and no clue was ever found to point to the spot or fix the date where and when the *Blenheim* foundered.'

According to a letter from an officer on board the *Harrier* sloop at the Cape of Good Hope, dated Table Bay 13 March, they lost sight of the *Blenheim* and *Java* in the afternoon of the 1st of the month, during a hard gale off Mauritius in position 20°21'S 64°11'E. The night was awful beyond description; it blew a perfect hurricane with a most tremendous sea. The *Blenheim* was in a very decayed state and was particularly bad in her hull. (*NC* vol 17, p506)

The *Java* was certainly badly manned, men having been taken from any and every available source, simply to man the vessel and this probably contributed to her loss. At least 950 men perished with the two ships, and it would appear that if Rear-Admiral Pellew actually did offer Troubridge alternative ships (which cannot now be proved), then the responsibility for the deaths of so many men must surely fall upon the latter. Since Troubridge's appointment effectively halved Pellew's command, thre was no love lost between the two admirals. In fact, there was a persistent rumour on the lower deck that Pellew had virtually driven Troubridge to sea, expecting his destruction.

The *Java* appears in *SNL*, 1 December 1807.

4 March, Blanche, 38 guns The *Blanche*, 38 guns, Captain Sir Thomas Lavie, was formerly the Spanish frigate *Amfitrite*, 36 guns, taken by the 80-gun *Donegal*, Sir R J Strachan, off Cadiz, on 25 November 1804. (*SNL*, February 1807)

The *Blanche* sailed from Portsmouth on 3 March 1807 and next morning made Portland Lights, distant about four leagues; they afterwards steered a west course until 8pm, then west by south half south. At 8pm it began to blow hard; and, from being under all sail, they reduced to close-reefed fore and main topsails, and got down topgallant yards. Ushant by their reckoning now bore SSW half W sixteen leagues. The captain left orders in writing to haul to the northward, the wind being ENE when the ship had run ten leagues, which Sir Thomas Lavie thought a good position to join Admiral Sir James Saumarez in the morning.

At 11pm Lt Apreece awoke the captain to say that it blew harder; on which he ordered the ship to be brought to the wind on the starboard tack, and the fore topsail to be taken in. The lieutenant had scarcely got out of the cabin before the vessel struck. Everybody was on deck in an instant; sails were clewed up and the anchors were let go; they rode a little until she parted from her anchors and was driven on the rocks.

The night was dark and cold, and there was no possibility of discriminating whether the rocks were distant from the land or connected with the shore; happily it proved the latter. The captain ordered the masts to be cut away and recommended the officers and men to stay by him and the ship to the last; a few hands got into the quarter boats, and they were no sooner on the water than they were dashed to pieces; it was about high water; and while the tide flowed the ship lay tolerably easy, until it began to fall, when tremendous breakers covered them.

The captain remained by the wheel until the vessel divided amidship, when he fell overboard seaward. The crew who were all on the side hauled him up immediately, and 'caressed him as their father'. In this state they lay about three hours when the water left the wreck sufficient for them to attempt a landing; and with the exception of a few they got safe on shore. At daylight not two pieces of wood were left together and the masts were shattered into shivers.

The crew who had saved nothing made a most shabby appearance. A cask of rum was the only thing found on the shore, which, after the captain was carried to a cottage, some were so imprudent as to broach, by which about fifteen died. They landed on a shocking coast, but every attention possible was paid to them. Having been marched about thirty miles, they arrived at Brest, where they were very comfortably lodged and fed in the Navy Hospital. Sir Thomas Lavie was accommodated at the house of the Commander-in-Chief, M Cefforelli, a perfect gentleman. Captain Lavie stated that it was his intention to put all the boys to school and to secure their maintenance while they continued in France. (*NC* vol 7, pp318-319)

Those saved from the wreck numbered: 26 officers; 180 seamen and 25 marines; while those lost numbered 45 including 20 marines. The crew were prisoners of war for seven years, but were released on the abdication of Napoleon.

On 2 June 1814 Sir T Lavie was tried for the loss of the *Blanche* on the coast of France near Abrevack in the month of March 1807, when on passage from Spithead to her station at Brest with the blockading squadron. Owing to the compasses being affected by the iron stanchions, cranks and arms under the half deck, the reckoning of the officers was in error. Captain Lavie and his officers were all honourably acquitted. (*NC* vol 31, p488; *MC* Duncan, 1808 ed, vol 6, p411 et seq)

9 March, Mary, transport The *Mary* transport, Captain Drysdale, sailed from England under convoy of the *Spartan* and on 9 March was wrecked a few miles east of Cadiz, with 25,000 stand of arms on board. The Spanish took possession of her but the *Beagle* gun brig came to an anchor near by and burnt the ship with her stores. See also 17 June 1808.

On board the *Mary* as passengers were the Countess of Strasoldo and Mrs Spencer-Smith, who were fortunate enough to arrive at Gibraltar on 19 March in a flag of truce vessel from Algeciras. (*Times*, 11 and 18 April 1807)

15 March, Leith, packet The *Leith* packet of Leith, from Hull to Leith, was lost at the mouth of the Humber on this Sunday night when all on board perished. (*Times*, 18 March 1807)

24 March, the kindness of St Valery Three of the fishermen of Hastings who were cast ashore on the coast of France in the late storm (18 February) returned safely home with their boat and nets a few days ago. As soon as they landed they delivered to Mr Milward a polite communication from the chief magistrate of St Valery, informing him that from motives of humanity towards these unfortunate people he had applied to the Minister of the Marine, and obtained permission for them to return to their country, by virtue of the passport which they would show him: 'that he would use his best endeavours to alleviate their sufferings whilst they remained in his district. That he had refitted their boat in which he hoped they would be safely carried back to their home, being amply provided with everything requisite for their subsistence on the voyage.' The whole of this is confirmed by the testimony of the fishermen who are full of gratitude for the kindness and attention shewn them by the inhabitants of St Valery. (*Times*, 24 March 1807)

24 March, Jupiter, transport The *Jupiter* transport ran on the Little Russel rock off the coast of Guernsey on this Tuesday evening and became a total loss. Forty survivors, men of the 56th Regiment, arrived at Portsmouth on 2 April in three Guernsey traders. The *Jupiter* was one of several transports on passage to Portsmouth with men of the 18th, 56th and 101st Regiments, who were to proceed on foreign service. (*Times*, 4 April 1807)

31 March, Eda, merchantman The brigantine *Eda*, from Lynn for London, laden with timber and planks, was lost upon the Shipwash sandbank, about fifteen miles from Harwich. (*Times*, 2 April 1807)

? March, Cesar, 18 guns A French 18-gun brig corvette, the *Cesar*, was taken in Verdon Roads in the Gironde on 15 July 1806 by a division of boats under the command of Lt E R Sibly, who received seven wounds for his part in the enterprise.

The vessel, now a Royal Navy ship, was driven on shore on the coast of the Gironde sometime during March and completely wrecked. More than fifty of her crew perished; the remaining forty-five being taken as prisoners of war. (*SNL*, 1806 and 1807; Norie, 1827 ed, p465)

15 April, a Portuguese Guineaman 'A letter from Barbados says: The only thing engaging the attention of the inhabitants here just now is a Portuguese Guineaman of 250 tons. The vessel left Angola for Para with 700 negroes on board and came to this place in distress, having thrown overboard 200 of her slaves to prevent the others from starving.' (*Times*, 15 April 1807)

18 April, capsize at Harwich On this Saturday afternoon, about 3pm, one of the companies of the 79th Regiment, with their wives and children, having to cross the ferry between Languard Fort and Harwich, took their passage in a large boat of eighteen tons burthen, the usual ferry being too small to contain them all. Shortly after quitting the beach the boat was overtaken by a violent squall of wind and capsized. No other vessel being at hand to help them, except for ten men, the whole perished. The company consisted in the main of highlanders and fifty-nine were drowned as well as the captain. The number of women and children could not be ascertained. On Sunday several of the bodies were washed on shore and taken to the fort to be owned. It was regrettable as most of the unfortunate men had distinguished themselves in Egypt. (*Times*, 22 April 1807)

16 May, Quebec, brig The American ship *Commerce*, laden with timber from Savannah for a market arrived at Plymouth on the morning of 7 June.

On 16 May she fell in with a large brig called the *Quebec*, of Quebec, a mere wreck with not a soul on board in position 45°21'N 31°20'W, supposed to have been plundered and deserted. Masts, bowsprits and pumps, all cut away even with the deck and not an inch of rope left on board. She appeared to be nearly a new vessel and had two feet of water in her hold. She was set fire to and destroyed. (*Times*, 10 June 1807)

29 May, Ganges, East Indiaman The East Indiaman *Ganges*, Captain T Harrington, was one of seven East Indiamen on passage to England under convoy of the 36-gun *Concorde* frigate. The *Ganges* had the misfortune on 21 May to part company from all the others except the ship *St Vincent*, Captain Jones. The *Ganges* had been in a leaky state for some time, which had necessitated that she should proceed only under easy sail.

Captain Harrington placed himself under the orders of Captain Jones who continued to keep his ship as near the *Ganges* as circumstances would permit until the moment she foundered in position 38°22'S 19°50'E, almost due south of Cape Aghulas. The vessel was carrying 209 persons, all of whom were taken on board the *St Vincent*; not a single life was lost. The ship's company, including men of the 77th Regiment working their passage home, behaved in the most exemplary manner.

The following is an extract from the logbook of the ship *Ganges*.

'Friday 29th May 1807. a.m. a light breeze and fair, the swell much gone down, but the ship still rolling dreadfully, and rendering it dangerous for the boats to take persons on board, whether astern or alongside. At ¼ past noon the *St Vincent* being still nearly four miles from us, there being seven feet water in the well, the stern post being now four inches off the deadwood,⁴¹ and the ship ungovernable by the helm, got the launch at all risks alongside, having in vain attempted to put the ladies on board of her out of the stern gallery, though the railing was cut away for the purpose. At ¾ past noon she left us with all the passengers, except a Mr Rolliston, of the Bombay civil establishment, who insisted in a manner most friendly to me, and the most honourable to himself, in remaining on board until my officers and self quitted the ship. At one p.m. the yawl left us with the sick people, and some others of the ship's company and soldiers of His Majesty's 77th Regiment still working at the pumps with unabated vigour and good will. At three p.m. eight feet water in the well and the ship sinking fast. At ½ past four, nine feet of water in the well, and seeing the launch on her return called the people up from the pumps. Down both cutters and sent them off as full as prudence would permit, with orders not to return. At five, the launch, yawl and one of the *St Vincent*'s boats came alongside, and by ½ past five had all left the ship again full of people, the third and fifth officers in charge of the launch and yawl. Immediately after the boat had quitted us, mustered the people, and there being 49 men still on board, again set the pumps to work, as the night was closing in fast, and the *St Vincent* still at some distance from us. At six p.m. in company with the chief officer, gunner and carpenter, visited the gun-room for the last time, found the head of the sternpost had forsaken the transom full six inches, the garboard seam of the counter two inches open, for six or seven feet down at least, the wood ends five inches off the stern-post, and all the timber gone at the heels. At ½ past eight p.m. the *St Vincent*'s boat and the yawl once again came alongside and then (and not till then) were the pumps finally quitted by my orders. Filled the two boats and despatched them, to return no more; five minutes afterwards the launch came up to us, and at ¾ past eight, accompanied by Mr Rolliston, the chief, fourth and sixth officers, and all that remained of the ship's company, I quitted the *Ganges* and twenty minutes later boarded the *St Vincent*.'

When the captain finally left the *Ganges*, she had ten feet of water in the well, had settled half way up her bends, was wholly ungovernable by the helm and the upper works generally were in motion. The ship foundered at noon the following day. (*NC* vol 18, p216 et seq)

17 June, Bowaniong, merchantman The Portuguese ship *Bowaniong*, Captain John Napremassena, on her voyage from Calcutta towards China, dropped her Bengal pilot at the end of April and stretched across the bay till 4 May, when in position 16°57′N 91°07′E the ship encountered a severe gale accompanied by a heavy swell, in which the ship laboured very much and became leaky. The gale increasing, it became necessary for the preservation of the ship to cut away the main and mizzen masts, yet with the masts gone and the gale further increasing she was exposed to the swell which broke over the hull with great force and frequency.

Three weeks later on 26 May at 8am the weather considerably moderated and the crew found almost the whole of their waterbutts stove in so that it became necessary, independent of their other wants, to go ashore for water. With what sail they could make they stood to the northward where they anchored off Saduha, at which place they obtained water and provisions but there were no facilities for ship repairing. On 16 June they stood out from Saduha, desirous of reaching either Cheduba Island or Chittagong. However, on the following day another gale occurred and the leak gaining in spite of all their exertions, they came to an anchor in a small somewhat sheltered bay at 6pm when the gale increasing, at 11pm the ship drove and soon struck on a narrow insulated rock, upon which it was evident she must soon go to pieces.

The captain ordered as many as possible into the longboat while others sought safety on spars, planks and hencoops, the captain meanwhile remaining on the wreck with five or six others trying to make a raft. At sunrise those in the long boat saw that the ship had gone to pieces and they were despondent. It was said afterwards that Captain Napremassena, a brave sailor, deserved a much better fate. It was noon before the longboat made the shore where the men were soon seized by natives and taken to the rajah by whom they were held as prisoners for four months during which time they experienced every privation and indignity.

On 17 October 46 of the men were released and provided with a small fishing boat, but cramped for room and exposed to the weather the men decided to once more go ashore, and walking without food or refreshment they arrived four days later at Chittagong, where James Bruce Laing, the judge and magistrate at Chittagong, succoured their distresses with zeal, liberality and money to help them to return to Calcutta.

Of the 60 men who had embarked at Calcutta 46 arrived at Chittagong, *viz* 9 Europeans, 2 Chinese, and 35 lascars. Those who died totalled 7: Captain Napremassena, 3 lascars, 2 Chinese and one Christian. Those detained at Ava by the rajah totalled 7. (*NC* vol 19, p395 et seq)

11 July, Charles, schooner   At midnight off Portland, Maine, the schooner *Charles*, Captain Adams, of Portland with eighteen passengers on board from Boston, Massachusetts, struck during a thick fog upon a reef of rocks a little to the west of the lighthouse. The vessel was thrown on her beam ends by the violence of the sea and some passengers were swept to their deaths by seas which broke over her.

The captain and three men managed to get ashore at 2am, but the captain endeavoured to get back on board to rescue his wife and he was lost in the attempt. One survivor said that when he left the wreck, four men, a woman and a boy, were in the shrouds, yet of the twenty-two persons on board only six survived. (*Times*, 14 September 1807)

30 July, Ann, brig   The brig *Ann* of Newcastle belonged to Messrs Lotheringtons, and was chartered to proceed from Newry in Ireland (where she was delivering her cargo) to Archangel in Russia. The navigation to this place, which is situated in the White Sea, is considered by skilful seamen to be one of the most difficult and dangerous in the world, and can only be performed with safety in the mild months of summer. The *Ann* was a good ship and had been at the above place before, under the command of Captain Robert Potter, who had effected the voyage from London to Archangel, and returned with a full cargo in three months, a proof of his consummate skill and perseverance.

On 17 July 1807 the *Ann* sailed from Newry but the opening prospect was gloomy; the season was far advanced and in a few days the wind blew in a most violent manner from SE with heavy rain, and almost impenetrable fogs, which drove them with irresistible force too far to the northward and westward.

After several days they managed to obtain by observation their bearings, position 71°N 10°W, and when the fog dispersed they found themselves surrounded by tremendous mountains of ice. With the gale then blowing it was not possible to tack to avoid the floes and one which struck and pierced the starboard bow threw the ship on to her beam ends, from which position she never recovered. The pumps were manned in an endeavour to keep the vessel above water and reach Jan Mayen Island, which the crew actually saw yet could not fetch, and the water being above the beams, the boats were hoisted out from the almost waterlogged vessel; because of the condition of the *Ann* the crew were able to procure only a very small supply of biscuit and water, which from the outset they decide to ration themselves to one glass of water and half a ship's biscuit a day.

They quitted the *Ann* on 30 July and shaped their course for Norway, 1400 miles away. During the twenty-two days they were in the open boats they suffered greatly, from the intense cold, from the lack of food and water, and from the bitter weather and the spray of the sea breaking over them. By the twenty-third day the condition of the men and boys was truly deplorable, several suffering from frostbite and exposure, but at this time when they were most despondent they were taken up by some Norwegian fishermen and towed into Christiansund.

The wrecked mariners were treated with the greatest humanity by the people of Christiansund, but as soon as they had recruited their strength they were marched to Drontheim as prisoners of war; while the two apprentices were returned to London where they both had both their legs amputated as a result of frostbite. The owners of the *Ann* used their exertions to remit the unhappy sufferers pecuniary aid; whilst all praise was given to the people of Norway who succoured them in their distress. (*MC* Duncan, 1808 ed, vol 5, p161 et seq)

12 September, Glasgow, merchantman The *Glasgow*, Captain McIvers, from Drogheda with bran and glue for Liverpool, was seen going down to the southward of Clogher Head and every soul perished. The vessel had sailed less than ten miles from Drogheda and as the tops of her masts were visible at low water it is possible that she sprang a leak and the crew had tried to run her ashore. (*Times*, 23 September 1807)

29 September, Golden Rule, merchantman The ship *Golden Rule*, Captain Austin, sailed from Wiscasset, Maine, with a cargo of timber on 8 September 1807. On the 29th she experienced a severe gale from the south-east, and at 8am they discovered she had sprung a leak and had four feet of water in her hold: at 9am it had increased to eight feet notwithstanding they had two pumps going and were throwing her deck load overboard, which they were enabled to do but slowly, from the sea driving the planks about the deck and wounding the crew.

By 10am the water had risen to twelve feet, the gale had increased, and the crew and all on board were quite exhausted, then going into the cabin they found she was welling fast. The main and mizzen masts were now cut away to prevent her upsetting, and she was quite clear of her deck load. By 11am she was full up to the main deck and all the bulkheads were gone.

It now occurred to the crew to endeavour to save some bread and Mr Boyd the first mate, with great resolution, went into the cabin and gave out some bread and two bottles of rum: but so rapidly did she fill, from the timber cargo shifting, that he was forced to leave through the skylight to save himself. Their small stock of provisions was put into the binnacle as a secure place but within a few minutes a tremendous sea struck them, carried away the binnacle and washed two men overboard. The waterlogged ship was kept before the wind during that night and next day another seaman died, this time of exposure.

The ship's deck was now blown up, her side stove and the crew had all but given themselves up, when on the 30th at noon they had the satisfaction to see a sail bear down for them. About 3pm she came alongside and proved to be the brig *George* of Portland; Captain Wildridge sent his longboat and took them from the wreck. (*NC* vol 19, pp58-59; *MC* Duncan, 1808 ed, vol 5, pp304-305)

10 October, Salisbury, transport The *Salisbury* transport, Captain Purdy, was one of several transports returning from the Copenhagen expedition, that were kept off Yarmouth for two or three weeks without the troops, their wives and children being allowed to land. As a direct consequence of this order the *Salisbury* was lost on the Long Sand (at the mouth of the Thames estuary), during the night of Tuesday 10 October, when 241 soldiers and part of the crew were drowned. Captain Purdy was fortunate enough to have been saved; but the number of women and children on the ship appears to have been unknown.

As late as 14 November 54 transports of the Baltic fleet were still missing; and those ships that had not been permitted to land their troops at Yarmouth, had to proceed to Portsmouth, and in so doing 1500 lives were lost, many more in fact than were lost in the battle at Copenhagen. (*Times*, 16 November 1807)

16 October, Pert, brig The *Pert* brig, Captain Donald Campbell, was lost on the Island of Margarita off the coast of Venezuela during a gale, when the master and ten men were drowned. The brig was formerly the *Buonaparte*, a French privateer. [Taken by the 18-gun sloop *Cyane*, Hon George Cadogan, off Mariegalante, 12 November 1804. (Norie, 1827, p507).] (*Times*, 6 January 1808)

20 October, Maria Elizabeth, galliot The *Halcyon* 18-gun sloop of war, Captain Pearce, fell in with the wreck of the galliot *Maria Elizabeth*, which had lost her bottom on one of the reefs of the Kattegat. All her masts were gone and, as no-one was found on board by the people of the *Halcyon* who boarded her, it was supposed that the entire crew had perished. (*Times*, 29 October 1807)

22 October, Alexander, transport Captain Russell, who arrived at Salem, Massachusetts, on 13 November 1807 from St Petersburg, communicates the following distressing account of the loss of the English transport *Alexander*:

'28th October, position 47°N 51°W, fell in with a boat having on board twenty-one living persons, among whom were a woman and child, apparently in a most distressed situation. After some conversation I took them on board, and from the most intelligent was informed they sailed from Monte Video on 9th August in the ship *Alexander*, Captain Richard Howard, an English transport ship, No. 421. That they sailed under convoy of the frigate *Unicorn* and *Thetis* sloop of war.

'There were about a hundred and ten persons on board of the *Alexander*; that on 20th October the ship being in a very leaky condition, they were under the necessity of carrying short sail, by which means they lost the convoy; and on the 22nd the leak increased to such a degree that with both pumps going and bailing at the hatchways they could not keep her free. The captain thought it advisable to quit the ship, took the small boat for his preservation, and rowed around the ship several times. Meantime the longboat was got ready and hoisted out but unfortunately bilged in going over the side. Thirteen sailors, fifteen soldiers, one woman and child, however, kept in the boat and found means to keep her from sinking. They had not got far off when the ship seemingly blew up and foundered immediately. This was about ten o'clock p.m. They afterwards spoke with the captain in the small boat, who told them to steer NE and NE by N, as that course would carry them near the coast of England, from which he said they were but a short distance. They had only four biscuits in the boat, three gallons of spirits, and one pound of raisins. They had been in the boat six days, during which seven soldiers died for want, two of whom lay dead in the boat when they came alongside; they had cut one man up and had eaten of his flesh; some remained in the boat when they saw the ship; but on seeing her they threw it overboard, Finding this to be the case, humanity claimed my assistance, and as the ship *Brutus* was still in sight (not being overstocked with provisions myself for so large a number), I thought it prudent to make a signal and lay-by till she came up. At one p.m. the *Brutus* came up and spoke. I informed the captain of this circumstance and wished him to take part of the people on board. He took eight of them but had no provisions for more. Accordingly I sent them on board, with liberty, if he chose, to take in the boat, it being a very fine one. He took the boat on board.

'From what these people observed it appears that their ship founder-ed between the 39th and 40th degrees of north latitude.' (*MC*, Duncan, 1808 ed, vol 6, p328 et seq) The *Times* 1 January 1808 printed the above article verbatim.

A hospital ship, the *Alexander* was very old. On board were sick and wounded of General Whitelocke's army, as well as some ladies, the widows of officers who were killed at Buenos Aires during the ill-fated British expedition to the River Plate. (*Times*, 16 November 1807)

The following were on board the *Alexander*: Lt Fairweather, agent of transports; Doctor Chambers, staff surgeon; Messrs Buxton and Buchanan, hospital mates; Mrs Captain Johnson, 36th Regiment, Mrs Willson, besides several others, names unknown, and about eighty wounded soldiers. (*Times*, 18 November 1807)

26 October, Subtle, schooner The Bermuda Islands are surrounded by the *Sea Venture* reef, so called from a ship of that name which was wrecked on the reef on 28 July 1609.

Almost 200 years later on 26 October 1807 *Subtle*, an 8-gun schooner commanded by Lt William Dowers, was wrecked off the NW end of Long Bar, on the western end of the reef, approximately in position 32°16'40"N 65°02'20"W. The crew saved themselves in the ship's boats. (*Findlay's North Atlantic Memoir*)

29 October, Rambler, merchantman The ship *Rambler* of Leith, James Norris master, cleared out of Thurso in September last for Picton (Nova Scotia) with emigrants. They left Stromness 1 October and on the 29th of the same month were wrecked near the Bay of Bulls in Newfoundland.

When the ship left Thurso she had 130 passengers, 14 seamen, the captain and surgeon. The only survivors were 3 passengers, the 2nd mate and 4 seamen, so that 138 persons perished. (*Times*, 6 January 1808)

31 October, Augustus Caesar, transport The transport *Augustus Caesar*, from Copenhagen for England with part of the German Legion on board, was run foul of by the *Inflexible*, 64 guns, during the night of 27 October, and after being dismasted, it was on the 31st driven upon the Dutch coast near Ter Hyde, where to avoid being wrecked, the captain brought the ship to an anchor. As soon as the officer at Ter Hyde discovered the vessel, he sent to the Minister of the War Department, who immediately dispatched some pieces of light artillery and a detachment of hussars and grenadiers, to compel the vessel to surrender. These troops having arrived, after a few discharges from the shore, the captain struck the flag.

However, the sea ran so high that all assistance was deferred until the next day when the weather being favourable the crew and troops were landed and conducted on the same day to the Hague; where upon their arrival the officers were lodged at the Hotel Parlement d'Angleterre, and the soldiers in barracks. The number taken prisoners of war consisted of one lieutenant colonel, two captains, three lieutenants, an ensign, a surgeon, a paymaster and 199 privates and drummers, as well as sixteen women and children. (*Times*, 18 November 1807)

6 November, James and Rebecca, transport At 10.30pm the transport ship No 42, named the *James and Rebecca*, of London, Captain Robert Rochester, was driven on to the rocks at Halzaphron during a violent gale when the ship became embayed.

The vessel was carrying besides the ship's company, about 180 of the 9th Light Dragoons who were returning from Montevideo. After she struck the ship went in two under a very high cliff, yet of 200 persons on board only 41 lost their lives. Mrs Lander, a widow, and Mrs Jordan, the wife of a surgeon were the only ladies on board and were both saved. The chief mate Mr Robert Mackay died four hours before the ship struck, most probably from gangrene as a result of a bruise or wound he received on board about ten days previously.

Those who perished were 28 men of the 9th Light Dragoons, 10 seamen, and 3 children; they were all interred in a large vault at the expense of Captain Rathbone. [The locality not given, but likely to have been St Keverne; and Captain Rathbone was probably a member of the 9th Light Dragoons as all the officers were saved.] (*SYM*, 16 November 1807)

12 November, Hero, transport The *Hero* transport arrived at Falmouth from Montevideo, having on board about 180 men of the 95th Regiment. 'They are generally in very good health, though they have been on shore only eight days in the past twelve months. They partake, poor fellows, of the extreme disgust which seems to be universally excited by disasters which they could not have merited,' referring to the conduct of General Whitelocke. (*SYM*, 16 November 1807)

20 November, Prince of Wales, packet The *Prince of Wales* packet, Captain Deans, sailed from Dublin for Liverpool on 19 November, but the following day was forced back by contrary winds. The ship however could not fetch the harbour and was driven on to the South Bull where she foundered within minutes.

The packet was carrying 120 volunteers for the 18th and 97th (the Queen's Own Germans) Regiments of Foot, as well as Captain Fitzgerald of the 6th and Captain Gregory of the 32nd. There were also other officers on board from various regiments. All these people perished, yet the master, crew and two ladies were saved, so we may assume they were in the deck house when the vessel struck, and took the only boat, whereas the others were below hatches. (*Times*, 26 and 28 November 1807)

20 November, Rochdale, brig The brig *Rochdale*, laden with provisions and having on board 265 persons in addition to the crew, probably sailed from Dublin in company with the *Prince of Wales* packet (*qv*) on the 19th, and like her was driven back by contrary winds. The vessel, unable to fetch Dublin harbour, was driven five miles south-eastward where she ran ashore under Sea Point near Black Rock, when all on board perished.

As the *Prince of Wales* packet was carrying volunteers for the Queen's Own German Regiment, so was the *Rochdale*; volunteers from the South Cork and Mayo Regiments. The embarkation return of the *Rochdale* was 265 persons, made up as follows: Major Gormoran of the 97th Foot; Lieutenants Long and Power; Ensign Way; 8 serjeants; 9 corporals; 173 rank and file; 42 women and 29 children. The number of persons in the crew appears to be unknown, but from this truly unfortunate vessel there was not a single survivor. (*Times*, 26 and 28 November 1807)

24 November, transport, No 203 A transport, No 203, from Copenhagen laden with sulphur was picked up by HMS *Ernest* off the Galloper sandbank, with no-one on board; having lost all her masts, bowsprit, cables and anchors. (*Times*, 26 November 1807). The Galloper sandbank is 30 miles NE of the North Foreland.

28 November, Boreas, 22 guns The *Boreas*, 22 guns, Captain Robert Scott, was standing towards Guernsey on the evening of 28 November, when about 6pm, with the wind blowing hard from the north-east, she ran upon the Hannois or Hannoveaux rocks. The story is here taken up by Captain Sir James Saumarez on 29 November.

'I received information of this unfortunate event about two o'clock this morning and immediately sent orders to the *Brilliant* and *Jamaica*,[42] the *Britannia* cutter, and one of the government scouts, to proceed off the Hannois and afford her every assistance: their lordships will be very much concerned to be informed, that on the tide's flowing, the vessel overset, and became a complete wreck at about two o'clock; and I am truly grieved to add that Captain Scott, with the officers and men, except those mentioned in the enclosed list, were lost with the ship. Lieutenant Bowick, with Lieutenant Wilson of the Royal Marines and six men, were sent off in the gig and landed in the western part of the island; about thirty others in the launch and large cutter were also landed and the boats returned to the ship, but have not been heard of, and there is every reason to fear were lost on nearing her.

'Through the great exertions of Lieutenant Colonel Sir Thomas Saumarez, in collecting the pilots and boatmen in the vicinity of Rorquains, about thirty seamen and marines were taken off the Hannois rocks at daylight, which I fear are the whole that have been saved.

'I have most sincerely to lament the loss of so many brave officers and men who have perished on this most melancholy occasion.'

The list referred to contained the names of seventy-seven men and boys, it would appear therefore that more than 100 perished. (*NC* vol 19, pp54-55)

8 December, Amicus, merchantman 'At four o'clock on Tuesday morning the 8th December, it blowing a tremendous gale of wind, with a heavy snow, the ship *Amicus*, Captain Simpson, of Hull, from St Petersburg with hemp, flax, tallow, &c. struck on the Holderness coast, half a mile to the south of the Sister Churches. At twelve o'clock the captain, who was an excellent swimmer, committed himself to the waves, with a rope, hoping to be able to gain the shore, but was overwhelmed by the breakers and perished in the attempt. The mate and another of the crew met a similar fate. The remaining part of the ship's company were seen by numerous spectators to be clinging to the rigging and wreck.

'After several ineffectual attempts a Mr Giles had recourse to the following: he procured a leaden half pound weight, and making a hole through it he fastened it to a long piece of whip-cord, and selected from the spectators the most athletic man to cast it at the wreck. After many fruitless trials, the man, following a receding wave, succeeded in throwing it across the vessel. The carpenter fastened the cord around his arm and was dragged through the surf to the shore, apparently lifeless, but afterwards recovered; the cord was again cast and a boy was rescued in the same manner. After this a person named John Greensides, notwithstanding the heavy surf, rushed through it to the vessel, and though he was hidden from the view of the spectators by tremendous waves, and could not swim, succeeded in gaining the wreck, and brought to land another boy; in his passage to the shore he was twice thrown down by the violence of the back water. He again returned to the wreck and at the hazard of his own saved the life of another seaman. At six o'clock four persons ventured through the waves to the ship, and brought away two others who died shortly after their gaining the shore.

The bodies of the captain and mate were washed ashore.' (*NC* vol 19, pp57-58)

29 December, Anson, 44 guns The *Anson*, 44 guns, Captain Charles Lydiard, had the reputation of being a bad seaboat. She had been built at Plymouth in 1781 as a 64-gun ship, but was cut down and made a razee of 44 guns in 1794. To the dismay of all who had to sail in her, she carried the same masts, rigging and sails, as when she was a Third Rate ship of the line, so she rolled very deep and was by no means calculated for such a station as the Black Rocks off Brest. (*NC* vol 19, p452)

The *Anson* sailed on 24 December from Falmouth to join the blockading squadron off Brest, and on the evening of the 27th the crew noticed the Île de Batz off Roscoff, at which time signs of an approaching gale were observed. The next morning with the Île de Batz still in sight and the gale increasing with every appearance of bad weather, Captain Lydiard determined to make Falmouth, his rendezvous in case of necessity, and accordingly shaped a course for the Lizard.

At noon all hands were upon deck, the sea running very high, two bow ports on the starboard side washed away by the violence of the sea, also a port abreast the main mast, by which means she shipped a great deal of water. By their reckoning at this time they imagined the Lizard north by west, eight or ten miles, and at about 12.30pm, when land was seen about two miles distant, the captain sent for the master to determine the situation of the ship, but from the thickness of the weather the land could not be recognised (it was Cuddan Point). The ship wore immediately and steered south-east by east until about 3pm when the master wished to run in again and make the land, supposed to be the Lizard, and, if they could make it out, proceed to Falmouth. They then wore, but the weather still very thick, they had a cast of the lead and having twenty-seven fathoms were convinced they were to the westward of the Lizard. The crew immediately wore ship again, made all sail, and stood out to the south-east.

Soon after 4pm, as the captain was going to dinner, he looked out of the quarter gallery, from whence he saw breakers close aboard, and a long way ahead the land; which he perceived to be the Lizard and he then knew that his ship was embayed. Every exertion was made to work the vessel off the lee shore, but with the gale then raging and a tremendous sea the *Anson* lost ground with every tack and at 5pm the crew furled everything and let go the best bower in twenty-five fathoms, veered away to two cables length, entirely to the clench. The topgallant masts were got upon deck, and she rode very well until 4am on Tuesday the 29th when the cable parted. The small bower was then let go and veered away to two cables length which brought her up to the clench also. The lower yards and topmasts were then struck and the anchor held until about 7.30am when the cable parted. The ship was then so close to the land that no alternative remained but to run her on shore. The fore topsail was set and the master Mr H Stuart ran the ship ashore on the sand which forms the bar between Loo Pool and the sea on Porthleven beach.

The *Anson* struck one hour after high tide and broached-to, broadside to the beach and heeled towards the shore. The main mast soon went by the board but injured no-one and was used as a floating bridge by the majority of those who were saved. Those who were too precipitate at landing generally lost their lives, whilst those who waited until 11am generally saved theirs. Several, including Captain Lydiard and the first lieutenant, were washed overboard and drowned. Two local men, one a methodist preacher and the other Mr Tobias Roberts, a shopkeeper of Helston, behaved with exemplary courage when they boarded the wreck and saved two women and a man from below decks. The number of persons saved from the wreck was about 250 and the number lost did not exceed 50, although this latter number was never accurately ascertained as many who were saved immediately scampered off. [On 4 January 1808 the *SYM* reported about 250 saved and 50 missing; and on 11 January the same paper reported that the number lost was not yet ascertained but was supposed to be about 30. (*Penzance report*, 31 December 1807; *Falmouth report*, 6 January 1808)]

On 1 January 1808 the body of Captain Lydiard was recovered and taken to Falmouth where interment took place the following day. At the funeral were Vice-Admiral Cotton and General Spencer together with the mayor and Corporation of Falmouth. A party of marines and the Oxford militia from Pendennis Castle fired three volleys over the grave. Some time later Captain Lydiard's body was removed to his family vault in the parish church of Haslemere, Surrey.

On 6 January 1808 a court martial was held on board the *Salvador del Mundo* in the Hamoaze at Plymouth to try the surviving officers and crew for the loss of the *Anson*. They were all honourably acquitted, except the master Mr H Stuart, who it was said did not fulfil the duties of his station; he was admonished. (*NC* vol 19, p451 et seq; *AR* 1808, Chr, p1; *Times*, 11 January 1808)

29 December, Antiope, transport The *Antiope* transport, Captain Molleny, with part of the 90th Regiment of Foot, sailed from Portsmouth on 20 December with a favourable wind for Cork. The weather for two days was very pleasant and after passing Scilly the vessel was becalmed for a further two days. On Christmas evening it began to blow very hard, and the gale increased to a hurricane, the sea rising to such prodigious heights as to alarm the most experienced sailor on board; with the situation rendered still more dangerous by a fog so thick that one end of the vessel could not be discovered from the other. Great quantities of water dashing over the deck and rushing down the hatchways, all hands wet to the skin and perishing with the cold, the pumps choked below, sails and rigging tearing and it was with extreme labour she was kept afloat by baling with buckets. The morning's light afforded a view of the Irish shore, but the wind then shifting prevented making any harbour on that coast, about two leagues distant. The sea ran so high that the captain and crew expected every moment to be their last, nor did they know exactly where they were. The ship put about again and experienced a dreadful sea; the people now five days without a change of clothing and starving with hunger, not being able to serve out provisions; yet this was trifling compared with what was yet to come. The vessel found her way into St Bride's Bay, in Pembrokeshire, where surrounded by prodigious and almost inaccessible cliffs she dashed upon a rock, not easily discovered. Their situation was now most alarming; not a boat could venture off to their relief, hundreds of people were viewing the vessel, yet without any means of affording the least assistance.

The main mast went by the board and took two poor fellows with it; while four others who tried to swim ashore were also lost. The soldiers and crew managed to get ashore on the evening of the 29th, but without anything but what they had on their backs. After they quitted the wreck some hardened wretches got on board and robbed the vessel.

The soldiers were taken to Haverfordwest and placed in very good quarters. In the midst of the scene, a soldier's wife was delivered of a very fine boy, and both were expected to do well. (*Times*, 29 January 1808)

1808

15 January, Sparkler, 14 guns Built at Warren's yard, Brightlingsea, the *Sparkler*, a 14-gun brig, was launched on 6 August 1804. Commanded by Lt James Samuel Aked Dennis, the vessel was driven ashore and wrecked off Terschelling during a gale. While the greater part of the crew were rescued and made prisoners of war; fourteen others, including Mr Richard Riley, midshipman; and Mr Eagersfield, clerk of the vessel, perished. (*NC* vol 19, p176)

15 January, Lord Keith, cutter The *Lord Keith* was a 10-gun hired (February 1804) cutter commanded by Lt Mitchell Roberts when it was driven ashore at Cuxhaven by the same gale which wrecked the *Sparkler*. The *Lord Keith* was taken possession of by the French, who managed to rescue the entire crew. (*SNL*, 1808)

18 January, Flora, 36 guns A 36-gun frigate, the *Flora*, was built at Deptford dockyard and launched on 6 May 1780. The vessel was commanded by Captain Loftus Otway Bland when she struck on the coast of Holland and was wrecked; yet although the ship had a crew of about 250 men, only nine were to lose their lives.

The following account of the loss of the *Flora* is taken from a letter written by an officer, dated Lewarden in Friesland, 26 January 1808: 'I am sorry to inform you that the *Flora* struck upon the Terschelling reef last Monday the 18th; and about nine o'clock that night succeeded in getting her off, but lost our rudder in the attempt; and after getting her to sea we could hardly keep her free with all the pumps, therefore was obliged the next day to run her on shore again about four o'clock that afternoon. After making rafts, fearing that if it came on to blow hard that night she would go to pieces, the captain, myself and others pushed off in the barge, that being the only boat we then had [the launch and jollyboat were lost when the rudder was unshipped], with about 130 of the crew on rafts, the rest choosing to stay by the ship; when after rowing 18 hours we landed on the island of Ameland, where they made us prisoners, and marched us here. After being four days and nights on board, the rest came on shore on some more rafts, and I believe all are saved. I have lost everything, as when I left the ship, though my bag was in my hand, I would not put it into the boat, as the captain would not his; nor indeed was it a time to think about any thing but one's life. Those we left on the wreck are in Harlingen.' (*NC* vol 19, p299; *SNL,* 1808; *MC* vol 5, pp302-303; *Times,* 19 March 1808)

31 January, Delight, 16 guns A 16-gun brig sloop built at Thorn's shipyard, Fremington, *Delight* was launched in June 1806.

On 31 January the vessel ran aground on the coast of Calabria when in chase of some enemy gunboats; the ship could not be got off and the following day the crew set fire to the vessel to prevent her falling into the hands of the enemy.

Cdr Philip Cosby Handfield and a visitor, Captain Thomas Seccombe of the 50-gun *Glatton*, both lost their lives, as did several of the crew, the remainder became prisoners of war. (*SNL,* 1808)

31 January, Leda, 38 guns *Leda*, a 38-gun frigate built at Chatham Dockyard, was launched on 18 November 1800.

Whilst commanded by Captain Robert Honyman, the ship was driven on shore by a gale and lost at the entrance to the harbour of Milford Haven, during the night of 31 January; then when the tide ebbed the crew scrambled ashore.

On 5 March 1808 a court martial was held at Plymouth on board the *Salvador del Mundo*, to try Captain Honyman, his officers and ship's company, for the loss of the *Leda*; they were honourably acquitted. (*SYM,* 14 March 1808; *SNL,* 1808)

10 February, Spy, 16 guns On this Wednesday evening, about 7.30pm, an explosion took place on board the *Spy*, a sloop of war, in ordinary at Sheerness, in consequence of some powder which had been embezzled taking fire. The forepart of the ship was materially damaged and nine men and a woman belonging to the *Charge* gunbrig were seriously burnt.

Nearby ships' crews helped to put the fire out and the sufferers were taken on board the *Sussex* hospital ship. (*Times*, 16 February 1808)

15 February, Raposa, 10 guns   The *Raposa* was a Spanish brig pierced for 16 guns but mounting only 10, when she was taken by three boats of the 36-gun *Franchise*, Captain Charles Dashwood, off Campeche in the Gulf of Mexico, on 7 January 1806.

Two years later, when commanded by Lt James Violett, the *Raposa* ran aground on a shoal near Cartagena on the north-west coast of Columbia; after which the vessel was fired by the crew to prevent her falling into the hand of the enemy. It would appear that the entire fifty-five man crew of the *Raposa* were rescued by ships of the enemy. (*SNL*, 1806 and 1808)

At a court martial assembled on board the *Arethusa* in Port Royal harbour, Jamaica, on 11 April, Captain Sir Charles Brisbane, president, for the trial of Lt James Violett, the officers and crew of the *Raposa* brig, for the loss of that vessel on 15 February near Cartagena; the Court having considered the circumstances attending the loss of the vessel, they were all honourably acquitted. (*NC* vol 20, p78)

? March, L'Hirondelle, 16 guns   L'Hirondelle was a French cutter mounting 14 guns when she was taken by the *Bittern*, an 18-gun sloop of war, Cdr Robert Corbet, in the Mediterranean on 28 April 1804. (*SNL*, 1807)

On 23 February 1808 *L'Hirondelle*, then mounting 16 guns and commanded by Lt Joseph Kidd, was wrecked near Tunis, and from a crew of about fifty men and boys there were only four survivors. (*SNL*, 1807 and 1811)

24 March, Muros, 22 guns   L'Alcide, 22 guns, was a French privateer taken on 8 March 1806 off Muros, twenty miles south-east of Cape Finisterre.

The British renamed the vessel *Muros* and she was captained by Alexander Duff when wrecked off Bahia Honda, on the north-west coast of Cuba, while attempting to destroy batteries in the neighbourhood of Havannah. The crew were rescued. (*SNL*, 1811)

25 March, Electra, 18 guns   Electra, an 18-gun brig built by Betts at Mistleythorn on the river Stour, was launched on 22 January 1806.

On 25 March *Electra*, Cdr George Barne Trollope, was stranded on the coast of Sicily, but was salvaged later the same year, taken to Malta and sold. (*SNL*, 1811)

26 March, Milbrook, schooner   A 16-gun schooner the *Milbrook*, built in 1797 at Redbridge on Southampton Water, was commanded by Lt James Leach when she was lost on the Burlings, near Lisbon, in a gale during the night of the 25th/26th. The crew were saved. (*SNL*, 1811)

6 April, Prussian merchantman A Prussian vessel laden with cork and 300 pipes of wine, from Oporto for London, was driven ashore and wrecked on Loo Bar in Mount's bay, near where the *Anson* was lost in December. Of the crew of eleven men seven lost their lives, as also did a young man of Gunwalloe parish, Joseph Hendy, a private in Captain Roger's company of the Royal Stannery Artillery, who lost his life while in the act of saving one of the crew. About thirty pipes of wine and some cork were later salvaged. (*SYM*, 11 April 1808)

7 April, Agatha, merchantman The following narrative of the loss of the ship *Agatha* of Lubeck, which was chartered at Liebau to carry passengers, including Lord Royston and Colonel Pollen with his wife and servants to Sweden was written by Mr Smith, the mate of the vessel, and because of its interest is taken verbatim from the *NC* vol 20, p215 et seq.

'On 2nd April at 2 p.m. sailed from Liebau, the wind at ENE and very fine weather, the loose ice lying about 2 versts [Russian measure, equivalent to 1168 yards] from the shore, but we got through it without doing the least damage to the vessel, at the rate of two miles an hour; then we got into clear water about 3 p.m. with the wind at ESE. Little wind and fine weather on the 4th; at 2 p.m. got sight of Oland, bearing by the compass 10° NW, distance eight or nine miles; at 4 p.m. got close in and perceived the ice lying about a mile from the shore. The wind was then about WSW and the colonel came to me and asked me if it was not possible to come to an anchor under the island? I told him no, for the ice would drift off with the wind and cut the cable; so he asked the captain what was the best to be done, and he said he would stand to the leeward till eight o'clock, and then come back to the island; but at eight he would not tack [a dangerous manoeuvre during a gale]. It then blew a gale of wind from the west, and a very high sea; the vessel made much water and the pumps were choked with the ballast, and the sailors would not bale but very little, by which means the water gained very fast, was partly over the ballast, and the wind was now at west-north-west. At twelve o'clock on the 6th Mr Pollen came to me and asked me what was best to be done; if the vessel was fit to keep the sea or not? I told him it was impossible for the vessel to live long if the sailors did not make better use of their baling, for there were already three feet water in the hold, and it still kept gaining on us, so I told him it was best to bear away for some port in Prussia to save the vessel and lives. "Yes" says Mr Pollen, "I think that is the best we can do." He then went to the captain and told him he thought it was necessary that we should bear away for some harbour. To which the captain readily complied, and recommended Liebau. But Mr Pollen objected to Liebau on account of Mr Bening's [or Benney's] coming away without a pass from Prussia. So he greed [*sic*] to go to Memel; for at Pillau there was too little water, and he said he had never been at Memel in his life. So he told Mr Pollen, if he would take the ship into Memel he would give me charge of her as soon as we came to the bar. At two in the morning of the 7th got sight of land, about fifteen miles to the leeward of Memel, and got close in on a lee shore through the captain's carelessness of running so far in the dark. We hauled the ship to by the wind on the larboard tack; at four got sight of Memel, which the captain taking to be Liebau, came and asked me what place it was. I told him it was Memel, which surprised him very much. I went down into the cabin and told Colonel Pollen I saw Memel; he immediately came on deck full of glee, and likewise Lord Royston and all the other gentlemen. Mr Pollen said to the captain "Now will you give the mate the charge of the vessel?" He told him "Yes, he would." At five I took charge of the vessel, to carry her into Memel harbour; at six came to the bar and the sea was very high, two seamen at the helm; as soon as the captain saw the sea breaking over the bar he was afraid and ran directly to the helm and put it hard a-port, and all my striving was in vain, against three of them; I begged for God's sake to put the helm the other way, and save our lives; but all was in vain, for in ten minutes she was on the south sand; the third time she struck she was full of water, and a dreadful sight soon presented itself to our view.

'The wind was then at west-north-west, a gale of a wind. There was a wooden house on deck; Lady Pollen, Mrs Barnes and her three children, and likewise three gentlemen, a servant, a Prussian boy, and a servant girl, got into this small place to save themselves from the sea. Colonel Pollen and I immediately began to clear the boat and the sailors would not assist us; he soon got the small boat out and three sailors got into her with the captain. Lord Royston would have got into the same but I stopped him, and the captain came out again; then as soon as they got away from the ship she turned over and the three sailors were drowned. Then we cleared the large boat, but before we got her out she was washed away from us by the sea. Then we could do nothing more than trust in God to send some assistance. About 9 p.m. [should be 9am] cut the mast to ease the vessel, but could not see the lifeboat come out of the harbour, which gave the gentlemen a bad heart; for the sea was very high and breaking right over all our heads, and it was so very cold that it was impossible for any man to hold himself fast. Colonel Pollen asked me if the round-house where the lady was would stand fast. I told him it would stand as long as the bottom of the ship and he said "That is right, we must all hold as fast as we can for the boat will soon be here." I then left him and went aft of the vessel.

'It was now half-past four, but still no boat to be seen, which we all thought long of her coming, for our situation was now dreadful to behold, and the vessel all underwater, except the round-house. Mr Benney cried out very much, but he was soon washed away, and after him. about ten o'clock, Lord Royston, Colonel Pollen, Mr Bailey, and Mr Baker, one sailor, and the lord's servant, were all washed away within three seas of each other. I saw the two servants washed away, and I got hold of them both but was obliged to let them go overboard, which grieved me very much. As for the lord and colonel, I never saw them after I left holding fast by the round house; when I jumped from the mizzen-rigging into the round house, and Mrs Pollen immediately says "Smith, where is my husband, is he safe?" I told her "Yes; he had got safe on shore in the ship's boat" which I believe gave them all good spirits, in hopes he would soon be coming in the lifeboat. I did not stop here ten minutes, before I went out again and espied the lifeboat coming; it was now eleven o'clock and all this while a most dreadful sea rolling over us. The captain and the two seamen were on the bowsprit with two dead sailors beside them. The boat came close to the vessel and filled with water went away. Now I thought we surely must all be lost. In half an hour's time she came back to the ship again and Captain Cope [Koop] and his two sailors got into her. I went into the round-house and took Mrs Barnes out in hopes to get her into the boat; but alas the sea was too strong for me, for we were both washed away twice by the strength of the sea; but I always recovered her again by the help of God. As for me, I was yet too weak to help myself, so I got her safe back to the round-house and went out myself, but was washed away a third time and the boat picked me out of the water. So I remember nothing more till between four and five in the evening when I found myself on shore at Memel. I asked the people if the boat had gone off again and they told me the captain said there were no more on board. What was intent for that I cannot tell.

'The boat went off six times that afternoon but never could come to the ship, the wind and sea were so very high. Now here they must pass a dreadful night, the sea rolling over their heads, and the cold very severe, by which one Mr Fock of Hamburgh died; about three the next morning the lifeboat went off twice and came back; the third time it got to the ship and brought back Mrs Pollen, Mr Halliday, Mr Perrero, and the servant of Mrs Pollen. Now here was left on board Mrs Barnes and two children, and a little Prussian boy, who belonged to Colonel Pollen; Mrs Barnes's servant girl, her youngest child, two months old, and Mrs Pollen's man-servant, assisting the girl into the boat, were all washed overboard together; the girl and child were brought on shore in half an hour after, but alas too late. Mrs Barnes remained on board six hours longer, alone, and the people in the life-boat said they saw her and the children washed overboard, which was a false report. I told the commodore of the pilots she was certainly yet alive, on which Captain Davison, an Englishman, jumped into the boat and went off and brought her safe on shore, with two children and the Prussian boy.

'Those lost from the wreck of the *Agatha* were: Lord Royston and his man-servant; Col. Pollen and man-servant; Mrs Barnes's man-servant, maid servant and youngest child; Mr Halliday's man-servant, Thomas D Bayley; Mr Becher; Mr Renny, and six seamen. Mr Focke died on board and was buried at Memel on the 13th. Mr Pereyra died on shore.

'Those saved from the wreck were: Mrs Barnes and two children; Mrs

Pollen and two servants; Mr Halliday, the captain and three seamen.' (*AR* 1808, Chr, p61 et seq; *Times*, 17 May and 8 June 1808)

The *Agatha* must have been a very tight ship for no apparent damage appears to have occurred to the deck house where all were safe until they ventured outside.

9 April, mutiny suppressed   A Third Rate 74-gun ship, the *Edgar* was built at Woolwich Dockyard in 1779 and carried a crew of 600 men and boys. (*NC* vol 1, p548)

On 9 April, and by adjournment on Monday the 11th, a court martial was held on board the *Salvador del Mundo* in Hamoaze for the trial of five mutineers of the *Edgar*, *viz* Henry Chesterfield captain of the main-top; John Rowlands, boatswain's mate; and George Scarr, Abraham Davis and Joseph Johnston, seamen; Rear-Admiral Sutton, president.

It appeared by the evidence of Lt Campbell that on 28 March last, when the ship lay in Cawsand Bay, he was acquainted while in the ward-room that the ship's company were assembling in a body on the quarter-deck; on going there they demanded with one voice 'fresh captain and officers', and some of them called out 'an answer and no mutiny'. Lt Campbell after remonstrating with them once or twice was obliged to order the marines to be drawn up on the quarterdeck and was on the point of directing them to fire when they thought fit to disperse. The five prisoners were seized and put in irons directly. In their defence the petty officers attempted to prove they were intimidated to go on the quarterdeck by the threats of the ship's company. Their sentences were as follows:

Chesterfield to receive 700 lashes around the fleet, on his bare back, and to be kept in solitary confinement in Marshalsea prison for two years.

Scarr, 500 lashes and one year's solitary. Rowland, 300 lashes.

Davis and Johnston, 200 lashes each. (*NC* vol 19, p347)

20 April, Widgeon, 8 guns   During a heavy snowstorm the 8-gun *Widgeon*, Lt George Elliot, was driven on to a dangerous lee shore at MacDuff, about 2.30am. In a very heavy sea the vessel soon bilged, yet the crew were more than fortunate and were all saved; but how they were saved appears to be unknown. (*SNL*, 1811)

22 April, Bermuda, 18 guns   An 18-gun sloop of war, the *Bermuda* was built in Bermuda, where she was launched in 1805. The ship was one of those vessels known as a Bermudian; they had a bad name, being too sharp built for the North Atlantic (Smyth). According to a contemporary account and published in the *Navy List* in 1811, the vessel, then commanded by Cdr William Henry Byam, with a crew of 120 men and boys was wrecked on the island of Providence in the West Indies, where the crew were saved.

Norie states that the vessel was lost on Memory Rock, Little Bermuda; but this should read Memory Rock, Little Bahamas Bank, position 26°57'N 79°06'40"W. (*Findlay's North Atlantic Memoir*, 1873 ed)

22 April, Perseverance The *Perseverance* sailed from Penang on 19 April bound to Pegue in company with two other ships and His Majesty's brig *Albatross*, and three days afterwards parted company; on this night between 10 and 11pm the gunner, a Manilla-man, and four Manilla sea-cunnies went on deck and knocked down and murdered Mr Baker, the chief mate; they then proceeded to the cabin of Mr Mathewson the second officer whom they also murdered.

'Captain Johnstone, awakened by the noise, came to the cuddy door, armed with a hanger [sword], at the moment the villains were about to enter; he wounded one of them slightly, but was quickly overpowered and disarmed; he then came on the quarterdeck, begging for mercy. – Alas! mercy was unknown to such vile wretches; the gunner indeed promised to spare him, but at the same instant one of the ruffians came behind him and with some weapon struck him on the back of the head; he fell, when another with a hatchet severed his head from his body.

'An Armenian passenger now came on deck, whom the villains instantly murdered; they then went below and murdered Mr Gorey the third officer, and Mr Palmer a gentleman of Calcutta, passenger for Pegue.

'The murderers then directed the lascars to remain quiet, and go into the hold, an order which these poor men readily obeyed. The only person whose life was at this time spared was an Armenian gentleman named Gregory Joahnes, from whose narrative this brief extract is taken.

'The villains now proceeded to plunder, breaking open Captain Johnstone's trunks, where they found nearly a thousand dollars and about seven hundred dollars belonging to the officers and passengers.

'They then hoisted out the yawl, putting into it the money and many valuable articles, and ordered into her the only persons they chose to save, viz. Mr Joahnes; the old Serang; Captain Johnstone's butler; a malay girl and two lascars; when, to complete these horrible transactions they set fire to the ship and abandoned her, leaving the lascars who were confined to the hold to perish in the flames. Mr Joahnes adds that he saw the ship all in flames and the following morning she had disappeared.

'The yawl proceeded for the nearest land, which was supposed to be Brothers Island, or Pulo Lancavy (Lancavy Island) and reached it in three days. Here Mr Joahnes escaped by hiding himself in the jungle, and after suffering great hunger and distress got a passage in a fishing prow to Quedah [Kedah]. The King of Quedah received him with great kindness and humanity, and finally sent him to Penang, where he arrived on 27th May.

'Letters from Penang of the 24th June state that two of the murderers, the gunner and one of the seacunnies had been apprehended at Malacca, where they were in close confinement, and would be sent to Penang. May the sanguinary villains meet with the punishment they deserve, and may this too horrid detail be the means of preventing a Manilla-man ever being, in future, received as part of the crew of a British vessel.' (Verbatim from *NC* vol 20, pp294-295)

18 May, Rapid, 14 guns   The *Rapid*, a 14-gun brig, was built at Davy's yard at Topsham and launched in 1804. The vessel was commanded by Lt Henry Baugh when an attempt was made to cut out two merchant ships at anchor in the Tagus. The ships were however protected by batteries, as a consequence of which the *Rapid* was sunk. [A shot from one of the batteries struck the *Rapid* between wind and water, when she went down almost immediately; but being a calm, boats belonging to the *Primrose* which was in company, saved the entire crew. (*Times*, 12 July 1808)] (*SNL*, 1808)

24 May, Astrea, 32 guns   The *Astrea*, a 32-gun frigate, was built at Fabian's yard, East Cowes, where the vessel was launched on 24 July 1781.
    While commanded by Captain Edmund Heywood the ship was wrecked off Anegada, one of the Virgin Islands in the West Indies. Except for four persons, the crew were saved. (*SNL*, 1811; *NC* vol 20, p44)

31 May, Manby's life-saving apparatus   A most interesting and highly important experiment was some time since made at Woolwich by Captain Manby of Yarmouth on a vessel at anchor in the Thames, upwards of 100 yards from the shore, before a committee of general officers of artillery, Admiral Losack, and several officers of the Royal Navy, for the purpose of effecting a communication with a ship stranded on a lee-shore, and to bring the crew in perfect safety from the wreck. A rope was projected from a royal mortar across the ship supposed to be stranded, by which was hauled on board by the crew a large rope, to be made fast to the mast-head, and kept at a proper degree of tension for a cot to travel on it, by a tackle purchase, that likewise admitted of the vessel rolling; at the same time a tailed block was sent to the ship, with a small rope rove through it; each end of the small rope was made fast to the end of the cot, which conveyed it to the ship, and brought a person in perfect safety to the shore.[43] The whole service was performed in a quarter of an hour. (*NC* vol 20, p360)

30 June, Capelin, schooner   A small 4-gun schooner, the *Capelin*, was built in 1804 and was commanded by Lt Josias Bray when she struck on a sunken rock while reconnoitring the harbour at Brest. The crew were saved by ships in company. (*SNL*, 1808)

10 July, Netley, 12 guns   *La Determinee*, a French 12-gun privateer brig, was captured in 1807, after which the vessel was purchased by the British government, renamed *Netley* and added to the strength of the Royal Navy.

The vessel, commanded by Lt Charles Burman, was wrecked while serving on the Leeward Islands station. Of her crew of about sixty men and boys, only nine survived. (*SNL*, 1808)

27 July, Pickle, schooner The *Pickle*, Lt Moses Cannadey, was a 10-gun schooner purchased by the government in 1805.[44] The vessel carrying despatches was entering Cadiz harbour when she grounded on a shoal and was lost. (*Times*, 17 August 1808)

30 July, Meleager, 36 guns *Meleager*, a 36-gun frigate, was built at Chatham Dockyard and launched 25 November 1806.

The vessel was commanded by Captain Frederick Warren when it was wrecked on Barebush Cay off the coast of Jamaica. Except for one midshipman and three seamen the crew were saved. (*SNL*, 1811)

? July, Mr Macdonald's wherry About the end of July a wherry belonging to Mr Macdonald of Balranald, manned with four men, and which had some cattle on board, sailed from North Uist for the island of Heisker (about 7½ miles off), which is the only island between the north of Scotland and America in that direction, and is visited but twice in the year. The day was very moderate and the wind fair when the vessel sailed; but when within two leagues of Heisker the wind became contrary and very tempestuous; the consequence was that the vessel foundered on a ridge of rocks which jutted out from the main island. Three of the hands perished as did all the cattle, except one cow, which together with the fourth man succeeded in scrambling up to the top of this rocky island.

In this dismal situation the man and his brute companion remained three days without any prospect of relief. On the fourth the cow dropped dead; in the interim, to preserve existence as long as possible, the man opened a vein in the cow and frequently sucked her blood; this source failing at her death, he cut out the tongue of the dead animal and mincing it down very small he supported his existence till the fifth day, on which to his great joy he spied an open fishing boat in the channel and hoisted, with all the strength that was left in him, his shirt as a signal of distress; the boat came and rescued him from his perilous situation. (*NC* vol 20, p218; *Times*, 2 September 1808)

4 August, Delphinen, 16 guns A 16-gun brig sloop the *Delphinen* was one of the vessels surrendered to the British at Copenhagen on 7 September 1807.

Almost a year later the vessel, commanded by Richard Harward (who survived the accident), was wrecked off the coast of Vlieland. *SNL* of 1808 contained no mention of the crew of ninety men and boys who became prisoners of war.

18 August, Rook, schooner   The *Rook*, Lt James Lawrence, was a small 4-gun schooner that carried a crew of about twenty-five men; she had been built at Sutton's boatyard at Ringmore, Shaldon.

The *Rook* sailed from Plymouth under the orders of Admiral Young on 24 June 1808 with despatches for the West Indies. After a fine passage she arrived at Jamaica from whence, after having waited a few days to refit and take in specie, she sailed for England on 13 August. For two days they were followed by a French schooner (which was pretty generally the case when a ship has any money on board, and of which intelligence was soon gained at some of the French islands), but whom they beat off. On 18 August at daylight they fell in with two French schooners and immediately cleared for action. On the largest vessel coming alongside with English colours and not answering when hailed, but immediately hoisting French colours, Lt Lawrence shot the French captain, when a most desperate action commenced; after an hour's hard fighting Lt Lawrence received his last wound by a musket-ball, and the *Rook* was immediately carried by boarding, the French officers repeatedly calling to their men to give no quarter.

Mr Stewart the master received seven cutlass wounds, of which he recovered but later died of yellow fever. Mr Donnelly the clerk was wounded in the groin but later recovered. Mr George, an officer in the Royal Artillery, who had served his country on the island of Jamaica for twenty years, and was related by marriage to Lt Lawrence, was induced to embark on the *Rook*, but was killed by the enemy on boarding. The survivors were stripped naked, put in their boat, and turned adrift; but by the exertions of four who were not wounded they reached land (but where is not specified), and were most hospitably received by the natives. The *Rook* was so much damaged that the enemy could not get her into port and therefore set fire to her. (*NC* vol 21, p62)

12 September, Swallow, brig   During this afternoon, the *Swallow* brig, Captain Milner, convoying eight sail of transports, arrived at Gijon to receive on board 2000 Merino sheep, presented by the Junta to His Majesty. (*AR* 1808, Chr, p103)

Soon after the *Swallow* came to an anchor, a boat put off from her with Captain Milner; the Hon Captain Herbert; Mr Creed, son of Mr Creed, navy agent, and seven seamen. Just as they were upon the bar a violent surf broke over them, filled the boat, and plunged the whole into the sea; the greater part, by taking hold of the boat, kept above water and supported themselves on oars and planks, till the boats which immediately put off from the shore picked them up. However, they were unable to save Captain Herbert and Mr Creed, who sunk before they arrived. These two gentlemen went out for the purpose of visiting the country.

Captain Herbert was the second son of the Earl of Caernarvon and a gentleman of respectable literary talents; he had lately published a volume of poems. (*NC* vol 20, p256)

25 September, Sisters, merchantman The ship *Sisters* from Greenock for St John, New Brunswick, was wrecked on sunken rocks about three leagues from Grand Manan Island; position 44°46'N, 66°53'W in the Bay of Fundy. Immediately she struck the stern boat was lowered and the captain and six seamen saved themselves; the remainder, the mate and fifteen other seamen were left to their fate, as it was impossible to render them any assistance. (*Times*, 28 November 1808)

3 October, Carnation, 18 guns The *Carnation*, 18 guns, Captain Charles Mars Gregory, fell in with the 16-gun French National brig *Le Palineure*, off Martinique, and after three hours hard fighting within pistol shot, was boarded and taken. Captain Gregory and nine of his crew were killed whilst a further thirty were wounded. The *Carnation* was so much shattered in the action that the French prize crew were not able to reach a port, but ran her ashore on Martinique, about 30 miles from Fort Royal (Fort de France), to which place the survivors of the *Carnation*'s crew were sent. After nine days they were exchanged and sent to Admiral Cochrane. During their stay at Fort Royal fifteen of those who had so nobly defended the *Carnation* died of their wounds. (*Times*, 7 January 1809)

But this was not the end of the matter. On 16 May 1809 the 74-gun *Belleisle* arrived at Portsmouth from the West Indies, and on the same day the *Times* printed: 'A court martial has been held in the West Indies on the master and surviving crew of the *Carnation* sloop of war, to account for the capture of that ship on 3rd October off Martinique by a French National brig. The result was that the master was acquitted, the sergeant of marines John Chapman was hanged, and twenty-six of the crew were sentenced to be transported to New South Wales for cowardice. The men under sentence of transportation are coming home prisoners on the *Belleisle*.'

[The *Palineure* was herself captured by the 32-gun *Circe*, Acting Captain Francis Augustus Collier, off the Diamond Rock, Martinique, on 31 October 1808.]

4 October, Greyhound, 32 guns A 32-gun frigate *Greyhound* was commanded by Captain the Hon William Pakenham [Captain Pakenham was to perish in the *Saldanha* on 4 December 1811 (*qv*)] when she was wrecked off Luconia (Luzon).

Only one seaman lost his life and Captain Pakenham together with his crew managed to make Manilla. They then proceeded in cartels for Penang; Captain Pakenham with 150 men on board the *Discovery*, which unfortunately fell in with two French frigates and was taken; the remainder sailed on board the *Diana*, which escaped and made Penang. (*Times*, 15 July 1809)

17 October, Hibernia, merchantman The ship *Hibernia*, Captain James, of and from Londonderry, bound to Newcastle (Delaware, a suburb of Philadelphia), and Philadelphia, with passengers, after being out four days was wrecked about 10pm on a ridge of rocks off the island of Islay. The masts were cut away and every effort made for the safety of those on board, which proved effectual, all were saved. On the same night, about a mile from the *Hibernia*, a large ship and a sloop, names unknown, were also wrecked and all on board these two vessels perished. (*Times*, 4 November 1808)

19 October, Chanticleer's boat Captain Charles Harford of HM sloop *Chanticleer*, aged about twenty-eight years, was drowned in Yarmouth Roads this evening. Captain Harford being unacquainted (having just arrived) with the rules of the Port Admiral, which prohibits boats landing or going off in foul weather after sunset, or when a certain flag is hoisted, was returning to his ship when a squall upset his boat. The captain, master, and Mr Poor, midshipman, continued on the keel of the boat from 6 to 9pm, when the captain and Mr Poor dropped off, the master however by his repeated cries was saved by boats which put off from the shore. (*NC* vol 20, p336)

24 October, Volador, 16 guns The 16-gun *Volador* was a Spanish privateer taken in 1807, bought by the British Admiralty and added to the Royal Navy.

On the night of the 23rd/24th the vessel was wrecked in the Gulf of Coro, Venezuela, whilst commanded by Cdr Francis George Dickens. Although only one man perished several others deserted. (Norie, 1827 ed) [Commander Dickens was to perish in the *Sylph* on 17 January 1815 (*qv*)]

25 October, Hindostan's boat General Murray, the Deputy Adjutant General of the army in Portugal, the man who signed the convention with the French General François Christophe Kellerman, Duke of Valmy, for the evacuation of Portugal, arrived at Plymouth on board the 54-gun *Hindostan* after a most tempestuous passage of eighteen days from Lisbon. (*SYM*, 31 October 1808)

The *Hindostan*, Captain Skinner, upon arrival from Lisbon anchored in Cawsand Bay. General Murray and his staff had intended to land at Dock but a violent squall occurred as their boat was crossing the Bridge, near Redding Point, and she was driven upon the rocks under Mount Edgcumbe and knocked to pieces. No lives were lost and both General Murray and Captain Skinner stripped, waded ashore, and proceeded through Mount Edgcumbe Park to Cremill Passage. (*Times*, 1 November 1808)

26 October, Crane, schooner The *Crane* built by Custance of Yarmouth was launched on 26 April 1806.

The vessel was a small armed schooner mounting 8 guns and was commanded by Lt Joseph Tindall, when weathering the gale in trying to work up the Hamoaze she unfortunately missed stays and went ashore on the rocks near Rusty Anchor, under the West Hoe, where she soon bilged and sunk; providentially the officers and crew were all saved. (*SYM*, 31 October 1808)

28 October, Russian squadron at Portsmouth 'The Russian admiral and officers remain in the command of their ships at Spithead without an Englishman on board of them; so that Spithead actually holds a fleet of our enemy, with every means to give battle at a moment's notice. That roadstead cannot be left without a squadron equal to the Russians lest they should escape. The Russian admiral will not quit his ship nor has he come on shore although hotels were prepared for him and his officers. He replied that he would not leave his men but would go with them to Russia.' (*Times*, 28 October 1808). Russia had become an enemy by virtue of the Treaty of Tilsit of the previous year which forced her into alliance with Napoleonic France.

29 October, Banterer, 22 guns The *Banterer*, a new ship of 22 guns, Captain Alexander Sheppard, on her voyage to Quebec took a pilot on board below the island of Bic in the St Lawrence river on 28 October and at 8pm they passed between the said island and the south shore with a fair wind; but it afterwards coming around to the westward, and the current not allowing them to regain the anchorage, they tacked for the north shore; not only to be ready to avail themselves of the northerly winds in the morning but also because the current there was more in their favour. After having tacked occasionally during the night, at 4am the helm was again put down, and on rising tacks and sheets, it was discovered that the ship was aground; as there was then a light breeze at west, the sails were all laid aback, the land (which they afterwards discovered to be Point Mille Vache, the current having set them considerably to the eastward of where they conceived themselves to be) being in sight from the larboard bow to the starboard beam, was apparently at a considerable distance.

The master now sounded around the ship and finding that the shoal lay on the starboard quarter and astern, which their sails were backing them on, they were furled; the stream anchor and cable got into the launch, and the boats ordered to tow her out two cables' length south-west of the ship, where the deepest water had been found; by this time the wind had increased to such a degree that they could not row ahead and having lost ground were obliged to let the anchor go in fifteen fathoms, a cable's length from the ship. On this anchor they hove occasionally as the flood made, and in the meantime got the spare topmasts over the side to make a raft to carry out a bower anchor, the boats being insufficient for that purpose; but the gale continued to increase, and the weather was so intensely cold that the accomplishment of it was rendered impracticable.

About 11.36am the stream cable being then taut ahead, the wind WSW with a very heavy sea, the ship canted suddenly around with her head to the southward, where they had deep water; the crew immediately set the courses, jib and driver, and had the most sanguine hopes of getting her off, but were disappointed, and as the ebb made, were obliged again to furl sails.

As the ship was then striking very hard with a heavy sea breaking over her in a body, her topmasts were cut away, not only to ease her but also to prevent their falling upon the deck; the crew also endeavoured to shore up the ship, but the motion was so violent that six parts of a five inch hawser were repeatedly snapped, with which they were lashing the shores through the main deck ports.

About 8pm, fearing the loss of the ship, a party of marines and boys, together with the sick and a quantity of provisions, were landed on the north shore of the St Lawrence; then the following morning the crew hove overboard the guns, shot and everything that could lighten the vessel, except for two guns which were kept for signal purposes. It was now the prevailing opinion that the ship would founder if got off, as the water flowed above the orlop deck, sand was coming up from the pumps, and the carpenter certain, that the ship could not swim. Those men who could be spared were now landed, that in the event of the ship going to pieces the boats might be the better able to save the rest. On the morning of the 31st the boats were employed in landing as many as possible through a dreadful surf; the captain, first lieutenant and a few others which the boats could not carry, remaining with the wreck. It was 11.30pm before the boats could return to the ship when all on board were sent ashore, except the jollyboat and crew in which the captain left the wreck at 2am on 1 November and landed through the surf with great difficulty.

On 3 November, the weather moderating, the jollyboat was despatched with the purser to the village of Trois Pistoles, about 45 miles distant, on the opposite side of the river, that he might find his way to Quebec (150 miles from Trois Pistoles) to procure relief and assistance.

During their stay near the wreck the men took every opportunity of going off to the vessel to salvage whatever they could, yet found only two casks of beef and some spirits. These excursions usually took between ten and twelve hours, the men being exposed to the cold and wet and without nourishment, from which and fatigue the men became every day more sickly, above twenty suffering frostbite while some thirty others perished in the timber.

On 20 November the survivors were relieved by the timely arrival of a small schooner with a fortnight's provisions from Quebec; and on the 24th by the arrival of the government schooner. On the 25th the men were taken by the latter vessel to the opposite bank where they boarded a transport which that day arrived and carried them to Halifax. (*NC* vol 22, p49 et seq)

At a court martial held on board HMS *Tourterelle*, in St George's Harbour, Bermuda, on the 28th and by adjournment on 30 January 1809 Captain Sheppard and the surviving officers, men and pilot were tried for the loss of the *Banterer* on 29 October between Port Neuf and Point Mille Vache in the St Lawrence.

The Court expressed the opinion that the loss of the ship was occasioned by the culpable neglect of the master, in not having repeated to the lieutenant who relieved him in the next watch, the orders he had received from Captain Sheppard to keep the lead going by the forecastle men, and to relieve them, in consequence of the very severe cold weather, every half hour; as also from the negligence and very culpable conduct of Lt Stephen C McCurdy, the officer of the middle watch, who not only permitted the pilot to quit the deck without his captain's knowledge, but likewise quitted it himself between the hours of two and four, without being relieved by any person whatever, and took with him to the gun room to drink grog the pilot's apprentice, the only midshipman, and the only quarter-master who were in the watch, where he remained upwards of a quarter of an hour; that Captain Sheppard appeared to have caused every possible exertion to be made to save the ship, and when that was found impracticable, to preserve the stores in which he was supported by the officers and men.

Lt McCurdy was sentenced to be dismissed from the navy as a lieutenant; Mr Robert Clegram the acting master was severely reprimanded; Captain Sheppard, the other officers, ship's company and the pilot were all acquitted. (*NC* vol 22, pp53-54)

7 November, Travers, extra ship   The *Travers*, Captain Collins, was an Extra Ship in the Honourable East India Company's service; at the time of her loss the ship had treasure on board 'to a large amount', besides 500 pipes of Madeira wine, and several valuable investments; and, in the whole, her loss, which is related in the following letter (here given in part) from Captain Collins to the Rt Hon Lord Minto, Governor General, was estimated at £150,000: 'I have to inform you of the loss of the *Travers*, under my command, on 7th November at five o'clock in the morning, on a rock detached from the Sunken Island, in position 15°38'N 94°20'E, Diamond Island bearing W by N distance about three miles; Sunken Island SW by S distant one mile and a quarter. Details of the catastrophe follow.

'About ten minutes before five o'clock a.m. on 7th November, when in our station on the starboard quarter of the *Monarch*, with the *Earl Spencer* in company, having hove the lead and got ground in twenty fathoms, mud and fine sand, I went to leeward and saw breakers on the starboard beam and a head. I immediately hauled the ship close to the wind, but unfortunately notwithstanding our exertions to clear the reef, we struck about five a.m. on a rock detached from Sunken Island, the other two ships passing considerably within hail. The cause of their escape, I believe, was from my hailing and firing guns. At this time the mizzen mast went fifteen feet above the board, the ship then bilged on the starboard side, and in about fifteen minutes we lost the rudder and the sternpost gave way. Finding it impossible to get the ship off, I ordered the main, fore mast, and spare anchors to be cut away, and threw overboard the starboard guns to ease her. I then sent an officer down to secure the packets, which I regret was impracticable, as the water was level with the gun deck, part of which had given way. As it was now daybreak, and we clearly could distinguish the ships standing on their course, we hoisted our ensign to the stump of our mizzen mast, with the union downwards: but not seeing that to have any effect, our only resource was now in our boats, which with the greatest exertions of the officers and crew, having no masts to which they could affix tackles, we were obliged to cut the gunwale down, to launch the long boat, and by dint of strength, a labour which was rendered doubly difficult by the uneasy state of the ship, the sea having by this time made a complete breach over her. By seven o'clock all the ladies, passengers and crew, with the exception of sixteen men were in the boats. The weather was so squally and a heavy sea running, I thought it not safe to allow more than ninety-three persons in the launch, she being so extremely deep, and eighteen in the cutter; but ordered the jollyboat back, though she was also very crowded, to endeavour to bring off as many of those remaining as possible; which I am sorry to say, from their obstinacy in persisting on not coming without their baggage, the officer was unable to effect, excepting three. When we put off our situation was still more distressing as Captain Hawes of the *Monarch*, the senior officer, followed by the *Earl Spencer* had gone to so great a distance that we could not discern the ships. I had in my pocket a compass, and steering WSW in about an hour and a half described them at a distance of about ten or eleven miles. The boats shipping much water, kept us constantly baling, which gave me at one time much apprehension, from the severity of the weather, of our not being able to reach them; but about eleven a.m. we were all safe on board the *Earl Spencer*.' (*NC* vol 21, pp516-517)

20 November, Glory, East Indiaman The *Glory*, an East Indiaman, Captain Beevor, is supposed gone to the bottom; on 22 November she was last seen by the *Phoenix*, East Indiaman, during a storm in the Indian Ocean. In the afternoon of the above day, between 4 and 5pm, the *Phoenix* then being at no great distance from the *Glory* observed that she was settling fast in the water and while the *Phoenix*'s crew were below decks at the pumps, in about half an hour the *Glory* disappeared. (*Times*, 21 December 1809)

On 22 December the *Times* printed a letter from Captain John Ramsden of the *Phoenix*: 'Now Sir, the truth is that the *Glory* was never seen from the *Phoenix* after 20th November, about half an hour after sunset (or as we term it, the 21st per log),[45] at which time, as far as we could judge, she was not in a dangerous state.' This is followed by a note written by the editor of the *Times* which stated that the article of the 21st was taken from the *Globe*.

28 November, Martha, merchantman The American ship *Martha*, Captain Beare, on her passage to India had two-thirds of her crew poisoned by eating fish caught on the voyage. (*Times*, 28 November 1808)

29 November, John and Thomas, merchantman One of the most distressing accidents for a number of years occurred on the western coast of Cumberland this Tuesday night. As the *John and Thomas* merchant vessel, the property of Mr Sewel of Workington, was attempting to enter Whitehaven harbour, the night being dark and the sea turbulent, she missed the mouth of the harbour and driving against the pier was dashed to pieces.

The vessel had sailed from Liverpool and was full of passengers all of whom, together with the crew, lost their lives. The beach next day presented a horrid spectacle. (*Times*, 13 December 1808)

5 December, Crescent, 36 guns The *Crescent* was a 36-gun frigate launched at the yard of Calhoun and Newland at Bursledon in September 1783. On 29 November 1808 the ship commanded by Captain John Temple and carrying a large supply of clothing for the sailors of the Baltic fleet sailed from Yarmouth, and at daylight on 5 December the coast of Norway was visible from the deck. The wind then south by west and south-south-west, the pilots steered the vessel south-east by east, and at 1pm sounded in twenty-five fathoms on the coast of Jutland near Robsnout.[46]

The pilots now steered the vessel east-south-east and at 2pm sounded in eighteen fathoms, whereupon they ordered the topsails close reefed, courses hauled up, and the ship hove to with her head to the southward; the weather at this time being remarkably thick. Shortly afterwards, when land was reported to have been seen from the lee-bow, the pilots stated that they knew where the ship was and that she would drift with safety. However, she dropped into less than ten fathoms but then continued in ten fathoms until 8pm when Captain Temple asked the pilots if they wished any alterations to be made. They replied, no alterations were requisite, and that the ship should continue on the same tack till the next morning. Unfortunately she struck about 10pm and most regrettably almost two miles off the coast, with a current setting to the eastward at the rate of three knots.

With the exception of the jollyboat all the boats were hoisted out; an anchor and cable got into the launch, for the other boats to tow, but from the rapidity of the current and the sea running high, they failed not only to tow the launch but were all driven with their crews to leeward where within an hour were lost sight of amongst the breakers, thus depriving those on board the *Crescent* of any hopes of survival. The wind now north-west blew directly on shore; the swell increasing and the ship striking very hard, the bower anchor was let go but the cable soon parted; the guns thrown overboard and the masts cut away, eased the ship very much. All hands were then employed in constructing a raft, which was made on the booms, by the different spars, and at 2pm the raft, or otherwise the *Forlorn Hope*, was launched from the booms, it had but a very indifferent appearance, having only four casks on each corner; more could not be obtained; three of those were soon washed away. The raft was ordered to be manned by the sick and part of the larboard watch (not an able seaman was on it), and given in charge of Lt Weaver of the Royal Marines. Everyone was supplied with a small line for the purpose of lashing themselves to the raft, yet during the half hour or so spent getting the men on to the raft several were washed away, whilst the others were almost perished with the cold, being frequently up to their waists in water. By good fortune the raft eventually made the shore with Lt Weaver, two midshipmen and about twenty seamen and marines. The jollyboat also reached the shore with eighteen more survivors; but their departure from the ship was more tragic. Numbers jumped overboard and endeavoured to get into the boat; those that were in were obliged to extricate the hands of the others in order to prevent the boat from being too full, as she was within eight inches of the water's edge.

Shortly after the jollyboat reached the shore the ship broke up and 220 souls perished. On board the *Crescent* were six women, one child and a passenger who all lost their lives as did Captain Temple. Of the sixty survivors it would appear that nineteen were from the boats that were driven ashore during the night. The survivors were taken from Rubjerg Knude to Aalborg in wagons, about thirty-two miles, and were treated very well.

At least one survivor, Mr Thomas Mason, the clerk of the *Crescent*, who had survived the loss of the *Anson* a year earlier, stated that their situation was truly dreadful, even worse than at the loss of his old ship. (*NC* vol 21, p64 and vol 22, p54 et seq; *Times*, 30 December 1808 and 17 January 1809; *SNL*, 31 January 1783, p6)

10 December, Jupiter, 50 guns   A Fourth Rate 50-gun ship the *Jupiter*, Captain Hon Henry Edward Reginald Baker, was wrecked upon a shoal near the Bayonne Islands, two small rocky islands situated in the Gulf of Bayonne, near Vigo. (*Times*, 10 January 1809)

On Wednesday 10 January 1809 a court martial was held on board the *Salvador del Mundo*, Admiral Young, in Hamoaze to try Captain Baker, his officers and ship's company, for the loss of the vessel. The Court adjudged the captain to be admonished, to act with more caution in future; Captain Baker not having endeavoured to obtain a pilot, or bring the ship to an anchor. (*NC* vol 21, p84)

At the time of her loss the *Jupiter* was quite an old vessel, having been built in Randall's shipyard, Rotherhithe, and launched 1778. (*NC* vol 1, p554)

18 December, Walpole, East Indiaman 'An East Indiaman the *Walpole* on her fifth voyage has gone on shore on the Mouse, one mile below Margate [the Mouse is actually 8 miles east of Shoeburyness]. Her main and mizzen masts are gone and with two hundred on board she lies with her head to the sea. There are hopes of saving all at low water.' (*Times*, 20 December 1808)

'The *Walpole* went on shore at ten o'clock, in the morning of the 18th off Fairness [Foulness] Point, and though the ship will be totally lost, yet all on board were saved and it is expected that the greater part of the cargo will also be saved. Mr Sutton the chief officer had his arm fractured by the wheel when the ship struck.' (*Times*, 21 December 1808)

Ramsgate, 21st. 'None of the *Walpole's* cargo has yet been landed, although several craft are around the vessel; she lays at low water, high and dry.' (*Times*, 23 December 1808)

'The *Walpole* continues discharging her cargo, at low water, in carts, and when the water is up, in boats, when the weather is moderate. The ship fills every tide.' (*Times*, 26 December 1808)

19 December, Tuee Gesustur, merchantman During the night of the 19th the Swedish ship *Tuee Gesustur* from Norden, laden with oats for London, struck on the Goodwin sands and was entirely lost. The crew saved themselves in the ship's boats and landed at Broadstairs. (*Times*, 23 December 1808)

21 December, Jane and Eleanor, brigs This was a bad night to be at sea; off the Dover coast a south-west gale was raging and with heavy snow it was so very dark that no object could be discerned.

The brig *Jane* of Carmarthen, Captain T Jenkins, from Limerick, with butter, feathers and hemp, for London, struck on a rock between South Pier Head and Shakespear's Cliff. The crew got on the masts via the rigging of the vessel while the captain got on the bowsprit. He was fortunate, for he was thrown off on to the beach, whereas all the others were washed off and drowned.

Very close to where the *Jane* was wrecked, the brig *Eleanor*, Captain Henderson, of Sunderland, laden with iron from Cardiff for London, was also wrecked, and all on board perished. (*Times*, 24 December 1808)

23 December, Fama, 18 guns A Danish brig mounting 18 guns, the *Fama*, was taken by the boats of the *Edgar*, Captain James McNamara, off Nyborg, on 9 August 1808. The vessel did not remain in British hands very long, for on 23 December the same year the brig then commanded by Lt Charles Topping was wrecked on Bornholm in the Baltic, during a snowstorm with nil visibility. The greater part of the crew were rescued by the Danes, but Lt Topping lost his life; he was quite young, having been appointed on 7 November 1806. (*SNL*, 1811)

26 December, Bustler, 12 guns   The *Bustler* was a 12-gun brig built by Ayles of Topsham and launched on 12 August 1805. In the morning of 26 December the ship then commanded by Lt Richard Welch ran ashore and was wrecked off Cap Gris Nez; the crew were saved. (*SNL*, 1811)

? December, cannibalism   'The *Monticello* arrived yesterday. About a fortnight ago she fell in with the wreck of a ship, which being laden with timber, was prevented from sinking. There was only one man alive on board, out of eleven that composed her crew, and shocking to relate this wretched being had preserved his existence by feeding on the bodies of his comrades.' (Times, 10 January)

1809

8 January, William, merchantman   The ship *William*, Captain Sinclear, from Demerara for London, was totally lost under St Levan signal house at Land's End on this Sunday morning. The master, mate and five seamen, lost their lives, but four men and a lad (the son of the owner), were saved by getting on a rock from which they were taken on Monday evening by means of a rope conveyed to them from the mainland. (*SYM*, 16 January 1809)

9 January, Morne Fortunee, schooner   *Morne Fortunee* was formerly a French privateer brig, mounting 12 guns, called the *Regulus*, which vessel was taken by the 44-gun *Princess Charlotte* on 13 December 1804. On 9 January 1809 the ship, then commanded by Lt John Brown, capsized in a squall off Martinique. Of her crew who numbered about fifty, only nineteen were saved. (*SNL*, 1811)

11 January, Magnet, 18 guns   *Magnet*, an 18-gun brig sloop, was built at Guillaum's yard Northam, where the vessel was launched on 19 October 1807. Commanded by Lt George Morris, the *Magnet*, escort of a small convoy, was driven with several other vessels by ice floes upon the flat marshy island of Saltholme, lying three miles off the coast at Copenhagen. Her crew were saved by ships in company. (*SNL*, 1811)

15 January, Pigeon, schooner   A small 2-gun schooner built in 1806, the *Pigeon* was commanded by Lt Richard Cox when she ran ashore during a snowstorm near Margate. The vessel quickly bilged and became a complete wreck. The crew lashed themselves to the rigging from which they were taken next morning. Two of them had however died of exposure. (*SNL*, 1811)

15 January, wounded from Corunna Extract of a letter from Dock (Devonport): 'The weather having moderated, early this morning the landing of the sick and wounded of our brave army proceeded with great alacrity; considerable numbers being brought ashore and conveyed to the hospitals. Their situation and wretched appearance was truly pitiable. Several were brought on shore dead, and some have died in the streets within the last three days on their way to the hospitals.

'It is impossible for me to portray the confusion and distress which has prevailed here the whole of the week. Women searching through the fleet for their husbands and relatives. Officers and men looking after wives, children and comrades. Nor can our loss be in any degree ascertained till a general muster takes place, and correct returns of the respective corps given in. I have, however, learnt from several intelligent officers who were present in the last engagement, that our loss in killed and wounded, and prisoners of war, and those who fell in fatigue and the want of proper food, does not fall short of nine or ten thousand men.' (*Times*, 28 January 1809). These were the wounded from the battle against Soult on 16 December 1808 during the retreat to Corunna.

18 January, Ann, brig The brig *Ann* arrived at Penzance in five days from Corunna, and landed Lt General Paget, Sir J Stewart, and two other officers. The news they brought was of a very unpleasant nature; our troops had re-embarked, but were obliged to leave their sick and wounded behind, and kill a number of horses to prevent their falling into the hands of the enemy, who were then within ten miles of Corunna. At the time of their departure from Corunna on the 14th our gallant army had arrived there and were embarking on board the transports that had come around from Vigo. (*SYM*, 23 January 1809)

19 January, Sheldrake's prize A letter dated Jersey 18 February 1809 contained the following statement:

'His Majesty's ship *Sheldrake*, Captain Thicknesse, having captured a large vessel off the coast of France, laden with about 300 quarters of wheat intended for the supply of the French army in Spain, Mr Hubbard, the master of the *Sheldrake*; a midshipman, and ten seamen, were put on board the prize, and two Frenchmen were suffered to remain with them.

'It was soon discovered that she was leaky, yet no danger was apprehended. She was spoke by the *Sheldrake* at nine o'clock in the evening of the day on which she was taken, when she was reported as being quite seaworthy. A short time afterwards, while the master and most of the crew were employed in stopping a leak that had been found in the cabin, the men at the pumps were alarmed by their becoming useless, the grain in the hold having been drawn into the suckers, which prevented them from working. Before those who were below could get upon deck, the ship went down head foremost, and every soul on board perished, except one man, who gives this melancholy account of the loss of his brave shipmates, and whose method of escape borders upon the miraculous: he was in the main-top when he discovered that the vessel was sinking; providentially a small boat was lying unfastened upon the deck, which floated from the deck as she sunk, and which he fortunately gained by swimming. He relates that he rowed about for some hours (as he imagines) near the place where she went down, hoping to save some of his comrades, but in vain. The *Sheldrake* picked him up next morning. The prize had sailed from Tercera the evening before she was captured.'

On this unfortunate occasion, Captain John Thicknesse wrote a letter to Captain Lloyd the commander of the Sea Fencibles on the coast of Lancashire, who was a friend of the late Mr William Hubbard. Dated 29 January 1809 it is quoted in part.

'On the morning of 19th January I fell in with a ship under French colours, apparently, by her papers bound to Bayonne, and laden with wheat. Poor Hubbard was accordingly sent with a midshipman and ten men to take charge of her and accompany me to Guernsey, then about fifteen leagues to leeward. At nine the same evening I hailed him to say I should heave-to at two in the morning until daylight; to which he replied "very well". I carried a top-light and an easy sail giving a strict charge to the officer of the watch not to lose sight of her. At ten the officer came down and acquainted me that the prize was lost sight of and that he had backed the main topsail. I went on deck immediately and burnt a blue light; on which it suddenly came on foggy. Therefore supposing the prize might pass me, I filled in half an hour and hove-to at two; and not seeing her at daybreak I bore away for Guernsey, trusting she was ahead. Sometime later a boat was discovered on our weather bow and painful to relate found her to be the prize's boat, with the only man who had escaped a watery grave. The prize had at ten the preceding evening sprung a sudden leak, which choked her pumps by the swelling of the wheat, and waterlogged her before they were the least aware of their imminent danger. When they found she was sinking everyone ran up the rigging; and the man who was saved, having observed the small boat floating off the booms, descended into her by the main stay and just pushed clear off the topgallant yardarm as it was disappearing. He called out as soon as he had recovered his surprise, but all was silent; and he assured me that every soul but himself went down on the rigging.' (*NC* vol 22, pp56-57)

20 January, Claudia, cutter The *Claudia*, a 10-gun cutter built in 1806, was commanded by Lt Anthony Bliss William Lord, when she was wrecked off the coast of Norway, exact position unspecified. The crew were saved. (*SNL*, 1811)

It would appear that the *Claudia* was wrecked during the night of the 19/20 January. The *NC* vol 21, p520 gives the following obituary. 'Died on

19th January 1809, Mr John Simmons the surgeon of HM ship *Claudia*, wrecked on the coast of Norway.'

22 January, Dispatch, transport, and Primrose, 18 guns At 4am the *Dispatch* transport of Shields, Captain Botley, with part of the 7th Light Dragoons, amounting in all with the crew to 100 persons, struck on the rocks at Coverack about one mile from the Manacles. She left Corunna on the 17th with Major Cavendish, Captain Duncanfield, Lt Waldegrave, and about 70 men of the 7th, together with 34 horses. When the ship struck the men were all in bed and consequently there were only six known survivors, one of whom was John Ravel, the farrier.

These brave fellows were the same as distinguished themselves so eminently under Lord Paget. (*SYM*, 30 January 1809)

Two hours after the *Dispatch* struck, and only one mile away, the 18-gun *Primrose*, sloop of war, Commander James Mein, on passage from Falmouth for Spain, with dispatches, struck on the Manacles about seven miles south of Falmouth. Of the crew who numbered about 125 there was only one survivor, a lad of seventeen years of age who had lashed himself to the stump of one of the masts where he remained for several hours until a boat neared him, threw a rope and brought him safely to shore.

A few days prior to the disaster the *Primrose* had sailed from Portsmouth with a fleet of transports, consisting of about 30 sail, destination unknown. (*NC* vol 21, pp62-63)

'The most melancholy spectacle that ever was, or we trust never will again be seen, passed through Helston to St Keverne on Tuesday 24th inst, several wagons laden with coffins to the amount of fifty, went through Helston to St Coverack, and from thence with a greater number, and with slow and solemn step, were conveyed to the churchyard of St Keverne, the bodies of the unfortunate fellows who had been crowned with honour and glory in the several skirmishes in Spain with the French Emperor's body-guards, from the edge of whose sword they had escaped the stroke of death, and near the shores of their native country met with a watery grave.' (*SYM*, 30 January 1809)

23 January, Rose, packet The *Rose* packet from Plymouth for Falmouth was wrecked on Looe Island when the crew and thirty-three passengers all lost their lives. (*SYM*, 30 January 1809; *Times*, 31 January 1809)

On this same day another vessel was seen to go down in Mount's Bay near Mullion Island, and every soul perished. She was presumed to have been a Dutch ship as 'a body resembling the Dutch features, a Dutch bible, and some wooden shoes having been washed ashore near where the vessel went down.' (*SYM*, 30 January 1809)

24 January, Admiral Gardner and Britannia, East Indiamen Whilst shipwrecked mariners were being interred at St Keverne yet others were losing their lives at the Downs. 'The effects of the gales this Tuesday were severely felt on the coasts of Britain. Great apprehensions were entertained for the fate of the East Indiamen proceeding through the Downs; yet nothing was known of their situation till the following morning, when a most distressing scene presented itself to the spectators from Deal. Three large ships were seen on the Goodwin Sands with only their fore masts standing, hoisting signals of distress, and the sea dashing over them mountains high. The crews were all collected on the poops waiting for that relief which the Deal boatmen seemed anxious to afford them. These men by their indefatigable exertions, and at the imminent hazard of their lives, reached the wrecks of the Indiamen and took out of the *Admiral Gardner* the whole of her crew.

'The boatmen from Ramsgate and Broadstairs joined those from Deal, and removed into their boats the people from the *Britannia*, previous to which this last ship had lost of her crew, three lascars and twenty-four seamen, and one died in one of the Deal boats from fatigue.

'Of the crew of the *Admiral Gardner*, four were lost; for in the night one of the seamen having been washed overboard, the third mate and three seamen volunteered their services to endeavour to pick him up in the ship's boat, which was never after heard of.

'Other accounts estimated the loss of the *Britannia* at only seven men.

'The boatmen were not in time to save a single man belonging to the third ship (a large brig), and all hands on board perished. There were proper pilots on board the Indiamen, but the violence of the weather baffled all their skill.

'The *Admiral Gardner* was the first vessel driven upon the sands; and as soon as the pilot of the *Britannia* found that that ship shoaled her water, he let go one anchor, and after that two more, but such was the violence of the gale, that she was driven on the sand with three anchors ahead.

'Vice-Admiral Campbell at daylight sent two gunbrigs, a lugger, and a cutter to anchor as near as possible in order to render the sufferers every assistance in their power. It was expected that if the weather moderated, a part of the cargoes might be saved. The loss was estimated at £200,000.' (*NC* vol 21, pp65-66)

24 January, the army at Corunna   A supplement to the *London Gazette* extraordinary contained the following release from the Admiralty Office; given here in part, it relates to the evacuation of Corunna by the British:

'18th January. The embarkation of the troops having occupied the greater part of last night, the army have been embarked to the last man, and the ships are now in the offing, preparatory to steering for England. The great body of the transports having lost their anchors, ran to sea without the troops they were ordered to receive, in consequence of which there are some thousands on board the ships of war.

'Several transports, through mismanagement, ran on shore. The seamen appeared to have abandoned them; two being brought out by the boats crews of the men of war, two were burnt and five were bilged.' (*NC* vol 21, pp83-84)

26 January, transports from Corunna During the last four days a great number of transports from Corunna have arrived at Falmouth with soldiers belonging to different regiments; some sick and wounded prisoners, belonging to the French Imperial Guards, have also been landed at Falmouth.

Two transports arrived this evening from Vigo, where the remains of the 4000 men who were detached to that port for embarkation; had arrived and embarked about 1000 short of their original number from fatigue, etc. (*SYM*, 30 January 1809)

26 January, the Corunna fleet The Plymouth report for this day reads: 'Came in the *Barfleur*, 98 guns, Rear-Admiral Sir Samuel Hood, Captain Linzee; *Tonnant*, 84 guns, Rear-Admiral the Hon. De Courcy, Captain Hancock; *Elizabeth*, 74 guns, Hon. Captain Curzon; *Zealous*, 74 guns, Captain Boys; *Norge*, 74 guns, Captain Rainier; *Implacable*, 84 guns, Captain McKenzie; *Victory*, 110 guns, Captain Serrell; *Mediator*, 44 guns; *Parthian*, 18 guns; *Unicorn*, 32 guns, Captain Hardyman; and *Cossack* of 18 guns; with one hundred and eleven sail of transports, having on board several thousand of the British troops from Corunna; and we are happy to say that part are put into Falmouth and the remainder passed up under convoy of the *Ville de Paris*, 110 guns, Captain Garden, and the *Endymion* for Portsmouth.

'Lieutenant Colonel Kerrison, who had his arm broke, is at the Pope's Head. He is in a fair way of recovery.' (*SYM*, 30 January 1809)

5 February, Carrier, cutter A small cutter mounting 10 guns, the *Carrier*, was commanded by Lt William Milner when the vessel was stranded on a sandbank off Boulogne. The crew rescued by the French had to endure five years as prisoners of war. (*SNL*, 1809)

9 February, Robert, cartel transport Letters were received at Plymouth from Captain Thorne of the cartel transport *Robert*, dated in the Downs. He stated that after he landed the French troops from Lisbon in Quiberon he was proceeding eastwards when he fell in with a French privateer, was taken, and carried into Calais. There, upon stating to the commandant of Calais his situation, and being in want of a cable and anchor, he was immediately presented with £70 in money as compensation for his detention, and provided with a new cable and anchor in exchange for old.

While he was there he observed twelve privateers from 12 to 16 guns fully manned by Danes, Americans, Irishmen and Englishmen, all ready for a start the moment the wind became fair. (*SYM*, 13 February 1809)

10 February, Barfleur's boat On Friday afternoon 10 February a boat with a crew of twenty-two persons belonging to the *Barfleur*, 98 guns, Captain Linzee, was upset in a heavy sea, when attempting to cross the Bridge of Rocks between Mount Edgcumbe and St Nicholas' Island, by which disastrous event seventeen persons were unfortunately drowned, among whom was Mr Foote, a lieutenant of marines, 21 years of age, son of the Rev Mr Foote of Torr; also Mr Le Mesurier, a master's mate. The remaining five, after floating by the aid of the oars about four hours, were picked up by the boats of the frigate *Emerald*. (*SYM*, 20 February 1809)

'It appears that the boat was proceeding from Cawsand Bay to the *Salvador del Mundo* in Hamoaze with two prisoners, John Bennet seaman, and William Jones carpenter's mate of the *Barfleur*, who were to take their trial next morning on a charge of having mutinously expressed their desire to have a new captain. Jones was among the drowned, as also were many of the witnesses; but Bennet was one of the five that were saved. Before the Court was formed the surviving prisoner had the option of postponing his trial but, although exhausted from lying in the water, he requested to be tried immediately. A long investigation took place when the Court adjudged that the charge was not proved, and the prisoner was acquitted. Many of the officers of the ship came forward and gave the prisoner an excellent character. It appeared in evidence that in consequence of a letter having been sent to the Admiralty against the captain, he turned the hands up, to inquire what complaint they had against him. The general answer was "A new captain". That the prisoner having sailed with Captain Linzee for some time was particularly asked his complaint and went the length of observing he did not wish to sail with the captain again. The prisoner read a written defence, which seemed to make a due impression on the Court. It is remarkable that the paper was in his pocket during the time he was in the water. We trust the unnecessary sacrifice of so many lives will not be suffered to pass unnoticed; this passage is so notoriously dangerous in bad weather that we hope steps will ere long be taken to prevent the fatal accidents that so frequently occur.

'The body of the unfortunate Lt Foote was picked up on the 13th and on the 16th an inquest was held on it; the jury returned a verdict, accidentally drowned.' (*NC* vol 21, pp161-162)

28 February, Proserpine, 32 guns The *Proserpine*, Captain Charles Otter, was a 32-gun frigate built in 1807. The vessel was taken and carried into Toulon by the French frigates, *Penelope* and *Pauline*, after a severe action during which the *Proserpine* suffered eleven killed and fifteen wounded. (*SNL*, October 1811, p79)

On 30 May 1814, after 5½ years as prisoners of war, Captain Otter, his officers and ship's company, were tried by court martial for the loss of the *Proserpine*, and her capture by a French squadron of two sail of the line and three frigates. The Court determined that the *Proserpine* was defended in a most gallant and determined manner, and was not surrendered until resistance was of no avail. Captain Otter, his officers and ship's company were honourably acquitted. (*NC* vol 31, p487)

? March, Harrier, 18 guns The *Harrier*, an 18-gun sloop of war, was built at Barnard and Roberts Yard at Deptford, and launched on 22 August 1804. The ship was commanded by Cdr John James Ridge when she parted from ships in company during a gale, when off the Île de France (Mauritius) in the Indian Ocean.

The vessel was never seen again, nor was any trace of her ever found; and another 125 seamen had perished with their ship. (*SNL*, 1809)

This was the same *Harrier* that was in company with the *Blenheim* and *Java* when both vanished in the Indian Ocean on 1 March 1807 (*qv*).

1 April, Lord Melville, merchantman A copy of a letter from Captain Brown of the ship *Lord Melville* to his owners Messrs John Campbell, Sen and Co Glasgow; reproduced here in part: 'It is with regret I inform you of the loss of your ship *Lord Melville*; she was burned at sea on 1st April 1809 in position 55°07'N 26°30'W. At three p.m. while writing in the cabin Mr Hutchon, a passenger on board, called down "The ship's on fire". I instantly ran to the deck and to my astonishment found it was the case; but neither of the mates nor any person on deck could tell me where the fire was or how it began. Every attempt was made to save the ship but all our efforts were fruitless, and at four p.m. the fire began rapidly to increase. Our situation then was beyond description, fifty puncheons of rum below deck and the magazine full of gunpowder. The latter we got emptied by one desperate effort, at the imminent risk of our lives.

'We then got the boats out for our future preservation and at five p.m. quitted the ship just as we stood, when we could no longer remain by her. I was informed that Jacob Anderson the boatswain had gone below with a candle while we were at dinner, and had been drawing off rum, which no doubt has been the cause of this melancholy business. He fell victim to it for his unpardonable conduct; we never saw him afterwards. At six o'clock both main and mizzen mast fell by the board and she blew up, a melancholy end to such a ship and cargo. Our situation then was beyond description: night coming on; twenty-six people in two small boats, fifteen in one and eleven in the other, and 650 miles from land. To all human appearance it was only the prolongation of a miserable existence. We parted from the small boat on the 3rd in the evening and never saw her again. During the time we were in the boat we were constantly wet with rain; the wind variable and sometimes a heavy sea; and we had nothing to live on but raw beef and water; biscuit we had none. On the 5th we fell in with the brig *Sally* of Whitehaven, Captain Anthony Grayson,who took us on board, and whose humanity to us will for ever stamp him as a man of feeling, for his fellow creatures in distress.' (*NC* vol 22, pp293-294)

The above was also printed verbatim in the *Times*, 26 June 1809.

17 April, Sparks and Rebecca, merchantman The ship *Sparks and Rebecca*, Captain Service, sailed from Liverpool for Malta on 16 April and was supposed to have foundered the following day, as the pilot did not return. Three bodies were later washed ashore and one was identified as the captain, not only by the clothes he was wearing but also by his having the bill of lading in one of his pockets. (*Times*, 7 July 1809)

30 April, Alcmene, 32 guns   On this day at 4.30pm the 32-gun frigate *Alcmene*, Captain Tremlett, standing into the Loire, following the 44-gun *Amelia* frigate, Hon Captain Irby, to reconnoitre the enemy's force struck on the Blanche Rock, off Nantes, owing to the ignorance of the pilot; and the tide then ebbing fast precluded the possibility of heaving her off; then at low water she bilged and broke her back. Happily the whole of her crew got safe on board the *Amelia* after first removing her stores and burning her to the water's edge. (*Times*, 15 May 1809)

14 May, fire in London docks This Sunday night a fire broke out in a vessel adjoining Billingsgate Dock in Lower Thames Street. The flames extended almost instantly to the other shipping and from them again to the line of warehouses running from the dock along Dyce Quay, etc. Notwithstanding the prompt assistance afforded by the engines, which reached the spot in a very short period from the commencement of the fire, its progress was very rapid. The range of warehouses filled with sugar, tar, oil, hemp, turpentine, tallow, etc, etc, were all successively consumed; the extensive warehouses of Ralph's Quay, Smart's Quay, Young's Quay and Dyce's Quay were entirely destroyed; Wiggon's Quay partly so.

The fire communicated in a gradual but rapid manner to the vessels next the shore but with a favourable tide, about 11pm several of the vessels were towed out, although with extreme difficulty. Four were completely burnt and about the same number damaged. A floating engine which was worked with great skill was of considerable service in preventing the extension of the flames along the river. The fire was said to have been caused in the following manner: A lamplighter imprudently struck his link [torch] when burning against a cask of spirits of turpentine, which it would appear must have been leaky, and the contents immediately took fire. A watchman then went to the lamplighter's assistance and the cask was pushed forward with the view of rolling it into the Thames. It took a different direction, however, and fell into a ship lying alongside the wharf. (*Times*, 15 and 16 May 1809)

15 May, Contest, gunbrig The *Times* printed the following article: 'The *Contest* gunbrig which arrived at Plymouth on Thursday (11th) got on shore in the night in Basque Roads [off La Rochelle], where she was soon dry, and remained so next morning at daylight, which being perceived by the enemy, they detached about five hundred men with muskets and field pieces to the beach to attack the vessel as she lay. The *Contest* could not get a gun to bear on them for more than an hour, till at length by great exertions she hoisted her guns over on the sand and with canister and grape shot soon cleared the beach of the enemy, many of whom were killed and the rest made a precipitate retreat.'

31 May, Unique, 12 guns The *Unique*, formerly *Le Duquesne*, a French gunbrig privateer mounting 12 guns, was taken on 23 September 1807 by the 38-gun *Blonde* frigate in the West Indies. On 31 May 1809 the *Unique* was lost when she was burnt by the French at Basseterre on the island of Guadaloupe. (*SNL*, 1812)

18 June, Sealark, schooner The *Sealark* was a schooner built at Wheaton's Yard at Brixham and launched on 1 August 1806. On 29 June 1809 the *Times* printed the following: 'The *Sealark* schooner has been upset on the coast of Holland and all hands on board, excepting one man, unfortunately perished.'

It may be noted that whereas *Steel's Navy List* of 1809 stated that the *Sealark* mounted 10 guns and was commanded by Lt B Banks at the time of the disaster, Clowes gives the name of the lieutenant as James Proctor and the number of guns mounted as 4, which probably reflects later research.

20 June, Agamemnon, 64 guns The 64-gun ship *Agamemnon* was built at Adam's Yard, Bucklers Hard, and launched on 10 April 1781. On 20 June 1809 the vessel, then commanded by Captain Jonas Rose, was wrecked in the River Plate when she struck a sandbank. The entire complement of 491 men and boys were saved; it was stated that many men wept when they were ordered to leave the old ship. (*SNL* and the *Times*, 12 September, both 1809)

25 June, Charwell, transport The transport brig *Charwell*, Captain Bigbie, with a detachment of the Royal Artillery and 2nd West India Regiment, and with a quantity of ordnance stores on board, was lost this day going into San Domingo, yet all on board were saved. (*Times*, 26 September 1809)

11 July, Solebay, 32 guns   The *Solebay*, 32 guns, Captain Edward Henry Columbine, was engaged in the reduction of Babaque Island in the Senegal river, about twelve miles above the bar when she took the ground and ultimately became a complete wreck, though no lives were lost and many stores were saved.

On 11 September a court martial was convened at Portsmouth to try Captain Columbine, his officers and ship's company, for the loss of the *Solebay*; they were all honourably acquitted, but it appeared that after she was on shore and before she was abandoned, four seamen belonging to her had been in a state of drunkenness. Michael Grace and Thomas Jones were each sentenced to receive 150 lashes; and Charles Nileus and Robert Storks to receive 50 lashes each; in addition to which the four were to be mulcted, or to forfeit all the pay due to them from 11 July last.

At the time the *Solebay* was lost she had been in company with the 18-gun *Derwent*, Commander Frederick Parker, who unfortunately lost his life on 7 July on the bar of the Senegal river. On 19 September, a court martial was held at Portsea on John Ashley, carpenter of the *Derwent*, for being drunk when ordered on duty at the capture of Senegal; so that he was incapable of leading his men to the attack of that place. He was sentenced to be dismissed the service, rendered incapable of serving as an officer again, and to be imprisoned six months in the Marshalsea prison.

The above court martial reports were both taken from *NC* vol 22, p243; these were themselves copied vertabtim from the *Times*, which however gave the trial dates as 28 and 29 August respectively.

3 August, Lark, 18 guns   The *Lark* was an 18-gun sloop of war, commanded by Robert Nicholas, the second son of Mr Nicholas, late MP for Cricklade and grandson of the late Admiral Sir Thomas Frankland, when she foundered during a gale off Cape Causada. There were only three survivors (120 died), and the substance of the depositions received from them, and given here, are taken from the *Times* of 22 November 1809.

Statement of William Dobson: 'The *Lark* anchored at Palenque in the evening of 2nd August and continued so till five o'clock the next morning when it came on to blow hard from the northward and obliged us to cut our best bower cable and stand out to sea, At about nine o'clock the foresail and fore topmast staysail blew to pieces in a most violent squall, which came rather ahead, and at the same time a tremendous sea broke over the larboard quarter, which completely filled the ship, when she fell over upon the starboard beam ends and instantly foundered. There was no other vessel in company. I immediately got hold of a piece of plank which I found in the water. In about an hour after I observed two men who proved to be John Gordon the cooper, and John Antonio a Spaniard, who were also on planks and we continued together until seven in the evening, when we were picked up by the *Moselle* [another 18-gun sloop].'

John Gordon stated that after the *Lark* had been struck by the sea he ran upon deck and observed the captain and officers standing upon the quarter deck; the captain gave orders to haul the foresail up, but the clue garnets gave way and the sail beat to pieces; at this time the ship was lying on her starboard beam ends and filling fast; in about five minutes after the sea struck her she sunk.

John Antonio states he jumped overboard and swam to a piece of plank; at this time the captain was close beside him in the water but he lost sight of him almost immediately afterwards and supposes him to have sunk. They all concur that none but themselves can possibly have been saved.

At the time of his death Captain Nicholas was 28 years of age. A few years previously, on the same station, died Captain Boyle Nicholas, who was another descendant of the family of Sir Edward Nicholas, Secretary of State to the two kings, Charles I and II.

A further account of the loss of the *Lark* was given in a letter from an officer of the 38-gun frigate *Hebe*, to the editor of the *NC* dated Sunday 6 August 1809, the *Hebe* then being off the city of Santo Domingo.

'We have just spoke the *Moselle*, Captain Boys, from whom we have learnt most dreadful news respecting the *Lark*, Captain Nicholas. It appears from a man on board, who with two others were picked up by the *Moselle* on Thursday evening, that the *Lark* was at anchor in Palanqua Bay, a few miles to the leeward of the city of Santo Domingo, on the 3rd inst. and on the commencement of the gale (which was about five o'clock in the morning) was obliged to cut away with a tomahawk, no axe being ready, and scudded under her foresail, and fore storm staysail, for about four hours; when, in attempting to lay-to (which was about nine o'clock, the period when it blew hardest) she broached to, (by the fore sheet, and staysail sheet, and tack giving way) and of course lost her way. A sea then struck her abaft, stove in her cabin windows, no dead light [solid shutters] being in, and almost filled her; another striking her almost at the same time on the beam, laid her on her beam ends, where she continued a few minutes, no-one being able to get an axe to cut away the masts &c. and then went down stern foremost.

'The man declared that he actually saw her keel as she lay on her beam ends before she went down, and saved himself by being on the jibboom.'

Then follows a log kept on board the *Hebe*, which was four or five miles from the *Lark* on Thursday 3 August 1809.

'A.M. At 1.30: squally, shortened sail. 3.45: fresh breeze and cloudy weather, in third reefs of topsails. 4: ditto weather. 4.20: strong breezes and cloudy, close reefed the topsails. 4.30: furled ditto and mainsail, gale increasing. 6: strong gales, with heavy rain, sent topgallant yards and masts on deck, in jibboom, and got the spritsail yard fore and aft. 8: ditto weather. 8.30: shipped several high seas, carried away the head rails, and guard iron, split the rudder coat, washed several pots away, and damaged a quantity of bread in the after gun-room. 10: set the storm staysails. 10.30: more moderate, in first reef of foresail, and set it.' (*NC* vol 25, pp213-214)

7 August, unnamed timber ship   The *SYM* carried a Plymouth report dated 3 August: 'Tuesday (1st) came in a large ship, with timber of great dimensions, supposed to be from New Brunswick. She was found abandoned by her master and crew, floating on the high seas waterlogged; from the circumstance of her being covered in barnacles inside and out, she is supposed to have been several weeks in that condition. She was picked up in the Atlantic Ocean five weeks since by the *Virago* gunbrig, and has been in tow of her ever since. She is now between the island (St Nicholas) and the main, stripping to go into harbour to be unladen.

'From a bottle, sealed, found in her well with a letter in it, it appears she belongs to Messrs Scott and Idle of London, was bound from New Brunswick to this dockyard with large timber, and is supposed to be worth £20,000. Her master and crew were taken up by the *Amelia*, 44-gun frigate, when she was in a sinking state, about two months since, and she had been tossing about ever since. She is now hauled alongside the Calder basin to be unloaded.'

12 August, Peace, merchantman   A large ship called *Peace*, belonging to London was lost on Saturday the 12th during the night near Salcombe and all the crew perished. The vessel was supposed to be from Spain and had a cargo of wine and nuts which together with the ship was totally lost. On Sunday the 13th eight men and a boy were picked up and interred at Salcombe. (*Times*, 15 August 1809)

13 August, Mr Murphy's boat   Mr Murphy's boat which conveyed passengers to and from the *Liverpool Packet*, at the Pigeon House, Dublin, went with passengers to the *Moira Packet*. Shortly afterwards, the vessel getting under sail with the boat lying alongside, the main beam struck the boat's mast and the five men on the boat were precipitated into the sea. Captain Roberts of the *Moira* put out the boat and picked up three. Mr Gibbons, one of the proprietors of the *Liverpool Packet* and a seaman named Farrel were drowned. (*Times*, 19 August 1809)

16 August, Meikle Ferry   A great number of people from Dornoch and other parts of Sutherland who were on their way to attend the Tain market on Wednesday last (16th), most imprudently crowded into the passage boat at the Meikle Ferry, to the number of at least 100 to 120, being considerably beyond its burthen. Unfortunately, from their anxiety to get across they were insensible to the danger to which they exposed themselves, and scarcely half way across the boat foundered and excepting for five persons, all were drowned. Mr McCulloch, sheriff substitute of Dornoch was said to be among the sufferers. (Inverness report of the 18th, quoted in the *Times*, 25 August).

On 1 September the *Times* quoted a further report which stated that the accident occurred because the boatmen were intoxicated and furthermore that the number of persons on board exceeded 140.

19 August, Jenny, collier The *Jenny* of South Shields, William Blagdon master and owner, was a collier on her passage to London when on Saturday night (19th) off Filey she was run foul of by a large sloop rigged vessel, supposed to be a Berwick smack. The *Jenny* foundered immediately and all hands except a mate and boy perished. A Mrs Hall sister of Mr Blagdon and her son aged eight were returning to London from visiting friends and they both died. (*Times*, 31 August 1809)

31 August, Foxhound, 18 guns The *Foxhound*, an 18-gun brig, was built at King's Yard, Dover, and launched on 30 November 1806. The ship was on her return passage from Halifax, Nova Scotia, when she went down in the Atlantic. Cdr James McKenzie, and his entire crew of about 120 men and boys perished, as the vessels in company were unable to render any assistance. (*SNL*, December 1812)

2 September, Minx, gunbrig The *Minx*, a gunbrig built in 1801 by Pitcher and Sons at Northfleet, was commanded by Lt George Le Blanc, and stationed off the Scaw as a lightship when taken by six Danish gunboats. (*SNL*, 1811). See also 10 December 1803.

3 September, Minerva, brig This morning the brig *Minerva* of Liverpool, Thomas Swainston master, from Portsmouth for Malta with 193 cases of sugar was driven on to the rocks a little to the eastwards of the Lizard where she was soon beaten to pieces, and where two members of the crew lost their lives. (*SYM*, 18 September 1809)

16 September, West Indies convoy A fleet of 44 vessels under convoy of the 74-gun *Captain* and 64-gun *Intrepid*, sailed from Martinique on 24 July, most destined for London.

On 27 August at 1.30am the ships experienced a violent gale for one hour when in position 41°N 42°W; and at daylight on the 28th 17 sail were to be seen in great distress, many dismasted. The *Henry*, which arrived at Plymouth on this day, lost her main and mizzen masts and had her rudder much damaged; every article on her deck was washed overboard and part of her cargo, consisting of 103 bags of cocoa, all the coffee, 15 hogsheads of sugar and 16 guns were obliged to be thrown overboard at the commencement of the gale. Several people were seen on wrecks, yet no assistance was possible and they were seen to go down. The *Express* cutter, together with several of the fleet, was supposed to have foundered during the gale as they were not afterwards heard of. (The *Express* was not lost.)

At the entrance to the Channel the *Henry* fell in with the fleet from Jamaica which had sailed on 20 July, under convoy of the 16-gun *Favourite* sloop of war, and which fleet together with the rest of the fleet from Martinique, only consisted of 14 sail. (*Times*, 19 and 20 September 1809)

24 September, dangers of the Bridge rocks Eleven men belonging to the *Tonnant*, who set off in a boat to join their ship in Cawsand Bay, at 12am on Sunday the 24th were all drowned on the ridge of rocks called the Bridge, which runs from St Nicholas Island to Mount Edgcumbe. The accident occurred on the ebb tide and as late as 7 October no bodies had been recovered, yet spars and oars belonging to the boat had been found. (*Times*, 3 and 9 October 1809)

The practice of suffering men to proceed in bad weather by this dangerous passage cannot be too strongly reprobated. Last year Lt Foote and sixteen seamen belonging to the *Barfleur* were sacrificed at this very spot, having been sent on a very squally day to convey three men to the *Salvador del Mundo* in Hamoaze to be tried on charges of which they were unanimously acquitted. (*Times*, 3 October, 1809). [In fact, it was 10 February 1809 and not three but two men were involved. The *Times* often made mistakes of this nature.]

?October, Dominica, gunbrig The gunbrig *Dominica*, formerly the French 14-gun privateer, *Tape a L'Oeil*, was captured by the British in 1807 and during this month of October was commanded by Lt Charles Welsh. The ship was cruising off Tortola, one of the Virgin Islands, when she was caught in a hurricane and capsized. Of her crew of fifty men and boys there were only three survivors; Lt Welsh was not one of them. (*SNL*, 1811)

3 November, Le Curieux, 18 guns The French brig *Le Curieux*, 18 guns, was taken at Fort Edward, Martinique, on 4 February 1804 by boats of the 74-gun *Centaur* led by Lt Robert Carthew Reynolds. The ship was bought by the British Admiralty the following year, and on 3 November 1809 the vessel then commanded by Lt the Hon G Moysey was wrecked in the West Indies (off Marie Galante Island). The crew were saved. (*SNL*, February 1807 and October 1811)

6 November, Diamond and Futty Allebhoy, merchantmen The following particulars are copied from an article in an Indian paper under the date of Bombay 9 December 1809:

'The *Diamond* and the *Futty Allebhoy* left Bassora (Basra) in company with the *Bassora Packet* on 29th October last, and after touching at Bushire proceeded on their voyage to this place. On 5th November it began to blow a hard gale: the weather at the same time hazy and the sea very high. At four o'clock next morning the *Diamond* found herself amongst breakers and shortly afterwards struck on the reef that lies on the NW end of the island of Nobflower [Nabiyu Farur]. An attempt was made to wear the ship, but the rudder going away she was driven on shore and laid on her beam ends. In about a quarter of an hour the *Futty Allebhoy* also struck, and shared the fate of the *Diamond*. Both vessels succeeded in getting all the crew and passengers on shore, with the exception of the Serang and one lascar belonging to the *Diamond*, who were drowned.

'In the afternoon, the waters having fallen, and the sea abated a good deal, Captain Benson of the *Diamond* went on board with a few of the best lascars, and the second officer, to try if they could save any of the treasure, provisions and clothes.

'They found the captain's trunks broken open, and a great many things missing; which they suspected to have been done by the arab horse keepers, whose conduct in other respects during the time of danger and calamity, is represented as having been very mutinous. A considerable part of the treasure, the packet, and a few clothes, with some bags of rice, and about twenty gallons of water, were brought on shore.

'Some of the horses were found alive; but it was impossible to get them out without cutting a hole in the ship's side; besides which, any attempt thus to save them, would only have exposed them to perish on shore for the want of fresh water. A few horses did indeed escape, from the ship and swam ashore; but in consequence of the total want of fresh water, they either died before the people quitted the island or were left there to perish.

'The sufferers had but a melancholy prospect before them; the whole number amounted to about 220 souls; the island on which they were cast was completely desolate, not a shrub or a drop of water to be found. They made large fires and slept around them during the night.

'To their great satisfaction, a ship appeared in sight the next morning, which turned out to be the *Bassora Packet*, that at the commencement of the gale had parted company. By the humane exertions of Captain Clement, who immediately went on shore to their assistance, they were all safely embarked on the packet before nightfall. It was found impossible to do anything effectual towards saving either vessel.' (*NC* vol 23, pp480-481)

? November, Glommen, 18 guns   The *Glommen*, 18 guns, Lt Charles Pickford, was formerly a Danish ship taken at the surrender of Copenhagen on 7 September 1807. The vessel was wrecked during a gale in Carlisle Bay, Barbadoes, where the crew were rescued by the 40-gun frigate *Gloire*. (*SNL*, October 1811)

7 December, Harlequin, armed ship   The *Harlequin*, a hired armed ship, sailed from Plymouth Sound during the afternoon of Tuesday 5 December, as convoy to a fleet of 27 sail. The wind was fair and remained so until the vessel struck near Seaford, at 4am on Thursday the 7th, when most were in their hammocks. Thinking the ship might be got off, the masts were soon cut away but the vessel bilged so that all efforts to save her were unavailing. An officer continued: 'Little did we think at the time we were so near the shore; all of us thought we had struck on a rock; and we immediately fired our guns and burnt blue lights till all were expended; yet the convoy continued to follow us and six of them struck; the rest hauled their wind and got safe off; those on shore soon went to pieces. Ours being the first vessel that struck, and nearest the shore, we lost only two lives, but many poor souls belonging to the other vessels perished, amounting in the whole to forty.' (*NC* vol 23, pp111-112)

13 December, Minerva   The ship *Minerva*, Captain Wheeler, from Virginia for Dublin, was lost in Douglas Bay (Isle of Man) with all her crew (the captain and steward excepted), together with the Kinsale pilot and two customs men. (*Times*, 25 December 1809)

13 December, Junon, 38 guns   In position 17°18'N 57°W the 38-gun frigate *Junon*, Captain John Shortland, at 5.30pm was engaged by the two French 40-gun frigates *La Renommee*, Cdr Roquebert, and the *Clorinde*, Captain St Cricq, having under their convoy the 40-gun frigates *La Seine* and *La Loire*, both armed *en flute*, yet mounting 20 guns apiece. With the *Junon* was the 16-gun *Observateur*, Cdr Frederick Wetherall and two transports under their convoy. After a most desperate resistance on the part of the *Junon*'s crew, the ensign was pulled down and the *Observateur* seeing the impossibility of preventing the taking of the *Junon*, hauled her wind and escaped; but the transports did not.

The *Junon* had commenced the action with 224 men of whom twenty, including Captain Shortland, were killed, and a further seventy were wounded. The damage to the *Junon* was such that the French deeming it impossible to carry her to Guadaloupe, only two days' sail away, set her on fire.

The *Junon* had not long been in the possession of the British; she had been captured in the West Indies on 10 February 1809. (*Times*, 6 February 1810; *SNL*, 1811)

14 December, Defender, gunbrig   The *Defender* was a gunbrig mounting 14 guns and commanded by Lt John George Nops, when she was driven ashore under Cob Point, near Folkestone, and became a total loss. The ship's crew, about fifty men, were saved. (*SNL*, 1811) (Cob, Cop or Copt Point is a headland one mile NE of Folkestone.)

18 December, Thomas, merchantman   During a severe north-easterly gale the ship *Thomas* from Curacao for Liverpool became embayed in Redwharf Bay, Anglesey, a lee shore, and within a few minutes completely went to pieces. Every soul on board, it was believed about thirty persons, perished. (*Times*, 25 December 1809)

? December, Contest, gunbrig The *Contest*, a gunbrig mounting 12 guns, was launched in June 1804. The ship was commanded by Lt John Gregory who with his entire crew perished, when the vessel foundered in the Atlantic, on her passage from America. (*SNL*, 1811) [This may have been as a direct consequence of the vessel grounding on 15 May of the present year (*qv*).]

? December, Pelter, gunbrig The *Pelter* gunbrig built at Deptford, was launched July 1804. The vessel, mounting 14 guns, was commanded by Lt William Evelyn and was on passage from Halifax, Nova Scotia, for the Leeward Islands, when she foundered in the Atlantic Ocean with the entire crew. (*SNL*, 1811)

27 December, unknown victim of fire At Plymouth, 31 December, arrived the *Shannon*, 38 guns, Captain Broke, from Basque Roads. On the night of the 27th a ship was discovered at some distance to be on fire, then about eight leagues to the westward of Ushant. The *Shannon* immediately stood towards her and a boat was lowered and sent off from that ship to save the people, yet on coming alongside it was found that she had burnt to the water's edge and had not a soul on board. From the state of the vessel it was supposed she must have been burning about fourteen hours; and as no boat was found near her, it is to be hoped that her crew may have landed on the French coast; it was not possible to ascertain to which nation she belonged, but there is reason to believe she was a light collier. (*Times*, 3 January 1810)

28 December, arms for Spain The Plymouth report this day read as follows: 'The *Amazon*, 38 guns, Captain Parker, which sailed for Corunna a few days since, has carried out for the use of the Spanish patriots, 10,000 stand of arms, and a proportionate quantity of musquet ball cartridges, fit for their calibre, which were manufactured in the laboratory of the gun-wharf at this port, where 400 children are daily employed in forming and filling ball cartridges for musquetry.' (*SYM*, Monday 1 January, 1810)

1810

6 February, Albion and Nesbery, merchantmen The brig *Shaw*, Captain Jackson, arrived at Liverpool on 9 April with the following melancholy account:

'On the 10th ult. in position 37°30'N 42°20'W a sail hove in sight at SE with only her fore mast and bowsprit standing. She proved to be the ship

Albion, Captain Kirby, of London from New Brunswick, which on 6th February was upset in a heavy gale of wind, but sometime after righted. The surviving part of the crew (the captain and two others, out of thirteen) were in such an emaciated state that they were not able to get into the boat when the *Shaw* came alongside, having been thirty-eight days in want of food; they had made a temporary wood hut well secured to the rigging but open at the top, and were found chewing the bark of a spruce spar which had been their principal support, and had been without water for several days. What added to their distress was that of seeing their fellow sufferers dying for want.

'On the 23rd ult. fell in with the brig *Nesbery* of Liverpool, in distress being struck by lightning on the 21st, which shattered her fore topmasts in such a manner as rendered them both useless, and caused her to make a quantity of water; kept in company with the brig till they made land. (*NC* vol 23, p486)

7 February, Achates, 10 guns   The *Achates*, a 10-gun brig, built by S and D Brent on one of their seven slips at Rotherhithe, was launched in February 1808. Two years later the vessel was commanded by Thomas Pinto when she was wrecked near Point de Antigue on the island of Guadaloupe. The crew were saved. (*NC* vol 31, p185; *SNL*, 1811)

15 February, Wild Boar, 10 guns   The *Wild Boar*, Commander Thomas Burton, a 10-gun sloop of war, was launched at Frindsbury, Rochester, July 1808. This vessel also had a short life, being wrecked 18 months later on the Runnelstone, approximately two miles south of Gwennap Head. (*NC* vol 25, p223; *SNL*, 1811) [*Wild Boar* went down almost at once and except for twelve who were drowned, the remainder of the crew were rescued by a Swansea brig which happened to be passing. (*SNL*, 1811)]

15 February, Tigris, East Indiaman   The *Tigris* East Indiaman was about to be paid off when a slop boat went alongside to supply the crew with clothing. Whilst the ship's company were purchasing, three of the seamen with the intention to desert seized the slop boat and were making for the shore; when Mr Upham the chief mate hailed the deserters and threatened to shoot them if they did not immediately return. No attention being paid to his threat he fired and killed one of the deserters; the other two were taken and put in irons on board the *Tigris*. The deceased was taken to the Castle and Falcon for a coroner's inquest to be held. Mr Upham the chief mate was held in confinement in the same tavern until a verdict was given. No locality is given in the article. (*Times*, 15 February 1810)

4 April, Cuckoo, schooner   The 8-gun schooner *Cuckoo*, Lt Silas Hiscutt Paddon, was driven ashore by a west-south-west gale at Galantzoog, near

Haarlem, during the night of the 4th; when the crew, rescued by the Dutch, surrendered to troops from Amsterdam. Lt Paddon was injured getting ashore. (*Times*, 17 April 1810; *SNL*, October, 1811)

15 April, San Juan Principe, frigate The subjoined letter, given here in part, was written from Gibraltar by Alexander Wilson, son of Mr Wilson, a watchmaker of Kelso:

'Gibraltar, 19th April 1810.

'On Sunday the 15th inst. I witnessed a scene of horror I never can forget. A Portuguese frigate the *San Juan Principe*, Captain R J F Lobo, was reported to be wrecked on the east coast, about four miles from the Spanish lines. About eight o'clock in the morning I could plainly perceive with a glass the vessel dismasted and a great number of men on board. A friend of mine, Mr Masser, and I immediately took horse and arrived on the beach about nine. We found the ship had almost at that instant gone to pieces and about two hundred men were floating on fragments of the wreck, and driving towards the mouth of a small river, which was swelled by the late rains. At the same time a most tremendous sea set in, which had raised the bank of sand at its mouth. I found I could ford the river about shoulder deep. Mr Masser followed me, as did some Spaniards. For two hours we were employed in snatching from a watery grave those unfortunates who were clinging to pieces of wreckage. With great difficulty I saved Captain Lobo, the second captain and a midshipman and Mr Masser saved the purser; these were the only officers saved. I dragged out a lieutenant, yet he expired on the beach.

'The crew consisted of 315 out of which there were 116 survivors. About half-past twelve, only nine persons remained on the wreck and with the assistance of people who arrived from the garrison four of these were saved. The sight was most dreadful; but the cause we had embarked upon nerved our arms.' (*NC* vol 25, pp215–216)

20 ? May, Margaret, merchantman The ship *Margaret*, Fairchild master, was overset on her passage from Naples to Salem. Fifteen of her crew escaped in the longboat and were saved. When the longboat quitted the wreck there were thirty-one persons still remaining on board. On 29 June in position 40°N 41°W the small boat of the *Margaret*, having Captain H Larcom of Beverley, Mr J Very and Mr E A Irvine of Salem, on board, was fallen in with and picked up by Captain Davis, in the *General Johnson*, from Lisbon for Gloucester, Massachusetts. The following account was given by Captain Larcom:

'The longboat quitted the *Margaret* on Monday 21st May at noon. The yawl was left adrift, having been attached to the stern of the longboat, but was recovered by one of the sailors, who swam to it and brought it back to the wreck, where they fastened her shattered parts together in the best manner they could. The people on board then proceeded to establish some order, to give the more efficiency to their exertions for self preservation. A scaffold with a covering was erected on the quarter rails and provisions and water secured and dealt out. The first week they had plenty of salt meat, pork, hams, flour, water, &c. They also caught a turtle, and having found a tinder box in the chest, kindled a fire and made soup, which gave them all a good warm dinner, but the last they ever cooked; for in the gale of wind on Sunday 27th May the upper deck of the ship was ripped open by the violence of the sea, the stern broken off, and their provisions and water swept away. On this Captain Larcom and four others took to the yawl, crazy as she was, keeping a painter fast to the wreck; the other twenty-six went forward to the bowsprit with two gallons of wine and a little salt meat; and another stage was raised upon the bows, to live on.

'After the upper deck and the stern were gone the vessel rose considerably, so that the water was only knee-deep on the lower deck. They were able with a boat-hook to collect from below hams &c. but for the want of water these were of little benefit. The wine above-mentioned was all the drink they had for seven days; they then with great labour procured a pipe of brandy from the lower hold, which proved immediately fatal to many of them; for their great thirst prompted them to drink too freely of it, and fourteen perished the succeeding night. One (a black man) had perished two days before, and another died the day after.

'During their lying in this wretched condition, their miseries were aggravated by seeing no less than four sail of vessels pass at a distance; the first of these was on the third day after the longboat had left them, and was so near that the yawl was despatched to intercept her, but in vain, she approached nigh enough to see the men moving upon deck but not to attract their notice, and was obliged to return unsuccessful.

'Seventeen days had now passed away, without relief, and Captain Larcom suggested moving the boat further northward, as being more in the track of vessels; there were only three on board the wreck who were in a situation to take any interest in it, and these thought their chances as good to remain, as to venture off in such a shattered boat without provision. Captain Larcom, however, and the four that were with him (Irvine, Very, Layth and John Treadwell all of Salem) determined on this expedient, and accordingly set a little sail and steered north-west, having some pork, brandy and a quadrant on board. They left the wreck, by observation in latitude 39°12'N. Using the brandy sparingly they derived some support from it; the pork they could not eat for want of water. After ten or twelve days sailing it rained and they saved some water by soaking their handkerchiefs and wringing them into a box; they also made a dip net of their handkerchiefs and caught some small fish which they split and dried. Yet their fatigue was excessive; they experienced rough weather and were obliged to bail incessantly, so that they nearly wore the bottom through.

The 16th day after leaving the wreck Mr Treadwell died; and on the 21st day Mr Layth. At different times they had seen three vessels pass in the offing without themselves being observed. At length on the 23rd day after leaving the wreck Captain Larcom espied a vessel about four miles distant, which gave them renewed hope. By good fortune they were to windward and they laid their course so as to meet her directly in her path. It proved to be the schooner *General Johnson*, Captain S L Davis, for Gloucester, on board of which they were well received, and 22 days later on the evening of Saturday 21st July they were landed at that place.'(*NC* vol 24, p316 et seq)

24 May, Fleche, 16 guns The *Fleche*, Cdr George Hewson, formerly a French 16-gun sloop of war, was wrecked off the mouth of the Elbe during a gale. The crew were saved. (*NC* vol 25, p223)

24 May, Racer, cutter The *Racer*, a 10-gun cutter built at Baker's Yard, Sandgate, and launched on 24 April 1810, was commanded by Lt Daniel Miller when wrecked on the coast of France near Gravelines. The crew were rescued and taken as prisoners of war. (*SNL*, 1811) [It may be noted that a copy of *Steel's Navy List* for 1811 has two entries for the loss of the *Racer*, one of which states that the vessel was lost in November 1810; but that was the month news arrived in England that the vessel was lost in May and the crew were prisoners-of-war.]

25 ? May, Young Edward, collier A few nights since, the wind blowing a perfect hurricane and the seas running mountains high, the brig *Young Edward* of Dover, Court master, a collier laden with coals, the vessel was driven ashore at Wainfleet on the coast of Lincolnshire and soon went to pieces. The crew got safely to land in the boat, yet the captain wishing to save every little he could, wished to venture once more to the ship, and five other captains volunteered to go with him. They put off in a boat, but upset before they reached the wreck, and the whole were drowned. (*Times*, 31 May 1810)

26 May, Mary, merchantman Came into Plymouth the *Catherine* from Madeira for London with wine. She brings an account of the wreck of the *Mary*, Captain McDoual from Glasgow, which vessel ran ashore on a reef at Teneriffe. The supercargo, a passenger and eleven seamen were drowned, the remainder managed to save themselves in the ship's boat. (*Times*, 29 May 1810)

29 May, saluting accident Today, Tuesday, during the firing of a Royal Salute, from one of the men-of-war lying in Plymouth Sound, in commemoration and honour of the restoration of the monarchy, a 12-pounder shot was fired. It passed over Plymouth Hoe and although at the time the

Hoe was crowded with spectators to see the firing, the ball providentially passed over their heads. The shot then continued its course over the town and passed into an upper room of a house in Pike Street where it struck and shivered to pieces a beam and then fell spent in How's Lane, just behind Pike Street.

This was the fifth occasion in as many years that a shot had been fired from an English man-of-war into the town of Plymouth. (*Times*, 2 June 1810)

? May, Diana, gunbrig   The *Diana* gunbrig, 14 guns, commanded by Lt William Kempthorne, was wrecked on Rodriguez Island (19°40′S 63°25′E) in the Indian Ocean, when, although the crew were saved, the exact date of loss appears to be unknown. (*NC* vol 25, p223)

29 May, desertion punished   Penzance report: 'The evening before last a midshipman and four seamen came into town and said they belonged to the *Crocus* brig, which had struck on the Wolf Rock and they were the only survivors. Yesterday the *Crocus* arrived and the midshipman and three seamen were taken and sent on board the ship.' (*SYM*, 4 June 1810)

On 11 June a court martial was held on board the *Salvador del Mundo* in Hamoaze for the trial of Mr G B Ramsey, a midshipman belonging to the *Crocus* brig of war, for deserting with a boat's crew when on duty. Mr Ramsey, while the *Crocus* was cruising off Land's End, was sent with a boat's crew to fetch sand to scrub the decks, when they drew the boat up on the beach and deserted.

The charge was fully proved and the Court sentenced Mr Ramsey to be imprisoned two years in the Marshalsea prison, to be mulct of all his pay, declared unworthy and incapable of ever serving as an officer in His Majesty's navy; and, at the expiration of his imprisonment, to serve before the mast. (*NC* vol 24, p82)

John Barnes, a seaman, was tried for deserting with Mr Ramsey, and for making use of mutinous expressions, when taken by the purser and first lieutenant. He was sentenced to receive 200 lashes.

Another court martial was held the same day on Joseph Dempsey, a marine of the *Medusa*, a 32-gun frigate, for desertion. He was sentenced to receive only fifty lashes on board his own ship, in consequence of his former good character. (*NC* vol 24, p82)

10 August, Lively, 38 guns   Particulars of the loss of the *Lively*, a 38-gun frigate, carrying Admiral Boyles and commanded by Captain George M'Kinley, were given in a letter from an officer of that ship, dated St Paul's Bay 18 August 1810.

'I am sorry to inform you that on 10th August, standing in towards the land about seven miles from Vallette (*sic*), we had the misfortune to be wrecked [at the entrance to St Paul's Bay]. Fortunately, none of the officers or crew were lost. It blew a very heavy gale, which obliged us to cut away our masts in order to save the people. Our fatigue has been very great, being cast away on a barren place. We are trying to get her off; but I think our labour will be in vain as the water is three feet above the lower deck. We are at present in tents, erected at a castle about half a mile from the ship. On our passage one of our convoy sprung a leak, and we were obliged to take the crew on board our ship; so that there were two wrecks before we reached Malta.'

Among the articles saved from the wreck were a number of boxes of dollars. (*NC* vol 24, p474; *Times*, 4 and 9 October 1810) [Clowes and other modern sources give the date the *Lively* was lost as 26 August; perhaps taken from the *NC* vol 25, p223, which gives the same date; yet the letter from St Paul's Bay is explicit.]

24 August, debacle at Grand Port A British frigate squadron comprising *Nereide*, 36 guns, taken 22 December 1797, commanded by Captain Nisbet Josiah Willoughby; *Sirius*, 36 guns, launched 12 April 1797, commanded by Captain Samuel Pym; *Magicienne*, 32 guns, taken 1782, commanded by Captain Lucius Curtis; and *Iphigenia*, 36 guns, built in 1808, commanded by Captain Henry Lambert blockaded a French force of the *Bellona*, 48 guns; *Minerve*, 52 guns; *Victor*, sloop of 20 guns; and *Ceylon*, captured Indiaman of 30 guns, in Grand Port, Isle of France (Mauritius). Captain Pym, in the *Sirius*, accompanied by the *Nereide*, *Magicienne*, and *Iphigenia*, made an attempt to capture them, which in the onset, promised the most complete success; but it failed from the intricacy of the harbour. In standing in to the attack, the *Sirius* and *Magicienne* grounded on an unknown sandbank; and after the most strenuous exertions had been used in vain to get them off, were blown up by their own crews the following morning the 25th. The *Nereide* alone gained her station, but having sustained the united fire of the enemy's vessels, she was compelled to surrender, after a most severe engagement during which she suffered 100 killed and wounded including her commander, who nobly refused to quit his wounded ship-mates, although a boat was sent from the *Sirius* to bring him off. The French loss was 37 killed and 112 wounded. The *Iphigenia* after the action, having landed the crews of the *Sirius* and *Magicienne* on the Isle de la Passe (a small fortified place at the entrance of Port South East, taken from the French a few days previously), remained to protect them; but on 28 August, being destitute of water and provisions, was compelled to surrender, together with the crews of two frigates, and the whole of the forces on the island, to four French frigates by which they were blockaded. (*NC* vol 25, pp223-224)

31 August, Union, merchantman The ship *Union*, Captain Watson, from

Jamaica for Charleston, was driven on shore on Tybee Sands, 15 miles east-south-east of Savannah. (*Times*, 29 October 1810)

1 September, Mary, brig   At 2am the brig *Mary*, of and for Bristol from Demerara, was totally lost off the Sker Weather, near the Mumbles; the master and three men were saved, but two other men and an apprentice were lost. (*Times*, 4 September 1810)

9 October, Hawke, merchantman   From London for Africa the ship *Hawke*, Captain Whitesides, foundered off Beachy Head, when all the crew perished. (*Times*, 25 October 1810)

19 October, Isabella, schooner   The *Isabella*, a Spanish schooner from Teneriffe for London, was lost in Tralee Bay, but the article contained no information of the crew. (*Times*, 29 October 1810)

19 October, Britannia, sloop   The *Britannia* sloop on her passage from London for Boston on Friday night 19 October struck on a sunken wreck near the Shipwash and foundered immediately afterwards. The vessel struck with such violence as to tear away the whole of her stern frame; and she filled and sunk with such rapidity as scarcely to allow the master and mate to gain the topmast head for safety; the remainder of the crew, three boys, were washed from the shrouds and perished. The master and mate succeeded in lashing themselves to the topmast with the pennant halyards, and in that situation were preserved, the vessel grounding in such a depth of water as at low mark just washed the crosstrees; and upon these, at such times, they supported themselves by standing, but were driven to the topmast head again on the return of high water. Having continued in this wretched situation from 8pm on Friday, till the same hour on Sunday morning, they were relieved by a passing ship and landed at Yarmouth. (*NC* vol 24, pp474-475)

24 October, Adamant, merchantman   'The *Adamant*, Hedley, of New-castle, sailed on 26th July 1810 from Oban with 80 passengers for Prince Edward's Island, and landed them safely. She took in a cargo of timber and left the island on 13th October, the wind being NNW turning to windward into the Gut of Canso, where she cast anchor. On the 15th weighed at five a.m. wind variable, and got to the mouth of the Gut that night when it came on to blow very hard from the NE with very foggy weather. On the 19th, the storm increasing, the vessel upset, and remained about twenty minutes with her masts in the water, when she righted as far as the lee-edge of the deck, her larboard gunwale remaining constantly under. The boats and other things on deck were swept away; the sea, being very high, had a free passage down the hatchways, and washed the provisions out of the cabin windows. The crew, 13 in number, were all lashed, and had nothing to subsist on but a little raw beef (of which they were each allowed two ounces per day) and a small quantity of rum. The water-casks being all stove by the violent motion of the vessel, they were obliged to drink their own urine. By the 23rd four of the crew had miserably perished and were thrown into the sea. On the 24th they came within sight of land, which proved to be Sable Island, on the outer bar of which, on the north side, the vessel struck about two p.m. that day; she lost her rudder, but did not go to pieces. Here they remained two days longer. On the 25th four more of the crew died. The people of the island appeared with a boat on the 26th, which had been brought overland in a cart for their relief. They were conveyed to a house two miles from the shore and in a week had recovered their strength. The four bodies left in the ship were decently interred in one grave, and an inscription placed thereon. Three of the survivors arrived at Shields in the *Free Briton*. They left the island on 23rd June having lived there more than seven months. The other two, Mr Thomas Ridley the owner, and the captain, put to sea from the island in an open boat, a considerable time before, and being taken up by some ship at sea, got home some time since. Sable Island was settled by the governor of Halifax about ten or twelve years ago, but there were not more than eight persons living on it when the crew left.' (*AR* 1811, Chr, p100 et seq)

30 October, plague at Gibraltar   The ship *Hope* arrived at Plymouth from Gibraltar, from whence she sailed on the 11th with a dozen other vessels, under convoy of the *Ramana* cutter. She brought advice that two transports with German deserters from the French army had arrived at Gibraltar from Carthagena with the plague on board. The *Whitby* was supposed to be one of the transports, on board of which the master and thirty-one of the crew and passengers were dead, and in the other transport seventeen had died. The commander of the garrison at Gibraltar has as a consequence, interdicted all communications with Spain, for 40 days. (*Times*, 2 November 1810)

? October, La Desiree, 14 guns   Letters from the Cape of Good Hope state the wreck in October of a French corvette, *La Desiree*, mounting 14 guns and with a crew of 112 men on the coast of Madagascar. *La Desiree* sailed from the Isle of France for Europe with a valuable freight. Of the ship's crew thirty-four survived, only to be taken into slavery by the natives. (*Times*, 15 January 1811)

? October, Union, merchantman   The ship *Union*, Captain Worrall, from Cadiz for London, was wrecked near Kidwelly in Carmarthen Bay, when all her crew lost their lives. (*Times*, 29 October 1810)

2 November, Magdelena, frigate, and Polemo, brig of war On 8 November 1810 Captain Robert Mends of the 38-gun frigate *Arethusa* wrote the following letter to His Excellency, the Captain-General, and the Superior Junta of Galicia:

'Illustrious Gentlemen, on the 2nd inst. in the evening the wind began to blow fresh, with heavy squalls, and sea from the NNE right in the harbour of Vivero, which continued to increase in a very alarming degree. About twelve o'clock at night the weather became very tempestuous, at which time the *Magdelena*, Spanish frigate, parted her cable, and driving on board the *Narcissus*, English frigate, completely dismasted her. The fall of the masts killed the surgeon and two marines and wounded several others. As the *Magdelena*'s masts were standing she was driven by the wind clear of the *Narcissus* (now a perfect hulk), or both ships must have sunk together, not having any other anchor to let go. No possible means remaining of my sending her relief owing to the darkness and the terrible weather which prevailed, she was unavoidably thrown upon the sand at the head of the harbour and dashed to pieces. The morning shewed us only the scattered remains of what she had been, in dreadful extent along the beach. Out of nearly five hundred people on board the vessel, two persons only have survived. Commodore Larouz; Captain Salseda her commander; and Colonel Hulfo commandant of artillery are amongst those who have perished. The *Polemo*, Spanish brig of war, has also suffered the same calamity and at the same time, only her commander and nine men surviving the destruction of their vessel out of nearly two hundred who were on board.

'Permit me to entreat that the condition of the many families who are thus involved in misery and want be most particularly recommended to the maternal care of the Spanish government.' (*NC* vol 24, p416)

Although the *Narcissus* was a complete wreck on 1 November, by the 12th she had arrived at Plymouth, having been convoyed home by the *Amazon*, another 38-gun frigate, as far as Falmouth; still it was a rough passage, for off Land's End in the violent gale of the 10th the *Narcissus* was near to foundering. (*Times*, 15 November 1810)

On arrival at Plymouth the crew gave their versions of the tragedy.

'The *Magdelena* drove and came athwart the hawse of the *Narcissus*, by which accident the *Narcissus* had her bowsprit carried away and parted one cable; soon after the accident the Spaniard attempting to get clear of the English vessel, the sea running so high, she swung around and carried away the masts of the *Narcissus* by the board, by the fall of which the surgeon and a marine were killed and several hurt. The *Magdelena* was then drifting about and the weather so bad it was not possible to get the sailors aloft to trim the sails and in consequence she soon after ran foul of the *Polemo*, a Spanish man-of-war brig and they drifted ashore on the rocks. Both went to pieces, no help was possible as no boat could live in such a gale. (*Times*, 16 November 1810)

'At midnight of the 1st November, blowing a heavy gale, the *Magdelena* parted her cables and drove on board us, carried away our bowsprit and all three masts, cut away one of our cables and we cut another. The sheet anchor was let go, which his anchor hooked and nearly cut our cable through. Fortunately we got at and cut his cable when he drove on shore and of five hundred on board only two were saved. The *Polemo* at the same time parted her cable and was totally lost, the captain and nine men being the only people saved.' (*Times*, 19 November 1810)

9 November, Conflict, gunbrig The *Conflict* gunbrig mounting 12 guns, built in 1801, had a crew of fifty men and boys, commanded by Lt Joseph B Batt. The vessel was cruising off the north coast of Spain in the Bay of Biscay in company with the *Arethusa*, a 38-gun frigate, when they were caught in a violent gale and towards nightfall the *Conflict* was seen to be in great distress. The vessel was never seen again and was presumed to have foundered with her entire crew. (*Times*, 15 January 1811; *SNL*, 1812)

10 November, Autumn, brig The brig *Autumn*, Thomas Day master, was wrecked on the Pye sandbank, near Harwich harbour when the crew perished. (*Times*, 14 November 1810)

10 November, canal boat disaster A report from Paisley, at 2pm:
'A few days ago a track-boat[47] from Paisley to Johnstone was launched, and daily since it had been filled with parties of pleasure. Today is a fair with us and every lad and lass who could muster eight pence must have a sail. About one hour ago, one p.m., she landed at the basin opposite Mr Barclay's with nearly one hundred on board (for she is sixty feet in length), and as many were on the breast ready to replace them; and who in spite of all remonstrance pressed in before she was cleared of the former load, in consequence of which she upset and plunged the whole, men women and children into the basin which is seven or eight feet deep of water. Three cabin passengers had narrow escapes. (*Times*, 16 November 1810)
'It is ascertained that 84 persons perished by the oversetting of the canal boat at Paisley; of whom 18 were below the age of 10; 49 from 10 to 20 years while 17 were above 20 years of age.' (*Times*, 19 November 1810)

14 November, Mary, merchantman The *Mary* of Dunbarton with a signal of distress flying was met with on the French coast by the 18-gun sloop of war *Cyane*, Captain Collier, who went on board the *Mary*. The severe gales had carried all her sails away and rendered her so unmanageable that the crew after every effort became so exhausted that they had lashed the helm a-lee and given her up to the mercy of the weather. One of the poor fellows lay dead on the deck, worn out by fatigue. She had been seventeen days from Dublin and was bound to London. The *Cyane* towed her to Portsmouth. (*Times*, 20 November 1810)

17 November, Downshire, packet   A report from Port Patrick read as follows: 'The wind has blown so strong in shore since Tuesday 13th that none of the packet boats could get to sea. This morning about eight o'clock a packet appeared from Donaghadee and with great difficulty delivered the Irish mail and received three English mails on board. This was effected by means of a rope as the boat that went off to her could not venture near, the sea ran so high; the three passengers therefore were obliged to submit to be relanded at Donaghadee. The packet which proved to be the *Downshire* had not gone a quarter of a mile when she was forced in against the cliffs and went to pieces in fifteen minutes. A passenger was lost and one crew member had a leg shattered between the vessel and the rocks, so badly, that amputation was necessary. One other young man suffered a blow from the boom but both seemed likely to recover. The mail bags were washed up an hour later.' (*Times*, 22 November 1810)

22 November, Aurora, merchantman   The *Aurora* barque of London on her passage from Quebec with a cargo of timber bound to Sheerness and Chatham, encountered a very heavy gale on 22 November in position 51°15'N 32°30'W in which all her boats were stove, nearly all her provisions and every article on deck washed overboard, and her bowsprit sprung; when the hardships of her unfortunate crew commenced the only article of provision left was a little bread, sufficient to supply their wants only for the short space of twenty-four hours, then at a distance of 1000 miles from Land's End. On the 26th following after enduring all the hardships imaginable for four days, during three of which they had been without food and reduced to a most deplorable state, being almost deprived of raiment, and their limbs frost-bitten, a more terrible gale of wind than that experienced on the 22nd came on, in which the vessel fell over on her broadside, which accident released from the horrors of an expected but untimely end, the first and second mates, two seamen and two boys, who were washed overboard and perished. The remainder of the crew consisting of the captain and three seamen were obliged to cling to the side of the wreck for the space of eight hours. During this period the main and mizzen masts, fore topmast and backstay went by the board, soon after which she again righted, but was full of water; however this afforded a retreat for the unfortunates, as they were then enabled to get into the fore top, where after some hours they secured themselves from the violence of the sea. The decks of the vessel then blew up and strange to tell these men endured all the horrors of starvation for the further space of seven days when on 2 December in position 47°50'N 23°30'W the ship *Maida* hove in sight and bore down on the *Aurora*, not perceiving at first that any of the crew remained on board. On nearing her some men were discovered in the fore top, and a boat was hoisted out to bring them off, when they had for eleven days kept themselves alive by sucking the ropes, which afforded them the water gathered there during the heavy rains. One of them appeared in a dead state, and the others were senseless; no intelligence could be obtained from them until within three or four days previous to the *Maida*'s arrival at Plymouth. Two English merchant brigs hove in sight, yet no notice was taken of their signal and both proceeded on their way. Captain Fleck and the two seamen were badly frostbitten and one seaman died soon after his arrival at Plymouth. (*Times*, 14 December 1810)

The above article was copied verbatim in the *NC* vol 25, pp216-217.

The *Times* of 13 December gave the following: Arrived the ship *Maida*, Captain Marshall, from Quebec with timber. On passage she fell in with a wreck which proved to be the *Aurora* of London, from Quebec with lumber and took therefrom Captain Afleck (*sic*) and two seamen.

The *SYM* of 17 December, which quoted a Plymouth report dated the 14th, said that the ship *Maida* arrived on Sunday 9 December and furthermore stated that the survivors were not expected to live.

26 November, disaster at Anholt A letter from Captain Maurice, Governor of Anholt (a British-occupied island off the Danish coast), to Vice-Admiral Sir James Saumarez, dated 3 December 1810, contains the following passage:

'On Monday 26th November a sloop anchored during the night close in with the beach; the wind on the next day blowing dreadfully hard, a bottle was picked up from her with a letter from Mr Irwin stating their perilous situation; it blew too hard to attempt relieving her. The next morning another letter came, still more lamentable; the lifeboat was launched and put off, and the life-shell thrown, both of which failed in getting to her. The *Centinel* was telegraphed to send a boat to render assistance, which succeeded in getting to her most delightfully, and four passengers got into the boat to go on board; when about ten yards from the sloop a sea turned her completely over, and melancholy to relate, the whole (eleven in number) perished in the waves; amongst them Mr Irwin, a merchant carrying on extensive trade at this island, and whose zeal in getting us supplies could not be excelled. His amiable disposition and gentlemanly manners had gained him the esteem of the whole garrison, and no one more deeply deplores his unfortunate end than myself; indeed the accident has caused a great depression in our spirits.' (*NC* vol 25, pp217-218)

9 December, Mandarin, 12 guns The 12-gun *Mandarin* was a Dutch vessel scuttled by the Dutch at the taking of Amboyna in 1810, but weighed later the same year. (Norie, 1827, p439)

In the hands of the British the *Mandarin* was to have a short life, her story being told in a letter from Penang dated 25 December 1810 and quoted in an East India paper; it follows:

'At Amboyna Captain Tucker, in the *Dover,* sent me [name not given] in the *Mandarin* prize ship with despatches for the admiral, and orders to procure stores and provisions at Penang for the *Dover,* which she was in great want of. I sailed on 2nd November and after a very fair passage for that time of the year [some 2000 miles] arrived in the Straits of Sincapour [*sic*] on 8th December; on the 9th in the morning beating through a narrow part of the channel, and having no chart but a very old one on a small scale, I stood too far over and unfortunately got on shore. It then blew a moderate breeze; I did everything in my power to get her off, but having no boat large enough to carry an anchor out, could not succeed. In a short time it came to blow extremely hard, and the tide had left her so much that to prevent her capsizing I ordered all the masts to be cut away. The wind and sea continued increasing which occasioned the ship to thump so hard that she began to make a great deal of water. I sent the boat on shore to a small island[48] with the despatches, and we collected all the spars we could and constructed a raft, which by five p.m. was complete. On board were nine women and three children, yet by seven o'clock everyone was ashore except four lascars who got intoxicated. At daylight, contrary to my expectations, the ship having kept together, I launched the boat and with much difficulty got on board. I found she had bilged during the night, was full of salt water and consequently all the fresh was spoiled. I sent a few pieces of salt beef and a few other things for the people on shore and remained by the wreck, with one European and four lascars. The wind increasing the boat could not return and we had to spend the ensuing night on board while the sea made complete breaches over her. At this critical moment it pleased the Almighty to send the *Chiffone* [British frigate of 36 guns] to our assistance; coming through the Straits and seeing our distressed situation, anchored, and sent a boat at once to our relief.' (*NC* vol 26, pp209-210)

18 December, Pallas and Nymphe, frigates   The *Pallas*, 32 guns, Captain George Paris Monke, and the *Nymphe*, 36 guns, Captain Edward Sneyd Clay, were lost at the entrance to the Firth of Forth, in consequence of their mistaking a lime kiln, burning at Broxmouth, for the light on the Isle of May, and the Isle of May light for the Bell Rock.[49] A heavy sea and a strong gale from north-north-east got up in the evening, when both vessels returning from a cruise in the North Sea were shaping a regular course for Leith Roads, then at 10.30pm, with the ships making ten knots, both ran aground on the rocks to the eastward of Dunbar, where while the *Pallas* was wrecked at the Vault, about one mile to the east of the town, the *Nymphe* took the ground about four miles from Dunbar near Skateraw.

It would appear that all on board the *Nymphe* escaped with their lives but the *Pallas* was in a different situation; she had struck about a cable's length from the shore and inside ten minutes had 13 feet of water in her hold. With the sea making a complete breach over the ship her masts were cut away, yet when daylight came the first object the crew saw was the bottom of the vessel containing the iron ballast separated from the upper works, and at some distance from the remainder of the ship. It became every man for himself, and when a Portuguese sailor jumped overboard and swam ashore several others followed but five perished in the attempt. It was 11am before a lifeboat managed to get alongside and then made two successful trips; on the third she was manned in part by five sailors of the *Pallas* and with a total of forty persons on board, including Captain Monke, she overset, yet only one person was drowned and altogether only nine crew members died.

Of the survivors about 150 were taken to the home of the Duchess of Roxburghe, Broxmouth Park, where they received every attention.

On Saturday 26 January 1811 a court martial was held in the Downs to try Captain Clay, his officers and ship's company for the loss of the *Nymphe*. They were all acquitted, except Mr G Scott master and Mr C Gascoigne pilot, who appeared to the Court to have been very incautious in asserting in a positive manner the light seen to have been the light on the May Island, and the Court did adjudge them to be severely reprimanded. (*NC* vol 25, p54 et seq and p170; *SNL*, 1812; *AR* 1810, Chr, p294; *Times*, 22, 25 and 26 December 1810)

19 December, Satellite, 16 guns　The *Satellite*, a 16-gun sloop of war, commanded by the Hon Willoughby Bertie, sailed from Spithead on Monday 17 December to join the ships that were cruising off St Vaast-la-Hougue. On Wednesday following at 6pm she was in company with the *Vautour*, Captain Lawless. It was then blowing very hard and in the course of the night the gale increased excessively, blowing in most tempestuous squalls. In one of these sudden gusts (which have been experienced both at sea and on shore in a most extraordinary degree this winter) she, it is supposed, upset, and every soul on board perished. The next morning her boats, some spars etc which were upon her deck were picked up by the *Vautour*; but no other vestige of her has ever been seen. The vessel had a crew of about ninety men and boys. (*AR* 1810, Chr, pp294-295)

The Hon Captain Bertie was son of the previous, and brother of the then, Earl of Abingdon.

By a subsequent account Mr Richard Cornby, surgeon, Mr R S Kempster, master's mate, Messrs A G Babington and William Brooke, midshipmen, who were stated to have been on board the *Satellite*, when she was last mustered, and who it was presumed had perished in that unfortunate ship, are safe. The midshipmen had been removed to the *Danemark* just before the *Satellite* sailed, and the surgeon was on shore on leave. (*NC* vol 25, p148)

21 December, Sarah, merchantman   Between 3 and 4pm of 21 December, about three hours before the time of high water, a vessel was observed close in shore, a little to the west of Redness Point near Whitehaven, in a very dangerous situation, the tempest having increased to a hurricane. Crowds of people hastened to the spot, numbers of lanterns were shewn, and several fires kindled amongst the rocks. The unfortunate men (ten in number) aboard the vessel were distinctly seen at intervals; but the roaring of the winds and the waves were great, that nothing else could be heard, nor could any assistance whatever be given. The vessel had grounded with her head to the sea and had two anchors out. After a most awful and afflicting suspense, a little before 9pm she went to pieces, and all on board perished, except one man who was washed on shore, lashed to part of the stern. She proved to be the *Sarah*, Captain Carmont of and for Liverpool, from America laden with timber, and had been thirteen weeks upon her passage. (*NC* vol 25, p217)

22 December, Minotaur, 74 guns   The *Minotaur*, 74 guns, Captain John Barrett, was lost on the Haak Sands at the mouth of the Texel on the night of 22 December. She left Gothenburg on the 15th, in company with the *Plantagenet* and *Loire* with sixty sail of ships under convoy, in tempestuous weather. The following Dutch official statement of her loss, all that had yet appeared, is deserving of notice.

'Amsterdam, 25th December.

'To his Excellency, the Minister of Marine and Colonies.

'Sir, in the absence of Vice-Admiral de Winter, Count of Huessen, I have the honour to inform your Excellency that the English ship the *Minotaur*, of 74 guns, with a crew of 590[50] men, and commanded by Captain John Barrett, was wrecked on the Haak's Bank on the night of the 22nd inst. Captain Musquetie, commander in the Texel Roads, sent at daybreak on the 23rd the aviso and pilot boat the *Dunker*, to reconnoitre the vessel that had been wrecked, but the wind and heavy sea prevented her from approaching the vessel. She had lost her masts, and was under water from about half-way up the bowsprit to behind the main mast. The waves broke over the remainder of her.

'One hundred and ten of the crew, notwithstanding, succeeded in saving themselves in the boats. They landed behind the Texel Island, near the village of Koog, where they were made prisoners of war by the troops stationed in that quarter. Among the prisoners was a lieutenant, the surgeon, and eight midshipmen. The *Minotaur* was on her way from the Baltic to Yarmouth, in company with the *Plantagenet*, a ship of the line, from which she was separated by the storm which drove her on the Haaks.

'I have the honour to be,

'C Langereld, Chief of Staff of the Third Maritime District of the North Coast.' (*NC* vol 25, p56)

A further report from Amsterdam, dated 29 December:

'On the 25th four men got ashore on a small piece of the wreck of the *Minotaur*, which was lost on the Haak Sands. According to accounts, the captain and sixty or seventy men who had got into a boat were unfortunately swamped close in with the ship. Among those who previously got to land is the 2nd lieutenant Mr Snell, as also the mate, a passenger and four men of the American ship *Charles*, Captain Woodward, from Memel for New York, which ship had been taken in the Baltic and sent for the Port of London.' (*Times*, 5 January 1811)

Three and a half years later on 30 May 1814 (when the prisoners of war had returned to England), a court martial was held on board the *Gladiator* in Portsmouth harbour to try Lt Snell, Mr Thompson, the master, and the few surviving members of the crew of the *Minotaur*, for the loss of the vessel on her passage from the Baltic to the Downs. 'It appeared that the loss of the ship was caused by an error in the reckoning of the pilots as to the ship's situation, they presuming her to be near Smith's Knowl, when at the time she struck she was sixty miles from that shoal. The court passed a sentence of acquittal on all the officers and ship's company. We are sorry to say that it appeared in evidence the Dutch might have saved the people if they had attended to the urgent requests of those who were fortunate enough to land first.' (*NC* vol 31, pp486-487)

25 December, Aimable, 32 guns The *Aimable*, a French 32-gun frigate, was taken in the Mona Passage between Santo Domingo and Puerto Rico on 19 April 1782 by the squadron of Sir Samuel Hood.

The *Aimable* ran on shore in Berwick Bay on the morning of the 25th. The ship was running at nine knots for May Island, when the pilot mistook the lime kiln light on shore (the same was the cause of the loss of the *Nymphe* and the *Pallas*) for the light of the May and altered the ship's course accordingly. The officer of the watch shortened sail immediately on seeing the light, but she took the ground one and a half hours later. (*Times*, 1 January 1811)

25 December, Monkey, gunbrig The *Monkey*, a gunbrig mounting 14 guns, was built by Nicholsons at their Rochester shipyard and launched in 1801.

On 25 May 1814 a court martial was held on board the *Gladiator* in Portsmouth harbour to try the surviving officers and ship's company of the *Monkey* for the loss of that vessel on Christmas Day 1810 on the coast of France near Belle Isle. It appeared in evidence, she had been greatly distressed by a continual series of gales of wind for nine days previous to her loss, during which time she could not make any observation of her situation, and that in the night time she was thrown miraculously between the two high rocks which sheltered the people from the effects of the heavy sea then running; that Lt Fitzgerald her commander jumped overboard and was swimming ashore when a heavy sea lifted the vessel close to him, and from his shrieks it was supposed his legs were jammed between the ship and the rocks; he immediately sunk and the receding waves washed him away. The officers and men were all acquitted. (*NC* vol 31, p486)

28 December, Elizabeth, country ship The *Elizabeth*, though not chartered to the East India Company, was nevertheless destined for Madras and Bengal, and laden with a cargo of iron, copper, lead, beer, glass and other sundry goods. A medium-sized, three masted vessel of 650 tons burthen, the *Elizabeth* was commanded by Captain Hutton and sailed from the river (Thames) on 26 October for Portsmouth to join the East Indies fleet. However, in consequence of the weather then prevailing the ship was unable to fetch Portsmouth and put into Cork, where she remained for nine days awaiting the weather to moderate, then on 17 December she sailed for her destination.

On board the ship was a total of 380 persons, of whom 30 were passengers, 100 were seamen and 250 were lascars; out of this whole number there were to be but 22 survivors. One account gave the number on board ship as 403, while a report in the *NC* vol 25, p149 stated that among the drowned were 8 black women servants and about 347 lascars. It may be that most of the seamen on the *Elizabeth* were lascars.

No sooner had the ship left Cork than she was once again over-powered by violent gales and driven up Channel as far as the South Foreland where she came to an anchor. It was now Thursday evening 27 December, 10 days since leaving Cork and two months since sailing from London, and now some distance off the South Foreland the *Elizabeth* parted her cables and drifted into Calais Roads, where she knocked off her rudder and sustained other damage. The ship then drove upon the outer edge of Dunkirk brake (the Breebauck), Dunkirk steeple bearing south by west, with the vessel at this time lying three leagues to the north-east of Dunkirk harbour. The *Elizabeth*, armed with ten 16-pounders (*sic*), was observed at daylight making signals of distress and firing minute guns, yet all attempts to send assistance to the ship proved fruitless, the wind blowing furiously from NNE and the sea in a frightful state of agitation. Hopes were entertained that at the ebb something might yet be done; but such hopes were in vain; it being absolutely impossible to send out any sort of boats, notwithstanding all the efforts that were made.

In the meantime the ship had lost her main and mizzen masts and soon after disappeared, leaving only the fore mast to be seen, which was covered with people. Three boats were seen directing their course towards the coast but only two succeeded in reaching Fort Risban, where twenty-two persons were landed with the assistance of the garrison. The survivors were well received by the inhabitants of the town and the Europeans were on various occasions allowed to leave prison and dine with such of the inhabitants as invited them.

On 28 January 1811 the *Times* published a letter ostensibly written by Captain Hubert Eastwick to the French Minister of Marine and Colonies requesting that the survivors be exchanged for a similar number of French prisoners held in England. The letter included the statement: 'The merchant vessel the *Elizabeth* of which I had the command'; the letter then goes on to say that the *Elizabeth* sailed from Cork on 19 December. [The *NC* vol 25, p150 has a footnote: The French commissary appears to be in a mistake. Captain Hutton was the commander of the *Elizabeth*; and Captain Eastwick, we believe, was a passenger. 'The only persons saved,' says the report at Lloyds, 'were Captain Eastwick, Captain Jackson, Mr Baker 2nd officer, Mr Laird 3rd officer, Mr Ediz free mariner, Mr Haywood and 15 lascars.']

General O'Meara, the commandant of Dunkirk, with the consent of Buonaparte, liberated the survivors who were landed from a cartel at Dover on 30 January 1811, on exchange for an equal number of French prisoners.

Whether or not the French prisoners ever made it to France, the author has been unable to discover, but the *Times* of Wednesday 6 March 1811 gave the following:

'The *Elizabeth* cartel arrived at Dover on Monday 4th from off Calais, whither she proceeded from Chatham with eighteen French prisoners of war, in lieu of those sent from Dunkirk belonging to the *Elizabeth* East Indiaman, but was not permitted to approach the harbour as the batteries fired at her and an eighteen pounder shot struck and went through the cartel, providentially without doing any harm.' (*NC* vol 25, p148 et seq; *Times*, 1 and 28 January and 6 March 1811)

The names of the Europeans landed at Dover appear below, and are also given in *NC* vol 25, p151, which gives the additional information that Captain Jackson was a doctor attached to the 24th Native Infantry.

29 December, Hoylake, lifeboat The *Hoylake* lifeboat, in attempting to succour and relieve the people on board the ship *Traveller*, driven on shore in the Mersey, was overwhelmed by a dreadful sea, and eight out of her crew of ten were drowned. The bodies were all found the same day and carried to their respective homes. The deceased were all neighbours and lived in a small village called Hoose, near Hoylake, in the most brotherly kindness. They had always displayed the greatest promptitude and alacrity in assisting vessels in distress. They left large families, totally unprovided for. (*AR* 1811, Chr, p4)

29 December, Fleur de la Mer The 10-gun schooner *Fleur de la Mer*, commanded by Lt John Alexander, was struck by mountainous seas which broke completely over her when midway between the Gulf of Maracaibo and San Domingo. The vessel started to take water, and to lighten her the best bower was cut away. Next morning, the water gaining on the pumps, the guns and shot that could be got at were thrown overboard, yet it availed nothing. The ship began to settle fast and during the afternoon the crew took to the boats and abandoned the vessel. They were then taken up by an American ship in their convoy and landed in Jamaica. (*Times*, 18 March 1811)

1811

3 January, evidence of shipwreck   Two hundred and ten tubs [probably from a French ship or smuggler that had gone down with all hands] of brandy were picked up at sea on this day by the custom-house officers of Brighton who lodged them in the customs-house at Shoreham. (*Times*, 9 January 1811)

5 January, boat accident in Lough Swilly   A melancholy accident occurred on Lough Swilly when a boat with a midshipman and eleven seamen, returning to one of the frigates lying near Buncrana, was overset. The midshipman and seven seamen were drowned. The remaining four swam ashore with difficulty.

This morning also a large Dutch ship performing quarantine off Margate drove from her anchors, and after making several attempts to gain the harbour, went on shore in Westgate Bay when, it not being possible to afford them any assistance, all the crew perished. (*AR* 1811, Chr, p2)

8 January, Romulus and the wreckers   A most daring attempt was made by a party of country people of Clonderalaw Bay to take possession of the American ship *Romulus*, on the night of 8 January. They assembled at about 10pm to the amount of between 200 and 300, and commenced a firing of musketry, which they kept up at intervals for three hours; when finding a steady resistance from the crew and guard of yeomanry, which had been put on the vessel on her first going ashore, they retired. The shot they fired appeared to have been cut from square bars of lead about half an inch in diameter. One of these miscreants dropped and was carried away by his companions. (*AR* 1811, Chr, p4)

13 January, Cumberland, merchantman   This Sunday night the ship *Cumberland*, Barrett master, arrived in the Downs from Quebec, under a jury fore mast and bowsprit, having pitched her bowsprit and fore mast away in a heavy gale of wind off the Newfoundland Banks.

From 7pm till 8am on the Sunday she was attacked by four French lugger privateers, between Dover and Folkestone, the first of which hailed to know if he wanted a pilot; Captain Barrett having suspicion of her, replied in the negative; immediately after another privateer ordered him to lay his main yard aback, and the whole of them commenced a fire of musketry, and two of them ran alongside and boarded the *Cumberland*; previous to which the captain had ordered all the ship's crew into the cabin, they being armed with their boarding pikes; as soon as about twenty men came on board the captain ordered the ship to be sheered off from the privateers, leaving the Frenchmen no good retreat, and on the ship being boarded, the privateers ceased firing; in the meantime the ship's company rushed forward and cleared the deck; the greater part of the boarders being killed, and the remainder jumping overboard. Immediately after another came alongside and told the captain they would give no quarter; on hearing this the ship's company cheered them; and they were boarded and cleared in like manner. This was repeated three times afterwards, with the like success on the part of the ship's crew, and their taking three prisoners, two of whom were wounded, and one later died of his wounds. Immediately after this Captain Barrett discharged three of his carronades loaded with round and canister shot; the first was seen to carry away the main mast of one of the privateers, and the second carried away the bowsprit of another, and it was supposed destroyed many of the men, as they were heard to cry out, and the shots were heard to strike the vessel. They then made off and the *Cumberland* proceeded for the Downs. 'We are sorry to say Mr Coward, chief mate, is wounded in the shoulder, and that one man on board the *Cumberland* has died of his wounds. The loss on the part of the enemy is supposed to be nearly sixty. Captain Barrett killed three himself, one of which he was obliged to put his foot on to extricate his pike.'

This is supposed to be the most gallant defence made by any merchant ship during the war, as her crew consisted of only 26 men, and those of the privateers according to the prisoners statements amounted to 270 men.

The Lords of the Admiralty have, as a mark of their satisfaction at the gallantry exhibited on this occasion, expressed their intention to grant each of the crew of the *Cumberland* a protection from the impress for a period of three years. (*AR* 1811, Chr, pp6-7)

19 January, Jason, merchantman A dreadful accident happened a few days earlier on board the *Jason*, a vessel of Boston, lying about four miles from the town, in a part of the Deeps (a channel on the west side of the Wash) called Clay-hole. Mr Massam the master was on business in Boston; but before he quitted the vessel he had carefully locked up the cabin in which were some swivel cartridges and a quantity of gunpowder. The mate of the vessel, to relieve the tedium of waiting for a wind, imprudently broke open the door during the master's absence, took some powder, and went from the vessel to shoot waterfowl, leaving on board a boy about fourteen years of age. The youth thus left amused himself by getting a handful of gunpowder and throwing it in small quantities into a fire on board; but having it is supposed scattered some between the cabin and the fireplace, the flame ran along the train, and in an instant, by the tremendous explosion of all the

powder kept for the guns which the *Jason* carried, the whole stern of the
vessel was swept away and she sank with a full cargo of oats on board.
Providentially the boy was not hurt by the explosion and was taken from
the sinking vessel by a boat which was put off from the *Tre Madoc* lying
near. (*AR* 1811, Chr, pp7-8)

22 January, Orion derelict Today, Tuesday, the *Tarantula* privateer arrived
at Fowey from an unsuccessful cruise off Cape Finisterre. On Friday last in
the Bay of Biscay she fell in with a large ship, dismasted and waterlogged;
and on boarding ascertained her to be the *Orion*, laden with timber and
lumber, supposed from America. They found one man dead in the companion and were preparing to go between decks when they were assailed by
the most horrid stench, which obliged them to relinquish their design and
abandon the wreck. The hold of the *Orion* appeared full of water but she
was tolerably clear between decks. The stench no doubt proceeded from the
bodies of the unfortunate crew who had perished on board her, but whether
through fatigue or hunger could not be ascertained. The man in the companion appeared to have been dead about one week. (*AR* 1811, Chr, p8)

31 January, unidentified wreck off Anglesey After weathering a dreadful
storm on Thursday 31 January the revenue cutter *Defence*, Captain Fishley,
in cruising the next day on the coast of Anglesey discovered a wreck near
the creek of Cambyr. After the most minute inquiry Captain Fishley could
only learn that her sails (or some remnants of them) were marked Robert
Kitson, sailmaker, Maryport, in a circle. She had apparently been from
Dublin in ballast; and the remains of her spars and rigging indicate her to
have been a fine stout well-found vessel. Nine of her crew were seen to
perish. She had struck on a ledge some distance from shore. No bodies were
found nor anything to trace what she really was. (*AR* 1811, Chr, p21)

13 February, Pandora, 18 guns During the night of 13 February the 18-gun
Pandora, Cdr John Macpherson Ferguson, struck on the Scaw reef, a shoal
off the coast of Jutland in the Kattegat which is surrounded by unpredictable
currents. In less than five minutes she lost her rudder, in consequence of
repeatedly striking the ground with great force in a heavy sea, and within
one hour she was nearly filled with water: previous to which the crew cut
away the masts in order to lighten the vessel; but the wind being extremely
high the sea broke over her with great fury, and every moment threatened
to be their last. The wind was piercingly cold and part of the crew perished
from exposure. Next morning some of the survivors contrived to cut a hole
in the weather side of the deck which was above water, and by that they
were enabled to get down below, one by one, out of the severe weather.
About three in the afternoon of the 14th some boats were observed coming
off from the shore to their assistance, but the sea running very high they

dare not approach the wreck. The surviving crew were so reduced as to be unable to launch their own boats which were covered in ice, which bore the appearance of marble of great thickness. However, in the course of the night the wind abated and the next morning being quite calm a number of boats came off and took the men from the wreck. The crew were made prisoners of war; but the Danes treated them with all possible hospitality. Twenty-nine sailors were lost due to the severity of the weather. (*AR* 1811, Chr, p19; *NC*, vol 26, pp151-152)

16 February, Amethyst, 36 guns Between midnight and 1am the 36-gun *Amethyst* frigate, Captain Jacob Walton, drifted on to the rocks, about a quarter of a mile to the southward of Mount Batten in Plymouth Sound. Being under sailing orders she was lying at single anchor and her drifting was not discovered until it was too late to drop another to bring her up. Guns, as signals of distress, were fired, but such was the violence of the wind and weather that no effectual assistance could be rendered her until a few hours later, when yard craft and boats from the shipping proceeded to the frigate.

Messrs Richard Crosby, John Davis, and Michael Bruce, masters of the *Lavinia, Diana,* and *Jane* transports, and Thomas Pope, foreman to Mr Blackburn of Turnchapel, were the first four who volunteered to go in a boat; they succeeded in getting alongside the wreck, and brought on shore 15 or 16 men. Mr Thomas Pope then left the boat, and William Robson (a seaman belonging to the *Lavinia*) went in his place; they reached the wreck a second time and returned with 17 or 18 men; they went off the third time but the people from the frigate anxious to get on shore overloaded the boat, and when about midway between the wreck and the shore it unfortunately overset and it is supposed about thirty perished. Mr Crosby and his lad were miraculously saved on part of the wreck and finally succeeded in getting on board the ship; Mr Davis got on a rock near the shore and was washed off two or three times, the surf so high it was impossible to give him assistance: he was providentially driven on shore at last by the waves, though nearly exhausted; poor Mr Bruce was never seen more. Of unimpeachable good character and morals, he left a wife and six children to lament his untimely death.

After the *Amethyst* went on shore arrangements were formed by the means of lumps, (lighters used for mooring) and casks, to the amount of 250, to float her; the weather, however, proving unfavourable, it was found expedient to rip her up.

The body of Mr James Harrison, a midshipman of the *Amethyst*, was picked up on 25 February and interred in Stoke Damerel churchyard, Dock. (*NC* vol 25, pp 295-296)

On 19 and 20 March a court martial was held on the *Salvador del Mundo* in Hamoaze for the trial of Captain Walton, his officers and ship's company, for the loss of the *Amethyst*. The court did adjudge Captain Walton to be severely reprimanded; and the master to be severely reprimanded, and to serve in a Sixth Rate for twelve months. The rest of the officers and crew were acquitted. (*NC* vol 25, p260)

18 February, Otter, 18 guns The 18-gun sloop of war *Otter*, Lt John Davies, had been launched in 1805 and with a crew in excess of 100 was stationed at the Cape of Good Hope. (*Steel's List of the Royal Navy*, 1 December 1807)

This vessel arrived at Plymouth from the Cape and on their passage home the crew had suffered the greatest privations owing to want of fuel to cook their provisions. They consumed two of their boats and all the spare timber they had and when that was expended they were compelled to eat their beef and pork raw. (*Times*, 18 February 1811)

21 February, John and Jane, transport The loss of the *John and Jane* transport is recorded in a letter from an officer of the *Franchise*, an ex-French 40-gun frigate captured in May 1803.

'The *Franchise*, with the Mediterranean convoy, amongst which were several transports having the 11th Regiment on board, sailed from Plymouth, with the wind at SE on the 19th inst., the signal being made by the admiral to weigh. The same evening it fell calm and continued so the greater part of the 20th, when the wind veered to the SW blowing fresh. It was too late to get into Falmouth and the necessary convoy signal was made to stand to sea. At three in the morning of 21st February it was judged necessary to go on the starboard tack, and the signal was made for that purpose. After giving the vessels ten minutes to effect it, the *Franchise* put up her helm; in the act of wearing, several vessels were seen, but from the extreme darkness of the night it was impossible to judge on what tack they were, though it was presumed from the time given they were on the starboard one. At once the lookout men forward, of whom there were six, reported "a vessel ahead" – she was cleared by shifting the helm; another was discovered instantly afterwards, and before the ship could answer her helm, going then about the rate of nine knots, she struck the unfortunate *John and Jane* transport, stem on, nearly amidships, and dreadful to relate she almost immediately went down. A few were saved by clinging to the *Franchise*'s ropes. The *Franchise* suffered little or no damage; and had the *John and Jane* shown lights in answer to the signal made, there can be no doubt but the catastrophe would not have happened. There cannot be the least blame attached to any of the *Franchise*'s officers; and their exertions to save the unfortunate sufferers were great.

'Drowned: officers and soldiers, 197; women 15; children 6; and seamen 6; total drowned 224.

'PS. In addition to the above, it is painful to relate that the same night the *Wellington* ordnance transport, bound to Cadiz, was run down by an American ship and instantly sunk. The mate and five hands were saved; the American lost his foremast and bowsprit.' [The captain and six seamen of the *Wellington* lost their lives. (*NC*, vol 28, p331)]

The *Franchise* had struck the *John and Jane* with her cutwater, right on the beam, which stove her to pieces and she filled instantly. The rigging of the *John and Jane*, being foul of the *Franchise*'s bowsprit, kept the wreck under the weather bow, by which means several were saved. About 4am the convoy signal was made to rendezvous at Falmouth, where the *Franchise* arrived at 2pm.

Another officer of the *Franchise*, at anchor in Carrick Roads, wrote:

'At three o'clock this morning the weather being uncommonly dark, squally and raining, in the act of wearing this ship ran on board a transport brig, and from the velocity with which we were going at the time the shock was so great that we very nearly cut her in two and she sank under our bows in less than five minutes.

'On striking her, we immediately proceeded to throw all aback, to prevent our going completely over her; she however went down almost immediately, but many of the unfortunate crew clung to the wreck of the masts and spars, which fortunately were entangled in the rigging of our bowsprit.

'Ropes were thrown to them, to which they fastened themselves, and by this means a few were saved. I offered to be lowered in one of the boats, to go to their assistance; so indeed did some of the other officers, but Captain Allen thought the boats would certainly be lost, and would not therefore let them be lowered. The darkness of the night, the howling of the wind, the cries of the poor fellows in the water, together with the view of several bodies lying on the wreck of the spars, presented a scene of indescribable horror.

'Out of 252 souls, 224 perished.'

The disaster is further illustrated by the following extract of a letter from a survivor of the *John and Jane*.

'I was officer of the middle watch which in consequence of the state of the weather, and of an order on the subject, had not been turned up. I was in bed, undressed, but not asleep (about three o'clock in the morning of the 21st), when I was alarmed by the report of a gun from the commodore's ship (the *Franchise*, Captain Allen). The report was so loud that I knew she must be very near us. I ran on deck, nearly naked, and found our vessel standing on her larboard tack, with part of the crew aloft reefing sails, the wind blowing a violent gale. At the same time seeing the *Franchise* running down upon us very fast, as convinced me of our imminent danger, I ran below to alarm my brother officers, all of whom were in bed. I returned upon deck immediately after the *Franchise* had struck our vessel nearly amidship, almost dividing her. Those below joined me in a few moments, with the exception of Captain Grigsby, who was prevented, perhaps, by the rushing in of the water. A moment later a second shock from the *Franchise* separated the transport; and with the greatest difficulty, after succeeding in fastening a rope round me, I was dragged aboard the frigate.' (*NC* vol 25, p296 et seq; *SYM*, 25 February, 4 and 11 March, 1811; *Times*, 26 and 27 February, and 16 March 1811)

25 February, Shamrock, schooner   *Shamrock*, an 8-gun schooner, commanded by Lt Wentworth Parsons Croke, was lost one mile to the west of Cape St Mary (approximately 36°55'N 7°48'W) during the night, due to an error in her reckoning. Her crew saved themselves by walking ashore using the mast as a bridge. (*SNL*, 1811)

26 February, unidentified brig on the Manacles   From Falmouth, a report dated 28 February gave the following: 'The tops of the masts of a brig appearing a little above the water, were seen for the first time yesterday, near the Manacle Rocks, about three leagues from this harbour. It is unknown what vessel it is.

'The crew must have perished, and it is supposed she sank on the preceding night.' (*SYM*, 4 March 1811)

6 March, Thistle, schooner   *Thistle*, an 8-gun schooner, commanded by Lt George M'Pherson, was wrecked on Manasquan beach, about thirty miles south of Sandy Hook, near New York. Six of her crew, including four small boys (probably powder monkeys), perished with their vessel. (*Times*, 15 April 1811)

6 March, boat accident in Carrick Roads   'A melancholy accident occurred last night in Carrick Roads; a transport's boat was going off from the town to the Roads, about nine o'clock, with the master of a transport, several seamen, five soldiers of the 11th Regiment (some of whom had been saved from the wreck of the *John and Jane*, run down by the *Franchise*), in all fifteen persons. In passing through the fleet the boat went too near the head of one of the vessels, and was overset by the rising of the cable, occasioned by the motion of the vessel in a rolling sea. Before assistance could be afforded the whole were drowned.' (*SYM*, 11 March 1811; which paper quoted a Falmouth report of 7 March)

? March, self-mutilation   A black seaman of the *Bittern* entered last week on board the *Essex* United States frigate at Plymouth, saying he was an American citizen: presently the Lieutenant of the *Bittern* came alongside the *Essex* and asked Captain Smith if he had not a black seaman on board? He answered in the affirmative, and ordered the man on deck. The black not being able to produce any papers of his citizenship Captain Smith very

politely gave him up to the Lieutenant of the *Bittern*: but the seaman going below to fetch his clothes seized a hatchet, laid his left hand on a gun and chopped it off close to the wrist. (*Times*, 23 March 1811; *AR* 1811, Chr, p34, 23 March). See also entry for 1 September 1812.

13 April, Hercules, merchantman The *Hercules*, Captain Chase, of Saco, Maine, owned by D Cutts and A Stevens, sailed from Liverpool on 17 February 1811 for Philadelphia with a cargo of dry goods. When 55 days out, she sprung a leak at 4am and at 7pm the water then over her main deck, the crew left her in the boat. Next day the boat was taken up by a brig from New York for Lisbon. Nine days later she fell in with the British frigate *Guerriere*, bound to Bermuda, the captain of which kindly offered to take on board the whole of the crew, or as many as chose to go with him. Captain Chase, Mr G Russell, mate, the second mate, and one seaman chose to remain on board the brig; four young men, seamen, all belonging to Saco, and without protection, went on board the frigate and were landed at Bermuda; but on their arrival there, no opportunity presenting itself for the United States, Captain James Richard Dacres of the *Guerriere* kindly offered them a passage in his ship to Halifax; prior to her sailing however an opportunity offered to proceed to North Carolina, where they safely arrived. The captain of the frigate furnished the brig with provisions enough to replenish what had been expended by the crew of the *Hercules*, and enough to supply those who chose to stay on board to carry them to Lisbon. (*NC* vol 26, p152)

16 April, last word from the Gobiten, brig The following melancholy detail has been cast ashore, enclosed in a box, near Rosehearty, Scotland, and directed 'To the Finder'. Perhaps a greater instance of presence of mind than that evinced, under such circumstances, by the writer, was scarcely ever known:

'North Sea, 18th April 1811. On board the *Gobiten*, from Gesle.

'In distress, being near to sink, as the brig has sprung a leak two days ago, and the water always increasing, notwithstanding all our attempts to prevent it, we have now come very near the last moments of our lives, wherefore we beg him or her, who may find this letter, to inform the public of our misfortune. The brig *Gobiten*, Captain Aberg, went from Hull the 14th inst., in order to seek for Gottenburg, but having come at the middle of Dogger, the wind, which previously was fair, went easterly, when the brig got the leak, notwithstanding the sails were shortened in a proper manner. We have been obliged to cut the masts, but all seems in vain. Except Charles John Shelberg, a passenger, the crew consists of the following, viz. Lindquist, from Gesle; Schlee, Sjosburg, Holtz, all three from the Swedish Pomeranias; Asoluud, from Sundswall; Hellberg, from Calmar.' (*NC* vol 25, p400)

20 April, disaster on the Erdre A tow-boat, which set out from the suburbs of Barbin, on the River Erdre, laden with goods and passengers, the greater part of whom were females, upset half a league above Nantes; nine persons only, including the two boatmen were saved. On the same evening a boatman fell into the river in a fit and was drowned. He had previously saved two persons from the boat which was overset. Next day thirty bodies were taken out of the river. (*AR* 1811, Chr, p48; *Times*, 6 May 1811)

25 April, Royal George's barge The barge of the 100-gun *Royal George* was overset on the Bridge of Rocks in Plymouth Sound and four of the eleven men on board were drowned. (*SYM*, 29 April 1811)

2 May, Dover, 38 guns, and Chichester, storeship Two ships, the *Dover*, a 38-gun frigate, Lt Charles Jenneris, acting captain, in the place of Captain Edward Tucker, and the *Chichester*, storeship, William Kirby master, were both driven on shore during a violent gale in Madras Roads, yet only two persons perished. (*SNL*, 1812)

The *Dover* had not long returned from her successful expedition against the Spice Islands (the Moluccas), for which the officers and crew (if preserved) will have to share very considerable prize money. (*NC* vol 26, p336) The *Chichester* was formerly the French corvette *Var*, 26 guns, captured on 15 February 1810.

5 May, Cecilia, merchantman The ship *Cecilia*, belonging to Appledore, in the Port of Barnstaple, of the burthen of about 180 tons, whereof John Tetherly was master, bound from Waterford to London, with a cargo of provisions, struck on a reef of rocks, within the Port of Plymouth, on the morning of the 5th, stove in her starboard bow, and immediately filled with water; soon after which she fell over and became a total wreck; the master and seven persons were washed off the said wreck and drowned. William Barnard, mate, and William Marshal, mariner, were the only persons saved. (*NC* vol 25, p400)

24 May, Adventure, merchantman The *Adventure*, Captain Snowden, of Whitby from Leith, for Quebec, was lost in the Gulf of St Lawrence; the crew were saved. (*NC* vol 26, p152)

'The *Adventure* of Whitby, lost 24th May 1811, in the Gulph of Saint Lawrence, on her passage from Leith to Quebec, was the identical ship which sailed around the world with Captain Cook.' (*NC* vol 32, p308)

26 May, Alacrity, 18 guns The *Alacrity*, 18 guns, Cdr Nisbet Palmer, was taken by the *Abeille* French corvette of 20 guns, after a severe action off Bastia, in the island of Corsica, when the *Alacrity* suffered 15 killed and 20 wounded. (*SNL*, 1812)

On 30 May 1814 a court martial was convened to try the surviving officers and ship's company for the loss of the vessel. The Court, from the circumstances related, agreed that the capture of the *Alacrity* was caused by Captain Palmer her commander, and nearly all the other officers, being killed or wounded early in the action, and the captain not returning on deck after having his wound dressed by the surgeon; that no blame was imputable to the surviving officers and ship's company, but that the whole of the conduct of Mr James Flexman the boatswain, was marked by great zeal and courage, particularly in not leaving the deck, although he was wounded. They were all acquitted. (*NC* vol 31, p486)

6 June, La Revanche du Cerf, privateer A French privateer *La Revanche du Cerf* was set on fire as she lay at anchor at Norfolk, Virginia, and burned to the water's edge. The account given by two boys who were left on board is that two boats came alongside manned by about fifteen armed persons, who took them out of the cabin, tied their hands behind their backs, and then proceeded with a tub which had fire in it, to the hold, and set fire to the vessel. It is supposed to have been committed by persons whose property had been formerly taken by the privateer. (*AR* 1811, Chr, p62)

28 June, Firm, 14 guns The *Firm*, a 14-gun brig, commanded by Lt John Little, was, with the boats of HMS *Fylla*, going into attack two French gunbrigs which they had chased inshore the evening before. Lt Little, finding the water shoal, wore around for the purpose of standing out, when the *Firm* grounded on a bank in the Bay of St Jean Thomas, in Concale Bay near St Malo. All efforts to get her off proving ineffectual, she was set on fire by the crew, in the face of the enemy. Not a man was hurt and they were all taken to Jersey in the *Fylla*.

Lt Little is very unfortunate, this being the third time this war he has lost his possessions. He was a passenger in the *Lady Hobart* packet when she struck an iceberg off Newfoundland, and was one of only two lieutenants saved from the wreck of the *Athenienne*. (*Times*, 9 July 1811). See also 20 June 1803 and 20 October 1806.

3 July, 209 people in a 50-ton schooner 'A schooner of about fifty tons arrived at St John's, Newfoundland, from Waterford, having been upwards of fifty days at sea. When she left Ireland with passengers and crew there were no less than two hundred and nine persons on board, thirty-seven of whom died before getting to St John's, and twelve or fifteen since her arrival; a number more are not expected to survive. It was from want of water and provisions that the unfortunate people lost their lives. Had they been out for one or two days more, most of them would have died. When they were landed, I never beheld such a melancholy sight. The magistrates have ordered a prosecution against the captain and owner of the schooner.' (*AR* 1811, Chr, p96)

19 July, Prince of Wales, packet   The packet *Prince of Wales*, Captain Proctor, with mails and passengers from the Bahamas and Britain, left Port Royal on 8 July under convoy of His Majesty's schooner *Barbara*, Lt Douglas. In the night of 16 July she lost sight of her convoy; and about 1.30am on the Friday following (the 19th), having been driven from her course by a strong current while going at the rate of five or six miles per hour, she got on Saltpond Reef on the south-west side of Heneagua (Great Inagua), one of the Bahama Islands. The moon, which was seen at intervals through hazy clouds, afforded sufficient light to discover rocks on every side, and all attempts to extricate the vessel from this dangerous situation were rendered abortive. There was now little wind, a boat was lowered and passengers and mail conveyed ashore. A few days later the schooner *Paragon*, Captain Knowles of Long Island, anchored off the spot where they were; and in the course of the day the Spanish schooner *La Perla*, Captain Pedro Blanco Casariego, from Cartagena bound for Cadiz, put in for water.

These two vessels afforded accommodation for the whole, and sailed on 23 July for Crooked Island. where *La Perla* arrived at 5pm on the 24th, and the *Paragon* on the 26th. This was one of those shipwrecks when no lives were lost. (*NC* vol 27, pp47-48)

23 July, Tartar, fishing smack   This morning as the fishing smack *Tartar* of Derbyhaven was drifting in the Channel with her nets shot, WNW from Peel, a heavy gale of wind came on, with a rough sea, which caused them to haul their train of nets on board; and in the act of hauling, she drifted down on a boat ahead of her, and took the point of her boom into her hull. Before the crew perceived any damage the water was over the ballast: the leak increasing fast, in less than ten minutes she went down; the crew, seven in number, providentially escaped in the punt. The other boat's crew, judging the boat and men went down together, made the best of their way home with the lamentable news of their fate to their families. But providence still had them in tow. They lay in the small boat, comparatively like a tub, eight feet keel, and five feet beam; and to prevent the sea from breaking in, they ranged their arms along the gunnels.

At daylight the brig *Lively* of Greenock, Captain M'Kenzie, for Gibraltar, hove in sight to leeward, the punt drifting in her headway, and when within pistol-shot, the men one and all gave a great shout, which was heard by the captain, but the sea ran so hollow, he could not perceive them; apprehending something wrong below, or a man overboard, he called all hands on deck; at the second shout the sailors were astonished at not seeing any vessel near them; and on the third one of the sailors running up the rigging perceived a number of men on the water, to his great astonishment, not seeing anything under them, as the state they lay in, with their arms near the water's edge, prevented him; with the greatest difficulty they were hoisted on board the brig one after the other. Some time after the *Prince of Wales* cutter, Captain Wallace, hove in sight, and by a signal from the brig was soon alongside. Captain Wallace immediately steered direct for the Isle of Man, and landed them safe in Derbyhaven, 'to the inexpressible joy of their despairing families.' (*AR* 1811, Chr, pp95-96)

6 August, William, brig The brig *William*, John Bateman master, bound from London for Selby, was proceeding up the Humber when the tide flowing swiftly caused her to ground on the Whitton Sand. The vessel then swung around by the strength of the tide and fell on her broadside. When the tide ebbed she was left perfectly upright but six or eight feet deep in the sand. The captain's wife, his two children and a female passenger were drowned. (*AR* 1811, Chr, p86)

9 August, Happy Return 'Lost near Shields, the *Happy Return*, of Whitby; the crew were saved. This was the oldest ship in the trade between Whitby and Newcastle; having been built in 1688, the year of the Revolution.' (*Times*, 16 August 1811)

13 August, Thames boat accident About 9pm this Tuesday evening, as six sailors were returning from Chelsea College, where they had been convey-ing invalids, either through carelessness or intoxication, the boat was driven against the centre arch of London Bridge, with such violence as to upset and four of the sailors were drowned. The other two swam ashore. (*Times*, 16 August 1811)

14 August, Mrs Bentley's ordeal A court martial took place on 23 October 1811 on board the *Salvador del Mundo* in Hamoaze for the trial of Lt William Gibbons, commanding His Majesty's schooner *Alphea*, on account of the treatment experienced by one Mrs Grace Bentley, the wife of a corporal of marines, who was in August last by Lt Gibbon's order put and left on the warping buoy, between the island and the main; and for a breach of the 33rd Article of War. On 14 August Lt Gibbons went on board the *Alphea*, to proceed to sea, and enquired what women were on board. He was told Corporal Bentley's wife, whom he had given positive orders should not come into the ship. Lt Gibbons desired a boat to be manned to take her on shore; upon which the woman commenced the most violent abuse of the lieutenant, which induced him to say to the men, 'put her no farther than the buoy; put her on the buoy.' She was there a quarter of an hour, when a boat from the shore took her off. Lt Gibbons in his defence admitted the fact; he thought no injury could arise to her from it; did not know she was pregnant; the buoy was so large that he and sixteen others had stood on it.

The Court thought that the treatment experienced by Grace Bentley, pursuant to Lt Gibbons' orders, was highly improper and reprehensible, but that the said Lt Gibbons had not been guilty of a breach of the 33rd Article of War. The Court did, in consequence, adjudge him to be dismissed the command of His Majesty's schooner *Alphea*. (*NC* vol 27, p250)

[On 24 April a writ of enquiry was executed at the Town Hall, Plymouth by the special appointment of the Under Sheriff of Devon, for ascertaining the damages in an action brought by Mrs Bentley against Lt Gibbons. The jury gave her a verdict for £500. (AR 1812, Chr, p61)]

18 August, Tartar, 32 guns   The *Tartar* frigate, 32 guns, Captain Joseph Baker, was standing into Dago Island (Hiiumaa) off the coast of Estonia, when the ship grounded and sprang a leak but fortunately floated off. Regardless of every effort on the part of the crew the water continued to rise and the vessel had eventually to be grounded on a small islet, Kahar, about mid-way between Dago Island and the Isle of Worms (Vormsi) in the Muhu Strait, where on the 23rd the vessel was set on fire by the crew, who were then taken up by the *Ethalion* frigate.

On 23 October a court martial was held at Portsmouth to try Captain Baker, his officers and crew for the loss of the *Tartar*. They were all honourably acquitted. (*NC* vol 26, p255 and vol 27, p251)

2 October, unnamed brig   A brig, name unknown, was observed in great distress between Portreath and Hayle, and about 10am she went on shore a little to the eastwards of Hayle bar; and shortly afterwards the captain, a Looe man called Davis; together with the mate and two boys, were all four washed overboard and drowned. Two men, all that remained of the crew, were observed by persons on the beach, to get into the rigging, one on the fore mast, the other on the main mast. In this dreadful situation they continued for some time, every sea breaking over them. The main mast soon went by the board carrying with it the unfortunate seaman who had apparently lashed himself to it. Just at this time a native of St Ives, a very good swimmer, stripped on the beach and plunged into the sea, then running mountains high, carrying with him the end of a rope, which he proposed to fasten around the man on board. He had nearly reached the vessel when the end of the rope slipped from him, and he was seen for some time struggling to gain the wreck of the main mast, to which the seaman still clung, and at length he reached it. On seeing the danger to which all three were now exposed a young Hayle man, called Burt, succeeded in getting the rope to the first adventurer, who fastened it around the seaman on the main mast, and having also fastened a rope to him from the ship the seaman was drawn ashore by the spectators. The seaman on the fore mast was likewise rescued; and lastly, their intrepid deliverers. (*NC* vol 26, p322)

5 October, Lynn ferry This day was a Saturday, and about 7pm the ferry boat from South Lynn for Lynn Regis started with eleven passengers and the ferryman. They being principally working men, were anxious to get home and although the boat was small, for occasional use only, they persisted in getting in to the above number. The tide coming rapidly up and the wind being full against them, made such a rough sea that the boat overset and all on board drowned. Eight bodies were picked up on the Sunday. (*Times*, 14 October 1811)

14 October, Pomone, 38 guns The *Pomone* was a 38-gun frigate, built in 1805, and commanded by Captain Robert Barrie, when she sailed from Constantinople, where she had been joined by Sir Harford Jones, late Ambassador to Persia, who had travelled overland to Constantinople, to join the ship. (*Times*, 17 October 1811)

At 7pm this Monday the *Pomone* returning from the Mediterranean struck on a sunken rock about two cables length SW from the Needles Point. Her momentum carried the ship over the rocks and she was driven ashore a few yards from the Point. The crew were saved by pilot vessels from Yarmouth, Isle of Wight, which were on the scene within an hour; assisted also by boats from the *Tisiphone* guard ship. The guns and principal stores were saved but not all the specie. The ship was carrying 55,000 dollars, but 4000 were taken out of a chest broken open by crew members who also stove in the spirit casks soon after the ship had struck, and drank themselves into a state of extreme intoxication. (*Times*, 4 November 1811)

On 25 October a court martial was holden at Portsmouth to try Captain Barrie, his officers and ship's company for the loss of the *Pomone*. The Court agreed that no blame was imputable to Captain Barrie, but that his conduct throughout was marked by great judgement, both as an officer and a seaman; that the conduct of Mr James Storroch the master was highly blameable in not having taken the accurate bearings of Hurst lighthouse, before he attempted to take the ship through the passage, and in not having paid sufficient attention to the observations of Captain Barrie, as to the said lighthouse; but that no blame was imputable to the other officers and ship's company. However, it appeared to the Court that Barnard Lowry, a private marine belonging to the ship, became intoxicated after her loss. The Court therefore adjudged Captain Barrie to be most fully acquitted; the said Mr James Storroch to be severely reprimanded; and the said Barnard Lowry to receive fifty lashes; but in consideration of the generally good conduct of Barnard Lowry, they recommended him to mercy; the Court adjudged the other officers, and the rest of the ship's company, to be also most fully acquitted. (*NC* vol 26, pp320-321 and vol 27, pp250-251)

22 October, Egmont's boat A party of marines and sailors of the 74-gun *Egmont* lying off Deal were on shore to attend the funeral of a marine officer belonging to the ship, who died a few days since in hospital; and upon their returning to the ship about 5pm had actually come alongside, when through some unaccountable accident, the boat upset and out of fifty-one seamen and marines who were on board thirteen were lost. The lieutenant of marines who was with the party was one of the sufferers. Every exertion was made by the boats of the *Egmont* and the *Armada* to render assistance, in which they fortunately succeeded in saving many lives, as otherwise the whole must have perished. (*AR* 1811, Chr, p121; *Times*, 25 October 1811)

The approach of November was to signal again the advent of the worst storms of the year. No part of northern Europe was to escape, and many ships out of the convoy of 250 which left Gothenburg on 25 October were to founder with their entire crews.

24 October, Ellen, merchantman   Arrived at the Cove of Cork on 6 November the ship *Ellen* of Glasgow, Thomas Ritchie master, from Martinique, Dominica and Antigua, with a cargo for Glasgow, after encountering one of the most violent storms during the three days 24 to 26 October when in latitude 51°N, which carried away her bowsprit, fore mast, main topmast, shattered the head of the rudder, and the seas running mountains high stove the boat over her stern, swept everything off the quarterdeck and obliged the lee guns to be thrown overboard. In this perilous situation, the vessel being totally unmanageable and unable to effect repairs owing to the violence of the gale until the night of Sunday 3 November; when by the unceasing efforts of Captain Ritchie and crew, aided by Andrew O'Shea and his son, and Lt Stephens of the 15th Regiment of Foot, the vessel and cargo were providentially brought into Cove harbour late on Monday evening 4 November.

The weather was so bad that HMS *Fortunee*, Captain Vansittart, was unable to beat out of Cove harbour on the 4th and 5th and during the whole of this period the most severe gales in living memory were experienced by the inhabitants. (*Times*, 13 November 1811)

26 October, Solomon and Hebe, merchantmen   On Saturday afternoon 2 November the *Fly* sloop of war arrived in Sandford Bay, Peterhead, having in tow the *Solomon*, Christopher Gromon master, from Riga for Newcastle with a cargo of hemp. She had drifted, dismasted and without her bowsprit or boats, from 26 October at the mercy of the sea, and not a man could venture on deck. On 2 November the *Fly*, Lt Highman, without any boat, having lost the whole of them in the storm, went alongside, and with great difficulty took her in tow and into Peterhead.

On Sunday afternoon 3 November HMS *Pylades* also arrived at Peterhead towing a large vessel loaded with wood, which she found at sea with no person on board, her main mast gone, her decks torn up and the ship full of water. She was supposed to be the *Hebe* of London, Captain

Showar, from Memel. The *Pylades* had also the crew of a large vessel on board, twenty-six in number, which she had in tow but was obliged to cut adrift on Friday morning 1 November.

At 1am on 5 November the *Pylades* was at anchor in Sandford Bay moored by chain cables, which snapped in a sudden squall and the sloop drifted ashore at the harbour mouth. To save the vessel the crew cut away the masts and were thereafter employed in clearing away the wreckage. (Aberdeen report of 6 November; quoted in the *Times* on 15 November 1811)

27 October, Russian galliot　At 1am a Russian galliot, lately stranded at Montrose, and which had been carried up the river and laid on the beach, drifted out to sea with a strong ebb tide and was completely wrecked on the Ness. The vessel was a prize to the *Tartar* frigate. (*Times*, 8 November 1811)

28 October, Dispatch, merchantman　The loss of the *Dispatch* of New York, Captain Elijah Smith, on her passage from Kronstadt to Dartmouth, is given here by her First Officer (name not given):

'Sailed from Kronstadt on 26th September with a cargo of iron, hemp and flax and arrived at Wingo Sound (Gothenburg) on 23rd October. Sailed from thence on the 25th in company with a large fleet.[51] At about eleven o'clock a.m. on the 26th, sea account [see Note 45], near the commander of the convoy, who was then under close reefed fore topsail, main and fore staysails. At one o'clock p.m. on the 27th lost sight of him. At three o'clock p.m. the ship labouring very much hove to under mizzen staysail; and at six o'clock a.m. on the 28th, while laying to, a sea struck her, which carried away her bowsprit, figurehead and cutwater, and started the main stem, when it was found necessary to keep the pumps going. At noon sounded the well, and found six feet of water in the hold; and then at four o'clock p.m. cut away the main mast. We continued at the pumps during the night but the water still gained. At six o'clock a.m. on the 29th cut away the fore mast, anchors from the bows etc. One hour later a British gunbrig passed ahead without noticing us as the weather was hazy. At nine o'clock a.m. a brig under Swedish colours passed to leeward, almost within hailing distance. The signal of distress hoisted in our mizzen shrouds, but the unfeeling Swede continued his course. At three o'clock p.m. on this day, finding the pumps ineffectual and the water between the decks, it was resolved to get the boats out if possible and abandon the ship; got the cutter out but she was instantly stove to pieces. Next attempt was the longboat which was successful and at four o'clock p.m. of the 29th the crew totalling sixteen and Mrs Smith, wife of the Captain, got into the longboat, the Naze of Norway bearing north-east, distant about seventy miles. Shortly after leaving the ship a sea broke over the boat but by using five buckets in baling, soon got her free again, and then threw everything overboard except the clothes on our backs, in order to lighten the boat. At about eight p.m. descried a ship close to us, which proved to be the *Alfred* of Portsmouth, New Hampshire, James Greensuch commander, who humanely received us on board, but James Curtis Second Officer was drowned in the attempt, the sea running so high. The gale continued without abatement until the 31st, when it moderated for a short time, which gave us an opportunity for cooking, having ate raw meat before. On 1st November saw a vessel bottom upwards and on the 2nd saw another dismasted, rudder gone and stern stove in, with a piece of canvas over the companion hatchway. On the 3rd arrived at Stromness where Captain Atweld of the ship *John* gave Mr Smith, his wife and self (First Officer) a passage to Liverpool, where we arrived on 14th November.' (*Times*, 28 November 1811)

30 October, Fancy, gunbrig   The gunbrig *Fancy* with a crew of 50, commanded by Lt Alexander Sinclair, went down off Montrose with all hands. Refer to Appendix B.

30 October, gales on the Scottish east coast   The Edinburgh report of 4 November gave details of various disasters which befell several of the ships which left Gothenburg on 25 October. No sooner had the ships sailed than seven of them were taken by the Danes.

Early on Wednesday morning 30 November, during a violent storm, a vessel was seen at anchor at Montrose, apparently a ship without main or mizzen masts. At 10am she broke from her anchor and got under way; but being unable to clear the Redhead, ran on shore at Ethie Haven in Lunan Bay, where she became a complete wreck. The ship proved to be the *Catherine*, Captain Evers, burthen 252 tons, from St Petersburg to London, laden with flax, iron and tallow. The gale came on soon after the ships had left Gothenburg, and to save the *Catherine* the crew had to cut away her masts, when five of the crew who were clearing away the wreckage were swept off the deck by a huge sea but providentially another sea washed two of the men back on board. The other three found a watery grave.

On this same day at 3am a large ship was driven ashore in Sandford Bay, Peterhead; where the crew of seventeen were saved by the exertions of the seamen and fishermen of that place. The ship of 400 tons burthen proved to be the *Concordia* of Lubec, Captain Thomas Cupper (Cooper?), from Memel for London with timber. On the evening of the 25th the Naze of Norway bearing north-east, a hard gale came on from east-south-east; the *Concordia* laboured much, the water gaining on the pumps until the vessel became waterlogged, when it was found necessary to cut away the main and mizzen masts to prevent the ship falling on her beam ends, the gale continuing with great violence till she was driven ashore.

Again on this same day, at 10am, another ship appeared off Peterhead with the main and mizzen masts gone; steering for Scotstown or Rattray

Head, where she must inevitably have gone to pieces, and all on board have been drowned. When north of the town the inhabitants fired three signal guns, one of which being heard on board the vessel had the desired effect of making her lay about and stand for the Bay, where she got ashore, after with difficulty clearing the Heads. The seamen at the risk of their own lives went out and brought the crew safely to land, with the exception of one man who was washed overboard when she struck. This ship, a foreigner, also from Memel for London with timber, was not so large as the *Concordia* but was of the same convoy. It was the *Enigheden*, Lars Lunberg master. The cargo being timber would be saved, but owing to the continuance of the gales and high tides it was doubtful if the ships could be salvaged.

Yet again on this same day another large ship passed Peterhead, running to the northward, and from the situation in which she was seen great apprehension was entertained for her safety, as also for that of many others of the same fleet, several of which the crews of the above ships had seen to founder. One or two other vessels ran ashore to the north of Peterhead. (*Times*, 8 November 1811)

4 November, James, sloop   During the night of Monday the 4th the sloop *James*, from Larne for Lancaster laden with flint struck upon a point of rocks about a mile and a half to the north of Port Patrick and went to pieces. The crew, four men, a woman and a boy, were all lost. (*Times*, 28 November 1811)

7 November, Trojan, schooner   The *Trojan*, a richly laden American schooner, detained by the *Armide*, was ordered to Hamoaze for safety on account of the rough weather. When she came abreast of the citadel, by a gust of wind she missed stays and went ashore on the Dutton rocks; she soon fell over and went to pieces; the people were all saved, the ship and cargo lost. (*Times*, 12 November 1811)

14 November, Unity, merchantman   The *Unity*, Captain Hardy, from Miramichi, New Brunswick, appeared in Lancaster Bay late on Thursday evening 21 November, in distress. On 14 November when in position 51°N 14°W, she experienced a heavy gale which carried away her bulwarks, and cleared the decks; the night after, the gale continuing, on Friday at 10pm she was struck by a sea which carried away her main mast and washed four of the crew overboard, one of whom, William Walker the carpenter, regained the ship; the other three, James Whitfield, Thomas Martindale and James Postlethwaite, perished. She immediately shipped five feet of water in her hold. On the Sunday following the gale began to moderate when they made the land; and by the exertions of Captain Hardy and the remainder of the crew she arrived at Glasson on Friday afternoon 22 November. (*Times*, 28 November 1811)

15 November, Fort George ferry   'Between one and two o'clock this afternoon during a strong gale from south-west accompanied with rain, the small ferry boat with four boatmen, nine or ten passengers and a pony, set out from Fort George for Fortrose. They proceeded about third ferry (five or six hundred yards) when they were seen to suddenly go down, and a number were then seen clinging to the wreck which drifted towards the garrison. Within twenty minutes the pony had made his way as far as the breakers, a man grasping the crupper in his left hand and exerting the right and his feet in swimming. The pony found bottom with his fore hoofs and seemed incapable of further exertion, while the man by the violence of the surge was forced from his hold, and quite encumbered with greatcoat, boots, etc., would have perished had not Mr Ferguson, Paymaster of the 78th Regiment, rushed in to his assistance and rescued him from his perilous situation. He is a Mr Henderson from Caithness. By this time the wreck had drifted within forty yards or so of the west point of the fort, with seven or eight persons on the keel, oars, etc. Some of them called out most piteously to those attempting to assist them from the shore; but at last getting into a violent eddy six or seven of them were successively washed from their holds and sunk to rise no more. A man and a woman still kept by the mast, which was floating alongside the wreck and in this affecting situation, the man setting up the most heart-rending shrieks, they drifted down the Frith, till nearly past the garrison, when William Skilling, a private in the 78th, swam out with the end of a rope to make fast to the wreck, but which was unfortunately too short. Encouraged however by his commanding officer Lt Colonel M'Leod, who was on the beach using every exertion which humanity could suggest, Skilling proceeded to the wreck, where he endeavoured to push the mast with those attached to it before him to the shore, but which noble attempt was frustrated by the mast's being fast to the wreck by a rope,which he could not disengage. In the meantime however a ship's boat from the pier which, to the imminent danger of the crew, had been got around the point, soon came up and succeeded in bringing the man and woman ashore. The man's name is John Angus, a sailor, and a native of Thurso. The woman was taken up lifeless.'

The reporter continues:

'I have spoken with Angus and Henderson; the account they give is, Angus wished to apply the rudder to the boat but was prevented by a ferryman. About third ferry, the wind being very strong against them, a rower on the lee side became exhausted; when a man getting wet by water breaking in at the bow, came backward to the stern, which circumstance, adding to the interruption of the rowers, a good deal of sea rushed in on the stern. The major part of them wished to return, and began putting the boat round to leeward which was opposed by Angus who begged them to put back by the stern or about to windward and at the same time rushed forward to seize an oar but was prevented by his wife laying hold of him, at which moment a wave made fairly over the boat, her side being to the storm. They remained some minutes in this alarming state and then resolved on clearing themselves of the pony. On this Mr Henderson threw up the bridle, laid hold of the crupper and set out for the shore. He had not proceeded many yards when the animal attempted to return to the wreck; on this he struck it on the side of the head with his disengaged hand and succeeded in putting him in the direction of the garrison; he looked back and saw the people on the wreck. Corroborated by Angus, who adds, that a few minutes after Mr Henderson left them a heavy sea overturned the boat keel uppermost, but he cannot tell how he got hold of the mast.' (*AR* 1811, Chr, pp130-131; *Times*, 27 and 29 November 1811)

15 November, Marston, merchantman The *Marston*, Pearson master, of Whitehaven, was lost during the night of the 15th, a little to the southward of St Bee's Head, when all seven persons on board perished. The captain and mate were brothers. (*Times*, 28 November 1811)

18 November, Isabella, merchantman The ship *Isabella* arrived at Hull from London in distress. She had taken potash for ballast, and springing a leak, the potash choked the pumps, so that the only way of saving her was by sending the men into the hold to bale the water out. As a consequence of this operation eight of them were terribly burnt, particularly in the arms and legs. Five of them were most dangerously injured and the rest, although terribly injured, are in a fair way of recovery. (*Times*, 28 November 1811)

25 November, Brilliant Star, merchantman The Letter of Marque, *Brilliant Star*, Captain John Craft, of 13 guns and 27 men, belonging to Mr Baily of Plymouth, was lost on the Black Rocks near Brest about 3am on Monday 25 November. She had sailed from Plymouth about 2pm on Saturday the 23rd with a cargo of blubber and pilchards for Malta, and her loss appears to have been solely owing to her very superior sailing, which much deceived the mariners as to the latitude they were in. In consequence of it having become very cloudy and dark within a few hours previous to the accident, an extra hand was put on the lookout, where he had not been long before he saw the breakers about half a cable's length ahead. The ship was going before the wind at the time and the man at the helm was instantly called to, to put it hard down, which was immediately complied with, when the promptness of the helmsman, in doing his duty, they shot by three of these dreadful rocks; but the fourth and fatal one was too near to be avoided and they ran upon it. All the crew but one got into the boats, although the vessel went down in less than a quarter of an hour after she struck; doubts however were entertained for the safety of eight seamen, all Swedes, who got into the jollyboat and headed for Brest. The captain, and the remainder, took to the longboat in which they were for two days; when the *Rhin* frigate hove in sight and took them on board, where they remained some time, when the captain ordered them to be put on a schooner, bound for London, which vessel they left a few hours later in the Channel in a gale; they again took to their boat and arrived at Plymouth next morning. (*NC* vol 27, p48; *Times*, 5 December 1811)

25 November, Diana's prize   'The boats of the *Diana*, a 36-gun frigate, together with the boats of the *Growler* gunbrig, cut out a French brig on the coast of France and put on board her, Mr Andrews midshipman; Mr Bolem quartermaster; and Mr Nicholas Winstanly (or Winstand), the captain's steward to navigate the vessel to Plymouth. Four of the original crew were left on board. They were James Martin a black; Manuel Joachim a Portuguese; John Hockey Martin an Irishman; and John Mellington a boy aged seventeen, an American.

'The brig lost sight of the *Diana* and bore away for a French port, hoping for protection; but the next day was seen again by the *Diana* which again retook her; but the British were not to be found in the ship, and from the conduct of the prisoners, on being questioned, it was supposed they had been murdered and thrown overboard. Enquiry will, no doubt, be made into this atrocious murder.'[52] (*SYM*, 9 December 1811)

'On 12th December a court martial was held on board the *Salvador del Mundo* in Hamoaze when the four members of the original crew were found guilty of mutiny and murder, and sentenced to be hanged on board such ship as the Lords of the Admiralty shall direct.' (*SYM*, 16 and 23 December)

'On Saturday 21st December the four mutineers and murderers on board the *Diana*'s prize were hanged on the fore yardarm of the *Diana* in Plymouth Sound. A boat from each man-of-war, manned and armed, rowed around the *Diana* during the awful ceremony. The mutineers were very penitent and acknowledged the justice of their sentences.' (*SYM*, 30 December 1811)

4 December, revenue cutter's boat   This evening in Whitstable Bay seven men belonging to the *Scorpion* revenue cutter stationed there left the vessel in the long galley, on the lookout for smugglers, and have not since been heard of, but the boat, oars, some hats and an ammunition box have been found on shore, and hence it is inferred that all on board perished. (*Times*, 13 December 1811)

4 December, Saldanha, 36 guns   The loss of the *Saldanha*, a 36-gun frigate built in 1809, is given in a report from Rathmelton (Ramelton) dated 6 December.

'His Majesty's ship *Saldanha*, Captain the Hon William Pakenham, sailed from Cork on 19 November to relieve His Majesty's ship *Endymion* off Lough Swilly. Having reached that harbour, she, with the *Endymion* and *Talbot*, sailed on the 30th, with an intention it is said of proceeding to the westward. On 3rd December it blew very hard from the north-west; the wind continued to increase till the 4th; and in the evening and night of that day it blew the most dreadful hurricane that the inhabitants of this part of the country ever recollect. At about ten o'clock at night, through the darkness and the storm, a light was seen from the signal towers passing rapidly up the harbour, the gale then blowing nearly right in. This light was, it is supposed, on board the *Saldanha*; but this is only conjecture, for when the daylight discovered the ship (a complete wreck in Ballyna Stoker Bay, on the west side of the harbour), every soul on board had already perished, and all the circumstances of her calamitous loss thus perished with her. It is stated in some of the accounts that the ship first struck on some rocks near the entrance of the harbour, and that the wind drove and the tide floated her to the distant place where the wreck came ashore; but this also can only be conjecture; and whether well-founded or otherwise, is now of little consequence.' (*Times*, 18 December 1811)

Captain Pakenham was brother to the Earl of Longford, Lady Wellington, and the Hon Colonel Pakenham, Deputy Quartermaster-General of the army in Portugal. The bodies of Captain Pakenham and about 200 of the crew were said to have been washed ashore and were to be interred in a neighbouring burial ground. (*NC* vol 27, pp42, 43 and 88; *AR* 1811, Chr, pp139-140)

On 14 December the *Times* quoted a letter written by a midshipman of the *Talbot*: 'At 12 o'clock (noon) on Saturday 30th November we weighed and made sail from Lough Swilly in company with the *Saldanha*. On Sunday it blew hard from the north and gradually increased until Wednesday it was blowing a hurricane with snow. The *Saldanha*'s lights were visible in passing Tannet Point [Fanad Head?] at half-past nine p.m., the wind blowing fair for the lough. It was believed that the ship struck on Swilly Rock [Swilly More off the Doaghbeg coast], after which the wind and tide shifted the wreck on shore in Ballymasclacken Bay. The shell of the vessel is fifty yards off at low watermark. The *Saldanha* had a complement of 280, but it was not known how many were on board. One man got to land, but was so weak he died in a few minutes.' [The *Saldanha* had a crew of 274, yet not all were on board when the disaster occurred. The Times of 18 December has the names of 21 persons who were left behind at Cork on board the hospital ship *Trent* when the *Saldanha* sailed.]

A sequel to the disaster occurred on 28 August 1812.

'At an early hour in the morning a bird was observed on a tree at a gentleman's house at Byrt; a clown who lived about the house as a servant, mistook it for a hawk and shot it, when it proved to be a beautiful green parrot, and had around its neck a gold ring, on which was engraved "Captain Pakenham, of His Majesty's ship *Saldanha*." A person in an adjoining field was listening to the bird when it was shot and thought it was attempting to speak either the Spanish or French language. What seems extraordinary is that the bird had not been seen in any part of the country before that morning, though the vessel from which it must have escaped was lost on 4th December last off Lough Swilly. The place where it was killed was about twenty miles from the wreck. Poor Poll and a dog were the only survivors from that ill-fated ship and her gallant crew.' (*Belfast Newsletter; AR* 1812, Chr, p131)

The following notice appeared in *NC* vol 25, p352.

'Obituary. 19th March at Lough Swilly, Captain John Stuart of HMS *Saldanha*, 2nd son of the late Hon. General Sir Charles Stuart KB and nephew of the Marquis of Bute and the Lord Primate of Ireland.'

Captain Pakenham was unfortunate enough to be his successor for nine months only; indeed, very unfortunate, for Captain Pakenham had been appointed to the 32-gun frigate *Aquilon* (*NC* vol 25, p172), but the *Aquilon* was part of the Baltic fleet and did not arrive at Yarmouth, Norfolk, until 31 October 1812.

The *Times*, 2 November 1812, has an article.

15 December, Polly, brig   On 20 June 1812 Captain Wyse of the ship *Modesty* which arrived at Waterford on 20 July 1812; spoke the wreck of the brig *Polly* of Boston in position 31°56′N 37°40′W and took off two men who had subsisted 190 days on the wreck, during which period they had eaten one of their companions. The *Polly* sailed from Boston on 12 December 1811, bound to Santa Cruz in the West Indies. On the 15th she sprung a leak, carried away all her masts, and upset, by which Mr J S Hunt, supercargo, and a negro girl were lost. The brig afterwards righted, but of the crew which including passengers consisted of nine persons, seven perished on the wreck, and the other two must have shared the same fate, had they not been taken up by Captain Wyse. (*Times*, 29 July 1812)

An extract from the journal of the ship *Fairy*, from Bahia for Liverpool dated Friday 19 June 1812, shows that she sailed in company with the *Modesty*; the extract follows: 'At six p.m. saw a wreck to the eastward of us; bore down for it and boarded it; found two men (one of them the Captain, William Leslie Cazuneau) still alive; they informed us, that they made 191 days since they left Boston, bound to Santa Cruz; the brig (called the *Polly*) had upset on the third day, but being laden with lumber, and some provisions, would not sink; as soon as they had cut away the masts she righted. They had existed partly on the beef and pork they could fish up from the cargo, and afterwards on the fish they caught; they had even been obliged to eat some part of one of their shipmates who had died, had cut up the rest of his body and put it into pickle to serve in case of necessity; the two we found were all that remained of a crew of nine; they had raised a temporary place in the forecastle to keep them dry and cook their provisions; they produced fire by rubbing violently together two pieces of shingle; and when it did not rain they procured fresh water by distillation from salt water and managed to make eight quarts a day. (*NC* vol 28, p198)

24 December, Fancy, gunbrig   *Fancy* was supposedly lost this day, but was last seen on 30 October and already presumed lost by 11 November.

24 December, disaster to the Baltic fleet   If we exclude Admiral Graves' fleet of 1782, then perhaps the most disastrous week in the history of the Royal Navy had arrived. On this Christmas Eve and Christmas Day three British ships went to the bottom taking with them more than 2000 men, in addition to many women and children. On this day the *St George* and the *Defence* were both wrecked off the coast of Jutland; then on the following day the *Hero* was lost on the Haaks, off the Texel. The narrative of incidents in their sequence follows.

The *St George*, 98 guns, was built at Portsmouth dockyard and came off the stocks in 1785. During the autumn of 1811 she was the flagship of Rear-Admiral Robert Carthew Reynolds, whose flag captain was Daniel Oliver Guion.

The *Defence* was a much older vessel having been built at Devonport dockyard and launched in 1763; she mounted 74 guns and was commanded by Captain David Atkins. Both vessels were part of the Baltic fleet returning to England, the whole being under the command of Admiral Sir James Saumarez, who had given orders to Reynolds not to delay the departure of the last homeward bound convoy on any account beyond 1 November. (Statement of the Hon C Yorke, First Sea Lord of the Admiralty, House of Commons, 17 January 1812)

According to his instructions Admiral Reynolds got the convoy in Matvik (56°10′N 14°58′E) under weigh on 1 November; and it was late in the same day when the ships began to arrive off Hano. Yet some, even then, had not left Matvik; then on the following morning when the wind came from the south several merchant ships of the 150 strong fleet (*NC* vol 27, p45), returned to Matvik for safety. Eventually, however, the convoy sailed from Hano Bay on 9 November and in the evening of the 10th came to an anchor between Moen Island and Dars Head (Darsser Ort). On the 12th the ships anchored off Nysted (Nystadt); so far all was well, but during the night of the 15th a severe gale came on, the fleet was dispersed and many ships returned to Matvik.[53] A large ship which nearly broke from her anchors, drove athwart the hawse of the *St George*, which ship parted her cables and lost her rudder when she tailed on the *Rodsand*, and the crew had to cut away the masts to save the vessel. However, by the 19th the *St George* had topmasts rigged for jury masts and the *Cressy* had supplied her with a temporary Pakenham rudder made of cable; then with repairs temporarily effected, the convoy, now only 72 ships, sailed for Wingo Sound, via the

Fehmarn Belt and the Great Belt, arriving at Wingo on 1 December, already
a month late. Yet here another 16 days were spent further securing the jury
masts of the *St George* and attending to her rudder. Still, the ships sailed on
the 17th, and on the 20th, early in the morning, the *St George*, *Defence*, and
Cressy, which latter two ships had been ordered to accompany the *St George*
to England, parted from the rest of the fleet; excepting the *Bellette* sloop
which had also been placed under Admiral Reynold's orders.

Captain Pater of the *Cressy* later stated that on the morning of the
21st they were close in with Salo Beacon (on the south end of Salo Island,
57°49'N 11°37'E), and it was proposed to anchor in that harbour during the
ensuing night: but a strong breeze coming in from NNE they continued on
all night through the Sleeve, the *St George* making five knots. At 11am on
the 22nd the land about Hanstholm bore SSW distance seven leagues. The
ships now stood to the westward with moderate weather all night, wind
about N by W. On the 23rd, at 9am, Captain Pater asked permission to take
the *St George* in tow, but was refused, and an hour later it came on to blow
a strong gale. At 11am the *St George* took in her topsails and courses, the
ship standing to the NE with a view to open the Sleeve. The whole of the
23rd she drifted so much to leeward as to oblige the *Cressy* to bear up three
or four times in a watch to keep up to leeward of her; and at 10.30pm Captain
Pater, seeing no possibility of clearing the land on the larboard tack, wore
ship, and by carrying a press of sail, had the good fortune to weather the
Horn Reef. At the time the *Cressy* wore, the *St George* and the *Defence* were
left with their heads on shore ENE under storm mizzen staysail and trysail,
with the land to the southward of Bovbjerg upon their lee beams and drifting
on shore at the rate of three knots.

The following narrative of John Anderson, one of the survivors of
the *St George*, was sent to Admiral Reynolds' family:

'On 21st December, lying off Salls (Salo), wind at WSW made signal
for a pilot, who came on board. The wind chopped round to the N by E
stood off to sea, and shaped a course for England.

'Sunday 22nd, the wind north by west we continued our course.
Monday evening the wind came round to the WNW blowing a strong gale,
with a heavy sea, and then at nine o'clock, lost sight of the *Defence*; and half
an hour later the *Cressy* passed us to leeward, and stood to the southward.
About eleven o'clock the wind changed to NNW; at twelve the admiral
made signal to wear and stand to the westward; we tried to hoist the jib, but
it was blown away before it was half way up; after it was gone, hands were
sent to loose the fore topsail; it was no sooner gone from their arms, before
it was blown away. All our head sails being gone, we got the hammock
cloaths (*sic*) in the fore rigging, which however had no effect. Then got a
nine inch hawser and bent it to the spare anchor, the stock and one fluke
being gone.

'Then taking the opportunity of a lull, let go the anchor and put the helm down, trying to club-haul her, and get her round on the other tack, but the hawser catching the heel of the rudder, carried it away. All we had to trust to then was our anchors. We immediately sent two watches below to arrange the cables, and kept one watch on deck to strike the lower yards and topmasts; finding we only had twelve fathom, let go the best bower, but by the time it was gone, she struck [between S Nissum and Husby, to the north of the Horn Reef]. This was between five and six of the morning of the 24th; orders were then given to cut away the masts, and sent hands down to the pump; but finding she gained so much water, all hands were obliged to fly to the poop, where they continued from the 24th, till we left the ship on the 25th, when the whole that remained were either dead or dying very fast. The sea ran so high, it was impossible for boats to live to come to our assistance: two yards being all we had left, we made a raft alongside; we then got on it, some lashed and others not; those who were not were swept off by the first sea.

'The admiral remained in his cabin till the 24th; when the sea came in he was obliged to be hoisted through the skylight on the poop, where he and Captain Guion lay close to each other; at half-past three on the 25th he died, the captain lying alongside of him.

'Those who were lashed, myself and three others, got on shore, but so weak as not to be able to get off without assistance. Seven got on shore afterwards, on planks or pieces of wreck as the ship broke up. On coming to our senses we could muster only eleven men.'

A report from Lemvig, dated 6 January 1812, stated that the Pakenham rudder was too weak to govern the *St George* during a North Sea gale; that the admiral, captain, and about 500 of the crew lay dead on the deck from exposure; and that twelve got ashore alive, including the admiral's secretary, although he died shortly afterwards. Two days later, with the wind offshore, two Englishmen (apparently survivors), went to the wreck which lay 300 fathoms offshore, to recover the bodies of the admiral and captain, but found the deck had been washed away by the sea, yet both ends of the ship were still visible, supposed broken right athwart and held together by the ammunition and guns in her bottom. The same report said that a great number of bodies had been washed ashore between South Nissum and Husby. (Husby Church 56°17'N 8°11'E; *Times*, 7 February 1812) [The men of the *St George* and the *Defence* were buried in the sand dunes where they came ashore, ever since known as 'dead men's dunes.' A prohibited area extends one mile from the coast from Nyminde Gab to a point twelve miles north of Hvide Sande.]

The *St George* had a crew of about 740, but this did not include the women and children, nor the pilots; and as there were eleven survivors, we may assume that at least 740 perished with the ship.

Joseph Page, a seaman of the *Defence* and one of the six people who got on shore alive, gave his account of the loss of the ship; which is given here as it was written, but am or pm have been corrected:

'On Monday 23rd December 1811 at 12 p.m. (noon), bent the storm staysails, and hauled up the fore topsail; it was then blowing a strong gale from WSW, the *St George* and *Cressy* in company to leeward. At one, took in the fore topsail, and lay-to under close reefed main topsail. At three p.m. split the main topsail; wind WNW; unbent the main topsail and sent it down on deck; got a fore topsail ready for bending, but having no other main topsail on board, Captain Atkins would not allow it to be bent, for fear of losing it; it was put under the poop awning in readiness, when the weather should moderate. We next hove-to under storm staysails, at nine-thirty; the *Cressy* wore and stood under our stern to the southward. Our Captain ordered to see all clear for wearing; at the same time asking Mr Baker [1st Lieutenant of *Defence*] if the *St George* had wore; and was answered, "No". He then said he would stand on with her, or would not wear till she did. We saw no more of the *Cressy*. At twelve a.m. (midnight), the watch and idlers turned up to wear ship. At half-past twelve the captain told Mr Baker he would not wear till the *St George* did, but would stay by her. Saw the *St George* burning a blue light to leeward. At two-thirty split the main staysail; hauled down the fore staysail, and lay-to under the mizzen staysail; blowing a hard gale from the NW. At four-thirty the 1st Lt ordered me (captain of the fore-top) to send four men into the top, and went up myself; to attend the backstays and overhaul the fore buntlines etc. Just as I got to the top, the ship struck very easy, and looking to leeward I saw the breakers. I mentioned to Ralph Teazie (one of the men saved) that the ship had struck, and just then falling into a trough of the sea, she struck heavy fore and aft. The fore staysail was about half hoisted; the sea making a fair breach over her, washed the men to leeward, rendering them unable to hoist it up. Just as the 1st Lt ordered the masts to be cut away, the main mast, mizzen mast, and fore topsail yard went over the side; about five minutes after, the fore mast went. The sea breaking her, the dismal shrieks of the people, the guns breaking adrift, and crushing the men to death, rendered the whole a dreadful scene. I saw the carpenter's wife, with a little girl in her hand, endeavouring to get on the quarterdeck, when a tremendous sea broke in, which washed her, with many of the people, down the hatchway. The captain was then on the poop, holding on by the howitzer, standing before the mizzen mast. The boats were laying on the lee gangway, all dashed to pieces except the pinnace, with about twenty men in her, and she was immediately washed overboard and lay bottom up. I now jumped overboard, and got on the mizzen-top, and the ship parted by the chesstree and gangway (48 years old and went to pieces within half an hour). By the heave of the sea, and rolling of the ship, the sheet anchor was driven athwart the forecastle, and killed several men. The sea was now making a fair breach between the forecastle and quarterdeck; the booms were washed away, with nearly a hundred men holding on by them. I with several others, was washed off the top; I now made the best of my way from one part of the wreck to another, till I got on the booms, on which at this time, were about forty men. When the sea coming again, made a clear sweep, except three or four. I got on the raft again, (booms lashed together), and spoke to John Brown, and told him I thought we were drawing near the land, he told me, yes, he believed we were. There were then about twenty men on the raft; but on reaching the shore, six only remained. Two Danes, who were on the beach, came to our assistance; my foot was at this time jammed in among the small spars. John Brown and Ralph Teazie, finding I was not able to get off the raft, were coming to assist me, but the Danes told them, as well as we could understand, to sit down, for they were stronger than us, and would try to get me off the raft; one Dane made three attempts before he could get to me; the third time he was washed over head and ears; but got hold of my foot, wrenched it out, and took me on shore. He then took me to a little shed, to wait for the carts, most of us being unable to walk; in the course of ten minutes a great number of carts, and gentlemen on horseback, came down to the beach. They put us in two different carts, and drove us to Sheltoz, a small village on the road. the man who drove us spoke to a woman on the road, and asked if she had any liquor. She took a bottle from her pocket, and made each of us take a drink, *which I believe was the principle of the safety of our lives.* We soon arrived at a house in the village, where we stript, had dry clothes given us, and were put to bed; it was then about eleven o'clock, as near as I can guess; the Danes were very near to us. When I came to myself, I found Thomas Mullins in bed with me; he came on shore sometime after me on a piece of the wreck. About five o'clock, a gentleman who could speak English, came to the bedside where me and Mullins was, and told us there was an officer brought up to the house, and asked if we were able to get up and see if we knew him. We told him "yes", and with the assistance of the people, went to the barn, and found it to be our captain. On Sunday the 29th he was put into a coffin, and buried in Sheltoz Churchyard. David M'Robb and John M'Cormic were buried alongside of him. We remained there till the 15th January, when our captain was taken up and carried to Rizkum, where we fell in with the survivors of the *St George*; they were at that time burying the boatswain of Anholt. We then buried our cap- tain, with the honours of war. The *St Georges* told us they were going to be sent home.'

Names of the survivors: Joseph Page, writer of the narrative; John Brown; Ralph Teazie; John Platt; Thomas Mullins; and David M'Cormic, who came ashore alive, but died going up in the cart. (*NC* vol 27, p44 et seq, vol 28, p113 et seq, vol 28, p210 et seq). There were, therefore, only five survivors out of a crew of 600 men and boys, in addition to whom, were an unknown number of women and infants.

The loss of the *St George*'s masts in the Fehmarn Belt is assigned as the original cause of the misfortune; but some intelligent mariners assert that it was a fault both in these ships and the *Hero* (see below) not to have stood, immediately after clearing the Skager Rack, over to the English coast, as the merchantmen from the Baltic usually do. (*AR* 1811, General History, p101)

The *Defence* first took the ground (not according to Joseph Page), and on signal being given by her of the accident, the *St George* immediately let go her anchor, but in bringing up with the anchor, she took the ground abaft, so that her forepart, which had deeper water, and was confined down by the cable was, in a short time, under water. (*AR* 1812, Chr, p1)

24 December, Hero, 74 guns   The following is a narrative by a person on board the *Grasshopper*, an 18-gun brig, Commander Henry Fanshawe, of the circumstances attending the loss of that vessel and the *Hero*, 74 guns, Captain James Newman Newman.

'On 18th December we sailed from Wingo Sound in company with HM ships *Hero, Egeria* and *Prince William*, armed ship, with a convoy of 120 sail or more. The *Egeria* and *Prince William*, with the greater part of the convoy, separated from us in the tremendous weather we had shortly after leaving the Sleeve, and on the 23rd we found ourselves in company with the *Hero* and about eighteen sail, mostly transports. At half-past eleven on that day Captain Newman made sail to come within hail, when he told us, as he conceived we were near the Silver Pitts,[54] he should steer SW after noon, which was done; and at the close of the day, we steering that course, running at the rate of nine knots, at about ten o'clock that night signal was made to alter course to port two points, which was repeated by us. At this time only four of the convoy were in sight and they were shortly lost sight of in a heavy squall of snow and sleet. At half-past three the hands were turned up, the ship being in broken water, we found we were on a sandbank, the pilots imagining it to be Smith's Knoll [off Winterton]. The captain instantly ordered the brig to be steered SSE, thinking to get out to sea, but she continued striking so hard for a length of time that we had almost given her up for lost, when suddenly and very fortunately, we fell into three fathoms water, upon which the captain caused an anchor to be let go. We again perceived the *Hero* (as we then thought) also at an anchor, though she fired guns and burnt blue lights; but, when day broke, we had the mortification of witnessing a most horrific scene; the *Hero* was totally dismasted; and on her larboard beam ends, with her head to the NE about a mile from us, upon the Haek's [Haake] Sand, as we then found we were inside of it, off the Texel Island: the ship's company were all crowded together on the poop and forecastle. As soon as the daylight had well appeared she hoisted a flag of truce and fired a gun, which we repeated, and very shortly after saw a lugger, two brigs, and several small vessels, plying out of the Texel to our assistance; but owing to the flood tide having made, and the wind blowing a perfect gale at NNW the lugger was only able to come within two or three miles of us by two o'clock in the afternoon. In the meantime we hoisted out our boats, and made an attempt to get near the *Hero*, but the surf was so high that it was all ineffectual, and we were under the cruel necessity of seeing so many of our brave countrymen perishing, without being able to render them any assistance. The *Grasshopper* at the same time was constantly striking very hard, though everything had been thrown overboard to lighten her, except the guns, upon which it was feared she would have bilged. The master was then sent to sound in every direction, for a passage to make our escape by (though I have since found out, that an escape was totally impossible); but quarter less three, and two fathoms and a half were the only soundings he could meet with. The captain, therefore, with the opinion of the officers, agreed, that we had no chance of saving ourselves, but by surrendering to the enemy, who were at this time, as I have before mentioned, coming to our assistance, and that of the *Hero*, from whose wreck, I am sorry to say, not one soul has been saved. At close of day, finding the weather threatening to be worse, and the brig striking so repeatedly, we cut the cable and ran for the port in view; when we approached the lugger, which was at this time anchored, she sent a pilot to us, who took us into the Texel (Niewe Diep), where we surrendered to the Dutch squadron, under the command of Admiral de Winter, who I must in justice say, has behaved to us in the most humane and attentive manner. They also used every means in their power to save the crew of the *Hero*; but the badness of the weather rendered it totally impossible.

'We lost only one man, Mr King the pilot, who was killed by a capstern bar, which flew out as we were heaving in cable to put service in the hawse.' (*AR* 1812, Chr, p2 et seq). *Hero* lost 600 men; there were no survivors.

'The *Hero* had been launched at Perry's Dock, Blackwall, on Thursday 18th August 1803; and never upon a similar occasion was noticed so great a concourse of spectators as were assembled to witness the pleasing scene.

'Before she was launched the riggers had furnished her with jury masts, temporary sails, yards, rigging and everything necessary to navigate her down the river, so that her appearance was infinitely more interesting than those ships which were launched as hulks.

'The head is ornamented with an heroic warrior, richly carved, in the Roman costume, surrounded by trophies, laurel leaves, and emblems of victory, the whole having the rake with her stem, which has been studied to give the figure a better effect upon the cutwater. The stern is plain but neat, allegorical figures richly carved, representing Plenty, Victory, Fame, &c. support the quarters. Admiral Lord Hood in his twelve oared barge rowed to the spot and expressed his satisfaction. Persons of the first distinction were present, and a line of carriages was formed from Blackwall almost to Limehouse.

'Mr Perry, upon the occasion, invited a select party of friends to his house, where an elegant cold collation and wine were prepared for their reception, which they partook of and drank to the future prosperity of the *Hero*.' (*NC* vol 10, p166)

25 December, Hawke's boat On the evening of Wednesday 25 December Lt Dumaresque of the *Hawke* sloop of war, lying off Calshot Castle, where she brought up to attend on His Royal Highness the Duke of Clarence, came to Southampton, rowed up the river from the ship by six men, to dine with Admiral Ferguson. After he had taken his dinner he embarked in the same boat for the purpose of returning to the *Hawke*; a breeze springing up, they found it eligible to set the sail, in doing which the mast fell, and overpowering the sailors upset the boat; and the whole party, with a man of the name of Shirlock, a musician, whom Lt Dumaresque had taken into the boat, at the request of the men to amuse them during the holidays on board, were plunged into the river. The sequel is a melancholy detail: Lt Dumaresque, Mr Shirlock and five sailors out of six were drowned; the other swam ashore. The accident happened between Netley and Weston (Woolston). (*NC* vol 27, pp104-105)

1812

28 January, Manilla, 36 guns The *Manilla*, a 36-gun frigate, Captain John Joyce, was wrecked on the Haaks during the night of the 28th and the three letters, here given in part, from Admiral de Winter to the Dutch Minister of Marine and Colonies, give the sequence of events during which time the Dutch rescued 243 officers and men from the ship.

'Texel, 30th January 1812
'Monseigneur,
'I have the honour of reporting to your excellency that on the 28th at nine in the evening we from time to time heard reports of cannon accompanied by rockets.

'These signals of distress determined the commanding officer to send immediately fishing boats, and boats belonging to the squadron to tender assistance; but the violence of the sea upon the bank, occasioned by a strong gale from ESE forced them to return at three in the morning.

'As day broke a large three masted vessel upon the Haak was perceived, continuing to make signals of distress. All the fishing boats and boats belonging to the squadron set out at daylight, and as the weather has become more favourable, it is hoped the crew will be saved.

'It is supposed this vessel is a frigate, undoubtedly the one which all this month has appeared, with one or two brigs, off this coast.'

'Texel, 31st January

'The boats which set out at daybreak on the 29th approached the ship; but at a cable's distance the sea was so strong, and the sands had collected to such a degree that the boats struck violently upon them and immediately the row boats became useless; nevertheless, the chief pilot Duynheer risked the sacrificing of his life to save some men, and ventured on the shallows and sunken rocks, whilst the English, having made a raft by tying empty barrels together, let it down. This bold measure placed Duynheer in a situation to receive 35 men, all sailors, and two pilots. The boat was already half filled with water, and it was with difficulty she withdrew from so critical a situation. One of the enemy's sailors expired in the boat and two are dangerously wounded.

'Six boats are anchored within the Haak to take advantage of the least change in the weather. The brig *Ferreter* was at anchor all day but returned in the evening. All the boats with decks which are in the Texel are in a state of readiness.

'On the 31st in the morning, it blowing from the southward very fresh, the frigate again began to fire, and the boats have returned to renew their efforts.

'On the night she struck the captain endeavoured to have an anchor carried out, but did not succeed, and lost in attempting it three boats and thirty-six men. From the morning of the 29th, the French flag has been hoisted and the English pulled down; during all that day three enemy ships were observed from Calands Oog. The prisoners are marched for Amsterdam.'

'Texel, 1st February

'I have the honour of concluding my report of the Shipwreck of the enemy's frigate, the *Manilla*. The boats succeeded in saving all the people on board the frigate; they are on board the squadron to proceed to Amsterdam.

'Three of the boats belonging to the frigate, which were believed to have been lost in carrying out the anchor, have arrived upon Texel Island with some men. A small part of the prisoners' clothes have been saved, it being with considerable difficulty that the crew were taken off. The ship cannot be got off and will be destroyed by the sea.

'I bring to your notice the exemplary conduct of the Lieutenant de Vaisseau Jacob Verveer who commanded pilot Duynheer's boat and who achieved with the greatest risk of perishing himself, the rescue of thirty-five men from off the raft.' (*NC* vol 27, p416 et seq, with a full list of the 243 saved)

In consequence of the drunkenness of the gunner, John Tyrell, a spark emitted from a blue light (a warning signal), falling on a salt box, which contained some cartridges, an explosion was caused which destroyed nine men, blew up the forecastle deck, and wounded twelve more. (*NC* vol 32, p220 et seq)

31 January, Laurel, 38 guns The *Laurel*, a 38-gun frigate, Captain Samuel Rowley, arrived in Quiberon Bay on the evening of 30 January and was immediately placed under the orders of Admiral Somerville of the *Rota* frigate to sail in company with her and the *Rhin* frigate, Captain Malcolm, in pursuit of three French frigates.

The next morning at 7am, with the wind blowing fresh from the south by east, and the rain falling heavily at intervals, the commodore made signal to weigh, but from the violence of the weather, the anchor was hove up with great difficulty.

The commodore now decided to take the northern and unfortunately the most hazardous passage out of Quiberon; the passage situated between Houat and a rock called the Teigneuse, to which the rock gives its name. At 9.25am the Teigneuse rock bore NE by E, the ships steering W by S at the rate of eight knots; tide setting WNW, nearly four knots. The only rock the ships had then to pass was the Govivas; a small sunken rock, which has at low water, only 4½ feet. The tide, which was at the spring, was fifteen feet, and it still had two hours to ebb.

On entering the passage, the thickness of the weather completely obscured the marks near the Morbihan, and the cross bearings were only at times visible.

The *Laurel* was now hauled up WSW; the *Rhin* being within half a cable's length, close on the weather quarter; the commodore a little on the *Laurel*'s lee, distant about half a mile. At this moment *Laurel* struck on the Govivas, and, from her way through the water, and the rapidity of the tide, it may easily be imagined with what force. Captain Rowley immediately ordered the *Rhin* to be hailed, which, letting go her head sheets, and luffing in stays, struck, but fortunately got off without any damage. The *Rota*, in most imminent danger, passed between the Govivas and Les Trois Peres, a passage used only by small craft and fishermen: her escape was miraculous. Meanwhile, on the *Laurel*, they hove all aback, and the ship dropped aft into deep water. The best bower was let go but soon parted; the small one was then let go and after carrying away all the stopper was brought up by the clench. At this instant the crew saw the whole of the false keel, and part of the main, floating alongside. The sails were furled; the well sounded, and six feet water reported in the hold; the chain pumps were manned, yet, in less than ten minutes the water was up to the lower deck and the ship was settling bodily down.

To save the lives of the crew the cable was cut, the fore sail set, and the ship was run on a ridge of rocks called Les Trois Peres, about a mile off shore. Before the masts were cut away the boats were lowered and kept clear; at which time two French batteries opened fire and completely enfiladed the ship. With the quarterdeck guns now under water, and the well-directed fire of the French, the decision was taken to surrender. Captain Rowley ordered the boats with a total of 98 officers, men and boys, ashore, when upon reaching the beach the fire of the enemy ceased. The French did not allow the boats to return to the ship, but two hours later the weather cleared and those left on board the *Laurel* had the pleasure of seeing the boats of the *Rhin* and *Rota* pulling towards them and by 5.15pm all were taken off and the frigate abandoned.

In a letter from Molini the Prefect at L'Orient, to the Minister of Marine and Colonies, dated 2 February, he stated that the *Laurel* struck on the Govivas at 10am at which time the weather was very foggy and the sea extremely rough; he then goes on to say that 96 men were saved and made prisoners of war. (*NC* vol 27, p228 et seq)

26 February, Pekin, merchantman The American ship *Pekin* of Philadelphia on her homeward bound passage from Canton was wrecked on 26 February in the Strait of Sunda. The captain and crew were saved by the British sloop of war *Procris*, which was in company. Three days later the British frigates *Cornelia* and *Bucephalus* came into the Strait, and finding the wreck abandoned got her off the rocks and took, her round to Batavia. At Ormus Island they hauled her on shore, took out the greater part of her cargo, and sold the remainder with the vessel for $12,000. The salvage was settled by arbitration: two-thirds to the owners and one-third to the Royal Navy. (*Times*, 14 September 1812)

29 February, Fly, 16 guns The *Fly* was a brig sloop mounting 16 guns commanded by Commander Henry Higman, when she struck on the Knobber Reef, a narrow spit of sand and large boulders which dries at its inner end, extends 4½ miles E from the eastern end of the island of Anholt, the accident being attributed to an error in the pilot's judgement. The ship's crew were saved by boats belonging to the Baltic Fleet. (*SNL*, 1812)

3 March, Conquestador, 74 guns The French newspapers carried a report dated Croisic, 4 March: 'Yesterday evening, about seven o'clock, guns being fired every minute, informed us that a ship had got aground upon the coast, and was in danger of perishing. In consequence of the bad weather it was impossible to send out any vessel to her assistance. Measures were immediately taken by the Under Commissioner of Marine, Proux, to reconnoitre the vessels if the wind abated, and receive the unfortunate men who should be thrown upon the coast. The night being extremely dark, and the sea running very high, it was requisite to wait till high water to put to sea and approach the vessel, so as to be able to reconnoitre her at break of day. Signal guns of distress were fired without intermission.

'On the 4th, about three in the morning, the boats which the preceding night had received notice to hold themselves in readiness, were afloat, and M. Proux embarked himself, followed by the Custom-house boats and twenty-two others, including the fishing boats from Turballe.

'At break of day M. Proux perceived that the ship in danger was a large one, to all appearance English, and that her situation had become less alarming. M. Proux immediately signalled the boats to lie to, and wait till he could better judge of the situation of the ship; but the boat *La Sentinelle* from Croisic, not having perceived this signal, and by its superior sailing being alongside the sloop, could not avoid going on board. At daylight M. Proux saw the ship was out of danger, the guns ceased firing, a launch left her, and sailed towards Hoedic Island, the enemy's usual station, which determined him to direct all boats to proceed with him to Croisic and Turballe. About eight in the morning all the boats had returned to port, and were immediately followed by *La Sentinelle*.

'The master of *La Sentinelle*, later said that the English captain, the Right Hon. Lord William Stuart, pressed him to go on board, and after thanking him for the measures adopted to save his crew, informed him he was out of danger and requested the name of the person who directed the succours which were sent him. He then requested the master to convey a letter and inclosed in a box his own pair of pistols, bearing his arms and crest, as a pledge of his gratitude, to be given to M. Proux. The master and crew of *La Sentinelle* received some biscuit and rum for breakfast. One of the Frenchmen saw upon the deck of the 74-gun *Conquestador*, an American captain, who spoke French, and informed him, he had been taken near the entrance of Bourdeaux, in the ship *Febronia* of 800 tons, 16 guns, and 80 men.' (*NC* vol 27, p303 et seq)

On 16 April 1812 a court martial convened and continued by adjournment to the 17th for the purpose of inquiring into the circumstance of HMS *Conquestador*, having struck on a shoal, at the east end of Quiberon Bay called 'Le Four', on the evening of 3 March last, and to try her commander, Lord William Stuart, and the other officers of the *Conquestador*, for not having taken care in the steering and conducting of His Majesty's said ship; and for having, through wilfulness, negligence, and other default, run the said ship on the said shoal or sand; and for having hazarded the said ship, contrary to the 26th Article of War.

In his defence, his Lordship stated, 'I cannot but deem it, from my own observation, as well as from the information of others, a novel proceeding for an accident of this nature, to be made the subject of inquiry in the first instance.'

Lord William Stuart and the other officers of the *Conquestador* were severally and fully acquitted. (*NC* vol 28, p340 et seq)

4 March, Fly, packet   On the morning of 5th March several bodies were found on the north shore near Liverpool; after a severe gale the previous night. Part of the stern of a vessel was washed ashore on which was the name *Fly*, a packet from Newry to Liverpool. From the best information available, the number of persons on board was not less than 40 all of whom perished. (*AR* 1812, Chr, p32)

26 March, Charles, brig The brig *Charles*, Captain Durdle, laden with bale goods for St John's, Newfoundland, left Liverpool on 15 or 18 March, and on the 26th fell in with the ice, accompanied by a heavy swell, which forced the brig with some violence against it, so that her planks were started and she began to settle. The captain and crew, eight in number, had scarcely time to quit her when she went down and in this deplorable situation they continued for nineteen days, fourteen of which, they were among the ice. During this time the chief mate, the second mate, and three men died. The captain, one man and a boy, the only survivors, were picked up by the schooner *Margaret*, John Brake, master, from Halifax, and carried into St John's on 16 April. They were in a pitiable state, and great praise was given to Captain Brake, for his attention to the sufferers. (*Times*, 11 June 1812)

3 May, Apelles and Skylark, sloops of war The two sloops of war, the 14-gun *Apelles*, Captain Charles Robb, and the 16-gun *Skylark*, Commander James Boxer, were both wrecked to the southward of Boulogne, in thick weather during a gale. The crew of the *Skylark* burnt the vessel to prevent her being taken by the enemy; but the *Apelles*, which was captured and refloated, was later retaken by the British under a severe fire from land-based batteries, for three hours. In each case the pilots were blamed in part, for the loss of the vessel.

Of the several men who were lost from the *Apelles*, perhaps the most unfortunate was Captain Robb, who was washed overboard and drowned while assisting to throw the guns overboard, to lighten the vessel. (*NC* vol 29, p264; *SNL*, 1812)

12 May, Irlam, merchantman This Sunday morning, the weather being thick and hazy, the ship *Irlam* (a letter of marque), from Barbadoes to Liverpool, laden with sugar and cotton, and having on board part of the 16th Regiment of Foot, commanded by Captain Hall, consisting of 10 officers, 62 rank and file, and 32 women and children, struck on the Tuskar Rock (off the south-east coast of County Wexford); the unhappy sufferers had just time to get into the boats, some half-dressed, others almost naked, when she filled with water, and in a short time went to pieces. The only means by which the passengers and crew could save their lives was to seek refuge on the rock, which was almost inaccessible at that side, the summit being not less than 30 feet from the surface of the water. This they were able to accomplish with the assistance of a number of men (providentially there for the purpose of laying the foundation of a lighthouse), who effected the task by drawing the men up from the boats, one by one, with a rope fastened around the waist, and placing the children in a bag made fast to the end of the rope. At this time a brig hove in sight, and lay-to, when seven of the officers, the ladies, the master, and a number of sailors and soldiers, were conveyed on board by the frequent returning of the boat. During this time, it began to blow with increased violence, and the vessel was compelled to get under weigh, leaving on the rock three officers, 16 privates, one woman, the mate and 12 seamen, who, after remaining there for two days and nights, were on Monday evening brought to Wexford. The officers lost property to a considerable amount. One gentleman had plate on board worth £300. The mate lost a box containing 200 guineas, the fruit of many years toil. (*Wexford Journal*; quoted in *AR* 1812, chr, p77)

14 May, Tribune, transport The *Tribune* transport was dashed to pieces on Pindee Point reef, and many wounded British soldiers, together with 250 French prisoners of war, unfortunately perished. (*NC* vol 29, p155)

    The writer has been unable to trace Pindee Point, but an East Indies fleet sailed from Bengal for England on 18 March 1812, and arrived at St Helena on 7 July. This fleet would have passed Pinda Shoal, the extreme east of which is in position 14°15′S 40°50′39″E, about 14 May, so this could therefore be the shoal on which the *Tribune* was wrecked; but this is only an educated guess. (*Findlay's Indian Ocean Pilot*, 1870 ed)

10 June, Campbell Macquarrie, merchantman The ship *Campbell Macquarrie*, of Calcutta, Captain Siddons, was wrecked on Macquarrie Island in the far South Pacific Ocean. Captain Siddons, together with his officers and crew, managed to save themselves and get ashore on the island, where, however, they were stranded until 11 October, when they were taken off by the brig *Perseverance*, belonging to Port Jackson.

    The cargo of 1650 seal skins was lost. (*Times*, 6 December 1813)

18 June On this day the Congress of the United States of America formally declared war against Britain.

8 July, Exertion, 12 guns The 12-gun brig *Exertion*, Lt James Murray, was lost by getting aground on a mudbank in the River Elbe. The crew who saved themselves in the boats of the vessel, afterwards returned and set fire to the ship, to prevent her falling into the hands of the French. (*SNL*, 1812)

11 July, Encounter, 12 guns The *Encounter* (Lt James Hugh Talbot) was another 12-gun brig; and in company with the *Tuscan* sloop of war was endeavouring to capture some enemy privateers, when, after a severe action, she grounded on a shoal off San Lucar de Barrameda, a few miles north of Cadiz. When the tide ebbed, the vessel was left high and dry and was boarded by the enemy, but was nevertheless believed to have been a complete wreck. (*SNL*, 1812).

23 August, Chubb, schooner His Majesty's schooner *Chubb* (not *Cherub*, as reported in *NC*), mounting 4 guns and commanded by Lt Samuel Nisbett, upset during a gale off Halifax, Nova Scotia, and every soul on board perished. (*NC* vol 28, p248)

1 September, an 'atrocious and unmanly' act On 19 October 1812 a court martial was held on William Gaiter, landman, on board HM ship *Coquette*, in Portsmouth harbour for maiming himself by chopping off his left hand at the wrist joint, on the evening of 1 September. The Court agreed that the charge had been proved and holding in great abhorrence the commission of so atrocious and unmanly an act, by which his country is deprived of his effective services; did adjudge him to be employed in the most menial situation, on board such ship of HM as the Commander in Chief of HM ships and vessels at Spithead and in Portsmouth harbour, or the Lords Commissioners of the Admiralty, shall from time to time direct, and to be rendered unworthy for ever hereafter of being employed in any situation superior to landman in the Royal Navy. (*AR* 1812, Chr, p129). See also 23 March 1811.

8 September, Laura, schooner A 12-gun schooner *Laura*, Lt Charles Newton Hunter, was off Cape May when she was engaged by a French privateer, *Diligence*, and taken after a severe action. Her commander was wounded and while he was being attended to, a seaman surrendered the vessel; for which trouble he received seven years transportation. Prior to the action, the *Diligence* had taken, on 22 August, the 4-gun schooner *Whiting*, Lt Lewis Maxey. (*SNL*, 1812)

27 September, Barbadoes, 28 guns The 28-gun Sixth Rate ship *Barbadoes*, Captain Thomas Huskisson, was formerly a French privateer *Le Brave*, taken during May 1803 and presented in 1804 by the inhabitants of Barbadoes, to the Royal Navy. The ship sailed from Bermuda on 15 September with three vessels under her convoy for St John's, Newfoundland. About 10pm on Sunday the 27th, the wind blowing hard with a heavy sea and hazy weather, the ship struck on the north-west bar of Sable Island, and notwithstanding every exertion, was lost. Two of the convoy, the schooner *Emeline* with a cargo of sugar, and the sloop *Swift* with rum, also went to pieces. The frigate lost only one man, while all on board the merchant vessels were saved. The cargo of the *Swift* was saved, as was also part of the provisions of the frigate, which was reputed to have been carrying £60,000 in specie for Halifax dockyard. (*Times*, 29 October 1812; *SNL*, 1812)

29 September, President Adams, merchantman The American ship *President Adams* was on 29 September wrecked on the coast of China. The vessel and cargo were valued at $300,000. The day after the wreck 200 boats, in which were 1500 Chinese fishermen, came alongside and plundered the ship of the specie and every movable article; during which time they began fighting and killing each other for the money. The crew were in danger of being massacred; but they ultimately succeeded in getting one of the boats of the natives for $800 to carry them to Macao, which they reached in three days. (*Times*, 17 May 1813)

6 October, Nimble, cutter   'A court martial has been holden on 20th October on board the *Zealous* in Hawke Roads [in the Humber], on Lt John Reynolds, late commander of the *Nimble* cutter, the officers and crew, for the loss of the said vessel, at half-past two a.m. on 6th October, on a sunken rock six or seven miles south by west of Salo Beacon.'

The Court agreed 'that the loss of the said cutter was occasioned by sufficient allowance not being made for the very strong currents prevailing on that part of the Swedish coast, by which it appears she had been driven considerably to the northward and eastward of her reckoning; and it appearing that some degree of blame is imputable to Lt J Reynolds, the commander, and to Mr J Pyle, the pilot, for not coming on deck at half-past one o'clock, and taking measures to ascertain the position of the cutter, after she had been tacked, and the land having been unexpectedly discovered, the Court do adjudge the said Lt J Reynolds, and Mr Pyle the pilot, to be reprimanded, and the latter to be mulct three months' pay; and were of the opinion that no blame attaches to the rest of the officers and ship's company.' (*SNL*, 1812)

This court martial also appeared in the *Times*, 5 November 1812.

8 October, Avenger, 16 guns   The *Avenger* was a 16-gun sloop of war, commanded by Cdr Urry Johnson, when she was wrecked on the Chain Rock during the night, as she tried to enter St John's harbour, Newfoundland. The crew were saved. (*SNL*, 1812; Norie, 1827 ed, p472)

11 October, Centinel, 14 guns, and convoy   The *Centinel* gunbrig, mounting 14 guns and commanded by Lt William Elletson King, with part of the homeward bound Baltic fleet, was on this day wrecked off the north-east point of the island of Rugen, on the shoals lying off Cape Arkona. The division of the convoy which got on shore amounted to 22 vessels, of which a frigate and five ships were floated before the morning of the 12th. The crews of eight merchantmen set their ships on fire and were taken on board vessels that had escaped the danger. Eight other merchantmen, within reach of the coastal guns, fell into the hands of the enemy. The crews of all the vessels were saved and the captain and crew of the *Centinel* arrived at Yarmouth on board the 32-gun *Aquilon* frigate, on 31 October. (*Times*, 2 November 1812)

29 October, Regent, merchantman 'The ship *Regent*, which had taken in from Jutland a cargo of rape seed of the value of £10,000, was at Heligoland driven on her anchor during a gale, when she then bilged.' (*Times*, 7 November 1812)

? October, Magnet, 16 guns The 16-gun *Magnet*, sloop of war, Captain Ferdinand Moore Maurice, was formerly a French privateer, *Le Joseph*, taken in 1809.

The *Magnet* sailed from Spithead on 14 August 1812, in company with the 74-gun *San Domingo*, Vice-Admiral Sir John Borlase Warren [C-in-C North America], Captain Hotham, from which vessel the *Magnet* parted during a violent storm.

A fortnight later the *San Domingo* arrived at Halifax, Nova Scotia; yet the *Magnet* did not, and was therefore presumed to have gone down with the entire crew of 95 men and boys.

Captain Maurice was brother to Captain James Wilkes Maurice, whose fame stood high for the noble defence he made at Anholt and the Diamond Rock, the latter at Martinique. (*NC* vol 28, p173)

6 November, Three Friends, sloop On the evening of Wednesday 6 November as the sloop *Three Friends* of Youghall, James Campbell master, was coming out of Southampton, she was captured off Start Point by a French privateer, *La Juliette*, Louis Marancourt of St Malo captain.

On finding the cargo to consist of bricks and hoops, orders were given to scuttle and sink the sloop; but on Captain Marancourt's perceiving among Mr Campbell's papers a certificate from his masonic lodge, the Frenchman countermanded his orders for sinking the vessel, entertained him with great hospitality, gave him a paper, by which the sloop and cargo were to be his, and made him promise under his hand that he would endeavour to procure the release of a certain French captain, now in Dartmouth prison, which Mr Campbell is resolved on taking the necessary steps to obtain. (*Times*, 25 November 1812)

20 November, Plymouth passage boat This Friday evening, about 5pm, as one of the passage boats which pass from Mutton Cove quay, Plymouth Dock to Cremill Passage, was endeavouring to head a Portsmouth sloop that was going out of Hamoaze, the bowsprit of the latter passed through the sail of the former, and in a moment the boat was shivered in a hundred pieces. There were on board eleven women, a boy and two boatmen. The most dreadful shrieks instantly announced the unexpected catastrophe, and a number of boats pulling to the spot, with a promptitude that deserves much praise, the whole were preserved from a watery grave, though the tide was then running down with such velocity through Hamoaze, as nearly to sink the buoys. (*Times*, 25 November 1812)

24 November, Belette, 18 guns   The *Belette*, 18-gun sloop of war, commanded by Lt David Sloane, had been appointed to lead a Russian fleet through the south-west passage of Anholt, when she was wrecked off Lessoe Island in the Kattegat. The *Belette* had a crew of 120 men and boys, but of this number there were only five survivors. (*NC* vol 28, p507)

27 November, Southampton, 32 guns   Captain Sir James Lucas Yeo of HM's late ship, the 32-gun *Southampton*, arrived at Portsmouth on 9 February; he came passenger in the 18-gun *Brazen*, Captain Stirling.

The *Southampton*, having captured the United States brig *Vixen*, of 14 guns and 130 men, was on passage with her prize to Jamaica, and going through the Crooked Island Passage, on the night of 27 November, they both ran on a reef, which extends eight or nine miles from one of the points of Conception Island. The *Southampton* bilged soon after she struck; her prize was under water in a few hours. The crews were all saved. The reef was not known to the Bahama pilots, one of the best of whom was on board the *Southampton*. It is now known as Southampton Reef.

A court martial was held on 13 February 1813 to try Sir James Yeo for the loss of his ship; when the Court agreed that the loss of the *Southampton* was caused by a strong westerly current driving her on a reef near the island of Conception, not laid down in the charts, and very imperfectly known; and that no blame was imputable to Sir James Yeo, his officers and ship's company for their conduct, and did adjudge them to be acquitted. (*NC* vol 29, p170)

29 November, storm off Gibraltar   On this day a most violent storm came on at Gibraltar from the SE in which many vessels were lost. Nine sail, part of a convoy from Malta, were driven on shore in Catata Bay at the back of the Rock, and all on board perished except one gentleman and his servant, who had been passengers. Seventeen more vessels were driven on shore in the bay, several of which were American prizes. One of them, a transport name unknown, with 36 officers and men, invalids, on board, was lost with all on board. The *Iphigenia*, Captain F Pellew, 36 guns, parted two cables and was nearly lost in Orange Grove, and the *Barfleur*, 98 guns, Captain Sir Edward Berry, arrived from off Toulon with six feet of water in her hold. The article then continues, apparently written by the gentleman above:

'I left Alicante on 25th November in the Spanish ship *San Joseph*, in company with 28 other vessels and a moderate breeze from SW. On the 29th the wind changed to east, increased to hurricane force, and the weather became so thick that the convoy mistook Gibraltar for the opposite shore and all except one vessel were wrecked. Myself and servant were the only survivors of 42 on board our vessel. I was saved by some Genoese boatmen who carried me to a Spanish guardroom.' (*Times*, 19 January 1813; also in AR 1813, Chr, p6)

1 December, eleventh-hour reprieve Today at Dock (Devonport), Gaetano
Cuyano a seaman belonging to the *Sybille*, 44 guns, and lately sentenced to
die for drunkenness and striking a superior officer, was brought up with the
usual ceremony, to suffer. A halter was placed around his neck, but, instead
of a gun being fired, which was fully expected (a signal for his being launched
into eternity), a reprieve was read, granted by the Prince Regent. (*Times*, 4
December 1812)

1 ? December, unknown transport The transport ship *Dawn* arrived from
Lisbon with sick and wounded soldiers. 'She reports in position 42°N 10°W,
during a violent storm she passed a large ship which appeared full of men
and in a sinking state, and which in all probability went down soon after.
Some uneasiness has been excited lest this should be one of the transports
that sailed with the Lifeguards.' (*Times*, 11 December 1812)

5 December, Caledonia, transport The *Caledonia*, a transport with troops
from Portsmouth for Cadiz, was towed into Penzance by HM's brig
Wizard, which vessel fell in with the transport about thirteen leagues off
Land's End; and but for the assistance rendered by HM's brig, and a pilot
boat from Mount's Bay, the *Caledonia* would probably have foundered.
The troops on board the transport were for the 9th, 67th and 87th Regiments
of Foot. A part of them had been taken out by the *Nemesis* frigate off Cape
Finisterre, and directions given for the *Caledonia* to return to Falmouth.
This was probably the troopship seen in distress by the *Dawn* transport.
(*Times*, 16 December 1812)

5 December, Plumper, 12 guns A 12-gun brig, the *Plumper*, commanded
by Lt James Bray, was lost at 4am during a violent gale, when she struck on
a ledge near Dipper Harbour, in the Bay of Fundy. Of the sixty or so people
on board forty-two perished, among them, all the passengers and officers
except a Mr Hall. Among the passengers lost were Dr and Mrs Wright, Mr
Cunningham and Mr Crawford, the latter of the Commissary Department;
Mr Crawford's son was also lost.
    The *Plumper* had sailed from Halifax, Nova Scotia, for St John, New
Brunswick, with Mr Crawford carrying £70,000 for the procurement of
arms. The specie was lost with the ship. (*Times*, 9 January 1813) [The author
has been unable to trace Dipper harbour, but has reason to believe the
Plumper went down off Point Lepreau, Charlotte County, New Bruns-
wick.]

13 December, Three Friends, brig HMS *Kent*, a 74-gun Third Rate ship of
the line, arrived at Plymouth from the Mediterranean during the night of 23
December.
    On the 15th she picked up at sea the English brig *Three Friends*, laden

with fruit, Mr S Whiley master, from Messina for London, on board of which the *Kent* put a scratch crew who sailed her to Plymouth, where she arrived on the 26th. The brig had been captured on the 13th by *La Mignitonpaise*, a French privateer of 16 guns and 150 men, from St Malo, who had plundered the vessel, taken out her crew, and abandoned her with only a dog on board.[55] The brig's crew were placed in the schooner *Badajos* into which the Frenchmen had put the crews of several other vessels, which they had captured and destroyed. The *Badajos*, in her turn, was then taken in the Channel by the *Pickle* schooner, and being from the Mediterranean, they were both put under quarantine. (*Times*, 28 and 29 December 1812)

17 December, a fate worse than pressing About 3am this Thursday the new raised men on board the *Neptune* tender lying in Belfast Lough broke through the press room and took possession of the vessel. After confining the crew of the tender below, and securing the hatches, they lowered the boats, and twenty-six chiefly impressed men, effected their escape and proceeded towards the shore. Owing however to the tempestuous weather, or their ignorance of the channel, it is supposed the boats struck on the banks, and the men, attempting to wade to land, it is feared have all perished, as at daylight one of the boats was found on shore, with two bodies lying near it. Six hats and several bundles of clothes were also picked up. (*AR* 1812, Chr, p152)

18 December, Alban, cutter The *Alban*, a 10-gun cutter, Lt William Sturges Key, was driven from her station off the coast of Holland, and being forced on shore at Aldborough in Suffolk became a complete wreck. Out of a crew of 56 men only one seaman, a man named Newton, was saved. The surgeon, Mr Thompson, came on shore with some life in him, but died immediately afterwards. There were also three women and two children on board, of whom one woman, the servant of Mrs Key, was saved. The following particulars of the loss of this vessel are stated by a man, a spectator of this deplorable catastrophe. He said that the cutter had been cruising, or was going to cruise, on the coast of Holland; that owing, it is supposed, to the ignorance of the pilot, she had struck on a sandbank, when they were obliged to throw the guns overboard, and cut away their mast, after which they were driven, on this Friday morning, at 8am, on the beach in front of the town of Aldborough. The surf was so high that no boat could be put off; but the beach being steep, the vessel was thrown up very high, and the tide retreating, the people of the town were soon able to reach the vessel. Though all the crew seemed to be safe at eight, by nine there were only three remaining alive: a young man, a woman (servant of Mrs Key), and the surgeon, who unaccountably jumped overboard at the time relief was given to them, and was lost. As the cutter did not go to pieces, the great loss of lives seemed to have been occasioned by the state of intoxication of the men, some of whom were found drowned in the vessel; it was difficult otherwise to account for such a melancholy catastrophe. (*AR* 1812, Chr, p152; *Times*, 21 and 25 December 1812)

19 December, a Gorleston yawl This morning, a Gorleston yawl with eight men went out to some ships in Yarmouth Roads, and in returning for the pier, upset, and seven of the eight were drowned. One of their companions, standing on the pier, threw them a rope, and being entangled in it, fell from off the pier and was drowned also. They have all left families. (*Times*, 22 December 1812)

30 December, Fortitude, brig A shipwreck took place in consequence of the extinction of the light on the Smalls [a rocky group of islands off the Pembrokeshire coast, 20 miles south-west of St David's Head]. On 17 December, the brig *Fortitude*, of London, John Owen master, sailed from hence with a cargo for Liverpool. At 8am on the 29th she sailed from Scilly, and about 2am the following day, she struck in a hard gale upon the Smalls, amidst total darkness. Finding the vessel sinking, the longboat was got out into which the master and nine of the crew went; six others took the jollyboat, and just as the vessel sunk, succeeded in getting clear of her. Unfortunately, the vessel fell over before the longboat could get sufficiently clear, and by all the screams and cries of those on board her, which were heard by the others in the dark, there is no doubt that they all perished. The six men in the jollyboat, after struggling with the sea till 11am, were picked up by the *Diligence* custom-house cutter. They were landed at Milford, and a subscription set on foot for their relief. (*Times*, 5 January 1813)

30 December, dockyard incident This afternoon, about 5pm, the following shocking accident occurred in the dockyard of Woolwich. A machine used for the purpose of bending and seasoning ship timber, unfortunately burst in consequence of being overcharged. Eight individuals lost their lives and fourteen were dangerously hurt, several of them having their legs and thighs broken. The premises in which the machine stood, were destroyed; and the explosion is represented as being most terrific. Several of the men, it is said, have left wives and families. (*Times*, 1 January 1813)

1813

1 January, Sarpedon, 10 guns For the Royal Navy the year 1813 commenced badly. The *Sarpedon*, a 10-gun brig, Commander Thomas Parker, had a crew of about 75 men and boys when she was wrecked, it was believed, on the coast of Norway. The master of a Danish vessel reported seeing an English brig on the rocks near Schulten on the coast of Norway; at the time, this was supposed to have been the *Sarpedon*, but as there were no survivors it would have been difficult to prove. (*SNL*, 1813)

1 January, Euphrates, East Indiaman   The *Euphrates*, an East Indiaman, Captain Herbert, was lost off Dondra Head, the southernmost point of Ceylon, on her outward bound voyage to China. Her crew were saved. (*Times*, 17 May 1813)

2 January, Hawker, merchantman   Arrived at Greenock, the ship *Hawker*, Captain Phillips, one of the Honduras homeward bound fleet which sailed from hence on 12 September, under convoy of the *Frolic*, an 18-gun brig, Captain Thomas Whinyates. However, the convoy was dispersed on 18 October, when the *Frolic* fought an action with the American 18-gun corvette *Wasp*, Captain Jacob Jones, five days out from the Delaware, and unfortunately the *Frolic* was captured by the American.[56]

About the middle of November, the *Hawker* made Tory Island, since when she was baffled by contrary winds and driven as far north as latitude 59°N. The crew, from extreme exertion, and the scarcity of provisions, consequent on this long protracted voyage, were driven to desperation and the greater part mutinied. A plot was laid to poison the captain, in order to get possession of the vessel, which proved abortive. A plan was then laid to assassinate him, but was happily discovered by one of their number. From the deplorable condition to which they were reduced, fifteen of the crew died. The remainder, captain, mate, steward, three men and four boys, arrived in a more or less exhausted condition. The *Hawker* had been out 112 days, without making any port until she arrived at Greenock. (*Times*, 9 January 1813)

5 January, Charles, brig   About 11pm the brig *Charles*, Captain Graham, bound to the coast of Africa, struck on a reef of the Tongui Rocks, about five miles from the shore, and twenty miles south of the River Gambia. The natives, a tribe of Mandingoes, attacked the wreck in great numbers, considering her as a lawful prize. The captain and one of the passengers were killed. The Rev Leopold Buscher, missionary of the Church Missionary Society for Africa and the East, was on board with his wife and seven other persons attached to the mission. Notwithstanding every exertion of the crew and missionaries, assisted by a force dispatched with the utmost promptitude by Major Chisholm, commandant of Goree, but a small part of the cargo was saved, the rest being plundered by the natives. Every attention was paid to the missionaries in their distress by Major Chisholm, and by Lt Colonel McCarthy, Governor of Senegal. One of their party died and was buried in Goree; the rest hired a Spanish vessel to convey them to the Society's settlements in the Rio Pongas, whither they were bound. (*AR* 1813, Chr, p3)

7 January, Ferret, 18 guns   The 18-gun *Ferret*, sloop of war, Commander Francis Alexander Halliday, sailed from Leith Roads on Wednesday 6

January and was wrecked the following day on Newbiggin Point, due, it was said, to the neglect of her pilot. The crew were saved. (*Times*, 13 January; *SNL*, 1813)

8 February, Isabella, brig Extract of a letter from Buenos Ayres, dated 3 April:

'On 30th March a boat of about seventeen feet keel arrived at this place, with six persons on board. The following is the account they have given: They sailed from New South Wales, on board the brig *Isabella*, George Highton, master, on 4th December last; they made the land about Cape Horn on 2nd February, and Falkland's Islands on 7th of the same month. In the morning of the 8th, about one o'clock a.m. the vessel struck on the rocks, and was wrecked. The crew and passengers got on shore on a desert isle, forming one of the group of the Falkland's Islands, and the weather being moderate, they were enabled to save from the vessel the provisions and stores. On 23rd February, having raised the longboat, and decked her, it was agreed that a part of the unhappy sufferers should embark in her, for the purpose of arriving at some inhabited place, where the means might be procured of sending a vessel to bring away the other part of the crew and passengers. The six men who arrived here accordingly put to sea on 23rd February, and after a voyage of upwards of 450 leagues on the ocean, they arrived in this river, without having seen the land for 36 days. Nothing but the protection of the Almighty could have preserved them from the inclemency of the weather, considering the great fatigue they must have endured, both in mind and body, and so long a navigation in seas almost proverbial for storms. On the first intelligence of the event, Captain Heywood, of His Majesty's ship *Nereus*, gave instructions to Lieutenant W D'Aranda, commander of the *Nancy* brig of war, to prepare for sea, and to proceed to the relief of the unhappy sufferers; it is expected she will sail about 9th April. It appears there were 55 souls on board the *Isabella* at the time she was wrecked, among whom were the following passengers: Captain Drury, 73rd Regiment, wife and family; Mr Holt, (Irish rebel), wife and family; Sir Henry Hayes; 3 female returned convicts; 3 marines and their wives.

'The following have arrived here: Captain Brooks, master of a merchant vessel; Lieutenant Lundie (army); a marine and three seamen.' (*AR* 1813, Chr, pp25-26)

The sequel appeared in the *Times* on 29 January 1814. It was written by an officer of the *Nancy*, yet his name was not given.

'We yesterday arrived in this roadstead [Buenos Aires], after encountering a series of the most tempestuous weather I ever experienced; we, from unceasing perseverance have executed the important service sent upon. The Anieers [*sic*] islands upon which we discovered the wrecked people are dangerous in the extreme, and surrounded by innumerable and extensive reefs; upon one of which we had a most miraculous escape; had the vessel gone to pieces, not a soul would have been saved, from the steepness of the shore and heavy surf.

'We were a month upon our passage, and three and twenty in returning, and had constant gales during our stay at the islands. The weather was so piercing cold with snow and hail, that the crew could not keep the deck or perform the least duty, and we were all but a complete wreck when we returned. It was with great difficulty we patched her up to bring us here. She is now past going to sea and our seamens limbs and sinews are so dreadfully contracted, that I fear some of them will be in a similar situation. I am just going to take a boat-load to the hospital.

'We found on the islands the unhappy people we went in search of, 48 in number, except two American seamen; but from our long passage there, and the prospect of another one back, we should not have been able, for want of provisions, to bring them all away, had we not most fortunately captured an American, on board of which we put thirty-three and took ourselves fifteen. The American arrived safe at Rio Janeiro as soon as we did at Buenos Ayres.

'Sir H Hayes, Bart., Captain Drury of the 73rd Regiment, his wife and two children, were amongst those brought off, also the master of the vessel in which they were wrecked.'

The letter from the *Nancy* went on to speak in the highest terms of the unwearied exertions of her commander, Lt D'Aranda. (*Times*, Saturday 29 January 1814)

12 February, Killybegs fishing fleet For some time past, herring fishing had been extremely good in and around the harbour of Killybegs (Little Churches). On the night of Friday, the 12th, a fleet of boats induced by the prospect of greater success ventured too far from the shore and encountered on their return a strong gale, when many of the most deeply laden unhappily perished with their crews, amounting to between 40 or 50 souls.

A letter dated the 13th, from Killybegs, stated: 'A number of fishing boats were lost in the dreadful storm of last night, in Bruckless Bay, and all the crews perished; supposing to number about eighty persons. Fifty bodies have been found.' (*Dublin report* of 15 February, quoted in the *Times* on 24 February 1813).

17 February, Nimrod, merchantman The *Nimrod*, Captain Jack, from Honduras, was totally lost near Beachy Head, when the master, 2 mates and 9 seamen perished. (*Times*, 20 February 1813)

21 February, Rhodian, 10 guns A 10-gun sloop of war, the *Rhodian*, Commander John George Boss, was lost on Little Plumb Point, at the entrance to the harbour of Kingston, Jamaica, during a gale. Her crew were saved. (*SNL*, 1813)

24 February, Peacock, 18 guns The United States 20-gun corvette *Hornet* (eighteen 32-pounder carronades and two long twelves), Captain James Lawrence, beating around the Carobana Bank, off Cape Carobana (6°49'20"N 58°11'30"W), got sight of the British 18-gun brig *Peacock*, (sixteen 24-pounder carronades and two long sixes), Commander William Peake.

'It was now half-past three p.m., and the *Hornet* continuing to turn to windward, by twenty minutes past four the stranger was made out to be a large man-of-war brig, and soon after he showed English colours.

'As soon as her captain was satisfied that the vessel approaching was an enemy, the *Hornet* was cleared for action, and her people went to quarters. The ship was kept close by the wind, in order to gain the weather gauge, the enemy still running free. At five ten, feeling certain that he could weather the Englishman, Captain Lawrence showed his colours and tacked. The two vessels were now standing towards each other, with their heads different ways, both close by the wind. They passed within half pistol-shot at 5.25, delivering their broadsides as the guns bore; each vessel using the larboard battery. As soon as they were clear, The Englishman put his helm hard up, with the intention to wear short round, and get a raking fire at the *Hornet*, but the manoeuvre was closely watched and promptly imitated, and firing his starboard guns, he was obliged to right his helm, as the *Hornet* was coming down on his quarter, in a perfect blaze of fire. The latter closed, and maintaining the admirable position she had got, poured in her shot with such vigour, that a little before 5.40, the enemy not only lowered his ensign, but he hoisted it union down, in the fore-rigging, as a signal of distress. His main mast soon after fell.

'Mr J T Shubrick was sent on board to take possession. This officer soon returned with the information that the prize was the enemy's sloop of war, *Peacock*, 18, Captain Peake, and that she was fast sinking, having already six feet of water in her hold. Mr Conner, the 3rd Lt of the *Hornet*, and Mr B Cooper, one of her midshipmen, were immediately despatched with boats, to get out the wounded, and to endeavour to save the vessel. It was too late for the latter, though every exertion was made. Both vessels were immediately anchored, guns were thrown overboard, shot-holes plugged, and recourse was had to the pumps, and even to bailing, but the short twilight of that low latitude soon left the prize crew, and all the prisoners were not yet removed. In the hurry and confusion of such a scene, and while the boats of the *Hornet* were absent, four of the prisoners lowered the stern boat of the *Peacock*, which had been thought too much injured to be used, jumped into it, and pulled for the land, at the imminent risk of their lives. [They eventually made Demerara.]

'The *Peacock* settled very easily but suddenly, in 5½ fathoms, and three of the *Hornet*'s people together with nine of the *Peacock*'s, who were below rummaging the vessel, went down with the ship. Four more of the latter saved themselves by running up the rigging into the fore-top, which remained out of water after the hull had got to the bottom.

'In this short encounter, the *Peacock* had her captain and 4 men killed, and 33 wounded. The *Hornet* had 1 man killed, and 2 wounded.' (Fenimore Cooper, *History of the Navy of the United States of America*, 1839, p227 et seq; W James, *Naval Occurrences*, 1817, pp200-201)

25 February, Linnet, 14 guns The *Linnet* gunbrig, 14 guns, commanded by Lt John Treacy, was captured by the French 44-gun frigate *La Gloire*, in the 'Chops of the Channel' [actually off Madeira] and carried into Brest.

On 31 May 1814 Lt Treacy and his ship's company were tried by court martial for the loss of the vessel. When first discovered, the enemy were to windward and from her superior sailing soon came within hail, and ordered the *Linnet* to strike. Instead of doing so, the *Linnet* crossed her bow and received her broadside. Then having the weather gage, the *Linnet* endeavoured by a press of sail, to work to windward, and obtained considerably the weather gage of *La Gloire*, but some long shots carried away the fore-yard, gaff and bowsprit, which compelled Lt Treacy to strike. The *Linnet* also lost her flying jibboom. The Court, in passing an honourable acquittal on Lt Treacy and his ship's company, complimented him for his judicious and seamanlike manoeuvres, for his courage and judgement, and for his endeavours to disable the enemy. (*NC* vol 31, p487)

22 March, Captain, 74 guns This night, at 11pm, a fire broke out on board the *Captain*, 74 guns, lately converted into a hulk, and moored off the Jettyhead, in Plymouth Dock. When the fire was first discovered, the *San Josef*, 112 guns, was moored to the hulk, but the lashings were cut, hawsers got out and the *San Josef* quickly towed away. The fire which had its seat in the small galley under the forecastle quickly spread, and by 2am the internal parts were so completely ignited, that they presented the appearance of iron in a state of red heat, without losing their original shape and connexion. At this period, the spectacle was one of the most magnificent, but awful, sights that can be conceived. All attempts to scuttle her by the common means being found impracticable from the intense heat, two fieldpieces and carronades were conveyed as near as possible in dockyard launches, and discharged at intervals more than 200 shots, which penetrated between wind and water, but without effect; for as the hulk became more buoyant by the operation of the flames, she rose considerably, and the shot-holes appeared above water. This novel species of bombardment was rendered peculiarly grand by the attendant echoes, and continued until 4am, when, being nearly consumed to the water's edge, her bow gradually drooped, the water poured through her port-holes, and she majestically glided to the bottom.

It appeared only two lives were lost: the cook of the hulk, and a black man belonging to the *San Josef*, were found to be missing, and were presumed to have perished in the flames. (*NC* vol 29, p333 et seq)

'As no means exist at Plymouth dockyard of subduing a fire of such magnitude, the *Captain, though floating in the very element, required to extinguish flames when breaking out in buildings on shore*, was left, like the *Boyne* [see 1 May 1795] upon a former occasion (and as all other ships must be left, until *floating engines be provided, a prey to the flames*), for it is well known that the engines supplied to ships of war are of little use but to wash their decks or sides with.' (*NC* vol 35, p219)

2 April, Asia, country ship   The ship *Asia*, of Bombay, from Batavia, foundered in position 10°S 85°E. The crew took to the boats, but only one officer Mr Patton, and twenty-nine lascars reached Quedah on 15 May. (*Times*, 10 February 1814)

17 April, transport's boat   Lt Handley, of the 9th Light Dragoons, was unfortunately lost in the harbour of Lisbon, by the upsetting of the boat in which his cousin, Captain Handley and himself were conveying the standards of the regiment to the Commanding Officer's transport. The serjeant-major was lost at the same time, but Captain Handley was saved. (*Times*, 17 May 1813)

18 April, St Johannes, merchantman   The *St Johannes*, Captain De Groote, from Seville for London, was wrecked on the Isle of Purbeck, but it was expected that her cargo of fruit would be saved. (*SYM*, 26 April, 1813)

30 April, Nancy, brig   The *Nancy* brig, loaded with moorstone, from Plymouth for London, in the gale at east, at low water pierced a hole in her bottom and went down. The passengers and crew were all saved. (*Times*, 4th May 1813)

30 April, Black Sea tragedy   Letters from Constantinople mention the following incident: 'Mr Levy, an English gentleman, well known and highly esteemed in Russia, was lately drowned in the Black Sea, together with Count Fogessiera, a Piedmontese nobleman, two orderly dragoons of the 20th Regiment, and a servant, on their route to join Sir Robert Wilson, with the rest of the crew of the vessel, one Greek only excepted. Mr Levy was on his return from Constantinople, whither he had been dispatched by Sir Robert Wilson, at the critical period of the retreat of the French from Moscow. The Count had also been the bearer of dispatches to the same quarter. In their anxiety to rejoin Sir Robert they could not be induced to postpone their passage till the weather moderated, and met their fate near Varna, after being many days at sea. Besides his friends, dragoons and servants, Sir Robert lost much valuable and curious property.

'The ravages of the plague had been dreadful: 250,000 are computed to have perished by this scourge. It had, at the date of these advices, entirely ceased.' (*AR* 1813, Chr, p34)

The above also appears in *SYM*, 3 May 1813.

10 May, an 'act of intrepidity' 'An act of intrepidity was performed at Portsmouth which merits commemoration. Three officers of the Inverness militia were in a pleasure-boat, and when sailing between the prison ships, a sudden current of wind upset the boat, which, having heavy ballast immediately sunk. Two of the officers could swim, and they kept themselves upon the surface until boats took them up; but the other was in the most imminent danger of drowning. A French prisoner of war on board the *Crown*, named Morand, the moment he saw the officer struggling, jumped off the gangway into the water, and, by putting his feet under the officer's body, as he was sinking, raised him to the surface, and then held him fast till further assistance was obtained. A proper representation has been made to government, and, no doubt, one part of the brave fellow's reward has been a release from his present situation.' (*AR* 1813, Chr, p38)

31 May, an act of stupidity   At Upton-upon-Severn, eight young men, consisting of a corporal, fifer, and four recruits of the 2nd Regiment of Foot, and two watermen named Pumphry and Oakley, took a fisherman's boat, intending to go to Hanley Quay, and back by water. They were returning from Hanley Quay to Upton, when Pumphry, who was conducting the boat, said he would frighten the recruits a little, and began rocking it. The water came in one side, and the recruits, being alarmed, immediately rushed to the opposite, which so overbalanced the boat that it was instantly filled with water. Oakley and the fifer swam ashore, then procured another boat, and rowed after their companions, who by the force of the current had been carried a considerable distance. They succeeded in picking up one of the recruits, who was saved, but the other five were drowned. (*AR* 1813, Chr, p39)

21 June, Persian, 18 guns 'On 21st June 1813 HM brig *Persian* was wrecked on that dangerous shoal called Silver Cays; where the *Stirling Castle*, 64 guns, was wrecked in 1780, during a hurricane, which was particularly distressing, only fifty of her crew being saved (450 perished). In the case of the *Persian*, 123 escaped on a raft and in the boats to Old Cape François, after 48 hours peril and fatigue.' (*NC* vol 35, p248)

'The loss of the *Persian* was occasioned either by a strong southerly current setting at the rate of four miles an hour; or the shoals called the Silver

Cays being laid down in the Admiralty charts 20 miles to the southward.'
(*SNL*, 1814)

Some reports stated the *Persian* was lost on 16 June.

Findlay's North Atlantic Memoir, 1873, states on p74: 'The north-east side of Silver Cay Bank is extremely dangerous, having a cluster of rocky heads, extending 18 miles, and even with the water.' (Silver Cay Bank 20°30′N 69°40′W)

2 July, Daedalus, 38 guns   *Daedalus*, a 38-gun frigate, Captain Murray Maxwell, made the island of Ceylon near Point de Galle, with her convoy on 1 July. On 2nd, about 8am, going very fast through the water, all hands were aroused and alarmed, in consequence of the ship touching the ground, and then sticking fast; everyone rushed on deck, when the distressing truth too evidently appeared. The ship had struck and grounded on a shoal. Signals were immediately made to the convoy which saved them from sharing the fate of the frigate. *Daedalus* remained on the shoal for twenty minutes, rolling a great deal, and while the boats were ascertaining the deepest water, the ship gathered way; sail was immediately set, and she once more floated. Whilst aground, the false keel was seen to come up alongside and several splinters separate from her, yet it was thought the damage extended no further.

For some time, the principal injury was suspected to be far aft, and not much under the water-mark: the cabin and aftermost guns were run forward to bring the ship by the head for the purpose of getting at the leak, but without effect. Soon the order was given to throw all the guns over-board, with their shot etc, which was done with the greatest expedition.

The carpenters now declared the leaks to be far underwater, about the keel and sternpost; and the rudder was found to work so much, that it was thought judicious to get it unshipped, which was very soon done, and brought alongside.

The lower piece of the sternpost was, at this time, observed to be gone; the water gaining considerably on the pumps though actively worked, and approaching the orlop deck. A sail, prepared with oakum and tar, was now got over the stern, for the purpose of stopping the leaks, which were now discovered, but, only to show their extent, with the impossibility of stopping them. They were on both sides, very far aft; and where the sternpost fell out, a stream rushed in nearly as large as a man's body.

The state of the ship was now nearly hopeless; the leaks were too numerous and large to be remedied in the smallest degree by any means, the ship's crew, nearly exhausted by unremitting labour for eight hours at the pumps, and seeing the water, in spite of their exertions, rising to the lower deck, began to flag.

Nothing remained untried to save the ship, yet without success. The crew were now put into the different boats in waiting, and taken on board the nearest Indiamen. Captain Maxwell remained till everyone was in the boats, and, about 6pm, he took a final leave of her. Shortly afterwards she fell on her beam ends, and continued so nearly a minute, then righted showing only her quarterdeck above water, then gradually disappeared. (*NC* vol 31, pp165-166)

22 August, Colibri, 16 guns   HM brigs *Moselle* and *Colibri* put into Port Royal, near Savannah, Georgia, about 20 August. Whilst at anchor, a gale came on which shifted the sandbanks at the entrance of the harbour. The *Colibri*, in attempting to find her way out, struck on one of the banks and in less than three hours was completely lost. The *Moselle* was sufficiently astern to cast anchor in time to avoid the bank, and Cdr Kinsman, of the latter ship, was thus fortunately enabled to save Cdr John Thompson of the *Colibri* and his crew of 140 men and boys.

After some days at anchor, in danger of suffering the same fate on the fifth day the *Moselle* succeeded in getting out to sea and was safe in the Chesapeake on the 5 September.

At a subsequent court martial, Cdr Thompson was honourably acquitted for the loss of his ship. (*Times*, 22 October 1813)

We may note that *Steel's Navy List*, 1813; Norie, 1827, p473; and Clowes also, each give the place of loss of the *Colibri* as Port Royal, Jamaica, yet the ship was not on the Jamaica station, it was on the American station, as was the *Moselle*. (*NC* vol 29, p122)

26 August, Laurestinus, 22 guns   The *Laurestinus*, a 22-gun Sixth Rate, was lost on the Silver Cays off Great Abaco in the Bahamas, during the hurricane of 26 August. Captain Graham and all the crew, excepting one man, were saved. (*Times*, 2 November 1813)

The *Laurestinus*, formerly named *Laurel*, was built by Bode and Good at Bridport where the vessel was launched on 2 June 1806. Whilst commanded by Captain John Charles Woollcombe, the *Laurel* was captured off Mauritius by the French 36-gun *Cannonière* on 12 September 1808, after a severe engagement during which the *Laurel* suffered eight killed and twenty wounded. The French renamed the ship *Esperance* and on 12 April 1810 the vessel was retaken by the British 32-gun *Unicorn*, Captain Alexander Robert Kerr from the Isle of France. (*SNL*, 1812)

Once again the name was changed, this time to *Laurestinus*.

SNL 1817, and Norie, 1827, each show the commander of the *Laurestinus* as Alexander Gordon, yet *NC* vol 29, p122, shows Cdr Gordon as being on the 18-gun *Rattler*, and Cdr Graham on the *Laurestinus*. This is followed by 'Alexander Gordon appointed to the *Chesapeake*.' (*NC* vol 30, p444)

1 September, William Miles, merchantman   The *William Miles* and the

Sarah, both vessels of heavy burthen, had left King Road within two days of the lowest neap tides; they left the Road with their full cargoes, and both arrived within a few minutes of each other, at the entrance of the basin. The *William Miles* pointed to the upper lock, and had entered within two yards of her stern, when a press gang from the receiving vessel in the river made its appearance on the sides of the lock.

The ship was immediately deserted; and having entered the lock when the tide was ebbing, and being a burthensome ship, with a remarkable convexity in her hold, upon the reflux of the tide, she was suspended between the sides of the lock, the bottom of which forms the sides of a circle, and from the weight of her cargo she immediately bilged.

Her cargo of rum was saved and about 100 hogsheads of sugar, and of course her sails, masts, rigging and stores. The loss was considerable. (*Times*, 9 September 1813) [A plan suggested by Mr Hillhouse, for removing the *William Miles* West Indiaman from the lock of the Cumberland Basin, Bristol, in which she was bilged has fortunately succeeded, and the vessel has been brought safely into dock. (*SYM* 4 October 1813)]

10 September, Alpheus, schooner A 10-gun schooner, *Alpheus*, Lt Thomas William Jones, fought a desperate close action for three and a half hours off Start Point, with the French 14-gun privateer *Renard*; at the end of which time the *Alpheus* blew up and all forty of her crew perished. (*SNL* 1813)

We may note that a close perusal of the *SYM* for the months of September and October 1813 revealed nothing of this tragedy.

21 September, Goshawk, 16 guns The 16-gun brig sloop *Goshawk*, Cdr Hon William John Napier, was built at the shipyard of Wallis, at Blackwall, where the vessel was launched July 1809.

In chase of an enemy ship the *Goshawk* stood in too close to Barcelona, and the wind dying away, with a heavy swell setting on shore, *Goshawk* grounded and Cdr Napier had of necessity to fire the sloop to prevent its falling into enemy hands. The crew saved themselves in the boats, only to become prisoners of war. (*Times*, 14 December 1813)

27 September, Bold, 14 guns *Bold*, a 14-gun brig, Cdr John Skekel, was a new vessel, built by Tyson and Blake at Bursledon on the Hamble and launched June 1812.

The vessel was lost on Prince Edward Island, owing to a strong current for which allowance had not been made. The crew were saved. (*AR* 1813, Chr, p83)

?October, Vautour, 16 guns *Vautour* was a sloop taken on the stocks at Flushing in August 1809 during the Walcheren campaign, and removed to Chatham where the vessel was completed and launched on 15 September

1810. The sloop, Cdr Paul Lawless, vanished with her crew of 120 in this month, at the time when the wreck of an unidentified naval sloop was washed up at Portreath.

15 October, Abeona, collier The collier *Abeona*, Captain Beedle, with coals from Sunderland, of and for Boston, was driven upon Wainfleet sands and wrecked. A passenger, an able seaman and a boy were lost. The master and the rest of the hands escaped. (*Times*, 28 October 1813)

21 October, Caesar, merchantman Early this morning, during a severe storm at east by south, a large dismasted ship struck upon Sal Martin rock, about three sea miles east by south of Ballywalter. Robert Adair, J Boyd, D Alexander, W Niblock (Nielock), and J Erskine put to sea in a small boat with the laudable aim of rescuing the crew, but within a few yards of the beach, the boat overset and the five were drowned. They were all from the village of Ballywalter. Their boat was washed ashore at 3am. At 5pm another boat endeavoured to reach the vessel but having failed in the attempt, nevertheless managed to return to the shore. The ship was the *Caesar* of Greenock, Captain McLarty, on her voyage from that port to join a convoy at Cork. She had a valuable cargo principally of soft goods. Three of the crew drifted from the ship in the longboat, and were drowned. The remainder got on shore about 5am on the 22nd. A Macmann, coast surveyor and Mr Mullhollan, coast officer, with a party of revenue boatmen, have a strong guard of Donaghalee and Grey Abbey Yeomanry at Ballywalter, and Messrs Miller and Lemon, coast officers at Ballyhalbert, have Lt MacNeill with a detachment of the Lough Militia to assist in protecting whatever property may come ashore from the rapacity of the plunderers.
    A sloop was also wrecked at Ballyhalbert early on 21 October and all the crew drowned. (*Times*, 29 October 1813)

30 October, Rose in June, lugger Saturday evening, 30 October, the *Rose in June* lugger sailed from Dover, with a crew of eight, for the purpose of procuring herrings, but in the storm which came on the whole of the men perished. The boat and nets were found on the Brake, bottom upwards. Six of the men were married. (*Times*, 4 November 1813)

5 November, Tweed, 18 guns *Tweed* was an 18-gun sloop of war, built by Iremonger of Littlehampton who launched the vessel in January 1807. Her end was to prove disastrous for many of her 120 crew.
    The *Tweed* sailed from Portsmouth at the latter end of September, with a small convoy for Newfoundland; and after a most boisterous and unpleasant passage, arrived upon the coast on 5 November, but amidst very thick fogs, which prevailed for several days, and prevented the most accurate observer from ascertaining the precise situation of the ship. At 6am, while

it was supposed they were yet at a distance from land, she struck on a rock in Shoal Bay.

Many of the crew instantly jumped upon the rock; but the greater part indulging hopes that by exertion she might be got off, remained in her. These hopes, however, it soon appeared, were not to be realised, for the ship drifted further on, and in such a situation that threatened to cut off all chance of escape from destruction. A cable was , therefore, conveyed to the people upon the rock, and as each man fastened one end of it round his body, he was dragged through the water upon the rock. Many however dreading the danger of this only remaining alternative, from a fear of being dashed against the rugged protuberances of the rock, stayed in the ship till she went to pieces. Captain Mather was among the last of the persons saved. Of those who were thus saved, several died of fatigue, or lost their way afterwards in the woods. (*AR* 1813, Chr, p100).

Note: *SNL* 1813 gives the number of survivors as fifty-two.

The *NC* vol 31, p62 states that besides the purser and surgeon being lost, sixty-five of the crew also perished.

6 November, Woolwich, storeship The *Woolwich*, 44 guns, Captain Thomas Ball Sullivan, armed *en flute* and being used as a storeship, was driven by stress of weather onto a shoal lying off the coast of Barbuda, one of the Lesser Antilles. The crew were saved. (*SNL* 1813)

10 November, Atalante, 18 guns *Atalante*, an 18-gun sloop of war, Cdr Frederick Hickey, en route from New London, Connecticut, with despatches for Halifax, Nova Scotia, struck on the Blind Sisters, off Cape Sambro, a ridge of rocks within fourteen miles of the land and twenty-one miles from Halifax. Although within twelve minutes the ship had become a complete wreck, the crew managed to save themselves in the ship's boats. (*NC* vol 31, p20)

4/10 December, convoy for Wellington 'The Paris papers state that four English vessels laden with oxen, sheep, etc., for the supply of Wellington's army, were wrecked on the 4th inst. between Teste and Mimizan. The greater part of the cattle perished in the sea; but such as remained alive were sent to Bayonne, for the use of the French army. French fishermen state that ten other vessels of the same convoy were lost up to the 10th inst., on the coast between Mimizan and Bayonne, making a total of fourteen wrecked. The ships formed part of the convoy which sailed from Cork under protection of the *Castilian* (Royalist), Captain James Gordon Bremer [*NC* vol 29, p85] and the *Tartarus*, Captain J Pascoe. They were laden with provisions, horses and reinforcements for the army of Wellington, and on the voyage met a storm which separated them and it would appear cost the loss of the greater part of the convoy.' (*Times*, 27 December 1813)

11 December, Mutine's boat   This evening a boat belonging to the *Mutine* brig came ashore at Dover, with the pilot. The vessel being under orders for Portsmouth, to be paid, several of the officers and people, who had been left ashore at Deal, came round by land for the purpose of joining her, and, taking advantage of the boat being ashore, the whole of them left Dover Harbour to proceed to the brig. But, whether from the darkness of the night, or some other cause, the boat did not reach the vessel, but was driven on the rocks at Cop Point, Folkestone, and, it is reported, that the purser, surgeon, and seven seamen were drowned; two lieutenants and five seamen saved themselves by clinging to the rocks. (*AR* 1813, Chr, p99). See also 14 December 1809.

15 December, Fortune, hoy   The *Fortune*, a Portsmouth hoy, belonging to Plymouth, John Davis, master, was this Wednesday night wrecked on the Shag Stone, between Plymouth Sound and the Mewstone when most of the passengers perished; seven only were saved out of forty or more, the number not being correctly ascertained. (*Times*, 20 December 1813)

17 December, William Pitt, merchantman   'Captain James Callander, long time resident at the Cape of Good Hope and well acquainted with the circumjacent coasts, to the bays eastward of the Cape, lately volunteered his services in HMS *Stag*, to search for the wreck of the ship *William Pitt*, thought to have been lost a little to the westward of Algoa Bay. Considerable anxiety respecting the fate of this ship having been excited in the public mind, we subjoin an extract of a letter from an officer on board the *Stag*, which seems to render but too probable the opinion, that she has been lost at sea. In fact, since this article has been prepared for the press, a paper has been printed by order of the House of Commons, wherein this *William Pitt*, of 572 tons, built at Liverpool 1803, is stated officially to have been lost off Algoa Bay, 17th December, 1813, on her third voyage, homeward-bound.

'Cape Town, 11th February.

'I am just arrived in the *Stag* frigate, having been three weeks down the coast eastward, as far as the Great Fish river (Rio Infante), in search of the wreck of a ship, which we can scarcely doubt is that of the *William Pitt*, Captain Butler, from Batavia. Prior to our departure, the *Morley* transport arrived here from Algoa Bay, bringing with her the top of a box, directed to the *William Pitt*, at Gravesend, dated Saturday 21st February 1813 [the 21st was a Sunday], to the care of Mr Raspinson, waterman; as also another, directed, "Mrs Crawford and John Crawford, Esq." Mr and Mrs Crawford and two children, are known to have been passengers in the *William Pitt*. There also drifted ashore near Algoa Bay, a chest, probably that of the captain's steward, having in the front and on the centre plank, the words *William Pitt*; also some of the poop-deck planks, with cot screws in them, apparently ripped from the beams with great violence. Her bulkheads and venetian blinds, the furniture of the cabin under the poop, small bedsteads, the remnant of a small boat, together with dead sheep and pigs, have also drifted on shore near Algoa Bay. As a ship was there seen passing to the westward on the 17th of last month, and in the night of the 18th five guns were heard in the Bay of St Francis, a gale blowing from the west, and the night very dark and raining, it is thought she must have been in the bay, and suffered this damage by shipping heavy seas, by which the articles above-mentioned were washed overboard. No traces, however, appear of a wreck, as no ropes, masts, sails, nor casks, have been seen. I have, however, little doubt in my mind, that the ship is lost, and, I fear, all on board must have perished. If she were at anchor near the bay when she suffered so much damage, she probably sunk at her moorings; or if, by any chance, she got out to sea, she has probably foundered; which last supposition I think the more natural, from no human bodies having floated on shore along with the sheep and pigs. About three days ago, one hundred letters arrived from Algoa Bay, part of the mail of the *William Pitt*, all directed for London, in a shattered state, and some without covers; also invoices of part of her cargo, open without cover, having all been washed about among the sand on the beach: duplicates were sent by the *Lord Eldon*.' (Hydrographer, *Naval Chronicle*; NC vol 32, pp68-69)

1814

14 January, Queen, transport 'The *Queen* transport No.332, Carr master, has been driven on Trefugis Point and beaten to pieces. She had brought home from the British army on the Continent 325 sick and invalided soldiers, 63 women and 58 children; besides whom she had on board six French officers, prisoners of war, and a crew of twenty-one men, making a total of 473 persons. The soldiers were all artillery men, except about twenty, who belonged to the 30th Regiment. One hundred men and four women, with great difficulty, got ashore; and all the rest, three hundred and sixty-nine in number, perished with the ship.' (*NC* vol 31, p62). The *Queen* was of 340 tons burthen. (*SYM* 24 January 1814)

The *Times* also printed the report and added: 'The *Queen*, from Lisbon, with 360 men, women and children; the men mostly invalided artillery men, went down in a hurricane at south-east.' (*Times*, 21 January 1814)

Next day the *Times* revised the account: 'The transport, *Queen*, No.332, Carr master, brought home 325 sick and invalid soldiers, 63 women and 58 children, from the British army on the Continent; she also had on board six French officers, prisoners of war and twenty-one crew, total 473 persons. The ship was lying in Carrick Roads, Falmouth, and was well moored. At the start of the gale, the ship rode hard, and about five o'clock on Friday morning, she parted her cables and drove ashore on Trefusis Point. One hundred and four got ashore, three hundred and sixty-nine perished. Some bodies were picked up at Penryn and a great number at Flushing. The soldiers were nearly all artillery men. Only 32 belonged to the 30th Regiment of Foot.

'The *Queen* went to pieces in ¾ of an hour.' (*Times*, 22 January 1814)

On 2 February the *Times* printed a revised list of the passengers: 8 officers, 185 NCOs and men, 63 women and 59 children were on board ship. Of these, 5 officers, 109 men and 10 women and children were saved.

16 January, Queen Charlotte, packet   In the harbour of San Sebastian at noon, a gale suddenly arose from the north-west, and at 4pm the *Queen Charlotte* packet parted from her anchor, and was retained by a small anchor and cable for half an hour; but before others of a sufficient strength could be got out, she was driven ashore at 5pm and about 10 or 10.30pm, went to pieces. Every exertion was made by the agent for packets at Passages, Mr Sebright, to afford assistance to the crew. A party of artillery drivers were immediately marched down to the beach by their officers and were ordered by Major Dyer to act as guard and prevent confusion; the crew of a gunboat, with several seamen of transports, also attended. It was, however, found impossible to send boats to her from the mole, on account of the night; and although, by the exertions of the packet-agent, a boat was brought round on men's shoulders from the mole to the beach, it proved impracticable to use it. The surgeon swam on shore at an early period; and the master and two men were picked up from the wreck. The others who were on board, seventeen in number, including Captain Mudge, the commander, met with a watery grave. The remainder of the crew had, luckily for them, received permission to go on shore the previous day, and had not been able to rejoin the vessel. (*NC* vol 31, pp166-167)

On 9 February the *Times* also recorded the above.

17 January, disaster to the Kilkeel fishing fleet   'On the morning of Monday's night (17th) fifty boats manned with six men each proceeded from Kilkeel to sea to fish; the sea being calm, the wind light and variable, a little snow on the ground, and light snow showers. About eleven o'clock the day brightened, and shortly after the sun had a muddy appearance through a heavy cloud; at the same time an unusual swell, accompanied with wind, set in from the south, so strong, that the inhabitants on shore were struck with horror for the approaching fate of the men at sea. About twelve o'clock the boats made every exertion to gain the shore at Annalong [the only shelter on that part of the coast], yet when about half-way, a dreadful storm overtook them. On their arrival off the harbour, signals were made to prevent them coming in there. Two only succeeded in landing out of six who made the attempt, the rest met a watery grave.

'The remainder of the boats proceeded along the shore, and were driven in at sundry places, some filled at sea, some were upset and others wrecked on shore. Mourne has suffered a loss of twenty-seven of its inhabitants, many of whom have left large and helpless families. On the same day, fishing off Annalong were two wherries (Clontarf hookers) and five boats from Newcastle, Dundrum Bay; and of the latter crews, thirteen men were drowned. Their bodies were recovered.

'A week earlier, on 10th January, several fishing boats were surprised off the Warren Point [Carlingford Lough] coast by a sudden storm. The vessels were upset and at least forty men perished. Lt Chesney of the Royal Artillery swam boldly out in the midst of a tremendous sea and saved the lives of some men, at the imminent peril of his own. At the same time five merchant vessels were wrecked off the Kilkeel coasts and the shoreline was covered with their wrecks.' (*Times*, 28 January 1814)

19 January, Robert and Ann, transport A Hull report of 14 February gave the following:

The *Robert and Ann* transport, of this port, was driven out of St Jean de Luz, near Biarritz, in a violent gale on 19 January and totally lost. The crew were all lost except for the captain and a Swedish seaman, who were on shore at the time. (*Times*, 17 February 1814)

20 January, Savage, 16 guns 'A court martial has been holden on Captain William Bissell, of the *Savage*, for the purpose of enquiring whether, from the wind and weather, the *Savage* should have been in the situation in which she was run on-shore, off the island of Guernsey, on 20th January 1814, and to try Captain Bissell for all the circumstances of that accident, and for his previous proceedings. Captain Bissell's narrative stated, that, on 20th January at six a.m. after having experienced much bad and thick weather, the wind constantly shifting, and not having seen the land for three days, the *Savage* got on-shore off Rock North, the north end of Guernsey; and had not the anchor been let go immediately, every soul on board would have perished, as the dawn of day shewed that the ship was entirely surrounded with rocks. In this alarming situation, and it blowing a gale of wind, there were but feeble hopes of saving a single life, other than relying on the merciful interposition of Providence! At the imminent risk of their lives, John Robin, and four other pilots, came off to the ship, when by the exertions used, she was taken into a place called Great Harbour, Guernsey, as the only alternative remaining; but there, on dropping anchor, she did not bring up, but drifted on-shore, in that confined harbour which abounds with rocks. The next day, the weather moderated, which enabled her to be moved to the Pier Head, Guernsey, and ultimately to this port [name not given] to be repaired.

'The Court was of opinion, that the *Savage* should not have been in the situation in which she was run on-shore, and that it was occasioned by her standing too long to the southward, and by great neglect of heaving the lead, and keeping a regular reckoning, from the time of taking her last departure from the land; and that blame was imputable to Captain William Bissell, for not having attended to those duties himself, and for not having taken proper care that they were regularly performed by the other officers, more particularly by Charles Leach, master, and did adjudge the said Captain William Bissell to be dismissed from the command of His Majesty's sloop *Savage*. The Court further agreed that it was indispensably necessary to call the attention of their Lordships to the conduct of the said Charles Leach, both with respect to the accident that has happened to His Majesty's said sloop, and the wilful perjury committed by him in his evidence on the trial. Rear-Admiral Foote, President.' (*SNL* May 1814, p84)

20 January, Venus, brig The brig *Venus* of Yarmouth was driven on shore in the tremendous gale of the 20th, half a mile to the southward of that pier; her large draught of water prevented her approaching nearer the land than 200 yards. Every effort to rescue the crew by the ordinary methods was attempted without success. At last the naval officer of the signal station brought the apparatus invented by Captain Manby down to the beach. At the second fire the shot with the line attached to it was thrown from the mortar over the vessel. The facility with which the crew were then disengaged from their danger was admirable, and deserves detail. By the line with which communication had been gained a hawser was drawn from the ship (in which it was made fast) to the shore, and distended by the efforts of the numerous spectators; the crew were then brought to land, one by one, in a sling that passed from the ship to the shore, by lines reaching to either; and ran, with ease along the hawser, by a ring, called a grummet. The storm was of such extreme severity that if the crew had not been thus saved, the poor wretches, supposing them to have escaped drowning, must have frozen to death.

The above article appeared not only in the *NC* vol 31, p113, but also in the *Times*, verbatim, on 12 February 1814; which, however, continued: 'When this ingenious method of rescue from shipwreck was first proposed several years ago the conviction on my mind, of its adequacy to its object, was intuitive. Its efficacy has now been proved by repeated instances of successful application; yet its general adoption is delayed, at the time when the crew of the *Venus*, consisting of nine is saved by it on the eastern, the *Queen* transport [see 14 January 1814] is wrecked on the western coast, under the same circumstances, within a few yards of the land and safety, and 300 perish.

'Is it only a fashionable error that we owe our national glory and independence to our seamen; and is the grief that is expressed at every disastrous shipwreck, mere affectation! This irony is not overstrained if the importance of our seamen be a political maxim, and our sorrow at their loss be sincere, why are the means of precaution neglected? and, with them, the first consolation to which the mind recurs under affliction at loss, the consolation that everything, which could have been done in prevention, has been done. I wish to be answered.' Needless to say, the *Times* writer was not answered.

29 January, Holly, schooner At 4am His Majesty's schooner, *Holly*, in a violent gale, parted her cables, and ran on the rocks under the Mount of St Sebastian. Her commander, Lt Samuel Sharpe Treacher, Mr Crane, the surgeon, and about four others, were washed overboard, and seen no more: the rest were saved. (*NC* vol 31, p167)

? January, troopship losses During January and February several troop transports were lost on the Haake Sandbank off the Texel. These shipwrecks were not well documented, principally because there were few, if any, survivors. *NC* vol 31, p167 and the *Times* of 18 February each published a Harwich report of 16 February:

The *Beresford* transport, Hope master, and the *Nancy* (marked W), Potter master, each carrying troops from the Downs to Holland, were both lost on the Haake Sand. From the former vessel forty-two were saved; but all the troops on board the *Nancy* perished. These tragedies can come as no surprise, if we read extracts of a letter from an officer of the 21st Regiment of Foot, dated 14 January 1814; and published in the *Times* on Saturday 19 February 1814: 'The 2nd division of the 21st arrived safe at Helvoetsluys on the evening of the 8th inst. after a teazing voyage of ten days. We were beating on and off the coast of Holland for a whole week. Unfortunately, neither the captain of the convoy, nor any of the masters of transports were at all acquainted with the Dutch shore; and not having a pilot on board we were certainly in a dangerous situation. On the 5th we stood in as near as possible, and fired the whole day for a pilot boat, but to no purpose. At this time the *Malta* [84 guns, ex-French *Guillaume Tell*] was in very shallow water, and the master dreading a lee shore, during the night, and in such weather thought proper to stand out to sea, the *Nightingale* and *Tiger* [*Tigre*, 80 guns, ex-French] casting anchor. During the afternoon the wind increased to a smart gale and blew straight in-shore. The *Tiger* parted from her anchor, and by mere chance drifted into the river, and made Helvoet; and the sloop of war, with the greatest difficulty, rode out the storm.'

27 January, Maria, schooner A Plymouth report read: 'The schooner *Maria* of Dublin from St Ubes to that port was upset in a gale; the crew were picked up by the *William Fenning*, and landed in Plymouth.' (*Times*, 1 February 1814)

13 March, John Palmer, country ship The country ship *John Palmer* from Bengal and the Île de Bourbon, laden chiefly with cotton, in company with other vessels, called at St Helena, at which place she took on passengers for England; among whom were Colonel Wade, his wife and three children; Lt Wade, and Mrs Edwards and four children. The *John Palmer*, Captain Reid, sailed from St Helena, in company with the *Henry Wellesley* and several other ships bound for England, on 3 February, and parted company on the 18th of the month off the Western Isles (Azores).

On 13 March the ship was wrecked off Ovar, near Oporto, when all on board perished. (*Times*, 28, 31 March and 1 April 1814)

11 March, Lord Dundas, packet The smack *Lord Dundas*, packet, Captain Leisk of Aberdeen, went down with all on board off Rattray Head. The crew consisted of four persons and there was also on board the wife of a ship's master and her child, who were passengers; the body of the child was washed ashore. (*Times*, 11 March 1814)

31 March, 'friendly fire' An action took place near Lisbon, between the *Duke of Montrose* packet, and the *Primrose*, a British sloop of war. From the *Duke of Montrose*'s log it appears that the action commenced at 7.30pm and lasted broadside to broadside within half pistol shot, till 8.45pm, when the *Primrose* attempted to carry the *Duke of Montrose* by boarding which was gallantly resisted and so much damaged as to oblige her to haul off at 9pm. The *Primrose* again came down and recommenced the action which was continued with the same spirit as previously until 9.50pm, when the *Primrose* hailed and asked what ship she was. The loss on board the packet is Lt and Adjutant Andrews of the 60th Regiment (a passenger), and the master killed and ten men wounded.

On the *Primrose* the loss was her master and four seamen killed and eighteen wounded. (*AR* 1814, Chr, p27)

31 May, Inveterate, 12 guns Lt Norton and crew of the *Inveterate* were tried by court martial for the loss of that vessel on the coast of France, near Étaples. The evidence related that in a heavy gale of wind the vessel drifted ashore, notwithstanding every exertion was made to prevent her falling to leeward. Lt Norton was consequently acquitted. (*NC* vol 31, p487)

The *NC* article then stated that the *Inveterate* was wrecked in February; yet omitted to say that it was in 1807, on 18 February, *qv*. Lt Norton and his surviving crew members [four had died in the wreck] had been held prisoners of war for more than seven years.

28 June, Leopard, 50 guns A report from Greenock dated 30 July gave the following: 'Arrived and passed to Port Glasgow yesterday, the *Charlotte*, Captain Duncanson, from Shadeack New Brunswick, in 38 days. On 2nd July off the east end of Anticosta was boarded by an officer from HM ship *Leopard*, then lying on a rock inshore and bilged. This happened on 28th

June at eleven p.m. The *Leopard* sailed from England about eight weeks previously with a large fleet carrying troops and stores for Quebec, which were all dispersed except one transport which ran on shore at the same time but fortunately got off. The whole crew and troops were saved and on the island with a large part of the stores. On the 9th, off the island of Belle Isle, the *Charlotte* fell in with the *Crocodile* frigate, and gave information to the captain of the situation of the *Leopard*. (*Times*, 3 August 1814)

'The transport which sailed from Cork, and was supposed to have been lost on her passage to Quebec, with 487 soldiers and 248 women and children on board, has been heard of. The *Crocodile* frigate, on approaching the desolate island of Anticosta, observed a part of the crew of the transport on shore, where she had been wrecked; and succeeded in bringing away the survivors, who had been on the island 37 days.' (*AR* 1814, Chr, p102)

2 July, Devonshire, East Indiaman 'The *Devonshire* East Indiaman, bound to China, upset at her moorings in Sanger Bay (Sagar Bay), during a violent squall on 2nd July; she had nearly the whole of her cargo on board and unfortunately twenty-nine persons lost their lives. This account is brought by the *Wellington* East Indiaman, which ship arrived in the Downs on 8th December 1814.

'The *Wellington* parted from the *Lord Castlereagh*, extra ship, off the Cape, where she arrived 20th July; at which time the *Lord Castlereagh* sprung a leak, threw half her cargo overboard and went back to Bombay.' (*Times*, 9 December 1814)

25 August, Mars, merchantman The following is an extract from a letter written by Captain Joseph Williamson of the ship *Mars*, dated Cove of Cork, 27 August:

'This day at two p.m. I arrived here in the *Orbit* of Liverpool, Captain Peers, he having picked me and my ship's company up at sea. On Thursday night the 25th inst. Waterford bearing NNE distance about six leagues, while sitting in the cabin with Mr Kelsey (passenger), the mate came down at nine o'clock and said there was a strong smell of fire. I instantly went on deck and found the watch that was below in the forecastle had come upon the deck almost suffocated; and at that time there was no smoke from any other part of the vessel. We began throwing water down the forecastle, and cutting a hole in the deck, to try if we could find where the fire was, when the smoke issued from the steerage in such volume, that we were likely to be suffocated, and could scarcely see one another on deck. I concluded the fire must be in the main hold, and immediately ordered the boats to be got out, and to break the main hatches open, to see if we could find the fire there, as it was impossible for any person to go below in the steerage or forecastle; and such was the rapidity of the flames that before we could get the longboat out they were issuing six feet through the main hatchway. It was with the greatest difficulty we succeeded in getting the boat over the side, as the vessel was a few minutes afterwards, in flames from the fore hatchway to the cabin doors. It is impossible for me to describe the horrors of the sight of the vessel, and the frantic state of the female passengers, who got out of bed on the first alarm, and came on deck. There was no time to get either water, provisions, or anything in the boat; and had it not been that providence threw a vessel in our way, we must have been turned on the sea without any kind of sustenance, some without covering, in an open boat. The *Orbit* hove in sight, hove-to, and took us on board, it then being about ten o'clock.

'By what means the vessel took fire, God only knows, as there had been no light whatever, either in the forecastle or steerage that night, and there was no fire in either of these places until after it broke through the main hatchway; and for any person to have communication with the hold was impossible, without being known, as the vessel was bulk headed up fore and aft. My opinion is, with that of the crew and passengers, that it must have been from aquafortis or other combustible matter that might have been shipped in a clandestine manner under a fictitious name, as from the time the smoke was first perceived until we were on board the *Orbit*, did not exceed one hour.'

The letter was sent to Messrs Ellis and McNeill, whom we may assume were the ship's owners. (*NC* vol 33, pp112-113; *Times*, 9 September 1814)

9 October, Wasp, sloop of war   On this day the USS *Wasp* informed the Swedish brig *Adonis* she was standing for the Spanish Main. The *Wasp* was never seen again and another 140 seamen had perished. (J Fenimore Cooper, *History of the Navy of the USA*, 1839, vol 2, pp338-341)

10 October, Baring, transport   In consequence of a severe gale coming on , on 10 October, the fleet under convoy of the *Sultan*, 74 guns, was directed to put into Bear Haven; the *Baring* transport, a fine ship, upwards of 700 tons, having on board eighteen officers and more than 200 men of the 40th Regiment of Foot, under the command of Major Shelton, lay-to for a pilot off the mouth of the Haven, but so near to the rocks that she drove upon them on the left side of the entrance, and after striking several times, lost her rudder, she then became unmanageable, drifted across the Haven and struck on the rocks of Bear Island, carrying away her bowsprit.

Through the exertions of the officers, the men were kept below, until the water was ankle deep upon the deck; every endeavour was then used to get them on shore, as the ship was found to be sinking fast; in the confusion many of them jumped overboard, there being no boats near, and several were drowned; 18 or 20 were thought missing, perhaps safe on the island. From the vessel filling so fast, and the exertions of every officer being required in saving the men, it was impossible for them to recover any part of their baggage; they have lost almost everything and many of the men are in a state of nakedness.

With the assistance of the boats belonging to the *Sultan* and *Shamrock*, the officers succeeded in getting the men on shore before dark. By the 15th the *Baring* was underwater and it was feared nothing could be recovered. It was providential that she did not remain where she struck in the first instance, as every soul would have perished, there being a heavy surf and no possibility of the men getting on the rocks had they jumped overboard, added to which, not a boat could get near her, the wind and tide setting into the Haven at the time. (*Times*, 8 November 1814)

11 October, Lady Lowther, merchantman The *Lady Lowther* of Port Carlisle, proceeding from Liverpool to Carlisle, laden with a general cargo, struck on a gravel bank off Seaton Point, near Workington, though a few minutes before, the line was sounded in six fathoms. The crew had barely time to launch their boat before the *Lady Lowther* went down. It was with great difficulty that the crew reached the shore as the sea often washed over them. (*Times*, 29 October 1814)

18 October, Champion and Sovereign, transports The *Champion* transport arrived at Quebec on 3 November from Portsmouth, under convoy of the 50-gun *Liffey*, a Fourth Rate frigate. The *Champion* was taken on 9 October by the American privateer *Mammoth*, after an action of one hour and twenty minutes, when the *Champion*'s guns were all disabled and her rigging much cut. During the ensuing forty-seven hours she was plundered to a considerable extent of her cargo, water and provisions, and then given up, leaving Captain Kirby to proceed where he pleased; providentially, to the wreck of the *Sovereign* transport on St Paul Island in the Cabot Strait.

The transport ship *Sovereign*, bound from England to Quebec, was wrecked on 18 October on the island of St Paul, in the Gulph of St Lawrence. She had on board 9 officers and186 soldiers of the 49th, 58th and 81st Regiments, 2 servants and 21 women and children, together with the captain, mate, and 19 seamen; total 239 persons, yet out of this whole number, only 27 were saved. Sailing at 7 knots, at 7pm, the lookouts saw the rock on which she struck, just three minutes before so doing. Only two days later the *Champion*'s crew observed smoke coming from the island, which induced Captain Kirby to approach it; they then perceived signal flags of distress, in consequence of which they hove-to and rescued the survivors. (Taken from the *Quebec Mercury*, 8 November 1814, and quoted in the *Times*, 19 December 1814)

20 October, Mervina, merchantman The *Mervina*, Captain Evans, from Peterborough was totally lost on Falster in the Baltic about this date. The crew were saved.

About this same date the *Active*, Captain Zachor, from Liverpool, was totally lost on Laeso Island. (*Times*, 26 November 1814)

8 November, Thetis, merchantman   The ship *Thetis* of Yarmouth, laden with hemp and iron, was totally lost on Darmet Sands, where the crew were saved. (*Times*, 26 November 1814)

25 November, Clifton, merchantman   The following is a copy of a letter from Captain Osborne to Mr John Osborne, Workington, giving an account of the loss of the *Clifton* of Workington, and the melancholy fate of her crew:

'Sidney, Cape Breton, 20th May 1815

'I am sorry to inform you of the loss of the *Clifton*. I left Chaleur Bay on 21st November last. and got on shore on the 25th, about six a.m. 18 miles to the NE of Cape St George, Newfoundland. The first stroke she gave knocked the rudder off, and we all got on shore in the afternoon, where we remained until the 28th, without anything to eat or drink.

'On that day it was more moderate, and we got on board again; got the boat ready, and provisions, to look for inhabitants. It came on to blow very strong that night, and we had to remain on board till the 30th, when I thought it best to get all the provisions on shore, for fear the vessel would go to pieces.

'On 12th December the mate and five hands took the boat to seek inhabitants. On the 16th they returned without finding any. At the same time W Gile and W Hailwood, apprentices, went off unknown to me: I expect they would find inhabitants, as I have since been informed there are some at the head of St George's Bay.

'Finding it impossible to travel, and not knowing where to look for inhabitants, but thinking that St Peter's Island would be the nearest inhabited place (and it being impossible for us to take provisions with us to last until we got there), I determined that we should go upon an allowance, and remain there until the spring, expecting the commencement early in March, but in that I was mistaken. We had a very severe winter, almost perished with hunger and cold.

'We agreed to live on six ounces of beef a day. We had very little bread, only about a cwt, and it was wet. We had a very good stock of potatoes, but they too got wet in getting them on shore, and the greater part of them wasted by the frost. We had four potatoes apiece served out as long as they lasted, which was till the latter end of February. On 30th December the cook died; he was a native of Africa.

'In the winter we got the longboat decked and on 20th April launched her down on the ice. On the 23rd the ice broke, and the wind being fair, we made sail from our weary abode. At eight o'clock got in between the ice, and stuck so fast that we could not get out. On the 24th, blowing very hard from the NNE and snowing, the ice stove in two planks of the longboat's bow. Fortunately, having the jollyboat with us we all got into her. It became moderate in the course of an hour, and froze very hard. It was one of the coldest nights I ever experienced.

'On the 25th William Hayton, Henry Touhunter, and William Crompton, died, the latter belonging to Newcastle. The 26th, John Durham of Whitehaven, and Thomas Chapman of Ulverston, carpenter, died. The 27th, Joseph Atkinson died, and on the 28th, John Cannon. We were still on the ice, and drifting out to sea. On the 30th, drifting close past the Bird islands, we hauled the boat up on a large island of ice. On 3rd May, I am sorry to inform you, I buried Joseph Losh.

'On the 5th in the morning we were between St Paul's Island and Cape Breton. The weather clearing up, and the ice breaking, we got the jollyboat off, and pulled in towards Cape North. Finding we could not get within two miles of the shore for ice, we stood to the SE, twenty miles round the ice and landed the next night, one man, a boy and myself; the man being nearly exhausted. I got a fire on shore, having tinder and matches with me. As soon as I got warmed, I found great pain in my feet; J Makinson the same. The bay being still full of ice, we could not reach any inhabitants. On the 12th Thomas Walstaff of Exeter died. I kept him in the boat, to make use of him, but fortunately the ice cleared away on the 14th, and we arrived here on the 15th. Thus, out of fourteen, only John Makinson (the boy) and myself are remaining. Our legs swell very much, but we expect to be better soon.' (*NC* vol 34, pp53-54)

28? November, unknown vessel The *Hope*, Captain Collins, on the 28th, SW of Milford, picked up a piece of boom and a piece of mainsail, of a vessel of 70 or 80 tons burthen; at the same time some casks and pieces of wreckage were seen. The same day off Milford Islands, was picked up a writing desk, supposed to belong to Captain Graham of the 23rd Regiment of Welch Fusiliers; there was a cheque in the desk drawn on Phillips and Starbock, Milford, dated February 1813; also a letter from a gentleman in London, to Captain Gosport, September 1814. There were also leases or copies of leases and a will in the desk. (*Times*, 5 December 1814).

Apparently the name of the vessel was not known nor does it appear there were any survivors.

3 December, Catherine, sloop 'The sloop *Catherine* of Grangemouth, 36 tons, laden with oats, sailed from Dundalk on 25th November; next day sprung a leak and during a fresh gale put into Ramsey where she got repaired. On Saturday the 3rd sailed with wind at southeast for her destination. About seven o'clock that evening, during a severe gale from south-southeast with much rain, when within two leagues of the Irish shore, the sloop leaked so much that pumping could not avail, and she became waterlogged, her cargo shifted and the vessel became unmanageable. While close in with the Long Rock of Ballywalter, the master and crew, three in all, went into the boat, but the violence of the surf upset her before they could get on the rock and one of the crew perished. The captain and surviving seaman with much difficulty got on the rock where they remained ten hours during high water, immersed three feet deep until Sunday morning when their cries were heard by a farmer, who brought them ashore in his boat, exhausted with fatigue, and used them with hospitality.

'The coast officer proceeded to render assistance, but owing to a south-east wind which drove the wreck to sea after the sloop had struck, the cargo was lost, together with the captain's money, charts, clothes, etc.' (*Times*, 17 December 1814)

12 December, Jenne Adelle, brig   In a violent gale during the night of 12 December the French brig *Jenne Adelle*, from Oporto for Havre le Grace, laden with oranges, was wrecked on the Mewstone, south-east of Plymouth. The mate and two seamen were washed ashore on the Mewstone and saved, but her captain (Laval) and three seamen drowned. Mewstone is an island rock, about a mile from the main, and the three poor fellows were many hours before a boat could venture out to take them off, which was at last done at very great risk, as the boat was swamped at the first attempt. This vessel was seven days from Oporto, during which time she experienced nothing but heavy gales of wind and the crew did not know they were near land, not having been able to make an observation during the voyage. (*Times*, 16 December 1814)

On 19 December the *SYM* stated that the *Jenne Adelle* struck at 4am, and Calmady Esq went out in the boat at the risk of his life to save the men.

13 December, British Queen, packet   The *Bee* cutter which sailed from Ramsgate on Friday 17 December for Ostend put into Margate Roads the following evening, having picked up off the North Foreland part of the stern of the *British Queen*, Margate packet, which is supposed to have sailed from Ostend on the 16th. (*Times*, 20 December 1814)

The *British Queen* left Ostend at 2pm on Tuesday the 13th with a fair wind. There were about nineteen people on board, including an hostle [ostler]. Two of the youths drowned were sons of Mrs Laming, widow of the owner of the vessel. (*Times*, 24 December 1814)

13 December, Providentia, brig   At 4am the brig *Providentia* of London, with a valuable cargo for Cadiz, parted her cable in the mouth of Catwater, and went on shore on the rocks at Teats Hill, near Queen Anne's Battery, Plymouth. 'Her rudder and sternpost have gone and although part of the cargo has been landed, yet she cannot be got off until the next high springs.' (*Times*, 16 December 1814)

A later Plymouth report of the same date stated that the *Providentia* from Hamburg had been unladen, yet could still not be got off.

13 December, Sophia, galliot　A galliot under Swedish colours is in Whitsand Bay with signals of distress and dismasted; said to be laden with sugar and cotton from Liverpool for Stralsund. Pilots have been sent off to her, and it is hoped she will be brought in. (*Times*, 16 December 1814)

The Swedish galliot *Sophia*, from Liverpool for Hamburg, with sugar and coffee, that has been riding to her anchors in Whitsand Bay since the 13th dismasted, was on the 15th driven on shore and by the 19th she had gone to pieces, with very little of the cargo saved. (*Times*, 20 December 1814)

14 December, 'highly blamable' conduct　The *Anna* of London fired several guns this afternoon; several pilots went off, when they were informed it was for the amusement of the master. Such conduct is highly blamable during a gale. (*Plymouth report*, quoted in the *Times* on 17 December 1814)

16 December, unnamed galliot　A Dutch galliot, laden with coffee and sugar, went on shore in Bigbury Bay. The crew were saved. (*Times*, 20 December 1814)

27 December, Betsy, sloop　A Greenock report of 20 January 1815:

'The sloop *Betsy* of Portrush, from hence, laden with tallow and coals for Newry, was wrecked during a gale upon the east side of Copeland Island [at the entrance to Belfast Lough]. It contained no news of the crew.' (*Times*, 25 January 1815)

1815

12 January, General Wellesley, East Indiaman　Loss of the prize ship *General Wellesley* from London, bound to India with a very valuable cargo, prize to the privateer brig *Yankee* of Bristol, Rhode Island, together with about 50 or 60 of her crew, is given in a letter from Charleston, S.C. dated 14 January:

'About one o'clock on Thursday last (12th) a ship was observed passing close in with our bar, from the northward, under a press of sail, with a signal for a pilot flying at her fore topmast head: and at the same time a very large ship in the offing, apparently a frigate of the first class, or a 74, endeavouring to cut her off from the south channel; soon after the first vessel had run down behind the land near the Light House, the ship of war hove to, and afterwards stood off to the eastward under her topsails. The general opinion at the moment was that the ships had crossed the bar and would soon be in sight, standing up for the town; but this hope was disappointed, and in the evening information was brought up by a small pilot-boat that the ship was ashore on the South Breakers, and that the sea was breaking around her in such a manner as rendered it impossible for them to board her. In this situation she was observed to remain at sun-down. During the night the wind blew fresh at N.E. and the ship went to pieces.

'Last evening Captain Cansler, Sailing Master of the US Navy, attached to the flotilla service, came up from below, and has furnished the following:

'On hearing that a ship was ashore near the bar, Captain C left town in an open boat in order to render any assistance which might be in his power, but on getting below, the weather was so boisterous, and night coming on, he found it impossible to approach her; it was therefore determined to join the flotilla of barges lying at the back of Cumming's Point until daylight next morning, when they would endeavour again to reach the wreck. During the night information was brought them overland from the Light House, that the prize master and twelve men had landed there from the ship, and that about sixty souls still remained on board her, principally Lascars or Sepoys.

'As soon as it was light in the morning Captain Cansler proceeded with all the boats attached to the barges to the wreck, but, dreadful to relate, on approaching where she lay, scarcely anything was to be seen above water; a part of the fore-chains remained, and several of the unfortunate creatures were lashed to it; seven of whom were taken off alive, two white seamen and five Lascars. All the rest, mounting to upwards of fifty, had been washed overboard and perished when the ship went to pieces during the night.

'The ship was the *General Wellesley* from London, bound to the East Indies, with a very valuable cargo, consisting of 18,000 bars of iron, besides a quantity of dry goods, brandy, porter, &c. She was one of a fleet of about thirty sail, all of which were in sight when she was taken; they were under the convoy of a 74 and a storeship, having on board three or four hundred soldiers. She was captured about 6th or 7th December in position 4°30′N 25°W, was a fine ship, coppered to the bends. Had seen no men of war until chased on shore on Thursday by a 74.

'Three or four trunks were brought ashore by the prize master when he landed; and some boxes containing valuables were taken out by the privateer. It is the opinion of the prize master, that had a decked boat come alongside them on the Thursday afternoon, property to the value of $20,000 might have been saved, as well as the lives of upwards of fifty of our fellow creatures, who have thus unfortunately perished. One of the two white seamen who perished was the boatswain of the prize.

'If something is not soon done to remedy the evils complained of by those approaching our bar, the revenue, and this city particularly, will suffer severely. Within two months two fine ships with very valuable cargoes have been lost upon our bar. In the first instance there was no enemy in pursuit, and had there been a pilot on board the vessel she might have been brought back into port in safety. In the latter case, she was closely pressed by an enemy's vessel, and the tide being one-third ebb, it was impossible to bring the ship over the bar; yet, if the ship must have been lost, with proper assistance a great portion of the cargo might have been saved.' (*NC* vol 33, pp303-304)

17 January, Sylph, 18 guns The *Sylph* sloop of war, rated at 18 guns and carrying 22, commanded by Cdr George Dickens, had a crew amounting, with himself and officers to 117 souls of whom 111 perished. On Tuesday 17 January at 2am, previous to the snow storm, the weather being thick and night dark, the wind at NE standing to the northward under close reefed topsails, the vessel struck on Southampton bar, at Shinecock Bay, or Canoe Place, five miles west of the town, and soon beat over and drove head onwards to within a few rods of the shore. From the height of the surf and violence of the sea, as the storm approached and increased, it was impossible to get to the vessel. The crew were all safe, sixty of them in the tops and on the rigging, until 8.30am, when the purser parted with the captain in the mizzen top and came to the windward gunwale, which was then as high out of water as her tops. Directly after, a tremendous sea capsized the ship and broke her in two between the fore and main masts, the fore part rolled over and lies keel upwards, and the after part, split lengthwise, went to pieces and drifted to the leeward.

The crew being thus dashed into the sea were chiefly drowned immediately. A few were seen on spars and pieces of the wreck, and every exertion was made by the spectators on shore to save them. The purser, Mr William Parsons, with two of the seamen, were taken off the spars about 2pm, and three more sailors, some time after, were saved from the wreck by a boat. The snow came on about noon, and the storm raged with great violence throughout the day.

The next morning the bodies of the 2nd Lt and three seamen were found on shore at Southampton and buried; and fifteen others drifted up with part of the wreck, as far west as Babylon, near Fife Island inlet. (*New York Gazette*, 26 January 1815; quoted in *NC* vol 33, p231)

18 January, Bengal, East Indiaman The following is a copy, in part, of a letter from Captain George Nicholls of the *Bengal* East Indiaman, 950 tons, dated Cape Town, 5 April 1815: 'The *Bengal* had, by dint of great exertion, completed her lading and joined the first fleet at Point de Galle, Ceylon; from whence they were to have sailed on 19th January, under convoy of the *Malacca* frigate; my passengers were all on board, and all was clear and ready for starting.

'The spirit-room had been unstowed on the forenoon of the 18th to examine a small leak which was observed to proceed from it; the defect was discovered, rectified, and the place again secured.

'Owing to there not being sufficient space in the spirit-room, four or five casks of liquor had been stowed in the gunroom and covered with bags of rice for security and as a measure of precaution, the gunner was directed to look at these, and ascertain if they were all safe, and he since reported them to have been all tight and dry.

'The largest cask, however, containing about 20 or 25 gallons of rum, and standing on its end, did not seem, as the gunner thought, to have its bung firmly in, and he struck it a blow to drive it further into the cask; yet, instead of going in, the bung flew out, and the spirit gushing forth caught fire, from a candle in a lanthorn which he held in his hand at the time. All was instantly in flames; and though every possible exertion was promptly made to arrest the progress of the flames, in less than an hour the ship was so far destroyed, that she sunk a blazing ruin.

'The ship's company behaved admirably, they were to a man orderly and obedient; not a man quitted the ship or relaxed from duty to the last moment.

'The number of sufferers was unhappily great, I fear upwards of twenty, principally occasioned by the sinking of boats alongside, although some perished in consequence of the dreadful rapidity with which the fire swept through the ship. Captain Newell of the *Alexander* [Extra ship]; Mr Barker, second mate of the *Surrey*; Mr Miller, midshipman of the *Bengal*; together with the master and a lieutenant of the *Malacca*, were all drowned. It is, after this melancholy detail, some consolation to reflect that all the females and helpless children were saved.

'I escaped at the last moment and did not preserve a single article excepting the clothes in which I stood, not even a paper was there saved from the general ruin.' (*NC* vol 33, pp497-498)

27 January, Queen Charlotte, West Indiaman   On this Friday evening the *Queen Charlotte*, a West India vessel, bound from Greenock to Jamaica, was driven ashore during a strong gale of wind, accompanied with a heavy fall of snow, among the islands of Scilly, where she was lost with three passengers and one seaman. Fourteen of the crew, having lashed themselves to a mast, were hurled upon a desolate rock, where they remained, during the night, without food, without clothing, and exposed to the severities of the most inclement weather, the sea making frequent breaches over them.

On Saturday the 28th the crews of numerous boats from the islands attempted to rescue the men from their perilous position; but so resistless was the force of the storm, that after many ineffectual endeavours, they were compelled to return, and the distressed mariners were obliged to pass another dreadful night in that exposed situation, and under the severest privations.

With the dawn of the Sabbath, some prospect of saving the unhappy people appeared; and the most resolute exertions were consequently made by the islanders. The crew of a stout rowing boat, after braving every danger, succeeded in reaching the perilous place, and in effecting the preservation of five of the almost-famished men. Encouraged by this success they made a second essay, when having rescued a poor Negro and being in the act of securing several others of the crew, a heavy wave, bursting with tremendous violence upon the boat, overwhelmed it, and hurried two of the gallant islanders into eternity.

The loss of their brave associates did but check for a moment the generous spirit of the natives. They renewed their humane exertions; and, by indefatigable perseverance, happily succeeded, with the aid of providence, in saving fourteen lives.

The persons who perished in their laudable endeavours to save the crew were Charles Jackson and James Tregarthen, two pilots belonging to Scilly. The former has left a widow, who is on the point of becoming a mother, to deplore his loss; the latter, recently emancipated from a French prison, after a captivity of nearly nine years, had but just returned to the arms of his wife, and a family of eight young children, when he was, by this lamentable catastrophe, torn from them a second time, never to return. (*NC* vol 33, p410)

28 January, Mercury, merchantman During a severe gale the ship *Mercury* of Blyth was driven upon the rocks near Tynemouth-haven. The Northumberland lifeboat went off to her and succeeded in taking the crew on board, yet they nearly all perished, as the swell was so dreadful that oars could not be used and the lifeboat struck several times, until the ship's master rushed among the broken water and managed to push her off; while in the meantime hundreds of spectators lined the shore, expecting every minute to see them perish. The ship's masts were all gone by the following morning and it was expected that the ship, built at Lynn in 1747, would soon vanish for ever. It was said at the time that either Admiral Lord Collingwood or Nelson had, at one time, served on this ship. (*Times*, 10 February 1815)

26 February, Statira, 38 guns Arrived at Falmouth on the morning of 15 April was the *Freeling* packet, Captain Bell, with mails from Jamaica, after a passage of 41 days.

She brought news that the ship *General Heathcote* had arrived at Jamaica from Bermuda and reported the loss of the *Statira*, a 38-gun frigate, on a sunken rock near Heneagua Bay (Great Inagua in the Windward Passage). Captain Spelman Swaine and his crew were saved and arrived at Jamaica in the *General Heathcote*.

From the above it would appear that the *Statira* was acting as convoy to the *General Heathcote*, in addition to which Great Inagua lies almost on the direct passage from Bermuda to Jamaica. (*Times*, 19 April 1815)

27 March, Alexander, East Indiaman A report from Weymouth read as follows: 'It has blown a hard gale of wind the whole of yesterday and last night; from the SSW, and it is with heartfelt regret that I inform you of the loss of the *Alexander* East Indiaman, from Bombay for London; she was thrown on shore, on the beach, two miles west of Portland, and I am sorry to add that the captain, crew and passengers are lost, except four lascars and a woman. The ship is gone to pieces and very little of her cargo can be saved.' (*Times*, 29 March 1815). This is not the ship mentioned in 18 January 1815.

Two days later the *Times* printed a Weymouth report of the 29th:

'Very little of the cargo saved. There have been taken up from the wreck the bodies of 39 lascars and 7 Europeans; amongst the latter Captain Campbell; Captain or Lieutenant Brooks; Lieutenant Hodges; Mr Jackson and two children; Mr Black, chief mate; Antonio, gunner's mate, but the above only are at present recognised.'

This was then followed by a Weymouth report of 30 March:

'The *Alexander*, laden with cotton, coffee and sugar, was driven ashore opposite the village of Wyke, by a south-west gale at two o'clock a.m. on Monday 27th March, and by four o'clock a.m. was a complete wreck. There were on board 150 persons, all of whom perished except four Malays and one Persian. From Portland to Abbotsbury the beach was littered with wreckage and the bodies of those who had perished. E Henning Esq. deserves special thanks as he provided wearing apparel, etc. for the survivors, which was sent to them at the Passage House.'

The *Bombay Courier* of 22 October 1814 contained a list of passengers, including Dr and Mrs Dunbar, Major Ramsey, and Master J Elphinstone. (*SYM*, 3 April 1815)

A monument erected in the churchyard of Wyke Regis reads:

'To record the melancholy wreck of

'THE SHIP ALEXANDER,

'This monument is erected by C Forbes, Esq., MP London, and the owners of the said ship, which, on her voyage from Bombay to London, was totally lost in the West Bay, on the night of 26th March 1815, when all the crew and passengers, consisting of more than 140 souls, unhappily perished, with the exception of five lascars.

'The following are the names of the persons whose bodies were found, and buried immediately adjoining this spot:

'Lewis Auldjo, Commander; Mr Brown, Chief Officer; Major Jackson, Captain Campbell, Lieutenant Wade, Mrs Auldjo, Mrs Dunbar, Miss Toriano, two Misses Deverells, Miss Jackson, Master Russel, Master Jackson, and Miss Elphinstone.'

The remains of Mr Dunbar were found subsequent to the interment of the above-mentioned, and buried in Portland. The body of Mrs Jackson was taken up near Lyme, in this county (Dorset), and there buried.

The under-mentioned also perished on this melancholy occasion, and their bodies have not been found:

Major Ramsey, Lts Bennet and Baker, Mrs Deverell, Miss Jackson, Master Deverell, Mr Bowman; 2nd, 3rd, and 4th mates; a European woman servant, and an invalid of artillery. (*NC* vol 35, p382)

27 March, Java, East Indiaman   The storm, which was fraught with such tragic consequences for the crew and passengers of the *Alexander*, was also responsible for the dispersal of the homeward-bound East India fleet. Another East Indiaman, homeward-bound, was the *Java*, 1175 tons, and during the night of 27 March, the *Java* was driven on shore on the rocks near the South Foreland, but by the assistance of the boatmen of Deal, the ship was got off with loss of her rudder, anchor and other damage. Next morning the ship started to drive once again; this time, from the Downs to within half a mile of the Goodwins, yet by cutting away her main and mizzen masts, the ship was brought up once more, and rode out the ensuing night in safety. (*Times*, 30 March 1815)

6 April, justifiable homicide   On 8 April an inquest was held before Joseph Whiteford, Esq, coroner, on the bodies of seven American prisoners of war, at the depot at Dartmoor (Princetown gaol), who came to their deaths in consequence of the military firing on them on Thursday the 6th, to prevent their escape from the prison. The jury after two days' investigation, returned a verdict of *Justifiable Homicide*. This affray appears to have been of a very serious nature: the prisoners, in consequence of the conclusion of peace, conceived themselves entitled to their immediate liberty; and not finding this to be the case, they became impatient, and determined to effect their escape by force. They armed themselves with knives and every weapon they could procure, and proceeded to attack the guards, who, in their own defence, were under the necessity of firing on them, by which the above seven prisoners were killed, and thirty-five others wounded. (*AR* 1815, Chr, p28)

16 April, Streatham, East Indiaman   Mr George Sheriff, 4th officer of the *Streatham* East Indiaman, 819 tons, and 4th son of Mr Sheriff of Munge-swells, East Lothian, was drowned on 16 April when off the Cape Verde Islands on passage to India, owing to the boat being upset, in which he had gone to save a man who had fallen overboard. (*NC* vol 34, p352)

Page 352 also gave the following: 'Lately was drowned in the Medway by the upsetting of one of the boats of HMS *Iphigenia*, which was conveying two sick men to the *Superb* hospital ship, Mr Alexander Milne, assistant surgeon of that ship; with Mr Milne perished the two sick men.'

30 April, Penelope, troopship   The *Penelope* was a 36-gun frigate, built at Bucklers Hard in 1798 (*NC* vol 1, p558); armed *en flute*, the vessel was being used as a troopship commanded by Cdr James Galloway at the time she was wrecked. A letter from Quebec, dated 27 May 1815, written by one of the surviving officers of the ship, imparts the following narrative of her loss in a storm of snow, when on passage to Quebec:

'We sailed from Spithead on 31st March, and had a favourable passage to the Banks of Newfoundland, where we met with immense quantities of ice, thick fogs, and strong south-east winds, the ice increasing as we drew near the Gulph, and at length we were frozen up for twelve hours near Cape North; with the thermometer eighteen degrees below the freezing point. When the ice loosened to permit the ship to move, all sail was set, and we got her out; the frost was frequently so intense as to preclude all possibility of working the ship; the ropes were so enlarged by the ice, that the sails which were not set were completely frozen into a solid body. On 27th April we had moderate weather, the frost was considerably gone, and we entered the Gulph of St Lawrence. On the 28th we passed between Brion and Magdelen Islands; on the 29th, sailed through great quantities of field-ice, the sea at the time appearing as one entire sheet, but not sufficiently strong to stop the ship's way. We soon after saw the coast of Lower Canada, about Cape Rozeare, wind north.

'On the 30th we stood to the eastward till the ship broke off to the southward of east; at three p.m. we tacked and stood for the Canada shore, at sunset laying a good course to clear the land, which was set by the master and first lieutenant; the supposed distance three or four leagues; the weather thick and cloudy, inclinable to snow, and very cold; the lead was kept going, the master was ordered not to quit the deck, and to make all the watch keep a good lookout. At eight p.m. we sounded in seventy-one fathoms; at half-past eight, while the line was passing forward, the captain and first lieutenant were looking at the chart, the ship going about four knots, when she was felt to strike the rocks, the atmosphere extremely dark and snowing! The helm was immediately put down, and the sails thrown aback: she came to about two points, and remained fast: the boats immediately lowered down, and the stream anchor taken out on the starboard quarter and let go in six fathoms; which was effected with great difficulty, owing to a current (unknown to us) setting in from the south-east. We cut away the bower anchors and threw the foremost ones overboard, there being three and a half fathoms aft. On our heaving round we found the anchor did not hold, the wind, too, increasing from the north-east with heavy snow, and extremely cold. The crew, with great difficulty and exertions of the officers, were kept at the necessary work; some of them actually got into their hammocks! The topmasts were got over the side, with six pigs of ballast at their heel to keep the ship upright, if possible; but the motion was so violent, the lashings were soon carried away. Great hopes, however, were entertained of getting the ship off in the morning, had the sea kept down, but, unfortunately, it increased fast: by midnight she was striking very heavy, and making water rapidly. Provisions were ordered to be got up, but before daylight the water was in the lower deck. All hopes of saving the ship being now given up, the masts were cut away to ease her; they fell in-shore which prevented the hull from heeling out. The master was now sent away in the cutter, with a small hawser, to make fast to the shore if possible; but the surf was so great, and it breaking over large ridges of rocks, the boat was swamped and stove long before she got near the shore, and the crew with great difficulty were saved. Three successive attempts were made with the other boats, one of which was the lifeboat, in which the purser was sent with the public despatches, which were saved. As none of the boats returned, the prospect of those on board became very alarming; the ship by this time (1st May) striking very heavy, it was impossible to stand upon the deck; the quarter-deck beams were giving way, and the sea was breaking into the captain's cabin, which destroyed the few bags of bread that were stowed there for safety. The pinnace being the only boat alongside, and in great danger of being stove, the captain was advised to go in her; he appeared much exhausted and fatigued, and apparently unable to assist himself into the boat, from severe rheumatic pains. He was lowered out of one of the quarter-ports, and with as many men as she could safely carry, took another rope to try and reach the shore; but she had scarcely cleared the lee of the ship, when a sea filled her, the next sea threw her upon a rock, when all were thrown out of her; but with the assistance of oars, and by swimming. they all got to the shore: the snow to the edge of the water was then four feet deep, and those on shore were obliged to haul the others up; the weather extremely cold with severe frost, and blowing hard; the gig and jollyboat were still on board, and after great difficulty, the gig was got alongside from the stern, when the first and second lieutenants, with eighteen men, got on shore in her better than any other of the boats. The gig succeeded in bringing on shore another party, but was unfortunately upset in the surf, and stove; the people were saved, though some of them were very drunk.

'The jollyboat being on the booms could not be launched; about forty of the crew were still on board; and when they saw all hopes of being saved cut off, by the boats being all swamped on shore, they made most lamentable cries. We had still hopes of some of them being saved, by getting on shore on pieces of the wreck, which some attempted, but perished: our prospects on shore were truly miserable; nothing to be seen but high mountains, covered with snow. Some hands were employed collecting wood to endeavour to make a fire, which was accomplished after several hours perseverance; the consequences, had we not succeeded, must have been fatal, as the clothes on our backs were actually freezing. A party was employed in making tents with branches of trees and wet blankets; others looking for provisions found about sixty pieces of pork, and that, with melted snow, was the only meat and drink to be obtained. Several cases of wine, belonging to Major General Conran, which were stowed in the wardroom, were driven on shore, found by some of the crew, who then drank to such excess that they were discovered almost frozen to death. Many of the men were frostbitten in the feet and hands, some have lost their toes, and ten have been left in hospital at Quebec.

'The whole of that day we were truly miserable; the cries of the poor sufferers on the wreck were beyond description, and when night approached, it was still more dreadful; they were often heard to call the captain and the several officers by name, to send them assistance; which, I am sorry to say, it was not in human power to give. About midnight, three tremendous crashes and loud screams were distinctly heard, and shortly after all was silent; from the darkness of the night nothing could be seen; at daylight the ship was observed to be in three separate pieces, and all on board perished, except David Bruce, seaman, who with great difficulty got on shore almost lifeless. The wreck appeared one entire body of ice, so severe was the frost that night; nothing but very large fires saved us from perishing, we having no dry clothes. The ship breaking up, the spirits floated on shore, which the crew soon found, and before the officers knew it, there was scarcely a sober man to be seen: many were so drunk to such a degree, that they laid lifeless in the snow. All the rum that could be found was stove, preserving a sufficient quantity to be used in a proper manner.

'The next day about forty-eight men deserted, after plundering some of their shipmates, and every trunk that was washed on shore. Some have since been found dead by the Canadians. With the remaining part of the crew the boats were hauled up, which we begun to repair in the best way we could; sails were made from a lower and topmast studding sail, which was drove on shore; a cask of flour was also found, a part of which was made into dough. On the third day a Canadian boat was passing, when the captain ordered her to be detained; they informed us of three transports lying in Gaspee Bay, and the captain determined to proceed to that port. With the assistance of the cooking utensils found in the Canadian boat, all the pork that could be found was cooked, and served out to the different boats, which was a very short allowance for two days. On the sixth day of our misery (the weather moderate) the boats were launched, and all hands embarked, sixty-eight persons in all, including two women; the wind, favourable but light; with rowing and sailing we got to Great Fox River that night, where we were hospitably entertained with potatoes and salt at a Canadian's hut. Next morning we sailed for Gaspee Bay, and reached Douglas Town in the evening. After three days' rest we walked nine miles over the ice, to where the transports lay, leaving the sick at Douglas Town. Seven days after we got on board, the ice broke up, we dropped down to Douglas Town and embarked the sick, one of whom had died, and two deserted. The next morning we sailed for Quebec, where we arrived on the 23rd. Seventeen of the crew that deserted got on board the three transports at Gaspee, but hearing of the captain's arrival at Douglas Town they set off again; an equal number had returned to the wreck, and it was reported that fifteen of them were found dead in the snow, and were buried by the Canadians.

'It is much to be lamented, that here, as in similar cases of shipwreck, the seamen in general appear to have no regard to their own or fellow creatures' preservation, but the moment they got hold of any spirits, they made themselves intoxicated with it.' (*NC* vol 34, p154 et seq)

The *Times* devoted one paragraph to the loss of the *Penelope*, which reads: 'The *Penelope*, Captain Galloway, was unfortunately wrecked on the night of 30th April, about three leagues eastward of the Magdalen River, when upwards of forty of the crew perished.[57] The captain, purser and Captain Murray, Aide-de-Camp to Lieutenant General Sir G Murray, arrived here [Quebec] in the *Ann* transport, the remaining officers and crew came in the *Belvedere* and *Cygnet* transports. The public despatches were the only things saved from the wreck.' (*Times*, 8 August 1815)

30 May, Arniston, transport   The following narrative is taken from the surviving crew, relative to the loss of the *Arniston* transport, wrecked near Cape L'Aghullas, on the evening of 30 May 1815.

'Charles Stewart Scott, late Carpenter's mate of the *Arniston* transport, and others, assert, to the best of their knowledge, that she sailed from Point de Galle on or about 4th April, under convoy of His Majesty's ship *Africaine* and *Victor* brig, with six Indiamen. About the 26th May, parted company from the convoy, owing to stress of weather, having blown away most of her sails. Other sails were then bent, but the weather continued very squally, with a heavy sea. On the 29th, about seven a.m. the land was discovered right ahead, bearing about north by west, a long distance off; the wind then south-south-east. About half-past four p.m. still blowing very strong, hauled to the wind on the larboard tack, under a close-reefed main topsail, and stood on till half-past two a.m. On the 30th, then supposing the land seen was near Table Bay, the hands were turned up. Bore up, steering north-west and set the fore sail, intending to run for St Helena. Continued on till ten a.m. when the land was discovered nearly ahead; turned the hands up, and hauled the ship close to the wind on the larboard tack; still blowing very hard, made all sail (having topsails and courses set), stood on till near noon, when breakers were discovered on the lee bow; wore ship, and hauled to the wind on the other tack; stood on till two p.m. then wore and hauled to the wind on the larboard tack, continuing on till near four o'clock, when breakers were seen (proved L'Aghullas Reef), which we could not weather on either tack, being completely embayed; clewed up the sails and cut away three anchors, the two bower cables parted shortly after, when Lt Brice, Agent for Transports, recommended the captain to cut the sheet cable, and run the ship on shore, the only chance of saving the peoples' lives; the cable was then cut, and the ship put before the wind; in about eight minutes after she struck forward, the ship heeling to the windward; cut away the guns in order to heel her the other way, which could not be effected, consequently she soon began to break up; about eight o'clock the masts went, and the ship in a very short time was quite in pieces; many people were drowned below, in consequence of her heeling to the windward, and others clung to the wreckage, endeavouring to reach the shore, about a mile and a half distant. Out of the whole crew and passengers, consisting of near three hundred and fifty persons, only six men reached the shore, with great difficulty upon planks, being much bruised by floating wreckage and the surf, which was very high. At daylight the next morning, the sternpost was the only part of the ship to be seen; the beach was covered with wreck, stores, &c. and a number of dead bodies (which were buried by the survivors), and among them were Lord and Lady Molesworth, the Agent, and Captain, with some children. Next day 1st June, considering ourselves to the westward of Cape Point, it was agreed to coast (walk) the beach to the eastward, which we continued to do for four days and a half, subsisting on shell-fish from off the rocks, but fearing we had taken a wrong direction, it was agreed to return to the wreck, and we accomplished it in three days and a half, where we remained six days, subsisting chiefly on a cask of oatmeal which was driven on shore; by drying it in the sun we experienced great relief. The pinnace had been thrown ashore bilged, which we proposed to repair in the best manner circumstances would allow, and endeavour to coast along shore; at that time, the 14th June, being at work in the boat, we were fortunately discovered by a farmer's son, John Swarts (who was out shooting), and humanely carried by him to his father's house, where we remained with every comfort he could afford us for a week, and then set off for Cape Town, where we arrived on Monday evening, 26th June.

'Before we left the country, we were informed that 331 bodies, thrown on shore, had been interred near the beach.'

(Signed) Charles Stewart Scott, and Party.

'This declaration was made before me at Cape Town the 27th day of June 1815, of which this is a true copy.'

(Signed) J Meres Lieutenant RN, Resident Agent for Transports

A list of officers and passengers who perished on board the *Arniston* transport follows, so far as can be recollected by the survivors.

OFFICERS:

Lieutenant Brice RN, Agent	4th Mate, Robinson
Captain George Simpson	Doctor Gunter
1st Mate, Thomas Bull	Boatswain, John Barrett
2nd Mate, William Young	Carpenter, John Finlay
3rd Mate, Gibbs	Gunner, Thomas Gowan

PASSENGERS:

Lord and Lady Molesworth, with a boy of about seven, under their care

Four children (boys) belonging to an officer of the 73rd Regiment at Columbo

Captain Stoddart (Royal Scots)

Mrs James with two children, belonging to Point de Galle

Mrs Taylor, an officer's widow

Miss Twisselton, daughter of the Clergyman at Columbo

Mr Gordon and son, about five years old

Ordnance Store-keeper

Lieutenant Callendar, 19th regiment

Invalids from the 19th, 22nd, 56th, 69th, 84th, and Royal Scots, with 14 women, including passengers, and 25 children, and near 100 seamen from the different men of war in India, in the whole, about 350 people.

Note: Captain Whyms of the 19th Regiment died on board about six weeks after leaving Ceylon.

SURVIVORS:

C S Scott, carpenter's mate	William Fisk, seaman
Philip Shea, seaman	Thomas Mansfield, ditto
William Drummond, ditto	John Lewis, ditto

The above has been taken verbatim in its entirety from the *Naval Chronicle*, vol 34, p429 et seq.

Perhaps the major cause of the loss of the *Arniston* occurred on the morning of the 29th, when the crew assumed that the land seen in the distance was near Table Bay. The *NC* gives the following:

'These different resemblances of the Table Mountain at the Cape of Good Hope, when bearing from north-by-west to north-north-east from Cape Infanta, led the unfortunate ship *Arniston*, into error, having seen these mountains on the day before, being cloudy, dark, rainy weather, had not a distinct view, and run as they supposed, a sufficient distance to have passed the Cape of Good Hope, while they were yet to the east of Cape Aquilias (Cape L'Alghullas), and bore up north-west for St Helena, which course, brought them directly into this Bay, where the rocky and shoal water extends in many parts two leagues off shore. This serious loss was owing to the neglect of sounding before they bore north-west; had they taken this precaution, the loss of nearly four hundred lives would have been prevented, by finding themselves in soundings of from 55 to 65 fathoms, which would have immediately convinced them, that they were to the east of the Cape of Good Hope, instead of being entirely out of soundings. Had they been only four leagues to the westward of the Cape, and had they been ignorant of this remarkable circumstance, finding themselves in that depth of water, they would have naturally sounded the many hours they were running in north-west, and would have discovered that they were running on shore, by shoaling the water so fast as they must have done on that course.

'The six only survivors, who arrived in Cape Town, declared that no attempt to sound had been made that day, until they saw land, then it was too late, being only about two leagues from the shore, and found that they could not clear the land on any tack, consequently anchored in rocky ground, which cut two cables; and about four p.m. judging that which they were then riding by would share the same fate, cut it, and made some sail, and endeavoured to run on shore into more safety, but, unfortunately,' the ship was immediately among the rocks, upwards of two miles off shore, when she immediately heeled with her decks off to seaward, by which unfortunate circumstance, the whole were in a short time no more, the sea raging high, broke into the ship, filled her, and broke her into thousands of pieces before it was dark.' (*NC* vol 38, p338 et seq)

4 June, 'victims of imprudence' 'Five young women and six young men, amongst whom were two sailors, went on a cruise of pleasure, in a boat with sails, without oars. The sailor who had the management, being intoxicated, imprudently ventured outside Hayle harbour, on the ebb tide, in a most dangerous situation, being almost half a mile eastward of the bar. In endeavouring to return against the wind and tide, which was impracticable, the boat was upset, and the whole party was plunged into the water. One young man regained a place in the boat, which was soon righted, and drifted far to the east.

'Captain Dodd of the steam passage-vessel was very fortunately entering the mouth of the harbour at the time, in his boat, which he directly steered to the spot, and made every exertion to rescue these victims of imprudence from a watery grave; he succeeded in saving one of the girls and one of the sailors; the others were taken up lifeless. Captain Dodd ordered the bodies to be carried to a public house, which was not far off, and sent for a surgeon. But the owner of the house refusing to admit the bodies, it was found necessary to call on a magistrate, who speedily attended, and with the surgeon, superintended the efforts made to restore animation, which they continued for several hours, but we are sorry to say, without success. It is to be regretted that the directions given by Captain Dodd to those who conveyed the bodies to the public house, were not attended to, as the heads, in place of being raised and supported, were suffered to hang down. *It cannot be too generally known that this circumstance alone was sufficient to frustrate all future efforts for the restoration of animation*. It should also be observed that inns are licensed for public accommodation, and must, at any time, be opened for the reception of persons who may suffer accidents of any kind. By the above melancholy event, eight persons, four young women and four young men, lost their lives; three of the former were sisters.' (*NC* vol 33, p469 et seq)

The above also appeared in the *SYM*, of which the following is a verbatim copy:

'On Saturday the 3rd inst. came into the harbour of Hayle, near St Ives, a schooner (yacht), constructed and worked on a new construction, called the *Thames*, commanded by Captain George Dodd; it was fitted up in Scotland, and is not only an elegant but valuable vessel, and is propelled by the power of STEAM. She had performed some extraordinary feats at sea against wind, waves and tide, and she came into Hayle to wait for moderate weather to double the Landsend (*sic*) to proceed to London. This curiosity attracted the notice of the neighbourhood on Sunday, a day too often dedicated to pleasure and amusement; a party of young men and women engaged a boat to go out to view this phenomenon, and after they had satisfied their curiosity the young men, too foolishly inclined for a frolic, proposed to proceed to sea to give the girls a sprinkling, but unfortunately they were unacquainted with the nature of the tides, and the current, and they had not proceeded far before the boat was drawn into a heavy swell in the sea, which rendered her unmanageable, and a great wave broke into her, and filled her, and immediately a heavy swell succeeded, which upset her, and threw eleven young persons into the sea. Eight out of the eleven met with a watery grave, and the other three were saved by holding by the boat 'till assistance reached, and preserved them. Six of the bodies were shortly after picked up, and means were employed to restore animation, but without effect; the other two bodies have not been found. The eight unfortunate young persons, who were thus dedicating the Sabbath to pleasure, instead of attending their church, were two brothers of 24 and 26; three sisters, fine young women, 13, 16, 25; and a young man 27, all of the parish of Phillack; a young woman of the parish of Lelant, 16 years of age, and a sailor 24, belonging to a vessel then lying in the harbour of Hayle.' (*SYM*, 12 June 1815)

On 10 June the *Plymouth and Dock Telegraph* printed the following item of news:

'The *Thames*, steam boat, has excited no little curiosity in this port. She last came from Greenock, and in her passage along the Cornish coast the fishermen and others, who perceived her rapidly gliding on without masts or sails, and vomiting forth flame and smoke from her bows, conceived her to be a sea devil and made a precipitate retreat. She is about 100 tons, and consumes when at sea a ton of coal in twelve hours. Her general rate of motion in smooth water is about seven miles an hour; but in rough weather she would be soon overwhelmed, or prevented from making any progress. She is intended to ply between London and Margate.'

4 June, Dundee, pinnace This Sunday forenoon one of the pinnaces plying between Dundee and Newport, in Fife, suddenly sunk, about half a mile from the latter port; out of 23 or 24 persons supposed to have been on board, only seven were saved. (*Times*, 9 June 1815)

1816

Although the Napoleonic Era terminated with the Battle of Waterloo on 18 June 1815, it was not until the following January and February that the British troops, their wives and children were brought back to England, where they arrived after incurring all the difficulties and hazards of a winter's march and passage. Then when they arrived, no adequate reason could be conceived for not putting these troops and their families into the nearest and most convenient quarters; yet, instead of so doing, they were embarked once again and sent to the extremities of the kingdom, to Plymouth and Sunderland – they were landed at Dover; whilst a third part were embarked and sent to Ireland. And it is to these latter, unfortunate troops, returning from the battlefield of Waterloo, that we will now direct our attention. It was said that to save money the government intended to disembody the militia in Ireland immediately, and these unfortunate veterans were being sent out to relieve them. (*NC* vol 35, p221)

On 26 January 1816 the *Times* printed a Ramsgate report dated 24 January: 'The 59th and 62nd Regiments arrived this morning from Deal and embarked on board four large transports; they will proceed for Ireland, with their several officers, this evening's tide, if the weather continues moderate.' This does not appear to be strictly correct, as *NC* vol 35, p222 states the two regiments were crowded into three common sized transports; and we know that the *Lord Melville* had on board 479 persons exclusive of her crew. (*Times*, 8 February 1816)

However, on Thursday 25 January 1816 the ship *Lord Melville*, the brig *Seahorse*, and the *William Pitt* all three sailed from Ramsgate carrying detachments of the 59th and 62nd Regiments of Foot. (*NC* vol 35, p403)

The fourth vessel mentioned above may have been the *Boadicea*, transport No 561, J Gibson master, with a detachment of the 82nd Regiment of Foot, bound for Cork; whether or not this was so, the fact remains that of the four ships mentioned here, three were to go down, two of them with grave consequences.

They were the *Lord Melville*, *Seahorse*, and the *Boadicea*, which all went down on the same day, 30 January 1816; and although it is outside the Napoleonic era, our book would not be complete without our knowing what happened to one thousand veterans of Waterloo, their wives and children.

30 January, Seahorse, transport   The following account of the loss of the *Seahorse*, a transport brig, was received from an officer at Waterford; it was written by Mr James Gibb, the vessel's master, who was fortunate enough to survive the disaster.

'26th January. Sailed from the Downs.

'28th. Off the Lizard in the evening; wind south.

'29th. Blowing fresh from the south-west. Made Bally-cotton

Islands, about five p.m. The mate, going aloft to look at the land, fell from the rigging and was killed. Hauled up for Kinsale light, but the weather coming on thick and hazy, and blowing very hard, hauled our wind on the larboard tack.

'The ship falling off, wore her round on the starboard tack. At daylight (30th), drifting fast upon Mine Head, set the mainsails and shook out a reef of the topsails. At ten a.m. off Newton Head, the fore topmast went, and afterwards, the mainsail split; finding the ship drifting very fast on a lee-shore that I could not weather the land, about Brownstown Head; furled sails, and brought up with both anchors and two and a half cables on end; but the sea making a fair breach over us, and the anchors coming home, we drifted on shore, and in an hour and a half went to pieces.' (*Times*, 7 February 1816)

The above was then followed by a report from Tramore, dated 31 January.

'Yesterday presented a melancholy sight near this place. A transport had been seen for some considerable time approaching the harbour, and at length having crossed it to anchor near the shore within the opposite land, her distressed and dangerous situation being evident, crowds gathered from Tramore and the surrounding country, on the beach. After a short period, her anchors having dragged, she drifted to the beach, and having struck in a tremendous surf, unspeakable horror soon followed. The ship being soon broken, the shore became scattered with bodies, a few straggling survivors, and all manner of wreckage. Much exertion was made by several spirited individuals, but particularly by Mr Hunt of Tramore, who was instrumental in saving many. The severity of the day, and the disadvantage of an ebb instead of a flood tide, added greatly to the calamity. Benumbed with cold, the poor sufferers fell speedy victims to their deplorable fate.

'About one half of the 59th Regiment had embarked in this transport at Deal, their number about three hundred of whom sixteen were officers. About twenty-four, including four officers, were saved. The regiment was coming from France, and had shared in the glories of Waterloo. The loss of the mate early in the day probably occasioned the deplorable loss, as he was well acquainted with the coast. Lieutenant Henry Allen of Deal, going to join the *Tonnant*, was a young naval officer of great merit who directed the ship for some time with boldness and skill; yet he too was swept away and lost.'

The number of persons lost or saved, remains open to question. Captain Gibb's list gives:

Soldiers lost. 12 officers, 267 men
Soldiers saved. 4 officers, 20 men
Seamen lost. 14
Seamen saved. Mr James Gibb (master), 2 seamen
Women and children lost. 31 women, 42 children

Women and children saved. None

Passengers lost. Lieutenant Henry Allen, going to the 80-gun *Tonnant*, was the only passenger.

The above list was printed in the *Times* on 7 February, and on the 8th the *Times* printed a report from Ramsgate, dated the 6th, which purported to give an apparent embarkation list; although the *Seahorse* sailed from Deal. It read as follows: 'Embarked on the *Seahorse* were 14 officers, 266 men, 33 women and 31 children.'

In addition to the second list, we have to add the crew of the ship which totalled seventeen men; but whichever list we believe to be correct, we are left with more then 350 people on the brig, and it may be readily assumed that the vessel was overladen.

30 January, Lord Melville, transport What follows is an extract from a letter by Colonel Darley who was on board at the time of the disaster; it is dated Kinsale, 1 February 1816.

'Upon making the land, about eleven o'clock a.m. on the 30th ult., having laid-to the previous night, it blowing nearly a gale of wind, a heavy sea running, and the atmosphere so thick and hazy, that, upon discerning the land, we found ourselves nearly embayed. The master bore up to weather what was universally supposed the entrance into Cove, but which proved to be the Old Head of Kinsale; and after every exertion to weather that Point, and run the ship into Kinsale harbour, he was compelled to bear away for some friendly looking strand, upon which he might run up the vessel, and await the going out of the tide, in the hopes of saving the lives of so many souls, very justly not holding in competition the ultimate security of the ship. In endeavouring most ardently to effect this object, the vessel was irrecoverably driven upon a bed of rocks by the violence of the gale, distance between three and four hundred yards of the shore, the tide then making in. No time was lost in passing a rope from the ship to the shore, and cutting away the fore and main masts, to ease the tremendous shocks of the ship against the rocks, by which her bottom was almost immediately stove in, and several feet of water in her cabin. At this time it was about three o'clock p.m. our situation becoming most critical by the violence of the sea breaking into the cabin, and over the stern, together with her continual dashing against the rocks, a boat was manned for the ladies on board to endeavour making the shore: two officers' wives with their servants, soldiers of the 59th Regiment, a serjeant's wife and child of the 59th Regiment, six of the crew, together with Captain Radford of the 62nd Regiment (who was in a weak state of health), got into the boat, and made for the shore; but distressing to add, they had not reached half-way when the boat was swamped, and with the exception of one sailor, all perished.

'Nothing possibly remained for those on board but to await, with hope of preservation, the falling of the tide, when, should the vessel keep together, it was determined to lash a long spar from the bow to the nearest dry rock, and pass every person over it, to make good their way along the range of rocks that extended to the shore. Between ten and eleven o'clock the attempt appeared practicable, and to my greatest satisfaction, succeeded beyond our utmost hopes. After the lapse of some time, every individual having happily descended from the ship without any accident, Lieutenant Harty, of the neighbouring signal-station, with a party of men, after the most praise-worthy exertions, had arranged those men along the rocks with lighted sticks, affording the most essential assistance, and thereby preventing the loss of the lives of several, who would otherwise have certainly fallen into the many large recesses of deep water that encompassed and obstructed our progress to the main land, and over which the breakers occasionally washed. Every person having at last safely reached the shore, Lieutenant Harty, with equal promptitude, had arranged for their being distributed among the neighbourhood cabins, and they were marched off accordingly, to return early next morning for the purpose of endeavouring to get out the arms and accoutrements: nothing however could possibly be effected towards that end by the early return of the tide. The few men who were enabled to return on board, reported the almost total destruction of all the baggage from the sea it was swimming in, and the pillaging that took place after the troops were got on shore. Finding the day advancing and the men in need of repose, I directed their proceeding to Kinsale, leaving two officers' parties from the 59th and 62nd Regiments to remain in protection of the ship, conjointly with a party from the Limerick militia. I beg leave to express the very great support and active assistance that has been afforded by Governor Browne, Collector of Customs Meade, and the magistrates and gentlemen of Kinsale.

'From the brig that has been wrecked (*Boadicea*), with part of the 82nd Regiment on board, I understand that out of 280 only 60 have been saved, and two officers.'

Lt General Lord Forbes.   EDWARD DARLEY, Lieutenant Colonel
                                 and Major 62nd Regiment

Embarked on the *Lord Melville* Transport, of the 2nd Battalion the 62nd Regiment:
     One Colonel, 1 Captain, 2 Lieutenants, 2 Ensigns, 75 rank and file, 1 servant, 6 women and 2 children. Total 90.

Embarked on the *Lord Melville* Transport, of the 2nd Battalion the 59th Regiment:
     Three Captains, 8 Lieutenants, 3 Ensigns, 260 rank and file, 2 servants, 83 women and 30 children. Total 389. (*Times*, 8 February 1816)

Whereas the above article was penned by Colonel Darley, a passenger on the *Lord Melville*, we now have a copy of a letter written by Captain Thomas Arman of the *Lord Melville*, to the owners in London, in which he details the difficulties which beset him and his crew when the ship became embayed; although lengthy, it is given here abridged, and has been taken from the *NC* vol 35, p403 et seq.

'I sailed from Ramsgate on Thursday 25th January in company with the *Seahorse* and *William Pitt*, who had part of the same regiment as myself, but parted company in steering down the Channel. On Monday morning the 29th I doubled the Scilly Islands, and at 6 a.m. St Agnes light bore SE and shaped my course to make the Old head of Kinsale, the wind then blowing strong from the south-west, and the ship running 9½ and 10 knots, with every appearance of bad weather approaching. About noon the wind and sea encreased very much; sent down topgallant yards and struck the masts, got in cabin dark-lights; close reeved the topsails, and reeved the courses; made all the other sails fast, got the gaff down, and doubly secured the boats, &c. for a gale, which appearances fully convinced me would be heavy, though little thought the consequences would prove so destructive.

'At four p.m. it became pitch dark, and we furled the fore and mizzen topsails. At six p.m. thinking it no longer prudent to scud, with such an iron-bound shore at no more than forty miles distance under my lee, furled the foresail, and hove-to under close reeved topsail with ship's head to westward, and lay-to as easy as might be expected in such dreadful weather. Ar midnight I wore with her head to the eastward, and the ship then laboured very much, and some heavy, though chase, seas struck us. At three a.m. on Tuesday morning, I wore with our head to the westward again, and observed two lights at some distance from each other to leeward. At four the wind seemed to lull a little, and I could at intervals distinguish some stars. At six the gale came, if possible, with increased violence, and the weather continued so hard, that it was not until nine a.m. that I could discern what the lights were, when I observed them to be two brigs. I then bore up, set the foresail, having been hove-to something longer than fourteen hours. At eleven a.m. I supposed myself to be about ten miles from land, and although the weather seemed rather cloudy, I had no doubt but we might see that distance at least, and the wind being to the westward of south, I could haul off if necessary; however, neither the men at the mast head nor any on deck could see anything like it. I now felt very uneasy in my own mind, when a little after noon (sun obscured) the breakers and land appeared all in an instant to those on deck, but could not be perceived from aloft. I immediately braced the yard up, and brought the ship to the wind on the starboard tack, set the mizzen topsail, mizzen staysail, and fore topmast staysail, and afterwards got the main and fore tacks well aboard.

'By this time the sky was quite clear, and I too soon found myself completely embayed between the Seven Heads and the Old Head of Kinsale, the sea running so high, that when the ship fell in the trough between the billows, the sails fell to the masts, and by the ship lurching so to windward, deadened her way, until the wind, which blew a hurricane, catched the sails with a terrible force over the waves again. The land then on our weather quarter, with breakers far outside of that, and the ship drifted very fast, broad on in the bight; and although she looked up near to the south-east, I readily saw there was no possibility of our weathering the head. I, therefore, hauled the courses snug up, got the anchors clear, and ranged the cables on deck. I now communicated our situation to Colonel Darley, 62nd, and Captain Fuller, 59th, who together with the other officers, prevented the confusion that could have arisen. I then stood up on the quarter rail, abreast the men at the wheel, which was put a-weather, and gave direction for clewing up the fore and main topsails. I called the sailors from the anchors, and directed them to brace the yard sharp up, and we again set the fore topsail, and with mizzen topsail and mizzen staysail, brought to on the starboard tack; we had been in broken water some time, and I considered the tide was only half flood by the shore. I conned the ship in, under a reef that the sea broke over, and at half-past three she struck, sent the pumps up, knocked the rudder off, and made all aloft sheer again. I still pressed the sail on her, and we ran a full length higher up before she filled with water, which was shortly up to the 'tween-deck beams.

'I now got some of my brave fellows in the quarter-boat, and gave them the end of a deep sea line, with strict directions how, and where, to haul the end of a thicker rope; this they got safe on shore, but soon got it entangled among the rocks, so that it did not prove of that service which my expectation pointed out. The boat now came off again towards the ship, and although I called to them not to come alongside, or they would lose their lives, they still persisted, and there they remained, until filled with fourteen persons, and just as they shoved off they were overwhelmed by a sea, which threw them half way on shore, and all perished, except one seaman who was washed on shore, and has now recovered.

'We now cut away the masts which required some management to get them clear of so many men on the deck; however, we succeeded, as I have heard of no accident. The sea had made such progress in the stern, as to wash down all the bulkheads and soldiers' bed places, and with the officers' baggage, became a confused and broken mass in the fore part of the ship, and I could perceive from the stumps of the masts that the bottom was gone.

'It was now high water, six p.m., our upper works still held fast; it was pitch dark for two hours when at length a sea came and completely overwhelmed us fore and aft with such a crash beneath as cannot be conceived. As soon as I could take breath, and the drift of the surf permitted me to look, I saw we had been thrown upon a large cragged rock with a chasm on each side. I cheered all around me, and assured them the tide was beginning to ebb, and our situation was better than before; and though some heavy seas came over us, yet there was none strong enough to lift the whole body any more. At ten p.m. the heads of the rocks began to show themselves, and the water began to ebb inside the ship; I sent one of my faithful fellows, Robert Piers, carpenter, down into the cabin, who fished out some bottles of famous ale, and of which Colonel Darley and all the officers and others around, cheerfully partook.

'It now drew fast on to low water, and I was doubtful whether the rocks would dry, so as to get over the bows by ladders I had already fixed. We therefore got a rough spar which lay on the main deck, sixty feet long, and launched it over the bows, and while one end lay on the rocks, the other rested between the cat and knight heads, and about midnight we commenced disembarking, about four hundred and fifty people, among whom were upwards of sixty women and children, had got safe on shore, and were conducted over the rocks by a private gentleman, Mr James Gibbons, and Lieutenant Harty RN who went before them with lighted clumps of wood in their hands. At Mr Gibbons' house we got a most friendly reception and every refreshment we wanted.

'With the remainder of my crew, I have done the last services for my poor fellows who lost their lives in the boat, by having them interred and reading the funeral service over them.'

30 January, Boadicea, transport   A report from Dublin dated 2 February gave the following: 'A gentleman who arrived yesterday from Kinsale has favoured us with the following particulars of the loss of two transports, near the Old Head, off that town. It is with heartfelt sorrow that we announce them to the public.

'On Tuesday evening last, these two vessels were observed to be embayed between the Old Head of Kinsale and the Seven Heads, the wind blowing a gale from the south-east. They adopted every expedient to weather the Old Head, but in vain; the peril of their situation increased every moment, and towards dusk an account was brought to Kinsale, that the ship would in a short time be on shore, and that the brig had dropped her anchors, in the hope of riding out the gale. On receipt of this distressing communication, Collector Meade, with a decision and promptness equally creditable to him as a public officer and a man of humanity, ordered an officers' party of the Limerick militia, under the direction of Mr Pratt, the port-surveyor, to the Old Head, to afford every assistance and protection to these unfortunate vessels. Mr Spiller Newman, a respectable gentleman of Kinsale, who holds a revenue situation, although indisposed, accompanied Mr Pratt and the military to the Old Head. They had to cross the ferry of Kinsale, and then march five or six miles through by-roads to get to the place of their destination. When they arrived, they found the ship, the *Lord Melville*, already ashore; but the brig *Boadicea*, being at anchor, and further off shore, had, to all appearance, much greater chance of escape than the ship. She was distinctly seen by the revenue officers and military party, with a light at her topmast, till after midnight. The light and vessel then disappeared altogether. It still blew a tremendous gale of wind right on the shore, the sea ran mountains high, the rain poured down in torrents, and the night was pitch dark. Under these circumstances, the most gloomy apprehensions for the fate of the brig were entertained by the party from Kinsale. When the morning dawned, these apprehensions seemed too well grounded, as the brig had disappeared altogether. However, after a diligent search for some time along the shore, her fragments were discovered among the rocks which lie between the two strands of Garretts-town, where she had been driven after parting from her anchors during the night. Upon approaching the wreck, a most heart-rending scene of misery, desolation, and death, presented itself to the view. The vessel seemed to be a confused mass of timber, planks and boards, broken to pieces, and intermixed with piles of dead bodies – men, women and children. Near to the wreck was a rock somewhat elevated above the surface of the water, and upon this were seen about eighty or ninety poor human creatures, who had scrambled to it from the vessel, and were still alive. The people on the shore communicated to them, as well as they could, that their only chance of safety was in remaining where they were until low water; but either through impatience of the misery of their situation, or from the impulse of despair, near thirty of them plunged into the sea, and endeavoured to gain the shore, but in vain, as most of them perished in the attempt. About fifty remained on the rock until low water, and were all saved.'

'The brig was a transport, and had a detachment of the 82nd Regiment on board, bound for Cork. Yesterday morning, the Sovereign of Kinsale, Governor Browne, and Collector Meade, were most actively employed procuring clothing, provisions, and medical assistance, for the poor suffering survivors. From the cordial co-operation which they received from the inhabitants of Kinsale, they have no doubt been enabled to afford the most timely and effectual relief.' (*Times*, 7 February 1816)

The *Cork Advertiser* office issued the following: 'We have just been put in possession of the official return of the loss of lives in the late shipwreck of the *Boadicea*, which completes the statements relative to this melancholy event.

'2 lieutenants; 1 assistant surgeon; 8 serjeants; 158 rank and file; 13 women and 16 children. Total lost, 198.

'Total embarked, 283 men including NCO's all of the 82nd Regiment, and 3 men of the 35th Regiment, 2 of whom were saved. There were also on board 7 officers, 14 women and 17 children.' (*Times*, 8 February 1816)

With regard to the figures quoted above, it should be noted that John Meade, the Collector of customs, wrote to Lord Forbes on 1 February, 'it is impossible as yet to be exact as to the numbers , as several of them who were injured are in cabins about the place.' (*Times*, 8 February 1816)

Yet one thing is certain: the passengers and crew on board the *Lord Melville* were more fortunate than the people on the other vessels, perhaps because it was a larger ship; but however that may be, all who remained on board the vessel survived, including 116 women and children. The only loss of life occurred when the ship's boat was lost and in this instance we have the names of the twelve who were so ill-starred as to be the only persons to perish, out of the 500 or so who were on board. Their names are: Mrs Mancor, wife of Captain Mancor; Mrs Fawson, wife of Captain Fawson; Mrs Weld, wife of Serjeant Weld; and Mary Weld, her daughter; Privates John Wheatley and Richard Mooney, both of the 59th; and servants of the two officers' wives. (*Times*, 8 February 1816)

Charles Taylor, steward; John Thompson, seaman; John Brown, seaman; William Bennet, seaman; Benjamin Bell, apprentice; all the foregoing interred; and William Brown, seaman, whose body was not recovered. One seaman was saved but his name was not published. (*NC* vol 35, p406)

It would appear then that of our troops returning from the Battlefield of Waterloo, 350 persons, including 70 women and children, perished with the *Seahorse*, and probably another 250, including about 30 women and children on the *Boadicea*; furthermore, it would seem that no woman or child escaped alive from either shipwreck.

So ends what has proved to have been a most disastrous period of maritime history.

NOTES – INTRODUCTION

1. '*Ville de Paris* was commanded by a most experienced seaman, who had made 24 voyages to and from the West Indies, and had been pitched upon to lead the fleet through the Gulph; yet she was buried in the ocean with all on board; more than 800 people.' (*NC* vol 5, p398). It refers to Captain George Wilkinson: see William Burney, *Naval Heroes of Great Britain*, London, 1806.

2. The French corvette *Atalante*, 16 guns, 125 men, taken on 10 January 1797, had on board a mooring chain weighing 12 tons, each link weighing 76lbs. (*Times*, 14 & 18 January 1797). See *Pylades*, 26 October 1811.

3. Old cordage which, when picked apart, forms oakum.

4. See also 7 February 1795, 29 September 1799 and 5 January 1802.

5. Captain Manby of Yarmouth was awarded the above Society's Gold Medal on 31 May 1808. (*NC* vol 20, p21). On 14 June 1811 Mr Wilberforce had a motion carried for an address to the Prince Regent, praying he would order Captain Manby's invention to be stationed on different parts of the coast; the House making good the expense. (*AR* 1811, p518 et seq)

6. Fifteen cases of other Elgin marbles arrived at Plymouth on board the *Diana* frigate on 13 August 1802. On the 13th, three of the cases were opened: 'One contained a beautiful Grecian statue of a Centaur; a second, one of 21 brass guns on curricle carriages; and a third, two shafts of pillars of exquisite workmanship, apparently Egyptian. Most of these curiosities were collected amidst the ruins of Corinth and Athens.' (*NC* vol 8, pp172-173)

7. Captain R R Bligh, who hailed from an old Looe family, was a son of Richard who served as a lieutenant of the *Rainbow* frigate with Captain (afterwards Lord) Rodney in 1749. (Ralfe, 1828). He is not to be confused with William Bligh of the *Bounty* mutiny.

NOTES – PART I

8. Shewn as a French loss in *SNL*, 1793, which gives the date of loss as 26 November. Named after Scipio Africanus, the great Roman general who defeated Hannibal at Zama, 201BC, and ended the Second Punic War.

9. Italian mile = 1467 yards. A mile was originally the Roman linear measure of one thousand paces, reckoned to have been 1618 yards.

10. As late as 1820, the best petty officers were allowed to have their wives on board, about one for every hundred men. (Smyth) See also 4 April 1799.

11. River Erme. With the wind then in the SW quarter, the *Pigmy* would have been embayed and was most probably wrecked at low tide at or near Fernycombe Beach.

12. Sixteen years later, on 24 July 1810, the *Times* printed this letter in full

on p3. Sir William Essington KCB died on 12 July 1816. He had not been employed since serving under Lord Gambier at Copenhagen. (*NC* vol 36, p87)

13. The cause was most likely to have been typhus, the agent lice or ticks.

14. It is likely that the transport was also carrying the dragoons' horses and this would surely have contributed to the disaster. See also *Viceroy*, 21 December 1797, and *Mariner*, 24 December 1798.

15. On 10 January 1762 the French National frigate *Zenobie*, 22 guns, 210 men, sailed from Havre de Grace. On the 12th during a violent storm the officers were obliged to run the vessel ashore, 'on the Peninsula of Portsland.' The 71 survivors, almost all wounded by floating debris, were robbed of the very little they possessed by the natives of the place, but were succoured by Mr Traver, the Commander of Portland. (*AR* 1762, Chr, p76 et seq)

16. The *Commerce* was at first mistaken for a transport of the same name, which had a detachment of the Royal Irish Artillery on board. (*Times*, 23 December 1795)

17. The *Naval Chronicle* contains errors on p171. The reports dated 19, 20 and 21 July belong to p174 and are really 19, 20 and 21 August.

18. The *Prince* was believed to have been the first vessel on which the experiment was tried of sawing a ship into two parts and then extending her, in this instance by 17ft. (*NC* vol 1, p546)

19. The Paternosters lie approximately 250 miles west of Kalaotoa, so it is more likely that the *Ocean* struck on one of the Tiger islands.

20. An old Dutch silver coin in general use in the Dutch East Indies, in which accounts used to be kept; its value was 19 or 20 fanams, or 192 doits, one doit equalling half a farthing. The Rix-dollar therefore equalled two English shillings at that time.

21. America was then engaged in what was called her 'quasi-war' with France – undeclared but not 'phoney' – and *Planter*'s assailant was a French privateer.

22. Jeziret Tumb, position 26°16′N 55°19′E, 165ft high, of level outline and two miles across. (Findlay, *Indian Ocean Pilot*, 1870 ed)

23. Steel's *Naval Chronologist* of 1801 claims *Trincomalee* blew up in the Strait of Babel Mandeb (position 12°30′N 43°10′E), but this cannot be so. The Strait is 1500 miles from the Quoins (position 26°30′N 56°32′E), therefore we may assume the *Chronologist* confused it with the Strait of Hormuz, near where *Trincomalee* was really lost.

24. The Dutch 20-gun frigate *Valk* was one of the ships taken possession of by the squadron of Vice-Admiral Mitchell, without firing a shot, in the Zuyder-Zee on 30 August 1799. This was the only success of the disastrous Anglo-Russian invasion of the Netherlands led by the Duke of York. The army was forced into a negotiated withdrawal, and as detailed

here suffered further losses from natural causes to add to those inflicted by the enemy.

25. *NC* vol 10, p367 alludes to a volume lately published, titled *Walks and Sketches at the Cape of Good Hope*. It purports to give an eyewitness account of the loss of the *Sceptre*, which with other ships was bound to the *eastward* – hardly to be believed if the *Sceptre* was carrying trophies taken at Wellesley's great Indian victory over Tipu Sultan at Seringapatam.

NOTES – PART II

26. 'Interest' in the eighteenth-century system of patronage meant influence or connections.

27. The *Guardian* was built by Batson at Limehouse and was launched on 23 March 1784. After the iceberg incident the ship was taken to Table Bay and beached on 8 February 1790. The ship was sold there exactly one year later. (See also *AR* vol 32, p254). Note that there is a monument in St Paul's Cathedral to Lt Riou who was cut in half by a cannon ball when commanding the 36-gun *Amazon* at Copenhagen 2 April 1801. (Norie, 1827, p360; *AR* 1801, Chr, p15; *SNL*, January 1783)

28. Cape Lookout is marked by a red tower, 150ft high, standing 2½ miles NNE of the point of the Cape. From Cape Lookout the shoals extend nearly in a SSE direction to the distance of 3 leagues from the lighthouse. A shoal having only 14ft water on it lies S by E ½ E distant 10½ miles from Cape Lookout lighthouse and about 2¼ miles to the southward of the extreme south point of the 3 fathom edge of the shoal that extends 7 miles to the south of Cape Lookout. (Findlay, *North Atlantic Memoir*, 1873).

29. *L'Aventuriere* (corvette), 12 guns: cut out in the night of 3 August 1798 from the port of Corigio near the island of Bas, by the boats of the *Melpomene*, 44 guns, Sir Charles Hamilton, and *Childers*, 14 guns, Lieutenant J O'Bryen, under the command of Lieutenant Shortland. (Norie, 1827, p415)

30. At one time the Lema, Kaipong and Wanshan Islands were altogether known as the Ladrones; whereas today only the Wanshan Islands may be known by that name. They should not be confused with the Ladrones, which since the Second World War are commonly known as the Mariana Islands, situated in approximately 16°N 145°E.

31. Suvarndrug or Soowurndroog Fort lies SSE from Bankot approximately 17°45′N 73°00′E. It was one of the piratical Mahratta forts erected in 1662 and was taken in 1755 by Commodore James. (Findlay, *Indian Ocean Pilot*, 1870 ed)

NOTES – PART III

32. The *Investigator*, originally the collier *Xenophon*, was a three-masted ship with one deck, purchased by the government and altered at Pitcher's Yard at Limehouse Hole to the specification of the Navy. (*SNL*, May 1803, p9)

33. The *NC* vol 11, p338 gives a Bombay report of 31 December: 'The *Bridgewater* from Botany Bay was spoke off Cape Cameron by the *Fame*, Captain Allison, arrived here on the 25th inst. from Bengal. By her we learn that the *Cato*, and a ship unknown, which sailed in company with the *Bridgewater*, were lost with every person on board in some Straights to the eastward.'

34. To anchor with a spring involves causing a smaller cable or hawser to be passed out of a stern or quarter port, and taken outside of the ship forward, in order to be bent or fastened to the ring of the anchor intended to be let go, for the purpose of bringing the ship's broadside to bear in any given direction. (James, 1826 ed)

35. In 1983 the wreck of the *Magnificent* was located, and artefacts found at the site were deposited with the French Government.

36. Formerly a French privateer ship of 30 guns and 240 men, *La Blonde* was taken on 17 August 1804 by the 40-gun *La Loire*, Captain F L Maitland, 49°30'N 12°20'W.

37. Allowing for an error of one degree in longitude, the *Betsey* most probably struck on Fiery Cross Reef, although the given position is very close to Sin Cowe Island. (*Findlay's China Sea Pilot*)

38. The *Times* did not carry the story of the loss of the *Hibernia*'s launch, but on 23 January the paper published a Plymouth report dated 20 January, which read: 'A report is prevalent of the loss of the *Impetueux*'s launch, but little credit is attached to it as the *Impetueux* was in Falmouth a few days since, and no accounts have been received from her of so unfortunate an accident.' The reporter simply had the wrong vessel.

39. Admiral Villeneuve was the French Commander in Chief at the Battle of Trafalgar; he died on 26 April just one week after returning to France. The three admirals who had commanded at the Battle of Trafalgar all died within six months of the engagement. The English admiral, Nelson, was killed outright; Admiral Gravina, the Spanish admiral died of wounds received and the French admiral possibly by his own hand. An account of the manner in which Admiral Villeneuve is believed to have died is given in *NC* vol 15, pp428-429.

40. Possibly meaning a timber bilge keel common in craft designed to take the ground regularly, but the word was also applied to a fixed fender down a ship's side to protect it.

41. The fine section of the underwater hull right aft.

42. *Brilliant*, 28 guns, built 1777. *Jamaica*, 26 guns, formerly the French

La Percante, taken by the *Intrepid*, 64 guns, Hon C Carpenter, off Porto-Plata, West Indies, February 1796.

43. An illustration of the device is to be found in an oil painting by J M W Turner entitled 'Lifeboat and Manby Rocket Apparatus going to a stranded vessel making a signal of distress, 1827' in the Victoria and Albert Museum, London. Even after this demonstration the establishment of a lifesaving service on the coastline of Britain was a long way off, although some local initiatives were made under the patronage of Lloyd's.

44. Built in 1800 under the name *Sting*, she was purchased and renamed in 1802. She was best known as the vessel that brought the news of Trafalgar and the death of Nelson to Britain.

45. Traditionally, a ship's log was written from noon on one day to noon on the following day; so that the ship's mornings were dated one day later than those on land. The Royal Navy was in the process of converting to the midnight-to-midnight system used on land, nominally introduced in 1805, but the HEIC was obviously still using the traditional sea-day.

46. Colloquial English rendition of Rubjerg Knude. There is a tablet in the disused Romanesque church at Maarup, about 2½ miles distant, to the sailors of the *Crescent*, who perished, as well as to the memory of the men of the *St George* and the *Defence* who lost their lives on 24 December 1811 (*qv*).

47. A boat towed by a line from the bank.

48. Red Island or Pulo Patampong is a mere islet or rock 20 ft high, lying about three miles south-west of Raffles lighthouse. It is not to be confused with the island of the same name in the northern part of the Durian Strait.

49. Bell Rock, or Inch Cape, a reef 12 miles SE of Arbroath, completely covered at high water. Tradition says that the Abbot of Arbroath caused a bell to be suspended here to warn sailors of the hidden danger. A lighthouse was erected upon the reef by Robert Stevenson in 1807-1810.

50. 'We have been informed that she had not more than 470 men on board, being short of her complement.' (*NC*, vol 25, p56). If this is so, then excluding women and children, 360 persons perished with the ship.

51. A total of 250 merchant ships, under convoy of the *Courageux*, 74 guns, and three or four smaller ships of war.

52. There are many instances on record of British ships being taken by the French and then retaken by members of the original crew, who either killed the Frenchmen or drove them overboard; then when the British arrived in England they were feted as heroes, not as so many murderers. Three examples immediately come to mind: *Townley*, 4 July 1799 (*NC* vol 2, p251); *Beaufoy*, 5 November 1799 (*NC* vol 2 p544); *Marquis of Granby*, 23 November 1799 (*NC* vol 3, p76).

53. On 21 November Captain Dashwood, on board the 36-gun *Pyramus* in Matvik harbour, wrote to Admiral Saumarez: 'The ships which have returned are all entirely without a single bower anchor or cable and are now riding within the inner harbour, some; made fast to trees or rocks, others with their streams or kedges. All their masters are necessarily absent, some at Karlshamn and others at Karlskrona, to endeavour to get their wants supplied, but which, I fancy, will be found very difficult. I understand it will take 16 or 18 days to bring anchors and cables from Karlskrona as they must come by land, and the roads are very bad. There are not above 10 at Karlshamn, and it is very doubtful whether so many can be purchased at Karlskrona.' (*Saumarez Papers*, Navy Records Society 1968)

54. The Silver Pitts are in the channel at the mouth of the Humber, by the Bull Sand, 180 miles from the Haake (Malham, p417). An apparent error occurred in *NC* vol 32, p220, which has Silver Pits (*sic*) 80 miles from the Haake.

55. A ship is derelict either by consent or by compulsion, stress of weather, etc., and yet, to save the owner's rights, if any cat, dog, or other domestic animal be found on board alive, it is not forfeited. The owner may recover, on payment of salvage, within a year and a day; otherwise the whole may be awarded. (Smyth, *Sailor's Word Book*, 1867 ed)

56. Of the 91 men and 18 boys, with which she commenced the action, the *Frolic* lost 15 killed, and Lt Charles M'Kay, and the master, John Stephens, mortally wounded; and Captain Whinyates, Lt Frederick B Wintle, and 43 men wounded. *Frolic* was retaken the same day, by the 74-gun *Poictiers*, Captain Sir J P Beresford. (Norie, 1827, p472)

57. The *Penelope*, armed *en flute*, was a transport carrying soldiers as well as her crew. There were 284 persons on board, yet as we have seen, only 68 survived. Most were either frozen to death or otherwise died of exposure.

APPENDICES

A: CAUSES OF THE LOSS OF SHIPS AT SEA, BY WRECK OR OTHERWISE

(Copied from the *Nautical Magazine* of 1841, pp49-50)

1. Short complement of men.
2. Deficiency of materials and stores.
3. Deficiency of water and provisions.
4. Bad materials - anchors, chains, boats, spars, sails, cordage, &c.
5. Bad quality of water and provisions.
6. Teetotality - coffee instead of rum, &c.
7. Bad condition of the ship from age, want of repairs, caulking, and looking properly to.
8. Bad construction of the ship, out of trim, &c.
9. Incapacity of masters and others.
10. Presence of captains' wives, and other women.
11. Insanity.
12. Inability of men, or crews, from sickness, maims, exhaustion, &c.
13. Drunkenness, revelry, &c.
14. Discipline, too lax or too severe.
15. Mutiny or insubordination.
16. A dead-and-alive set; no devil on board.
17. Discord and dissension: the devil let loose.
18. Deaths, desertions, and discharges.
19. Fire.
20. Collision.
21. Upsetting in a squall, &c.
22. Shifting of cargo, &c.
23. Consternation - the ship on her beam-ends, on fire, water-logged, &c.
24. Shipping of seas, foundering by stress of weather, &c.
25. Springing a leak by starting a butt-end, &c.
26. Deep lading, crowded stowage on deck, &c.
27. Striking on rocks, grounding on shoals, &c.
28. Driving on a lee shore.
29. Impressment at sea, detention and deviation.
30. Incorrectness of charts, compass, &c.
31. Want of care: bad dead-reckoning.
32. Want of vigilance: bad look-out.
33. No latitude by observation, on account of fogs, &c.
34. No flying the blue pigeon [nickname for the sounding lead]: no regard to lights, bells, drums, &c.

35. Capture or destruction by an enemy or pirate.
36. Struck or blown up by lightning.
37. Masts, &c., rolled or pitched away.
38. Driving with a foul anchor: a kink in the cable, &c.
39. Parting a cable.
40. Staving of boats, carrying away of masts, splitting of sails, &c.
41. Sleeping on watch, drowsiness of helmsman.
42. Breaking adrift of floating-lights, &c.
43. Mistaking of headlands, lights, &c.
44. Sinking or destroying a ship purposely.
45. Rising of prisoners, convicts, &c.
46. Fool-hardihood - guns run out when blowing hard upon a wind, press of sail with a crank ship, &c.
47. Carrying away topmasts from neglect of breast backstays, after going about.
48. Broaching to when weathering a headland in a gale of wind.
49. Incapacity of persons having charge, as pilots.
50. Abandonment of ship without sufficient causes, in case of wreck, officers leaving their juniors in command, with orders to land the treasure, the men &c.

B: FANCY GUNBRIG

Although Clowes, Norie and *Steel's Navy List* each state the *Fancy*, a 14-gun brig, was lost in the Baltic on 24 December 1811, this does not appear to be correct. It would seem that each copied the date and place either from *Steel's Navy List* or from one another.

Doctor Fereday, the noted historian, has been able to provide the writer with the following information, in the form of two official letters written by Vice-Admiral W A Otway.

The first letter, to John W Croker, Secretary to the Admiralty, is referenced ADM 1/694 (Leith 1811) H 781, 14 November 1811:

'I am sorry to have to acquaint you... that I entertain very serious apprehension for the safety of the *Fancy* gunbrig, as she has not been heard of since the very severe easterly gale of the 26th, 27th and 28th ult. She sailed in company with the Fleet from Wingo Sound, and on the former of the above days was left in charge of the ships bound to Dundee, only four are survived, and of the others several are missing.

'The *Fancy* was a very fine vessel of her class, well manned, and commissioned by an able and excellent officer, Lieutenant Alexander Sinclair. [We may note that Lt Sinclair was an Orcadian and therefore was most likely a very fine sailor.]

'I am Sir, etc. etc.'

The second letter, to Sir Richard Bickerton, is referenced ADM 1/694 (Leith 1811) H 795, 25 November 1811:

'...The loss of the *Fancy* is the more distressing as, from the length of time she has been on this station, Commander, Officers and most of the men are married and have families here (Leith). She was last seen on the 30th ult. off Montrose during the heavy Eterly (*sic*) gale, carrying a great press of sail, endeavouring to clear the land. As none of her wreck has been seen, she probably foundered.'

So this indicates her being lost off Montrose on 30 October 1811.

C: LETTER FROM CAPTAIN R R BLIGH TO PHILIP STEPHENS, ESQ, SECRETARY TO THE LORDS OF THE ADMIRALTY

'On board the *Marat*, at Brest

'23rd November 1794

'Sir,

'The arrival of the *Canada* must long since have informed their Lordships of my misfortune, in losing His Majesty's ship *Alexander*, late under my command, having been taken by a squadron of French ships of war, consisting of five of 74 guns, three large frigates, and an armed brig, commanded by Rear-Admiral Neilly. Farther (*sic*) particulars and details I herewith transmit you, for their Lordships' information. We discovered this squadron on our weather-bow, about half-past two o'clock, or near three in the morning, on the 6th inst., being then in latitude 48 deg. 25 min. North, 7 deg. 53 min. West, the wind then at West, and we steering North-East; on which I immediately hauled our wind, with the larboard tacks on board, and without signal, the *Canada* being close to us. We passed the strange ships at about half a mile distant, but could not discover what they were. Shortly after, we bore more up, let the reefs out of the top-sails, and set steering sails.

'About five o'clock, perceiving, by my night-glass, the strange ships to stand after us, we crowded all the sail we could possibly set, as did the *Canada* and hauled more to the Eastward. About daybreak the *Canada* passed us, and steering more to the Northward than we did, brought her on our larboard bow. Two ships of the line and two frigates pursued her; and three of the line, and one frigate, chased the *Alexander*. About half past seven o'clock the French ships hoisted English colours.

'About a quarter past eight o'clock we hoisted our colours, upon which the French ships hauled down the English, and hoisted theirs; and drawing up within gunshot, we began firing our stern chaces at them, and received their bow chaces. About nine o'clock, or shortly after, observing the ships in pursuit of the *Canada*, drawing up with her, and firing at each other their bow and stern chaces, I made the *Canada*'s signal to form ahead for our mutual support, being determined to defend the ships to the last extremity; which signal she instantly answered, and endeavoured to put it in execution, by steering towards us. But the ships in chase of her, seeing our intentions, hauled more to starboard, to cut her off, and which obliged her to steer the course she had done before. We continued firing our stern chaces at the ships pursuing us, till near eleven o'clock, when three ships of the line came up, and brought us to close action, which we sustained for upwards of two hours, when the ship was become a complete wreck, the main yard, spanker-boom, and three topgallant yards shot away, all the lower masts shot through in many places, and expected every minute to go over the side; all the other masts and yards were also wounded, more or less, nearly the whole of the standing and running rigging cut to pieces, the sails torn into ribbands, and her hull much shattered, and making a great deal of water, and with difficulty she floated into Brest. At this time the ships that had chased the *Canada* had quitted her, and were coming fast up to us, the shot of one of them at the time passing over us. Thus situated and cut off from all resources, I judged it advisable to consult my officers, and accordingly assembled them all on the quarterdeck; when, upon surveying and examining the state of the ship (engaged as I have already described), they deemed any further resistance would be ineffectual, as every possible exertion had already been used in vain to save her; and therefore they were unanimously of opinion, that to resign her would be the means of saving the lives of a number of brave men. Then, and not till then (painful to relate), I ordered the colours to be struck: a measure which, on a full investigation, I hope and trust their Lordships will not disapprove. Hitherto I have not been able to collect an exact list of the killed and wounded, as many of the former were thrown overboard during the action, and, when taken possession of, the people were divided, and sent on board different ships; but I do not believe they exceed forty, or thereabout. No officer above the rank of boatswain's mate was killed. Lieutenant Fitzgerald of the marines, Messrs Burns, boatswain, and M'Curdy, pilot, were wounded, but are in a fair way of doing well.

'The cool, steady, and gallant behaviour of all my officers and ship's company, marines as well as seamen, throughout the whole of the action, merits the highest applause: and I should feel myself deficient in my duty, as well as in what I owe to those brave men, were I to omit requesting you will be pleased to recommend them, in the strongest manner, to their Lordships' favour and protection; particularly Lieutenants Godench, Epworth, Carter, West, and Daracott: Major Tench, Lieutenants Fitzgerald and Brown of the marines; Mr Robinson, the master, together with the warrant and petty officers, whose bravery and good conduct I shall ever hold in the highest estimation. I have hitherto been treated with great kindness and humanity, and have not a doubt but that I shall meet with the same treatment during my captivity.

'I am, with great respect, Sir,
'Your most obedient and most humble servant,
'R R Bligh
'Philip Stephens Esq., Secretary to the Admiralty.'

D: LIGHTNING CONDUCTORS

Whilst British merchant and naval vessels of the period 1793-1815 were not regularly protected against lightning, it is of interest to note that the Americans, owing to the confidence they reposed in the celebrated Franklin, had long since employed lightning conductors on some of their ships; they being the first people to do so. In the Royal Navy lightning conductors were available, but were only fitted at the express request of the captain.

The French also were not backward in this respect, and volume one of the *NC*, published early in 1799, contained an abridged translation of a memoir by Jean Baptiste Le Roy, in the *Histoire de L'Academie des Sciences* for 1790, published in 1797, of a tour made to the different sea ports of France, to erect lightning conductors on the various magazines, and to cause them to be placed on ships.

'In the autumn of 1784, M Le Roy received orders from the Minister of the Marine, to visit Brest with citizen Billiaux, to place lightning conductors on the powder magazines as they had done on the gallery of the Louvre and Belle Vue.

'While the work was progressing, M Le Roy was employed in causing a conductor to be made for the *Etoile Galley* of 700 tons, destined for America, and commanded by Lieutenant Voutron. This well-informed officer, who clearly perceived the utility of conductors, had requested one from M Le Roy, who anxious to oblige him, fixed one on his vessel, on 18th November 1784. This was the first fixed conductor which had ever been placed on a French ship.

'This conductor was formed of a chain of copper rings, continued along the part of the rigging employed to steady the main topmast, and from thence, by means of metal plates sufficiently thick, a communication was formed between the conductor and the sea. This conductor was broken in a storm but set to rights again; however, this accident caused M Le Roy to alter parts of its construction, and at length he made some that were divided in a line of continuation down the mast, in such a manner, that though connected they would not suffer so much from the motion or flexing of the mast in rough weather, and would also be better enabled to stand against it. His endeavours met with much success; and those which were afterwards placed on ships remained uninjured.' (*NC* vol 1, p197 et seq)

E: KEITH'S REEF

The very existence of those formidable shoals, the Esquirques and Keith's Reef, was treated in the navy almost as chimerical, till the period of the Egyptian expedition in 1801, which drew such a considerable portion of English shipping to the coast of Africa that the fact became notorious; and this problem of hydrography was afterwards fatally and fully demonstrated by the loss of the *Athenienne*. It was not until this tragedy had occurred that the reefs were surveyed and properly charted.

Keith's Reef is a contiguous ledge of shelving rocks, which till the above surveys had taken place, was deemed to form part of the Esquirques, but is in fact seven miles east from their northern end. It is steep-to, except on the south side, whence there extends a sandy spit. Although no sensible alteration was found in the depth of water at the full moon, yet a strong south-east wind has been observed, on approaching the rocks, to shoal the water almost nine feet. The water is so clear that the bottom is said to be distinctly seen in twenty-five fathoms.

The spot where the *Athenienne* was wrecked bears from the north castle of Martimo Island south 78½°W, difference of longitude 54′01″. The latitude of the north end of the reef is 37°49′.

The variation of the compass off the Esquirques was nineteen degrees east in 1802. (*NC* vol 25, pp294-295)

F: VICE-ADMIRAL SIR WILLIAM PARKER

Vice-Admiral Sir William Parker was tried on 21 November 1801 at Portsmouth by court martial on a charge of having authorised his son-in-law, Captain Bingham, to cruise in the *America*, 64 guns, beyond the limits of his (Admiral Parker's) command on the Halifax station, with the view, as it was insinuated, of making prizes.

If the *America* had returned safely, there would probably have been no complaint; but she was lost.

A Court of Inquiry sat upon Captain Bingham and acquitted him of all blame; but a question arose as to how that ship came to be in that part of the world. Admiral Parker was called upon to answer it. After hearing the whole case on both sides, the Court was of the opinion that the Admiral was justified in sending the *America* and *Cleopatra* to the West Indies but was indiscreet in the detailed instructions for their return within the limits of their station. The Court declared the general character of Sir William to be such as to preclude the idea of his having been influenced by any motive not connected with the good of His Majesty's service and therefore honourably acquitted him. (*AR* 1801, Chr, pp42-43)

The story of the court martial appears in *NC* vol 6, pp420-421, but the fact of Captain Bingham being the son-in-law of Admiral Parker was omitted from the article, which included the following: 'Sir William made a defence so forcible, convincing, and exculpatory, as impressed the whole Court, not only with a complete conviction of his innocence, but also of his having acted upon principles dictated by an ardent desire to serve the country. His sentiments were given with a particular perspicuity, without any artifice of logical arrangement or rhetorical figure. He made no appeal to the passions. All he delivered was dictated by truth: in language captivating from its simplicity, and irresistibly persuasive from its energy, manliness and sincerity.'

Sir William Parker died on 31 December 1802, at his seat at Ham, near Richmond, Surrey. (*NC* vol 9, p81)

G: LOSS OF HMS GARLAND

Findlay, 1870 ed, p396 states the *Garland* was wrecked in Santa Lucia Bay, which bay is formed by a chain of rocky islets extending about one and a half miles north and south, at from a half to one mile offshore.

The entrance to the anchorage is from the northward, but there are some very dangerous patches in the bay, as well as to the northward of the northern island. It was on one of these latter patches that the *Garland* was lost.

Santa Lucia Bay, which is about fifteen miles to the north of Fort Dauphin, appears to be a very dangerous place.

The position given by Captain Owen, for the north islet, is latitude 24°44′42″S longitude 47°14′09″E.

H: LOSS OF THE 26th LIGHT DRAGOONS

Whilst it is by no means certain that the ship which carried the 26th Regiment of Light Dragoons was the *Fowler*, we nevertheless have two versions of the disaster which befell the unfortunate soldiers and their families.

The following story appeared in the *Times* on Tuesday 2 February 1796, and is perhaps open to question:

'At Porthleven a large transport said to be from Cork for Portsmouth with 26th Regiment of Dragoons, between five and six hundred men and officers went down a cable's length of the shore and every soul perished. Several dead horses and two children were washed ashore.

'Nine men from Brague, called wreckmen, joined themselves by a rope and attempted to reach her when the ship was going down, when a sudden gust and a dreadful sea coming over them, their rope broke and they were never seen more.'

The second version of the tragedy appeared in the *SYM*, and is an extract from a letter sent from Falmouth and dated 28 January. (*SYM*, 1 February 1796)

'On Monday night last a vessel foundered in Mount's Bay, near Penzance; she is supposed to have struck on a sunk rock, called the Wellow [this can only be the Runnel or Rundle Stone which lies about two miles south of Gwennap Head], about two miles from the shore. Some horses and soldiers' cloaths having washed on shore in Mount's Bay on Monday, give rise to a supposition, that the vessel was a transport belonging to Admiral Christian's fleet. Every person on board must have perished. The number of buttons of the soldiers' clothes washed on shore is 26; they very probably belonged to the 26th Light Dragoons, which sailed with Admiral Christian.

'Ten miners who were busy on a rock, in plundering the things which were driven on shore, were suddenly forced off by a sea, and never seen afterwards.'

GLOSSARY

Anchor *Best bower* and *small bower* – the two stowed furthest forward or near to the bows, the *best bower* being the anchor on the starboard bow, the *small bower* the one on the larboard bow. *Sheet anchor* – of the same size and weight as either of the bowers but was kept in reserve to be deployed in emergencies. *Stream anchor* – a smaller one used for temporary mooring and *Kedge anchor* – the smallest of all, used for *kedging* (*qv*).

Anker A liquid measure varying considerably; that of Rotterdam having a capacity of 10 wine gallons. *Anker* was also the name of the cask holding wine or brandy.

Armed *en flûte* See *flute*.

Athwart hawse The situation of a ship when driven by the wind, tide, or other accident, across the stem of another, whether they bear against, or are at a small distance from, each other, the transverse position of the former with respect to the latter being principally understood.

Bare poles Having no sails set.

Barge The 2nd largest boat of a man-of-war, often the captain's personal transport.

Belay To make fast; to fasten a running rope around a cleat or belaying pin.

Bembridge Ledge The rocks, which are sometimes visible at neap tides, lie a little to the northward of the Foreland on the Isle of Wight. It was here that the East Indiaman *Henry Addington* was lost during a fog on 9 December 1798, *qv*.

Bend the cable To fasten the cable to the anchor, etc.

Bend the sails To make fast the sails to the yards.

Bends The strongest planks in a ship's side; the wales.

Bight Any part of a rope between the ends; also a collar or an eye formed by a rope.

Bitts Large upright pins of timber, with a cross-piece, over which the bight of the cable is put. Also smaller pins to belay ropes, etc.

Blackstakes A roadstead in the River Medway, above Sheerness.

Braces Ropes fastened to the yardarms to brace them about.

Bring to To check the course of a ship by arranging the sails in such a manner that they counteract each other, and keep the ship nearly stationary; when she is said to *lie by* or *lie to*, having, according to the sea-phrase, some of her sails aback, to oppose the force of those which are full.

Broach, to When the violence of the wind, or a heavy sea upon the quarter, the ship is forced up to windward of her course or proper direction in defiance of the helm.

Bulkheads Partitions in the ship.

Bumkin A short boom or beam of timber projecting from each bow of a ship, to extend the clew or lower edge of the foresail to windward.

Cabin dark lights Same as dead lights.

Cable A large rope by which means the ship is secured to the anchor.

Cable's length A measure of 120 fathoms or 240 yards.

Carronade A short cannon of large bore.

Cartel A ship carrying prisoners of war being returned under flag of truce; or an agreement to do the same.

Cat-head A strong projection from the fore castle on each bow, furnished with sheaves or strong pulleys, and to which the anchor is lifted after it has been hove up to the bow by the capstan.

Chain-cables 'Are not new; Caesar found them on the shores of the English Channel. In 1818 I saw upwards of eighty sail of vessels with them at Desenzano, on the Lago di Garda.' (Smyth, 1867 ed). They were divided into parts 15 fathoms in length, connected by shackles, any one of which could be slipped in emergency; at each 7½ fathoms a swivel was inserted, but later dispensed with.

Chain-pump This is composed of two long metal tubes let down through the decks somewhat apart from each other, but joined at their lower ends, which are pierced with holes for the admission of water. Above the upper part of the tubes is a sprocket wheel worked by crank handles; over this wheel, and passing through both tubes, is an endless chain, furnished at certain distances with bucket valves or pistons, turning round a friction roller. The whole, when set in motion by means of the crank handles, passing down one tube and up the other, raises the water very rapidly.

Chains Properly called *Chain-wales* or *Channels*. Broad and thick platforms projecting horizontally from the ship's side, to which they are fayed and bolted, abreast of and somewhat abaft the masts. They are formed to project the chain-plate, and give the lower rigging greater spread, free from the topsides of the ship, thus affording greater security and support to the masts, as well as to prevent the shrouds from damaging the gunwale, or being hurt by rubbing against it. By 1860 they were discontinued in many ships, the eyes being secured to the timber heads, and frequently within the gunwale to the stringers or lower shelf-pieces above the water-way. *In the chains* applies to the leadsman who stands on the channels between the two shrouds to heave the hand-lead.

Chasse-Maree A French lugger.

Chess-tree A piece of wood bolted perpendicularly on each side of the ship near the gang-way, to confine the clew of the mainsail; for which purpose there is a hole in the upper part, through which the tack passes, that extends the clew of the sail to windward.

Chommery Colloquial for *Chasse-Maree*.

Clew garnet Fore or main *clew garnet* is a rope running double from nearly the centre of the fore or main yard, to the clews or corners of the sail, where the tack and sheet are affixed, and is the principal means of clewing up or taking in the sail.

Close hauled The arrangement or trim of a ship's sails when she endeavours to make a course in the nearest direction possible towards that point of the compass from which the wind blows.

Coehorn or Cohorn. A small portable mortar, which fired a shell weighing 8½lbs by means of a charge of 3¾oz of black powder.

Country ship A local trader in the East Indies, usually based in India and sometimes in native ownership.

Courses A name by which the fore, main and driver sails are usually distinguished.

Crank, groggy or **groggified** The quality of a ship which, for want of a sufficient quantity of ballast or cargo, is rendered incapable of carrying sail, without being exposed to the danger of oversetting.

Dead-lights Storm shutters for a cabin window.

Dogger, Dutch A two-masted fishing vessel.

Driver A large fore-and-aft sail set on the mizzen between a gaff and boom; called also *spanker*.

Embayed Landlocked with a lee shore.

Extra ship A ship temporarily chartered to the East India Company, but not specifically built for the trade; usually smaller than the East India-men proper.

Fear-nought Stout fire-resistant felt woollen cloth, used for port-linings, hatchway fire-screens etc. Same as dreadnought.

Fetch To arrive at.

Floating anchor A simple machine consisting of a fourfold canvas, stretched by two cross-bars of iron, rivetted in the centre, and swifted at both ends. It is made to hang perpendicularly at some distance below the surface, where it presents great resistance to being dragged through the water, diminishing a ship's leeward drift in a gale where there is no anchorage.

Floating coffin A term for the old 10-gun brigs. (See *Frapping a ship*.)

Flogging the glass Where there is no ship time-piece, the watches and half-hour bells are governed by a half-hour sand-glass. The run of the sand was supposed to be quickened by vibration, hence some weary soul towards the end of his watch was said to flog the glass.

Flute A Dutch cargo ship with a narrow stern and heavy tumblehome (the curving-in of the topsides so that the ship was broader at the waterline than at deck level). For warships, *en flûte* referred to a state in which the ship was partially disarmed, usually while acting in an auxiliary capacity such as troopship, transport or hospital ship.

Forepeak The contracted part of a ship's hold, close to the bow.

Formicas Clusters of small rocks. See 13 December 1800.

Fothering Is usually practised to stop a leak at sea. A heavy sail is closely thrummed with yard and oakum, and drawn under the bottom; the pressure of the water drives the thrumming into the apertures. If one does not succeed others are added, using all the sails rather than lose the ship.

Frapping a ship The act of passing four or five turns of a large cable laid rope round a ship's hull when it is apprehended that she is not strong enough to resist the violence of the sea. This expedient is only made use of for very old ships, and then only temporarily. St Paul's ship was 'undergirded' or frapped.

Galliot A Dutch cargo ship; the rig was also used for bomb vessels in some navies.

Gammon The lashing of the bowsprit.

Gang-casks Small barrels used for bringing water on board in boats, somewhat larger than breakers, and usually containing 32 gallons.

Gangway The platform on each side of the skid-beams leading from the quarterdeck to the forecastle, and peculiar to deep-waisted ships, for the convenience of walking expeditiously fore and aft; they were fenced on the outside by iron stanchions and ropes, or rails, and in vessels of war with a netting, in which part of the hammocks are stowed. In merchant ships it was frequently called the gang-board.

Gant-lope or **Gauntlope** (commonly pronounced **Gantlet**) A race which a man was sentenced to run, in the navy or army, for almost any offence. The ship's crew, or a certain division of soldiers, were disposed in two rows face to face, each provided with a knotted cord, or *knittle*, with which they severely struck the delinquent as he ran between them, stripped down to the waist. This was repeated according to the sentence, but seldom beyond three times, and constituted *'running the gauntlet.'* (Refer to 18 March 1806)

Gasket A canvas band or plaited rope used to lash the sails to the yards when furled.

Glass Used in the plural to denote the passage of time. One 'glass' equals one half-hour. *To flog or sweat the half-hour glass:* to turn the sand-glass before the sand has quite run out, and thus gaining a few minutes in each half-hour, make the watch too short. *Half-minute and Quarter-minute glasses:* to ascertain the rate of the ship's speed, measured by the log.

Glazed powder Gunpowder of which the grains, by friction against one another in a barrel worked for the purpose, have acquired a fine polish, sometimes promoted by a minute application of black-lead; reputed to be very slighter weaker than the original, and somewhat less liable to deterioration.

God-send Any unexpected piece of good fortune.

Grab A two- or three-masted vessel of the Malabar coast.

Great gun An old name for a cannon.

Gripe By carrying too great a quantity of after-sail, a ship inclines too much to windward, and requires to be kept a-weather, or to windward. Also the fore end of the keel.

Gun-shot A ship was within gun-shot of another, when she was within a mile or a mile and a quarter of her.

Gun-stone A stone used as shot for a gun.

Gunwale The wale or upper edge of a ship's side, next the bulwarks.

Halyards A rope or purchase for lowering or raising a yard, etc.

Hammock A swinging sea-bed, the undisputed invention of Alcibiades. 'At present the hammock consists of a piece of canvas, 6 feet long and 4 feet wide, gathered together at the two ends by means of clews, formed by a grommet and knittles, whence the *head-clew* and *foot-clew*. The hammock is hung horizontally under the deck, and forms a receptacle for the bed on which the seamen sleep. There are usually allowed from 14 to 20 inches between hammock and hammock in a ship of war. In preparing for action, the hammocks, together with their contents, are all firmly corded, taken upon deck, and fixed in various nettings, so as to form a barricade against musket-balls.' (Smyth, 1867 ed)

Hand To hand a sail is to furl it.

Hawse-holes The holes through which the cables pass.

Heneaga or Heneague Great Inagua.

Hogged Spoken of a ship having a droop at both the bow and stern.

Hogshead A cask containing 63 old wine gallons.

Hoveller A boatman acting as a non-certificated pilot, or doing any kind of occasional work on the coast. A small coasting vessel.

Iron bound coast A coast where the shores are composed of rocks which mostly rise perpendicularly from the sea and have no anchorage nearby; they are therefore dangerous for vessels to borrow upon; that is, to approach closely either to land or wind, to hug a shoal or coast in order to avoid an adverse tide.

Jollyboat The smallest boat of a man-of-war.

Kedging Moving the ship by carrying out a small anchor and cable in a boat, and then hauling in using the capstan or windlass.

Knight-heads Two short thick pieces of wood, formerly carved like a man's head, having four sheaves in each, one of them abaft the fore mast, called *fore-knight*, and the other abaft the main mast, called *main-knight*.

Labour Pitch and roll heavily.

Langrage *Ad hoc* ammunition made up of old iron, nails, etc. Also called langrel and langrishe.

Large Applied to the wind, when it crosses the line of a ship's course in a favourable direction; particularly on the beam or points aft; hence, to *sail large* is to sail before the wind so that the sheets are slackened and flowing.

Larboard or port The lefthand side of the vessel when looking forward from the stern.

Lascar A navtive sailor in the East Indies.

Launch The largest boat of a man-of-war.

League A measure of distance: 3 nautical miles or 3041 fathoms.

Letter of Marque A commission to allow merchant ships to commit acts of war against enemy vessels, and by extension used of the ship herself. Although privateers required such a commission, they cruised specifically to capture enemy ships, whereas the term 'Letter of Marque' tended to be confined to ships on cargo-carrying voyages that might make a capture if the opportunity arose.

Luconia This is a corruption of Luzon, the largest of the Philippines (Findlay's *Directory for the Navigation of the Indian Archipelago, China and Japan*, 1870 ed, p815). Malham's *Gazetteer* states: 'Luconia, more usually known under the name of Manilla, which is only the port of the island of Luconia.' (Malham, 1795 ed, p69)

Lumper A docker.

Mast coat A conical canvas fitted over the wedges round the mast, to prevent water coming down from the decks.

Musket-shot distance From 300 to 400 yards.

Offing Implies out at sea, or at a good distance from the shore, generally thought of as that part of the sea rather more than halfway between the shore and the horizon.

Ordinary A ship in ordinary is in reserve.

Orlop The deck where the cables were stored; the deck below the lowest gundeck.

Pay To pay a ship's bottom is to paint it with tar.

Pinnace The third boat of a man-of-war; primarily a pulling boat but could also carry sail.

Pipe A large cask containing two hogsheads.

Pistol-shot distance About 50 yards.

Poop A deck above the ordinary deck in the after part of the ship.

Pooped Said of a ship when the stern is broken in by the sea, or when a sea strikes the stern.

Press of sail As much as can be carried.

Quarter That part of a ship's side which lies towards the stern, or which is comprehended between the aftmost end of the main chains and the side of the stern, where it is terminated by the quarter pieces.

Quintal A hundredweight.

Razee A ship-of-war cut down by reducing the number of gundecks.

Reef To reduce a sail by tying a portion of it to the yards.

Run of the ship The aftermost part of a ship's bottom.

Scranny-picker A beachcomber, looking for God-sends.

Scud To run before a gale under canvas enough to keep the vessel ahead of the sea; as, for instance, a close-reefed main topsail and foresail; without canvas she was said to scud under bare poles, and was likely to be pooped.

Scuppers Apertures cut through the waterways and sides of a ship at proper distance, and lined with metal, in order to carry the water off the deck into the sea.

Sea-cunny Lascar steersman.

Sheathing Underwater protection against fouling and the pernicious effects of the worm, initially of thin boards and later of copper. In 1613 a junk of 800 or 1000 tons was seen in Japan all sheathed in iron; lead was tried in Europe in the seventeenth century, but a definitive answer was copper; by 1783 warships of every class were coppered, but not all merchant ships.

Sheet A rope fastened to the leeward corner of a sail to extend it to the wind.

Sloop of War A small warship, usually brig or ship rigged, carrying from 10 to 18 guns captained by an officer of Commander rank.

Snow A vessel like a brig, but having the boom mainsail traversing on the trysail mast, instead of hooped to the main mast.

Spanker The after-sail of a ship or barque, so called from its flapping in the breeze; see also *driver*.

Spring, to anchor with a Before letting go the anchor, to cause a smaller cable or hawser to be passed out of a stern or quarter port, and taken outside of the ship forward, in order to be bent or fastened to the ring of the anchor intended to be let go, for the purpose of bringing the ship's broadside to bear in any direction.

Spring a mast, yard, or any other spar When it becomes rent or split by an overpress of sail, heavy pitch or jerk of the ship in a rough sea, or by too slack rigging.

Stand on To keep on the same course.

Starboard The right side of the vessel, looking forward from the stern.

Start, as to start a butt-end To move suddenly from its position due to the action of the sea.

Strike To lower anything, as the ensign or topsail in saluting, or the yards, topgallant masts and topmasts in a gale.

Studding sail A narrow sail set temporarily at the leeches of a square sail when the wind is light.

Sweep An oar of great length used during a calm or to escape an enemy.

Syrang In the East Indies, a native boatswain or captain of a lascar crew.

Tartan A Mediterranean vessel with a lateen sail.

Thole pin A pin in the side of a boat to keep the oar in place.

Thwart A bench for rowers placed athwart the boat.

Tierce One-third of a pipe; 42 old wine gallons.

Tight or taut Words applied to a ship in good condition.

Tindal A lascar petty officer.

Top A platform set at the top of a mast.

Trade wind A wind blowing steadily towards the thermal equator and deflected westwardly by the eastward rotation of the earth.

Warp To move a vessel by hauling on warps, that is, ropes, hawsers or chains, to other ships, to anchors sunk in the bottom, or to certain stations on shore.

Water-logged Full of water and therefore unmanageable and log like.

Wear or veer ship To change a ship's course from one tack to the other by turning her stern through the wind.

Weather a ship, headland, etc To sail to windward of it. The weathergage implies the situation of one ship to windward of another when in action, etc.

Western Isles The Azores.

Wherry A shallow light boat; sharp at each end and built for speed.

Wingo Island On the coast of Sweden. It is 4 leagues to the south of Calf Sound, where ships take pilots for Gothenburg one way and Aahus the other.

Xebec A small lateen rigged vessel, often used by Algerine corsairs.

BIBLIOGRAPHY

Baltic Pilot, vols 1, 2 and 3

Berman, Bruce D, *Encyclopaedia of American Shipwrecks* [1972]

Brenton, Edward Pelham, *The Naval History of Great Britain*, 2 vols [1823/24]

Burney, W, *Naval Heroes of Great Britain* [1806]

Clowes, Sir William Laird, *The Royal Navy*, 7 vols [1897-1903]

Colledge, J J, *Ships of the Royal Navy* [1969]

Commissioned Sea Officers of the Royal Navy, 3 vols [1660-1815]

Cooney, David W, *A Chronology of the United States Navy* [1965]

Cooper, J Fenimore, *The History of the Navy of the United States of America* [1839]

Dalyell, Sir G J, *Shipwrecks and Disasters at Sea*, 3 vols [1812]

Dictionary of National Biography

Dodsley's Annual Register, General Index to; from its commencement in 1758 to 1819 [1826]

Dodsley's Annual Register, 1758-1816

Duncan, *Mariner's Chronicle*, 6 vols [1805-1812]

Dundonald, Thomas Cochrane, Earl of, *The Autobiography of a Seaman*, 2 vols [1860]

Falconer, William, *A Universal Dictionary of the Marine* [1780]

Fereday, R P, *Saint-Faust in the North 1803-1804*

Fereday, R P, *The Orkney Balfours*

Findlay, Alexander George, *A Directory for the Navigation of the Indian Archipelago, China and Japan* [1870]

Findlay, Alexander George, *Indian Ocean Pilot* [1870]

Findlay, Alexander George, *North Atlantic Memoir* [1873]

Gold, Joyce, *The Naval Chronicle*, 39 vols [1799-1818]

International Journal of Nautical Archaeology, various

James, W, *Naval Occurrences* [1817]

James, William, *The Naval History of Great Britain*, 6 vols [1822]

Lecky, E S, *The King's Ships* [1913]

Malham, John, *The Naval Gazetteer* or *Seaman's Complete Guide*, 2 vols [1795]

The Mariner's Mirror

Marshall, John, *Royal Naval Biography*, 6 vols [1823]

McArthur, John, *Principles and Practice of Naval and Military Courts-martial*, 2 vols [1813]

Naval and Military Record

Naval Magazine or *Maritime Miscellany*, vol 2 [1800]

Norie, J W, *The Naval Gazetteer, Biographer and Chronologist* [1827]
North Sea Pilot (East), No 55 and Amendments
Plymouth and Dock Telegraph
Ralfe, J, *Naval Biography*, 4 vols [1828]
Saumarez Papers, Navy Records Society [1968]
Sherbourne and Yeovil Mercury or *Western Flying Post*
Smyth, Admiral W H, *Sailor's Word-Book* [1867]
Steel's Naval Chronologist of the War, February 1793-1801
Steel's Original and Correct List of the Royal Navy, various
Steel's 'A Complete List of the Royal Navy'. For 1797, embodied in the
    above for June 1797; and for 1803, embodied in the above for May
    1803
The *Times*
The *Times*, Palmer's Indexes to
Van der Molen, S J, *The Lutine Treasure*, Adlard Coles, London

INDEX

INDEX